Puritan Reformed Spirituality

Puritan Reformed Spirituality

Joel Beeke

EVANGELICAL PRESS

EVANGELICAL PRESS

Evangelical Press
Faverdale North Industrial Estate, Darlington, DL3 0PH England
email: sales@evangelicalpress.org

Evangelical Press USA
PO Box 825, Webster, NY 14580 USA
email: usa.sales@evangelicalpress.org

www.evangelicalpress.org

First published 2004, © Reformation Heritage Books

Printed in the United States of America

British Library Cataloguing in Publication Data available

ISBN 0 85234 629 8

With heartfelt appreciation for

John R. Beeke

and

James W. Beeke

brothers in the flesh, in mind, in heart, and in Christ;
born for adversity and sharers of joy unspeakable.

Foreword

Spirituality is a subject much on the minds of people today. With its prevailing secularism and materialism, modern culture has failed to satisfy its consumers. Many are coming to realize the truth of what Moses said to the children of Israel, "Man doth not live by bread only" (Deut. 8:3). With Christ in His Sermon on the Mount, they ask, "Is not the life more than meat, and the body than raiment?" (Matt. 6:25). The result is a new interest in discovering and nurturing the inward, spiritual dimensions of human life.

Historic Christianity has always shared this interest. Fundamental to the Christian faith is the conviction that "God is a Spirit" (John 4:24), and that human beings are made in the image of God (Gen. 1:26-27). Assessing the state of fallen man, the apostle Paul declared that men are "alienated from the life of God through the ignorance that is in them, because of the blindness of their heart" (Eph. 4:18). Christ Himself declared, "Except a man be born again, he cannot see the kingdom of God" (John 3:3).

The cultivation of spiritual life has been addressed in different ways by different Christian traditions. Roman Catholicism has offered a spirituality of ritualism and sacramental administration, and alternatively, the disciplines of monastic life and the pursuits of mysticism. The Wesleyan Methodist tradition, the Holiness movement, and more recently, Pentecostalism and the charismatic movement have offered a spirituality with less ceremonial or intellectual content and a great deal more emotion and subjectivism.

The problem with most spirituality today is that it is not closely moored in Scripture and too often degenerates into unbiblical mysticism. In contrast, Reformed Christianity has followed a path of its own, largely determined by its concern to test all things by Scripture and to develop a spiritual life shaped by Scripture's teachings and directives. Reformed spirituality is the outworking of the conviction that "all scripture is given by inspiration of God, and is profitable for doctrine, for reproof, for correction, for instruction in righteousness" (2 Tim. 3:16). In dependence upon the Holy Spirit, it aims to achieve what John Murray called "intelligent piety," wedding scriptural knowledge and heartfelt piety. Of the preachers, scholars, and writers who fostered this kind of biblical spirituality, none have excelled the Puritans of England and their contemporaries in Scotland and the Netherlands. Their legacy excels in basing all spirituality, experience, and affections on the Bible.

The dual emphasis of nurturing both the mind and the soul is sorely needed today. On the one hand, we confront the problem of dry Reformed orthodoxy, which has correct doctrinal teaching but lacks emphasis on vibrant, godly living. The result is that people bow before the doctrine of God without a vital, spiritual union with the God of doctrine. On the other hand, Pentecostal and charismatic Christianity offers emotionalism in protest against a formal, lifeless Christianity, but it is not rooted solidly in Scripture. The result is that people bow before human feeling rather than before the Triune God.

This book promotes biblical spirituality through a study of the Reformed and Puritan heritage. The first three chapters deal with various aspects of Calvin's spirituality, while the next five show spiritual dimensions of the Puritans, specifically in the work of William Ames (chapter 6) and Anthony Burgess (chapter 8). Chapters 9–12 consider the Puritan spirituality of the Scottish tradition through the lives of John Brown of Haddington, Thomas Boston, and Ebenezer and Ralph Erskine. Chapter 13 introduces the spirituality of the Dutch Second Reformation, followed by studies of some of its leading representatives (chapters 14–16): Willem Teellinck, Herman Witsius, and Theodorus Jacobus Frelinghuysen. The book concludes with studies on justification by faith alone, holiness, and Reformed experiential preaching (chapters 17–19), all of which focus on Puritan spirituality.

Chapter 13 of this book was given as an address for the Interdisziplinäres Zentrum für Pietismusforschung in Halle, Germany in 1997. It has not been previously printed in a periodical or book. Other chapters have been revised and/or expanded, and all of them have been edited from their original printing. I wish to thank heartily the following sources for permission to reprint: Chapter 1, *The Cambridge Companion to John Calvin*, edited by Donald K. McKim (Cambridge: University Press, 2004), 125–52; chapter 2, *Calvin and Spirituality*, edited by David W. Foxgrover (Grand Rapids: CRC Product Services, 1999), 13–30; chapter 3, *Reformation and Revival* 10, 4 (fall, 2001):107–32; chapter 4, *Reformed Spirituality: Communing with Our Glorious God*, edited by Joseph A. Pipa, Jr. and J. Andrew Wortman (Taylors, S.C.: Southern Presbyterian Press, 2003), 73–100; chapter 5, *Trust and Obey*, edited by Don Kistler (Morgan, Penn.: Soli Deo Gloria, 1996), 154–200; chapter 6, *The Devoted Life: An Invitation to the Puritan Classics*, edited by Randall C. Gleason and Kelly M. Kapic (Downers Grove, Ill.: InterVarsity, 2004); chapter 7, *Whatever Happened to the Reformation?*, edited by Gary L.W. Johnson and R. Fowler White (Phillipsburg, N.J.: Presbyterian & Reformed, 2001), 229–52, 320–25; chapter 8, *The Answer of a Good Conscience* (Westminster Conference papers, London: Tentmaker, 1998), 27–52; chapter 9, *The Systematic Theology of John Brown of Haddington* (Ross-shire: Christian Focus, and Grand Rapids: Reformation Heritage Books, 2002), e–x; chapter 10, *Complete Works of Thomas Boston* (Stoke-on-Trent, England: Tentmaker, 2002), 1:I–1 to I–16; chapters 11–12, *The Beauties of Ebenezer Erskine* (Ross-shire: Christian Focus, and Grand Rapids: Reformation Heritage Books, 2001), i–liii, 617–22; chapter 14, *The Path of True Godliness by Willem Teellinck* (Grand Rapids: Baker, 2003), 11–29; chapter 15, *An Analysis of Herman Witsius's Economy of the Covenants* (Ross-shire: Christian Focus, 2002), iii–xxi; chapter 16, *Forerunner of the Great Awakening: Sermons by Theodorus Jacobus Frelinghuysen* (Grand Rapids: Eerdmans, 2000), vii–xxxviii; chapter 17, *Justification by Faith Alone*, edited by Don Kistler (Morgan, Penn.: Soli Deo Gloria, 1995), 53–105; chapter 18, *Reformation and Revival* 4, 2 (1995):81–112; chapter 19, *Feed My Sheep: A Passionate Plea for Preaching*, edited by Don Kistler (Morgan, Penn.: Soli Deo Gloria, 2002), 94–128.

Each chapter is an independent unit with the exception of chapters 11 and 12. Consequently, footnotes in each chapter record sources without reference to previous chapters. Chapters that were originally written as introductions for books are not footnoted. Where antiquarian sources are quoted, spelling is updated. Repetition between the independent chapters has been kept to a minimum. Also, a few chapters address ministers directly in their applications, as they were first delivered as addresses at ministers' conferences. Bibliographies are appended for chapters 1, 4, 11–12, and 16, for those who wish to pursue further study.

I dedicate this book to my two older brothers, John and James, who "love our Lord Jesus Christ in sincerity" (Eph. 6:24) and model for me the essence of Puritan Reformed spirituality. They are gifts of God to me—real friends who have proven themselves to be faithful spiritual brothers in prosperity and adversity. I cannot express in words what they mean to me.

I also thank the following friends for coauthoring chapters with me: Ray B. Lanning (chapter 5), Jan van Vliet (chapter 6), Randall Pederson (chapters 9 and 10), and Cornelis Pronk (chapter 16). I thank Phyllis TenElshof, Ray Lanning, Kate Timmer, and Kristen Meschke for their able proofreading, and Gary and Linda den Hollander for their conscientious typesetting. I am deeply grateful to the seminary students who have heard many of these chapters in lectures and have assisted me "as iron sharpens iron." I am also grateful to the staff and board of Reformation Heritage Books for their faithful support and dedication. Thanks, too, to my loving flock, Heritage Netherlands Reformed Congregation of Grand Rapids, Michigan, without whom the pastoral tone of this book would not have been possible. Above all, I owe an enormous debt to my dear wife, Mary, and our three children, Calvin, Esther, and Lydia, for their loving sacrifices over the years as this book was being written.

If God uses this book to help some see more clearly the vision and value of the spiritual Puritan Reformed tradition, and especially to move us more deeply into intimate friendship with Himself through our Elder Brother, the Lord Jesus Christ, my joy will be full. *Soli Deo Gloria!*

March, 2004

Joel R. Beeke
2919 Leonard N.E.
Grand Rapids, Michigan 49525

Table of Contents

List of Illustrations

Calvin on Piety

John Calvin's *Institutes* have earned him the title of "the preeminent systematician of the Protestant Reformation." His reputation as an intellectual, however, is often seen apart from the vital spiritual and pastoral context in which he wrote his theology. For Calvin, theological understanding and practical piety, truth and usefulness, are inseparable. Theology first of all deals with knowledge—knowledge of God and of ourselves—but there is no true knowledge where there is no true piety.

Calvin's concept of piety (*pietas*) is rooted in the knowledge of God and includes attitudes and actions that are directed to the adoration and service of God. In addition, his *pietas* includes a host of related themes, such as filial piety in human relationships, and respect and love for the image of God in human beings. Calvin's piety is evident in people who recognize through experiential faith that they have been accepted in Christ and engrafted into His body by the grace of God. In this "mystical union," the Lord claims them as His own in life and in death. They become God's people and members of Christ by the power of the Holy Spirit. This relationship restores their joy of fellowship with God; it recreates their lives.

The purpose of this chapter is to show that Calvin's piety is fundamentally biblical, with an emphasis on the heart more than the mind. Head and heart must work together, but the heart is more important.[1] After an introductory look at the definition and goal of piety in Calvin's thinking, I will show how his *pietas* affects the theological, ecclesiological, and practical dimensions of his thought.

The Definition and Importance of Piety

Pietas is one of the major themes of Calvin's theology. His theology is, as John T. McNeill says, "his piety described at length."[2] He is determined to confine theology within the limits of piety.[3] In his preface addressed to King Francis I, Calvin says that the purpose of writing the *Institutes* was "solely to transmit certain rudiments by which those who are touched with any zeal for religion might be shaped to true godliness [*pietas*]."[4]

For Calvin, *pietas* designates the right attitude of man towards God. This attitude includes true knowledge, heartfelt worship, saving faith, filial fear, prayerful submission, and reverential love.[5] Knowing who and what God is (theology) embraces right attitudes toward Him and doing what He wants (piety). In his first catechism, Calvin writes, "True piety consists in a sincere feeling which loves God as Father as much as it fears and reverences Him as Lord, embraces His righteousness, and dreads offending Him worse than death."[6] In the *Institutes,* Calvin is more succinct: "I call 'piety' that reverence joined with love of God which the knowledge of his benefits induces."[7] This love and reverence for God is a necessary concomitant to any knowledge of Him and embraces all of life. As Calvin says, "The whole life of Christians ought to be a sort of practice of godliness."[8] Or, as the subtitle of the first edition of the *Institutes* states, "Embracing almost the whole sum of piety & whatever is necessary to know of the doctrine of salvation: A work most worthy to be read by all persons zealous for piety."[9]

Calvin's commentaries also reflect the importance of *pietas*. For example, he writes on 1 Timothy 4:7-8, "You will do the thing of greatest value, if with all your zeal and ability you devote yourself to godliness [*pietas*] alone. Godliness is the beginning, middle and end of Christian living. Where it is complete, there is nothing lacking . . . . Thus the conclusion is that we should concentrate exclusively on godliness, for when once we have attained to it, God requires no more of us."[10] Commenting on 2 Peter 1:3, he says, "As soon as he [Peter] has made mention of life he immediately adds godliness [*pietas*] as if it were the soul of life."[11]

Piety's Supreme Goal: Soli Deo Gloria

The goal of piety, as well as the entire Christian life, is the glory of God—glory that shines in God's attributes, in the structure of the world, and in the death and resurrection of Jesus Christ.[12] Glorifying God supersedes personal salvation for every truly pious person.[13] Calvin writes thus to Cardinal Sadolet: "It is not very sound theology to confine a man's thought so much to himself, and not to set before him, as the prime motive for his existence, zeal to illustrate the glory of God.... I am persuaded that there is no man imbued with true piety who will not consider as insipid that long and labored exhortation to zeal for heavenly life, a zeal which keeps a man entirely devoted to himself and does not, even by one expression, arouse him to sanctify the name of God."[14]

That God may be glorified in us, the goal of piety, is the purpose of our creation. It thus becomes the yearning of the regenerate to live out the purpose of their original creation. [15] The pious man, according to Calvin, confesses, "We are God's: let us therefore live for him and die for him. We are God's: let his wisdom and will therefore rule all our actions. We are God's: let all the parts of our life accordingly strive toward him as our only lawful goal."[16]

God redeems, adopts, and sanctifies His people that His glory would shine in them and deliver them from impious self-seeking.[17] The pious man's deepest concern therefore is God Himself and the things of God—God's Word, God's authority, God's gospel, God's truth. He yearns to know more of God and to commune more with Him.

But how do we glorify God? As Calvin writes, "God has prescribed for us a way in which he will be glorified by us, namely, piety, which consists in the obedience of his Word. He that exceeds these bounds does not go about to honor God, but rather to dishonor him."[18] Obedience to God's Word means taking refuge in Christ for forgiveness of our sins, knowing Him through His Word, serving Him with a loving heart, doing good works in gratitude for His goodness, and exercising self-denial to the point of loving our enemies.[19] This response involves total surrender to God Himself, His Word, and His will.[20]

Calvin says, "I offer thee my heart, Lord, promptly and sincerely." This is the desire of all who are truly pious. However, this desire can only be realized through communion with Christ and participation in Him, for outside of Christ even the most religious person lives for himself. Only in Christ can the pious live as willing servants of their Lord, faithful soldiers of their Commander, and obedient children of their Father.[21]

Theological Dimensions

Piety's Profound Root: Mystical Union
"Calvin's doctrine of union with Christ is one of the most consistently influential features of his theology and ethics, if not the single most important teaching that animates the whole of his thought and his personal life," writes David Willis-Watkins.[22]

Calvin did not intend to present theology from the viewpoint of a single doctrine. Nonetheless, his sermons, commentaries, and theological works are so permeated with the union-with-Christ doctrine that it becomes his focus for Christian faith and practice.[23] Calvin says as much when he writes, "That joining together of Head and members, that indwelling of Christ in our hearts—in short, that mystical union—are accorded by us the highest degree of importance, so that Christ, having been made ours, makes us sharers with him in the gifts with which he has been endowed."[24]

For Calvin, piety is rooted in the believer's mystical union (*unio mystica*) with Christ; thus this union must be our starting point.[25] Such a union is possible because Christ took on our human nature, filling it with His virtue. Union with Christ in His humanity is historical, ethical, and personal, but not essential. There is no crass mixture (*crassa mixtura*) of human substances between Christ and us. Nonetheless, Calvin states, "Not only does he cleave to us by an indivisible bond of fellowship, but with a wonderful communion, day by day, he grows more and more into one body with us, until he becomes completely one with us."[26] This union is one of the gospel's greatest mysteries.[27] Because of the fountain of Christ's perfection in our nature, the pious may, by faith, draw whatever they need for their sanctification. The flesh of Christ is the source from which His people derive life and power.[28]

If Christ had died and risen but was not applying His salvation to believers for their regeneration and sanctification, His work would have been ineffectual. Our piety shows that the Spirit of Christ is working in us what has already been accomplished in Christ. Christ administers His sanctification to the church through His royal priesthood so that the church may live piously for Him.[29]

Piety's Major Theme: Communion and Participation
The heartbeat of Calvin's practical theology and piety is communion (*communio*) with Christ. This involves participation (*participatio*) in His benefits, which are inseparable from union with Christ.[30] The *Confessio Fidei de Eucharistia* (1537), signed by Calvin, Martin Bucer, and Wolfgang Capito, supported this emphasis.[31] However, Calvin's communion with Christ was not shaped by his doctrine of the Lord's Supper; rather, his emphasis on spiritual communion with Christ helped shape his concept of the sacrament.

Similarly, the concepts of *communio* and *participatio* helped shape Calvin's understanding of regeneration, faith, justification, sanctification, assurance, election, and the church. He could not speak of any doctrine apart from communion with Christ. That is the heart of Calvin's system of theology.

Piety's Double Bond: The Spirit and Faith
Communion with Christ is realized only through Spirit-worked faith, Calvin teaches. It is actual communion not because believers participate in the essence of Christ's nature, but because the Spirit of Christ unites believers so intimately to Christ that they become flesh of His flesh and bone of His bone. From God's perspective, the Spirit is the bond between Christ and believers, whereas from our perspective, faith is the bond. These perspectives do not clash with each other, since one of the Spirit's principal operations is to work faith in a sinner.[32]

Only the Spirit can unite Christ in heaven with the believer on earth. Just as the Spirit united heaven and earth in the Incarnation, so in regeneration the Spirit raises the elect from earth to commune with Christ in heaven and brings Christ into the hearts and lives of the elect on earth.[33] Communion with Christ is always the result of the Spirit's work—a work that is astonishing and experiential rather than comprehensible.[34] The Holy Spirit is thus the link that binds the believer to Christ and the channel through which Christ is communicated to the believer.[35] As Calvin writes to Peter Martyr: "We grow up together with Christ into one body, and he shares his Spirit with us, through whose hidden operation he has become ours. Believers receive this communion with Christ at the same time as their calling. But they grow from day to day more and more in this communion, in proportion to the life of Christ growing within them."[36]

Calvin moves beyond Luther in this emphasis on communion with Christ. Calvin stresses that, by His Spirit, Christ empowers those who are united with Him by faith. Being "engrafted into the death of Christ, we derive from it a secret energy, as the twig does from the root," he writes. The believer "is animated by the secret power of Christ; so that Christ may be said to live and grow in him; for as the soul enlivens the body, so Christ imparts life to his members."[37]

Like Luther, Calvin believes that knowledge is fundamental to faith. Such knowledge includes the Word of God as well as the proclamation of the gospel.[38] Since the written Word is exemplified in the living Word, Jesus Christ, faith cannot be separated from Christ, in whom all God's promises are fulfilled.[39] The work of the Spirit does not supplement or supersede the revelation of Scripture, but authenticates it, Calvin teaches. "Take away the Word, and no faith will remain," Calvin says. [40]

Faith unites the believer to Christ by means of the Word, enabling the believer to receive Christ as He is clothed in the gospel and graciously offered by the Father.[41] By faith, God also dwells in the believer. Consequently, Calvin says, "We ought not to separate Christ from ourselves or ourselves from him," but participate in Christ by faith, for this "revives us from death to make us a new creature." [42]

By faith, the believer possesses Christ and grows in Him. Furthermore, the degree of his faith exercised through the Word determines his degree of communion with Christ.[43] "Everything which faith should contemplate is exhibited to us in Christ," Calvin writes.[44] Though Christ remains in heaven, the believer who excels in piety learns to grasp Christ so firmly by faith that Christ dwells within his heart.[45] By faith, the pious live by what they find in Christ rather than by what they find in themselves.[46]

Looking to Christ for assurance, therefore, means looking at ourselves in Christ. As David Willis-Watkins writes, "Assurance of salvation is a derivative self-knowledge, whose focus remains on Christ as united to his body, the Church, of which we are members."[47]

Piety's Double Cleansing: Justification and Sanctification
According to Calvin, believers receive from Christ by faith the "double grace" of justification and sanctification, which, together, provide a twofold cleansing.[48] Justification offers imputed purity, and sanctification, actual purity.[49]

Calvin defines justification as "the acceptance with which God receives us into his favor as righteous men."[50] He goes on to say that "since God justifies us by the intercession of Christ, he absolves us not by the confirmation of our own innocence but by the imputation of righteousness, so that we who are not righteous in ourselves may be reckoned as such in Christ."[51] Justification includes the remission of sins and the right to eternal life.

Calvin regards justification as a central doctrine of the Christian faith. He calls it "the principal hinge by which religion is supported," the soil out of which the Christian life develops, and the substance of piety.[52] Justification not only serves God's honor by satisfying the conditions for salvation; it also offers the believer's conscience "peaceful rest and serene tranquility."[53] As Romans 5:1 says, "Therefore, being justified by faith, we have peace with God through our Lord Jesus Christ." This is the heart and soul of piety. Believers do not need to worry about their status with God because they are justified by faith. They can willingly renounce personal glory and daily accept their own life from the hand of their Creator and Redeemer. Daily skirmishes may be lost to the enemy, but Jesus Christ has won the war for them.

Sanctification refers to the process in which the believer increasingly becomes conformed to Christ in heart, conduct, and devotion to God. It is the continual remaking of the believer by the Holy Spirit, the increasing consecration of body and soul to God.[54] In sanctification, the believer offers himself to God as a sacrifice. This does not come without great struggle and slow progress; it requires cleansing from the pollution of the flesh and renouncing the world.[55] It requires repentance, mortification, and daily conversion.

Justification and sanctification are inseparable, Calvin says. To separate one from the other is to tear Christ in pieces,[56] or like trying to separate the sun's light from the heat that light generates.[57] Believers are justified for the purpose of worshipping God in holiness of life.[58]

Ecclesiological Dimensions

Piety through the Church
Calvin's *pietas* is not independent of Scripture nor the church; rather, it is rooted in the Word and nurtured in the church. While breaking with the clericalism and absolutism of Rome, Calvin nonetheless maintains a high view of the church. "If we do not prefer the church to all other objects of our interest, we are unworthy of being counted among her members," he writes.

Augustine once said, "He cannot have God for his Father who refuses to have the church for his mother." To that Calvin adds, "For there is no other way to enter into life unless this mother conceive us in her womb, give us birth, nourish us at her breast, and lastly, unless she keep us under her care and guidance until, putting off mortal flesh, we become like the angels." Apart from the church, there is little hope for forgiveness of sins or salvation, Calvin wrote. It is always disastrous to leave the church.[59]

For Calvin, believers are engrafted into Christ and His church, because spiritual growth happens within the church. The church is mother, educator, and nourisher of every believer, for the Holy Spirit acts in her. Believers cultivate piety by the Spirit through the church's teaching ministry, progressing from spiritual infancy to adolescence to

Interior of the Cathedral of Geneva

full manhood in Christ. They do not graduate from the church until they die.[60] This lifelong education is offered within an atmosphere of genuine piety in which believers love and care for one another under the headship of Christ.[61] It encourages the growth of one another's gifts and love, as it is "constrained to borrow from others."[62]

Growth in piety is impossible apart from the church, for piety is fostered by the communion of saints. Within the church, believers "cleave to each other in the mutual distribution of gifts."[63] Each member has his own place and gifts to use within the body.[64] Ideally, the entire body uses these gifts in symmetry and proportion, ever reforming and growing toward perfection.[65]

Piety of the Word
The Word of God is central to the development of Christian piety in the believer. Calvin's relational model explains how.

*Calvin preaching his farewell sermon in
expectation of banishment.*

True religion is a dialogue between God and man. The part of the dialogue that God initiates is revelation. In this, God comes down to meet us, addresses us, and makes Himself known to us in the preaching of the Word. The other part of the dialogue is man's response to God's revelation. This response, which includes trust, adoration, and godly fear, is what Calvin calls *pietas*. The preaching of the Word saves us and preserves us as the Spirit enables us to appropriate the blood of Christ and respond to Him with reverential love. By the Spirit-empowered preaching of men, "the renewal of the saints is accomplished and the body of Christ is edified," Calvin says.[66]

Calvin teaches that the preaching of the Word is our spiritual food and our medicine for spiritual health. With the Spirit's blessing, ministers are spiritual physicians who apply the Word to our souls as earthly physicians apply medicine to our bodies. Using the Word, these spiritual doctors diagnose, prescribe for, and cure spiritual disease in those plagued by sin and death. The preached Word is used as an instrument to heal, cleanse, and make fruitful our disease-prone souls.[67] The Spirit, or the "internal minister," promotes piety by using the "external minister" to preach the Word. As Calvin says, the external minister "holds forth the vocal word and it is received by the ears," but the internal minister "truly communicates the thing proclaimed…that is Christ."[68]

To promote piety, the Spirit not only uses the gospel to work faith deep within the souls of His elect, as we have already seen, but He also uses the law. The law promotes piety in three ways:

1. It restrains sin and promotes righteousness in the church and society, preventing both from lapsing into chaos.

2. It disciplines, educates, and convicts us, driving us out of ourselves to Jesus Christ, the fulfiller and end of the law. The law cannot lead us to a saving knowledge of God in Christ; rather, the Holy Spirit uses it as a mirror to show us our guilt, shut us off from hope, and bring us to repentance. It drives us to the spiritual need out of which faith in Christ is born. This convicting use of the law is critical for the believer's piety, for it prevents the ungodly self-righteousness that is prone to reassert itself even in the holiest of saints.

3. It becomes the rule of life for the believer. "What is the rule of life which [God] has given us?" Calvin asks in the Genevan Catechism. The answer: "His law." Later, Calvin says the law "shows the mark at which we ought to aim, the goal towards which we ought to press, that each of us, according to the measure of grace bestowed upon him, may endeavor to frame his life according to the highest rectitude, and, by constant study, continually advance more and more."[69]

Calvin writes about the third use of the law in the first edition of his *Institutes,* stating, "Believers…profit by the law because from it they learn more thoroughly each day what the Lord's will is like…. It is as if some servant, already prepared with complete earnestness of heart to commend himself to his master, must search out and oversee his master's ways in order to conform and accommodate himself to them.

Moreover, however much they may be prompted by the Spirit and eager to obey God, they are still weak in the flesh, and would rather serve sin than God. The law is to this flesh like a whip to an idle and balky ass, to goad, stir, arouse it to work."[70]

In the last edition of the *Institutes* (1559), Calvin is more emphatic about how believers profit from the law. First, he says, "Here is the best instrument for them to learn more thoroughly each day the nature of the Lord's will to which they aspire, and to confirm them in the understanding of it." And second, it causes "frequent meditation upon it to be aroused to obedience, be strengthened in it, and be drawn back from the slippery path of transgression." Saints must press on in this, Calvin concludes. "For what would be less lovable than the law if, with importuning and threatening alone, it troubled souls through fear, and distressed them through fright?"[71]

Viewing the law primarily as an encouragement for the believer to cling to God and obey Him is another instance where Calvin differs from Luther. For Luther, the law is primarily negative; it is closely linked with sin, death, or the devil. Luther's dominant interest is in the second use of the law, even when he considers the law's role in sanctification. By contrast, Calvin views the law primarily as a positive expression of the will of God. As Hesselink says, "Calvin's view could be called Deuteronomic, for to him law and love are not antithetical, but are correlates."[72] The believer follows God's law not out of compulsory obedience, but out of grateful obedience. Under the tutelage of the Spirit, the law prompts gratitude in the believer, which leads to loving obedience and aversion to sin. In other words, the primary purpose of the law for Luther is to help the believer recognize and confront sin. For Calvin, its primary purpose is to direct the believer to serve God out of love.[73]

Piety in the Sacraments

Calvin defines the sacraments as testimonies "of divine grace toward us, confirmed by an outward sign, with mutual attestation of our piety toward him."[74] The sacraments are "exercises of piety." They foster and strengthen our faith, and help us offer ourselves as a living sacrifice to God.

For Calvin, as for Augustine, the sacraments are the visible Word. The preached Word comes through our ears; the visible Word, through our eyes. The sacraments hold forth the same Christ as the preached Word but communicate Him through a different mode.

In the sacraments, God accommodates Himself to our weakness,

Calvin says. When we hear the Word indiscriminately proclaimed, we may wonder: "Is it truly for me? Does it really reach me?" However, in the sacraments God reaches out and touches us individually, and says, "Yes, it's for *you*. The promise extends to *you*." The sacraments thus minister to human weakness by personalizing the promises for those who trust Christ for salvation.

God comes to His people in the sacraments, encourages them, enables them to know Christ better, builds them up, and nourishes them in Him. Baptism promotes piety as a symbol of how believers are engrafted into Christ, renewed by the Spirit, and adopted into the family of the heavenly Father.[75] Likewise, the Lord's Supper shows how these adopted children are fed by their loving Father. Calvin loves to refer to the Supper as nourishment for the soul. "The signs are bread and wine which represent for us the invisible food that we receive from the flesh and blood of Christ," he writes. "Christ is the only food of our soul, and therefore our heavenly Father invites us to Christ, that refreshed by partaking of him, we may repeatedly gather strength until we shall have reached heavenly immortality."[76]

As believers, we need constant nourishment. We never reach a point

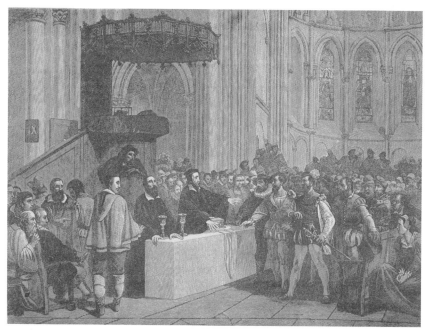

Calvin refusing the Lord's Supper to the Libertines, in St. Peter's Cathedral, Geneva.

where we no longer need to hear the Word, to pray, or to be nurtured by the sacraments. We must constantly grow and develop. As we continue to sin because of our old nature, we are in constant need of forgiveness and grace. So the Supper, along with the preaching of the Word, repeatedly reminds us that we need Christ, and we need to be renewed and built up in Him. The sacraments promise that Christ is present to receive us, bless us, and renew us.

For Calvin, the word *conversion* doesn't just mean the initial act of coming to faith; it also means daily renewal and growth in following Christ. The sacraments lead the way to this daily conversion, Calvin says. They tell us that we need the grace of Christ every day. We must draw strength from Christ, particularly through the body that He sacrificed for us on the cross.

As Calvin writes, "For as the eternal Word of God is the fountain of life so his flesh is the channel to pour out to us the life which resides intrinsically in his divinity. For in his flesh was accomplished man's redemption, in it a sacrifice was offered to atone for sin, and obedience yielded to God to reconcile him to us. It was also filled with the sanctification of the Holy Spirit. Finally having overcome death he was received into the heavenly glory."[77] In other words, the Spirit sanctified Christ's body, which Christ offered on the cross to atone for sin. That body was raised from the dead and received up into heaven. At every stage of our redemption, Christ's body is the pathway to God. In the Supper, then, Christ comes to us and says: "My body is still given for you. By faith you may commune with me and my body and all of its saving benefits."

Calvin teaches that Christ gives Himself to us in the Supper, not just His benefits, just as He gives us Himself and His benefits in the preaching of the Word. Christ also makes us part of His body as He gives us Himself. Calvin cannot precisely explain how that happens in the Supper, for it is better experienced than explained.[78] However, he does say that Christ does not leave heaven to enter the bread. Rather, in the Holy Supper, we are called to lift up our hearts to heaven, where Christ is, and not cling to the external bread and wine.

We are lifted up through the work of the Holy Spirit in our hearts. As Calvin writes, "Christ, then, is absent from us in respect of his body, but dwelling in us by his Spirit, he raises us to heaven to himself, transfusing into us the vivifying vigor of his flesh just as the rays of the sun invigorate us by his vital warmth."[79] Partaking of the flesh of Christ is a spiritual act rather than a carnal act that involves a "transfusion of substance."[80]

The sacraments can be seen as ladders by which we climb to heaven. "Because we are unable to fly high enough to draw near to God, he has ordained sacraments for us, like ladders," Calvin says. "If a man wishes to leap on high, he will break his neck in the attempt, but if he has steps, he will be able to proceed with confidence. So also, if we are to reach our God, we must use the means which he has instituted since he knows what is suitable for us. God has then given us this wonderful support and encouragement and strength in our weakness."[81]

We must never worship the bread because Christ is not *in* the bread, but we find Christ *through* the bread, Calvin says. Just as our mouths receive bread to nourish our physical bodies, so our souls, by faith, receive Christ's body and blood to nourish our spiritual lives.

When we meet Christ in the sacraments, we grow in grace; that is why they are called a means of grace. The sacraments encourage us in our progress toward heaven. They promote confidence in God's promises through Christ's "signified and sealed" redemptive death. Since they are covenants, they contain promises by which "consciences may be roused to an assurance of salvation," Calvin says.[82] The sacraments offer "peace of conscience" and "a special assurance" when the Spirit enables the believer to "see" the Word engraved upon the sacraments.[83]

Finally, the sacraments promote piety by prompting us to thank and praise God for His abundant grace. They require us to "attest our piety toward him." As Calvin says, "The Lord recalls the great bounty of his goodness to our memory and stirs us up to acknowledge it; and at the same time he admonishes us not be ungrateful for such lavish liberality, but rather to proclaim it with fitting praises and to celebrate [the Lord's Supper] by giving thanks."[84]

Two things happen in the Supper: the receiving of Christ and the surrender of the believer. The Lord's Supper is not eucharistic from God's perspective, Calvin says, for Christ is not offered afresh. Nor is it eucharistic in terms of man's merit, for we can offer God nothing by way of sacrifice. But it is eucharistic in terms of our thanksgiving.[85] That sacrifice is an indispensable part of the Lord's Supper which, Calvin says, includes "all the duties of love."[86] The Eucharist is an *agape* feast in which communicants cherish each other and testify of the bond that they enjoy with each other in the unity of the body of Christ.[87]

We offer this sacrifice of gratitude in response to Christ's sacrifice for us. We surrender our lives in response to the heavenly banquet God spreads for us in the Supper. By the Spirit's grace, the Supper enables us

John Calvin

as a royal priesthood to offer ourselves as a living sacrifice of praise and thanksgiving to God.[88]

The Lord's Supper thus prompts both piety of grace and piety of gratitude, as Brian Gerrish has shown.[89] The Father's liberality and His children's grateful response are a recurrent theme in Calvin's theology. "We should so revere such a father with grateful piety and burning love," Calvin admonishes us, "as to devote ourselves wholly to his obedience and honor him in everything."[90] The Supper is the liturgical enactment of Calvin's themes of grace and gratitude, which lie at the heart of his piety.[91]

In the Lord's Supper, the human and divine elements of Calvin's piety are held in dynamic tension. In that dynamic interchange, God moves toward the believer while His Spirit consummates the Word-based union. At the same time, the believer moves toward God by contemplating the Savior who refreshes and strengthens him. In this, God is glorified and the believer edified.[92]

Piety in the Psalter

Calvin views the Psalms as the canonical manual of piety. In the preface to his five-volume commentary on the Psalms—his largest exposition of any Bible book—Calvin writes: "There is no other book in which we are more perfectly taught the right manner of praising God, or in which we are more powerfully stirred up to the performance of this exercise of piety."[93] Calvin's preoccupation with the Psalter was motivated by his belief that the Psalms teach and inspire genuine piety the following ways:

- As the revelation from God, the Psalms teach us about God. Because they are theological as well as doxological, they are our sung creed.[94]
- They clearly teach our need for God. They tell us who we are and why we need God's help.[95]
- They offer the divine remedy for our needs. They present Christ in His person, offices, sufferings, death, resurrection, and ascension. They announce the way of salvation, proclaiming the blessedness of justification by faith alone and the necessity of sanctification by the Spirit with the Word.[96]
- They demonstrate God's amazing goodness and invite us to meditate on His grace and mercy. They lead us to repent and to fear God, to trust in His Word, and to hope in His mercy.
- They teach us to flee to the God of salvation through prayer and

show us how to bring our requests to God.[97] They show us how to pray confidently in the midst of adversity.[98]

- They show us the depth of communion we may enjoy with our covenant-keeping God. They show how the living church is God's bride, God's children, and God's flock.

- They provide a vehicle for communal worship. Many use first-person plural pronouns ("we," "our") to indicate this communal aspect, but even those with first-person singular pronouns include all who love the Lord and are committed to Him. They move us to trust and praise God and to love our neighbors. They prompt reliance on God's promises, zeal for Him and His house, and compassion for the suffering.

- They cover the full range of spiritual experience, including faith and unbelief, joy in God and sorrow over sin, divine presence and divine desertion. As Calvin says, they are "an anatomy of all parts of the soul."[99] We still see our affections and spiritual maladies in the words of the psalmists. When we read about their experiences, we are drawn to self-examination and faith by the grace of the Spirit. The psalms of David, especially, are like a mirror in which we are led to praise God and find rest in His sovereign purposes.[100]

Calvin immersed himself in the Psalms for twenty-five years as a commentator, preacher, biblical scholar, and worship leader.[101] Early on, he began work on metrical versions of the Psalms to be used in public worship. On January 16, 1537, shortly after his arrival in Geneva, Calvin asked his council to introduce the singing of Psalms into church worship. He recruited the talents of other men, such as Clement Marot, Louis Bourgeois, and Theodore Beza, to produce the Genevan Psalter. That work would take twenty-five years to complete. The first collection (1539) contained eighteen Psalms, six of which Calvin put into verse. The rest were done by the French poet, Marot. An expanded version (1542) containing thirty-five Psalms was next, followed by one of forty-nine Psalms (1543). Calvin wrote the preface to both of those, commending the practice of congregational singing. After Marot's death in 1544, Calvin encouraged Beza to put the rest of the Psalms into verse. In 1564, two years before his death, Calvin rejoiced to see the first complete edition of the Genevan Psalter.[102]

The Genevan Psalter is furnished with a remarkable collection of 125 melodies, written specifically for the Psalms by outstanding musicians, of whom Louis Bourgeois is the best known. The tunes are melodic, distinctive, and reverent.[103] They clearly express Calvin's convictions that piety is best promoted when priority is given to text over tune, while recognizing that Psalms deserve their own music. Since music should help the reception of the Word, Calvin says, it should be "weighty, dignified, majestic, and modest"—fitting attitudes for a sinful creature in the presence of God.[104] This protects the sovereignty of God in worship and conduces proper conformity between the believer's inward disposition and his outward confession.

Psalm-singing is one of the four principle acts of church worship, Calvin believed. It is an extension of prayer. It is also the most significant vocal contribution of people in the service. Psalms were sung in Sunday morning and Sunday afternoon services. Beginning in 1546, a printed table indicated which Psalms were to be sung on each occasion. Psalters were assigned to each service according to the texts that were preached. By 1562, three Psalms were sung at each service.[105]

Calvin believed that corporate singing subdued the fallen heart and retrained wayward affections in the way of piety. Like preaching and the sacraments, Psalm-singing disciplines the heart's affections in the school of faith and lifts the believer to God. Psalm-singing amplifies the effect of the Word upon the heart and multiplies the spiritual energy of the church. "The Psalms can stimulate us to raise our hearts to God and arouse us to an ardor in invoking as well as in exalting with praises the glory of his name," Calvin writes.[106] With the Spirit's direction, Psalm-singing tunes the hearts of believers for glory.

The Genevan Psalter was an integral part of Calvinist worship for centuries. It set the standard for succeeding French Reformed psalm books as well as those in English, Dutch, German, and Hungarian. As a devotional book, it warmed the hearts of thousands, but the people who sang from it understood that its power was not in the book or its words, but in the Spirit who impressed those words on their hearts.

The Genevan Psalter promoted piety by stimulating a spirituality of the Word that was corporate and liturgical, and that broke down the distinction between liturgy and life. The Calvinists freely sang the Psalms not only in their churches, but also in homes and workplaces, on the streets and in the fields.[107] The singing of Psalms became a "means of Huguenot self-identification."[108] This pious exercise became a cultural emblem. In short, as T. Hartley Hall writes, "In scriptural or metrical versions, the Psalms, together with the stately tunes to which they were early set, are clearly the heart and soul of Reformed piety."[109]

Practical Dimensions

Although Calvin viewed the church as the nursery of piety, he also emphasized the need for personal piety. The Christian strives for piety because he loves righteousness, longs to live to God's glory, and delights to obey God's rule of righteousness set forth in Scripture.[110] God Himself is the focal point of the Christian life[111]—a life that is therefore carried out in self-denial, particularly expressed in Christ-like cross-bearing.[112]

For Calvin, such piety "is the beginning, middle, and end of Christian living."[113] It involves numerous practical dimensions for daily Christian living, which are thoroughly explained in Calvin's *Institutes,* commentaries, sermons, letters, and treatises. Here is the gist of what Calvin says on prayer, repentance, and obedience, as well as on pious Christian living in Chapters 6-10 of Book 3 of the *Institutes* of 1559.[114]

Facsimile of Calvin's handwriting.

Prayer

Prayer is the principal and perpetual exercise of faith and the chief element of piety, Calvin says.[115] Prayer shows God's grace to the believer even as the believer offers praises to God and asks for His faithfulness. It communicates piety both privately and corporately.[116]

Calvin devoted the second longest chapter of the *Institutes* (Book 3, Chapter 20) to prayer, providing six purposes for it: To fly to God with every need, to set all our petitions before God, to prepare us to receive God's benefits with humble gratitude, to meditate upon God's kindness, to instill the proper spirit of delight for God's answers in prayer, and to confirm His providence.[117]

Two problems are likely to surface with Calvin's doctrine of prayer. First, when the believer obediently submits to God's will, he does not necessarily give up his own will. Rather, through the act of submissive prayer, the believer invokes God's providence to act on his behalf. Thus, man's will, under the Spirit's guidance, and God's will work together in communion.

Second, to the objection that prayer seems superfluous in light of God's omniscience and omnipotence, Calvin responds that God ordained prayer more for man as an exercise of piety than for Himself. Providence must be understood in the sense that God ordains the means along with the ends. Prayer is thus a means to receive what God has planned to bestow.[118] Prayer is a way in which believers seek out and receive what God has determined to do for them from eternity.[119]

Calvin treats prayer as a given rather than a problem. Right prayer is governed by rules, he says. These include praying with:

- a heartfelt sense of reverence
- a sense of need and repentance
- a surrender of all confidence in self and a humble plea for pardon
- a confident hope.

All four rules are repeatedly violated by even the holiest of God's people. Nevertheless, for Christ's sake, God does not desert the pious but has mercy for them.[120]

Despite the shortcomings of believers, prayer is required for the increase of piety, for prayer diminishes self-love and multiplies dependence upon God. As the due exercise of piety, prayer unites God and man—not in substance, but in will and purpose. Like the Lord's Supper, prayer lifts the believer to Christ and renders proper glory to God.

That glory is the purpose of the first three petitions of the Lord's Prayer as well as other petitions dealing with His creation. Since creation looks to God's glory for its preservation, the entire Lord's Prayer is directed to God's glory.[121]

In the Lord's Prayer, Christ "supplies words to our lips," Calvin says.[122] It shows us how all our prayers must be controlled, formed, and inspired by the Word of God. Only this can provide holy boldness in prayer, "which rightly accords with fear, reverence, and solicitude."[123]

We must be disciplined and steadfast in prayer, for prayer keeps us in fellowship with Christ. We are reassured in prayer of Christ's intercessions, without which our prayers would be rejected.[124] Only Christ can turn God's throne of dreadful glory into a throne of grace, to which we can draw near in prayer.[125] Thus, prayer is the channel between God and man. It is the way in which the Christian expresses his praise and adoration of God, and asks for God's help in submissive piety.[126]

Repentance
Repentance is the fruit of faith and prayer. Luther said in his *Ninety-Five Theses* that all of the Christian life should be marked by repentance. Calvin also sees repentance as a lifelong process. He says that repentance is not merely the start of the Christian life; it *is* the Christian life. It involves confession of sin as well as growth in holiness. Repentance is the lifelong response of the believer to the gospel in outward life, mind, heart, attitude, and will.[127]

Repentance begins with turning to God from the heart and proceeds from a pure, earnest fear of God. It involves dying to self and sin (mortification) and coming alive to righteousness (vivification) in Christ.[128] Calvin does not limit repentance to an inward grace, but views it as the redirection of a man's entire being to righteousness. Without a pure, earnest fear of God, a man will not be aware of the heinousness of sin or want to die to it. Mortification is essential because, though sin ceases to reign in the believer, it does not cease to dwell in him. Romans 7:14-25 shows that mortification is a lifelong process. With the Spirit's help, the believer must put sin to death every day through self-denial, cross-bearing, and meditation on the future life.

Repentance is also characterized by newness of life, however. Mortification is the means to vivification, which Calvin defines as "the desire to live in a holy and devoted manner, a desire arising from rebirth; as if it were said that man dies to himself that he may begin to live to

God."[129] True self-denial results in a life devoted to justice and mercy. The pious both "cease to do evil" and "learn to do well." Through repentance, they bow in the dust before their holy Judge, then are raised to participate in the life, death, righteousness, and intercession of their Savior. As Calvin writes, "For if we truly partake in his death, 'our old man is crucified by his power, and the body of sin perishes' (Rom. 6:6), that the corruption of original nature may no longer thrive. If we share in his resurrection, through it we are raised up into newness of life to correspond with the righteousness of God."[130]

The words Calvin uses to describe the pious Christian life (*reparatio, regeneratio, reformatio, renovatio, restitutio*) point back to our original state of righteousness. They indicate that a life of *pietas* is restorative in nature. Through Spirit-worked repentance, believers are restored to the image of God.[131]

Self-denial

Self-denial is the sacrificial dimension of *pietas*. The fruit of the believer's union with Jesus Christ is self-denial, which includes the following:

1. The realization we are not our own but belong to God. We live and die unto Him, according to the rule of His Word. Thus, self-denial is not self-centered, as was often the case in medieval monasticism, but God-centered.[132] Our greatest enemy is neither the devil nor the world, but ourselves.

2. The desire to seek the things of the Lord throughout our lives. Self-denial leaves no room for pride, lasciviousness, and worldliness. It is the opposite of self-love because it is love for God.[133] The entire orientation of our life must be toward God.

3. The commitment to yield ourselves and everything we own to God as a living sacrifice. We then are prepared to love others and to esteem them better than ourselves—not by viewing them as they are in themselves, but by viewing the image of God in them. This uproots our love of strife and self and replaces it with a spirit of gentleness and helpfulness.[134] Our love for others then flows from the heart, and our only limit to helping them is the limit of our resources.[135]

Believers are encouraged to persevere in self-denial by what the gospel promises about the future consummation of the Kingdom of God. Such promises help us overcome every obstacle that opposes self-renunciation and assist us in bearing adversity.[136]

Furthermore, self-denial helps us find true happiness because it helps us do what we were created for. We were created to love God above all and our neighbor as ourselves. Happiness is the result of having that principle restored. Without self-denial, as Calvin says, we may possess everything without possessing one particle of real happiness.

Cross-bearing

While self-denial focuses on inward conformity to Christ, cross-bearing centers on outward Christlikeness. Those who are in fellowship with Christ must prepare themselves for a hard, toilsome life filled with many kinds of evil, Calvin says. This is not simply due to sin's effect on this fallen world, but is because of the believer's union with Christ. Because His life was a perpetual cross, ours must also include suffering.[137] We not only participate in the benefits of His atoning work on the cross, but we also experience the Spirit's work of transforming us into the image of Christ.[138]

Cross-bearing tests piety, Calvin says. Through cross-bearing we are roused to hope, trained in patience, instructed in obedience, and chastened in pride. Cross-bearing is our medicine and our chastisement; it reveals the feebleness of our flesh and teaches us to suffer for the sake of righteousness.[139]

Happily, God promises to be with us in all our sufferings. He even transforms suffering associated with persecution into comfort and blessing.[140]

The Present and Future Life

Through cross-bearing, we learn to have contempt for the present life when compared to the blessings of heaven. This life is nothing compared to what is to come. It is like smoke or a shadow. "If heaven is our homeland, what else is the earth but our place of exile? If departure from the world is entry into life, what else is the world but a sepulcher?" Calvin asks.[141] "No one has made progress in the school of Christ who does not joyfully await the day of death and final resurrection," he concludes.[142]

Typically, Calvin uses the *complexio oppositorum* when explaining the Christian's relation to this world, presenting opposites to find a middle way between them. Thus, on the one hand, cross-bearing crucifies us to the world and the world to us. On the other hand, the devout Christian enjoys this present life, albeit with due restraint and moderation, for he is taught to use things in this world for the purpose that God intended them. Calvin was no ascetic; he enjoyed good literature, good food, and the beauties of nature. But he rejected all forms of earthly excess. The believer is called to Christlike moderation, which includes modesty, prudence, avoidance of display, and contentment with our lot,[143] for it is the hope of the life to come that gives purpose to and enjoyment in our present life. This life is always straining after a better, heavenly life.[144]

How, then, is it possible for the truly pious Christian to maintain a proper balance, enjoying the gifts that God gives in this world while avoiding the snare of over-indulgence? Calvin offers four guiding principles:

1. Recognize that God is the giver of every good and perfect gift. This should restrain our lusts because our gratitude to God for His gifts cannot be expressed by a greedy reception of them.
2. Understand that if we have few possessions, we must bear our poverty patiently lest we be ensnared by inordinate desire.
3. Remember that we are stewards of the world in which God has placed us. Soon we will have to give an account to Him of our stewardship.
4. Know that God has called us to Himself and to His service. Because of that calling, we strive to fulfill our tasks in His service, for His glory, and under His watchful, benevolent eye.[145]

Obedience

For Calvin, unconditional obedience to God's will is the essence of piety. Piety links love, freedom, and discipline by subjecting all to the will and Word of God.[146] Love is the overarching principle that prevents piety from degenerating into legalism. At the same time, law provides the content for love.

Piety includes rules that govern the believer's response. Privately, those rules take the form of self-denial and cross-bearing; publicly, they are expressed in the exercise of church discipline, as Calvin implemented in Geneva. In either case, the glory of God compels disciplined obedience. For Calvin, the pious Christian is neither weak nor passive but dynamically active in the pursuit of obedience, much like a distance runner, a diligent scholar, or a heroic warrior, submitting to God's will.[147]

In the preface of his commentary on the Psalms, Calvin writes: "Here is the true proof of obedience, where, bidding farewell to our own affections, we subject ourselves to God and allow our lives to be so governed by his will that things most bitter and harsh to us—because they come from him—become sweet to us."[148] "Sweet obedience"—

Calvin welcomed such descriptions. According to I. John Hesselink, Calvin described the pious life with words such as *sweet, sweetly, sweetness* hundreds of times in his *Institutes,* commentaries, sermons, and treatises. Calvin writes of the sweetness of the law, the sweetness of Christ, the sweetness of consolation in the midst of adversity and persecution, the sweetness of prayer, the sweetness of the Lord's Supper, the sweetness of God's free offer of eternal life in Christ, and the sweetness of eternal glory.[149]

He writes of the sweet fruit of election, too, saying that ultimately this world and all its glories will pass away. What gives us assurance of salvation here and hope for the life to come is that we have been "chosen in Christ before the foundation of the world" (Eph. 1:4).[150] "We shall never be clearly persuaded…that our salvation flows from the wellspring of God's free mercy until we come to know the very sweet fruit of God's eternal election."[151]

Conclusion
Calvin strove to live the life of *pietas* himself—theologically, ecclesiastically, and practically. At the end of his *Life of Calvin,* Theodore Beza wrote, "Having been a spectator of his conduct for sixteen years,…I can

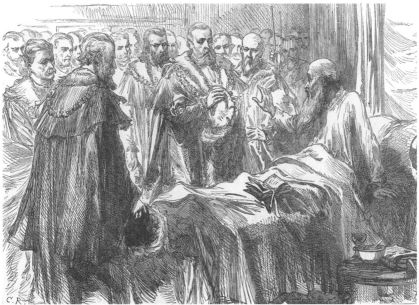

Calvin addressing the Geneva city council for the last time.

Guillaume Farel's last visit with Calvin on his deathbed.

now declare, that in him all men may see a most beautiful example of the Christian character, an example which it is as easy to slander as it is difficult to imitate."[152]

Calvin shows us the piety of a warm-hearted Reformed theologian who speaks from the heart. Having tasted the goodness and grace of God in Jesus Christ, he pursued piety by seeking to know and do God's will every day. He communed with Christ; practiced repentance, self-denial, and cross-bearing; and was involved in vigorous social improvements.[153] His theology worked itself out in heart-felt, Christ-centered piety.[154]

For Calvin and the Reformers of sixteenth-century Europe, doctrine and prayer, as well as faith and worship, are integrally connected. For Calvin, the Reformation includes the reform of piety (*pietas*), or spirituality, as much as a reform of theology. The spirituality that had been cloistered behind monastery walls for centuries had broken down; medieval spirituality was reduced to a celibate, ascetic, and penitential devotion in the convent or monastery. But Calvin helped Christians understand piety in terms of living and acting every day according to God's will (Rom. 12:1-2) in the midst of human society. Through Calvin's influence, Protestant spirituality focused on how one lived the Christian life in the family, the fields, the workshop, and the marketplace.[155] Calvin helped Protestants change the entire focus of the Christian life.

Calvin's teaching, preaching, and catechizing fostered growth in the relationship between believers and God. Piety means experiencing sanctification as a divine work of renewal expressed in repentance and righteousness, which progresses through conflict and adversity in a Christ-like manner. In such piety, prayer and worship are central, both privately and in the community of believers.

The worship of God is always primary, for one's relationship to God takes precedence over everything else. That worship, however, is expressed in how the believer lives his vocation and how he treats his neighbors, for one's relationship with God is most concretely seen in the transformation of every human relationship. Faith and prayer, because they transform every believer, cannot be hidden. Ultimately, therefore, they must transform the church, the community, and the world.

---

[1] Serene Jones, *Calvin and the Rhetoric of Piety* (Louisville: Westminster/John Knox Press, 1995). Unfortunately, Jones exaggerates Calvin's use of rhetoric in the service of piety.

[2] Cited in John Hesselink, "The Development and Purpose of Calvin's *Institutes*," in *Articles on Calvin and Calvinism, vol. 4, Influences upon Calvin and Discussion of the 1559 Institutes,* ed. Richard C. Gamble (New York: Garland, 1992), 215-16.

[3] See Brian A. Gerrish, "Theology within the Limits of Piety Alone: Schleiermacher and Calvin's Doctrine of God" (1981), reprinted in *The Old Prestantism and the New* (1982), chap. 12.

[4] John Calvin, *Institutes of the Christian Religion* [hereafter, Inst.], ed. John T. McNeill and trans. Ford Lewis Battles (Philadelphia: Westminster Press, 1960), 1:9.

[5] Cf. Lucien Joseph Richard, *The Spirituality of John Calvin* (Atlanta: John Knox Press, 1974), 100-101; Sou-Young Lee, "Calvin's Understanding of *Pietas*," in *Calvinus Sincerioris Religionis Vindex*, ed. W.H. Neuser & B.G. Armstrong (Kirksville, Mo.: Sixteenth Century Studies, 1997), 226-33; H.W. Simpson, "*Pietas* in the *Institutes* of Calvin," *Reformational Tradition: A Rich Heritage and Lasting Vocation* (Potchefstroom: Potchefstroom University for Christian Higher Education, 1984), 179-91.

[6] *John Calvin: Catechism 1538*, ed. and trans. Ford Lewis Battles (Pittsburgh: Pittsburgh Theological Seminary), 2.

[7] Inst., Book 1, chapter, 2, section 1. Hereafter the format, 1.2.1, will be used.

[8] Inst. 3.19.2.

[9] *Institutes of the Christian Religion: 1536 Edition,* trans. Ford Lewis Battles, rev. ed. (Grand Rapids: Eerdmans, 1986). The original Latin title reads: *Christianae religionis institutio total fere pietatis summam et quidquid est in doctrina salutis cognitu necessarium complectens, omnibut pietatis studiosis lectu dignissimum opus ac recens editum (Joannis Calvini opera selecta,* ed. Peter Barth, Wilhelm Niesel, and Dora Scheuner, 5 vols. [Munich: Chr. Kaiser, 1926-52], 1:19 [hereafter, *OS*]. From 1539 on the titles were simply *Institutio Chris-*

tianae Religionis, but the "zeal for piety" continued to be a great goal of Calvin's work. See Richard A. Muller, *The Unaccommodated Calvin: Studies in the Foundation of a Theological Tradition* (New York: Oxford University Press, 2000), 106-107.

[10] *Calvin's New Testament Commentaries,* ed. David W. Torrance and Thomas F. Torrance, 12 vols. (Grand Rapids: Eerdmans, 1959-72), *The Second Epistle of Paul the Apostle to the Corinthians, and the Epistles to Timothy, Titus and Philemon,* trans. Thomas A. Smail (Grand Rapids: Eerdmans, 1964), 243-44. Hereafter, *Commentary* [on text].

[11] For the roots of Calvin's piety, see William J. Bouwsma, "The Spirituality of John Calvin," in *Christian Spirituality: High Middle Ages and Reformation,* ed. Jill Raitt (New York: Crossroad, 1987), 318-33.

[12] Inst. 3.2.1; Calvin, *Ioannis Calvini opera quae supersunt omnia,* ed. Wilhelm Baum, Edward Cunitz, and Edward Reuss, *Corpus Reformatorum,* vols. 29-87 (Brunsvigae: C.A. Schwetschke and Son, 1863-1900), 43:428, 47:316. Hereafter, *CO.*

[13] *CO* 26:693.

[14] *OS* 1:363-64.

[15] *CO* 24:362.

[16] Inst. 3.7.1.

[17] *CO* 26:225; 29:5; 51:147.

[18] *CO* 49:51.

[19] *CO* 26:166, 33:186, 47:377-78, 49:245, 51:21.

[20] *CO* 6:9-10.

[21] *CO* 26:439-40.

[22] "The *Unio Mystica* and the Assurance of Faith According to Calvin," in *Calvin Erbe und Auftrag: Festschrift für Wilhelm Heinrich Neuser zum 65. Geburtstag,* ed. Willem van't Spijker (Kampen: Kok, 1991), 78.

[23] E.g., Charles Partee, "Calvin's Central Dogma Again," *Sixteenth Century Journal* 18, 2 (1987):194. Cf. Otto Gründler, "John Calvin: Ingrafting in Christ," in *The Spirituality of Western Christendom,* ed. Rozanne Elder (Kalamazoo, Mich.: Cistercian, 1976), 172-87; Brian G. Armstrong, "The Nature and Structure of Calvin's Thought According to the *Institutes:* Another Look," in *John Calvin's Magnum Opus* (Potchefstroom, South Africa: Institute for Reformational Studies, 1986), 55-82; Guenther Haas, *The Concept of Equity in Calvin's Ethics* (Waterloo, Ontario: Wilfred Laurier University Press, 1997).

[24] Inst. 3.11.9. Cf. *CO* 15:722.

[25] Howard G. Hageman, "Reformed Spirituality," in *Protestant Spiritual Traditions,* ed. Frank C. Senn (New York: Paulist Press, 1986), 61.

[26] Inst. 3.2.24.

[27] Dennis Tamburello points out that "at least seven instances occur in the *Institutes* where Calvin uses the word *arcanus* or *incomprehensibilis* to describe union with Christ" (2.12.7; 3.11.5; 4.17.1, 9 31, 33; 4.19.35; *Union with Christ: John Calvin and the Mysticism of St. Bernard* [Louisville: Westminster/John Knox, 1994], 89, 144). Cf. William Borden Evans, "Imputation and Impartation: The Problem of Union with Christ in Nineteenth-Century American Reformed Theology" (Ph.D. dissertation, Vanderbilt University, 1996), 6-68.

[28] *Commentary* on John 6:51.

[29] Inst. 2.16.16.

[30] Willem van't Spijker, "*Extra nos* and *in nos* by Calvin in a Pneumatological Light," in *Calvin and the Holy Spirit,* ed. Peter DeKlerk (Grand Rapids: Calvin Studies

Society, 1989), 39-62; Merwyn S. Johnson, "Calvin's Ethical Legacy," in *The Legacy of John Calvin,* ed. David Foxgrover (Grand Rapids: Calvin Studies Society, 2000), 63-83.

31 *OS* 1:435-36; Willem van't Spijker, "*Extra nos* and *in nos* by Calvin in a Pneumatological Light," 44.

32 Inst. 3.1.4.

33 Inst. 4.17.6; *Commentary* on Acts 15:9.

34 *Commentary* on Ephesians 5:32.

35 Inst. 3.1.1; 4.17.12.

36 "Calvinus Vermilio" (#2266, 8 Aug 1555), *CO* 15:723-24.

37 CR 50:199. Cf. Barbara Pitkin, *What Pure Eyes Could See: Calvin's Doctrine of Faith in Its Exegetical Context* (New York: Oxford University Press, 1999).

38 *Institutes* 2.9.2; *Commentary* on 1 Peter 1:25. Cf. David Foxgrover, "John Calvin's Understanding of Conscience" (Ph.D. dissertation, Claremont, 1978), 407ff.

39 *The Commentaries of John Calvin on the Old Testament,* 30 vols. (Edinburgh: Calvin Translation Society, 1843-48), on Genesis 15:6. Hereafter, *Commentary* on text. Cf. *Commentary* on Luke 2:21.

40 Inst. 3.2.6.

41 Inst. 3.2.30-32.

42 Inst. 3.2.24; *Commentary* on 1 John 2:12.

43 *Sermons on the Epistle to the Ephesians,* trans. Arthur Golding (1577; reprint Edinburgh: Banner of Truth Trust, 1973), 1:17-18. Hereafter, *Sermon* on Ephesians text.

44 *Commentary* on Ephesians 3:12.

45 *Sermon* on Ephesians 3:14-19.

46 *Commentary* on Habakkuk 2:4.

47 "The Third Part of Christian Freedom Misplaced," in *Later Calvinism: International Perspectives,* ed. W. Fred Graham (Kirksville, Mo.: Sixteenth Century Journal, 1994), 484-85.

48 Inst. 3.11.1.

49 *Sermons on Galatians*, trans. Kathy Childress (Edinburgh: Banner of Truth Trust, 1997), 2:17-18. Hereafter, *Sermon* on Galatians text.

50 Inst. 3.11.2.

51 Ibid.

52 Inst. 3.11.1; 3.15.7.

53 Inst. 3.13.1.

54 Inst. 1.7.5.

55 *Commentary* on John 17:17-19.

56 Inst. 3.11.6.

57 *Sermon* on Galatians 2:17-18.

58 *Commentary* on Romans 6:2.

59 Inst. 4.1.1, 4.1.3-4; cf. Joel R. Beeke, "Glorious Things of Thee Are Spoken: The Doctrine of the Church," in *Onward, Christian Soldiers: Protestants Affirm the Church,* ed. Don Kistler (Morgan, Pa.: Soli Deo Gloria, 1999), 23-25.

60 Inst. 4.1.4-5.

61 *Commentary* on Psalm 20:10.

62 *Commentary* on Romans 12:6.

63 *Commentary* on 1 Corinthians 12:12.

64 *Commentary* on 1 Corinthians 4:7.

[65] *Commentary* on Ephesians 4:12.

[66] *Commentary* on Psalm 18:31; 1 Corinthians 13:12; Inst. 4.1.5, 4.3.2.

[67] *Sermons of M. John Calvin, on the Epistles of S. Paule to Timothie and Titus,* trans. L.T. (1579; reprint facsimile, Edinburgh: Banner of Truth Trust, 1983), 1 Timothy 1:8-11. Hereafter, *Sermon* on text.

[68] *Calvin: Theological Treatises,* ed. J.K.S. Reid (Philadelphia: Westminster Press, 1954), 173. Cf. Brian Armstrong, "The Role of the Holy Spirit in Calvin's Teaching on the Ministry," *Calvin and the Holy Spirit,* ed. P. DeKlerk (Grand Rapids: Calvin Studies Society, 1989), 99-111.

[69] *Selected Works of John Calvin: Tracts and Letters,* ed. Henry Beveridge and Jules Bonnet (1849; reprint Grand Rapids: Baker, 1983), 2:56, 69.

[70] *Institutes of the Christian Religion: 1536 Edition,* 36.

[71] Inst. 2.7.12. Calvin gleans considerable support for his third use of the law from the Davidic Psalms (cf. Inst. 2.7.12 and his *Commentary on the Book of Psalms,* trans. James Anderson, 5 vols. [Grand Rapids: Eerdmans, 1949]).

[72] "Law—Third use of the law," in *Encyclopedia of the Reformed Faith,* ed. Donald K. McKim (Louisville: Westminster/John Knox, 1992), 215-16. Cf. Edward A. Dowey, Jr., "Law in Luther and Calvin," *Theology Today* 41, 2 (1984):146-53; I. John Hesslink, *Calvin's Concept of the Law* (Allison Park, Pa.: Pickwick, 1992), 251-62.

[73] Joel Beeke and Ray Lanning, "Glad Obedience: The Third Use of the Law," in *Trust and Obey: Obedience and the Christian,* ed. Don Kistler (Morgan, Pa.: Soli Deo Gloria, 1996), 154-200; W. Robert Godfrey, "Law and Gospel," in *New Dictionary of Theology,* eds. Sinclair B. Ferguson, David F. Wright, J. I. Packer (Downers Grove, Ill.: InterVarsity Press, 1988), 379.

[74] Inst. 4.14.1.

[75] Inst. 4.16.9; Ronald S. Wallace, *Calvin's Doctrine of the Word and Sacrament* (London: Oliver and Boyd, 1953), 175-83. Cf. H.O. Old, *The Shaping of the Reformed Baptismal Rite in the Sixteenth Century* (Grand Rapids: Eerdmans, 1992).

[76] Inst. 4.17.8-12.

[77] Ibid.

[78] Inst. 4.17.24, 33.

[79] Inst. 4.17.12.

[80] *CO* 9:47, 522.

[81] Inst. 4.14.18.

[82] *Commentary* on 1 Corinthians 11:25.

[83] *Commentary* on Matthew 3:11; Acts 2:38; 1 Peter 3:21.

[84] *OS* 1:136, 145.

[85] Inst. 4.18.3.

[86] Inst. 4.18.17.

[87] Inst. 4.17.44.

[88] Inst. 4.18.13.

[89] "Calvin's Eucharistic Piety," in *The Legacy of John Calvin,* ed. David Foxgrover (Grand Rapids: CRC, 2000), 53.

[90] *OS* 1, 76.

[91] Brian A. Gerrish, *Grace and Gratitude: The Eucharistic Theology of John Calvin* (Minneapolis: Fortress Press, 1993), 19-20.

[92] Lionel Greve, "Freedom and Discipline in the Theology of John Calvin, William

Perkins and John Wesley: An Examination of the Origin and Nature of Pietism" (Ph.D., dissertation, Hartford Seminary Foundation, 1975), 124-25.

93 *CO* 31:19; translation taken from Barbara Pitkin, "Imitation of David: David as a Paradigm for Faith in Calvin's Exegesis of the Psalms," *Sixteenth Century Journal* 24: 4 (1993):847.

94 James Denney, *The Letters of Principal James Denney to His Family and Friends* (London: Hodder & Stoughton, n.d.), 9.

95 See James Luther Mays, "Calvin's Commentary on the Psalms: The Preface as Introduction," in *John Calvin and the Church: A Prism of Reform* (Louisville: Westminster/John Knox Press, 1990), 201-204.

96 Allan M. Harman, "The Psalms and Reformed Spirituality," *Reformed Theological Review* 53, 2 (1994), 58.

97 *Commentary* on the Psalms, 1:xxxvi-xxxix.

98 Ibid., Psalm 5:11, 118:5.

99 Ibid., 1:xxxix. See James A. De Jong, "'An Anatomy of All Parts of the Soul': Insights into Calvin's Spirituality from His Psalms Commentary," in *Calvinus Sacrae Scripturae Professor* (Grand Rapids: Eerdmans, 1994), 1-14.

100 *Commentary* on the Psalms, 1:xxxix.

101 John Walchenbach, "The Influence of David and the Psalms on the Life and Thought of John Calvin" (Th.M. thesis, Pittsburgh Theological Seminary, 1969).

102 More than 30,000 copies of the first complete, 500-page Genevan Psalter were printed by over fifty different French and Swiss publishers in the first year, and at least 27,400 copies were published in Geneva in the first few months (Jeffrey T. VanderWilt, "John Calvin's Theology of Liturgical Song," *Christian Scholar's Review* 25 [1996]:67. Cf. *Le Psautier de Genève, 1562-1685: Images, commentées et essai de bibliographie,* intro. J.D. Candaus (Geneva: Bibliothèque publique et universitaire, 1986), 1:16-18; John Witvliet, "The Spirituality of the Psalter: Metrical Psalms in Liturgy and Life in Calvin's Geneva," in *Calvin's Study Society Papers, 1995-1997,* ed. David Foxgrover (Grand Rapids: CRC, 1998), 93-117.

103 Unlike Luther, Calvin tried to avoid mixing secular tunes with sacred singing and believed that all Psalm-singing must be in the vernacular. The grounds for liturgical Psalm-singing are found in the evidence of Scripture and in the practices of the ancient church, Calvin said (VanderWilt, "John Calvin's Theology of Liturgical Song," 72, 74).

104 Preface to the Genevan Psalter (1562) (Charles Garside, Jr., *The Origins of Calvin's Theology of Music: 1536-1543* [Philadelphia: The American Philosophical Society, 1979], 32-33).

105 Cf. *John Calvin: Writings on Pastoral Piety*, ed and trans. Elsie Anne McKee (New York: Paulist Press, 2001), Part 3.

106 *CO* 10:12; cited in Garside, *The Origins of Calvin's Theology of Music,* 10.

107 Witvliet, "The Spirituality of the Psalter," 117.

108 W. Stanford Reid, "The Battle Hymns of the Lord: Calvinist Psalmody of the Sixteenth Century," in *Sixteenth Century Essays and Studies,* ed. C.S. Meyer (St. Louis: Foundation for Reformation Research, 1971), 2:47.

109 "The Shape of Reformed Piety," in Robin Maas and Gabriel O'Donnell, *Spiritual Traditions for the Contemporary Church* (Nashville: Abingdon Press, 1990), 215. Cf. Reid, "The Battle Hymns of the Lord," 2:36-54.

110 Inst. 3.6.2.

[111] Inst. 3.6.3.

[112] Inst. 3.7, 3.8.

[113] *Commentary* on 1 Timothy 4:7-8.

[114] This section was first translated into English in 1549 as *The Life and Conversation of a Christian Man* and has been reprinted often as *The Golden Booklet of the True Christian Life.*

[115] See R.D. Loggie, "Chief Exercise of Faith: An Exposition of Calvin's Doctrine of Prayer," *Hartford Quarterly* 5 (1965):65-81; H.W. Maurer, "An Examination of Form and Content in John Calvin's Prayers" (Ph.D. dissertation, Edinburgh, 1960).

[116] Due to space limitations, prayer is considered here in its personal dimension, but for Calvin prayer was also of vast importance in its communal aspect. See McKee, ed., *John Calvin*, Part 4, for a selection of individual and family prayers Calvin prepared as patterns for Genevan children, adults, and households, as well as a number of prayers from his sermons and biblical lectures. Cf. Thomas A. Lambert, "Preaching, Praying, and Policing the Reform in Sixteenth Century Geneva" (Ph.D. dissertation, University of Wisconsin-Madison, 1998), 393-480.

[117] Inst. 3.20.3.

[118] Inst. 3.20.3.

[119] Charles Partee, "Prayer as the Practice of Predestination," in *Calvinus Servus Christi,* ed. Wilhelm H. Neuser (Budapest: Pressabteilung des Raday-Kollegiums, 1988), 254.

[120] Inst. 3.20.4-16.

[121] Inst. 3.20.11.

[122] Inst. 3.20.34.

[123] Inst. 3.20.14; Ronald S. Wallace, *Calvin's Doctrine of the Christian Life* (London: Oliver and Boyd, 1959), 276-79.

[124] *Commentary* on Hebrews 7:26.

[125] Inst. 3.20.17.

[126] Greve, "Freedom and Discipline in the Theology of John Calvin," 143-44. For how Calvin's emphasis on prayer impacted the Reformed tradition, see Diane Karay Tripp, "Daily Prayer in the Reformed Tradition: An Initial Survey," *Studia Liturgica* 21 (1991):76-107, 190-219.

[127] Inst. 3.3.1-2, 6, 18, 20.

[128] Inst. 3.3.5, 9.

[129] Inst. 3.3.3; Randall C. Gleason, *John Calvin and John Owen on Mortification: A Comparative Study in Reformed Spirituality* (New York: Peter Lang, 1995), 61.

[130] Inst. 3.3.8-9.

[131] John H. Leith, *John Calvin's Doctrine of the Christian Life* (Louisville: Westminster/ John Knox Press, 1989), 70-74.

[132] Inst. 3.7.1.

[133] Inst. 3.7.2.

[134] Inst. 3.7.4-5.

[135] Inst. 3.7.7; Merwyn S. Johnson, "Calvin's Ethical Legacy," in *The Legacy of John Calvin,* ed. David Foxgrover (Grand Rapids: CRC 2000), 74.

[136] Inst. 3.7.8-10.

[137] Richard C. Gamble, "Calvin and Sixteenth-Century Spirituality," in *Calvin Studies Society Papers,* ed. David Foxgrover (Grand Rapids: CRC, 1998), 34-35.

[138] Inst. 3.8.1-2.

[139] Inst. 3.8.3-9.

[140] Inst. 3.8.7-8.

[141] Inst. 3.9.4.

[142] Inst. 3.9.5.

[143] Wallace, *Calvin's Doctrine of the Christian Life,* 170-95.

[144] Inst. 3.9.3.

[145] Inst. 3.10.

[146] Greve, "Freedom and Discipline in the Theology of John Calvin," 20.

[147] Leith, *John Calvin's Doctrine of the Christian Life,* 82-86.

[148] Battles, *The Piety of John Calvin,* 29.

[149] I. John Hesselink, "Calvin, Theologian of Sweetness" (unpublished paper delivered as The Henry Meeter Center for Calvin Studies Spring Lecture, March 9, 2000), 10-16.

[150] For Calvin on assurance, see Randall Zachman, *The Assurance of Faith: Conscience in the Theology of Martin Luther and John Calvin* (Minneapolis: Fortress Press, 1993); Joel R. Beeke, "Making Sense of Calvin's Paradoxes on Assurance of Faith," in *Calvin Studies Society Papers,* ed. David Foxgrover (Grand Rapids: CRC, 1998), 13-30, and *The Quest for Full Assurance: The Legacy of Calvin and His Successors* (Edinburgh: The Banner of Truth Trust, 1999), 39-72.

[151] Inst. 3.21.1.

[152] In *Selected Works of Calvin,* ed. and trans. Henry Beveridge (Grand Rapids: Baker, 1983), 1:c. For piety in Calvin's own life, see Ford Lewis Battles, *The Piety of John Calvin* (Grand Rapids: Baker, 1978), 16-20.

[153] Merwyn Johnson, "Calvin's Ethical Legacy," 79-83.

[154] Cf. Erroll Hulse, "The Preacher and Piety," in *The Preacher and Preaching,* ed. Samuel T. Logan, Jr. (Phillipsburg, N.J.: Presbyterian and Reformed, 1986), 71.

[155] Hughes Oliphant Old, "What is Reformed Spirituality? Played Over Again Lightly," in *Calvin Studies VII,* ed. J.H. Leith (Davidson, N.C.: n.p., 1994), 61.

2

Making Sense of Calvin's Paradoxes on Assurance of Faith

John Calvin's doctrine of the assurance of faith is replete with paradoxes that have often been misunderstood, even by Calvin scholars. For example, William Cunningham (1805-1861), a staunch Calvinist scholar, writes, "Calvin never contradicted himself so plainly and palpably as this [when], in immediate connection with the definition given from him of saving faith, he had made statements, with respect to the condition of the mind that may exist in believers, which cannot well be reconciled with the formal definition."[1]

After briefly presenting Calvin's understanding of faith and assurance and their paradoxical relationship, I will focus on four principles from which Calvin operates. Each will help make sense of Calvin's apparent contradictions on assurance. Combined, these principles confirm the thesis that Calvin actually developed a scriptural doctrine of assurance that confirms initial and ongoing spiritual experiences in the life of faith.[2]

Nature and definition of faith
Calvin's doctrine of assurance affirms the basic tenets of Martin Luther and Ulrich Zwingli and discloses emphases of his own. Like Luther and Zwingli, Calvin says faith is never merely assent (*assensus*), but involves both knowledge (*cognitio*) and trust (*fiducia*). He affirms that knowledge and trust are saving dimensions of the life of faith rather than notional matters. For Calvin, faith is not historical knowledge plus saving assent, as some of his successors would teach, but faith is a saving and certain knowledge joined with a saving and assured trust.[3]

Calvin held that knowledge is foundational to faith. Knowledge rests upon the Word of God, which is essentially the Holy Scriptures as well as the gospel and its proclamation.[4] Faith originates in the Word of God. Faith rests firmly upon God's Word; it always says amen to the Scriptures.[5] Hence, assurance must be sought *in* the Word and flows *out of* the

Ulrich Zwingli

Word.[6] Assurance is as inseparable from the Word as sunbeams are from the sun.

Faith is also inseparable from Christ and the promise of Christ, for the totality of the written Word is the living Word, Jesus Christ, in whom all God's promises are "yea and amen."[7] Faith rests on scriptural knowledge, and on promises that are Christ-directed and Christ-centered. True faith receives Christ as He is clothed in the gospel and graciously offered by the Father.[8]

Thus, true faith focuses upon the Scriptures in general, and particularly the promise of the grace of God in Christ. Calvin makes much of the promises of God as the ground of assurance, for these promises are based on the very nature of God, who cannot lie. Since God promises mercy to sinners in their misery, faith relies upon such promises.[9] The promises are fulfilled by Christ; therefore Calvin directs sinners to Christ and to the promises as if they were synonyms.[10] Rightly understood, faith rests on and appropriates the promises of God in Christ made known in Scripture.[11]

Since faith takes its character from the promise on which it rests, it takes on the infallible stamp of God's very Word. Consequently, faith possesses assurance in its very nature. Assurance, certainty, trust—such is the essence of faith.

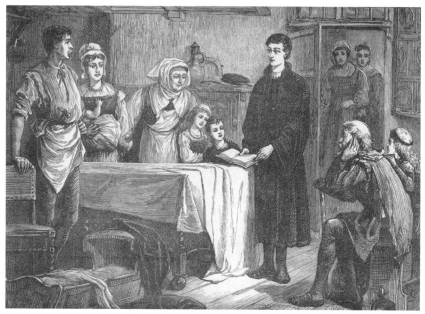

Young Calvin expounding the Bible to a family at Bourges.

This assured and assuring faith is the Holy Spirit's gift to the elect. The Spirit persuades the elect sinner of the reliability of God's promise in Christ and grants faith to embrace that Word.[12]

In short, for Calvin, assuring faith necessarily involves saving knowledge, the Scriptures, Jesus Christ, God's promises, the work of the Holy Spirit, and election. God Himself is the assurance of the elect. Assurance is gratuitously founded upon God.[13]

Consequently, Calvin's formal definition of faith reads like this: "Now we shall possess a right definition of faith if we call it a firm and certain knowledge of God's benevolence toward us, founded upon the truth of the freely given promise in Christ, both revealed to our minds and sealed upon our hearts through the Holy Spirit."[14] In essence, Calvin stresses that faith is assurance of God's promise in Christ and involves the whole man in the use of the mind, the application to the heart, and the surrendering of the will.[15]

Assurance of the essence of faith
More specifically, Calvin argues that faith involves more than objectively believing the promise of God; it involves personal, subjective assurance. In believing God's promise to sinners, the true believer

recognizes and celebrates that God is gracious and benevolent to him in particular. Faith is an assured knowledge "of God's benevolence toward us…revealed to our minds…sealed upon our hearts."[16] Faith embraces the gospel promise as more than impersonal abstraction; it is inseparable from personal certainty. Calvin writes, "Here, indeed, is the hinge on which faith turns: that we do not regard the promises of mercy that God offers as true only outside ourselves, but not at all in us; rather that we make them ours by inwardly embracing them."[17]

Thus, as Robert Kendall notes, Calvin repeatedly describes faith as "certainty (*certitudino*), a firm conviction (*solido persuasio*), assurance (*securitas*), firm assurance (*solida securitas*), and full assurance (*plena securitas*)."[18] While faith consists of knowledge, it is also marked by heartfelt assurance that is "a sure and secure possession of those things which God has promised us."[19]

Calvin emphasizes also throughout his commentaries that assurance is integral to faith.[20] He says that anyone who believes but lacks the conviction that he is saved by God is not a true believer after all. He writes:

> Briefly, he alone is a true believer, who convinced by a firm conviction that God is a kindly and well-disposed Father toward him, promises himself all things on the basis of his generosity; who, relying upon the promises of divine benevolence toward him, lays hold on an undoubted expectation of salvation…. No man is a believer, I say, except him who, leaning upon the assurance of his salvation, confidently triumphs over the devil and death.[21]

Calvin says that true believers must and do know themselves to be such: "Let this truth then stand sure—that no one can be called a son of God, who does not know himself to be such…. This so great an assurance, which dares to triumph over the devil, death, sin, and the gates of hell, ought to lodge deep in the hearts of all the godly; for our faith is nothing, except we feel assured that Christ is ours, and that the Father is in him propitious to us."[22] In exegeting 2 Corinthians 13:5, Calvin even states that those who doubt their union to Christ are reprobates: "[Paul] declares, that all are reprobates, who doubt whether they profess Christ and are a part of his body. Let us, therefore, reckon that alone to be right faith, which leads us to repose in safety in the favour of God, with no wavering opinion, but with a firm and steadfast assurance."

That kind of statement prompted a charge of incautiousness by William Cunningham and Robert Dabney.[23] A culling of Calvin's *Institutes*, commentaries and sermons, however, also presents a formidable number of equally intense, qualifying statements.

Faith and assurance versus unbelief

Throughout his lofty doctrine of faith, Calvin repeats these themes: unbelief dies hard; assurance is often contested by doubt; severe temptations, wrestlings, and strife are normative; Satan and the flesh assault faith; trust in God is hedged with fear.[24] Calvin freely acknowledges that faith is not retained without a severe struggle against unbelief, nor is it left untinged by doubt and anxiety. He writes: "Unbelief is, in all men, always mixed with faith.... For unbelief is so deeply rooted in our hearts, and we are so inclined to it, that not without hard struggle is each one able to persuade himself of what all confess with the mouth, namely, that God is faithful. Especially when it comes to reality itself, every man's wavering uncovers hidden weakness."[25]

According to Calvin, faith ought to be assuring, but no perfect assurance exists in this life. The believer will not be fully healed of unbelief until he dies. Though faith itself cannot doubt, faith is constantly harassed with the temptation of doubt.[26] The Christian strives for, but never wholly attains, uninterrupted assurance.

Calvin does allow for varying degrees of faith. Though secondary sources often downplay it, Calvin uses such concepts as "infancy of faith," "beginnings of faith," and "weak faith" more frequently even than Luther.[27] All faith begins in infancy, Calvin says. He writes: "The forbearance of Christ is great in reckoning as disciples those whose faith is so small. And indeed this doctrine extends generally to us all; for the faith which is now full grown had at first its infancy, nor is it so perfect in any as not to make it necessary that all to a man should make progress in believing."[28]

Expounding faith's maturation process more than its secret beginnings or final realization, Calvin asserts that assurance is proportional to faith's development. More specifically, he presents the Holy Spirit not only as the initiator of faith, but also as the cause and maintainer of its growth.[29] Faith, repentance, sanctification, and assurance are all progressive.[30]

In expounding John 20:3, Calvin seems to contradict his assertion that true believers know themselves as such when he testifies that the disciples were not aware of their faith as they approached the empty tomb: "There being so little faith, or rather almost no faith, both in the disciples and in the women, it is astonishing that they had so great zeal; and, indeed, it is not possible that religious feelings led them to seek Christ. *Some seed of faith, therefore, remained in their hearts, but quenched for a time, so that they were not aware of having what they had.* Thus, the Spirit of God often works in the elect in a secret manner" [emphasis mine].[31]

This prompts us to ask, How can Calvin say that assertions of faith are characterized by full assurance, yet still allow for the kind of faith that lacks assurance? The two concepts appear antithetical. Assurance is free from doubt, yet not free. It does not hesitate, yet can hesitate; it contains security, but may be beset with anxiety. The faithful have assurance, yet waver and tremble.

Making sense of antinomies
Calvin operated from four principles that address this complex issue. Each helps make sense of his apparent contradictions.

• Faith and experience
First, consider Calvin's need to distinguish between *the definition of faith* and *the reality of the believer's experience.* After explaining faith in the *Institutes* as embracing "great assurance," Calvin writes:

> Still, someone will say: "Believers *experience* something far different: In recognizing the grace of God toward themselves they are not only tried by disquiet, which often comes upon them, but they are repeatedly shaken by gravest terrors. For so violent are the temptations that trouble their minds as not to seem quite compatible with that certainty of faith." Accordingly, we shall have to solve this difficulty if we wish the above-stated doctrine to stand. Surely, while we teach that faith *ought* to be certain and assured, we cannot imagine any certainty that is not tinged with doubt, or any assurance that is not assailed.[32]

Later, Calvin writes: "And I have not forgotten what I have previously said, the memory of which is *repeatedly renewed by experience*: faith is tossed about by various doubts, so that the minds of the godly are *rarely* at peace."[33]

Those quotations, and other writings (most notably when dealing with the sacramental strengthening of faith[34]), indicate that, though Calvin is anxious to define faith and assurance together, he also recognizes that the Christian gradually grows into a fuller faith in God's promises. This recognition is implicit in Calvin's use of expressions such as "full faith" in God's promises, as though he is distinguishing between the exercise of faith and what he calls "full faith." In short, Calvin distinguishes between the "ought to" of faith and the "is" of faith in daily life. He writes: "By these words Paul obviously shows that there is no *right faith* except when we dare with tranquil hearts to stand in God's sight. This boldness arises only out of a sure confidence in divine benevolence and salvation. This is so true that the word *faith* is very often used for confidence.... When anything is defined we should…seek its very integrity and perfection. Now this is not to deny a place for growth."[35]

Calvin's definition of faith serves as a recommendation about how his readers ought "habitually and properly to think of faith."[36] Faith should always aim at full assurance, even if it cannot reach perfect assurance in experience. In principle, faith gains the victory (1 John 5:4); in practice, it recognizes that it has not yet fully apprehended (Phil. 3:12-13).

Nevertheless, the practice and experience of faith—weak as it sometimes may be—validates that faith which trusts in the Word. Calvin is not as interested in experiences as he is in validating Word-grounded faith. Experience confirms faith, Calvin says. Faith "requires full and fixed certainty, such as men are wont to have from things experienced and proved."[37] Both the object of faith and the validation of faith by experience are gifts of God that confirm His gracious character by means of His Word.

Thus, bare experience (*nuda experientia*) is not Calvin's goal, but experience grounded in the Word, flowing out of the fulfillment of the Word. Experimental knowledge of the Word is essential.[38] For Calvin, two kinds of knowledge are needed: knowledge by faith (*scientia fidei*) that is received from the Word, "though it is not yet fully revealed," and the knowledge of experience (*scientia experentiae*) "springing from the fulfilling of the Word."[39] The Word of God is primary to both, for experience teaches us to know God as He declares Himself to be in His Word.[40] Experience not consonant with Scripture is never experience of true faith. In short, though the believer's experience of true faith is far weaker than he desires, there is an essential unity in the Word between faith's perception (the *ought-to* dimension of faith) and experience (the *is* dimension of faith).

• Flesh versus spirit
The second principle that helps us understand Calvin's ought-to/is tension in faith is the principle of flesh versus spirit. Calvin writes:

> It is necessary to return to that division of flesh and spirit which we have mentioned elsewhere. It most clearly reveals itself at this point. Therefore the godly heart feels in itself a division because it is partly imbued with sweetness from its recognition of the divine goodness, partly grieves in bitterness from an awareness of its calamity; partly

rests upon the promise of the gospel, partly trembles at the evidence of its own iniquity; partly rejoices at the expectation of life, partly shudders at death. This variation arises from imperfection of faith, since in the course of the present life it never goes so well with us that we are wholly cured of the disease of unbelief and entirely filled and possessed by faith. Hence arise those conflicts, when unbelief, which reposes in the remains of the flesh, rises up to attack the faith that has been inwardly conceived.[41]

Like Luther, Calvin sets the ought-to/is dichotomy against the back-drop of spirit/flesh warfare.[42] Christians experience this spirit/flesh tension acutely because it is instigated by the Holy Spirit.[43] The paradoxes that permeate experiential faith (e.g., Romans 7:14-25 in the classical Reformed interpretation) find resolution in this tension: "So then with the mind [spirit] I myself serve the law of God; but with the flesh the law of sin" (v. 25). Hence Calvin writes: "Nothing prevents believers from being afraid and at the same time possessing the surest consolation.... Fear and faith [can] dwell in the same mind.... Surely this is so: We *ought* not to separate Christ from ourselves or ourselves from him. Rather we *ought* to hold fast bravely with both hands to that fellowship by which he has bound himself to us."[44]

Calvin sets the sure consolation of the spirit side-by-side with the imperfection of the flesh, for these are what the believer finds within himself. Since the final victory of the spirit over the flesh will only be fulfilled in Christ, the Christian finds himself in perpetual struggle in this life. His spirit fills him "with delight in recognizing the divine goodness" even as his flesh activates his natural proneness to unbelief.[45] He is beset with "daily struggles of conscience" as long as the vestiges of the flesh remain.[46] The believer's "present state is far short of the glory of God's children," Calvin writes. "Physically, we are dust and shadow, and death is always before our eyes. We are exposed to a thousand miseries...so that we always find a hell within us."[47] While still in the flesh, the believer may even be tempted to doubt the whole gospel.

The reprobate do not have these struggles for they neither love God nor hate sin. They indulge their own desires "without fear of God," Calvin says. But the more sincerely the believer "is devoted to God, he is just so much the more severely disquieted by the sense of his wrath."[48] Assurance of God's favor and a sense of His wrath only appear contrary, however. In reality, a reverential spirit of fear and trembling helps to establish faith and to prevent presumption, for fear stems from a proper sense of unworthiness while confidence arises from God's faithfulness.[49] This spirit/flesh tension keeps the believer from indulging in the flesh, and from yielding to despair.[50] The believer's spirit will never utterly despair; rather, faith grows on the very brink of despair. Strife strengthens faith. It makes the believer live circumspectly, not despondently.[51] With the help of the Holy Spirit, heavenly faith rises above all strife, trusting that God will be faithful to His own Word.

Even as he is tormented with fleshly doubts, the believer's spirit trusts God's mercy by invoking Him in prayer and by resting upon Him through the sacraments. By these means, faith gains the upper hand in its struggles with unbelief. "Faith ultimately triumphs over those difficulties which besiege and . . . imperil it. [Faith is like] a palm tree [that] strives against every burden and raises itself upward."[52]

In short, Calvin teaches that from the spirit of the believer rise hope, joy, and assurance; from the flesh, fear, doubt, and disillusionment. Though spirit and flesh operate simultaneously, imperfection and doubt are integral only to the flesh, not to faith. The works of the flesh often attend faith but do not mix with it. The believer may lose spiritual battles along the pathway of life, but he will not lose the ultimate war against the flesh. Prayer and the sacraments help the spirit of faith gain the ultimate victory.

• Germ of faith vs. consciousness of faith

Thirdly, despite the tensions between definition and experience, spirit and flesh, Calvin maintains that faith and assurance are not so mixed with unbelief that the believer is left with probability rather than certainty.[53] The smallest germ of faith contains assurance in its very essence, even when the believer is not always able to grasp this assurance due to weakness. The Christian may be tossed about with doubt and perplexity, but the seed of faith, implanted by the Spirit, cannot perish. Precisely because it is the Spirit's seed, faith retains assurance. The assurance increases and decreases in proportion to the rise and decline of faith's exercises, but the seed of faith can never be destroyed. Calvin says: "The root of faith can never be torn from the godly breast, but clings so fast to the inmost parts that, however faith seems to be shaken or to bend this way or that, its light is never so extinguished or snuffed out that it does not at least lurk as it were beneath the ashes."[54]

Calvin thus explains "weak assurance in terms of weak faith without thereby weakening the link between faith and assurance."[55] Assurance is normative but varies in degree and constancy in the believer's consciousness of it. Therefore, in responding to weak assurance, a pastor should not deny the organic tie between faith and assurance but should urge the pursuit of stronger faith through the use of the means of grace by the Spirit.

• Trinitarian framework

Through a fourth sweeping principle, namely, a Trinitarian framework for the doctrine of faith and assurance, Calvin spurs forward the doubt-prone believer. As surely as the election of the Father must prevail over the works of Satan, the righteousness of the Son over the sinfulness of the believer, and the assuring witness of the Spirit over the soul's infirmities, so surely faith shall and must conquer unbelief.

Calvin's arrangement of Book III of the *Institutes* reveals the movement of the grace of faith from God to man and man to God. The grace of faith is from the Father, in the Son, and through the Spirit, by which, in turn, the believer is brought into fellowship with the Son by the Spirit, and consequently is reconciled to the Father.

For Calvin, a complex set of factors establishes assurance, not the least of which is the Father's election and preservation in Christ. Hence he writes that "predestination duly considered does not shake faith, but rather affords the best confirmation of it,"[56] especially when viewed in the context of calling: "The firmness of our election is joined to our calling [and] is another means of establishing our assurance. For all whom [Christ] receives, the Father is said to have entrusted and committed to him to keep to eternal life."[57]

Decretal election is a sure foundation for preservation and assurance; election is not coldly causal. As Gordon Keddie notes: "Election is never seen, in Calvin, in a purely deterministic light, in which God…is viewed as 'a frightening idol' of 'mechanistic deterministic causality' and Christian experience is reduced to either cowering passivity or frantic activism, while waiting some 'revelation' of God's hidden decree for one's self. For Calvin, as indeed in Scripture, election does not threaten, but rather undergirds, the certainty of salvation."[58]

Such a foundation is possible only in a christocentric context; hence Calvin's constant accent on Christ as the mirror of election "wherein we must, and without self-deception may, contemplate our own election."[59] Election turns the believer's eyes from his hopeless inability to meet any conditions of salvation to focus on the hope of Jesus Christ as God's pledge of undeserved love and mercy.[60]

Through union with Christ, "the assurance of salvation becomes real and effective as the assurance of election."[61] Christ becomes ours in fulfillment of God's determination to redeem and resurrect us. Consequently, we ought not to think of Christ as "standing afar off, and not dwelling in us."[62] Since Christ is for us, truly contemplating Him is seeing Him form in us what He desires to give us, Himself above all. God has made Himself "little in Christ," Calvin states, so that we might comprehend and flee to Christ alone who can pacify our consciences.[63] Faith must begin, rest, and end in Christ. "True faith is so contained in Christ, that it neither knows, nor desires to know, anything beyond him," Calvin says.[64] Therefore, "we ought not to separate Christ from ourselves or ourselves from him."[65] Union with Christ merges objective and subjective assurance; to look to Christ alone for assurance means also to look to ourselves in Christ as His body. As Willis-Watkins notes, "It would be entirely hypothetical for faith to focus on ourselves apart from Christ—and it would be entirely hypothetical for faith to focus on Christ apart from his body.... Assurance of salvation is a derivative self-knowledge, whose focus remains on Christ as united to his body, the Church of which we are members."[66]

In this christological manner, Calvin reduces the distance between God's objective decree of election and the believer's subjective lack of assurance that he is elect. For Calvin, election answers, rather than raises, the question of assurance. In Christ, the believer sees his election; in the gospel, he hears of his election.

Nevertheless, Calvin is acutely aware that a person may think that the Father has entrusted him to Christ when such is not the case. It is one thing to underscore Christ's task in the Trinitarian salvific economy as the recipient and guardian of the elect; the center, author, and foundation of election; the guarantee, promise, and mirror of the believer's election and salvation. But it is quite another to know how to inquire about whether a person has been joined to Christ by a true faith. Many appear to be Christ's who are strangers to Him. Says Calvin: "It daily happens that those who seemed to be Christ's fall away from him again.... Such persons never cleaved to Christ with the heartfelt trust in which certainty of salvation has, I say, been established for us."[67]

Calvin never preached to console his flock into false assurance of salvation.[68] Many scholars minimize Calvin's emphasis on the need for a subjective, experiential realization of faith and election by referring to Calvin's practice of approaching his congregation as saved hearers. They misunderstand. Though Calvin practiced what he called "a judgment of charity" (i.e., addressing as saved those church members who maintain a commendable, external lifestyle), he also frequently asserted that only a minority receive the preached Word with saving faith. He says: "For though all, without exception, to whom God's Word is preached, are taught, yet scarce one in ten so much as tastes it; yea, scarce one in a hundred profits to the extent of being enabled, thereby, to proceed in a right course to the end."[69]

For Calvin, much that resembles faith lacks a saving character. He thus speaks of unformed faith, implicit faith, the preparation of faith, temporary faith, an illusion of faith, a false show of faith, shadow-types of faith, transitory faith, and faith under a cloak of hypocrisy.[70]

Self-deception is a real possibility, Calvin says. Because the reprobate often feel something much like the faith of the elect,[71] self-examination is essential. He writes: "Let us learn to examine ourselves, and to search whether those interior marks by which God distinguishes his children from strangers belong to us, viz., the living root of piety and faith."[72] Happily, the truly saved are delivered from self-deception through proper examination directed by the Holy Spirit. Calvin says: "In the meantime, the faithful are taught to examine themselves with solicitude and humility, lest carnal security insinuate itself, instead of the assurance of faith."[73]

Even in self-examination, Calvin emphasizes Christ. He says we must examine ourselves to see if we are placing our trust in *Christ alone*, for this is the fruit of biblical experience. Anthony Lane says that for Calvin self-examination is not so much "Am I *trusting* in Christ?" as it is "Am I trusting in *Christ*?"[74] Self-examination must always direct us to Christ and His promise. It must never be done apart from the help of the Holy Spirit, who alone can shed light upon Christ's saving work in the believer's soul. Apart from Christ, the Word, and the Spirit, Calvin says, "if you contemplate yourself, that is sure damnation."[75]

Thus, Calvin's line of reasoning proceeds like this: (1) The purpose of election embraces salvation. (2) The elect are not chosen for anything in themselves, but only in Christ. (3) Since the elect are in Christ, the assurance of their election and salvation can never be found in themselves or in the Father apart from Christ. (4) Rather, their assurance is to be found in Christ; hence, communion with Him is vital.

The question remains, however: How do the elect enjoy such communion, and how does that produce assurance? Calvin's answer is pneumatological: The Holy Spirit applies Christ and His benefits to the hearts and lives of guilty, elect sinners, through which they are assured by saving faith that Christ belongs to them and they to Him. The Holy Spirit especially confirms within them the reliability of God's promises in Christ. Thus, personal assurance is never divorced from the election of the Father, the redemption of the Son, the application of the Spirit, and the instrumental means of saving faith.

The Holy Spirit has an enormous role in the application of redemption, Calvin says. As personal comforter, seal, and earnest, the Holy Spirit assures the believer of his adoption: "The Spirit of God gives us such a testimony, that when he is our guide and teacher our spirit is made sure of the adoption of God; for our mind of itself, without the preceding testimony of the Spirit, could not convey to us this assurance."[76] The Holy Spirit's work underlies all assurance of salvation, without detracting from the role of Christ, for the Spirit is the Spirit of Christ who assures the believer by leading him to Christ and His benefits, and by working out those benefits within him.[77]

The unity of Christ and the Spirit has sweeping implications for the doctrine of assurance. Most recent scholars minimize Calvin's emphasis on the necessity of the Spirit's work in assuring a believer of God's promises. The *ground* of assurance supposedly is God's promises, in Christ, and/or in the Word of God, whereas the *cause* of assurance is the Spirit, who works it in the heart. Cornelis Graafland argues, however, that this distinction is too simplistic, since the Spirit always works as the Spirit of Christ. Hence the objective and subjective elements in assurance cannot be so readily separated; objective salvation in Christ is bound to subjective sealing by the Spirit. Graafland concludes that "Christ in and through His Spirit is the ground of our faith."[78]

Moreover, for Calvin, a believer's objective reliance upon God's promises as the primary ground for assurance must be subjectively sealed by the Holy Spirit for true assurance. The reprobate may claim God's promises without experiencing the feeling (*sensus*) or consciousness of those promises. The Spirit often works in the reprobate, but in an inferior manner. Calvin says the minds of the reprobate may be momentarily illumined so that they may seem to have a beginning of faith; nevertheless, they "never receive anything but a confused awareness of grace."[79]

On the other hand, the elect are regenerated with incorruptible seed.[80] They receive subjective benefits that the reprobate never taste.

They alone receive the promises of God as truth in the inward parts; they alone receive the testimony that can be called "the enlightening of the Spirit"; they alone receive experiential, intuitive knowledge of God as He offers Himself to them in Christ.[81] Spirit-worked faith in the promises of God effects union with Christ.[82] Calvin says the elect alone come to "be ravished and wholly kindled to love God"; they are "borne up to heaven itself" and "admitted to the most hidden treasures of God."[83] "The Spirit, strictly speaking, seals forgiveness of sins in the elect alone, so that they apply it by special faith to their own use."[84] The elect alone come to know special faith and a special inward testimony.

According to Heribert Schutzeichel, a Roman Catholic theologian, Calvin's emphasis on special faith and a special testimony is reminiscent of the Council of Trent's insistence that assurance is always revealed in a special manner.[85] For the Council of Trent, however, assurance is special and rare; for Calvin, assurance is special and normative, for it is part of the essence of faith.[86] For Trent, assurance is separate from the Word; for Calvin, assurance is always involved with the Word. The Spirit's assuring testimony does not add to the Word through some mystical vision or audible voice;[87] rather, it accompanies the Word. The Spirit's seal is a personal testimony, by means of the gospel, that God's promises are for the believer personally. Says Calvin: "Assurance...is a thing that is above the capacity of the human mind, it is the part of the Holy Spirit to confirm within us what God promises in his Word."[88] The reprobate never experience such assurance, for they never taste the union of the objective truth of God's promise and the subjective sealing of the Spirit.

Ultimately, however, when distinguishing the elect from the reprobate, Calvin speaks more about what the Spirit does *in us* than what Christ does *for us*, for here the line of demarcation is sharper. He speaks much of inward experience, of feeling, of enlightenment, of perception, even of "violent emotion."[89] Though aware of the dangers of excessive introspection, Calvin also recognizes that the promises of God are sufficient only when they are brought by the Spirit within the scope, experience, and obedience of faith.[90]

To summarize Calvin's position, all three members of the Trinity are involved in the believer's assurance of faith. Moreover, the work of Christ and the Holy Spirit are complementary. When Calvin replies to Pighius that "Christ is a thousand testimonies to me," he is saying that Christ is an overwhelming, foundational, and primary source of assurance for him precisely because of the Spirit's application of Christ and

His benefits to him. Again, when Berkouwer says that Calvin's *Institutes* never tire "of repeating the warning against every attempt at gaining assurance apart from Christ and His cross,"[91] this must be understood in terms of the work of the Spirit, since no one can ever be assured of Christ without the Spirit.[92] The Holy Spirit reveals to the believer through His Word that God is a well-disposed Father, and enables him to embrace Christ's promises by faith.

Conclusion

These four principles operative in Calvin—faith and experience, flesh versus spirit, the germ of faith versus the consciousness of faith, and the Trinitarian framework—allow us to draw several conclusions:

First, Calvin's concept of faith includes assurance in the essence and quintessence of faith, without demanding that the believer feel assurance at all times. Many Calvin scholars, including William Cunningham, have overlooked that concept. Cunningham says the only way to remove the apparent contradiction from Calvin is to proceed "upon the assumption that the definition was intended not so much to state what was essential to true faith and always found in it, as to describe what true faith is, or includes, in its most perfect condition and its highest exercise."[93] But for Calvin, assurance is both essential for faith and contained in all its exercises, regardless of the believer's consciousness of it.

Second, through this combination of principles, any radical discontinuity between Calvin and the Calvinists with regard to faith and assurance must be rejected. Despite varying emphases, Calvin and the Calvinists agree that assurance may be possessed without always being known.[94] When Calvin defines faith as including assurance, he is not contradicting the Westminster Confession's distinction between faith and assurance, for he and the Confession do not have the same concern in mind. Calvin is defining faith in its assuring character; the Confession, what assurance is as a self-conscious, experimental phenomenon.[95]

Third, though Cunningham rightly asserts that Calvin did not work out all the details of the relationship of faith and assurance, he, Robert Dabney, and Charles Hodge go too far in saying Calvin's doctrine is contradictory or ignorant of the issues that would surface in the century to come.[96] Though the spiritual climate of the seventeenth century would vary considerably from the sixteenth, a thorough study of Calvin on the faith-assurance relationship reveals a tightly knit, integrated doctrine that is true to Scripture and experience. Calvin's emphasis on assurance throughout his *Institutes*, commentaries, and sermons proves that the issue of personal assurance was very much alive in his generation. Phrases such as "this is how to come to assurance," "this is the kind of assurance we have," and "this is where our assurance rests," show that Calvin is speaking to an audience who knew little assurance.[97] He is addressing individuals newly delivered from the bondage of Rome, which had taught that assurance was heretical. By teaching that assurance ought to be normative, though unbelief will not die easily, Calvin aims to build assurance in the church on solid, biblical grounds. He says unbelief is only a disease and an interruption of faith that will not have dominion over faith on a daily basis, nor shall it ultimately triumph.[98] Rather, God "wishes to cure the disease [of unbelief] so that among us he may obtain full faith in his promises."[99] Because it is of God, faith must triumph, for God will use even doubts and assaults to strengthen faith. Through faith's perpetual triumphs in God, Calvin encourages children of God who frequently doubt by pointing them Godward to find the assuring principle of faith.

---

[1] *Reformers and the Theology of the Reformation* (1856; repr. London: Banner of Truth Trust, 1967), 120. Cf. Robert L. Dabney, *Lectures in Systematic Theology* (1871; repr. Grand Rapids: Zondervan, 1972), 702; Paul Helm, *Calvin and the Calvinists* (Edinburgh: Banner of Truth Trust), 25-26; Cornelis Graafland, *De zekerheid van het geloof: Een onderzoek naar de geloofsbeschouwing van enige vertegenwoordigers van reformatie en nadere reformatie* (Wageningen: H. Veenman & Zonen, 1961), 21-22n.

[2] Works that deal exclusively with Calvin's doctrine of faith and assurance include S. P. Dee, *Het geloofsberijp van Calvijn* (Kampen: J. H. Kok, 1918); W. E. Stuermann, "A Critical Study of Calvin's Concept of Faith" (Ph.D. dissertation, University of Tulsa, 1952); K. Exalto, *De Zekerheid des Geloofs bij Calvijn* (Apeldoorn: Willem de Zwijgerstichting, 1978); Victor A. Shepherd, *The Nature and Function of Faith in the Theology of John Calvin* (Macon, Ga.: Mercer University Press, 1983).

Though Luther's struggles in attaining faith and assurance, documented copiously by himself and others, are well-known, J. H. Merle D'Aubigne provides evidence that Calvin's "chamber became the theatre of struggles as fierce as those in the cell at Erfurth" (*History of the Reformation in Europe in the Time of Calvin* [London: Longman, Green, Longman, Roberts & Green, 1863], 1:522). Cf. Calvin's preface to his commentary on the Psalms (*Calvin's Commentaries* [repr. Grand Rapids: Baker, 1979], 4:xxxvii-xlix [hereafter: *Commentary*]); C. Harinck, "Geloof en zekerheid bij Calvijn," *De Saambinder* 68 (1990) #38:5-6; H. J. Couvee, *Calvijn en Calvinisme: Een studie over Calvijn en ons geestelijk en kerkelijk leven* (Utrecht: Kemink en Zoon, 1936), 70-95.

[3] John Calvin, *Institutes of the Christian Religion,* [hereafter: Inst.], ed. by John T. McNeill and trans. by F. L. Battles (Philadelphia: Westminster Press, 1960), Book 3, chapter 2, section 14 (hereafter: 3.2.14). For Calvin's Latin works, see *Opera quae supersunt omnia*, ed. by Guilielmus Baum, Eduardus Cunitz, and Eduardus Reuss,

vols. 29-87 in Corpus Reformatorum (Brunsvigae: C. A. Schwetschke et filium, 1863-1900; hereafter: *CO*).

[4] For Calvin, the "word of the Lord" can also refer to the spoken word, especially to the "proclamation of the grace of God manifested in Christ" (Inst. 2.9.2; *Commentary* on 1 Peter 1:25). Cf. David Foxgrover, "John Calvin's Understanding of Conscience" (Ph.D. dissertation, Claremont, 1978), 407ff.

[5] *Commentary* on John 3:33; Psalm 43:3. Cf. Exalto, *De Zekerheid des Geloofs bij Calvijn*, p. 24. Edward Dowey mistakenly dichotomizes the Scriptures and assurance when he asserts that the center of Calvin's doctrine of faith is assurance rather than the authority of the Scriptures. For Calvin, the separation of the Word of God from assurance is unthinkable (*The Knowledge of God in Calvin's Theology* [New York: Columbia University Press, 1965], 182).

[6] *Commentary* on Matthew 8:13; John 4:22.

[7] *Commentary* on Genesis 15:6; Luke 2:21.

[8] Inst. 3.2.32.

[9] Inst. 3.2.29, 41. *Commentary* on Acts 2:39.

[10] Inst. 3.2.32; *Commentary* on Romans 4:3, 18; Hebrews 11:7, 11.

[11] Inst. 3.2.6; 3.2.15; *Commentary* on 1 John 3:2.

[12] Inst. 3.2.16.

[13] *Commentary* on Romans 8:16; 1 Peter 1:4; Hebrews 4:10.

[14] Inst. 3.2.7.

[15] Cf. Inst. 1.15.7; 3.2.8; A. N. S. Lane, "Calvin's Doctrine of Assurance," *Vox Evangelica* 11 (1979):42-43, 52n; Robert Letham, "Saving Faith and Assurance in Reformed Theology: Zwingli to the Synod of Dort" (Ph.D. dissertation, University of Aberdeen, 1979), 2:70n.

[16] Inst. 3.2.7.

[17] Inst. 3.2.16; cf. 3.2.42.

[18] Robert T. Kendall, *Calvin and English Calvinism to 1649* (New York: Oxford University Press, 1979), 19; cf. Inst. 3.2.6, 3.2.16, 3.2.22.

[19] Inst. 3.2.41; 3.2.14.

[20] *Commentary* on Acts 2:29 and 1 Corinthians 2:12.

[21] Inst. 3.2.16.

[22] *Commentary* on Romans 8:16, 34; Inst. 3.2.2.

[23] Cunningham, *Reformers*, 119ff.; Robert L. Dabney, *Discussions: Evangelical and Theological* (1890; repr. London: Banner of Truth Trust, 1967), 1:216ff.; idem, *Systematic Theology*, 702, 709.

[24] Inst. 3.2.7; *Commentary* on Matthew 8:25; Luke 2:40.

[25] Inst. 3.2.4, 3.2.15.

[26] Inst. 3.2.18-20.

[27] Cf. Inst. 3.2.17-21; *Commentary* on Galatians 4:6.

[28] Ibid., 89-90.

[29] Inst. 3.2.33ff.

[30] Inst. 3.2.14, 3.3.9; *Commentary* on John 2:11; 1 John 5:13. Stuermann correctly notes that though Calvin was no perfectionist, the idea of growth and development is ubiquitous in his writings ("A Critical Study of Calvin's Concept of Faith," 117).

[31] Cf. Inst. 3.2.12.

[32] Cf. Inst. 3.2.16-17; emphasis mine.

[33] Cf. Inst. 3.2.51, emphasis mine.

[34] Cf. esp. Inst. 4.14.7.

[35] Inst. 3.2.15, 3.3.8.

[36] Helm, *Calvin and the Calvinists*, 26.

[37] Inst. 3.2.15.

[38] Inst. 1.7.5.

[39] Cf. Charles Partee, "Calvin and Experience," *Scottish Journal of Theology* 26 (1973): 169-81 and W. Balke, "The Word of God and *Experientia* according to Calvin," in *Calvinus Ecclesiae Doctor* (Kampen: Kok, 1978), 23ff., for Calvin's understanding of experience. Balke points out that Calvin's writings are full of expressions such as *"experientia docet, ostendit, clamat, confirmat, demonstrat, convincit, testatur"* (ibid., 20).

[40] Inst. 1.10.2.

[41] Inst. 3.2.18.

[42] Cf. C. A. Hall, *With the Spirit's Sword: The Drama of Spiritual Warfare in the Theology of John Calvin* (Richmond: John Knox Press, 1970).

[43] Cf. Shepherd, *Faith in the Theology of John Calvin*, 24-28.

[44] Inst. 3.2.24, emphasis mine.

[45] Inst. 3.2.18, 3.2.20.

[46] *Commentary* on John 13:9.

[47] *Commentary* on 1 John 3:2.

[48] *Commentary* on Psalm 6:6.

[49] Inst. 3.20.11.

[50] Inst. 3.2.17.

[51] Inst. 3.2.22-23.

[52] Inst. 3.2.17.

[53] Cf. Graafland, *Zekerheid van het geloof,* 31n.

[54] Inst. 3.2.21.

[55] A. N. S. Lane, "The Quest for the Historical Calvin," *Evangelical Quarterly* 55 (1983):103.

[56] Inst. 3.24.9.

[57] Inst. 3.24.6.

[58] Gordon J. Keddie, "'Unfallible Certenty of the Pardon of Sinne and Life Everlasting': the Doctrine of Assurance in the Theology of William Perkins," *Evangelical Quarterly* 48 (1976):231; cf. G. C. Berkouwer, *Divine Election*, trans. Hugo Bekker (Grand Rapids: Eerdmans, 1960), 10ff.

[59] Inst. 3.24.5; cf. John Calvin, *Sermons on the Epistle to the Ephesians* (repr. Edinburgh: Banner of Truth Trust, 1973), 47; idem, *Sermons from Job* (Grand Rapids: Eerdmans, 1952), 41ff.; *CO* 8:318-321; 9:757.

[60] Inst. 3.24.6; William H. Chalker, "Calvin and Some Seventeenth Century English Calvinists" (Ph.D. dissertation, Duke, 1961), 66.

[61] Wilhelm Niesel, *The Theology of Calvin*, trans. Harold Knight (1956; repr. Grand Rapids: Baker, 1980), 196. Cf. Inst. 3.1.1; Shepherd, *Faith in the Theology of John Calvin*, 51.

[62] Inst. 3.2.24.

[63] *Commentary* on 1 Peter 1:20.

[64] *Commentary* on Ephesians 4:13.

[65] Inst. 3.2.24.

[66] David Willis-Watkins, "The Third Part of Christian Freedom Misplaced, Being an Inquiry into the Lectures of the Late Rev. Samuel Willard on the Assembly's

Shorter Catechism," in *Later Calvinism: International Perspectives*, ed. W. Fred Graham (Kirksville, Mo.: Sixteenth Century Journal, 1994), 484-85.

[67] Inst. 3.24.7.

[68] Cf. Cornelis Graafland, "'Waarheid in het Binnenste': Geloofszekerheid bij Calvijn en de Nadere Reformatie," in *Een Vaste Burcht*, ed. K. Exalto (Kampen: Kok, 1989), 65-67.

[69] *Commentary* on Psalm 119:101. More than thirty times in his *Commentary* (e.g., Acts 11:23 and Psalm 15:1) and nine times within the scope of Inst. 3.21-24, Calvin refers to the fewness of those who possess vital faith.

[70] Inst. 3.2.3, 5, 10-11. For Calvin on temporary faith, see "'Temporary Faith' and the Certainty of Salvation," *Calvin Theological Journal* 15 (1980):220-32; Lane, "Calvin's Doctrine of Assurance," 45-46; Exalto, *De Zekerheid des Geloofs bij Calvijn*, 15-20, 27-30.

[71] Inst. 3.2.11.

[72] *Commentary* on Ezekiel 13:9. David Foxgrover shows that Calvin relates the need for self-examination to a great variety of topics: knowledge of God and ourselves, judgment, repentance, confession, affliction, the Lord's Supper, providence, duty, the kingdom of God, etc. ("John Calvin's Understanding of Conscience," 312ff.). Cf. J. P. Pelkonen, "The Teaching of John Calvin on the Nature and Function of the Conscience," *Lutheran Quarterly* 21 (1969):24-88.

[73] Inst. 3.2.7.

[74] "Calvin's Doctrine of Assurance," 47.

[75] Inst. 3.2.24.

[76] *Commentary* on Romans 8:16 and 2 Corinthians 1:21-22. Cf. Inst. 3.2.11, 34, 41; *Commentary* on John 7:37-39; Acts 2:4; 3:8; 5:32; 13:48; 16:14; 23:11; Romans 8:15-17; 1 Corinthians 2:10-13; Galatians 3:2, 4:6; Ephesians 1:13-14, 4:30; *Tracts and Treatises*, 3:253ff.; J. K. Parratt, "The Witness of the Holy Spirit: Calvin, the Puritans and St. Paul," *Evangelical Quarterly* 41 (1969):161-68.

[77] Inst. 3.2.34.

[78] "Waarheid in het Binnenste," 58-60.

[79] Inst. 3.2.11.

[80] Inst. 3.2.41.

[81] Inst. 1.4.1; 2.6.4, 19.

[82] Balke, "The Word of God and *Experientia* according to Calvin," 26.

[83] Inst. 3.2.41.

[84] Inst. 3.2.11.

[85] *Katholische Beitrage zur Calvinforschung* (Trier: Paulinus-Verlag, 1988).

[86] *Tracts and Treatises*, 3:135ff. Cf. Michael A. Eaton, *Baptism with the Spirit: The Teaching of Dr Martyn Lloyd-Jones* (Leicester: InterVarsity Press, 1989), 44-55.

[87] *Commentary* on Acts 7:31; 9:15; 23:11.

[88] *Commentary* on 2 Corinthians 1:22.

[89] "Too few scholars have been willing to recognize the intensely experiential nature of Calvin's doctrine of faith" (M. Charles Bell, *Calvin and Scottish Theology: The Doctrine of Assurance* [Edinburgh: Handsel Press, 1985], 20).

[90] Inst. 3.1.1. Cf. Randall C. Zachman, *The Assurance of Faith: Conscience in the Theology of Martin Luther and John Calvin* (Minneapolis: Fortress, 1993), 198-203.

[91] *Faith and Perseverance*, trans. Robert Knudsen (Grand Rapids: Eerdmans, 1958), 61.

[92] Inst. 3.2.35.

[93] *Reformers,* 120; cf. Gerrit H. Kersten, *Reformed Dogmatics,* trans. J. R. Beeke and J. C. Weststrate (Grand Rapids: Eerdmans, 1983), 2:404.

[94] *Commentary* on John 20:3. Cf. Peter Lewis cited in Errol Hulse, *The Believer's Experience* (Haywards Heath, Sussex: Carey Pub., 1977), 128-29.

[95] *Westminster Confession of Faith,* ch. 18. Cf. Sinclair Ferguson, "The Westminster Conference, 1976," *The Banner of Truth* no. 168 (1977):20.

[96] Cunningham, *Reformers,* p. 120; Dabney, *Discussions,* 1:216; Charles Hodge, *Exposition of 1 and 2 Corinthians* (repr. Wilmington, Del.: Sovereign Grace, 1972), 367.

[97] Inst. 3.2.22.

[98] Inst. 3.2.24.

[99] Inst. 3.2.15.

3

John Calvin: Teacher and Practitioner of Evangelism

Many scholars would take issue with the title of this chapter. Some would say that Roman Catholicism kept the evangelistic torch of Christianity lit via the powerful forces of the papacy, the monasteries, and the monarch while Calvin and the Reformers tried to extinguish it.[1] But others would assert that John Calvin, the father of Reformed and Presbyterian doctrine and theology, was largely responsible for relighting the torch of biblical evangelism during the Reformation.[2]

Some also credit Calvin with being a theological father of the Reformed missionary movement.[3] Views of Calvin's attitude toward evangelism and missions have ranged from hearty to moderate support on the positive side,[4] and from indifference to active opposition on the negative side.[5]

A negative view of Calvin's evangelism is usually a result of:

- A failure to study Calvin's writings prior to drawing conclusions,
- A failure to understand Calvin's view of evangelism within his own historical context, and/or
- Preconceived doctrinal notions about Calvin and his theology. Some critics naively assert that Calvin's doctrine of election virtually negates evangelism.

To assess Calvin's view of evangelism correctly, we must understand what Calvin himself had to say on the subject. Second, we must look at the entire scope of Calvin's evangelism, both in his teaching and his practice. We can find scores of references to evangelism in Calvin's *Institutes*, commentaries, sermons, and letters. Then we can look at Calvin's evangelistic work (1) in his own flock, (2) in his home city of Geneva, (3) in greater Europe, and (4) in mission opportunities overseas. As we shall see, Calvin was more of an evangelist than is commonly recognized.

Calvin: Teacher of Evangelism

How was Calvin's teaching evangelistic? In what way did his instruction obligate believers to seek the conversion of all people, those within the church as well as those in the world outside it?

Along with other Reformers, Calvin taught evangelism in a general way by earnestly proclaiming the gospel and by reforming the church according to biblical requirements. More specifically, Calvin taught evangelism by focusing on the universality of Christ's kingdom and the responsibility of Christians to help extend that kingdom.

The universality of Christ's kingdom is an oft-repeated theme in Calvin's teaching.[6] Calvin says all three persons of the Trinity are involved in the spreading of the kingdom. The Father will show "not only in one corner, what true religion is...but he will send forth his voice to the extreme limits of the earth."[7] Jesus came "to extend his grace over all the world."[8] And the Holy Spirit descended to "reach all the ends and extremities of the world."[9] In short, innumerable offspring "who shall be spread over the whole earth" will be born to Christ.[10] And the triumph of Christ's kingdom will become manifest everywhere among the nations.[11]

How will the triune God extend His kingdom throughout the world? Calvin's answer involves both God's sovereignty and our responsibility. He says the work of evangelism is God's work, not ours, but God will use us as His instruments. Citing the parable of the sower, Calvin explains that Christ sows the seed of life everywhere (Matt. 13:24-30), gathering His church not by human means but by heavenly power.[12] The gospel "does not fall from the clouds like rain," however, but is "brought by the hands of men to where God has sent it."[13] Jesus teaches us that God "uses our work and summons us to be his instruments in cultivating his field."[14] The power to save rests with God, but He reveals His salvation through the preaching of the gospel.[15] God's evangelism causes our evangelism.[16] We are His co-workers, and He allows us to participate in "the honor of constituting his own Son governor over the whole world."[17]

Calvin taught that the ordinary method of "collecting a church" is by the outward voice of men; "for though God might bring each person to himself by a secret influence, yet he employs the agency of men, that he may awaken in them an anxiety about the salvation of each other."[18] He goes so far as to say, "Nothing retards so much the progress of Christ's kingdom as the paucity of ministers."[19] Still, no human effort has the final word. It is the Lord, says Calvin, who "causes the voice of the gospel to resound not only in one place, but far and wide through the whole world."[20] The gospel is not preached at random to all nations but by the decree of God.[21]

According to Calvin, this joining together of divine sovereignty and human responsibility in evangelism offers the following lessons:

1. As Reformed evangelists, we must pray daily for the extension of Christ's kingdom. As Calvin says, "We must daily desire that God gather churches unto himself from all parts of the earth."[22] Since it pleases God to use our prayers to accomplish His purposes, we must pray for the conversion of the heathen.[23] Calvin writes, "It ought to be the great object of our daily wishes, that God would collect churches for himself from all the countries of the earth, that he would enlarge their numbers, enrich them with gifts, and establish a legitimate order among them."[24] By daily prayer for God's kingdom to come, we "profess ourselves servants and children of God deeply committed to his reputation."[25]

2. We must not become discouraged by a lack of visible success in evangelistic effort, but pray on. "Our Lord exercises the faith of his children, in that he doth not out of hand perform the things which he had promised them. And this thing ought specially to be applied to the reign of our Lord Jesus Christ," Calvin writes. "If God pass over a day or a year [without giving fruit], it is not for us to give over, but we must in the meanwhile pray and not doubt but that he heareth our voice."[26] We must keep praying, believing that "Christ shall manifestly exercise the power given to him for our salvation and for that of the whole world."[27]

3. We must work diligently for the extension of Christ's kingdom, knowing that our work will not be in vain. Our salvation obligates us to work for the salvation of others. Calvin says, "We are called by the Lord on this condition, that everyone should afterwards strive to lead others to the truth, to restore the wandering to the right way, to extend a helping hand to the fallen, to win over those that are without."[28] Moreover, it is not enough for every man to be busy with other ways of serving God. "Our zeal must extend yet further to the drawing of other men." We must do everything we are capable of to draw all men on earth to God.[29]

There are many reasons why we must evangelize. Calvin offers the following:

• God commands us to do so. "We should remember that the

gospel is preached not only by the command of Christ but at his urging and leading."[30]

- God leads us by example. Like our gracious God who wooed us, we must have our "arms extended, as he has, toward those outside" of us.[31]
- We want to glorify God. True Christians yearn to extend God's truth everywhere that "God may be glorified."[32]
- We want to please God. As Calvin writes, "It is a sacrifice well-pleasing to God to advance the spread of the gospel."[33] To five students who were sentenced to death for preaching in France, Calvin wrote, "Seeing that [God] employs your life in so worthy a cause as is the witness of the gospel, doubt not that it must be precious to him."[34]
- We have a duty to God. "It is very just that we should labor...to further the progress of the gospel," says Calvin;[35] "it is our duty to proclaim the goodness of God to every nation."[36]
- We have a duty to our fellow sinners. Our compassion for sinners should be intensified by our knowledge that "God cannot be sincerely called upon by others than those to whom, through the preaching of the gospel, his kindness and gentle dealings have become known."[37] Consequently, every encounter with other human beings should motivate us to bring them to the knowledge of God.[38]
- We are grateful to God. Those who are indebted to God's mercy are bound to become, like the psalmist, "the loud herald of the grace of God" to all men.[39] If salvation is possible for me, a great sinner, then it is possible for others. I owe it to God to strive for the salvation of others; if I do not, I am a contradiction. As Calvin says, "Nothing could be more inconsistent concerning the nature of faith than that deadness which would lead a man to disregard his brethren, and to keep the light of knowledge...in his own breast."[40] We must, out of gratitude, bring the gospel to others in distress, or appear ungrateful to God for our own salvation.[41]

Calvin never assumed that the missionary task was completed by the apostles. Instead, he taught that every Christian must testify by word and deed of God's grace to everyone he or she meets.[42] Calvin's affirmation of the priesthood of all believers involves the church's participation in Christ's prophetic, priestly, and kingly ministry. It commissions believers to confess Christ's name to others (prophetical task), to pray for their salvation (priestly task), and to disciple them (kingly task). It is the basis for powerful evangelistic activity on the part of the entire living church "to the world's end."[43]

Calvin: Practitioner of Evangelism

Calvin believed we must make full use of the opportunities God gives to evangelize. "When an opportunity for edification presents itself, we should realize that a door has been opened for us by the hand of God in order that we may introduce Christ into that place and we should not refuse to accept the generous invitation that God thus gives us," he writes.[44]

On the other hand, when opportunities are restricted and doors of evangelism are closed to our witness, we should not persist in trying to do what cannot be done. Rather, we should pray and seek for other opportunities. "The door is shut when there is no hope of success. [Then] we have to go a different way rather than wear ourselves out in vain efforts to get through it," Calvin writes.[45]

Difficulties in witnessing are not an excuse to stop trying, however. To those suffering severe restrictions and persecutions in France, Calvin wrote: "Let every one strive to attract and win over to Jesus Christ those whom he can."[46] "Each man must perform his duty without yielding to any impediment. At the end our effort and our labors shall not fail; they shall receive the success which does not yet appear."[47]

Let's examine Calvin's practice of evangelism in his own congregation, in his home city of Geneva, in Europe (particularly France), and in missionary efforts overseas (particularly Brazil).

Evangelism in the Congregation

Too often today we think of evangelism only as the Spirit's regenerating work and the sinner's consequent receiving of Christ by faith. In this, we reject Calvin's emphasis on conversion as a continuous process involving the whole person.

For Calvin, evangelism involved a continual, authoritative call to the believer to exercise faith and repentance in the crucified and risen Christ. This summons is a whole-life commitment. Evangelism means presenting Christ so that people, by the power of the Spirit, may come to God in Christ. But it also means presenting Christ so that the believer may serve Christ as Lord in the fellowship of His church and in the world. Evangelism demands building up believers in the most holy faith according to the five key tenets of the Reformation: Scripture alone, grace alone, faith alone, Christ alone, the glory of God alone.

Calvin was an outstanding practitioner of this kind of evangelism within his own congregation. His evangelism began with preaching. William Bouwsma writes, "He preached regularly and often: on the Old Testament on weekdays at six in the morning (seven in winter), every other week; on the New Testament on Sunday mornings; and on the Psalms on Sunday afternoons. During his lifetime he preached, on this schedule, some 4,000 sermons after his return to Geneva: more than 170 sermons a year." Preaching was so important to Calvin that when he was reviewing the accomplishments of his lifetime on his deathbed, he mentioned his sermons ahead of his writings.[48]

Calvin's intention in preaching was to evangelize as well as edify. On average, he would preach on four or five verses in the Old Testament and two or three verses in the New Testament. He would consider a small portion of the text at a time, first explaining the text, then applying it to the lives of his congregation. Calvin's sermons were never short on application; rather, the application was often longer than the exposition in his sermons. Preachers must be like fathers, he wrote, "dividing bread into small pieces to feed their children."

He was also succinct. Calvin's successor, Theodore Beza, said of the Reformer's preaching, "Every word weighed a pound."

Calvin frequently instructed his congregation on how to listen to a sermon. He told them what to look for in preaching, in what spirit they should listen, and how they should listen. His goal was to help people participate in the sermon as much as they could so that it would feed their souls. Coming to a sermon, Calvin said, should include "willingness to obey God completely and with no reserve."[49] "We have not come to the preaching merely to hear what we do not know," Calvin added, "but to be incited to do our duty."[50]

Calvin also reached out to unsaved people through his preaching, impressing them with the necessity of faith in Christ and what that meant. Calvin made it clear that he did not believe everyone in his flock was saved. Though charitable toward church members who maintained a commendable, outward lifestyle, he also referred more than thirty times in his commentaries and nine times in his *Institutes* (only counting references within 3.21 to 3.24) to the small numbers of those who receive the preached Word with saving faith. "If the same sermon is preached, say, to a hundred people, twenty receive it with the ready obedience of faith, while the rest hold it valueless, or laugh, or hiss, or loathe it," Calvin says.[51] He writes, "For though all, without exception, to whom God's Word is preached, are taught, yet scarce one in ten so much as tastes it; yea, scarce one in a hundred profits to the extent of being enabled, thereby, to proceed in a right course to the end."[52]

For Calvin, the most important tasks of evangelism were building up the children of God in the most holy faith, and convicting unbelievers of the heinousness of sin and directing them to Christ Jesus as the only Redeemer.

Evangelism in Geneva

Calvin did not confine preaching to his own congregation. He also used it as a tool to spread the Reformation throughout the city of Geneva. On Sundays, the Genevan Ordinances required sermons in each of the three churches at daybreak and 9 a.m. At noon, children went to catechism classes. At 3 p.m., sermons were preached again in each church.

Weekday sermons were scheduled at various times in the three churches on Mondays, Wednesdays, and Fridays. By the time Calvin died, a sermon was preached in every church each day of the week.

Even that wasn't enough. Calvin wanted to reform Genevans in all spheres of life. In his ecclesiastical ordinances, he required three additional functions besides preaching that each church should offer:

1. Teaching. Doctors of theology should explain the Word of God, first in informal lectures, then in the more formal setting of the Geneva Academy, established in 1559. By the time Calvin's successor, Theodore Beza, retired, the Geneva Academy had trained 1,600 men for the ministry.
2. Discipline. Elders appointed within each congregation were, with

Calvin re-enters Geneva.

View of the city of Geneva (1641), looking eastwards from the Rhone. The old city, centering on the cathedral of Saint-Pierre, is to the right of the illustration.

the assistance of the pastors, to maintain Christian discipline, watching over the conduct of church members and their leaders.
3. Charity. Deacons in each church were to receive contributions and distribute them to the poor.

Initially, Calvin's reforms met stiff local opposition. People particularly objected to the church's use of excommunication to enforce church discipline. After months of bitter controversy, the local citizens and religious refugees who supported Calvin won control of the city. For the last nine years of his life, Calvin's control over Geneva was nearly complete.

Calvin wanted to do more than reform Geneva, however; he wanted the city to become a kind of model for Christ's reign throughout the world. Indeed, the reputation and influence of the Genevan community spread to neighboring France, then to Scotland, England, the Netherlands, parts of western Germany, and sections of Poland, Czechoslovakia, and Hungary. The Genevan church became a model for the entire Reformed movement.

The Geneva Academy also assumed a critically important role as it quickly became more than a place to learn theology. In "John Calvin: Director of Missions," Philip Hughes writes:

Calvin's Geneva was something very much more than a haven and a school. It was not a theological ivory tower that lived to itself and for itself, oblivious to its responsibility in the gospel to the needs of others. Human vessels were equipped and refitted in this haven...that they might launch out into the surrounding ocean of the world's need, bravely facing every storm and peril that awaited them in order to bring the light of Christ's gospel to those who were in the ignorance and darkness from which they themselves had originally come. They were taught in this school in order that they in turn might teach others the truth that had set them free.[53]

Influenced by the Academy, John Knox took the evangelical doctrine back to his native Scotland. Englishmen were equipped to lead the cause in England; Italians had what they needed to teach in Italy; and Frenchmen (who formed the great bulk of refugees) spread Calvinism to France. Inspired by Calvin's truly ecumenical vision, Geneva became a nucleus from which evangelism spread throughout the world. According to the Register of the Company of Pastors, eighty-eight men were sent out between 1555 and 1562 from Geneva to different places in the world. These figures are woefully incomplete. In 1561, which appears to have been the peak year for missionary activity, the dispatch of only twelve men is recorded, whereas other sources indicate that nearly twelve times that number—no less than 142—went forth on respective missions.[54]

That is an amazing accomplishment for an effort that began with a small church struggling within a tiny city-republic. Yet, Calvin himself recognized the strategic value of the effort. He wrote to Bullinger, "When I consider how very important this corner [of Geneva] is for the propagation of the kingdom of Christ, I have good reason to be anxious that it should be carefully watched over."[55]

In a sermon on 1 Timothy 3:14, Calvin preached, "May we attend to what God has enjoined upon us, that he would be pleased to show his

Calvin threatened in the church of Rive.

Farel preaching in the market-place of Neuchâtel

grace, not only to one city or a little handful of people, but that he would reign over all the world; that everyone may serve and worship him in truth."

Evangelistic Efforts in France

To understand how Calvin promoted the Reformation throughout Europe, we need to look at what he did in France.

France was only partially open to Reformed evangelism. Religious and political hostilities, which also threatened Geneva, were a constant danger in France. Nonetheless, Calvin and his colleagues made the most of the small opening they had. The minutes of the Company of Pastors in Geneva deal with the supervision of the missionary efforts in France more than in any other country.[56]

This is how it worked. Reformed believers from France took refuge in Geneva. While there, many began to study theology. They then felt compelled to return to their own people as Reformed evangelists and pastors. After passing a rigorous theological examination, each was given an assignment by the Genevan Company of Pastors, usually in response to a formal request from a French church needing a pastor. In most cases, the receiving church was fighting for its life under persecution.

The French refugees who returned as pastors were eventually killed, but their zeal encouraged the hopes of their parishioners. Their mission, which, according to the pastors, sought "to advance the knowledge of the gospel in France, as our Lord commands," was successful. Reformed evangelistic preaching produced a remarkable revival. In 1555, there was only one fully organized Reformed church in France. Seven years later, there were close to 2,000.

The French Reformed pastors were on fire for God and, despite massive persecution, God used their work to convert thousands. This is one of the most remarkable examples of effective home missions work in the history of Protestantism, and one of the most astonishing revivals in church history.

Some of the French Reformed congregations became very large. For example, Pierre Viret pastored a church of 8,000 communicants in Nimes. More than ten percent of the French population in the 1560s— as many as three million—belonged to these churches.

During the St. Bartholomew's Day massacre of 1572, 70,000 Protestants were killed. Nevertheless, the church continued. Persecution eventually drove out many of the French Protestants, known as the Huguenots. They left France for many different nations, enriching the church wherever they went.

Not all of the refugee pastors were sent to French churches. Some went to Northern Italy, others to Antwerp, London, and other cities in Europe. Some even went far beyond Europe to Brazil. Regardless of where they went, their preaching was strong and powerful, and God frequently blessed their efforts.

Evangelism in Brazil
Calvin knew there were nations and people who had not yet heard the gospel and he keenly felt the burden. Though there is no record that he ever came into contact with the newly discovered world of Asian and African paganism, Calvin was involved with the Indians of South America through the Genevan mission to Brazil.

With the help of Gaspard de Coligny, a Huguenot sympathizer, and the support of Henry II, Nicolas Durand (also called Villegagnon) led an expedition to Brazil in 1555 to establish a colony there. The colonists included former prisoners, some of whom were Huguenots. When trouble erupted in the new colony near Rio de Janeiro, Villegagnon turned to the Huguenots in France, asking for better settlers. He appealed to Coligny as well as to Calvin and the church in Geneva. That letter was not preserved and there is only a brief summary in the account of the Company of Pastors of what happened.

Nonetheless, we have some insight into those events because of what Jean de Lery, a shoemaker and student of theology in Geneva who was soon to join the Brazilian colony, recorded in his personal journal.

Portrait of the French Calvinist leader, Gaspard de Coligny (1519-72). (Bibliothèque du Protestantisme, Paris. Photograph: Photographie Giraudon.)

He wrote, "The letter asked that the church of Geneva send Villegagnon immediately ministers of the Word of God and with them numerous other persons 'well instructed in the Christian religion' in order better to reform him and his people and 'to bring the savages to the knowledge of their salvation.'"[57] Responsibility for evangelism to the heathen was thus laid squarely at the feet of the church of Geneva.

The church's reaction, according to Jean de Lery, was this: "Upon receiving these letters and hearing this news, the church of Geneva at once gave thanks to God for the extension of the reign of Jesus Christ in a country so distant and likewise so foreign and among a nation entirely without knowledge of the true God."[58]

The Company of Pastors chose two ministers to send to Brazil. The Register succinctly notes: "On Tuesday 25 August [1556], in consequence of the receipt of a letter requesting this church to send ministers to the new islands [Brazil], which the French had conquered, M. Pierre Richer and M. Guillaume Charretier were elected. These two were subsequently commended to the care of the Lord and sent off with a letter from this church."[59] Eleven laymen were also recruited for the colony, including Jean de Lery.

Although Calvin was not in Geneva at this time, he was kept informed of what was happening and offered his advice in letters that were sent on to Villegagnon.

The work with Indians in Brazil did not go well. Pastor Richier wrote to Calvin in April 1557 that the savages were incredibly barbaric. "The result is we are frustrated in our hope of revealing Christ to them," he said.[60] Richier did not want to abandon the mission, however. He told Calvin that the missionaries would advance the work in stages and wait patiently for the six young boys who were placed with the Indians (the Tupinambas) to learn their language. "Since the Most High has given us this task, we expect this Edom to become a future possession for Christ," he added confidently. Meanwhile, he trusted that the witness of pious and industrious members of the Reformed Church in the colony would influence the Indians.

Richier was a striking witness of Calvin's missionary emphasis in four ways: (1) obedience to God in doing what is possible in a difficult situation, (2) trust in God to create opportunities for further witness, (3) insistence on the importance of the lives and actions of Christians as a means of witness, and (4) confidence that God will advance His kingdom.

The rest of the story is tragic. Villegagnon became disenchanted with Calvin and the Reformers. On February 9, 1558, just outside of Rio de Janeiro, he strangled three Calvinists and threw them into the sea. Believers fled for their lives. Later, the Portuguese attacked and destroyed the remainder of the settlement.

Thus ended the mission to the Indians. There is no record of any Indian converts. But when an account of the martyrs of Rio de Janeiro was published six years later, it began with these words: "A barbarous land, utterly astonished at seeing the martyrs of our Lord Jesus Christ die, will some day produce the fruits that such precious blood has been at all times wont to produce."[61] As Tertullian once wrote, "The blood of the martyrs is the seed of the church." Today, the Reformed faith is growing in Brazil among conservative Presbyterians through Reformed preaching, the Puritan Project, and various ministries that reprint Reformed and Puritan titles in Portuguese.

Clearly, Calvin was interested in spreading the gospel overseas, but that interest was limited by the following realities of the sixteenth century:

1. Time constraints. The Reformation was still so new in Calvin's time that he needed to concentrate on building up the truth in the churches. A mission church that is not built on foundational truth is not equipped to carry its message to foreign lands.

2. Work at home. Those who criticize Calvin, saying his evangelistic efforts failed to extend to the foreign mission field, are quite unfair. Did not Christ command his disciples to begin spreading the gospel in Jerusalem and Judea (home missions) and then move on to Samaria and the uttermost parts of the earth (foreign missions)? Obviously, the established church should be involved

in both home and foreign missions, but we err when we judge one more important than the other. A genuine spirit of evangelism sees need everywhere. It does not fall prey to the worldly spirit that "The farther from home, the better."

3. Government restrictions. Overseas mission work for the Reformers was virtually impossible because most of the governments in Europe were controlled by Roman Catholic princes, kings, and emperors. Persecution of Protestants was widespread. As Calvin wrote, "Today, when God wishes his gospel to be preached in the whole world, so that the world may be restored from death to life, he seems to ask for the impossible. We see how greatly we are resisted everywhere and with how many and what potent machinations Satan works against us, so that all roads are blocked by the princes themselves."[62]

Nearly every door to the heathen world was closed for Calvin and his fellow Reformers. The world of Islam to the south and east was guarded by Turkish armies, while the navies of Spain and Portugal prevented access to the recently discovered new world. In 1493, Pope Alexander VI gave the Spanish and Portuguese rulers exclusive rights to these areas, which were reaffirmed by popes and treaties that followed.

Going out into the world for Calvin and other Reformers didn't necessarily mean leaving Europe. The mission field of unbelief was right within the realm of Christendom. For the Genevan church, France and much of Europe were open. Strengthened by Calvin's evangelistic theology, believers zealously responded to the mission call.

Calvin did what he could to support evangelism on the foreign front. Despite its tragic failure, the pioneer Protestant project off the coast of Brazil from 1550 to 1560 evoked Calvin's wholehearted sympathy, interest, and continued correspondence.[63]

Calvin's Missionary Spirit and Election
Though Calvin's specific writings on missiology are limited, his *Institutes*, commentaries, sermons, letters, and life glow with a missionary spirit. It is abundantly clear that John Calvin had a heart for evangelism to extend the kingdom of our Lord Jesus Christ to the ends of the earth. It was Calvin's wish that "the kingdom of Christ should flourish everywhere." Establishing the heavenly reign of God upon earth was so important, Calvin said, that it "ought not only to occupy the chief place among our cares, but even absorb all our thoughts."[64]

All of this should dispel the myth that Calvin and his followers promoted inactivity and disinterest in evangelism. Rather, the truths of sovereign grace taught by Calvin such as election are precisely the doctrines that encourage missionary activity. Where biblical, Reformed truth is loved, appreciated, and rightly taught, evangelism and mission activity abounds.

Election encourages evangelistic activity, for God sovereignly links election with the means of grace (Acts 13:44-49). Election evokes mission activity characterized by a humble dependence on God for blessing. The doctrine of free grace is not a barrier to God-centered, God-glorifying evangelism; it is a barrier against a humanistic concept of evangelistic task and methods.[65]

Calvin never allowed election to limit the free offer of the gospel. He taught that since no one knows who are elect, preachers must operate on the principle that God wills all to be saved.[66] Election undergirds rather than limits evangelism. Election belongs to the special category of God's secret purposes, not to the evangelistic activity of the church. Consequently, the gospel must be preached to every sinner; the sinner's believing response to the free offer of salvation in Christ reveals whether or not he is elect. For though the gospel call comes to all who hear the Word, that call is only made effectual by the Holy Spirit in the elect.[67] God opens doors for the church that the gospel may go into all the world, and His elect will hear it and respond in faith.[68]

Election thus is the impetus and guarantor of the success of Reformed evangelism. As Isaiah 55:11 says, "My word...that goeth forth out of my mouth...shall not return unto me void, but it shall accomplish that which I please, and it shall prosper in the thing whereto I sent it."

Is it any wonder, then, that Calvin called election the church's heart, hope, and comfort? Totally depraved creatures such as you and I may hope in an electing God.

A Word of Encouragement

Calvin has been criticized for his supposed failure to support evangelistic efforts. We have seen that this is simply not so, and the lessons ought to give us encouragement.

For one, it tells us we ought to stay on task and worry less about what others say of us. If Calvin could not shield himself from critics even when he worked twenty hours a day, preaching, teaching, and writing, what does that say about our work for God's kingdom? If Calvin was not evangelistic, who is? Are we willing to confess with William Carey as we labor for the souls of sinners, "I had rather wear out than rust out"?

Perhaps some of us are tired. We fear we are wearing out without seeing fruit from our evangelistic efforts. We are burdened with work. Spiritual labor has produced spiritual weariness, which in turn has produced spiritual discouragement. Our eye has not dimmed, but our physical and spiritual energy has been seriously depleted by the constant giving of ourselves for the good of others.

That may be particularly true for those of us who are pastors. On Saturday evenings we are anxious because we do not feel adequately prepared for worship; our responsibilities have been too heavy. We have been overwhelmed with church administration, personal counseling, and correspondence. By Sunday evening we are completely drained. Unable to sustain our responsibilities, we labor under a continual sense of inadequacy. We lack family time; we lack private time with God. Like Moses, our hands grow heavy in intercession. Like Paul, we cry out, "Who is sufficient for these things?" (2 Cor. 2:16). The routines of daily ministry become overwhelming; we experience what Spurgeon called "the minister's fainting fits," and we wonder if we are being used by God after all. Our vision of ministry is sadly diminished.

In such times, we should follow Calvin's example. Some lessons from him include:

- Look more to Christ. Rest more in His perseverance, for your perseverance rests in His. Seek grace to imitate His patience under affliction. Your trials may alarm you, but they will not destroy you. Your crosses are God's way to royal crowning (Rev. 7:14).
- Take the long view. Seek to live in light of eternity. The Chinese bamboo tree appears to do absolutely nothing for four years. Then, during its fifth year, it suddenly shoots up ninety feet in sixty days. Would you say that this tree grew in six weeks or in five years? If you follow the Lord in obedience, you will generally see your efforts rewarded eventually. Remember, however, that God never asked you to produce growth; He only asks you to continue working.
- Realize that times of discouragement are often followed by times of revival. While we predict the church's ruin, God is preparing for her renewal. The church will survive through all time and come to glory while the ungodly will come to ruin. So gird up the loins of your mind and stand fast, for the Lord is greater than both Apollyon and the times. Look to God, not man, for the church belongs to God.
- Rely on God. Though friends may fail you, God will not. The Father is worthy. Christ is worthy. The Holy Spirit is worthy. Seeing

that you have a great high priest, Jesus, the Son of God, who rules from the heavens, draw near to Him in faith, and wait upon Him, and He will renew your strength. We are not all Calvins. Actually, none of us can be Calvins. But we can keep working by God's grace, looking to Jesus for daily strength. If Calvin, one man, did so much good for the cause of evangelism, shouldn't we ask God to also use our efforts, making them fruitful by His blessing?

Heed the advice of the Puritan, John Flavel, who wrote, "Bury not the church before she be dead." Pray more and look at circumstances less. Continue with double earnestness to serve the Lord when no visible result is before you. Endure hardship as good soldiers of Christ. Be willing to be counted fools for Christ's sake. Be sure that you are in God, for you may then be sure that God is in you.

In M'Cheyne's words, "Let your life speak even louder than your sermons. Let your life be the life of your ministry." Be exemplary on and off the pulpit, and leave the fruits of your ministry to our sovereign God who makes no mistakes and who never forsakes the work of His hands.

Finally, take heart from Calvin's approach to "the open door." Do we not err in spending our energies trying to pry open doors that God has closed? Shouldn't we rather pray more for new doors to open for our ministries? Shouldn't we ask for God's guidance in recognizing which doors are open and for His strength to walk through them? May God give us grace not to lead Him, but rather to follow Him in all our evangelistic efforts. Isn't the very heartbeat of Reformed evangelism to follow God rather than try to lead Him?

May the Lord Jesus be able to say of us what he said to the church in Philadelphia in Revelation 3:8, "I know thy works: behold, I have set before thee an open door, and no man can shut it: for thou hast a little strength, and hast kept my word, and hast not denied my name."

That is what Calvin's Reformed evangelism is all about, and that is what our evangelism must be all about. May God help us to be true to His Name, to be obedient to His Word, to look for the doors He will open before us, and to pray with Calvin: "May we daily solicit thee in our prayers, and never doubt, but that under the government of thy Christ, thou canst again gather together the whole world...when Christ shall exercise the power given to him for our salvation and for that of the whole world."[69]

---

[1] William Richey Hogg, "The Rise of Protestant Missionary Concern, 1517-1914," in *Theology of Christian Mission,* ed. G. Anderson (New York: McGraw-Hill, 1961), 96-97.

[2] David B. Calhoun, "John Calvin: Missionary Hero or Missionary Failure?," *Presbuterion* 5,1 (Spr 1979):16-33—to which I am greatly indebted in the first part of this article; W. Stanford Reid, "Calvin's Geneva: A Missionary Centre," *Reformed Theological Review* 42,3 (1983):65-74.

[3] Samuel M. Zwemer, "Calvinism and the Missionary Enterprise," *Theology Today* 7,2 (July 1950):206-216; J. Douglas MacMillan, "Calvin, Geneva, and Christian Mission," *Reformed Theological Journal* 5 (Nov 1989):5-17.

[4] Johannes van den Berg, "Calvin's Missionary Message," *The Evangelical Quarterly* 22 (1950):174-87; Walter Holsten, "Reformation und Mission," *Archiv für Reformationsgeschichte* 44,1 (1953):1-32; Charles E. Edwards, "Calvin and Missions," *The Evangelical Quarterly* 39 (1967):47-51; Charles Chaney, "The Missionary Dynamic in the Theology of John Calvin," *Reformed Review* 17,3 (Mar 1964): 24-38.

[5] Gustav Warneck, *Outline of a History of Protestant Missions* (London: Oliphant Anderson & Ferrier, 1906), 19-20.

[6] John Calvin, *Commentaries of Calvin* (Grand Rapids: Eerdmans, 1950ff.), on Psalm 2:8, 110:2, Matthew 6:10, 12:31, John 13:31. (Hereafter the format, *Commentary* on Psalm 2:8, will be used.)

[7] *Commentary* on Micah 4:3.

[8] John Calvin, *Sermons of M. John Calvin on the Epistles of S. Paule to Timothy and Titus,* trans. L. T. (Edinburgh: Banner of Truth Trust, 1983), sermon on 1 Timothy 2:5-6, 161-72.

[9] *Commentary* on Acts 2:1-4.

[10] *Commentary* on Psalm 110:3.

[11] T. F. Torrance, *Kingdom and Church* (London: Oliver and Boyd, 1956), 161.

[12] *Commentary* on Matthew 24:30.

[13] *Commentary* on Romans 10:15.

[14] *Commentary* on Matthew 13:24-30.

[15] John Calvin, *Institutes of the Christian Religion,* ed. John T. McNeill and trans. Ford Lewis Battles (Philadelphia: Westminster Press, 1960), Book 4, chapter 1, section 5. (Hereafter the format, Inst. 4.1.5, will be used.)

[16] *Commentary* on Romans 10:14-17.

[17] *Commentary* on Psalm 2:8.

[18] *Commentary* on Isaiah 2:3.

[19] Jules Bonnet, ed., *Letters of Calvin,* trans. David Constable and Marcus Robert Gilchrist, 4 vols. (Philadelphia: Presbyterian Board of Publication, 1858), 4:263.

[20] *Commentary* on Isaiah 49:2.

[21] *Commentary* on Isaiah 45:22.

[22] Inst. 3.20.42.

[23] *Sermons of Master John Calvin upon the Fifthe Book of Moses called Deuteronomie,* trans. Arthur Golding (Edinburgh: Banner of Truth Trust, 1987), sermon on Deuteronomy 33:18-19. (Hereafter *Sermon on Deuteronomy* 33:18-19.)

[24] Inst. 3.20.42.

[25] Inst. 3.20.43.

[26] *Sermon on Deuteronomy* 33:7-8.

[27] *Commentary* on Micah 7:10-14.

[28] *Commentary* on Hebrews 10:24.

[29] *Sermon on Deuteronomy* 33:18-19.

[30] *Commentary on* Matthew 13:24-30.

[31] John Calvin, *Sermons on the Epistle to the Ephesians,* trans. Arthur Golding (Edinburgh: Banner of Truth Trust, 1973), sermon on Ephesians 4:15-16.

[32] Bonnet, *Letters of Calvin*, 4:169.

[33] Bonnet, *Letters of Calvin*, 2:453.

[34] Bonnet, *Letters of Calvin*, 2:407.

[35] Bonnet, *Letters of Calvin*, 2:453.

[36] *Commentary* on Isaiah 12:5.

[37] Inst. 3.20.11.

[38] *Sermon on Deuteronomy* 33:18-19.

[39] *Commentary* on Psalm 51:16.

[40] *Commentary* on Isaiah 2:3.

[41] *Sermon on Deuteronomy* 24:10-13.

[42] Inst. 4.20.4.

[43] *Sermon on Deuteronomy* 18:9-15.

[44] *Commentary* on 2 Corinthians 2:12.

[45] Ibid.

[46] Bonnet, *Letters of Calvin*, 3:134.

[47] *Commentary* on Genesis 17:23.

[48] William Bouwsma, *John Calvin: A Sixteenth-Century Portrait* (New York: Oxford, 1988), 29.

[49] Leroy Nixon, *John Calvin, Expository Preacher* (Grand Rapids: Eerdmans, 1950), 65.

[50] John Calvin, *Opera quae supersunt omnia,* ed. Guilielmus Baum, Eduardus Cunitz, and Eduardus Reuss, in *Corpus Reformatorum* (Brunsvigae: C. A. Schwetschke et filium, 1895), 79:783.

[51] Inst. 3.24.12.

[52] *Commentary* on Psalm 119:101.

[53] Philip Hughes, *The Heritage of John Calvin,* ed. John H. Bratt (Grand Rapids: Eerdmans, 1973), 44.

[54] Ibid., 45-46.

[55] Bonnet, *Letters of Calvin*, 2:227.

[56] Robert M. Kingdon, *Geneva and the Consolidation of the French Protestant Movement* (Madison: University of Wisconsin Press, 1967), 31.

[57] R. Pierce Beaver, "The Genevan Mission to Brazil," in *The Heritage of John Calvin,* ed. John H. Bratt, 61.

[58] Ibid.

[59] Philip E. Hughes, ed. and trans., *The Register of the Company of Pastors of Geneva in the Time of Calvin* (Grand Rapids: Eerdmans, 1966), 317.

[60] Beaver, "The Genevan Mission to Brazil," 62.

[61] G. Baez-Camargo, "The Earlist Protestant Missionary Venture in Latin America," *Church History* 21, 2 (June 1952):144.

[62] *Commentary* on Genesis 17:23.

[63] Beaver, "The Genevan Mission to Brazil," 55-73.

[64] Bonnet, *Letters of Calvin*, 2:134-35.

[65] Van den Berg, "Calvin's Missionary Message," 179.

[66] Inst. 3.24.16-17.

[67] Ibid.

[68] Inst. 3.21.7.

[69] Cited in J. Graham Miller, *Calvin's Wisdom* (Edinburgh: Banner of Truth Trust, 1992), 221.

The Puritan Practice of Meditation

"Meditation applieth, meditation healeth, meditation instructeth."
–Ezekiel Culverwell[1]

Spiritual growth is intended to be part of the Christian life of believers. Peter exhorts believers to "grow in grace, and in the knowledge of our Lord and Saviour Jesus Christ" (2 Pet. 3:18). The Heidelberg Catechism says that true Christians are members of Christ by faith and partake in His anointing. By Christ's power, they are raised up to a new life and have the Holy Spirit given to them as an earnest; by the Spirit's power they "seek the things which are above" (Col. 3:1). Spiritual growth is only to be expected, since "it is impossible that those, who are implanted into Christ by a true faith, should not bring forth fruits of thankfulness."[2]

One hindrance to growth among Christians today is our failure to cultivate spiritual knowledge. We fail to give enough time to prayer and Bible-reading, and we have abandoned the practice of meditation. How tragic that the very word *meditation*, once regarded as a core discipline of Christianity and "a crucial preparation for and adjunct to the work of prayer," is now associated with unbiblical New Age spirituality. We rightly criticize those who engage in transcendental meditation and other mind-relaxing exercises because these practices are connected with false religions, such as Buddhism and Hinduism, and have nothing to do with Scripture. Such forms of meditation focus on emptying the mind to become detached from the world and to merge with the so-called Cosmic Mind—not to attach to, listen to, and to be active for a living, personal God. Yet, we can learn from such people the importance of quiet reflection and prolonged meditation.[3]

At one time, the Christian church was deeply engaged in biblical meditation, which involved detachment from sin and attachment to God and one's neighbor. In the Puritan age, numerous ministers preached and wrote on how to meditate.[4] In this chapter, we will look at the Puritan art of meditation, considering the nature, duty, manner, subjects, benefits, obstacles, and self-examination of meditation.[5] With the Puritans as mentors, perhaps we can recover the biblical practice of meditation for our time.

The Definition, Nature, and Kinds of Meditation

The word *meditate* or *muse* means to "think upon" or "reflect." "While I was musing the fire burned," David said (Ps. 39:3). It also means "to murmur, to mutter, to make sound with the mouth.... It implies what we express by one talking to himself."[6] Such meditation involved reciting to oneself in a low undertone passages of Scripture one had committed to memory.

The Bible often speaks of meditation. "Isaac went out to meditate in the field in the evening," says Genesis 24:63. Despite Joshua's demanding task of supervising the conquest of Canaan, the Lord commanded Joshua to meditate on the book of the law day and night so that he might do all that was written in it (Josh. 1:8). The term *meditation*, however, occurs more often in the Psalms than in all other books of the Bible put together. Psalm 1 calls that man blessed who delights in the law of the Lord and meditates on it day and night. In Psalm 63:6, David speaks of remembering the Lord on his bed and meditating on Him in the night watches. Psalm 119:148 says, "Mine eyes prevent the night watches, that I might meditate in thy word."[7]

Thinking, reflecting, or musing presupposes a subject on which to meditate. Formal meditation implies weighty subjects. For example, philosophers meditate on concepts such as matter and the universe, while theologians reflect on God, the eternal decrees, and the will of man.

The Puritans never tired of saying that biblical meditation involves thinking upon the Triune God and His Word. By anchoring meditation in the living Word, Jesus Christ, and God's written Word, the Bible, the Puritans distanced themselves from the kind of bogus spirituality or mysticism that stresses contemplation at the expense of action, and flights of the imagination at the expense of biblical content.

For the Puritans, meditation exercises both the mind and the heart; he who meditates approaches a subject with his intellect as well as his affections. Thomas Watson defined meditation as "a holy exercise of the mind whereby we bring the truths of God to remembrance, and do seriously ponder upon them and apply them to ourselves."[8]

Edmund Calamy wrote, "A true meditation is when a man doth so meditate of Christ as to get his *heart* inflamed with the love of Christ; so meditate of the Truths of God, as to be transformed into them; and so meditate of sin as to get his heart to hate sin." He went on to say that, in order to do good, meditation must enter three doors: the door of understanding, the door of the heart and affections, and the door of practical living. "Thou must so meditate of God as to walk as God walks; and so to meditate of Christ as to prize him, and live in obedience to him."[9]

Meditation was a daily duty that enhanced every other duty of the Puritan's Christian life. As oil lubricates an engine, so meditation facilitates the diligent use of means of grace (reading of Scripture, hearing sermons, prayer, and all other ordinances of Christ),[10] deepens the marks of grace (repentance, faith, humility), and strengthens one's relationships to others (love to God, to fellow Christians, to one's neighbors at large).

The Puritans wrote of two kinds of meditation: occasional and deliberate. "There is a *sudden, short, occasional meditation* of Heavenly things; and there is a *solemn, set, deliberate meditation*," Calamy wrote. Occasional meditation takes what one observes with the senses to "raise up his thoughts to Heavenly meditation." The believer makes use of what he sees with his eyes, or hears with his ears, "as a ladder to climb to Heaven." That's what David did with the moon and stars in Psalm 8, what Solomon did with the ants in Proverbs 6, and what Christ did with well water in John 4.[11] Thomas Manton explained: "God trained up the old church by types and ceremonies, that upon a common object they might ascend to spiritual thoughts; and our Lord in the new testament taught by parables and similitudes taken from ordinary functions and offices among men, that in every trade and calling we might be employed in our worldly business with an heavenly mind, that, whether in the shop, or at the loom, or in the field, we might still think of Christ and heaven."[12]

Occasional meditation—or "extemporal" meditation[13]—is relatively easy for a believer because it may be practiced at any time, any place, and among any people. A spiritually minded man can quickly learn how to spiritualize natural things, for his desires run counter to the worldly minded who carnalize even spiritual things.[14] As Manton wrote, "A gracious heart is like an alembic [distillation apparatus], it can distil useful meditations out of all things it meeteth with. As it seeth all things in God, so it seeth God in all things."[15]

Nearly every Puritan book on meditation mentions occasional meditation. Some Puritans, such as William Spurstowe, Thomas Taylor, Edward Bury, and Henry Lukin, wrote entire books of occasional meditations.[16]

Occasional meditation has its dangers, however. Bishop Joseph Hall warned that when left unbridled, such meditations could easily wander from the Word and become superstitious, as was the case in Roman Catholic spirituality.[17] One's imagination must be reined in by sacred Writ.

Puritans differed among themselves in how far to go with such meditation. In *The Pilgrim's Progress and Traditions in Puritan Meditation,* U. Milo Kaufmann said there were two divergent traditions in Puritan meditation. He said that Joseph Hall, a moderate Puritan in theological orientation though not in church polity, led the way in developing literature on meditation among the Puritans through his work, *Art of Divine Meditation,* first published in 1606. Hall reined in imagination in meditation by confining it to the content of the Word. That greatly influenced Isaac Ambrose and Thomas Hooker, who wrote in the 1650s, and John Owen and Edmund Calamy, who wrote a generation later. Kaufmann asserted that, unlike Roman Catholic writers, most Puritans were "not likely to meditate upon events in the life of Christ but rather upon doctrines or specific propositions of Scripture."[18]

According to Kaufmann, Richard Sibbes and Richard Baxter broke out of this tradition in recommending meditation on the sacraments and heaven. Sibbes, particularly, asserted that though the soul can receive much hurt from unbridled imagination, it can also "have much good thereby." Representing heavenly things in earthly terms, such as

Richard Sibbes   *Richard Baxter*

presenting the kingdom of heaven in terms of a banquet and union with Christ as a marriage, offered "a large field for our imagination to walk in. . .with a great deal of spiritual *gain*," Sibbes wrote.[19] Kaufmann believed that Baxter, in emphasizing imagination by comparing objects of sense with objects of faith, was moved by Sibbes's *The Soul's Conflict.* In turn, John Bunyan was encouraged to write *The Pilgrim's Progress,* in which he applied his imagination to a wide variety of topics affecting the believer's spiritual pilgrimage.[20]

Though Kaufmann's assessment has grains of truth, he has too little feeling for the Puritan fear of allowing imagination to have free reign beyond Scripture. The Puritans rightly feared the excesses of Anselm, Ignatius of Loyola, and other Roman Catholics in visualizing gospel stories—particularly the arrest, trial, crucifixion, and resurrection of Christ —to open imagination through the five senses.[21] Moreover, Kaufmann's negative assessment of Hall and Ambrose fails to take into account the remarkable freedom that both writers gave to scriptural imagination and use of the senses.[22] Hall's *Contemplations* and Ambrose's *Looking Unto Jesus* freely indulged in meditation without trespassing the boundaries of Scripture. That balance is critical in Puritan tradition and, as such, the Puritans serve as mentors on how we can use sanctified imagination.[23]

The most important kind of meditation is daily, deliberate meditation, engaged in at set times. Calamy said deliberate meditation takes place "when a man *sets apart*...some time, and goes into a private Closet, or a private Walk, and there doth solemnly and *deliberately meditate of the things of Heaven.*" Such deliberation dwells upon God, Christ, and truth like "the Bee that dwells and abides upon the flower, to suck out all the sweetness." It "is a reflecting act of the soul, whereby the soul is carried back to itself, and considers all the things that it knows" about the subject, including its "causes, fruits, [and] properties."[24]

Thomas White said deliberate meditation draws from four sources: Scripture, practical truths of Christianity, providential occasions (experiences), and sermons. Sermons are particularly fertile fields for meditation. As White wrote, "It is better to hear one Sermon only and meditate on that, then to hear two Sermons and meditate on neither."[25]

Some Puritans divided deliberate meditation into two parts: meditation that is direct and focuses on the meditated object, and meditation that is reflective (or "reflexive") and focuses on the person who is meditating. Direct meditation is "an act of the contemplative part of the understanding," whereas reflective meditation is "an act of conscience."

Direct meditation enlightens the mind with knowledge, while reflective meditation fills the heart with goodness.

Deliberate meditation can be dogmatic, having the Word as its object, or practical, having our lives as its object.[26] Thomas Gouge combined several aspects of deliberate meditation in writing, "A set and deliberate Meditation, is a serious applying of the mind to some spiritual or heavenly subject, discoursing thereof with thyself, to the end thine heart may be warmed, thine affections quickened, and thy resolutions heightened to a greater love of God, hatred of sin, etc."[27]

Richard Baxter said that "set and solemn" meditation differs from "occasional and cursory" meditation much as set times of prayer differ from spontaneous prayers uttered in the midst of daily business.[28] Both kinds of meditation are essential for godliness; they serve both the needs of the head and the heart.[29] Without heart application, meditation is no more than study. As Thomas Watson wrote, "Study is the finding out of a truth, meditation is the spiritual improvement of a truth; the one searcheth for the vein of gold, the other digs out the gold. Study is like a winter sun that hath little warmth and influence: meditation…melts the heart when it is frozen, and makes it drop into tears of love."[30]

The Duty and Necessity of Meditation

The Puritans stressed the need for meditation. They said that, first, God commands us to meditate on His Word. That should be sufficient reason alone. They cite numerous biblical texts (Deut. 6:7; 32:46; Ps. 19:14; 49:3; 63:3; 94:19; 119:11, 15, 23, 28, 93, 99; 143:5; Is. 1:3; Luke 2:19; 4:44; John 4:24; Eph. 1:18; 1 Tim. 4:13; Heb. 3:1) and examples (Melchizedek, Isaac, Moses, Joshua, David, Mary, Paul, Timothy). When we fail to meditate, we slight God and His Word and reveal that we are not godly (Ps. 1:2).

Second, we should meditate on the Word as a letter God has written to us. "We must not run it over in haste, but meditate upon God's wisdom in inditing, and his love in sending it to us," wrote Thomas Watson.[31] Such meditation will kindle our affections and love for God. As David said, " I will lift up my hands also to thy commandments, which I have loved, and I will meditate in thy statutes" (Ps. 119:48).

Third, one cannot be a solid Christian without meditating. As Thomas Manton said, "Faith is lean and ready to starve unless it be fed with continual meditation on the promises; as David saith, Ps. cxix. 92, 'Unless thy law had been my delight, I should then have perished in my affliction.'"[32] Watson wrote, "A Christian without meditation is like a soldier without arms, or a workman without tools. Without meditation the truths of God will not stay with us; the heart is hard, and the memory slippery, and without meditation all is lost."[33]

Fourth, without meditation, the preached Word will fail to profit us. Reading without meditation is like swallowing "raw and undigested food," wrote Scudder.[34] Richard Baxter added, "A man may eat too much but he cannot digest too well."[35]

Watson wrote, "There is as much difference between the knowledge of a truth, and the meditation of a truth, as there is between the light of a torch, and the light of the sun: set up a lamp or torch in the garden, and it hath no influence. The sun hath a sweet influence, it makes the plants to grow, and the herbs to flourish: so knowledge is but like a torch lighted in the understanding, which hath little or no influence, it makes not a man the better; but meditation is like the shining of the sun, it operates upon the affections, it warms the heart and makes it more holy. Meditation fetcheth life in a truth."[36]

Fifth, without meditation, our prayers will be less effective. Manton wrote, "Meditation is a middle sort of duty between the word and prayer, and hath respect to both. The word feedeth meditation, and meditation feedeth prayer; we must hear that we be not erroneous, and meditate that we be not barren. These duties must always go hand in hand; meditation must follow hearing and precede prayer."[37]

Sixth, Christians who fail to meditate are unable to defend the truth. They have no backbone and little self-knowledge. As Manton wrote, "A man that is a stranger to meditation is a stranger to himself."[38] "It is meditation that makes a Christian," said Watson.[39] "Thus you see the necessity of meditation," wrote Archbishop James Ussher, "we must resolve upon the duty, if ever we mean to go to heaven."[40]

Finally, it may also be added that such meditation is an essential part of sermon preparation. Without it, sermons will lack depth of understanding, richness of feeling, and clarity of application. Bengel's directive to students of the Greek New Testament captures the essence of such meditation: *"Te totam applica ad textum; rem totam applica ad te"* (Apply your whole self to the text; the whole matter of it, apply to yourself).

The Manner of Meditation

For Puritan authors, there were requisites and rules for meditation. Let us consider what they wrote about the frequency and time of meditation, preparation for meditation, and guidelines for meditation.

William Bates   *Thomas Gouge*

Frequency and Time

First, divine meditation must be frequent—ideally, twice a day, if time and obligations permit; certainly at least once a day. If Joshua, as a busy commander, was ordered by God to meditate on His law day and night, should we not also delight in meditating on God's truth every morning and evening? Generally speaking, the more frequently we meditate on the Triune God and His truth, the more intimately we will know Him. Meditation will also become easier. [41]

Lengthy intervals between meditations will hinder their fruit. As William Bates wrote, "If the bird leaves her nest for a long space, the eggs chill and are not fit for production; but where there is a constant incubation, then they bring forth: so when we leave religious duties for a long space, our affections chill, and grow cold; and are not fit to produce holiness, and comfort to our souls."[42]

Second, set a time for meditation and stick to that time, the Puritans advised. That will put brackets around duty and defend you "against many temptations to omission," wrote Baxter.[43] Let it be the most "seasonable time" for you, when you are most alert and not stressed by other obligations. Early morning is an excellent time, because your meditations then will set the tone for the remainder of the day (Ex. 23:19; Job 1:5; Ps. 119:147; Prov. 6:22; Mark 1:35). Still, for some, evenings may be more fruitful (Gen. 24:63; Ps. 4:4). The busyness of the day is behind them, and they are ready to rest in "the bosom of God by sweet meditation" (Ps. 16:7).[44]

Use the Lord's Day for generous doses of meditation time. In their

Directory for the Publique Worship of God, the Westminster divines advised "that what time is vacant, between, or after the solemn meeting of the congregation in public, be spent in reading, meditation, and repetition of sermons."[45] Thomas Gouge admonished, "Had you ever tasted of the sweetness of this duty of Divine Meditation, you would find little time for vain talk, and idle discourses, especially upon the Lord's day."[46] Baxter asked, "What fitter day to ascend to heaven than that on which our Lord did arise from earth, and fully triumph over death and hell, and take possession of heaven for us?"[47]

Use special times as well for meditation. According to the Puritans, those include the following: "1. When God doth extraordinarily revive and enable thy spirit. 2. When thou art cast into perplexing troubles of mind, through sufferings, or fear, or care, or temptations. 3. When the messengers of God do summon us to die; when either our grey hairs, or our languishing bodies, or some such-like forerunners of death, do tell us that our change cannot be far off."[48] 4. "When the heart is touched at a Sermon or Sacrament, or observing of any judgement or mercy, or act of Gods providence, [for then] it is best striking when the Iron is hot (Ps. 119:23)."[49] 5. "Before some solemn duties, as before the Lord's supper, and before special times of deep humiliation, or before the Sabbath."[50]

Third, meditate "ordinarily till thou dost find some sensible benefit conveyed to thy soul." Bates said that meditating is like trying to build a fire from wet wood. Those who persevere will produce a flame. When we begin to meditate, we may first garner only a bit of smoke, then perhaps a few sparks, "but at last there is a flame of holy affections that goes up towards God." Persevere "till the flame doth so ascend," Bates said.[51]

There will be times when the flame does not ascend. You must not then carry on indefinitely. "Neither yield to laziness, nor occasion spiritual weariness: the devil hath advantage upon you both ways," Manton wrote. "When you torture your spirits after they have been spent, it makes the work of God a bondage."[52]

Most Puritans did not advise a specific amount of time to be spent on meditation. However, James Ussher recommended at least one hour per week, and Thomas White suggested, "considering the parts of Meditation are so many, viz. Preparation, Considerations, Affections, Resolutions, etc. and none of them are to be past slightly over, for Affections are not so quickly raised, nor are we to cease blowing the fire as soon as ever it beginneth to flame, until it be well kindled, half an hour [each day] may be thought to be the least for beginners, and an hour for those that are versed in this duty."[53]

Preparation

Puritan writers suggested several ways to prepare for effective meditation, all of which depend "much on the frame of thy heart":

1. Clear your heart from things of this world—its business and enjoyments as well as its internal troubles and agitations. Calamy wrote, "Pray unto God not only to keep out outward company, but inward company; that is, to keep out vain, and worldly, and distracting thoughts."[54]

2. Have your heart cleansed from the guilt and pollution of sin, and stirred up with fervent love for spiritual things. Treasure up a stock of scriptural texts and spiritual truths. Seek grace to live out David's confession in Psalm 119:11, "Thy word have I hid in my heart, that I might not sin against thee."

3. Approach the task of meditation with utmost seriousness. Be aware of its weightiness, excellence, and potential. If you succeed, you will be admitted into the very presence of God and feel once again the beginning of eternal joy here on earth.[55] As Ussher wrote, "This must be the thought of thy heart, I have to do with a God, before whom all things are naked, and bare, and therefore I must be careful to not speak foolishly before the wise God, that my thoughts be not wandering. A man may talk with the greatest prince on earth, his mind otherwise busied. Not so come to talk with God; his eye is on the heart, and therefore thy chief care must be to keep the rudder of thy heart steady. Consider the three persons in the Trinity are present."[56]

James Ussher

4. Find a place for meditation that is quiet and free from interruption. Aim for "secrecy, silence, rest, whereof the first excludeth company, the second noise, the third motion," wrote Joseph Hall.[57] Once a suitable place is found, stick with that place. Some Puritans recommended keeping the room dark or closing one's eyes to remove all visible distractions. Others recommended walking or sitting in the midst of nature. Here one must find his own way.

5. Maintain a body posture that is reverent, whether it be sitting, standing, walking, or lying prostrate before the Almighty. While meditating, the body should be the servant of the soul, following its affections. The goal is to center the soul, the mind, and the body upon "the glory of God in the face of Christ" (2 Cor. 4:6).[58]

Guidelines

The Puritans also offered guidelines for the process of meditation. They said to begin by asking the Holy Spirit for assistance. Pray for the power to harness your mind and to focus the eyes of faith on this task. As Calamy wrote, "I would have you pray unto God to enlighten your understandings, to quicken your devotion, to warm your affections, and so to bless that hour unto you, that by the meditation of holy things you may be made more holy, you may have your lusts more mortified, and your graces more increased, you may be the more mortified to the world, and the vanity of it, and lifted up to Heaven, and the things of Heaven."[59]

Next, read the Scriptures, then select a verse or doctrine upon which to meditate. Be sure to pick out relatively easy subjects to meditate on at the beginning, the Puritans advised. For example, begin with the attributes of God rather than the doctrine of the Trinity. Consider subjects one at a time.

In addition, select subjects that are most applicable to your present circumstances and that will be most beneficial for your soul. For example, if you're spiritually dejected, meditate upon Christ's willingness to receive poor sinners and pardon all who come to Him. If your conscience troubles you, meditate on God's promises to give grace to the penitent. If you're financially afflicted, meditate on God's wonderful providences to those in need.[60]

Now, memorize the selected verse(s), or some aspect of the subject, to stimulate meditation, strengthen faith, and serve as a means of divine guidance.

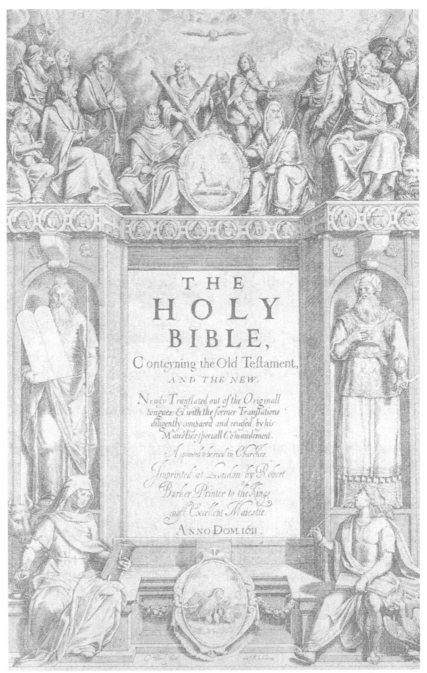

The title page of the first edition of the King James Version of the Bible.

Next, fix your thoughts on the Scripture or a scriptural subject without prying further than what God has revealed. Use your memory to focus on all that Scripture has to say about your subject. Consider past sermons and other edifying books.

Use "the book of conscience, the book of Scripture, and the book of the creature"[61] as you consider various aspects of your subject: its names, causes, qualities, fruits, and effects. Like Mary, ponder these things in your heart. Think of illustrations, similitudes, and opposites in your mind to enlighten your understanding and enflame your affections. Then let judgment assess the value of what you are meditating upon.

Here is an example from Calamy. If you would meditate on the subject of sin, "Begin with the description of sin; proceed to the distribution of sin; consider the original and cause of sin, the cursed fruits and effects of sin, the adjuncts and properties of sin in general and of personal sin in particular, the opposite of sin—grace, the metaphors of sin, the titles given to sin, [and] all that the Scripture saith concerning sin."[62]

Two warnings are in order. First, as Manton wrote, "Do not bridle up the free spirit by the rules of method. That which God calleth for is religion, not logic. When Christians confine themselves to such rules and prescriptions, they straiten themselves, and thoughts come from them like water out of a still, not like water out of a fountain."[63] Second, if your mind wanders, rein it in, offer a short prayer for forgiveness, ask for strength to stay focused, read a few appropriate Scriptures again, and press on. Remember that reading Scripture, meditation, and prayer belong together. As one discipline wanes, turn to another. Persevere; don't surrender to Satan by abandoning your task.

Next, stir up affections, such as love, desire, hope, courage, gratitude, zeal, and joy,[64] to glorify God.[65] Hold soliloquies with your own soul. Include complaints against yourself because of your inabilities and shortcomings, and spread before God your spiritual longings. Believe that He will help you.

Paul Baynes, in discussing meditations as a "private meanes" of grace, compared it first with the power of sight to affect the heart, then with the process of conception and birth: "Now look as after conception, there is a travail to bring forth and a birth in due season: so when the soul by thought hath conceived, presently the affections are tickled and excited, for the affections kindle on a thought, as tinder doth, when a spark lighteth on it. The affections moved, the will is stirred and inclined."[66]

Now, following the arousal of your memory, judgment, and affections, apply your meditations to yourself to arouse your soul to duty and comfort, and to restrain your soul from sin.[67] As William Fenner wrote, "Dive into thy own soul; anticipate and prevent thy own heart. Haunt thy heart with promises, threatenings, mercies, judgments, and commandments. Let meditation trace thy heart. Hale thy heart before God."[68]

Examine yourself for your own growth in grace. Reflect on the past and ask, "What have I done?" Look to the future, asking, "What am I resolved to do, by God's grace?"[69] Do not ask such questions legalistically but out of holy excitement and opportunity to grow in Spirit-worked grace. Remember, "Legal work is our work; meditation work is sweet work."[70]

Follow Calamy's advice, "If ever you would get good by the practice of meditation, you must come down to *particulars;* and you must so meditate of Christ, as to apply Christ to thy soul; and so meditate of Heaven, as to apply Heaven to thy soul."[71] Live out your meditation (Josh. 1:8). Let meditation and practice, like two sisters, walk hand in hand. Meditation without practice will only increase your condemnation.[72]

Next, turn your applications into resolutions. "Let your resolutions be firm and strong, not [mere] wishes, but resolved purposes or Determinations," wrote White. [73] Make your resolutions be commitments to fight against your temptations to sin. Write down your resolutions. Above all, resolve that you will spend your life "as becomes one that hath been meditating of holy and heavenly things." Commend yourself, your family, and everything you own to the hands of God with "sweet resignation."

Conclude with prayer, thanksgiving, and Psalm-singing. "Medita-

Edmund Calamy

John Lightfoot

tion is the best beginning of prayer, and prayer is the best conclusion of meditation," wrote George Swinnock. Watson said, "Pray over your meditations. Prayer sanctifies every thing; without prayer they are but unhallowed meditations; prayer fastens meditation upon the soul; prayer is a tying a knot at the end of meditation that it doth not slip; pray that God will keep those holy meditations in your mind for ever, that the savour of them may abide upon your hearts."[74]

Thank the Lord for assistance in meditation, or else Richard Greenham warned, "we shall be buffeted in our next meditation."[75]

The metrical versions of the Psalms are a great help in meditation. Their metrical form facilitates memorization. As God's Word, they are a proper subject for meditation. As a "complete anatomy of the soul" (Calvin), they afford abundant material and guidance for meditation. As prayers (Ps. 72:20) and as thanksgiving (Ps. 118:1), they are both a proper vehicle for meditation and a fitting way to conclude it. Joseph Hall wrote that he found much comfort in closing his meditations by lifting up his "heart and voice to God in singing some verse or two of David's Psalms—one that answers to our disposition and the matter of our meditation. In this way the heart closes up with much sweetness and contentment."[76] John Lightfoot added, "Singing God's praise is a work of the most meditation of any we perform in public. It keeps the heart longest upon the thing spoken. Prayer and hearing pass quick from one sentence to another; this sticks long upon it."

Finally, don't shift too quickly from meditation to engagement with things of this world, lest, as Thomas Gouge advised, "thereby thou suddenly quench that spiritual heart which hath in that exercise been kindled in thine heart."[77] Remember that one hour spent in such meditation is "worth more than a thousand sermons," Ussher said, "and this is no debasing of the Word, but an honour to it."[78]

The Subjects of Meditation
The Puritans suggested various subjects, objects, and materials for meditation. The number after each entry represents the number of Puritan writers I found who called for meditation on that subject. This list follows the traditional loci of Reformed systematic theology.

Prolegomena
    the sacred Word of God (3)
    the defense of Christianity (1)

Theology proper
> the nature and attributes of God (7)
> the works and providences of God (7)
> the glory of God as man's chief end (4)
> the majesty of God (3)
> the mercies of God (3)
> God as Creator (2)

Anthropology
> the sinfulness of sin and our personal sin (9)
> the corruption and deceitfulness of the heart (5)
> the fall in Adam and estrangement from God (4)
> the vanity of man (4)
> the value and immortality of the soul (3)
> the frailty of the body (2)
> the uncertainty of earthly comforts (1)
> the sin of covetousness (1)
> the contrast between God and man (1)

Christology
> the passion and death of Christ (8)
> the love of Christ (5)
> the person of Christ (4)
> the mystery and wonder of the Gospel (4)
> the natures of Christ (2)
> the offices of Christ (2)
> the life of Christ (2)
> the states of Christ (1)

Soteriology and the Christian Life
> the promises of God (7)
> self-examination for experiential evidences of grace (5)
> the rich privileges of believers (3)
> the grace and person of the Holy Spirit (3)
> the benefits of faith (2)
> sanctification (2)
> prayer (2)
> the commandments of God (2)
> the admonishments and threatenings of God (2)
> the danger of apostasy (1)
> the small number of the saved (1)

spiritual dangers (1)
love, joy, hope (1)
the Sabbath (1)
self-denial (1)

Ecclesiology
the ordinances of God (5)
the Lord's Supper (4)
baptism (2)
hearing and reading the Word (2)
the joys and sorrows of the church (1)
Eschatology
heaven (10)
death (8)
judgment (7)
hell (7)
eternity (5)

The Puritans called these subjects the plain, powerful, useful truths of God. Some Puritans, such as Joseph Hall, offered more detailed lists than others. Hall listed eighty-seven subjects upon which to meditate, as well as a paragraph with each on how to do so. They include:

> fame and greatness, ignorance, depravity, holy living, gossip, evil companions, God's promises, love of the world, contentment, hypocrisy, happiness, love of the world, companions, heaven and earth, work and pain, riches, heaven and hell, death, affliction, godly warfare, sin, success, growing in grace, pride, hatred of sin, prejudice, covetousness,

Joseph Hall

prayer, love, blasphemy, nobility, prayer, temptation, the use of means, worship, happiness, obedience, repentance, ambition, conceit, the shortness of life, self-examination, adversity, affliction, faith and philosophy, pleasure, sin, faithful friends, schism and truth, grief and worry, fear, the heathen and the Christian, the light of the eye, the mind and the heart, heartfelt religion, hurting ourselves, the heart and the tongue, the use of time, cares, providence, love, displeasure, friendship, bargain hunting, reproof, envy, worldly pleasures, following good examples, time, enjoyment, good works, fruitfulness, foolishness, doing good, hermitage, a happy life, heavenly correction, heavenly hunger, repentance, spiritual warfare, strength in trials, heavenly-mindedness, humility, death, purpose in life, good from evil, madness, and the practice of meditation itself.[79]

Clearly the Puritans believed some topics ought to be focused on more than others. This led John Owen to say, "If I have observed anything by experience, it is this: a man may take the measure of his growth and decay in grace according to his thoughts and meditations upon the person of Christ, and the glory of Christ's kingdom, and of His love."

For the Puritans, probably the most important theme for meditation was heaven—the place where God is supremely known and worshiped and enjoyed, where Christ is seated at the right hand of the Father, and where the saints rejoice as they are transcribed from glory to glory. "Meditation is the life of most other duties: and the views of heaven is the life of Meditation," wrote Baxter.[80] Heaven was the supreme subject for meditation for these reasons:

- Christ is in heaven now and our salvation consists of union through the Holy Spirit with Christ. He is our wisdom, righteousness, sanctification, and redemption. Christ, the center of heaven, ought to be the center of all our faith, hope, and love.
- We can only live as Christians in the present evil age if we have the mind of Christ—that is, if we are genuinely heavenly-minded, seeing our earth and this age from the perspective of heaven.
- Heaven is the goal of our pilgrimage. We are pilgrims on the earth, journeying in faith, hope, and love toward heaven to be with Christ.[81]

The Puritans taught that meditations on heaven and other subjects take priority on three occasions. First, special meditation is necessary in conjunction with worship, particularly with regard to the sermon. "God requires you to hear Sermons, requires you to meditate on the Sermons you hear," wrote Calamy.[82] As James Ussher wrote, "Every sermon is but a preparation for meditation."[83]

Good sermons not only inform the mind with sound doctrine but also stir up the affections. They turn the will away from sin and toward loving God and one's neighbor. Meditation enlarges and directs the affections through the reception of the Word of God in the heart from the mind. When people stop meditating on sermons, they stop benefiting from them.

Richard Baxter wrote, "Why so much preaching is lost among us, and professors can run from sermon to sermon, and are never weary of hearing or reading, and yet have such languishing, starved souls, I know no truer or greater cause than their ignorance and unconscionable neglect of meditation." Some hearers have spiritual anorexia, Baxter said, for "they have neither appetite nor digestion," but others have spiritual bulimia—"they have appetite, but no digestion."[84]

Conscientious Puritans often took sermon notes to help facilitate meditation. In my own congregation, an elderly Christian woman decided to emulate that practice. Every Sabbath evening she spent an hour on her knees with notes from the sermons of the day, praying and meditating her way through them. She often found this to be the best part of her Sabbath.

Second, to rightly receive the sacrament of the Lord's Supper, a believer is expected to meditate on the Lord Jesus as the sacrifice for his sin. As Thomas White wrote, "Meditate upon your preparatory, concomitant and subsequent duties: Meditate upon the love of God the Father, upon the love of God the Son, Jesus Christ, consider the excellency of his person, the greatness of his sufferings, and how valid they be to the satisfaction of God's Justice, and so likewise to consider of the excellency, nature, and use of the Sacrament."[85]

Calamy listed twelve subjects for meditations during the sacrament: "the great and wonderful love of God the Father in giving Christ; the love of Christ in giving himself; the heinousness of sin; the excellency of this Sacramental feast; your own unworthiness; your spiritual wants and necessities; the cursed condition of an unworthy receiver; the happy condition of those that come worthily; the Sacramental Elements [bread and wine]; the Sacramental actions [how the minister's actions represent Christ]; the Sacramental Promises; what retribution to make unto Christ for [the gift of His Supper]."[86] Some Puritan divines, such as Edward Reynolds, wrote entire treatises to help believers during the Lord's Supper.[87] John Owen showed how preparation for the Lord's Supper involved meditation, examination, supplication, and expectation.[88] Every believer was expected to share in that preparation.[89]

Third, every Sabbath was a special season for meditation. It was a time of spiritual nourishment for the God-fearing who stocked up on spiritual goods for the week to come. Hence, the Sabbath was fondly called "the market day of the soul."

Finally, Puritans such as Nathanael Ranew, who wrote extensively on meditation, gave various directions to believers, depending on their spiritual maturity. Ranew wrote chapters for "young Christians newly converted," "more grown and elder Christians," and for "old Christians." The older the Christian, the greater the expectation for more profound meditations.[90]

The Benefits of Meditation

The Puritans devoted scores of pages to the benefits, excellencies, usefulness, advantages, or improvements of meditation. Here are some of those benefits:

- Meditation helps us focus on the Triune God, to love and to enjoy Him in all His persons (1 John 4:8)—intellectually, spiritually, aesthetically.
- Meditation helps increase knowledge of sacred truth. It "takes the veil from the face of truth" (Prov. 4:2).
- Meditation is the "nurse of wisdom," for it promotes the fear of God, which is the beginning of wisdom (Prov. 1:8).
- Meditation enlarges our faith by helping us to trust the God of promises in all our spiritual troubles and the God of providence in all our outward troubles.[91]
- Meditation augments one's affections. Watson called meditation "the bellows of the affections." He said, "Meditation hatcheth good affections, as the hen her young ones by sitting on them; we light affection at this fire of meditation" (Ps. 39:3).[92]
- Meditation fosters repentance and reformation of life (Ps. 119:59; Ez. 36:31).
- Meditation is a great friend to memory.
- Meditation helps us view worship as a discipline to be cultivated. It makes us prefer God's house to our own.
- Meditation transfuses Scripture through the texture of the soul.
- Meditation is a great aid to prayer (Ps. 5:1). It tunes the instrument of prayer before prayer.
- Meditation helps us to hear and read the Word with real benefit. It makes the Word "full of life and energy to our souls." William

Bates wrote, "Hearing the word is like ingestion, and when we meditate upon the word that is digestion; and this digestion of the word by meditation produceth warm affections, zealous resolutions, and holy actions."[93]

- Meditation on the sacraments helps our "graces to be better and stronger." It helps faith, hope, love, humility, and numerous spiritual comforts thrive in the soul.
- Meditation stresses the heinousness of sin. It "musters up all weapons, and gathers all forces of arguments for to press our sins, and lay them heavy upon the heart," wrote Fenner.[94] Thomas Hooker said, "Meditation sharpens the sting and strength of corruption, that it pierceth more prevailingly."[95] It is a "strong antidote against sin" and "a cure of covetousness."
- Meditation enables us to "discharge religious duties, because it conveys to the soul the lively sense and feeling of God's goodness; so the soul is encouraged to duty."[96]
- Meditation helps prevent vain and sinful thoughts (Jer. 4:14; Matt. 12:35). It helps wean us from this present evil age.
- Meditation provides inner resources on which to draw (Ps. 77:10-12), including direction for daily life (Prov. 6:21-22).
- Meditation helps us persevere in faith; it keeps our hearts "savoury and spiritual in the midst of all our outward and worldly employments," wrote William Bridge.[97]

William Bridge

- Meditation is a mighty weapon to ward off Satan and temptation (Ps. 119:11,15; 1 John 2:14).
- Meditation provides relief in afflictions (Is. 49:15-17; Heb. 12:5).
- Meditation helps us benefit others with our spiritual fellowship and counsel (Ps. 66:16; 77:12; 145:7).
- Meditation promotes gratitude for all the blessings showered upon us by God through His Son.
- Meditation glorifies God (Ps. 49:3).[98]

In short, as Thomas Brooks wrote, "meditation is the food of your souls, it is the very stomach and natural heat whereby spiritual truths are digested. A man shall as soon live without his heart, as he shall be able to get good by what he reads, without meditation.... It is not he that reads most; but he that meditates most, that will prove the choicest, sweetest, wisest, and strongest Christian."[99]

The Obstacles of Meditation

Puritan leaders frequently warned people about hindrances to meditation. Here is a summary of their responses to such obstacles:

Obstacle #1: Unfitness or ignorance. Such say they "cannot confine their thoughts to an object." Their "thoughts are light and feathery, tossed to and fro."

Answer: Disability, ignorance, and wandering thoughts offer no exemption from duty. Your "loss of ability" does not imply God's "loss of right." Truth be told, you are probably unfit because you have neglected meditation and have not loved the truth. "Sinful indispositions do not disannul our engagements to God, as a servant's drunkenness doth not excuse him from work," Manton wrote.[100] Remedy your problem by getting "a good stock of sanctified knowledge" and by "constant exercise" of that knowledge, leaning all the while on the Holy Spirit for assistance. You will find meditation becoming easier and sweeter in due course.

Obstacle #2: Busyness. Such say "they are so harassed by the employments of this world, that they cannot spend time in this duty solemnly, and seriously."

Answer: True religion is not performed merely in leisure time. Great busyness should move us to more meditation, as we then have more needs to bring before God and upon which to meditate.

Obstacle #3: Spiritual lethargy. Such admit that though they may have good intentions, their soul is prone to divert itself from meditation.

Answer: Matthew 11:12 says heaven is the reward of "the violent

[who] take it by force." Why are you lazy in spiritual pursuits that can reap eternal rewards when you are not lazy in pursuing secular work in this world, which produces only temporary rewards? Spiritual "drowsiness shall clothe a man with rags" (Prov. 23:21). As Manton said, "It is better to take pains than to suffer pains, and to be bound with the cords of duty than with the chains of darkness."[101]

Obstacle #4: Worldly pleasures and friendships. Such say they don't want to be righteous overmuch and hence do not wish to abandon vain entertainment and friends.

Answer: "The pleasures of the world discompose our souls, and unfit our bodies for the duties of meditation…. Remember this, the sweetness of religion is incomparably more than all the pleasures of sense," wrote Bates.[102]

Obstacle #5: Adverseness of heart. Such say they don't like to be yoked to such a difficult task. Burdened with guilt, they fear being alone with God.

Answer: "Get your conscience cleansed by the hearty application of the blood of Christ," Manton advised, then yoke yourself to the means of grace, including meditation (Ps. 19:14).[103]

The consequences of omitting meditation are serious, Calamy warned. It leads to hardness of heart. Why do the promises and threatenings of God make so little impression on us? Because we fail to meditate upon them. Why are we so ungrateful to God for His blessings? Why do His providences and afflictions fail to produce godly fruit in our lives? Why do we fail to benefit from the Word and sacraments, why are we so judgmental of others, why do we so feebly prepare for eternity? Is it not largely due to our lack of meditation?[104]

We must discipline ourselves to meditate. Most Puritan pastors said that. Yet comparatively few people, even in Puritan times, saw this as their duty. "Many are troubled," wrote Baxter, "if they omit a sermon, a fast, a prayer in public or private, yet were never troubled that they have omitted meditation, perhaps all their life-time to this very day."[105]

Conclusion: Meditation as Self-Examination

Puritan meditation was more than a particular means of grace; it was a comprehensive method for Puritan devotion—a biblical, doctrinal, experiential, and practical art. Its theology was Pauline, Augustinian, and Calvinistic. Its subject matter was drawn from the book of Scripture, the book of creation, and the book of conscience. As William Bridge said,

"Meditation is the vehement or intense application of the soul unto some thing, whereby a man's mind doth ponder, dwell and fix upon it, for his own profit and benefit," which, in turn, leads to God's glory.[106]

Typically, Puritans concluded their treatises on meditation by calling readers to self-examination, which consists of:

(1) Trial

• Are your meditations motivated by the exercise of "a lively faith"? Real meditation is inseparable from the exercise of faith. Do you ever meditate as Samuel Ward describes: "Stir up thy soul in [meditation] to converse with Christ. Look what promises and privileges thou dost habitually believe, now actually think of them, roll them under thy tongue, chew on them till thou feel some sweetness in the palate of thy soul. View them jointly, severally: sometimes muse on one, sometimes of another more deeply. This is that which the Spouse calls walking into the Gardens and eating of the Fruits, which in plain terms, I call using of Faith, and living by Faith."[107]

• "Are these spiritual thoughts in thy heart, productive of holiness in thy life?" Remember, "To be weary of the thoughts of God is to degenerate into devils" (cf. James 2:19).[108]

(2) Reproof or exhortation

• To the unbeliever: When God made you a rational creature, did He intend that you should use your thoughts for selfish and sinful purposes? Why isn't God in all your thoughts? "Hast thou not a God and a Christ to think of? And is not salvation by him, and everlasting glory, worthy of your choicest thoughts? You have thoughts enough and to spare for other things—for base things, for very toys—and why not for God and the word of God?" Manton asked.[109]

• To the believer: Neglecting meditation should "strike us with fear and sorrow." How degrading it is to God when we turn our meditation from Him to sinful objects! If the farmer meditates upon his land, the physician upon his patients, the lawyer upon his cases, the storeowner upon his wares, shouldn't Christians meditate upon their God and Savior?[110]

The Puritans would say to us: "If you continue to neglect meditation, it will dampen or destroy your love for God. It will make it unpleasant to think about God. It will leave you open to sin so that you view sin as a pleasure. It will leave you vulnerable and fragile before trials and temptations of every kind. In short, it will lead to a falling away from God."[111]

"No holy duties will come to us," Ranew wrote, "we must come to them."[112] Let us heed Watson's exhortation, "If you have formerly neglected it, bewail your neglect, and now begin to make conscience of it: lock up yourselves with God (at least once a day) by holy meditation. Ascend this hill, and when you are gotten to the top of it, you shall see a fair prospect, Christ and heaven before you. Let me put you in mind of that saying of Bernard, 'O saint, knowest thou not that thy husband Christ is bashful, and will not be familiar in company, retire thyself by meditation into the closet, or the field, and there thou shalt have Christ's embraces.'"[113]

---

[1] Introduction to "Divine Meditations and Holy Contemplations," in *The Works of Richard Sibbes* (Edinburgh: Banner of Truth Trust, 2001), 184.

[2] *Heidelberg Catechism*, Questions 32, 45, 49, 64.

[3] Richard J. Foster, *Celebration of Discipline* (San Francisco: Harper & Row, 1978), 14-15.

[4] See bibliography attached.

[5] Few studies have been done on Puritan meditation. Louis Martz, who established the intimate connection between meditation and poetry, wrote a critical chapter on Richard Baxter's view of meditation (*The Poetry of Meditation* [New Haven: Yale, 1954]). U. Milo Kaufmann showed the importance of Puritan meditation in shaping Bunyan's *Pilgrim's Progress* (*The Pilgrim's Progress and Traditions in Puritan Meditation* [New Haven: Yale, 1966]). Barbara Lewalski sharpened the focus on the contributions of a distinctively Protestant form of meditation (*Donne's "Anniversaries" and the Poetry of Praise, the Creation of a Symbolic Mode* [Princeton: University Press, 1973] and *Protestant Poetics and the Seventeenth-Century Religious Lyric* [Princeton: University Press, 1979]). Norman Grabo effectively challenged Martz's thesis that Calvinistic thinking prevented Protestantism from developing the art of meditation until the mid-seventeenth century ("The Art of Puritan Devotion," *Seventeenth-Century News* 26, 1 [1968]:8). Frank Livingstone Huntley too neatly categorized Protestant meditation as philosophically Platonic, psychologically Augustinian, and theologically Pauline and Calvinistic in contrast to Roman Catholic meditation as Aristotelian and Thomistic (*Bishop Joseph Hall and Protestant Meditation in Seventeenth-Century England: A Study With the texts of* The Art of Divine Meditations *[1606] and* Occasional Meditations *[1633]* [Binghamton, N.Y.: Center for Medieval & Early Renaissance Studies, 1981]). Simon Chan provided a fresh historical appraisal of Puritan meditation, covering a larger body of texts than those previously examined and moving beyond a literary view ("The Puritan Meditative Tradition, 1599-1691: A Study of Ascetical Piety" [Ph.D. dissertation, Cambridge University, 1986]). He argued that Puritan meditation progressively moved in a more methodical direction in the second half of the seventeenth century. A book examining the theological and practical assessment of Puritan meditation has yet to be written.

[6] William Wilson, *OT Word Studies* (McLean, Va.: MacDonald Publishing Co., n.d.), 271.

[7] Cf. Psalm 4:4; 77:10-12; 104:34; 119:16, 48, 59, 78, 97-99.

[8] *Heaven Taken by Storm* (Morgan, Pa.: Soli Deo Gloria, 2000), 23. For similar defini-

tions by other Puritans, see Richard Greenham, "Grave Covnsels and Godly Observations," in *The Works of the Reverend and Faithfvll Servant of Iesvs Christ M. Richard Greenham,* ed. H. H. (London: Felix Kingston for Robert Dexter, 1599), 37; Thomas Hooker, *The Application of Redemption: The Ninth and Tenth Books* (London: Peter Cole, 1657), 210; Thomas White, *A Method and Instructions for the Art of Divine Meditation with Instances of the several Kindes of Solemn Meditation* (London: for Tho. Parkhurst, 1672), 13.

[9] *The Art of Divine Meditation* (London: for Tho. Parkhurst, 1634), 26-28.

[10] Cf. *Westminster Larger Catechism,* Q. 154.

[11] Calamy, *The Art of Divine Meditation,* 6-10.

[12] *The Works of Thomas Manton* (London: James Nisbet & Co., 1874), 17:267-68.

[13] Huntley, *Hall and Protestant Meditation,* 73.

[14] *The Art of Divine Meditation,* 14-15.

[15] *The Works of Thomas Manton,* 17:267. Cf., "A gracious heart, like fire, turns all objects into fuel for meditation" (*The Sermons of Thomas Watson* [Ligonier, Pa.: Soli Deo Gloria, 1990], 247).

[16] William Spurstowe, *The Spiritual Chymist: or, Six Decads Of Divine Meditations* (London: n.p., 1666); Thomas Taylor, *Meditations from the Creatures* (London, 1629); Edward Bury, *The Husbandman's Companion: Containing One Hundred Occasional Meditations, Reflections, and Ejaculations, Especially Suited to Men of that Employment. Directing them how they may be Heavenly-minded while about their Ordinary Calling* (London: for Tho. Parkhurst, 1677); Henry Lukin, *An Introduction to the Holy Scriptures* (London, 1669).

[17] Huntley, *Hall and Protestant Meditation,* 74.

[18] (New Haven: Yale, 1966), 126. Kaufmann quotes Thomas Hooker's strong rejection of imagination, "To preserve our minds from windy and vain imaginations, is to have our understandings fully taken up with the blessed Truths of God as our daily and appointed food" (*The Application of Redemption: The Ninth and Tenth Books,* 232).

[19] Cited in Kaufmann, 144-45.

[20] Ibid., 150-251.

[21] Peter Toon, *Meditating as a Christian* (London: Collins, 1991), 175-78; *The Spiritual Exercises of St. Ignatius,* trans. Anthony Mottola (New York: Doubleday & Co., 1964).

[22] Huntley, *Hall and Protestant Meditation,* 44-54.

[23] Cf. Peter Toon, *From Mind to Heart: Christian Meditation Today* (Grand Rapids: Baker, 1987), 99-100.

[24] *The Art of Divine Meditation,* 22-23; *Works of Greenham,* 38.

[25] White, *A Method and Instructions for the Art of Divine Meditation with Instances of the several Kindes of Solemn Meditation* (London: for Tho. Parkhurst, 1672), 17-20.

[26] *The Works of Thomas Manton,* 17:268.

[27] *Christian Directions, shewing How to walk with God All the Day long* (London: R. Ibbitson and M. Wright, 1661), 65.

[28] *The Saints' Everlasting Rest* (Ross-shire, Scotland: Christian Focus, 1998), 553. Cf. White, *A Method and Instructions for the Art of Divine Meditation,* 14.

[29] Henry Scudder, *The Christian Man's Calling* (Philadelphia: Presbyterian Board of Publication, n.d.), 103-104. Cf. *The Works of William Bates* (Harrisonburg, Va.: Sprinkle, 1990), 3:113-65.

[30] *Gleanings from Thomas Watson* (Morgan, Pa.: Soli Deo Gloria, 1995), 106.

31 *Sermons of Thomas Watson*, 238.

32 *The Works of Thomas Manton*, 17:270.

33 *Sermons of Thomas Watson*, 238.

34 *The Christian's Daily Walk*, 108.

35 *The Saints' Everlasting Rest*, 549.

36 *Sermons of Thomas Watson*, 239.

37 *The Works of Thomas Manton*, 17:272.

38 Ibid., 271.

39 *Sermons of Thomas Watson*, 240.

40 *A Method for Meditation: or, A Manuall of Divine Duties, fit for every Christians Practice* (London: for Joseph Nevill, 1656), 21.

41 *The Art of Divine Meditation*, 96-101.

42 *The Works of William Bates* (Harrisonburg, Va.: Sprinkle, 1990), 3:124-25.

43 *The Saints' Everlasting Rest*, 555.

44 *The Works of William Bates*, 126-27. Thomas Watson makes the strongest case for morning meditations (*Sermons of Thomas Watson*, 250-54).

45 See "Of the Sanctification of the Lord's Day," *Directory for the Publique Worship of God*.

46 *Christian Directions, shewing How to walk with God All the Day long* (London: R. Ibbitson and M. Wright, 1661), 66-67.

47 *The Saints' Everlasting Rest*, 560.

48 Ibid., 561-63.

49 William Fenner, *The Use and Benefit of Divine Meditation* (London: for John Stafford, 1657), 10.

50 *The Works of Thomas Manton*, 17:298.

51 *The Works of William Bates*, 3:125.

52 *The Works of Thomas Manton*, 17:299.

53 Ussher, *A Method for Meditation: or, A Manuall of Divine Duties, fit for every Christians Practice* (London: for Joseph Nevill, 1656), 30-31; White, *A Method and Instructions for the Art of Divine Meditation*, 29.

54 Calamy, *The Art of Divine Meditation*, 173.

55 *Heidelberg Catechism*, Q. 58.

56 *A Method for Meditation*, 32-33.

57 *Bishop Joseph Hall and Protestant Meditation*, 80-81.

58 *The Works of William Bates*, 136-39; Baxter, *The Saints' Everlasting Rest*, 567-70.

59 Calamy, *The Art of Divine Meditation*, 172.

60 Ibid., 164-68.

61 *The Works of George Swinnock* (Edinburgh: Banner of Truth Trust, 1998), 2:417.

62 Calamy, *The Art of Divine Meditation*, 178-84. Cf. Gouge, *Christian Directions, shewing How to walk with God All the Day long*, 70-73.

63 *The Works of Thomas Manton*, 17:281.

64 Baxter, *The Saints' Everlasting Rest*, 579-90.

65 Jonathan Edwards, *Religious Affections* (London: Banner of Truth Trust, 1959), 24.

66 *A Help to True Happinesse* (London, 1635).

67 *The Works of William Bates*, 3:145.

68 *The Use and Benefit of Divine Meditation*, 16-23.

69 Ussher, *A Method for Meditation*, 39.

70 *The Works of William Bridge* (Beaver Falls, Pa.: Soli Deo Gloria, 1989), 3:153.

71 Calamy, *The Art of Divine Meditation*, 108.

72 *The Sermons of Thomas Watson,* 269, 271.

73 *A Method and Instructions for the Art of Divine Meditation,* 53.

74 Ibid, 269.

75 *The Works of the Reverend and Faithfvll Servant of Iesvs Christ M. Richard Greenham,* 41.

76 *The Art of Meditation* (Jenkintown, Pa.: Sovereign Grace Publishers, 1972), 26-27.

77 *Christian Directions, shewing How to walk with God All the Day long,* 70.

78 *A Method for Meditation,* 43.

79 *The Art of Meditation,* 37-60. Due to its detail, I have not included Hall's list in my listing above.

80 *The Saints' Everlasting Rest,* 702.

81 Toon, *From Mind to Heart,* 95-96. For how to meditate on heaven, see White, *A Method and Instructions for the Art of Divine Meditation,* 281-94; Baxter, *The Saints' Everlasting Rest,* 620-52; *The Select Works of Thomas Case,* 1-232 (second book).

82 *The Art of Divine Meditation,* 4.

83 *A Method for Meditation,* 49.

84 *The Saints' Everlasting Rest,* 549-50.

85 *A Method and Instructions for the Art of Divine Meditation,* 88.

86 *The Art of Divine Meditation,* 88-96. Cf. *The Works of Thomas Manton,* 17:288-97.

87 "Meditation on the Holy Sacrament of the Lord's Last Supper," in *The Whole Works of the Right Rev. Edward Reynolds* (Morgan, Pa.: Soli Deo Gloria, 1999), 3:1-172.

88 *The Works of John Owen,* 9:558-63.

89 Cf. *Westminster Larger Catechism,* Questions 171, 174, 175.

90 *Solitude Improved by Divine Meditation* (Morgan, Pa.: Soli Deo Gloria, 1995), 280-321.

91 Calamy, *The Art of Divine Meditation,* 40-42.

92 *The Sermons of Thomas Watson,* 256.

93 *The Whole Works of the Rev. W. Bates,* 3:131.

94 *The Use and Benefit of Divine Meditation,* 3.

95 *The Application of Redemption,* 217.

96 *The Whole Works of the Rev. W. Bates,* 3:135.

97 *The Works of the Rev. William Bridge,* 3:133.

98 Cf. *The Whole Works of the Rev. Oliver Heywood,* 2:276-81.

99 *The Works of the Rev. Thomas Brooks,* 1:8, 291.

100 *The Works of Thomas Manton,* 6:145.

101 Ibid., 17:283.

102 *The Whole Works of the Rev. W. Bates,* 3:122-23.

103 *The Works of Thomas Manton,* 17:285. Cf. Hooker, *The Application of Redemption,* 230-40.

104 Calamy, *The Art of Divine Meditation,* 28-40.

105 *The Saints' Everlasting Rest,* 549.

106 *The Works of William Bridge,* 3:125

107 *A Collection of Sermons and Treatises* (London, 1636), 69-70.

108 *The Works of Thomas Manton,* 7:480.

109 Ibid., 6:145.

110 Calamy, *The Art of Divine Meditation,* 58-75.

111 Edmond Smith, *A Tree by a Stream: Unlock the Secrets of Active Meditation* (Ross-shire, Scotland: Christian Focus, 1995), 36.

112 *Solitude Improved by Divine Meditation,* 33.

113 *The Sermons of Thomas Watson,* 241-43.

5

The Didactic Use of the Law

Keep me from falsehood, let Thy law
With me in grace abide;
The way of faithfulness I choose,
Thy precepts are my guide.

I cleave unto Thy truth, O Lord;
From shame deliver me;
In glad obedience I will live
Through strength bestowed by Thee.[1]

The law of God directly or indirectly addresses the world and the life of every individual. Protestant theologians have written much about the various applications or uses of the law in the life of society at large and in the individual lives of both the unbeliever and the Christian. Classic Protestant theology posits a threefold use of the law: the *usus primus* ("first use"), or *civil* use of the law in the life and affairs of state and society; the *usus secundus* ("second use"), or *evangelical* use of the law as a teacher of sin in the experience or process of conversion unto God; and the *usus tertius* ("third use"), or *didactic* use of the law as a rule of thankful obedience on the part of the Christian.[2] It is this last or third use of the law that inspires the prayer of the psalmist cited above, for he knows that only God's law can direct him as he endeavors to live "in glad obedience" as a child of God.

This chapter briefly summarizes the first two uses of the law in order to examine its third use in the proper context of sanctification, which necessarily involves grateful obedience to God for His full-orbed salvation in Jesus Christ. The believer who is justified by faith alone, and adheres to the principle of "Scripture alone" *(sola scriptura)*, will thankfully and wholeheartedly trust and obey the Lord. This response of grateful obedience is fleshed out in a case study of the law's most controversial commandment—keeping the Sabbath day holy. All of this enables us to draw several significant conclusions about the Christian in his relationship to the third use of the law.

The Uses of the Law

The Civil Use of the Law

The first use of the law is its function in public life as a guide to the civil magistrate in the prosecution of his task as the minister of God in things pertaining to the state. The magistrate is required to reward good and punish evil (Rom. 13:3-4). Nothing could be more essential to this work than a reliable standard of right and wrong, good and evil. No better standard can be found than the law of God.

Here the Protestant Reformers were in complete accord. Concerning the restraint of sin, Martin Luther writes in his *Lectures on Galatians* (3:19), "The first understanding and use of the Law is to restrain the wicked.... This civic restraint is extremely necessary and was instituted by God, both for the sake of public peace and for the sake of preserving everything, but especially to prevent the course of the Gospel from being hindered by the tumults and seditions of wild men."[3] John Calvin concurs:

> The...function of the law is this: at least by fear of punishment to restrain certain men who are untouched by any care for what is just and right unless compelled by hearing the dire threats in the law. But they are restrained not because their inner mind is stirred or affected, but because, being bridled, so to speak, they keep their hands from outward activity, and hold inside the depravity that otherwise they would wantonly have indulged.[4]

The civil use of the law is rooted thoroughly in the Scriptures (most specifically in Romans 13:1-7) and in a realistic doctrine of fallen human nature. The law teaches us that the powers that be are ordained of God in order to administer justice—justice which necessarily includes being a terror to the workers of iniquity. The powers that be bear the sword; they possess a divinely conferred right of punishment, even of ultimate capital punishment (vv. 3-4).

This first use of the law, however, serves not only to prevent society from lapsing into chaos; it also serves to promote righteousness: "I exhort therefore, that, first of all, supplications, prayers, intercessions, and giving of thanks, be made for all men, for kings and for all that are in authority; that we may lead a quiet and peaceable life in all godliness and honesty" (1 Tim. 2:1-2). The "higher powers" must not only strive to intimidate evil, but also to provide a peaceable context in which the gospel, godliness, and honesty may prosper. This duty compels the state, the Reformers believed, to preserve certain rights, such as freedom of worship, freedom to preach, and freedom to observe the Lord's Day.

The implications of the first use of the law for the Christian are inescapable. He must respect and obey the state so long as the state does not command what God forbids or forbid what God commands. In all other cases, civil disobedience is unlawful. To resist authority is to resist the ordinance of God, "and they that resist shall receive to themselves damnation" (Rom. 13:2). This is critical to affirm in our day when even Christians are prone to be swept along with a worldly spirit of rebellion and contempt for authority. We need to hear and heed what Calvin writes:

> The first duty of subjects toward their magistrates is to think most honorably of their office, which they recognize as a jurisdiction bestowed by God, and on that account to esteem and reverence them as ministers and representatives of God…. [Even] in a very wicked man utterly unworthy of all honor, provided he has the public power in his hands, that noble and divine power resides which the Lord has by his Word given to the ministers of his justice and judgment.[5]

Of course, this does not imply that the believer forfeits his right to criticize or even condemn legislation which strays from the principles of Scripture. It does mean that a significant part of our "adorning the doctrine of God" involves our willing subjection to lawful authority in every sphere of life—be it in the home, school, church, or state.

The Evangelical Use of the Law[6]

Wielded by the Spirit of God, the moral law also serves a critical function in the experience of conversion. It disciplines, educates, convicts, curses. The law does not only expose our sinfulness; it also condemns us, pronounces a curse upon us, declares us liable to the wrath of God and the torments of hell. "Cursed is every one that continueth not in all things which are written in the book of the law to do them" (Gal. 3:10). The law is a hard taskmaster; it knows no mercy. It terrifies us, strips us of all our righteousness, and drives us to the end of the law, Christ Jesus, who is our only acceptable righteousness with God. "Wherefore the law was our schoolmaster to bring us unto Christ, that we might be justified by faith" (Gal. 3:24). Not that the law itself can lead us to a saving knowledge of God in Christ. Rather, the Holy Spirit uses the law as a mirror to show us our impotence and our guilt, to shut us up to hope in mercy alone, and to induce repentance, creating and sustaining the sense of spiritual need out of which faith in Christ is born.

Here, too, Luther and Calvin see eye-to-eye.[7] Typical of Luther's writings are his comments on Galatians 2:17:

> The proper use and aim of the Law is to make guilty those who are smug and at peace, so that they may see that they are in danger of sin, wrath, and death, so that they may be terrified and despairing, blanching and quaking at the rustling of a leaf (Lev. 26:36).... If the Law is a ministry of sin, it follows that it is also a ministry of wrath and death. For just as the Law reveals sin, so it strikes the wrath of God into a man and threatens him with death.[8]

Calvin is no less intense:

> [The law] warns, informs, convicts, and lastly condemns, every man of his own righteousness.... After he is compelled to weigh his life in the scales of the law, laying aside all that presumption of fictitious righteousness, he discovers that he is a long way from holiness, and is in fact teeming with a multitude of vices, with which he previously thought himself undefiled.... The law is like a mirror. In it we contemplate our weakness, then the iniquity arising from this, and finally the curse coming from both—just as a mirror shows us the spots on our face.[9]

This convicting use of the law is also critical for the believer's sanctification, for it serves to prevent the resurrection of self-righteousness—that ungodly self-righteousness which is always prone to reassert itself even in the holiest of saints. The believer continues to live under the law as a lifelong penitent.

This chastening work of the law does not imply that the believer's justification is ever diminished or annulled. From the moment of regeneration, his state before God is fixed and irrevocable. He is a new creation in Christ Jesus (2 Cor. 5:17). He can never revert to a state of condemnation nor lose his sonship. Nevertheless, the law exposes the ongoing poverty of his sanctification on a daily basis. He learns that there is a law in his members such that when he would do good, evil is present with him (Rom. 7:21). He must repeatedly condemn himself, deplore his wretchedness, and cry daily for fresh applications of the blood of Jesus Christ that cleanses from all sin (Rom. 7:24; 1 John 1:7, 9).

The Didactic Use of the Law

The third or didactic use of the law addresses the daily life of the Christian. In the words of the Heidelberg Catechism, the law instructs the believer how to express gratitude to God for deliverance from all his sin and misery (Question 2). The third use of the law is a subject that fills a rich chapter in the history of Reformation doctrine.

• Philip Melanchthon (1497-1560)
The history of the third use of the law begins with Philip Melanchthon, Luther's co-worker and right-hand support. Already in 1521, Melanchthon had planted the seed when he affirmed that "believers have use of the Decalogue" to assist them in mortifying the flesh.[10] In a formal sense, he increased the number of functions or uses of the law from two to three for the first time in a third edition of his work on Colossians published in 1534[11]—two years before Calvin produced the first edition of his *Institutes*. Melanchthon argued that the law coerces (first use), terrifies (second use), and requires obedience (third use). "The third reason for retaining the Decalogue," he writes, "is that obedience is required."[12]

By 1534, Melanchthon was using the forensic nature of justification as bedrock for establishing the necessity of good works in the believer's life.[13] He argued that though the believer's first and primary righteousness was his justification in Christ, there was also a second righteousness—the righteousness of a good conscience, which, notwithstanding

Philip Melanchthon

its imperfection, is still pleasing to God since the believer himself is in Christ.[14] The conscience of the believer, made good by divine declaration, must continue to use the law to please God, for the law reveals the essence of God's will and provides the framework of Christian obedience. He asserted that this "good conscience" is a "great and necessary godly consolation."[15] As Timothy Wengert asserts, he was no doubt encouraged to emphasize the connection between a good conscience and good works by his desire to defend Luther and other Protestants from the charge that they deny good works without at the same time robbing the conscience of the gospel's consolation. Melanchthon thus devised a way to speak of the necessity of works for the believer by excluding their necessity for justification.[16] Wengert concludes that by arguing from the necessity of knowing how we are forgiven, to the necessity of obeying the law, and to the necessity of knowing how this obedience pleases God, Melanchthon managed to place law and obedience at the center of his theology.[17]

• Martin Luther (1483-1546)

Unlike Melanchthon, who went on to codify the third use of the law in the 1535 and 1555 editions of his major work on Christian doctrine,[18] Luther never saw a need to formally embrace a third use of the law.

Martin Luther

Lutheran scholars, however, have debated at length over whether Luther taught in fact, though not in name, a third use of the law.[19] Suffice it to say, Luther advocated that though the Christian is not "under the law," this ought not be understood as if he were "without the law." For Luther, the believer has a different attitude to the law. The law is not an obligation, but a delight. The believer is joyfully moved towards God's law by the Spirit's power. He conforms to the law freely, not because of the law's demands, but because of his love for God and His righteousness.[20] Since in his experience the law's heavy yoke is replaced by the light yoke of Christ, doing what the law commands becomes a joyous and spontaneous action. The law drives sinners to Christ through whom they "become doers of the law."[21] Moreover, because he remains sinful, the Christian needs the law to direct and regulate his life. Thus Luther can assert that the law which serves as a "stick" (i.e., rod—second use) God uses to beat him to Christ, is simultaneously a "stick" (i.e., cane—which Calvin would call the third use) that assists him in walking the Christian life. This emphasis on the law as a "walking-stick" is borne out implicitly by his exposition of the ten commandments in various contexts—each of which indicates that he firmly believed that the Christian life is to be regulated by these commandments.[22]

Luther's concern was not to deny sanctification nor the law as a guiding norm in the believer's life; rather, he wished to emphasize that good works and obedience to the law can in no way make us acceptable with God. Hence he writes in *The Freedom of the Christian,* "Our faith in Christ does not free us from works, but from false opinions concerning works, that is, from the foolish presumption that justification is acquired by works." And in *Table Talk* he is quoted as saying, "Whoso has Christ has rightly fulfilled the law, but to take away the law altogether, which sticks in nature, and is written in our hearts and born in us, is a thing impossible and against God."[23]

• John Calvin (1509-1564)
What Melanchthon began to develop in the direction of a God-pleasing righteousness in Christ and Luther left somewhat undeveloped as a joyous action and a "walking-stick," Calvin fleshed out as a full-fledged doctrine, teaching that the primary use of the law for the believer is as a rule of life. Though Calvin borrowed Melanchthon's terminology, "third use of the law" (*tertius usus legis*), and probably gleaned additional material from Martin Bucer,[24] he provided new contours and content to

the doctrine and was unique among the early Reformers in stressing that this third function of the law as a norm and guide for the believer is its "proper and principal" use.[25]

Calvin's teaching on the third use of the law is crystal clear. "What is the rule of life which [God] has given us?" he asks in the Genevan Catechism, and replies, "His law." Later in the same catechism, he writes:

> [The law] shows the mark at which we ought to aim, the goal towards which we ought to press, that each of us, according to the measure of grace bestowed upon him, may endeavour to frame his life according to the highest rectitude, and, by constant study, continually advance more and more.[26]

Calvin wrote definitively of the third use of the law already in 1536 in the first edition of his *Institutes of the Christian Religion:*

> Believers...profit by the law because from it they learn more thoroughly each day what the Lord's will is like.... It is as if some servant, already prepared with complete earnestness of heart to commend himself to his master, must search out and oversee his master's ways in order to conform and accommodate himself to them. Moreover, however much they may be prompted by the Spirit and eager to obey God, they are still weak in the flesh, and would rather serve sin than God. The law is to this flesh like a whip to an idle and balky ass, to goad, stir, arouse it to work.[27]

In the last edition of the *Institutes,* completed in 1559, Calvin retains what he wrote in 1536, but stresses even more clearly and positively that believers profit from the law in two ways: first, "here is the best instrument for them to learn more thoroughly each day the nature of the Lord's will to which they aspire, and to confirm them in the understanding of it"; second, by "frequent meditation upon it to be aroused to obedience, be strengthened in it, and be drawn back from the slippery path of transgression. In this way the saints must press on." Calvin concludes: "For what would be less lovable than the law if, with importuning and threatening alone, it troubled souls through fear, and distressed them through fright? David especially shows that in the law he apprehended the Mediator, without whom there is no delight or sweetness."[28]

This predominantly positive view of the law as a norm and guide for the believer to encourage him to cling to God and to obey God ever more fervently is where Calvin distances himself from Luther. For Luther, the law generally denotes something negative and hostile—something usually listed in close proximity with sin, death, or the devil.

Luther's dominant interest is in the second use of the law, even when he considers the function of the law in sanctifying the believer. For Calvin, as I. John Hesselink correctly notes, "the law was viewed primarily as a positive expression of the will of God.... Calvin's view could be called Deuteronomic, for to him law and love are not antithetical, but are correlates."[29] For Calvin, the believer strives to follow God's law not as an act of *compulsory* obedience, but as a response of *grateful* obedience. The law promotes, under the tutelage of the Spirit, an ethic of gratitude in the believer, which both encourages loving obedience and cautions him against sin, so that he sings with David in Psalm 19:

Most perfect is the law of God,
Restoring those that stray;
His testimony is most sure,
Proclaiming wisdom's way.

The precepts of the Lord are right;
With joy they fill the heart;
The Lord's commandments all are pure,
And clearest light impart.

The fear of God is undefiled
And ever shall endure;
The statutes of the Lord are truth
And righteousness most pure.

They warn from ways of wickedness
Displeasing to the Lord,
And in the keeping of His word
There is a great reward.[30]

In summary, for Luther, the law *helps* the believer—especially in recognizing and confronting indwelling sin; for Calvin, the believer *needs* the law to direct him in holy living in order to serve God out of love.[31]

• The Heidelberg Catechism (1563)
Ultimately, Calvin's view of the third use of the law won the day in Reformed theology. An early indication of this strongly Calvinistic view of the law is found in the Heidelberg Catechism, composed a year or two before Calvin's death. Though the Catechism begins with an intense emphasis on the evangelical use of the law in driving sinners to Christ (Questions 3-18), a detailed exhortation on the prohibitions and re-

quirements of the law placed upon the believer is reserved for the final section which teaches "how I shall express my *gratitude* to God" for deliverance in Jesus Christ (Questions 92-115).[32] The Decalogue provides the material content for good works which are done out of thankfulness for the grace of God in His beloved Son.

- The Puritans

The Puritans carried on Calvin's emphasis on the normativity of the law for the believer as a rule of life and to arouse heartfelt gratitude, which in turn promotes genuine liberty rather than antinomian licentiousness.[33] To cite only a few of hundreds of Puritan sources available on these themes: Anthony Burgess condemns those who assert that they are above the law or that the law written in the heart by regeneration "renders the written law needless."[34] Typically Puritan is Thomas Bedford's affirmation for the need of the written law as the believer's guide:

> There must also be another law written in tables, and to be read by the eye, to be heard by the ear: Else…how shall the believer himself be sure that he doth not swerve from the right way wherein he ought to walk?… The Spirit, I grant, is the justified man's Guide and Teacher:… But he teacheth them…by the law and testimony.[35]

The Spirit's teaching results in Christians being made "friends" with the law, Samuel Rutherford quipped, for "after Christ has made agreement between us and the law, we delight to walk in it for the love of Christ."[36] That delight, grounded in grateful gratitude for the gospel, produces an unspeakable liberty. Samuel Crooke put it this way: "From the commandment, as a rule of life, [believers] are not freed, but on the contrary, are inclined and disposed, by [their] free spirit, to willingly obey it. Thus, to the regenerate the law becomes as it were gospel, even a law of liberty."[37] The Westminster Larger Catechism, composed largely by Puritan divines, provides the most fitting summary of the Reformed and Puritan view on the believer's relationship to the moral law:

> *Q. 97. What special use is there of the moral law to the regenerate?*
>
> A. Although they that are regenerate, and believe in Christ, be delivered from the moral law as a covenant of works, so as thereby they are neither justified nor condemned; yet, besides the general uses thereof common to them with all men, it is of special use, to shew them how much they are bound to Christ for his fulfilling it, and enduring the curse thereof in their stead, and for their good; and thereby to provoke them to more thankfulness, and to express the same in their greater care to conform themselves thereunto as the rule of their obedience.[38]

But how do the Reformation principles of gratitude work themselves out in actual practice as the believer seeks to obey the law as a rule of life? To this question we now turn in the form of a case study as we consider the moral law's most controversial commandment in our day—"Remember the sabbath day, to keep it holy" (Ex. 20:8).

The Fourth Commandment: A Case Study
Central to the concern fostered by Reformed Christianity to apply the moral law to Christian living has been the sanctification of the first day of the week as the Christian Sabbath. If there was any degree of ambiguity among the Reformers of the sixteenth century, it had utterly vanished when, in the midst of the seventeenth century, the Westminster divines assembled to write their Confession of Faith (Chapter 21):

> 7. As it is the law of nature, that, in general, a due proportion of time be set apart for the worship of God; so, in His Word, by a positive, moral, and perpetual commandment, binding all men, in all ages, He hath particularly appointed one day in seven, for a Sabbath, to be kept holy unto Him: which, from the beginning of the world to the resurrection of Christ, was the last day of the week; and, from the resurrection of Christ, was changed into the first day of the week, which, in Scripture, is called the Lord's Day, and is to be continued to the end of the World, as the Christian Sabbath.

> 8. This Sabbath is then kept holy unto the Lord, when men, after a due preparing of their hearts, and ordering of their common affairs beforehand, do not only observe an holy rest, all the day, from their own works, words, and thoughts about their worldly employments, and recreations, but also are taken up the whole time in the public and private exercises of His worship, and in the duties of necessity and mercy.[39]

This high view of the Sabbath won the day in Britain, North America, throughout the British Empire, and also in the Netherlands. Though it was a key concern of the Reformed Christians, Sabbath observance was embraced as a rule by Christians of nearly every denomination. In the wake of the powerful revivals of the mid-eighteenth and early nineteenth centuries, Sabbath-keeping was embraced by the general population as well.

This happy state of affairs prevailed throughout the nineteenth century and into the twentieth. Large urban centers such as Philadelphia and Toronto were known for the care with which the Sabbath was observed by their inhabitants. Until the end of the nineteenth century, some major railroads ceased operations on Sundays. Seaside resorts took such measures as banning all motor traffic from the streets on Sundays (Ocean Grove, N.J.) and the use of movie houses for public worship on Sunday evenings (Ocean City, N.J.).

Today's scene presents a vastly altered aspect. The forces of secularization and the rise of the leisure culture, obsessed with pursuing recreations of all kinds, have extinguished concern for Sabbath observance in the general population. Even more tragic is the steady erosion of conviction on the part of Christians. The greatest damage was done by modernism's attack on the authority of Scripture, thus undermining and overthrowing all biblical norms for living. However, Fundamentalism must also bear its share of the blame. Under the influence of Dispensationalism, a growing antinomianism developed in the most conservative circles of American Christians. The Old Testament in general, and the moral law in particular, came to be regarded as monuments of a bygone era. The result has been wholesale destruction of conviction regarding the Sabbath, even among Presbyterians who subscribe to the Westminster Standards—notwithstanding the jarring inconsistency involved!

Surely the time is ripe for Christians to look once more to God's Word for instruction regarding the fourth commandment and its claims upon us. If for no other reason, the study should be undertaken in view of the mounting evidence of the high degree of destructive stress lurking behind the appealing facade of the so-called "culture of leisure." Men are destroying themselves because they cannot say no, whether at work or at play. Great spiritual blessings are promised to those who subject themselves to the self-denying discipline of Sabbath observance.

The Sabbath as a Divine Institution

"The seventh day is the sabbath of the LORD thy God" (Ex. 20:10). These words remind us that the Sabbath is a divine institution in two senses. First, the weekly Sabbath is instituted by God's word of command. Secondly, God claims the day as His own: "the Sabbath of Jehovah thy God." The six days of the work week are ceded to man for his labor and leisure pursuits; not so the Sabbath, which God names as "my holy day" in Isaiah 58:13. Not to devote the day to the purposes and activities commanded for its sanctification is to rob God of that which belongs to Him.

This truth is reinforced by the words of the Lord Jesus Christ recorded by the first three evangelists (Matt. 12:8, Mark 2:28, and Luke 6:5) when He said, "The Son of man is Lord of the sabbath." At one blow, Christ asserts His full deity and identity with Jehovah and reaffirms the claim of God upon the hours of the weekly Sabbath, embracing the claim and restating it in His own name. The claim left its mark on the beliefs, practices, and usages of the Apostolic Church, so that by the end of that era, the Christian Sabbath was known as "the Lord's day" (Rev. 1:10).

The Sabbath as a Creation Ordinance

A common error is to assume that the Sabbath originates with the giving of the law at Sinai. Such a view ignores the fact that the Sabbath is not introduced as something new, but rather acknowledged as something ancient and historic that is now to be recalled and observed by God's people: "*Remember* the sabbath day, to keep it holy" (Ex. 20:8).

And what, specifically, is to be remembered in the pattern of six days of work punctuated by a day of holy rest? "In six days the LORD made heaven and earth, the sea, and all that in them is, and rested the seventh day: wherefore the LORD blessed the sabbath day, and hallowed it" (Ex. 20:11).

The biblical answer to the question of when was the Sabbath instituted, and by whom, is abundantly clear: the Sabbath was instituted by God at the very dawn of history. Of course, man was present, and significantly, it was the first full day of his life on earth (Gen. 2:1-3). Whether the pattern was perpetuated after that point or not is perhaps a matter of speculation, but the history of the Sabbath was not lost. All that was necessary at Sinai was to recall that history, and to charge the people to keep up the remembrance of it ever afterwards.

The Sabbath is therefore not strictly a Mosaic ordinance. Its origin is rooted in creation itself, and like marriage, the Sabbath is an institution of the highest significance to the human race. Its temporal blessings may be enjoyed by all mankind, and its spiritual blessings are promised to all who seek them, even to the "eunuchs" and "the sons of the stranger, that join themselves to the LORD" (Isa. 56:1-8).

The Sabbath as Redemptive Memorial

In the recapitulation of the ten commandments (Deut. 5:6-21), we discover that redemption does not alter or annul the requirement to keep the Sabbath holy. Rather, it only adds to the meaning of the day for those who are "the redeemed of the LORD." Just as, in the New Testament, slaves were to share fully with their masters in the blessing of the gospel, so it was a law in Israel that servants were to enjoy the rest provided for in the fourth commandment along with their masters: "that thy manservant and thy maidservant may rest as well as thou" (Deut. 5:14). To this is added the following reminder: "And remember that thou wast a servant in the land of Egypt, and that the LORD thy God brought thee out thence through a mighty hand and by a stretched out arm: therefore the LORD thy God commanded thee to keep the sabbath day" (v. 15). With these words the Sabbath assumes a new meaning and function as a memorial of the redemption from bondage which God wrought for His people. This added meaning reinforces the Sabbath as an institution among God's people.

Here also is an anticipation of the impact of Christ's death and resurrection on the Sabbath observance of His followers. So great was this climactic and decisive fulfillment of the promise of redemption, closely followed by the outpouring of the Spirit on the day of Pentecost, that from that time onward the Sabbath "was changed into the first day of the week, which, in Scripture, is called the Lord's Day, and is to be continued to the end of the world, as the Christian Sabbath" (WCF, 21:7).

The result is, as the apostle Paul writes in Hebrews 4:9, "There remaineth therefore a rest to the people of God." The Sabbath is with us still as a sign of something that is yet to be attained, experienced, and enjoyed in the eternal state. At the same time, because the word he uses for "rest" is *sabbatismos*, or "a keeping of a sabbath" (see KJV margin), the obligation to observe a weekly Sabbath continues under the gospel. Sabbath-keeping became, in fact, a mark of Christian discipleship in the age of the martyrs, as Maurice Roberts relates: "One question put to the martyrs before they were put to death was: 'Dominicum servasti?' (Do you keep the Lord's Day?)"[40]

The Sabbath as Eschatological Sign

The prophecy of Isaiah closes with the announcement of the promise of the new heavens and the new earth for God's people: "For, behold, I create new heavens and a new earth: and the former shall not be remembered, nor come into mind" (Isa. 65:17). In this new creation, the labor of God's people shall be wholly redeemed from the curse: "They shall not labour in vain, nor bring forth trouble; for they are the seed of the blessed of the LORD, and their offspring with them" (v. 23).

This new order of creation will abide as the consummation of the promise of redemption. Not only is the labor of God's people to be wholly redeemed from the curse; the Sabbath also will at last come into its own as the universal day for the worship of Jehovah. Such is the promise of God: "For as the new heavens and the new earth, which I will make, shall remain before me, saith the LORD, so shall your seed and your name remain. And it shall come to pass, that from one new moon to another, and from one sabbath to another, shall all flesh come to worship before me, saith the LORD" (Isa. 66:22-23).

In summary, the Sabbath stands as an institution as old as creation itself. It belongs to the order of things as they were at the beginning, before man's fall into sin. It is as universal as any other creation ordinance, holding the promise of blessing for all mankind. The promise of redemption and its fulfillment only add to the significance of the Sabbath as a day to be observed by the redeemed of the Lord. The Sabbath is a sign of the promise of redemption, both in its fulfillment now, and also the consummation which is yet to be. It is God's day, a holy day—a day for Christians to keep holy.

Christ and the Sabbath
The Sabbath is as much a feature of the New Testament landscape as of the Old. The question of the Sabbath and how it ought to be kept was an oft-revisited battlefield in the war of Christ against the Pharisees. So intense was His opposition to the Pharisees' ideas of Sabbath-keeping that many have concluded that Christ was opposed to the Sabbath itself, and would therefore be opposed to any continuation of Sabbath-keeping among His followers.

Such a conclusion ignores or conflicts with three key facts of the gospel records. First, Christ Himself kept the Sabbath faithfully (see Luke 4:16). Second, Christ declared that He had not come to destroy the law, and it follows therefore that He had not come to destroy or abolish the Sabbath (see Matt. 5:17). Third, Christ claimed the Sabbath as His own, as we have seen already: "The Son of man is Lord of the sabbath."

Christ's conflict with the Pharisees must be viewed therefore as a campaign not to destroy, but rather to reclaim and restore the Biblical institution of the Sabbath. Accordingly Christ embraced the Sabbath and claimed it as His own. Moreover, He declared that He personally will fulfill the promise of the Sabbath in the lives of His disciples: "Come unto me, all ye that labour and are heavy laden, and I will give you rest. Take my yoke upon you, and learn of me; for I am meek and lowly in heart: and ye shall find rest unto your souls" (Matt. 11:28-29). Even here Christ sounds the note of opposition to the Pharisees and their "yoke" of traditional proscriptions and prohibitions regarding the

Sabbath. Peter referred to this yoke, and declared it was one "neither our fathers nor we were able to bear" (Acts 15:10). Christ offers a very different yoke, and says, "My yoke is easy, and my burden is light" (Matt. 11:30). To take Christ's yoke is to become His disciple, just as to take that of the Pharisees was to become theirs. To those who embrace Christ with a true faith, He promises rest as the fulfillment of redemption, in sharp contrast to the denial of that rest to the unbelieving and disobedient Israelites (Ps. 95:10, 11).

This rest consists of putting an end to the fruitless toil of seeking to be justified by works of the law. Christ also lifts from our backs the burden of the guilt of all our sins. Nor is this all, for there is the promise of more to come when we have put off "this body of death" (Rom. 7:25, margin): "And I heard a voice from heaven saying unto me, Write, Blessed are the dead which die in the Lord from henceforth: Yea, saith the Spirit, that they may rest from their labours; and their works do follow them" (Rev. 14:13). With this in mind, the apostle reminds believers of "a promise being left us of entering into his rest" and adds this exhortation, involving a profound play on words: "Let us labour therefore to enter into that rest" (Heb. 4:1, 11).

The Christian and the Sabbath

How should the followers of Christ keep the Sabbath today? Many writers have offered answers to this question.[41] For the present purpose, however, we prefer to point to three rich sources of guidance: the fourth commandment itself; the prophet Isaiah; and the teachings and example of Christ Jesus our Lord.

The fourth commandment in its two canonical forms (Ex. 20:8-11 and Deut. 5:12-15) provides much instruction. First, we must lay aside our daily tasks and employments. We must do so individually, as families, as congregations, and as communities. Second, we must turn our minds and hearts to the great themes of Holy Scripture: the wonderful works of God as Creator, Redeemer, and Sanctifier. Third, we must engage in those activities which obtain, increase, and express knowledge of the holiness of God, and our own holiness in Christ. "Remember the Sabbath day, to keep it *holy*."

The prophet Isaiah lived in a day much like our own, a time of prosperity and general affluence. He has a clear word to say about the perils of such affluence, in the form of the "culture of leisure" that prosperity makes possible:

If thou turn away thy foot from the sabbath, from doing thy pleasure on my holy day; and call the sabbath a delight, the holy of the LORD, honourable; and shalt honour him, not doing thine own ways, nor finding thine own pleasure, nor speaking thine own words: then shalt thou delight thyself in the LORD; and I will cause thee to ride upon the high places of the earth, and feed thee with the heritage of Jacob thy father: for the mouth of the LORD hath spoken it (Isa. 58:13,14).

Here the prophet extends the ban on engaging in labor to include the pursuit of our personal recreations and leisure-time activities. Even the words we speak are to be regulated by the commandment. In return, the prophet promises a wonderful kind of spiritual liberty and enjoyment of God: "Then shalt thou delight thyself in the LORD!"

Finally, we must consider the teachings and example of the Lord Jesus Christ. He stamped the day with an indelible, Christian character when He said, "The Son of man is Lord of the sabbath day." Henceforth it was only right to speak of the *Christian* Sabbath. He reclaimed the day as an institution designed for the good and blessing of mankind when he reminded the Pharisees that "the sabbath was made for man, and not man for the sabbath" (Mark 2:27). He taught us thereby not to encumber the day with strictures that work against basic human needs. He further insisted that "it is lawful to do well" (Matt. 12:12) and "lawful…to do good" (Luke 6:9) on the Sabbath. Here he sanctions works of mercy and compassion done in His name and for His sake.

From Christ's example we learn diligently to attend the church of God, assembling on the Sabbath to hear God's Word (Luke 4:16). It is likewise a day on which the ministers of the Word are to devote themselves to teaching and preaching (Luke 4:31). It is a day to do good to our fellow members of the household of faith (Luke 4:38, 39) and to extend and receive the grace of Christian hospitality (Luke 14:1) as part of the fellowship of the saints appropriate to the day (see also Luke 24:29, 42). Finally, the Sabbath days are to be the great days for the manifestation and enjoyment of the grace of God revealed in the gospel—grace that opens our blind eyes, rebukes in us the fever of sin, sets us free from our sore bondage, triumphs over the devil and his host, restores what sin has caused to wither away, and heals all the sicknesses of our hearts and minds. It can fairly be said that everything Christ ever did on the Sabbath was aimed at this one thing: to reveal and proclaim the grace of God to sinners.

We conclude therefore that to omit or neglect the sanctification of the Christian Sabbath is to disobey God, break faith with the Lord Jesus, and rob ourselves of great blessing. Likewise, to keep the Sabbath as it ought to be kept, according to the teaching and example of our Lord, is a large part of living to the glory of God, and is nothing less than "to begin in this life the eternal sabbath" (Heidelberg Catechism, Question 103).

Conclusions

Biblical character of the third use of the law

Several important conclusions about the Christian's third use of the law can now be drawn.[42] First, the third use of the law is *biblical*. Old and New Testament scriptures teem with expositions of the law directed primarily at believers to assist them in the abiding pursuit of sanctification. The Psalms repeatedly affirm that the believer relishes the law of God both in the inner man and in his outward life.[43] One of the psalmists' greatest concerns is to ascertain the good and perfect will of God, and then to run in the way of His commandments. The Sermon on the Mount and the ethical portions of Paul's epistles are prime New Testament examples of the law being used as a rule of life. The directions contained in these portions of Scripture are intended primarily for those already redeemed, and seek to encourage them to reflect a theology of grace with an ethic of gratitude. In this ethic of gratitude the believer lives out of and follows in the footsteps of his Savior, who was Himself the Servant of the Lord and Law-Fulfiller, daily obeying all His Father's commandments throughout His earthly sojourn.

Contrary to antinomianism and legalism

Second, the third use of the law combats both *antinomianism* and *legalism*. Antinomianism (*anti*=against; *nomos*=law) teaches that Christians no longer have any obligation toward the moral law because Jesus has fulfilled it and freed them from it in saving them by grace alone. Paul, of course, strongly rejected this heresy in Romans 3:8, as did Luther in his battles against Johann Agricola, and as did the New England Puritans in their opposition to Anne Hutchinson. Antinominians misunderstand the nature of justification by faith, which, though granted apart from works of the law, does not preclude the necessity of sanctification. One of sanctification's most important constituitive elements is the daily cultivation of grateful obedience to the law. As Samuel Bolton graphically states, "The law sends us to the gospel, that we may be justified, and the gospel sends us to the law again to enquire what is our duty, being justified."[44]

. Antinomians charge that those who maintain the necessity of the law as a rule of life for the believer fall prey to legalism. Now it is possible, of course, that abuse of the third use of the law can result in legalism. When an elaborate code is developed for believers to follow, covering every conceivable problem and tension in moral living, no freedom is left for believers in any area of their lives to make personal, existential decisions based on the principles of Scripture. In such a context man-made law smothers the divine gospel, and legalistic sanctification swallows up gracious justification. The Christian is then brought back into a bondage akin to that of medieval Roman Catholic monasticism.

The law affords us a comprehensive ethic, but not an exhaustive application. Scripture provides us with broad principles and illustrative paradigms, not minute particulars which can be mechanically applied to every circumstance. Daily, the Christian must bring the law's broad strokes to bear on his particular decisions, carefully weighing all things according to the "law and testimony" (Isa. 8:20) while striving and praying all the while for a growing sense of Christian prudence.

Legalism and thankful obedience to God's law operate in two radically different spheres. They differ as much from each other as do compulsory, begrudging slavery and willing, joyous service. Sadly, too many in our day confuse "law" or "legal" with "legalism" or being "legalistic." Seldom is it realized that Christ did not reject the law when He rejected legalism. Legalism is indeed a tyrant and an antagonist, but law must be our helpful and necessary friend. Legalism is a futile attempt to attain merit with God. Legalism is the error of the Pharisees: it cultivates outward conformity to the letter of the law without regard for inward attitude of the heart.

The third use of the law steers a middle course between antinomianism and legalism. Neither antinomianism nor legalism are true to either the law or the gospel. As John Fletcher has perceptively noted, "Pharisees are no more truly legal than antinomians are truly evangelical."[45] Antinomianism emphasizes Christian freedom from the condemnation of the law at the expense of the believer's pursuit of holiness. It accents justification at the expense of sanctification. It fails to see that the abrogation of the law's *condemning* power does not abrogate the law's *commanding* power. Legalism so stresses the believer's pursuit of holiness that obedience to the law becomes something more than the fruit of faith. Obedience then becomes a constituent element of justification. The commanding power of the law for sanctification all but suffocates the condemning power of the law for justification. In the final analysis, legalism denies in practice, if not in theory, a Reformed concept of justification. It accents sanctification at the expense of justification. The Reformed concept of the third use of the law helps the believer safeguard both in doctrine and in practice a healthy balance between justification and sanctification.[46] Justification necessarily leads to and finds its proper fruit in sanctification.[47] Salvation is by gracious faith alone, and yet, cannot but produce works of grateful obedience.

Promotes spontaneous love

Third, the third use of the law promotes *love*. "For this is the love of God, that we keep his commandments: and his commandments are not grievous" (1 John 5:3). God's law is a gift and evidence of His tender love for His children (Ps. 147:19-20). It is not a cruel or hard taskmaster for those who are in Christ. God is no more cruel in giving His law to His own than is a farmer who builds fences to protect his cattle and horses from wandering into roads and highways. This was vividly illustrated recently in Alberta, where a horse belonging to a farmer broke through her fence, found her way to the highway, and was struck by a car. Not only the horse, but also the 17-year-old driver was killed immediately. The farmer and his family wept all night. Broken fences do irreparable damage. Broken commandments reap untold consequences. But God's law, obeyed out of Spirit-worked love, promotes joy and the rejoicing of the heart. Let us thank God for His law which fences us in to contented enjoyment of the green pastures of His Word.

In Scripture law and love are not enemies, but best of friends. Indeed, the essence of the law is love: "Thou shalt love the Lord thy God with all thy heart, and with all thy soul, and with all thy mind. This is the first and great commandment. And the second is like unto it, Thou shalt love thy neighbour as thyself. On these two commandments hang all the law and the prophets" (Matt. 22:37-40; cf. Rom. 13:8-10). Just as a loving subject obeys his king, a loving son obeys his father, and a loving wife submits to her husband, so a loving believer yearns to obey the law of God. Then, as we have seen, the dedication of the entire Sabbath to God becomes not a burden, but a delight.

Promotes authentic Christian freedom

Finally, the third use of the law promotes *freedom*—genuine Christian freedom. Today's widespread abuse of the idea of Christian liberty, which is only freedom taken as an occasion to serve the flesh, should not obscure the fact that true Christian freedom is both defined and protected by the lines drawn for the believer in the law of God. Where God's law limits our freedom, it is only for our greater good; and where God's law imposes no such limits, in matters of faith and worship, the Christian enjoys perfect freedom of conscience from all the doctrines and commandments of men. In matters of daily life, true Christian freedom consists in the willing, thankful, and joyful obedience which the believer renders to God and to Christ. As Calvin wrote of the consciences of true Christians, that they "observe the law, not as if constrained by the necessity of the law, but that freed from the law's yoke they willingly obey God's will."[48]

God's Word binds us as believers, but *His* alone. He alone is Lord of our consciences. We are truly free in keeping God's commandments, for freedom flows out of grateful servitude, not out of autonomy or anarchy. We were created to love and serve God above all, and our neighbor as ourselves—all in accord with God's will and Word. Only when we realize this purpose again do we find true Christian freedom. True freedom, Calvin writes, is "a free servitude and a serving freedom." True freedom is obedient freedom. Only "those who serve God are free…. We obtain liberty in order that we may more promptly and more readily obey God."[49]

> *I am, O Lord, Thy servant, bound yet free,*
> *Thy handmaid's son, whose shackles Thou hast broken;*
> *Redeemed by grace, I'll render as a token*
> *Of gratitude my constant praise to Thee.*[50]

This then is the only way to live and to die: "We are God's," concludes Calvin, "let us therefore live for him and die for him. We are God's: let his wisdom and will therefore rule all our actions. We are God's: let all the parts of our life accordingly strive toward him as our only lawful goal."[51]

---

[1] Psalm 119:29-32, metrical version, *The Psalter* (1912; reprint Grand Rapids: Eerdmans, 1995), No. 324:3-4.

[2] Many Reformed theologians, following Calvin, invert the first and second uses of the law.

[3] "Lectures on Galatians, 1535," *Luther's Works,* ed. Jeroslav Pelikan (St. Louis: Concordia, 1963), 26:308-309.

[4] *Institutes of the Christian Religion,* ed. John T. McNeill, trans. Ford Lewis Battles (Philadelphia: Westminster Press, 1960), Book 2, chapter 7, paragraph 10. (Hereafter, *Institutes* 2.7.10.)

[5] *Institutes* 4.20.22, 25.

[6] In selecting a term for this use of the law, we are aware of the many possibilities in the literature, but have chosen the term which best expresses the Reformed view of the relationship of the law and the gospel, to wit, that they are complementary and not antithetical. Here we are dealing with that work of the law which prepares the heart of the sinner to receive Christ freely offered in the gospel to sinners as the only Savior from the law's condemnation, curse, and punishment—i.e., with evangelical rather than legal convictions. The Puritans excelled in describing this distinction, stressing that legal conviction deals only with the consequences of sin whereas evangelical conviction grapples with sin itself and the need to be delivered from it by Christ. For example, Stephen Charnock wrote, "A legally-convinced person would only be freed from the pain [of sin], an evangelically-convinced person from the sin [itself]" (I.D.E. Thomas, *Puritan Quotations* [Chicago: Moody, 1975], 167).

[7] The only substantial difference between Luther and Calvin on the evangelical use of the law is that for Luther this is the law's primary use, whereas for Calvin the third use of the law is primary.

[8] *Luther's Works* 26:148, 150.

[9] *Institutes* 2.7.6-7.

[10] *The Loci Communes of Philip Melanchthon [1521],* trans. Charles Leander Hill (Boston: Meador, 1944), 234.

[11] *Scholia in Epistolam Pauli ad Colossense iterum ab authore recognita* (Wittenberg: J. Klug, 1534), XLVIII r, LXXXII v - LXXXIII v.

[12] *Ibid.,* XCIIII v.

[13] *Ibid.,* XVII r.

[14] *Ibid.,* XC v.

[15] *Ibid.,* L v.

[16] Timothy Wengert, *Law and Gospel: Philip Melanchthon's Debate with John Agricola of Eisleben over* Poenitentia (Grand Rapids: Baker, 1997), 200-204.

[17] *Ibid.,* 205-206.

[18] *Melanchthon on Christian Doctrine (Loci communes 1555),* trans. and ed. Clyde L. Manschreck (Oxford: University Press, 1965), 127.

[19] Cf. Hans Engelland, *Melanchthon, Glauben und Handeln* (Munich: Kaiser Verlag, 1931); Werner Elert, "Eine theologische Falschung zur Lehre vom tertius usus legis," *Zeitschrift für Religions- und Geistesgeschichte* 1 (1948):168-70; Wilfried Joest, *Gesetz und Freiheit: Das Problem des tertius usus legis bei Luther und die neutestamentliche Parainese* (Göttingen: Vandenhoeck & Ruprecht, 1951); Hayo Gerdes, *Luthers Streit mit den Schwarmern um das rechte Verständnis des Gesetzes Mose* (Göttingen: Gottiner Verlagsanstalt, 1955), 111-116; Gerhard Ebeling, *Luther: An Introduction to His Thought,* trans. R. A. Wilson (Philadelphia: Fortress, 1970); Eugene F. Klug, "Luther on Law, Gospel, and the Third Use of the Law," *The Springfielder* 38 (1974):155-69; A.C. George, "Martin Luther's Doctrine of Sanctification with Special Reference to the Formula *Simul Iustus et Peccator*: A Study in Luther's Lectures on Romans and Galatians" (Th.D. dissertation, Westminster Theological Seminary, 1982), 195-210.

[20] Cf. Paul Althaus, *The Theology of Martin Luther,* trans. Robert Schultz (Philadelphia: Fortress, 1966), 267.

[21] *Luther's Works* 26:260.

[22] See *On Good Works, The Freedom of the Christian, Small Catechism, Large Catechism, Disputations with Antinomians.*

23 Cited by Donald MacLeod, "Luther and Calvin on the Place of the Law," in *Living the Christian Life* (Huntingdon, England: Westminster Conference, 1974), 10-11.

24 Speaking of believers, Bucer taught that "Christ will indeed have freed [*liberasse*], but will not have loosed [*solvisse*] us from the law" (*Enarrationes* [1530], 158b; cf. 50a-51b). Francois Wendel suggests that the three functions of the law "recognized by Melanchthon" were "further accentuated by Bucer in his Commentaries" (*Calvin: The Origins and Development of His Religious Thought*, trans. Philip Mairet [New York: Harper & Row, 1963], 198). For example, Bucer wrote that the law "is in no sense abolished, but is so much the more potent in each one as he is more richly endowed with the Spirit of Christ" (*ibid.*, 204). Cf. Ralph Roger Sundquist, "The Third Use of the Law in the Thought of John Calvin: An Interpretation and Evaluation" (Ph.D. dissertation, Union Theological Seminary, 1970), 317-18.

25 For Calvin, the convicting use of the law is not its "proper" use for this was to drive a sinner to Christ, and the civic use was only an "accidental" purpose. Cf. Victor Shepherd, *The Nature and Function of Faith in the Theology of John Calvin* (Macon, Ga.: Mercer, 1983), 153ff.

26 *Selected Works of John Calvin: Tracts and Letters,* ed. Henry Beveridge and Jules Bonnet (1849; reprint Grand Rapids: Baker, 1983), 2:56, 69.

27 *Institutes of the Christian Religion: 1536 Edition,* trans. Ford Lewis Battles (Grand Rapids: Eerdmans, 1975), 36.

28 *Institutes* 2.7.12. Calvin gleans considerable support for his third use of the law from the Davidic Psalms (cf. *Institutes* 2.7.12 and his *Commentary on the Book of Psalms,* trans. James Anderson, 5 vols. [Grand Rapids: Eerdmans, 1949]).

29 "Law—Third use of the law," in *Encyclopedia of the Reformed Faith,* ed. Donald K. McKim (Louisville: Westminster/John Knox, 1992), 215-16. Cf. Edward A. Dowey, Jr., "Law in Luther and Calvin," *Theology Today* 41, 2 (1984):146-53; I. John Hesslink, *Calvin's Concept of the Law* (Allison Park, Pa.: Pickwick, 1992), 251-62.

30 *The Psalter,* No. 42.

31 W. Robert Godfrey, "Law and Gospel," in *New Dictionary of Theology,* eds. Sinclair B. Ferguson, David F. Wright, J. I. Packer (Downers Grove, Ill.: InterVarsity Press, 1988), 379.

32 *The Psalter,* 26-88.

33 Ernest F. Kevan, *The Grace of Law* (London: Carey Kingsgate, 1976) provides a thorough treatment of Puritan teaching on the believer's relationship to the law.

34 *Spiritual Refining: or a Treatise of Grace and Assurance* (London: A. Miller, 1652), 563.

35 *An Examination of the chief Points of Antinomianism* (London, 1646), 15-16.

36 *The Trial and Triumph of Faith* (Edinburgh: William Collins, 1845), 102; Samuel Rutherford in *Catechisms of the Second Reformation,* ed. Alexander F. Mitchell (London: James Nisbet, 1886), 226.

37 *The Guide unto True Blessedness* (London, 1614), 85.

38 *Westminster Confession of Faith* (Glasgow: Free Presbyterian, 1994), 180-81.

39 Ibid., 94-95.

40 "Sabbath Observance," *Banner of Truth,* no. 392 (May 1996):5.

41 In addition to treatises on the ten commandments and on the Westminster standards, see Thomas Shepard, *The Doctrine of the Sabbath* (London, 1655); John Owen, *An Exposition of the Epistle to the Hebrews,* ed. W. H. Goold (London: Johnstone & Hunter, 1855), vols. 3-4 on Hebrews 3-4; Jonathan Edwards, "The Perpetuity and Change of the Sabbath," in *The Works of Jonathan Edwards* (1834;

reprint Edinburgh: Banner of Truth Trust, 1974), 2:93-103; Robert Dabney, "The Christian Sabbath: Its Nature, Design, and Proper Observance," in *Discussions: Evangelical and Theological* (1890; reprint London: Banner of Truth Trust, 1967), 1:496-550; Matthew Henry, "A Serious Address to Those that Profane the Lord's Day," in *The Complete Works of Matthew Henry* (1855; reprint Grand Rapids: Baker, 1979), 1:118-33; W.B. Whitaker, *Sunday in Tudor and Stuart Times* (London: Houghton, 1933); Daniel Wilson, *The Divine Authority and Perpetual Obligation of the Lord's Day* (1827; reprint London: Lord's Day Observance Society, 1956); John Murray, "The Moral Law and the Fourth Commandment," in *Collected Writings* (Edinburgh: Banner of Truth Trust, 1976), 1:193-228; James I. Packer, "The Puritans and the Lord's Day," in *A Quest for Godliness* (Wheaton: Crossway, 1990), 233-43; Roger T. Beckwith and Wilfrid Stott, *The Christian Sunday: A Biblical and Historical Study* (1978; reprint Grand Rapids: Baker, 1980); Errol Hulse, "Sanctifying the Lord's Day: Reformed and Puritan Attitudes," in *Aspects of Sanctification* (Westminster Conference of 1981; Hertfordshire: Evangelical Press, 1982), 78-102; James T. Dennison, Jr., *The Market Day of the Soul: The Puritan Doctrine of the Sabbath in England, 1532-1700* (New York: University Press of America, 1983); Walter Chantry, *Call the Sabbath a Delight* (Edinburgh: Banner of Truth Trust, 1991).

[42] Cf. MacLeod, 12-13, to whom we are here indebted, for a helpful summary of observations on the normativity of the law for the believer.

[43] Cf. Psalm 119 for a remarkable example.

[44] Cited in John Blanchard, *Gathered Gold* (Welwyn, Hertforshire: Evangelical Press, 1984), 181.

[45] "Second Check on Antinomianism," in *The Works of John Fletcher* 1:338.

[46] For a more detailed description of the relationship of justification and sanctification, see Joel R. Beeke, "The Relation of Faith to Justification," in *Justification by Faith Alone,* ed. Don Kistler (Morgan, Pa.: Soli Deo Gloria, 1995), 82ff.

[47] Ernest F. Kevan, *Keep His Commandments: The place of Law in the Christian Life* (London: Tyndale Press, 1964), 28.

[48] *Institutes* 3.19.4.

[49] *Commentary* on 1 Peter 2:16.

[50] *The Psalter,* No. 426:9 (Psalm 116).

[51] *Institutes* 3.7.1.

6

The Learned Doctor William Ames
and *The Marrow of Theology*

When Abraham Kuyper, Jr. examined the antagonistic relationship between William Ames (1576-1633) and Johannes Maccovius (1588-1644), two theological teachers at Franeker, the Netherlands, he concluded that Ames had deviated from the Reformed position that Maccovius defended.[1] Robert T. Kendall goes so far as to say that through Ames's influence, "Calvin's doctrine of faith, for all practical purposes, was now dead and buried. Ames espoused a voluntaristic doctrine of faith within a tradition that had already been shaking off Calvin's influence anyway." Kendall goes on to conclude that "Ames's voluntarism appears to be the key to all he believes."[2]

Though Ames did make occasional statements that sounded as though he were a voluntarist who had strayed from the path of Reformed orthodoxy, scholars who charge Ames with voluntarism betray a lamentable lack of understanding of his entire work. Within the parameters of orthodox Reformed theology, Ames stressed that Christianity is a Spirit-worked, vital, heartfelt faith that produces a genuine Christian walk.

After a sketch of Ames's life and teaching career, we will show that an examination of the system and content of Ames's classic work, *The Marrow of Theology,* reveals that Ames was one of the first to build an entire system of Reformed covenant theology. Although a theology of covenant is discernible in Calvin and other Reformers, Ames went beyond them, turning a covenantal theology (i.e., covenant treated as an important aspect of theology) into a theology of the covenant (i.e., covenant as the overarching principle and framework of theology). Within the framework of covenant theology, Ames wedded doctrine and life to promote practical Puritan piety.

Biographical Sketch[3]
William Ames (Latinized as "Amesius") was born in 1576 at Ipswich, chief city of England's Suffolk County, then a center of the robust Puri-

William Ames

tanism introduced by William Perkins (1558-1602). John Winthrop (1588-1649), a zealous Puritan and the first governor of Massachusetts Bay, also hailed from Suffolk County.

Ames's father, also named William, was a well-to-do merchant with Puritan sympathies; his mother, Joan Snelling, was related to families that helped to found Plymouth Plantation in the New World. Since both parents died when he was young, he was reared by his maternal uncle, Robert Snelling, a Puritan from nearby Boxford. From childhood Ames was steeped in the vigorous Puritanism of his age and place.

Ames's uncle spared no expense for his education, sending him in 1593 to Christ's College at Cambridge University, known for its undiluted Puritanism and Ramist philosophy. Ames rapidly displayed his proclivity to learn. He was graduated with a Bachelor of Arts degree in 1598. In 1601, he received a Master of Arts degree, was elected Fellow at Christ's College and ordained to the ministry, and underwent a dramatic conversion experience under the "rousing preaching" of Master William Perkins, father of experimental Puritan theology.

Following this profound spiritual transformation, Ames declared that "a man may be *bonus ethicus*, and yet not *bonus theologus*, i.e., a well carriaged man outwardly, expressing both the sense and practise of religion in his outward demeanor: And yet not be a sincere hearted Christian."[4]

This personal experience became Ames's life-long concern and the center of all his thought, revealing itself in a practical, outward Christianity that expressed the inner piety of an obedient, redeemed heart.

With an emphasis on piety and opposition to any practice not explicitly regulated by Scripture, Ames quickly became the moral compass and conscience of the College. He viewed himself as Ezekiel's watchman (Ezek. 33), with a duty to warn students about sin and to promote a deeper faith and purity among the students. But this role was short-lived. With King James's edict of tolerance at the 1604 Hampton Court Conference, any Puritan activity at the colleges that involved criticism of the Church of England was suppressed. The church had reformed enough, the King said.

The Puritan party at Cambridge, however, continued their unrelenting opposition to the Elizabethan settlement. This violation of the King's edict had serious consequences. Puritan spokesmen were soon stripped of their degrees and dismissed. The establishment's coup culminated in 1609 with the appointment of Valentine Cary, who hated Puritanism, to the mastership rather than William Ames, who was far more qualified for the position. Cary had more ecclesiastical clout than Ames. With his appointment, Christ College's approach to Puritanism became decidedly antagonistic. Ames's rebukes of the Church of England and his refusal to wear priestly vestments such as the surplice were increasingly resented. On December 21, 1609, when Ames preached a sermon on St. Thomas's Day—an annual festivity at Cambridge which had become increasingly raucous over the years—and denounced gambling, administering the "salutary vinegar of reproof,"[5] the college authorities had him taken into custody and suspended his degrees.

Although Ames was not technically expelled, he reckoned that leaving was more appealing than facing the grim prospects of an unknown future in Cambridge, and "voluntarily" left his position as a Fellow. After a brief stint as city lecturer in Colchester, Ames was forbidden to preach by the bishop of London, George Abbott. In 1610, Ames decided to seek the freer academic and ecclesiastical climate of the Netherlands. There he remained in exile for the rest of his life.

Ames first went to Rotterdam where he met John Robinson, pastor of the English separatist congregation at Leiden. Some of the congregation's members were soon to establish Plymouth Plantation in the New World and become known as the Pilgrims. Ames could not persuade Robinson to abandon his separatist sentiments, namely, that the Puritan churches should separate "root and branch" from the Church of England, but did succeed in tempering some of his more radical views.

Following a brief stay in Rotterdam and Leiden, Ames was employed by Sir Horace Vere from 1611 to 1619 as military chaplain of the English forces stationed at The Hague. Here Ames wrote prolifically against the Arminianism that would soon precipitate an ecclesiastical crisis. That crisis among the Dutch was eventually addressed at an international Synod in the Dutch city of Dordrecht (1618-1619). Because of his expertise in addressing issues of the Arminian struggle, Ames, an Englishman and non-voting member of the Synod of Dort, was called to be chief theological advisor and secretary to Johannes Bogerman, the presiding officer. Members of the Synod of Dort ruled in favor of the historic Calvinist position on all five points raised by the Arminians, much to Ames's joy. Unwanted in England, he found himself here, at least, on the winning side.

An anti-Arminian purge in ecclesiastical, political, and academic circles followed the Synod of Dort's rulings and opened a professorship at Leiden University. Ames was elected to fill the chair, but the long arm of the English state prevailed. Ames, recently dismissed from his post in The Hague under pressure from the English authorities, found the post at Leiden University closed to him as well.

Ames married his second wife, Joan Fletcher, around 1618, who bore him three children, Ruth, William, and John. (His first wife, the daughter of John Burgess, Ames's predecessor in The Hague, died shortly after they married, leaving no children.) To support his family, he turned to private lecturing and tutoring university students for three years after the Synod of Dort. He ran a little private "house college," resembling on a small scale the Staten College presided over by Festus Hommius. Theological students lived in Ames's home and he taught them Puritanism and systematic theology according to the logical method of Petrus Ramus. He later developed some of these lectures into his famous *Marrow of Theology*.[6]

In 1622, officials at Franeker University, a relatively new institution in the remote province of Friesland, ignored the English authorities and appointed Ames as professor of theology. On May 7, 1622, Ames gave his inaugural address on the Urim and Thummim, based on Exodus 28:30. Four days after his inauguration as professor, he received the Doctor of Theology degree upon successfully defending 38 theses and four corollaries on "the nature, theory, and practical working of Conscience" before Sibrandus Lubbertus, senior professor on the faculty. In 1626, he was appointed Rector Magnificus, the highest honorary academic office in the university.

During his eleven year tenure at Franeker, Ames became known as the "Learned Doctor" who tried to "puritanize" the entire university. Ames acknowledged the university was orthodox in doctrine, but did not feel that a majority of the faculty and student body were sufficiently Reformed in practice. Their faith was not yet translated into proper Christian observance. The faculty, in particular, were, for Ames's thinking, too dependent on Aristotelian logic and inadequately emphasized human responsibility and the exercise of the human will in Christian living. Therefore, Ames once again organized a kind of rooming house or "college" in his house, within the university where tutorial sessions, lectures, and numerous theological discussions took place.[7] Ames's goal was "to see whether at least in our University I could in any way call theology away from questions and controversies obscure, confused, and not very essential, and introduce it to life and practice so that students would begin to think seriously of conscience and its concerns."[8] To that end, Ames, as Rector, promoted piety, enforced Sabbath observance, shortened Christmas and Easter holidays, and tightened student discipline. His puritanical reforms produced what was called "the Reformation" of the 1620s.

Through lecturing and prolific writing during his Franeker years, Ames maintained a strong anti-prelatic and anti-Arminian stance, but his greatest contribution was in theology and ethics, which he saw as a unified system that helped the Christian live a life of genuine piety. Here he wrote his two greatest works, *Medulla Theologie (The Marrow of Theology)* and *De Conscientia* ("Of the Conscience," translated in English as *Conscience with the Power and Cases Thereof*). In his system of theological and moral divinity, Ames incorporated the Ramist philosophy and method he had learned at Cambridge.

Ramism was a philosophy that sought to correct the artificial sophistry of the Aristotelianism of the day that was characterized by a breach between life and thought, between knowing and doing, and, in the case of the religious life, between theology and ethics. Ramism was developed by Petrus Ramus (1515-1572), a sixteenth-century French Reformed philosopher.[9] Ames incorporated the thought of this Huguenot into his own work, seamlessly weaving theology and ethics together into a program of obedient, covenant living.

Through his teaching, Ames established his own reputation as well as that of the academy where he taught. Students came from all over Europe to study under him. His most famous pupil was Johannes Cocceius, who would later carry covenant theology well beyond Ames's thought. Yet Ames was not content, for all was not well at the University. Some students and faculty members did not appreciate Ames's efforts to achieve deeper or further reformation. A clique of professors, led by Johannes Maccovius, sabotaged Ames's efforts. Moreover, continuing arguments between Ames and his Aristotelian colleague Maccovius spoiled the intellectual climate at Franeker, while the damp sea air of Friesland eroded Ames's health. Those problems, combined with his wife's desire to rejoin her countrymen, convinced Ames to look for a new place in which to serve.

In 1632, Ames accepted an invitation from his friend Hugh Peter to join him in co-pastoring the English-speaking Congregationalist church at Rotterdam. Ames was very attracted to the invitation because of Peter's design for an independent, covenant-centered congregation that strove for a purged membership of regenerate believers who truly practiced their faith. Ames had long argued for such Congregationalist principles within and outside Puritan circles.[10] He was also attracted to the idea of helping the church develop a Puritan college in Rotterdam.

In late summer of 1633, Ames finally headed south to Rotterdam. His tenure there was brief. In the fall, the Maas River breached its banks, and Ames, who was already unwell, became even sicker after his house was flooded. He died of pneumonia on November 11 at the age

The eighteenth-century English church at the Hague, the former Sacrament Chapel, where Ames preached.

of fifty-seven in the arms of his friend, Hugh Peter. To the end, he remained firm in faith and triumphant in hope.[11]

Shortly before his death, Ames had seriously considered joining his friend John Winthrop in New England, but God had another "New World" in mind for him. Though Ames had great influence on the theological and intellectual history of New England—particularly through the *Marrow*—he never arrived at its shores. Would he have become the first president of Harvard, as many historians have speculated?[12] In his history of New England, the Puritan Cotton Mather mused that the "angelical doctor" William Ames, "was *intentionally* a New England man, though not *eventually*."[13] Four years after Ames's death, his wife and children went to live in the Puritan settlement of Salem, Massachusetts. They brought Ames's library with them, which formed the nucleus of the original library for Harvard College, though fire later destroyed most of the books.

The Marrow of Theology
Although William Ames's *Marrow of Theology* was first published in Latin as *Medulla Theologiae* in 1627, its main ideas were expressed earlier than that. The theological lectures that Ames gave from 1619 to 1622 as tutor to the students at Leiden were reworked while he stood, as he put it, "idle in the marketplace." They were first released in Latin (1623) in fragmentary form from Franeker. Four years later, after Ames found financial security within the scholarly environment of the university, he finally finished what would become his landmark publication for which he is best remembered today.

The book was intended to serve as a useful compendium of theology for laypeople and theological students. It immediately earned recognition and acclaim in scholarly and ecclesiastical circles, and was quickly translated into many languages. The first English translations were published in 1642 and 1643.

Major Theme
The opening theme of the *Marrow* is remarkably simple and terse. "Theology is the doctrine of living to God," Ames writes. This statement, simple as it may appear, is loaded with meaning. Grounded in how Ames was raised, it found theological and scholarly articulation at Christ's College, and over time Ames developed it into a theological system.

The theology of this book is all about practical Christianity—a Christianity of the whole man, not just the intellect, will, or affections. It demonstrates Ames's passion that thought and life should represent a single system of practical, vital Christianity. Ames tried to show that theology does not deal primarily with statements about God, but rather with knowledge of how to live to God, i.e., "in accord with the will of God."

Ames centered theology more on *action* than on *knowledge*. For Calvin, theology focused on knowing God and knowing one's self, though active faith was never far behind knowledge. Only where God is known is there religion and piety, Calvin said. For Ames, knowing God was never the end or goal of theology; rather, the end was to bring the heart and will into subjection to God and His Word.[14] Practical Christianity was the centerpiece of theology.

In this regard, Ames was moving in a direction established by his mentor Perkins and reflecting the influence of Petrus Ramus, who said, "Theology is the doctrine of living well." Perkins saw theology as "the science of living blessedly forever." This blessed life, according to Perkins, is obtained via knowledge of God and knowledge of self. In this respect, Perkins's theology was a combination of the theology of Calvin and the methodology of Ramus. Ames, however, sought to distance himself from this view because of his concern that living blessedly could promote self-indulgence. After all, what constitutes the blessed life? What constitutes happiness? As John Dykstra Eusden put it: "For Ames the end of theology was never to produce blessedness, which he felt related chiefly to man's ultimate aspiration and desire. In search for his own blessedness, man could miss God, the very object of his living rightly."[15] For Ames, theology was the art of Christian living. This art doesn't exist in a vacuum, however; rather, it is informed and driven by a heartfelt desire to obey God. Theology prompts the exercise of Christianity.

Ames's emphasis on the will was one of the key points of the controversy with him and his Franeker colleague Maccovius. Maccovius emphasized the primacy of the intellect in the regenerate mind; i.e., the will is renewed through the intellect. The intellect is the *terminus a quo* (the point of departure of a process); the will is the *terminus ad quem* (the final goal of a process). But Ames held to the primacy of volition. Faith involves "an act of the whole man—which is by no means a mere act of the intellect," he wrote, but the act of the will in believing the gospel is that which, by the Spirit's grace, makes knowledge saving. Saving knowledge, therefore, differs from mere knowledge by involving the wholehearted commitment of the will. Ames writes, "Although faith always presupposes a knowledge of the gospel, there is nevertheless no saving knowledge in anyone...except the knowledge which follows this act of the will and depends upon it."[16]

This position differed from much of established orthodoxy in the early seventeenth century, which said that faith proceeded from knowledge. Consequently, Ames's position on faith and volition came under scrutiny by the orthodox Reformed. Interestingly, Gisbertus Voetius, a follower of Ames and a leader in developing the Reformed system of theology and piety in the post-Reformation Netherlands, declared that attributing salvation to the will was unheard of in Reformed theology, with the exception of Ames who was the only one he had known to defend that view publicly.[17]

By focusing on the will as the center of faith, Ames wanted to demonstrate that true piety takes place in a covenant relationship between the sinful creature and the redeeming Creator. Faith as an act of the will is a true mark of covenant obedience as the creature is asked to respond with faith and obedience to the covenant promises offered freely in Christ. Covenant theology is the heart of Ames's theological system.

Organization and Content

The *Marrow* is organized according to the Ramist system of dichotomies[18] in which the theme is pursued that theology, the doctrine of living to God, consists of, first, "faith" (Book 1, chapters 1-41, pages 77-216), or what one believes, and second, "observance" (Book 2, chapters 1-22, pages 219-331), or how one practices faith and does good works in obedience to God. Such works flow from and add life and meaning to faith. Those two major categories—faith and observance—comprise the fountainhead from which Ames's entire theological system flows. Understanding the concept of faith in Book 1 and its observance by way of the Calvinist call to good works in Book 2 leads Ames to explain his theological system through various dichotomies in which the marks of living to God are continually set forth.

After defining faith as "the resting of the heart on God" and setting forth faith as an act of the whole man, especially the will, Ames discusses the object of faith, which is God. Following his teaching on the knowledge and essence of God (Book 1, Chapters, 4-5; hereafter, 1.4, 5), Ames sets forth God's "efficiency," which he defines as the "working power of God by which He works all things in all things (Eph. 1:11; Rom. 11:36)" (1.6). He then discusses God's decree as the first exercise of God's efficiency (1.7). He establishes that everything happens because of God's eternal good pleasure as demonstrated in His creation and providence (1.8, 9). God's preserving grace extends over the created order, while the special government that God exercises toward humanity, the "intelligent creature," is the covenant of works (1.10). By violating this conditional covenant, humanity tragically fell into sin. That fall had serious and eternal consequences, including spiritual and physical death and the propagation of original sin (1.11-17).

But there is still hope. Condemnation is overturned by restorative grace through redemption. Through the person and work of Christ, fallen humanity can have renewed fellowship with God. All of this happens solely for God's good pleasure and out of His "merciful purpose" (1.18-23).

From the beginning, Ames's theology is built implicitly along covenantal lines. In chapter 24, titled "The Application of Christ," Ames's covenant theology becomes more obvious. The means through which the covenant of redemption between God and Christ comes to fruition is the covenant of grace, which the Scriptures call the "new covenant." In other words, the "application of Christ" is administered covenantally. After explaining how the new covenant differs from the old, Ames asserts that the essence of the covenant of grace continues through different historical dispensations until, finally, in the last day, believers will be swept up into glory, and the covenant of grace inaugurated at the fall will finally be consummated.

The covenant of grace is both *conditional*, for faith is required, and *absolute*, for, as Ames put it, "the condition of the covenant is also promised in the covenant." To Ames, as John von Rohr points out, "The promise of fulfillment of covenant conditions was itself covenant promise." Thus, in the final analysis, grace does all and the believer learns to rest on a promising, decreeing God.[19]

It is noteworthy that in Ames's theology the decrees of election and reprobation are not discussed until chapter 25. They do not appear in his earlier chapters on the decree of God (1.7) or on his government over intelligent creatures (1.10). Ames is satisfied to place the doctrine of predestination where Calvin put it: as part of the doctrine of assurance. For Ames, assuring grace belongs with his examination of the order of salvation, before moving through "union by calling," justification, adoption, sanctification, and glorification (1.26-30). This is the substance of his "application of the covenant of grace considered in itself."[20]

Ames then devotes two chapters to the *subject* of the application of redemption, which is the church. After considering the mystical, invisible church (1.31) and the instituted or visible church (1.32), he addresses the *way* or *means* of the application of redemption, devoting chapters to

Holy Scripture (1.34), the ministry (1.33, 35), the sacraments (1.36, 41), and ecclesiastical discipline (1.37).

Finally, Ames explains the *administration* of the application of redemption, i.e., how God administers the covenant of grace (1.38, 39, 41). He focuses on the chronology of covenant administration by dividing history into time periods, showing how there has been progression from "the imperfect to the more perfect" and "from the general and obscure to the more specific and clear" (1.38.2, 3). From Adam to Abraham, the covenant of grace was administered by general promises, such as Genesis 3:15 (1.38.14). From Abraham to Moses, the covenant was administered chiefly along a family line to Abraham and his posterity (1.38.20). From Moses to Christ, the church was in its childhood under the covenant and the ministry was "almost always an extraordinary one conducted by prophets" (1.38.12). From Christ's coming in the flesh all the way to His return on the clouds, the church freely receives the application of the covenant as a spiritual heir through the Spirit of adoption, rather than as an earthly child in the spirit of fear and bondage (1.38.8, 9; 1. 39.9). Upon Christ's return, "the application which has only been begun in this life will be perfected" (1.41.1).

Throughout Ames's Ramistic explanation of covenant administration in various time periods, he uniquely configures two major doctrines— "redemption by Christ" and the "application of redemption"—which flow out of God's restorative grace at the fall. He takes each element of the order of salvation and applies it to some fact or event in each covenantal time period that he has enumerated. By placing predestination in the order of salvation, Ames dovetails the eternal aspect of the life of the elect into the temporal and historical progression of redemptive history. The logical elements of the order of salvation are thus wrapped into the chronological periods of covenant administration through the history of salvation. Each period in salvation history is coordinated with a corresponding series of conditions or states of believers (1.30-39). In this way, Ames avoids the apparent incongruity between covenant and decree that has often dogged Reformed theology. He offers an internally consistent system of covenant theology that does justice to both God's decretal activity and His covenantal commitment.

We have seen that Ames's theological teaching begins with faith, which is explained in Book 1 of the *Marrow,* within a covenantal framework. Book 2 offers the second half of Ames's Ramist system of theology: the observance or obedience that accompanies faith. Obedience is accomplished through virtue and good works, and is manifested in religion (love to God) as well as justice and charity (love to neighbor). Here Ames explains how the first table of the law and its theological virtues are the foundation of religion and worship of God, while the second table of the law and its charitable virtues constitute the paradigm for interpersonal behavior. This blueprint for the Christian life is expressed by acting toward God and each other as the Ten Commandments prescribe (2.1-22).

At this point, we should note the relationship between the *Marrow* and *Conscience with the Power and Cases Thereof* (1630 in Latin, 1639 in English), which became a landmark in moral theology, passing through nearly twenty editions in one generation.[21] That these two volumes are unified is evident by their subject matter as well as by how *Conscience* naturally flows from and serves as a commentary, as it were, on Book 2 of the *Marrow*. Ames's stated intent is that "if there are some who desire to have practical matters better explained, especially those of the latter part of this *Marrow*, we shall attempt, God willing, to satisfy them in a special treatise, which I mean to write, dealing with questions usually called 'cases of conscience.'"[22] Given the importance of *Conscience* in Ames's system of thought and his own statement regarding its significance, we could not rightly understand this author if we did not consider this very significant work. That is why we will include a brief comment on *Conscience* in our explanation of the second part of Ames's *Marrow*.

The subject of Christian ethics was critically important to Ames. That is perfectly understandable, given what we know about Ames's emphasis on practical Christian living. If living to God in covenantal obedience is characterized by heart religion and vital piety, what should be done with the more difficult ethical questions concerning the Christian life? This concern is addressed in *Conscience,* a collection of five books that move from a highly theoretical treatment of the nature of conscience to very practical applications. The core content of this book first came to light in Ames's defense of the 38 theses and four corollaries connected with his promotion to the Doctor of Theology degree at Franeker University in 1622. Eight years after that defense, Ames published this undertaking as a multi-volume work on moral theology that filled a gap in the developing system of Reformed thought. Richard Baxter, who built his own *Christian Directory* on Ames's casuistry, said that Perkins did valuable service in promoting Reformed casuistry but Ames's work, though briefer, was superior. "Ames hath exceeded all," Baxter said.[23]

The first Book in *Conscience* defines conscience as "a man's judgment of himself, according to the judgment of God of him."[24] It offers a theoretical treatment of what constitutes conscience before going into detail about the working of conscience.

In Book 2, Ames describes what a case of conscience is: "a practical question, concerning which, the Conscience may make a doubt." This section explains sin, entry into the state of grace, the ongoing battle between flesh and spirit, and conduct in the Christian life. Book 2 could easily serve as a compendium of Reformed theology.

Book 3, titled "Of Man's Duty in General," asks about "the actions, and conversation of [man's] life." Ames says the sign of true obedience is submissively placing God's will ahead of the will of the creature, even when that will does not appear to work towards the creature's advantage. This is accomplished by exercising the disciplines of an obedient life—humility, sincerity, zeal, peace, virtue, prudence, patience, temperance—and by avoiding practices that hinder an obedient walk, such as drunkenness, sins of the heart, and sins of the tongue.

These three books take up about a third of *Conscience*. Following these preliminary matters of definitional statements and conceptual elaborations on conscience and obedience, Ames now concentrates on his real concern for ethics or moral theology by asking how cases of conscience are to be adjudicated. The simple answer is: by proper understanding and application of the moral law. This is where *Conscience* picks up the theme from Book 2 of the *Marrow*.

Books 4 and 5 elucidate the moral law regarding one's duty toward God and one's neighbor. Man's duty to God covers the entire spectrum of the obedient Christian walk, from love towards God in public and private worship to the keeping of the Sabbath. Ames discusses general topics such as the church, but he also covers specific topics such as prayer and singing. He properly prepares the reader for Book 5 on interpersonal relations by first settling any uncertainty the believer may have about his relationship to God. In Book 5, which has 57 chapters and is twice as long as book 4, Ames discusses cases of conscience that might come up in interpersonal relationships. He grounds all his teaching in the last six of the Ten Commandments.

Ames's writing is permeated with practical Christianity. He offers a blueprint for a walk of faith with the warm heart religion of the redeemed. He makes clear how crucial covenant obedience, as demonstrated by love for God and love for neighbor, is in the life of the redeemed. This is an appropriate conclusion to Ames's work on moral theology in Book 2 of the *Marrow* (observance), which is itself the logi-

Cotton Mather

cal concomitant to his formal theology elucidated in Book 1 (faith). These two volumes, along with Ames's commentary on the Heidelberg Catechism, show that Ames has left no stone unturned in his quest for the walk of faith. They demonstrate that the sovereign covenant love of a gracious God must be answered by the submissive covenant obedience of the redeemed child of God.

Influence

The Marrow of Theology was most influential in New England, where it was generally regarded as the best summary of Calvinistic theology ever written. It was required reading at Harvard and Yale well into the eighteenth century, when it was supplanted by Francis Turretin's *Institutes of Elenctic Theology*.[25] Thomas Hooker and Increase Mather recommended the *Marrow* as the most important book beyond the Bible for making a sound theologian. Jonathan Edwards made copious marginal notes on his own copy of the *Marrow,* and acknowledged his indebtedness to Ames.

Ames's influence in New England, however, went beyond his manual of theology. His ecclesiological writings laid the groundwork for non-separating Congregationalism in New England, a movement that maintained that the Congregational churches of Massachusetts Bay Colony ought to model reforming the Church of England rather than separating from it. The Cambridge Platform of 1648 in particular reflects Ames's thought. Then, too, his Puritan Ramism was eagerly embraced and became characteristic of New England Puritanism.[26] New England Puritans such as John Cotton, Increase Mather, and Cotton Mather quoted Ames more frequently than they quoted Calvin. Increase Mather said, "It is rare for a *scholastical wit* to be joined with an *heart warm in religion,* but in Ames it was so." Cotton Mather called Ames "that profound, that sublime; that subtle, that irrefragable—yea, that angelic doctor."[27]

Ames and his *Marrow* had their second greatest impact in the Netherlands. According to Matthias Nethenus, Voetius's colleague at the University of Utrecht, "In England, the study of practical theology has flourished marvelously, and in the Dutch churches and schools, from the time of Willem Teellinck and Ames it has ever more widely spread, even though all do not take to it with equal interest."[28] Keith L. Sprunger notes that Ames found the Dutch too intellectual and not sufficiently practical, and therefore promoted Puritan piety with some considerable success in an effort to "make Dutchmen into Puritans."[29] In addition to Voetius, he greatly impacted Peter VanMastricht (a Dutch pietist whose systematic theology Jonathan Edwards thought even surpassed that of Turretin's for usefulness), who drew heavily on Ames, especially in covenantal thinking and casuistry.

Nearly all of Ames's books were printed in the Netherlands, many in Latin for the international scholarly community. *The Marrow of Theology* and *Conscience with the Power and Cases Thereof* were soon both translated into Dutch and printed at least four times in the seventeenth century.[30] His ecclesiological writings, however, were not printed as often, suggesting that his theology and casuistry made more impact in the Netherlands than his congregationalist views.

Ironically, Ames was least influential in his homeland of England, although there, too, he was considered Perkins's most influential disciple and true heir. Ames's major works were widely circulated, and influenced English Calvinistic theology throughout the seventeenth century. His *Marrow of Theology* was particularly highly esteemed by the Puritans. Thomas Goodwin said that "next to the Bible, he esteemed Dr. Ames his Marrow of Divinity as the best book in the world."[31]

Conclusion: Grace and Obedience

As we review the life and teaching of Ames, we must ask: did Ames really depart from the mainstream of Reformed theology, as Kuyper and Kendall contend? The answer has to be in the negative. Ames was instrumental in contrasting Reformed thought with that of an orthodoxy that was beginning to lose its vitality. Covenantally based obedience is activism of a Christian sort. This sort of activism is not mere voluntarism. True, Ames's emphasis was on the will: "The true and proper subject of theology is the will."[32] But Ames, as a faithful son of the Reformation, continued to emphasize that "the final dependence of faith, as it designates the act of believing, is on the operation and inner persuasion of the Holy Spirit."[33]

Moreover, Ames's focus on the will should be seen for what it is: a combination of faith and observance in theological commitment. Ames worked this out in philosophical and theological battles with his Franeker colleagues, which demonstrates his attempts to reintroduce a vital piety to the stagnant church of the seventeenth-century Netherlands. Neither faith nor practice is adequate by itself. Faith divorced from practice leads to "cold orthodoxy," while an isolated emphasis on the will and on good works leads to Arminianism. The story of Ames's life, and the theme of his thought as evidenced in *Marrow of Theology, Conscience,* and other writings, is that he strove for proper balance between the two.[34] The key to this balance was to place obedience within the covenant.

Ames legitimized this covenant obedience as characterizing the Christian life with his system of covenant theology. Without this foundation, Ames's system would surely have collapsed, for voluntarism on its own has no biblical content. Ames demonstrated the biblical truth that although justification is by grace alone through faith alone, and never by works and obedience, the believer's response of obedience is absolutely vital to authentic covenant life and to Christianity itself.

While tenaciously holding to the one-sided, unconditional character of the covenant of grace, Ames also stressed the responsibility of the covenant child. He emphasized a life of covenant responsibility. Because faith is known by its works, obedience underlies the experiential life of the covenant child. This obedience is an informed piety, the alignment of doctrine with life, the intersection of orthodoxy with orthopraxy. With his system of covenant theology, Ames demonstrated that there is harmony, not contradiction, between grace and obedience. The formal structure of this obedience was a Christian life whose direction and content were set by the Ten Commandments.

The full impact of Ames's thought can only be correctly determined if his work is considered as a whole. Only when this is done can we see that the activism of Ames was not a reductionist voluntarism. Rather, it was the very epicenter of heart religion. It represented the desire to live a life of humble obedience in thankfulness for God's gracious condescension to His people in covenant.

The Marrow of Theology more clearly and systematically set forth "the gist of Puritan thought about God, the church, and the world" than any other Puritan book.[35] It is essential for understanding the Puritan view of covenant, sanctification, and activism, and is highly recommended for laypeople and theologians alike. It ought to be a part of every pastor's library and every church library, and is still worth consulting today.

---

[1] *Johannes Maccovius* (Leiden: D. Donner, 1899), 315-96. Abraham Kuyper, Jr. was the son of the famous Abraham Kuyper, Sr. (1837-1920), Dutch Reformed theologian and political leader who served as Prime Minister in the Netherlands from 1901 to 1905.

[2] Kendall, *Calvin and English Calvinism to 1649* (Oxford: Oxford University Press, 1979), 151, 154.

[3] The definitive biographical account of Ames is Keith L. Sprunger, *The Learned Doctor William Ames: Dutch Backgrounds of English and American Puritanism* (Chicago: University of Illinois Press, 1972), a revision of idem, "The Learned Doctor Ames" (Ph.D. dissertation, University of Illinois, 1963). Also helpful is Benjamin J. Boerkoel, Sr., "William Ames (1576-1633): Primogenitor of the *Theologia-Pietatis* in English-Dutch Puritanism" (Th.M. thesis, Calvin Theological Seminary, 1990). For briefer accounts of Ames's life and work, see Eusden's introduction in William Ames, *The Marrow of Theology,* trans. and ed. John H. Eusden (1968; reprint, Grand Rapids: Baker, 1997), 1-66; introduction by Lee W. Gibbs in William Ames, *Technometry* (Philadelphia: University of Pennsylvania Press, 1979), 3-17; Jan van Vliet, "William Ames: Marrow of the Theology and Piety of the Reformed Tradition" (Ph.D. dissertation, Westminster Theological Seminary, 2002), 15-40. The best Dutch sources are Hugo Visscher, *Guilielmus Amesius, Zijn Leven en Werken* (Haarlem: J.M. Stap, 1894); Willem van't Spijker, "Guilielmus Amesius," in *De Nadere Reformatie en het Gereformeerd Piëtisme* ('s-Gravenhage: Boekencentrum, 1989), 53-86.

Three biographical works on Ames were translated and edited by Douglas Horton, and published in one volume as *William Ames by Matthew Nethenus, Hugo Visscher, and Karl Reuter* (Cambridge: Harvard Divinity School Library, 1965). These include Matthias Nethenus, *Introductory Preface in Which the Story of Master Ames is Briefly Narrated and the Excellence and Usefulness of his Writings Shown* (Amsterdam: John Jansson, 1668), Hugo Visscher, *William Ames: His Life and Works* (Haarlem: J. M. Stap, 1894), and Karl Reuter, *William Ames: The Leading Theologian in the Awakening of Reformed Pietism* (Neukirchen: Neukirchener Verlag des Erziehungsvereins, 1940). Notes from these biographies reference Horton's volume. See also Horton, "Let Us Not Forget the Mighty William Ames," *Religion in Life* 29 (1960):434-42, and John Quick's (1636-1706) unpublished manuscript, "Icones Sacrae Anglicapae" at Dr. Williams's Library in London, which includes a chapter, "The Life of William Ames, Dr. of Divinity."

[4] *A Fresh Suit Against Human Ceremonies in God's Worship* (Rotterdam, 1633), 131.

[5] Horton, *Ames*, 4.

[6] Horton, *Ames,* 13.

[7] See Sprunger, *The Learned Doctor Ames,* chap. 4; idem, "William Ames and the Franeker Link to English and American Puritanism," in G. Th. Jensma, F.R.H. Smit, and F. Westra, eds., *Universiteit te Franeker, 1585-1811* (Leeuwarden: Fryske Academy, 1985), 264-85.

[8] Ames, "Paraenesis ad studiosos theologiae, habita Franekerae" (1623), trans. Douglas Horton as "An Exhortation to the Students of Theology" (1958).

[9] Sprunger, *Ames*, 107; Eusden, "Introduction" to *Marrow*, 37. Ramus was martyred in the St. Bartholomew's Day massacre in Paris.

[10] Ames, *Marrow*, Book One, Chapter XXXII, Paragraphs 6 and 15 (hereafter 1.32.6 and 15); cf. his *A Reply to Dr. Mortons Generall Defence of Three Nocent Ceremonies* (1622), *A Reply to Dr. Mortons Particular Defence of Three Nocent Ceremonies* (1623), and *A Fresh Suit against Human Ceremonies in Gods Worship* (1633). Increase Mather said that Ames gave us "perfect Congregationalism" (*A Disquisition concerning Ecclesiastical Councils* [Boston, 1716], v-vi).

[11] Sprunger, *The Learned Doctor Ames,* 247.

[12] Ames's disciple, Nathaniel Eaton, became Harvard's first president.

[13] Cotton Mather, *The Great Works of Christ in America or Magnalia Christi Americana*, 3d ed. (1853; reprint, Edinburgh: Banner of Truth Trust, 1979), 1:236.

[14] William Ames, *The Substance of Christian Religion: Or, a plain and easy Draft of the Christian Catechism, in LII Lectures* (London: T. Mabb for T. Davies, 1659), Q. 113.

[15] Eusden, "Introduction" to *Marrow,* 47.

[16] Ames, *Marrow,* 1.3.3-4.

[17] Voetius, *Selectarum theologicae* (Utrecht: Joannem à Waesberge, 1669), 5:289.

[18] For an outline of the entire book in a Ramist fashion, see Ames, "Method and Chart of the *Marrow,"* in *Marrow*, 72-73.

[19] Ibid., 1.24; John von Rohr, "Covenant and Assurance in Early English Puritanism," *Church History* 34 (1965):199-202.

[20] Ames, *Marrow,* 1.30.

[21] For Ames as a Puritan casuist, see George L. Mosse, *The Holy Pretence* (Oxford: Basil Blackwell, 1957), 68-87.

[22] Ames, "Brief Forewarning," *Marrow*, 70.

[23] *The Practical Works of Richard Baxter* (London: James Duncan, 1838), 1:3-4.

[24] Ames, *Conscience with the Power and Cases Thereof* (London, 1639; reprint, Norwood, N.J.: Walter J. Johnson, 1975), 1.1.preamble.

[25] S. E. Morison, *Harvard College in the Seventeenth Century* (Cambridge: Harvard University Press, 1936), p. 267.

[26] Keith L. Sprunger, "Ames, Ramus, and the Method of Puritan Theology," *Harvard Theological Review* 59 (1966):133-51.

[27] Mather, *Great Works of Christ in America*, 1:245, 236.

[28] Horton, *Ames,* p. 15.

[29] Sprunger, *The Learned Doctor Ames,* 260.

[30] C. W. Schoneveld, *Intertraffic of the Mind: Studies in Seventeenth-Century Anglo-Dutch Translation With a Checklist* (Leiden: E. J. Brill, 1983).

[31] Increase Mather, "To the Reader," in James Fitch, *The First Principles of the Doctrine of Christ* (Boston, 1679).

[32] Ames, *Marrow,* 1.1.9.

[33] Ibid., 1.3.12.

[34] See William Ames, *An Analytical Exposition Of Both the Epistles of the Apostle Peter* (London: E.G. for Iohn Rothwell, 1641).

[35] Douglas Horton, "Foreword" in Ames, *Marrow,* vii.

7

Evangelism Rooted in Scripture:
The Puritan Example

A great Puritan evangelist, John Rogers, warned his congregation against neglecting Scripture by telling them what God might say: "I have trusted you so long with my Bible…it lies in [some] houses all covered with dust and cobwebs, you care not to listen to it. Do you use my Bible so? Well, you shall have my Bible no longer." Rogers then picked up his Bible and started walking away from the pulpit. Then he stopped, fell on his knees, and took on the voice of the people, who pleaded, "Lord, whatever Thou dost to us, take not Thy Bible from us; kill our children, burn our houses, destroy our goods; only spare us Thy Bible, take not away Thy Bible." "Say you so?" the minister replied, impersonating God. "Well, I will try you a while longer; and here is my Bible for you. I will see how you use it, whether you will search it more, love it more, observe it more, and live more according to it." Thomas Goodwin was so moved by Rogers's dramatic presentation that when he left church he wept upon his horse's neck for fifteen minutes before he felt strong enough to mount it.[1]

John Calvin and his Puritan successors did not lack evangelistic zeal, as some have claimed. David Calhoun has defended Calvin's work as a teacher and practitioner of evangelism.[2] Similarly, I will show how the Puritans brought the gospel to others in a thoroughly scriptural manner.[3] First, I will define what I mean by Puritan evangelism, then show that the Puritan evangelistic message, based on Scripture, was doctrinal, practical, experimental, and symmetrical. Then I will examine the primary methods they used to communicate the gospel—a plain style of preaching and the practice of catechetical evangelism. Finally, we will see that the Puritans believed that the message and methods of evangelism were inseparable from the inward disposition of an evangelist. That disposition included a heartfelt dependence on the Holy Spirit and earnest prayer that God's Word and Spirit would bless all evangelistic efforts.

A look at the scriptural message, methods, and disposition of Puritan evangelism should convict us of our need to return to a scriptural foundation for all evangelism. As the Puritans adopted biblical principles of evangelism and became practitioners of them in their ministries, so we should embody these same principles in our teaching and work. We have much to learn from the Puritans about how to evangelize.

Puritan Evangelism Defined

Our use of the word *Puritan* includes those people who were ejected from the Church of England by the Act of Uniformity in 1662. The term, however, also applies to those in Britain and North America who, for several generations after the Reformation, worked to reform and purify the church and to lead people toward biblical, godly living con-

THE
BRITISH ISLES
DURING THE
CIVIL WAR
1642-1649

sistent with the Reformed doctrines of grace.[4] Puritanism grew out of at least three needs: (1) the need for biblical preaching and the teaching of sound, Reformed doctrine; (2) the need for biblical, personal piety that stresses the work of the Holy Spirit in the faith and life of the believer; and (3) the need for a restoration of biblical simplicity in liturgy, vestments, and church government, so that a well-ordered church life would promote the worship of the triune God as prescribed in His Word.[5] Doctrinally, Puritanism was a kind of broad and vigorous Calvinism; experientially, it was a warm and contagious kind of Christianity; evangelistically, it was tender as well as aggressive.[6]

Interestingly, "evangelism" was not a word the Puritans commonly used, but they were evangelists nonetheless. Richard Baxter's *Call to the Unconverted* and Joseph Alleine's *Alarm to the Unconverted* were pioneer works in evangelistic literature. Evangelism was, for these and other Puritans, a Word-centered task of the church, particularly of her ministers. They understood well the centrality of preaching, the role of the pastor, and the necessity of prayer in evangelism. They were truly "fishers of men," seeking to awaken the unconverted to their need of Christ, to lead them to faith and repentance, and to establish them in a lifestyle of sanctification.

The expression "Puritan evangelism," then, refers to how the Puritans proclaimed what God's Word teaches about the salvation of sinners from sin and its consequences. That salvation is granted by grace, received by faith, grounded in Christ, and reflective of the glory of God. For the Puritans, evangelism not only involved presenting Christ so that by the power of the Spirit people came to God through Him; it equally involved so presenting Christ that the believer might grow in Him, and serve Him as Lord in the fellowship of His church and in the extension of His kingdom in the world. Puritan evangelism involves declaring the entire economy of redemption by focusing on the saving work of all three Persons of the Trinity, while simultaneously calling sinners to a life of faith and commitment, and warning that the gospel will condemn forever those who persist in unbelief and impenitence.[7]

Characteristics of Puritan Preaching

In discussing the message of Puritan evangelism, we will focus on five distinctive characteristics of Puritan preaching and then consider how those characteristics differ from what is used in evangelistic preaching today.

Evangelist directing Christian to the wicket gate in Pilgrim's Progress.

1. Puritan Preaching Was Thoroughly Biblical

Puritanism was a Scripture-based movement, and the Puritans themselves were people of the living Book. They loved, lived, and breathed Scripture, relishing the power of the Spirit that accompanied the Word.[8] They regarded the sixty-six books of Scripture as the library of the Holy Spirit that was graciously bequeathed to them. The Puritan preacher found his message in God's Word. "The faithful Minister, like unto Christ, [is] one that preacheth nothing but the word of God," said Puritan Edward Dering.[9] John Owen agreed: "The first and principal duty of a pastor is to feed the flock by diligent preaching of the word."[10] As Miller Maclure noted, "For the Puritans, the sermon is not just hinged to Scripture; it quite literally exists inside the Word of God; the text is not in the sermon, but the sermon is in the text.... Put summarily, listening to a sermon is being in the Bible."[11]

Puritan Richard Greenham suggested eight ways to read Scripture: with diligence, wisdom, preparation, meditation, conference, faith, practice, and prayer.[12] Thomas Watson provided numerous guidelines on how to listen to the Word: Come to the Word with a holy appetite and a teachable heart. Sit under the Word attentively, receive it with meekness, and mingle it with faith. Then retain the Word, pray over it, practice it, and speak to others about it.[13] "Dreadful is their case who go loaded with sermons to hell," Watson warned. By contrast, those who respond to Scripture as a "love letter sent to you from God" will experience its warming, transforming power.[14] "Feed upon the Word," the Puritan preacher John Cotton exhorted his congregation.[15] Clearly, the Puritans sounded a clarion call to become intensely Word-centered in faith and practice.

No wonder, then, that a typical page of a Puritan evangelistic sermon contains five to ten citations of biblical texts and about a dozen references to texts. Puritan preachers were conversant with their Bibles; they memorized hundreds, if not thousands, of texts. They knew what Scripture to cite for any concern. "Long and personal familiarity with the application of Scripture was a key element in the Puritan ministerial makeup," Sinclair Ferguson writes. "They pondered the riches of revealed truth the way a gemologist patiently examines the many faces of a diamond."[16] They used Scripture wisely, bringing cited texts to bear on the doctrine or case of conscience[17] at hand, all based on sound hermeneutical principles.[18]

The evangelistic sermons of contemporary preachers often incorporate verses wrested out of context or a string of texts that do not belong together. Modern evangelism, in quest of a "simple gospel," favors a mere formula, a packaged presentation, instead of the whole counsel of God. Moreover, some preachers seem to have a better understanding of professional football and television programs, or of the teachings of Sigmund Freud and Paul Tillich, than they do of Moses and Paul.

If we are ever prone to be proud of our Bible knowledge, we ought to open any volume of John Owen, Thomas Goodwin, or Thomas Brooks, note how some obscure passage in Nahum is quoted followed by a familiar passage from John—both of which perfectly illustrate the point the writer is making—and then compare our knowledge to theirs. How can we explain this marvelous—for us, humbling—grasp of Scripture other than that these divines were ministers of the Word? These men obviously studied their Bibles daily, falling to their knees as God's Spirit burned the Word into their pastoral hearts. Then, as they wrote or preached their evangelistic messages, one scriptural passage after another would come to mind.

Our evangelistic efforts must be similarly grounded in the Bible. We must search the Scriptures more frequently and love the Word of God more fervently. As we learn to think, speak, and act more biblically, our messages will become more authoritative and our witness more effective and fruitful.

2. Puritan Preaching Was Unashamedly Doctrinal

The Puritan evangelist saw theology as an essentially practical discipline. William Perkins called it "the science of living blessedly for ever";[19] William Ames, "the doctrine or teaching of living to God."[20] As Ferguson writes, "To them, systematic theology was to the pastor what a knowledge of anatomy is to the physician. Only in the light of the whole body of divinity (as they liked to call it) could a minister provide a diagnosis of, prescribe for, and ultimately cure spiritual disease in those who were plagued by the body of sin and death."[21]

The Puritans, therefore, were not afraid to preach the whole counsel of God. They did not conciliate their hearers by lightening their messages with humorous stories or folksy anecdotes. They felt the awesome responsibility of handling eternal truth and addressing immortal souls (Ezek. 33:8). They preached the weighty truths of God, "As a dying man to dying men, / As never sure to preach again!"

For example, when the Puritans dealt with the doctrine of sin, they called sin "sin," and declared it to be moral rebellion against God that reaps eternal guilt. They preached about sins of commission and sins of omission in thought, word, and deed.[22] They linked sin with the fall of Adam and Eve in Paradise.[23] They taught in no uncertain terms that through that fall we inherit the depravity that makes us unfit for God, holiness, and heaven. "In Adam's fall, we sinned all," they affirmed. They stressed that the problem of sinners was twofold: a bad record, which is a legal problem; and a bad heart, which is a moral problem. Both make us unfit for communion with God. More than an outward reformation of life is needed to meet the demands of God; inward regeneration of heart through a triune God is essential for salvation (John 3:3-7).

The Puritans also preached the doctrine of God without equivocation. They proclaimed God's majestic being, His trinitarian personality, and His glorious attributes.[24] All of their evangelism was rooted in a robust biblical theism, unlike modern evangelism, which too often approaches God as if He were a next-door neighbor who can adjust His attributes to our needs and desires. While modern evangelism claims John 3:16 as its text, the Puritan would more likely cite Genesis 1:1, "In the beginning God," to show how everything that happened since is part of what God has designed for His own glory. The Puritans understood that the doctrines of atonement, justification, and reconciliation are meaningless apart from a true understanding of God who condemns sin, and atones for sinners, justifies them, and reconciles them to Himself.

Puritan evangelism also proclaimed the doctrine of Christ. "Preaching is the chariot that carries Christ up and down the world," wrote Richard Sibbes.[25] Preaching the whole Christ to the whole man,[26] Puritan preachers offered Him as Prophet, Priest, and King. They did not separate His benefits from His person or offer Him as a Savior from sin while ignoring His claims as Lord. As Joseph Alleine wrote in his model of Puritan evangelism,[27] *An Alarm to the Unconverted*,

> All of Christ is accepted by the sincere convert. He loves not only the wages but the work of Christ, not only the benefits but the burden of Christ. He is willing not only to tread out the corn, but to draw under the yoke. He takes up the commands of Christ, yea, the cross of Christ. The unsound convert takes Christ by halves. He is all for the salvation of Christ, but he is not for sanctification. He is for the privileges, but does not appropriate the person of Christ. He divides the offices and benefits of Christ. This is an error in the foundation. Whoever loves life, let him beware here. It is an undoing mistake, of which you have often been warned, and yet none is more common.[28]

Alleine shows us that the division of the offices and benefits of

Christ is not a contemporary invention. Throughout the ages man has rebelled against Christ as God offers Him—as Lord and Savior (Ps. 2). The true convert, however, is willing to receive a whole Christ, without limitations. He is willing to have Christ upon any terms; he is "willing to have the dominion of Christ as well as deliverance by Christ," Alleine said.[29] The Puritans would stand aghast at the present trend in modern evangelism that seeks merely to rescue sinners from hell, postponing their submission to the sovereign lordship of Christ until later.

Preaching Christ with winsomeness and grace was the greatest burden and most essential task of the Puritan evangelists.[30] They repeatedly presented Christ in His power, willingness to save, and preciousness as the only Redeemer of lost sinners. They did so with theological articulation, divine grandeur, and human passion. They extolled Christ to the highest, and abased man to the lowest. They were not worried about injuring the self-esteem of listeners. They were far more concerned about esteeming the triune God: the Father who created us with dignity in His image; the Son who restores that dignity to us through redemption and the adoption of sons; and the Holy Spirit who indwells us and makes our souls and bodies His temple. Self-esteem messages that do not center upon a triune God they would have viewed as "self-deceit" messages. We have nothing to esteem in ourselves apart from God, the Puritans said. Apart from His grace, we are fallen, wretched, unworthy, and hell-bound.

3. Puritan Preaching Was Experimentally Practical

Puritan preaching explained how a Christian experiences biblical truth in his life. Their "experimental"[31] preaching sought to explain, in terms of biblical truth, how matters ought to go and how they do go in the Christian life, and aimed to apply divine truth to the whole range of the believer's experience—in his walk with God as well as his relationship with family, the church, and the world around him. We can learn much from the Puritans about this type of preaching.

The experimental preaching of the Puritans focused on the preaching of Christ. As Scripture clearly shows, evangelism must bear witness to the record God has given of His only begotten Son (Acts 2:3; 5:42; 8:35; Rom. 16:25; 1 Cor. 2:2; Gal. 3:1). The Puritans thus taught that any preaching in which Christ does not have the preeminence is not valid experiential preaching. William Perkins said that the heart of all preaching was to "preach one Christ by Christ to the praise of Christ."[32]

In this Christ-centered context, Puritan evangelism was marked by a discriminating application of truth to experience. Discriminatory preaching defines the difference between the Christian and the non-Christian. It offers the forgiveness of sins and eternal life to all who embrace Jesus Christ as Savior and Lord by true faith, and likewise pronounces the wrath of God and eternal condemnation upon the unbelieving and impenitent. Such preaching teaches that if our religion is not experiential, we will perish—not because experience itself saves, but because Christ who saves sinners must be experienced personally as the Rock upon whom our eternal hope is built (Matt. 7:22-27; 1 Cor. 1:30; 2:2).

The Puritans were very aware of the deceitfulness of the human heart. Consequently, Puritan evangelists took great pains to identify the marks of grace that distinguish the church from the world, true believers from imposters and merely professing believers, and saving faith from temporary faith.[33] This kind of discriminatory preaching is extremely rare today. Even in conservative evangelical churches, head knowledge of scriptural truth is often a substitute for heart experience; or, what is equally unscriptural, heart experience is substituted for head knowledge. Experimental preaching calls for both head knowledge and heart experience; its goal, according to John Murray, is "intelligent piety."

Space does not permit me to show how the various stages of spiritual experience are neglected in today's preaching. We will focus instead on only the first step—conviction of sin.[34] In all periods of genuine revival and spiritual prosperity, including the Puritan era, a profound conviction of sin is common. That conviction is due to the Holy Spirit, whose first work in a sinner is to convince of sin (John 16:8). The more the Spirit works in a person, the more he is convicted of his unworthiness before God. The Spirit prompts such an awareness of God, that the sinner confesses along with Isaiah, "Woe is me! for I am undone; because I am a man of unclean lips...for mine eyes have seen the King, the LORD of hosts" (Isa. 6:5), and with Paul, "O wretched man that I am! who shall deliver me from the body of this death?" (Rom. 7:24). Does the lack of conviction of sin in much modern evangelism imply the absence of the Spirit whose convicting work is essential to salvation?

The church should take a fresh look at Scripture, the Puritans, and church history, which all show that God is pleased to work conviction through His Holy Spirit using men whose hearts He has broken and led to Christ, and who then go out to preach with hearts full of compassion for Christ-less sinners. In the words of John Willison, God raises up men "of large hearts" when He is going to save many people. We today need more biblical, holy, humble, prayerful, and heavenly ministers. When John the Baptist preached convictingly, people fled from the wrath to come (Matt. 3:1-12). When Peter preached convictingly on Pentecost, at least three thousand were pricked in their hearts (Acts 2:37). When God is pleased to raise and use such men to bring others to a conviction of sin there is something distinctive about their preaching. Such preaching purposefully aims to convict of sin, not just to alarm people, but to awaken them as sinners. Such preaching searches and, as Perkins put it, "rips up the consciences" of men and women, boldly calling sinners to heartfelt repentance.

By contrast, modern evangelism, dating in North America from Charles Finney, does not strive to bring sinners to repentance, partly because of its defective, Pelagian view of man and sin.[35] The Bible, however, abounds with teaching about sin as guilt, defilement, depravity, and corruption in the human heart. Too many evangelists today say too little about sin, perhaps because they have little sense of sin themselves and because they believe that the first task of evangelism is to win people to Christ by addressing their "felt needs"—the things people think they need to hear about, rather than real spiritual needs related to sin.

Some evangelists today who speak about the guilt of sin and man's need of forgiveness, do not go far enough. They do not teach that "the natural man"—the non-Christian—is so dead in trespasses and sins (Eph. 2:1-3) that, left to himself, he is not able to seek God and his forgiveness (Rom. 3:9-18). They overlook verses such as Romans 8:7, "The carnal mind is enmity against God: for it is not subject to the law of God, neither indeed can be"; and 1 Corinthians 2:14, "The natural man receiveth not the things of the Spirit of God: for they are foolishness unto him: neither can he know them, because they are spiritually discerned." Such texts are not relevant to evangelism, contemporary evangelists say, because "How can we speak of the sinner's depravity, then ask him to respond to the gospel?"[36] The error of such thinking is the premise that any teaching on human sinfulness that denies a person's ability to respond is a hindrance to evangelism. We must not forget the example of the prophet Ezekiel (Ezek. 37:1-14)—namely, how God commands His servants to preach to valleys of dry, dead bones, and that He blesses the preaching of His Word by breathing life into those bones and regenerating them by His Spirit.

The Puritan emphasis on conviction of sin is only the starting point for biblical, experiential, and practical evangelism. The ultimate aim of such preaching is to lead people just as they are, in all their sinfulness and need, to Jesus Christ, who alone can save them from eternal condemnation and present them holy before the Father.

4. Puritan Preaching Was Holistically Evangelistic

The Puritans used all of Scripture to confront the whole man. They did not merely pressure the human will to respond on the basis of a few dozen texts that emphasize the volitional aspect of evangelism.

Modern evangelism, convinced that the first aim of preaching is to call upon men to believe, stresses a decisional act of faith on the part of the sinner. It does not think the saving work of the Holy Spirit is necessary prior to faith. It holds that we believe in order to be born again, that faith precedes and effects regeneration. Faith is, of course, essential to salvation from beginning to end (e.g., Rom. 1:17; Heb. 11:6), and there is no time lapse between regeneration and the Spirit's implanting of saving faith in the heart of a sinner. Puritan evangelism, however, has a deeper and wider message to the unconverted.

Certainly the duty to respond to the gospel in faith is important, but so are other duties. There is the duty to repent—not just as a temporary feeling of sorrow, but as a full amendment of life. The Puritans preached that sinners are to "cease to do evil" (Isa. 1:16), and to "be holy as God is holy." They are to love God and His holy law with heart and mind and strength, and to let nothing stand in the way of obedience. They are to "strive to enter in at the strait gate" (Luke 13:24).[37]

Some church leaders would argue that such preaching leads to legalism. However, such preaching is justified on this ground: in the work of conversion God does not normally begin with a conscious decision of faith, but with conviction of sin and a sense of total helplessness to obey God's commands. Thus the Puritan evangelists preached about the legal obligations and liabilities under which sinners toil, before showing them the way of deliverance through faith in Christ's blood. They preached the law before the gospel in much the same way Paul wrote the first three chapters of Romans. The apostle first explains the holiness of God and His law so that the mouths of sinners are stopped and the whole world is found guilty before God. Likewise, the Puritans believed that, through a confrontation with the demands of the law, the Holy Spirit would bring sinners to know their helplessness before God and their need for salvation. Only to sinners who recognize their sinfulness will the gospel be meaningful.

The Puritans, then, were not afraid to use the law of God as an instrument of evangelism. When God is about to play the chord of grace in the soul, they taught, He usually starts with the bass note of the law. In order for man to come to Christ, he must first come to an end of his own righteousness.[38] "They held [that] the index of the soundness of a man's faith in Christ is the genuineness of the self-despair from which it springs," says Packer.[39]

This type of evangelism is clearly rooted in Scripture. John the Baptist preached repentance and holiness (Matt. 3:1-2) before he preached, "Behold the Lamb of God, which taketh away the sin of the world" (John 1:29). Jesus began His ministry with the same message. As Matthew 4:17 says, "From that time Jesus began to preach, and to say, Repent: for the kingdom of heaven is at hand." He continued that theme with individuals such as Nicodemus, saying, "Ye must be born again" (John 3:7), and with the rich young ruler, confronting him first of all with the commandments (Mark 10:19).

The message of the Bible and the Puritans is that the law has an evangelistic use.[40] Let man try to obey the law for salvation. At first he will think he can do it. Then he will learn that he cannot possibly be as holy as the law demands. Wielded by the Spirit, the law condemns him, pronounces a curse upon him, and declares him liable to the wrath of God and the torments of hell (Gal. 3:10). Finally, he will come to the desperate realization that only God can save him by changing his heart and giving him a new nature. The Spirit brings him to the end of the law, Christ Jesus, as the only righteousness acceptable with God (Gal. 3:24). Sinners who experience both this necessity and impossibility cry out in anguish for God to do what they cannot do themselves. In this way sinners have room made in them to receive the rich proclamation and application of the gospel; the Spirit of God then enables them to embrace Christ by faith.[41]

Modern evangelism differs from this in how it persuades men to embrace the gospel. Modern evangelists do not believe that the necessity of holiness is a suitable subject for the unconverted, so they do not present the gospel as a divine remedy for corrupt and impotent sinners. Puritans, by contrast, believed that the best news in the world for sinners who are truly convicted of sin is that deliverance from the power of sin is possible through faith in Christ. Such sinners need more than forgiveness or pardon; they want sin to be put to death in themselves forever. They want to live for the glory of God. They want to be holy as

God is holy. They want to be conformed to the character of the Father, the image of the Son, and the mind of the Spirit.[42]

Modern evangelism has lost sight of that motive. Holiness is treated as something separate from salvation. Thus the message that seeks to convince people to embrace Christ is generally an appeal to self-interest. It offers forgiveness with the assurance of heaven and the kind of happiness and satisfaction that is found in Christ, without mentioning fruits of sanctification such as self-denying humility and unconditional obedience. Thankfully, under defective preaching (by the mercy of God) some people are saved. But that does not make such preaching right. Such preaching often minimizes the difficulty of coming to Christ and overplays the temporal benefits of living life as a Christian. This type of preaching is an attempt to give men who have no conviction of sin an alternative reason to decide for Christ.

All of this leads us to conclude that the teaching of modern evangelism on the nature of faith and its relationship to regeneration fails the test of the Word of God. The Puritans taught that a "regeneration" that leaves men without the indwelling power of the Holy Spirit and without the practice of holy living is not what is promised in Scripture.[43] According to the Bible, a regenerate person is not simply changed in his religious opinions. A regenerate person is someone who has been given a new nature by the Holy Spirit. He is born of the Spirit to become spiritual (John 3:6). He has been recreated so all things are become new.[44] Such a person ceases to be self-centered and becomes God-centered. "They that are after the flesh do mind the things of the flesh; they that are after the Spirit, the things of the Spirit" (Rom. 8:5). The regenerate man loves God, loves holiness, loves the Bible, loves the godly, and loves the thought of going to heaven to commune with God and to leave sin behind forever.

The discrepancies between Puritan and modern evangelism should prompt us to revert back to the older message where the whole of Scripture is addressed to the whole man.

5. Puritan Preaching Was Studiously Symmetrical
There was in Puritan preaching both well-roundedness and good balance. Puritan preaching achieved this symmetry in four ways:

• First, it allowed Scripture to dictate the emphasis for each message. The Puritans did not preach sermons that were a kind of balancing act between various doctrines. Rather, they let the biblical text determine the content and emphasis of each message.[45] They preached a Bible text completely, whatever its theme, and so in time they would be sure to address every major theme of Scripture and every major doctrine of Reformed theology.

Nothing was left out of balance in the total range of the Puritans' frequent and lengthy sermons. In theology proper, they proclaimed God's transcendence as well as His immanence. In anthropology, they preached about the image of God in its narrower as well as its wider sense. In Christology, they exhibited Christ's state of humiliation as well as exaltation. In soteriology, they presented divine sovereignty and human responsibility as doctrines that do not need to be reconciled by our finite minds, since, as one preacher quipped, "friends need no reconciliation." In ecclesiology, they acknowledged the high calling of special offices (ministers, elders, and deacons) as well as the equally high calling of the general office of all believers. In eschatology, they declared both the glories of heaven and the horrors of hell.

• Second, Puritan preaching instilled appreciation for each scriptural doctrine. The typical member of a Puritan congregation could relish a sermon one week on Genesis 19:17 ("Escape for thy life") for its warning notes on fleeing wickedness and following God, and the next week savor a message on how difficult it is to follow God unless God draws us to Himself (John 6:44). Puritan pastors and people alike treasured the full scope of God's biblical truth rather than just their favorite passages or particular doctrines by which they rated each sermon.

• Third, Puritan preaching allowed for a wide variety of sermon topics. A carefully cultivated appreciation for all scriptural doctrine in turn allowed the Puritans to cover nearly every topic imaginable. For example, one volume of Puritan sermons includes the following messages:

–How may We Experience in Ourselves, and Evidence to Others, that Serious Godliness is more than a Fancy?
–What Are the Best Preservatives Against Melancholy and Overmuch Sorrow?
–How May We grow in the Knowledge of Christ?
–What Must We Do to Prevent and Cure Spiritual Pride?
–How May We Graciously Improve Those Doctrines and Providences That Transcend Our Understanding?
–What Distance Ought We to Keep, in Following the Strange Fashions of Apparel Which Come Up in the Days in Which We Live?
–How May We Best Know the Worth of The Soul?[46]

Modern evangelism, by contrast, is reductionistic—using only a few texts, expounding a limited range of themes, and bringing little if any doctrine to bear on the work of evangelism.

• Fourth, Puritan preaching was backed by right living. Puritan preachers lived what they preached. For them, balanced doctrine was inseparable from balanced living. Puritan ministers were teaching prophets, interceding priests, and governing kings in their own homes as well as their congregations and society. They were men of private prayer, family worship, and public intercession. They were living illustrations of Robert Murray M'Cheyne's words: "A holy minister is an awful weapon in the hand of God…. A minister's life is the life of his ministry."[47] Or as John Boys put it: "He doth preach most, that doth live best."[48]

One of the glaring faults in modern evangelism is its lack of balance in word and deed. Modern evangelism presents a gospel that is so stripped of the demands of Christ's lordship that it becomes cheap grace, and cheap grace produces cheap living.

We need to ask ourselves: Is our preaching, teaching, and evangelizing thoroughly scriptural, unashamedly doctrinal, experimentally practical, holistically evangelistic, and beautifully symmetrical?

The Method of Puritan Evangelism

Although evangelism differs to some degree from generation to generation according to gifts, culture, style, and language, the primary methods of Puritan evangelism—plain preaching and catechetical teaching—can teach us much about how to present the gospel to sinners.

1. Plain Preaching

The greatest teacher of the Puritan "plain style of preaching" was William Perkins. Perkins, often called the father of Puritanism, wrote that preaching "must be plain, perspicuous, and evident…. It is a byword among us: It was a very plain Sermon: And I say again, the plainer, the better."[49] And Cotton Mather wrote succinctly in his eulogy for John Eliot, a great Puritan missionary to the Indians, that his "way of preaching was very plain; so that the very lambs might wade into his discourses on those texts and themes, wherein elephants might swim."[50] The Puritan plain style of preaching avoided all that was not clear or "perspicuous" to an ordinary listener. Since the minister was first and foremost God's appointed interpreter of the Word, no oratorical interest should ever be allowed to obscure the gospel's truth and clarity. "A crucified style best suits the preachers of a crucified Christ," John Flavel noted.[51]

The Puritans used the plain style of preaching because they were evangelistic to the core—they wanted to reach everyone, to preach so that all might know the way of salvation. The first part of a Puritan sermon was exegetical; the second, doctrinal and didactic; and the third, applicatory.[52] The third part, often called the "uses" of the text, was quite lengthy and applied Scripture in various ways to various listeners.[53] Perkins gave distinct directions on how to shape Scripture's applications to seven categories of listeners: ignorant and unteachable unbelievers; teachable but ignorant people; knowledgeable but unhumbled people; the humbled who lack assurance; believers; backsliders; and "a mingled people"—that is, those who are a combination of several categories.[54] Puritan preachers addressed all seven types of people over a period of time, but not in each sermon. Each sermon at least included directions to believers and unbelievers. The unbeliever was usually called to examine how he was living and what behavior needed changing; then he was admonished to flee to Christ who alone could fulfill his needs. For the believer, "uses" usually contained points of comfort, direction, and self-examination.

Three characteristics associated with Puritan plain preaching need to be recovered by today's preachers.

• First, Puritan preaching addressed the mind with clarity. It addressed man as a rational creature. The Puritans loved and worshiped God with their minds. They viewed the mind as the palace of faith. They refused to set mind and heart against each other, but taught that knowledge was the soil in which the Spirit planted the seed of regeneration. Puritans thus preached that we need to think in order to be holy. They challenged the idea that holiness is only a matter of emotions.

The Puritans preached that a flabby mind is no badge of honor. They understood that a mindless Christianity will foster a spineless Christianity. An anti-intellectualistic gospel will spawn an irrelevant gospel that does not get beyond "felt needs." That's what is happening in our churches today. We've lost our Christian mind, and for the most part we do not see the necessity of recovering it. We do not understand that where there is little difference between the Christian and non-Christian in what we think and believe, there will soon be little difference in how we live.

• Second, Puritan preaching confronted the conscience pointedly. The Puritans worked hard on the consciences of sinners as the "light of nature" in them. Plain preaching named specific sins, then asked questions to press home the guilt of those sins upon the consciences of men, women, and children. As one Puritan wrote, "We must go with the stick of divine truth and beat every bush behind which a sinner hides, until like Adam who hid, he stands before God in his nakedness." They believed that was necessary because until the sinner gets out from behind that bush, he'll never cry to be clothed in the righteousness of Christ. So the Puritans preached urgently, believing that many of their listeners were still on their way to hell. They preached directly, confronting their hearers with law and gospel, with death in Adam and life in Christ. They preached specifically, taking seriously Christ's command "that repentance and remission of sins should be preached in his name" (Luke 24:47).

Modern evangelism is, for the most part, afraid to confront the conscience pointedly. We need to learn from the Puritans who were solemnly persuaded as they evangelized that the friend who loves you most will tell you the most truth about yourself. Like Paul and the Puritans, we need to testify, earnestly and with tears, of the need for "repentance toward God, and faith toward our Lord Jesus Christ" (Acts 20:21).

• Third, Puritan preaching wooed the heart passionately. It was affectionate, zealous, and optimistic. Puritan preachers did not just reason with the mind and confront the conscience; they appealed to the heart. They preached out of love for God's Word, love for the glory of God, and love for the soul of every listener. They preached with warm gratitude of the Christ who had saved them and made their lives a sacrifice of praise. They set forth Christ in His loveliness, hoping to make the unsaved jealous of what the believer has in Christ. The Puritans used every weapon they could—compelling preaching, personal pleading, earnest praying, biblical reasoning, joyful living—to turn sinners from the road of destruction to God. They believed that God would use their preaching as a weapon to conquer and a power to convert sinners. They knew from Scripture and by experience that only an omnipotent Christ can arrest a dead sinner wedded to his sinful lusts, divorce him from the primary love of his heart, make him willing to forsake his bosom sin, and turn him to God with full resolve to obey and honor Him and make Him his end and goal. They preached knowing that Christ, not our old Adamic nature, was sufficient for these things. "Preaching, therefore, ought not to be dead, but alive and effective so that an unbeliever coming into the congregation of believers should be affected and, as it were, transfixed by the very hearing of the word so that he might give glory to God," wrote William Ames.[55]

2. Catechetical Evangelism

Like the Reformers, the Puritans were catechists. They believed that pulpit messages should be reinforced by personalized ministry through *catechesis*—the instruction in the doctrines of Scripture using catechisms. Puritan catechizing was evangelistic in several ways.

Scores of Puritans reached out evangelistically to children and young people by writing catechism books that explained fundamental Christian doctrines via questions and answers supported by Scripture.[56] For example, John Cotton entitled his catechism, *Milk for Babes, drawn out of the Breasts of both Testaments*.[57] Other Puritans included in the titles of their catechisms such expressions as "the main and fundamental points," "the sum of the Christian religion," the "several heads" or "first principles" of religion, and "the ABC of Christianity." At various levels in the church as well as in the homes of their parishioners, Puritan ministers taught rising generations both from the Bible and from their catechisms. Their goals were to explain the fundamental teachings of the Bible, to help young people commit the Bible to memory, to make sermons and the sacraments more understandable, to prepare covenant

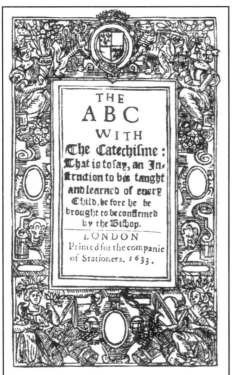

A typical title page of a seventeenth century catechism book for children

children for confession of faith, to teach them how to defend their faith against error, and to help parents teach their own children.[58]

Catechizing was a follow-up to sermons and a way to reach neighbors with the gospel. Joseph Alleine reportedly followed up his work on Sunday five days a week by catechizing church members as well as reaching out with the gospel to people he met on the streets.[59] Richard Baxter, whose vision for catechizing is expounded in *The Reformed Pastor*, said that he came to the painful conclusion that "some ignorant persons, who have been so long unprofitable hearers, have got more knowledge and remorse of conscience in half an hour's close disclosure, than they did from ten years' public preaching."[60] Baxter invited people to his home every Thursday evening to discuss and pray for blessing upon the sermons of the previous Sabbath.

Catechizing was evangelistic for purposes of examining people's spiritual condition, and for encouraging and admonishing them to flee to Christ. Baxter and his two assistants spent two full days each week catechizing parishioners in their homes. In addition to that, on Monday and Tuesday afternoons and evenings he catechized each of his seven family members for an hour per week. Those visits involved patiently teaching, gently examining, and carefully leading family and church members to Christ through the Scriptures. Packer concludes: "To upgrade the practice of personal catechising from a preliminary discipline for children to a permanent ingredient in evangelism and pastoral care for all ages was Baxter's main contribution to the development of Puritan ideals for the ministry."[61]

The hard work of the Puritan catechist was greatly rewarded. Richard Greenham claimed that catechism teaching built up the Reformed church and did serious damage to Roman Catholicism.[62] When Baxter was installed at Kidderminster in Worcestershire, perhaps one family in each street honored God in family worship; at the end of his ministry there, there were streets where every family did so. He could say that of the six hundred converts that were brought to faith under his preaching, he could not name one that had backslidden to the ways of the world. How vastly different was that result compared to the results of today's evangelists who press for mass conversions, then turn over the hard work of follow-up to others!

The Inward Disposition of the Puritan Evangelist
Finally, the Puritan evangelist brought to his work a unique inward disposition or frame of mind and soul. Commitment to godliness lay at the

heart of the Puritan vision. Thomas Brooks wrote, "A preacher's life
should be a commentary upon his doctrine; his practice should be the
counterpane [counterpart] of his sermons. Heavenly doctrines should
always be adorned with a heavenly life.

> *Preachers are the glass [the mirror], the school, the book,*
> *Where people's eyes do learn, do read, do look."*[63]

The Puritan evangelist had a heart to serve God, devotion to and care
for the people of God and the unsaved, devotion to the Scriptures and
ability to preach them, and a sense of dependency on the Holy Spirit
coupled with a life of prayerfulness. These last two qualities in particular are lacking in modern evangelism and need to be addressed.

First, the Puritans showed a profound dependence upon the Holy
Spirit in everything they said and did. They keenly felt their inability to
bring anyone to Christ as well as the magnitude of conversion. They
were convinced that both preacher and listener are totally dependent on
the work of the Spirit to effect regeneration and conversion when, how,
and in whom He will. The Spirit brings God's presence into human
hearts. He persuades sinners to seek salvation, renews corrupt wills, and
makes scriptural truths take root in stony hearts. As Thomas Watson
wrote, "Ministers knock at the door of men's hearts, the Spirit comes
with a key and opens the door."[64] And Joseph Alleine said: "Never think
you can convert yourself. If ever you would be savingly converted, you
must despair of doing it in your own strength. It is a resurrection from
the dead (Eph. 2:1), a new creation (Gal. 6:15; Eph. 2:10), a work of absolute omnipotence (Eph. 1:19)."[65]

Modern evangelists need to be persuaded that the Spirit's regenerating action, as John Owen wrote, is "infallible, victorious, irresistible,
and always efficacious"; it "removeth all obstacles, overcomes all oppo-
sitions, and infallibly produces the effect intended."[66] All modes of action that imply another doctrine are unbiblical. As Packer writes: "All
devices for exerting psychological pressure in order to precipitate 'decisions' must be eschewed, as being in truth presumptuous attempts to
intrude into the province of the Holy Ghost." Such pressures may even
be harmful, he goes on to say, for while they "may produce the outward
form of 'decision,' they cannot bring about regeneration and a change
of heart, and when the 'decisions' wear off those who registered them
will be found 'gospel-hardened' and antagonistic." Packer concludes in
a Puritan vein: "Evangelism must rather be conceived as a long-term
enterprise of patient teaching and instruction, in which God's servants

seek simply to be faithful in delivering the gospel message and applying it to human lives, and leave it to God's Spirit to draw men to faith through this message in his own way and at his own speed."[67]

Second, the Puritans saturated all their evangelistic efforts in prayer. They were "men of the closet," first of all. They were great preachers only because they were also great petitioners who wrestled with God for divine blessing upon their preaching. Richard Baxter said, "Prayer must carry on our work as well as preaching; he preacheth not heartily to his people, that prayeth not earnestly for them. If we prevail not with God to give them faith and repentance, we shall never prevail with them to believe and repent."[68]

And Robert Traill wrote, "Some ministers of meaner gifts and parts are more successful than some that are far above them in abilities; not because they preach better, so much as because they pray more. Many good sermons are lost for lack of much prayer in study."[69]

The well-known story of Puritan-minded Robert Murray M'Cheyne illustrates best what Traill means. An old sexton in M'Cheyne's church noticed the awe on the face of a visitor and invited him into his study. "Tell me," said the visitor, "having sat under this godly man's ministry, what is the secret of his success?" The sexton told the visitor to sit at M'Cheyne's desk. Then he asked the man to put his hands on the desk. Then to put his face in his hands and weep. Next the two men walked into the church sanctuary and ascended to the pulpit. "Lean over the

Robert Murray M'Cheyne

pulpit," the sexton said. "Now stretch out your hands and weep." "Now you know the secret of M'Cheyne's ministry."[70]

The church today desperately needs such preachers whose private prayers season their pulpit messages. The Puritan pastors jealously guarded their personal devotional time. They set their priorities on spiritual, eternal realities. They knew that if they ceased to watch and pray constantly they would be courting spiritual disaster. Faithful, steadfast, and sincere, they were God-fearing men who continually examined themselves and were painfully aware, as John Flavel said, "that a man may be objectively a spiritual [man], and all the while subjectively a carnal man."[71] They believed, as John Owen noted, "No man preacheth that sermon well that doth not first preach it to his own heart. . . . If the word do not dwell with power in us, it will not pass with power from us."[72] Unlike many modern evangelists, the quality of their spiritual life was uniformly high.[73]

Let us challenge one another! Are we, like the Puritans, thirsting to glorify the triune God? Are we motivated by biblical truth and biblical fire? Do we share the Puritan view of the vital necessity of conversion? Who among us will live godly in Christ Jesus like the Puritans? Who will go beyond studying their writings, discussing their ideas, recalling their achievements, and berating their failures? Who will practice the degree of obedience to God's Word for which they strove? Will we serve God as they served Him? "Thus saith the LORD, Stand ye in the ways, and see, and ask for the old paths, where is the good way, and walk therein, and ye shall find rest for your souls" (Jer. 6:16).

We must ourselves be conquered by the great and mighty truths of God. The time is short. Soon we will pray our last prayer, read Scripture for the last time, preach our last sermon, and witness to our last friend. Then the only thing that will matter will be the gospel. Surely on our deathbed a question uppermost in our minds will be: What kind of an evangelist have I been? Scripture tells us: "He that winneth many souls is wise" (Prov. 11:30). "And they that be wise shall shine as the brightness of the firmament; and they that turn many to righteousness as the stars for ever and ever" (Dan. 12:3).

---

[1] Allen C. Guelzo, "The Puritan Preaching Ministry in Old and New England," *Journal of Christian Reconstruction* 6, 2 (1980):24-25.

[2] David B. Calhoun, "John Calvin: Missionary Hero or Missionary Failure?," *Presbyterion* 5, 1 (1979):16-33. Cf. Samuel M. Zwemer, "Calvinism and the Missionary Enterprise," *Theology Today* 7, 2 (1950):206-216; Johannes van den Berg, "Calvin's

Missionary Message," *Evangelical Quarterly* 22 (1950):174-87; G. Baez-Camargo, "The Earliest Protestant Missionary Venture in Latin America," *Church History* 21, 2 (1952):135-45; Johannes van den Berg, "Calvin and Missions," in *John Calvin: Contemporary Prophet,* ed. J.T. Hoogstra (Grand Rapids: Baker, 1959), 167-84; Charles Chaney, "The Missionary Dynamic in the Theology of John Calvin," *Reformed Review* 17, 3 (1964):24-38; Philip E. Hughes, "John Calvin: Director of Missions," and R. Pierce Beaver, "The Genevan Mission to Brazil," in *The Heritage of John Calvin,* ed. John H. Bratt (Grand Rapids: Eerdmans, 1973), 40-73; W. Stanford Reid, "Calvin's Geneva: A Missionary Centre," *Reformed Theological Review* 42, 3 (1983):65-73; J. Douglas MacMillan, "Calvin, Geneva, and Christian Mission," *Reformed Theological Journal* 5 (1989):5-17.

[3] The best sources for a Puritan theology of evangelism and missions are Sidney H. Rooy, *The Theology of Missions in the Puritan Tradition. A Study of Representative Puritans: Richard Sibbes, Richard Baxter, John Eliot, Cotton Mather, and Jonathan Edwards* (Grand Rapids: Eerdmans, 1965), and James I. Packer, *A Quest for Godliness: The Puritan Vision of the Christian Life* (Wheaton, Ill.: Crossway, 1990), chps. 2, 10, 17-19. Cf. Francis G. James, "Puritan Missionary Endeavors in Early New England" (M.A. thesis, Yale, 1938); Ernst Benz, "Pietist and Puritan Sources of Early Protestant World Missions," *Church History* 20, 2 (1951):28-55; Johannes van den Berg, *Constrained by Jesus' Love: An Inquiry into the Motives of the Missionary Awakening in Great Britain in the Period Between 1698 and 1815* (Kampen: J.H. Kok, 1956); Alden T. Vaughan, *New England Frontier: Puritan and Indian, 1620-1675* (Boston: Little, Brown and Company, 1965); R. Pierce Beaver, *Pioneers in Mission* (Grand Rapids: Eerdmans, 1966); Charles L. Chaney, *The Birth of Missions in America* (South Pasadena, Calif.: William Carey Library, 1976); William S. Barker, "The Rediscovery of the Gospel: The Reformation, the Westminster Divines, and Missions," *Presbyterion* 24, 1 (1998):38-45.

[4] Richard Mitchell Hawkes, "The Logic of Assurance in English Puritan Theology," *Westminster Theological Journal* 52 (1990):247. For the difficulties in, and attempts at, defining Puritanism, see Ralph Bronkema, *The Essence of Puritanism* (Goes: Oosterbaan and LeCointre, 1929); Leonard J. Trinterud, "The Origins of Puritanism," *Church History* 20 (1951):37-57; Jerald C. Brauer, "Reflections on the Nature of English Puritanism," *Church History* 23 (1954):98-109; Basil Hall, "Puritanism: The Problem of Definition," in G. J. Cumming, ed., *Studies in Church History,* vol. 2 (London: Nelson, 1965), 283-96; Charles H. George, "Puritanism as History and Historiography," *Past and Present* 41 (1968):77-104; William Lamont, "Puritanism as History and Historiography: Some Further Thoughts," *Past and Present* 42 (1969):133-46; Richard Greaves, "The Nature of the Puritan Tradition," in R. Buick Knox, ed., *Reformation, Conformity and Dissent: Essays in Honour of Geoffrey Nuttall* (London: Epworth Press, 1977), 255-73; D.M. Lloyd-Jones, "Puritanism and Its Origins," *The Puritans: Their Origins and Successors* (Edinburgh: Banner of Truth Trust, 1987), 237-59; Packer, "Why We Need the Puritans," in *A Quest for Godliness,* 21-36; Joel R. Beeke, *The Quest for Full Assurance: The Legacy of Calvin and His Successors* (Edinburgh: Banner of Truth Trust, 1999), 82ff.

[5] Peter Lewis, *The Genius of Puritanism* (Hayward Heath, Sussex: Carey, 1975), 11ff.

[6] Rooy, *Theology of Missions in the Puritan Tradition,* 310-28.

[7] *The Complete Works of Thomas Manton,* ed. T. Smith. (1870; reprint Worthington, Pa.: Maranatha, 1980), 2:102ff.

166 Puritan Reformed Spirituality

8 See Joel R. Beeke and Ray B. Lanning, "The Transforming Power of Scripture," in *Sola Scriptura: The Protestant Position of the Bible*, ed. Don Kistler (Morgan, Pa.: Soli Deo Gloria, 1995), 221-76.

9 *M. Derings Workes* (1597; reprint New York: Da Capo Press, 1972), 456.

10 *The Works of John Owen*, ed. William H. Goold (1853; London: Banner of Truth Trust, 1965), 16:74.

11 *The Paul's Cross Sermons, 1534-1642* (Toronto: University of Toronto Press, 1958), 165.

12 "A Profitable Treatise, Containing a Direction for the reading and understanding of the holy Scriptures," in H[enry] H[olland], ed., *The Works of the Reverend and Faithfull Servant of Iesvs Christ, M. Richard Greenham* (1599; reprint New York: Da Capo Press, 1973), 389-97. Cf. Thomas Watson, "How We May Read the Scriptures with Most Spiritual Profit," in *Heaven Taken by Storm: Showing the Holy Violence a Christian Is to Put Forth in the Pursuit After Glory*, ed. Joel R. Beeke (1669; reprint Pittsburgh: Soli Deo Gloria, 1992), 113-129.

13 Ibid., 16-18, and Thomas Watson, *A Body of Divinity* (1692; reprint London: Banner of Truth Trust), 377-79.

14 Ibid., 379. "There is not a sermon which is heard, but it sets us nearer heaven or hell" (John Preston, *A Pattern of Wholesome Words*, quoted in Christopher Hill, *Society and Puritanism in Pre-Revolutionary England*, 2nd ed. (New York: Schocken, 1967), 46.

15 *Christ the Fountain of Life* (London: Carden, 1648), 14.

16 "Evangelical Ministry: The Puritan Contribution," in *The Compromised Church: The Present Evangelical Crisis*, ed. John H. Armstrong (Wheaton, Ill.: Crossway, 1998), 267.

17 E.g., *William Perkins, 1558-1602: English Puritanist. His Pioneer Works on Casuistry: "A Discourse of Conscience" and "The Whole Treatise of Cases of Conscience,"* ed. Thomas F. Merrill (Nieuwkoop: B. DeGraaf, 1966). These works earned Perkins the title of "the father of Puritan casuistry."

18 See Packer, *A Quest for Godliness*, 81-106; Leland Ryken, *Worldly Saints: The Puritans as They Really Were* (Grand Rapids: Zondervan, 1986), 143-49, 154; Thomas D. Lea, "The Hermeneutics of the Puritans," *Journal of the Evangelical Theological Society* 39, 2 (1996):271-84.

19 *The Works of William Perkins* (London: John Legate, 1609), 1:10.

20 William Ames, *The Marrow of Theology*, ed. John D. Eusden (1629; Boston: Pilgrim Press, 1968), 77.

21 *Compromised Church*, 266.

22 Burroughs, *The Evil of Evils* (1654; reprint Morgan, Pa.: Soli Deo Gloria, 1995). Cf. Ralph Venning, *The Plague of Plagues* (1669; reprint London: Banner of Truth Trust, 1965); Thomas Watson, *The Mischief of Sin* (1671; reprint, Morgan, Pa.: Soli Deo Gloria, 1994); Samuel Bolton, "Sin: the Greatest Evil," in *Puritans on Conversion* (Pittsburgh: Soli Deo Gloria, 1990), 1-69.

23 The most powerful Puritan work on the dread consequences of original sin is Thomas Goodwin, "An Unregenerate Man's Guiltiness Before God in Respect of Sin and Punishment," vol. 10 of *The Works of Thomas Goodwin* (1865; reprint Eureka, Calif.: Tanski, 1996). The classic doctrinal Puritan work on the subject is Jonathan Edwards, *Original Sin*, vol. 3 of *The Works of Jonathan Edwards* (1758; New Haven: Yale, 1970). The best secondary source on the Edwardsean view is

C. Samuel Storms, *Tragedy in Eden: Original Sin in the Theology of Jonathan Edwards* (Lanham, Md.: University Press of America, 1985). Thomas Boston's classic, *Human Nature in Its Fourfold State* (1720; reprint London: Banner of Truth Trust, 1964), focuses on the four states of innocence, depravity, grace, and glory, but his section on imputed and inherited depravity is especially poignant. He details how Adam's original sin broke man's relationship with God as well as each of the Ten Commandments.

24 The classic work on God's attributes is Stephen Charnock's massive *Discourses on the Existence and Attributes of God* (1682; reprint Grand Rapids: Baker, 1996). See also William Bates, *The Harmony of the Divine Attributes in the Contrivance and Accomplishment of Man's Redemption* (1674; reprint Harrisonburg, Va.: Sprinkle, 1985).

25 *The Complete Works of Richard Sibbes*, ed. Alexander B. Grosart (1862; reprint Edinburgh: Banner of Truth Trust, 1977), 5:508.

26 Thomas Taylor, *Christ Revealed: or The Old Testament Explained; A Treatise of the Types and Shadowes of our Saviour* (London: M.F. for R. Dawlman and L. Fawne, 1635) is the best Puritan work on Christ in the Old Testament. Thomas Goodwin, "Christ Our Mediator," vol. 5 of *The Works of Thomas Goodwin* (1865; reprint Eureka, Calif.: Tanski, 1996) ably expounds primary New Testament texts on the mediatorship of Christ. Alexander Grosse, *The Happiness of Enjoying and Making a True And Speedy use of Christ* (London: Tho: Brudenell, for John Bartlet, 1647) and Isaac Ambrose, *Looking Unto Jesus* (1658; reprint Harrisonburg, Va.: Sprinkle, 1988) are experiential Christology at its best. Ralph Robinson, *Christ All and In All: or Several Significant Similitudes by which the Lord Jesus Christ is Described in the Holy Scriptures* (1660; reprint Ligonier, Pa.: Soli Deo Gloria, 1992), Philip Henry, *Christ All in All, or What Christ is Made to Believers* (1676; reprint Swengel, Pa.: Reiner, 1976), and John Brown, *Christ: the Way, the Truth, and the Life* (1677; reprint Morgan, Pa.: Soli Deo Gloria, 1995) contain precious sermons extolling Christ in all His relations to believers. John Owen, *A Declaration of the Glorious Mystery of the Person of Christ* (1679; reprinted in vol. 1 of *Works of Owen*) is superb on the relation of Christ's natures to His person. James Durham, *Christ Crucified; or The Marrow of the Gospel in 72 Sermons on Isaiah 53* (1683; reprint, 2 vols., Glasgow: Alex Adam, 1792) remains unrivaled as a scriptural exposition of Christ's passion.

27 Joseph Alleine, *An Alarm to the Unconverted* (1671; reprint London: Banner of Truth Trust, 1959), 11. This book was reprinted again by Banner of Truth Trust in 1995 as *A Sure Guide to Heaven,* a title first used in 1675.

28 Ibid., 45.

29 Ibid., 45-46.

30 E.g., see ibid., 117-20; William Guthrie, *The Christian's Great Interest* (1658; reprint London: Banner of Truth Trust, 1969), 169-92; Richard Alleine, *Heaven Opened: The Riches of God's Covenant of Grace* (1666; Grand Rapids: Baker, 1979); Philip Doddridge, *The Rise and Progress of Religion in the Soul* (1744; Edinburgh: for Ogle, Allardice, & Thomson, 1819), 217-26.

31 "Christian Experience," *Banner of Truth*, No. 139 (Apr. 1975):6.

32 *Works of Perkins,* 2:762.

33 Thomas Watson, *The Godly Man's Picture* (1666; reprint Edinburgh: Banner of Truth Trust, 1992), 20-188, sets forth twenty-four marks of grace for self-examination.

34 For several thoughts in this section on conviction of sin, I am indebted to addresses given by Iain Murray, Donald Macleod, and Albert Martin.

[35] See Packer, *A Quest for Godliness*, 292-94; Iain Murray, *Revival and Revivalism: The Making and Marring of American Evangelicalism 1750-1858* (Edinburgh: Banner of Truth Trust, 1994), 228ff., and *Pentecost—Today? The Biblical Basis for Understanding Revival* (Edinburgh: Banner of Truth Trust, 1998), 33-53.

[36] Cf. Billy Graham, *The Holy Spirit: Activating God's Power in Your Life* (Waco, Tx.: Word, 1978).

[37] Cf. Joel R. Beeke, *Knowing and Living the Christian Life* (Grand Rapids: Reformation Heritage Books, 1997), 16-21.

[38] Thomas Hooker, *The Soul's Preparation for Christ: Or, A Treatise of Contrition, Wherein is discovered How God breaks the heart, and wounds the Soul, in the conversion of a Sinner to Himself* (1632; reprint Ames, Ia.: International Outreach, 1994), 121-55; Samuel Bolton, Nathaniel Vincent, and Thomas Watson, *The Puritans on Conversion* (Pittsburgh: Soli Deo Gloria, 1990), 107-113.

[39] *A Quest for Godliness*, 170.

[40] Joel R. Beeke and Ray B. Lanning, "Glad Obedience," in *Trust and Obey*, ed. Don Kistler (Morgan, Pa.: Soli Deo Gloria, 1996), 159-62.

[41] For a description of how faith embraces Christ, see Joel R. Beeke, "The Relation of Faith to Justification," in *Justification by Faith Alone*, ed. Don Kistler (Morgan, Pa.: Soli Deo Gloria, 1995), 68-78.

[42] Joel R. Beeke, *Holiness: God's Call to Sanctification* (Edinbrugh: Banner of Truth Trust, 1994), 11.

[43] William Whately, *The New Birth* (London, 1618); Stephen Charnock, "A Discourse of the Efficient of Regeneration," in *The Works of Stephen Charnock* (1865; reprint Edinburgh: Banner of Truth Trust, 1986), 3:166-306.

[44] "A Discourse on the Nature of Regeneration," ibid., 3:82-165.

[45] Cf. *The Wrath of Almighty God: Jonathan Edwards on God's Judgment against Sinners*, ed. Don Kistler (Morgan, Pa.: Soli Deo Gloria, 1996); *The Works of Jonathan Edwards*, 2:617-41; John H. Gerstner, *Jonathan Edwards on Heaven and Hell* (Grand Rapids: Baker, 1980).

[46] *Puritan Sermons 1659-1689: Being the Morning Exercises at Cripplegate*, ed. James Nichols (1682; reprint Wheaton, Ill.: Richard Owen Roberts, 1981), vol. 3.

[47] *Memoir and Remains of Robert Murray M'Cheyne*, ed. Andrew A. Bonar (London: Banner of Truth Trust, 1966), 282.

[48] *The Works of John Boys* (1629; reprint Morgan, Pa.: Soli Deo Gloria, 1997), 481.

[49] *The Works of Perkins*, 2:222. Cf. William Perkins, *The Art of Prophesying* (1606; revised ed., Edinburgh: Banner of Truth Trust, 1996), 71-72; Charles H. George and Katherine George, *The Protestant Mind of the English Reformation 1570-1640* (Princeton: Princeton University Press, 1961), 338-41.

[50] *The Great Works of Christ in America: Magnalia Christi Americana*, Book III (1702; reprint London: Banner of Truth Trust, 1979), 1:547-48. For a bibliography of Eliot's sermons and writings, see Frederick Harling, "A Biography of John Eliot" (Ph.D. dissertation, Boston University, 1965), 259-61.

[51] *The Works of John Flavel* (1820; reprint London: Banner of Truth Trust, 1968), 6:572.

[52] Perry Miller, *The New England Mind: The Seventeenth Century* (Cambridge: University Press, 1939), 332-33.

[53] Most Puritans preached from fifty to sixty minutes. They wrote out their sermons, particularly their application, in a much fuller way than they were actually preached.

54 *The Art of Prophesying,* 56-63.

55 *The Marrow of Theology,* 194.

56 See George Edward Brown, "Catechists and Catechisms of Early New England" (D.R.E. dissertation, Boston University, 1934); R.M.E. Paterson, "A Study in Catechisms of the Reformation and Post-Reformation Period" (M.A. thesis, Durham University, 1981); P. Hutchinson, "Religious Change: The Case of the English Catechism, 1560-1640" (Ph.D. dissertation, Stanford University, 1984); Ian Green, *The Christian's ABC: Catechisms and Catechizing in England c. 1530-1740* (Oxford: Clarendon Press, 1996).

57 London, 1646.

58 Cf. W.G.T. Shedd, *Homiletics and Pastoral Theology* (1867; reprint London: Banner of Truth Trust, 1965), 356-75.

59 C. Stanford, *Joseph Alleine: His companions and Times* (London, 1861).

60 Richard Baxter, *Gidlas Salvianus: The Reformed Pastor: Shewing the Nature of the Pastoral Work* (1656; reprint New York: Robert Carter, 1860), 341-468.

61 *A Quest for Godliness,* 305.

62 *A Short Forme of Catechising* (London: Richard Bradocke, 1599).

63 *Works of Thomas Brooks,* 4:24.

64 *A Body of Divinity,* 154.

65 *An Alarm to the Unconverted,* 26-27.

66 *Works,* 3:317ff.

67 *A Quest for Godliness,* 163-64.

68 *The Reformed Pastor,* 123.

69 *Works of Robert Traill,* 1:246.

70 Cf. John Flavel, "The Character of a True Evangelical Pastor," in *Works of Flavel,* 6:564-85.

71 Ibid., 6:568.

72 *Works,* 9:455, 16:76.

73 See Benjamin Brook, *The Lives of the Puritans,* 3 vols. (1813; reprint Pittsburgh: Soli Deo Gloria, 1994); Joel R. Beeke, "Meet the Puritans," *Banner of Truth* 52 (1986):44-45, 102-103, 156-57, 240-41, 292-93; 53 (1987):154-55, 184-85; William Barker, *Puritan Profiles* (Fearn, Ross-shire: Christian Focus, 1996).

8

Anthony Burgess on Assurance

When the Christian feels deserted by God, what should he do? If the evidence of God's saving work in the believer's life appears as "muddied waters, the proper duty of a godly man is to throw himself boldly upon the promise,…to go unto God, and rely upon him, in which sense Job said, Though he kill me, yet will I trust in him."[1] So said Anthony Burgess, one of the Westminster Assembly's most insightful writers on the comprehensive doctrine of assurance of faith.

After presenting the contemporary need for considering the subject of assurance of faith, I will introduce Burgess, then explain his views on assurance, which, as I will show, heartily support the eighteenth chapter of the Westminster Confession on assurance. Finally, I will present several conclusions that ought to influence scholarship today as well as our personal lives.

Contemporary Need for Considering Assurance

You may ask: Do we still need to wrestle with questions about assurance in our secular age? I believe we do. I believe that assurance is as critical a doctrine today as it ever has been. Here's why:

First, the fruits of genuine assurance are sorely lacking in the contemporary church. The church is crippled because of the absence of assurance, but, even worse, most of us are scarcely aware of it. We live in a day of minimal assurance. How do we know that? Assurance is known by its fruits: a thirsting after God; a life of close fellowship with God; a tender, filial relationship with God. Assurance is not a self-given but a Spirit-applied certainty that moves the believer to God through Christ. Assurance is the opposite of self-satisfaction and secularization. Assurance is God-centered; it does not rely on personal righteousness or service for justification. When assurance is vibrant, a concern for God's honor and the progress of His kingdom is present. Assured believers view heaven as their home. They long for the second advent of Christ and their translation to glory (2 Tim. 4:6-8).

Compared to the Reformers and post-Reformers, Christians today are impoverished in spiritual exercises. The desire for fellowship with God, the sense of the reality of heaven, and the relish of God's glory fall short of a former day. The church's emphasis on earthly good overshadows the conviction that she is traveling through this world on her way to God and glory. Clearly, assurance is at a low ebb (Heb. 11).

Second, assurance of faith is sorely needed today because assurance cannot be separated from genuine revival and conviction of sin. We should remember that every true revival has been connected with the recovery of assuring faith. How true that was of Martin Luther! Read Luther on Galatians. Did he not burn with indignation for the way the church left people uncertain about salvation? By contrast, Luther was filled with the assurance that flows out of the gospel. Search his writings and you will feel the power of what he is saying.

Another reason assurance revives in times of awakening is that the forerunner of every revival is conviction of sin. When sinners become bowed down with the burden of guilt, forgiveness in Christ becomes invaluable. That is why assurance is always brought to the foreground in the soul's time of real need.

Third, assurance is necessary if we are to be God-honoring Christians in a day of great secularization and apostasy. The gospel has always been difficult to live out in the world, but sometimes opposition to the gospel is especially intense. We are living in such a time; we are living in a bruising time. We are called to be lights on the hill in the thick of spiritual battle, while the devil promotes apostasy on all sides, especially within the church and educational institutions. To be lights on the hill, we need much assurance.

Fourth, the doctrine of assurance is sorely needed today because doctrine itself is largely despised. Few understand Martin Luther's assertion: "Doctrine is heaven." Assurance is the nerve center of doctrine put in *use*, as the Puritans would say. Assurance entwines itself with the work of the Spirit in every link of the chain of salvation, from calling to glorification. It is connected with the doctrines of sin, grace, atonement, and union with Christ. It is inseparable from the marks and steps of grace. It touches on the issue of divine sovereignty and human responsibility; is intimately connected with Holy Scripture; and flows out of election, the promises of God, and the covenant of grace. It is fortified by preaching, the sacraments, and prayer. Assurance is broad in scope, profound in depth, and glorious in height. One could almost write a systematic theology under the framework of assurance.

Finally, our difficulties are compounded today by our culture's emphasis on feeling. How we feel takes precedence over what we believe. This spirit has also infiltrated the church, most notably in the charismatic or Pentecostal movement, which appeals to emotion in reaction to a formal, lifeless Christianity. We profit little by criticizing the charismatic movement without understanding its worldwide appeal. That appeal is related to our lack of assurance of faith—an assurance which manifests itself in daily, godly living.

We are responsible for showing a better way. Happily, we do not have to start from scratch. Scriptural, Reformed, experimental faith properly marries head and heart knowledge, as well as faith and feeling. Numerous post-Reformation theologians and Puritan pastors wrestled with ascertaining the precise relationship between the Christian's faith and his personal assurance of salvation. Out of their labor for theological precision came a fine-tuned vocabulary that defined assurance in terms of its possibilities, kinds, degrees, foundations, experiences, means, obstacles, and fruits.

The Puritan doctrine of assurance was formally codified by chapter 18 of the Westminster Confession. The chapter contains four sections: 18.1 addresses the possibility of assurance; 18.2, the foundations of assurance; 18.3, the cultivation of assurance; 18.4, the renewal of assurance. We will consider chapter 18 primarily in relationship to the views of Anthony Burgess. Prior to examining those views, however, we need to take a look at Burgess's life and writings.

Anthony Burgess: A Pious Scholar

Anthony Burgess was a nonconformist clergyman and writer who lived in the mid-seventeenth century. He was the son of a schoolmaster at Watford in Hartfordshire, England. He entered St. John's College, Cambridge in 1623, and graduated with a master's degree. He then became a fellow at Emmanuel College, where he tutored John Wallis. Wallis, who also was a member of the Westminster Assembly, described his tutor as "a pious, learned, and able scholar, a good disputant, a good tutor, an eminent preacher, a sound and orthodox divine."[2]

Burgess served as vicar at Sutton-Coldfield in Warwickshire from 1635 to 1662, except for some years in the 1640s. During the civil war, Burgess fled to Coventry for safety from the king's army. The king's soldiers persecuted Puritan pastors with relish, often rifling their houses and forcing out their families. From Coventry, Burgess joined the Westminster Assembly of Divines, where he became known for theological discernment and piety. During his years in London, he frequently preached to Parliament and at Lawrence-Jury.

After the Westminster Assembly, Burgess returned to Sutton-Coldfield. He was ejected from there by the Uniformity Act of 1662 after the Restoration. He retired to Tamworth, Staffordshire, where he attended a parish church until his death.

Bishop Hacket of Lichfield supposedly begged Burgess to conform, noting his potential to be a university professor. Hacket's praise was based on his familiarity with Burgess's writings, which thoroughly analyze every subject addressed. During a fifteen-year span (1646-1661), Burgess wrote at least a dozen books based largely on his sermons and lectures. His writings reveal a scholarly acquaintance with Aristotle, Seneca, Augustine, Aquinas, Luther, and Calvin. He used many Greek and Latin quotations, but judiciously. He also reasoned in the plain style of Puritan preaching. The cultured scholar and experimental preacher combined in Burgess to produce astute, devotional warmth.

Several of Burgess's major works have a strong polemic emphasis. His first major treatise, *Vindiciae Legis* (1646), based on twenty-nine lectures he gave at Lawrence-Jury, vindicated the Puritan view of the moral law and of the covenants of works and grace in opposition to Roman Catholics, Arminians, Socinians, and, especially, Antinomians. Two years later Burgess wrote against the same opponents in his first volume on justification. His second volume on justification, which appeared six years later (1654), addressed the natural righteousness of God and the imputed righteousness of Christ. Those two volumes contain seventy-five sermons. His 555-page *Doctrine of Original Sin* (1659) drew the Anabaptists into the fray.

Burgess's works show that he was a faithful steward of the mysteries of God. In addition to being a formidable polemicist, Burgess excelled as an experimental writer. His treatises are discriminatory and applicatory. He masterfully separated the precious from the vile in *The Godly Man's Choice,* based on thirteen sermons on Psalm 4:6-8. His detailed exegesis in his 145-sermon work on John 17, in his 300-page commentary on 1 Corinthians 3, and in his 700-page commentary on 2 Corinthians 1, are marked by a heart-warming and heart-searching experimental emphasis. This fulfilled Burgess's goal to "endeavour the true and sound Exposition…so as to reduce all Doctrinals and controversals to practicals and experimentals, which is the life and soul of all."[3]

Burgess's *magnum opus,* a massive, two-volume work of nearly 1,100 pages, titled *Spiritual Refining* (1652-54), has been called an "unequaled anatomy of experimental religion."[4] The first volume, subtitled *A Treatise of Grace and Assurance,* contains 120 sermons; the second, subtitled *A Treatise of Sinne, with its Causes, Differences, Mitigations and Aggravations,* contains 42 sermons.

In the first section of the first volume, Burgess discussed assurance and refuted the antinomian error that internal marks of grace within a believer are no evidence of his justification. Sections two and three describe numerous signs of grace. The remaining nine sections of this volume discuss the work of grace in terms of regeneration, the new creature, God's workmanship, grace in the heart, washing or sanctifying grace, conversion or turning unto God, taking away the stony heart, God's Spirit within us, and vocation or calling. Throughout, Burgess separated saving grace from its counterfeits.

In the second volume of *Spiritual Refining,* Burgess focused on sin. He addressed the deceitfulness of the human heart, presumptuous and reigning sins, hypocrisy and formality in religion, the misguided conscience, and secret sins that often remain unrecognized. Positively, he explained the tenderness of a gracious heart, showing "that a strict scrutiny into a man's heart and ways, with a holy fear of sinning, doth consist with a Gospel-life of faith and joy in the Holy Ghost." His goal, Burgess stated, was to "unmask counterfeit Christians, terrify the ungodly, comfort and direct the doubting saint, humble man, [and] exalt the grace of God."[5]

Those volumes, written five to seven years after the Westminster Confession of Faith (1647), contain the essence of Burgess's views on assurance. Let us look at his views through the grid of the Westminster Confession's eighteenth chapter, which remains the greatest Reformed confessional statement ever written on assurance.

18.1: The Possibility of Assurance

Although hypocrites, and other unregenerate men, may vainly deceive themselves with false hopes and carnal presumptions of being in the favour of God, and estate of salvation (which hope of theirs shall perish): yet such as truly believe in the Lord Jesus and love Him in sincerity, endeavouring to walk in all good conscience before Him, may, in this life, be certainly assured that they are in the state of grace, and may rejoice in the hope of the glory of God, which hope shall never make them ashamed.

Chapter 18.1 of the Confession presents three possibilities in relation to assurance: the possibility of false assurance, the possibility of true assurance, and the possibility of a lack of true assurance. Burgess closely analyzed all three.

False assurance. Burgess was deeply convinced of the significance of the Confession's phrase "false hopes and carnal presumptions." That is shown in his detailed description of religious exercises that fall under the umbrella of historical or temporary faith, and in his seven-sermon exposition of Jeremiah 17:9, which says, "The heart is deceitful above all things, and desperately wicked: who can know it?"[6] Burgess cited parables, such as the two builders (Matt. 7:24-27) and the ten virgins (Matt. 25), to show the tragic possibility of deceiving oneself.[7] *"It is a most sad delusion for an ungodly or unregenerated man to be persuaded, his estate is an estate of grace, whereas indeed it is nothing but of sin and death,"* Burgess wrote. "We pity…a man…possessed with a devil turned into an Angel of light."[8]

In the sixth sermon of *Spiritual Refining*, "Shewing the Difference between true Assurance and Presumption," Burgess provided a typically Puritan example of discriminating preaching. He first warned that false assurance is common among those who claim to be Christians: "The greatest part of Christians are delivered up to such a carnal confidence [that they] are like that mad *Athenian* who thought all the Ships on the Sea were his. How many are there, who when they hear the exact Discoveries that are made of Grace, whereby they may evidently conclude, That they are for the present shut out of this Kingdom, do yet bless themselves, as if all were well with them!"[9]

True assurance and false assurance are vastly different, Burgess said. First, they differ in their "efficient cause or principle." False assurance is motivated by self-love and an outward belief in the gospel without any "apprehension of the depth of sin." Second, the grounds of false assurance arise from "a mere natural light and judgment about the state of regeneration," and from "outward comforts and plenty" enjoyed. Third, false assurance cannot identify with "the Manner and Method [by which] the Spirit of God doth usually work Assurance," which involves "serious Humiliation for sin, and feeling the burden of it…conflicts and doubts, and opposition of unbelief…[and] vehement and fiery assaults of Satan." Fourth, unfruitfulness exposes false assurance, such as little "diligent use of the means," no real inflaming of "the heart with love to God," and an inability to "keep up the heart under all discouragements and desolations." Fifth, false assurance is not accompanied by "the Companions or Concomitants" of true assurance, namely, "holy fear and trembling" as well as "Humility and lowliness of mind." Finally, false assurance will be shaken by some outward troubles rather than by sin, whereas true assurance remains strong in trials.[10]

After identifying false assurance, Burgess commented on remedies that the Holy Spirit can use to overthrow false assurance, even though "carnal presumers" are seldom "debased and humbled." Possible remedies include a powerful and searching ministry that pierces the soul, a strong and particular application of the law, a discovery of the fullness and necessity of Christ, a profound affliction, an experience of the dreadful deathbed of a carnal professor of Christianity, and a serious consideration of how mistaken we can be in other areas of our lives.[11]

True assurance. Chapter 18.1 of the Confession clearly says that assurance is possible for Christians, but it also stresses that assurance cannot be obtained apart from Christ. Every part of 18.1 connects assurance with Christ by saying, believe in *Him*; love *Him*; walk before *Him*. Assurance is interwoven with Christian believing, Christian loving, and fruits of faith in Christ. The essence of assurance is living in Christ.

Burgess demonstrated that possibility of assurance in a variety of ways: (1) biblical saints whose lives evidenced assurance; (2) many scriptures that show how Christians may attain assurance; (3) commands in Scripture, such as 2 Peter 1:10, that Christians seriously search for assurance; (4) "the Institution of Sacraments, as Signs and Seals particularly to Witness God's love to us"; (5) the exercises of divine graces, including "the joy and thankfulness" of God's people; (6) "signs of grace, whereby a man may discern what he is"; and, most importantly, (7) "the peculiar office and work attributed to God's Spirit…to witness with our spirit, to seal unto us" our salvation.[12]

Burgess repeatedly stated the importance of the Holy Spirit's role in assurance; without the Spirit, he said, there is no authentic assurance upon any grounds.[13] He wrote, "In all the acts of Faith, whether they be direct or reflex, the firmness and certainty of them doth more depend upon God's Spirit confirming us, than in the clearness of the argument."[14]

Lacking the consciousness of true assurance. Finally, chapter 18.1 and the writings of Burgess emphasized a third option: Believers may possess saving faith without the assurance that they possess it. Assurance augments the joy of faith, but it is not essential to salvation. Faith *alone* justifies through Christ *alone*; assurance is the conscious enjoyment of that justifying salvation.

Assurance is necessary for spiritual health but not absolutely necessary for salvation. Burgess devoted the first two sermons of *Spiritual Refining* to "How necessary and advantageous the Assurance of our being in the state of Grace is."[15] The advantages of assurance are so great that Burgess called assurance "Necessary": (1) "from the nature of faith," (2) "from God's glory," (3) to "have more Joy and Peace in our hearts," and (4) "in the usefulness of it, [for] hereby we shall be enlarged and quickened up to all holy Duties."[16] Nevertheless, assurance is "not of absolute necessity to salvation: Its not a necessary effect of our calling and election at all times."[17]

Burgess acknowledged that many believers lack full assurance. Though most believers have some degree of assurance, few attain a comfortable degree of assurance. Full assurance is difficult for most believers to attain.[18]

18.2: The Foundations of Assurance

This certainty is not a bare conjectural and probable persuasion grounded upon a fallible hope; but an infallible assurance of faith founded upon the divine truth of the promises of salvation, the inward evidence of those graces unto which these promises are made, the testimony of the Spirit of adoption witnessing with our spirits that we are the children of God, which Spirit is the earnest of our inheritance, whereby we are sealed to the day of redemption.

The Westminster Confession addresses the foundations of assurance in chapter 18.2. It is important here not to confuse the foundations or grounds of *assurance* with the foundations or grounds of *salvation*.[19] As John Murray said: "When we speak of the grounds of assurance, we are thinking of the ways in which a believer comes to entertain this assurance, not of the grounds on which his salvation rests. The grounds of salvation are as secure for the person who does not have full assurance as for the person who has."[20]

In this sense, 18.2 presents a complex ground of assurance,[21] including a primary, objective ground ("the divine truth of the promises of salvation") and one or two secondary, subjective grounds ("the inward evidence of those graces unto which these promises are made" and "the testimony of the Spirit of adoption witnessing with our spirits").

Divine promises in Christ. Burgess and most Puritans believed that God's promises in Christ are the primary ground for a believer's assurance. "It cannot be denied but that it is a more noble and excellent way to believe in the Promise," wrote Burgess, "than to believe upon the sense and evidences of Grace in us, yet this latter is also lawful and encouraged by God."[22] This emphasis on God's promises in Christ implies several things for a believer's experience of assurance.

First, the believer does not gain assurance by looking at himself or anything he has produced apart from God's promises, but primarily by looking to God's faithfulness in Christ as He is revealed in the promises of the gospel. The promises that lead to salvation are sufficient to lead the believer to assurance. When expounding the Luke 7 account of the woman who was forgiven and received assurance, Burgess wrote, "*As soon as ever she repented in her heart of her evil ways, and believed in Christ, her sins were forgiven her;* for so God doth promise; and this was before she came to Christ, but she cometh to Christ for the more assurance of pardon. . . . How could she come to know her sins were forgiven before Christ told her? I answer, By the promise of God made to every true penitent and believer: though this assurance of hers was imperfect, and therefore admitted of further degrees."[23]

Second, as assurance grows, God's promises become increasingly real to the believer personally and experimentally. Burgess wrote, "Where there is this experimental knowledge, that man's heart is as it were the Bible's counterpane. The Scripture is the original, and his heart is the copy of it, he can read over the Promises,... and can say, *Probatum est* [It is proven]."[24] Counterpane here is an archaic variant of counterpart, used in its technical, legal sense of being a duplicate or copy of the original. In this case, comparing what is in Scripture with what has been experienced in the heart, the believer may conclude, "My salvation is proven!"

Third, the Christ-centeredness of personal assurance is accented in God's promises, for Jesus Christ Himself is the "sum, fountain, seal, treasury of all the promises."[25] In Him, the promises of God are "yea, and Amen" (2 Cor. 1:20). Burgess wrote:

> *We must take heed that we do not so gaze upon ourselves to find graces in our own hearts as thereby we forget those Acts of Faith, whereby we close with Christ immediately, and rely upon him only for our Justification. . . .* The fear of this hath made some cry down totally the use of signs, to evidence our Justification. And the truth is, it cannot be denied but many of the children of God, while they are studying and examining, whether grace be in their souls, that upon the discovery thereof, they may have comfortable persuasions of their Justification, are very much neglective of those choice and principal Acts of Faith, whereby we have an acquiescency or recum-

bency upon Christ for our Acceptation with God. This is as if old *Jacob* should so rejoice in the Chariot *Joseph* sent, whereby he knew that he was alive, that he should not desire to see *Joseph* himself. Thus while thou art so full of joy, to perceive grace in thee, thou forgettest to joy in Christ himself, who is more excellent then all thy graces.[26]

Finally, though subjective phenomena may sometimes feel more sure than faith in God's promises, such experiences give less glory to God than divine promises apprehended directly by faith. Burgess said, "Trusting in God and in Christ, when we feel nothing but guilt and destruction in our selves, is the greatest honour we can give God, and therefore though the living by signs be more comfortable to us, yet the living by faith is greater honour to God."[27]

Thomas Brooks once wrote, "The promises of God are a Christian's *magna charta*, his chiefest evidences for heaven." He then offered nine ways "a person may know whether he has a real and saving interest in the promises or no."[28] Many of those ways deal with subjective fruits in the believer that flow out of a proper embrace of the objective promise.

Burgess agreed. The promises of God don't exist in a vacuum, he said. They are applied to the soul in assurance, and that application produces *"an holy and humble walking."* For proof, Burgess quoted 2 Corinthians 7:1, "Having therefore these promises, dearly beloved, let us cleanse ourselves from all filthiness of the flesh and spirit, perfecting holiness in the fear of God." Burgess concluded, "The more gracious then we perceive God to us, the more humiliation and debasement we find in our selves."[29]

Burgess and his colleagues consistently reminded believers that the objective promise embraced by faith is infallible because it is God's comprehensive and faithful covenant promise. Consequently, subjective evidence, though necessary, must always be regarded as secondary, for it is often mixed with human convictions and feelings even when it gazes upon the work of God. All exercises of saving faith apprehend to some degree the primary ground of divine promise in Christ.

Inward evidences verified by syllogisms. The Puritans coveted a life that showed Christ's presence in the believer. They were convinced that the grace of God within believers confirms the reality of faith. William Ames wrote, "He that doth rightly understand the promise of the covenant, cannot be sure of his salvation, unless he perceive in himself true Faith and repentance."[30] They often viewed that grace of God within believers in terms of syllogisms, which use the so-called reflex or reflective act of faith.[31] By the reflective act of faith, the Holy Spirit sheds light upon His work in the believer, enabling him to conclude that his faith is saving because its exercises have a saving character. Burgess wrote:

> There are first the *direct acts* of the soul, whereby it is carried out immediately to some object. And there are secondly *reflex acts*, whereby the soul considers and takes notice of what acts it doth. It's as if the eye were turned inward to see it self. The Apostle John expresseth it fully, *We know that we know*, 1 John 2:3. So that when we believe in God, that is a direct act of the soul; when we repent of sin, because God is dishonoured, that is a direct act; but when we know that we do believe, and that we do repent, this is a reflex act.[32]

Burgess and the Puritans talked about two closely related yet distinct syllogisms that fortify assurance—the practical syllogism (*syllogismus practicus*) and the mystical syllogism (*syllogismus mysticus*).[33] The practical syllogism was based on the believer's sanctification and good works in daily life. It emphasized that the believer's life of obedience confirmed his experience of grace. It went something like this. *Major premise*: According to Scripture, only those who possess saving faith will receive the Spirit's testimony that their lives manifest fruits of sanctification and good works. *Minor premise*: I cannot deny that by the grace of God I have received the Spirit's testimony that I manifest fruits of sanctification and good works. *Conclusion*: I have saving faith.

The mystical syllogism was based largely on the believer's internal exercises and progress in sanctification. It focused on the inward man and went something like this. *Major premise*: According to Scripture, only those who possess saving faith will so experience the Spirit's confirmation of inward grace and godliness that self will decrease and Christ will increase. *Minor premise*: I cannot deny that by the grace of God I experience the Spirit's testimony confirming inward grace and godliness such that self decreases and Christ increases. *Conclusion*: I am a partaker of saving faith.

The practical syllogism was based on texts such as 2 Peter 1:5-10 (virtue, knowledge, temperance, patience, godliness, brotherly love),[34] and verses in 1 John stressing the Christian walk. For example, "hereby we do know that we know him, if we keep his commandments" (2:3). "We know that we have passed from death unto life, because we love the brethren" (3:14). "By this we know that we love the children of God, when we love God, and keep his commandments" (5:2).

The mystical syllogism evidences itself in a variety of ways. "Sometimes *Fear of God* is a sign, sometimes *Poverty of Spirit*, sometimes *Hungering and thirsting after Righteousness*, sometimes *Repentance*, sometimes *Love*, and sometimes *Patience*," Burgess wrote. "So that if a godly man can find any one of these in himself, he may conclude of his Salvation and Justification."[35]

By the 1640s, Puritans were accepting the mystical syllogism on par with the practical syllogism.[36] Consequently, some Puritans, including Burgess, were fond of answering the great case of conscience, "How do I know whether or not I am a believer?", by offering a combination of signs that contained the good works of the practical syllogism as well as the steps of grace of the mystical syllogism. For example, after preaching eleven sermons on assurance, Burgess delivered eight messages on the true signs of grace and fifteen on the false signs of grace. True signs include obedience, sincerity, opposition against and abstinence from sin, openness to divine examination, growth in grace, spiritual performance of duties, and love to the godly. Signs that could fall short of saving grace include outward church privileges; spiritual gifts; affections of the heart in holy things; judgments and opinions about spiritual truth; great sufferings for Christ; strictness in religion; zeal in false worship; external obedience to the law of God; a belief of the truths of religion; a peaceable frame of heart and persuasion of God's love; outward success; prosperity and greatness in the world; and an abandonment of gross sins. The section on false signs concludes with a sermon on "the difficulty, and in some sense, impossibility of salvation, notwithstanding the easiness which men fancy to themselves thereof."

In a sermon on "the Lawfulness and Obligation of proceeding by way of Signs," Burgess raised and answered six objections against the use of syllogisms and the reflex act of faith. In the fifth objection he comes to the heart of the matter:

> A fifth doubt *may be from the difficulty, if not impossibility of any certainty by signs*: for take we any sign, suppose love of the brethren, that must be explained of such love as is because they are brethren, and of such a love as proceedeth from upright principles, and pure motives, and with many other qualifications, which will be as hard to know, as the inward root of grace itself....
>
> Now to this we answer these things: First, *That the Scripture giveth many Signs and Symptoms of grace*; So that if a man cannot find all, yet if he discover some, yea, if but one, he may assuredly gather all the rest are there, for the whole harmony and connexion of grace is compared to the image of God, which doth consist of all its due lineaments. . . .
>
> Secondly, *There is a two-fold Knowledge, one Distinct and Demonstrative,* which is *a priori*, from the cause to the effect, and that is, when we know the principles and root of grace within us, and so proceed to the effects

of it. The other is more *General*, and that is from the effect to the cause, and this is a knowledge *a posteriori*, we proceed from the streams to the fountain, and this kind of knowledge as it is most easy, so we are prone to, and the Spirit of God guideth us in this way, as being most suitable to our natures.

Thirdly, *Although a man may doubt of some Signs, yet it doth not follow he will doubt of all, because his temptation may be stronger about one Sign then another, and one Sign may be more easily perceived than another*; And so a godly man may argue from that which is less known, to the other that is more known.[37]

Burgess used the syllogism of the Spirit's work to help believers toward assurance by directing them, in the tradition of Theodore Beza and William Perkins, to grasp any link of the order of salvation to "press toward the mark for the prize of the high calling of God in Christ Jesus" (Phil. 3:14). Burgess said, "[Since] it is more difficult to find some [signs of grace] in ourselves than others, yet we are to proceed from those that are more facile, to those that are more difficult."[38]

Burgess was aware of possible "free-will" overtones in the reflex act of faith and took pains to keep it within the confines of the doctrines of grace by further analysis of the syllogism.

First, Burgess identified the syllogism as the work of the Spirit of God. All believers were forbidden to trust in their *own* trusting or the conclusions they drew from it, apart from the Spirit. Burgess insisted that we must not separate the Spirit's work from the syllogistic, reflex act of faith:

> We say not the Graces of God's Spirit, can or do witness of themselves, The sealing and witnessing is efficiently from the Spirit of God, they are only the means by which God's Spirit makes known itself. And therefore as colours, though they be the object of sight, yet they cannot actually be seen without light shining upon them: so neither are we able to behold the good things God hath wrought for us without the Spirit of God.... In Philosophy, reason makes the major and minor in any Syllogism; [but] in spiritual things, the Spirit of God enableth a man to make a whole Syllogism for a believer's comfort and establishment.[39]

Burgess concluded that if we desire to increase our assurance by employing the syllogism we must "above all pray to God for his Spirit, so to enlighten our eyes.... For the Spirit of God is the efficient cause of all this Certainty."[40]

Second, Burgess said the syllogism flowed out of the living Word, Jesus Christ, and was based on the written Word for its very framework. The reflex act of faith arises from the believer seeing Christ's distinguishing graces in himself as they conform to the Word of God. Burgess wrote: "When the Apostle commands us to *examine and prove ourselves*, it supposeth there is a sure Canon and Rule to go by, which is to measure and regulate those things we doubt of. And that is the Word of God.... Scripture-godliness is as different from the moral man's godliness as the Sun is from a Glow-worm."[41]

Third, Burgess said the syllogism and reflex act only have a secondary status. He wrote:

> Though the sight of thy graces be comfortable, yet that of Christ ought to be much more. These graces are but the handmaids and servants that wait upon Christ, they are but tokens from him, they are not himself: A man is not only to go out of his sins, but also out of his graces unto Christ. See Paul, Phil. 3. how excellently doth he debase all his own graces to be found in Christ. Let not therefore the desire after inherent righteousness make thee forget imputed righteousness: This is to take the friend of the Bridegroom for the Bridegroom itself; and for this end (without doubt) it is that the people of God are so often in darkness and have no light, see no comfortable sign or token of God's love unto them, that so they may stay themselves upon God.[42]

The Witnessing Testimony of the Spirit. The writers of the Westminster Confession knew that the part of assurance most difficult to understand was the witnessing of the Holy Spirit. They confessed that vast mysteries surrounded them when they spoke of that subject. One reason the assembly did not detail more specifically the Spirit's role in assurance was to allow for the freedom of the Spirit; a second reason was that the assembly wanted to allow freedom of conscience to those who differed about the finer details of the Spirit's testimony. Most of the members of the assembly had one of two emphases.

Burgess emphasized that the Spirit's witness coincides with assurance gleaned from inward evidences of grace. He asked, "*Whether this certainty God's Spirit works in the godly, in and through the graces of Sanctification, be the only witnessing and sealing that is? or, Whether there be not an immediate testimony of God's Spirit to the soul, either before or without those gracious fruits of holiness?...* For my part," he answered, "I think the former kind of witnessing, *viz.* by fruits of holiness, the only safe and sure way, and which the Scripture doth for the most part commend."[43]

Jeremiah Burroughs[44] and George Gillespie[45] agreed with Burgess. They said the witnessing testimony of the Holy Spirit in assurance referred exclusively to His activity in connection with the syllogisms, whereby He brings conscience to unite with His witness that the Christian is a child of God. According to this view, the witness of the Holy Spirit conjoins *with* the witness of the believer's spirit. Romans 8:15 and 8:16 are thus synonymous. Burgess wrote, "The meaning is, the Spirit of God *beareth witness unto us,* with those gifts and graces that are the fruit of the same Spirit. So that he speaks not of such an immediate Testimony,… but mediately by and with our spirits, being enlightened and sanctified: So that although the Spirit of God be the alone Author of this Assurance, yet it is in an ordinary way by the fruits of the Spirit."[46] He likewise interpreted the sealing "with the holy Spirit of promise" in Ephesians 1:13. He wrote, "They therefore who understand this sealing of the extraordinary and miraculous gifts of God's Spirit, hit not the mark, because there were not necessary signs of adoption, and also they were not bestowed upon every particular believer; we must therefore understand it of the sanctifying graces of God's Spirit.… Thus doth God the Father seal his children to him by furnishing them with all the graces of his holy Spirit, and by these they know they are of God."[47]

Burgess believed the secondary grounds of assurance did not break down, since the inward evidences of grace and the testimony of the Spirit are essentially one. If this were not so and the believer received assurance through the direct testimony of the Spirit, then there would be no need to pursue assurance through inward graces, for such a pursuit would be "to light a candle when the Sun shineth; but the testimony of the Spirit and the evidence of graces make up one complete witness, and therefore are not to be disjoined, much less opposed."[48] Thus, for Burgess, Spirit-enlightened syllogisms meant full assurance. He felt this view was important because it opposed mysticism and antinomianism, which tend to accent a direct testimony of the Spirit disjoined from the need to produce practical fruits of faith and repentance.[49]

Other divines of the assembly, such as Samuel Rutherford, William Twisse, Henry Scudder, and Thomas Goodwin, presented another emphasis. They said the witness of the Spirit described in Romans 8:15 contains something distinct from that of verse 16.[50] They distinguished the Spirit witnessing *with* the believer's spirit by syllogism from His witnessing *to* the believer's spirit by direct applications of the Word. As the New Testament commentator Heinrich Meyer showed, the former leaves in its wake the self-conscious conviction that "*I* am a child of God" and, on the basis of such Spirit-worked syllogisms, finds freedom to approach God as Father. The latter speaks the Spirit's pronouncement on behalf of the Father, "*You* are a child of God," and, on the basis of hearing of its sonship from God's own Word by the Spirit, approaches Him with the familiarity of a child.[51]

Those who accepted two secondary grounds of assurance differed as to whether the Spirit's testimony should be regarded as more durable than His syllogistic testimony and hence be placed practically on a higher level. Thomas Goodwin, for example, asserted that the direct witness of the Spirit supersedes the co-witnessing of the Spirit and the believer through the syllogisms.[52] Generally speaking, however, other Westminster Assembly divines did not view the direct testimony of the Spirit as superior to or independent of the syllogisms but as added to them. They agreed that the syllogistic way of reaching assurance is more common and safe than immediate assurance by the Spirit's direct witness. For example, Rutherford said the reflex act of faith is, as a rule, "more spiritual and helpful" than direct acts.[53] Burgess, giving some allowance for the second emphasis under certain conditions, put it this way: If the direct testimony be allowed, it is "more subject to dangerous delusions," for the reflex act "goeth upon a [more] sure ground, the fruits of mortification and vivification."[54]

Burgess summarized the view of those who differed in emphasis when he stated, "Some Divines do not indeed deny the possibility of such an immediate Testimony, but yet they conclude the ordinary and safe way, is, to look for that Testimony, which is by the effects, and fruits of God's Spirit."[55] Most of the assembly's divines agreed that, regardless of what you believe about the direct witness of the Spirit, it is hard to see that it is the most important kind of assurance, for Christians are called to live daily in the joy of assurance, and such assurance cannot be maintained on the basis of occasional experiences.

In every sense, however, the assembly's divines unitedly asserted that the Spirit's testimony is always tied to, and may never contradict, the Word of God. Only then can antinomianism be avoided, they said, and the freedom of the Spirit be protected.

For Burgess and the Westminster divines, the grounds of faith in God's promises, inward evidences of grace realized through syllogisms, and witness of the Spirit must be pursued to obtain as full a measure of assurance as possible. If any of these grounds are emphasized at the expense of others, the teaching of assurance loses balance and becomes dangerous. None of these men would teach that assurance is obtainable by trusting only in the promises, or only in inward evidences, or only in the witness of the Holy Spirit. Rather, they taught that the believer cannot truly trust the promises without the aid of the Holy Spirit, and that he cannot with any degree of safety look upon himself without the illumination of the Spirit.

Burgess wrote, "Two Graces ought to be conjoined which the Godly by their weakness make one oppose another; They are to believe firmly on God's promise, and yet to be humble in themselves; They are to rejoice, and yet with trembling; when thy confidence devoureth an holy trembling, then take heed of presumption; When thy fear devoureth thy Faith and Joy, then take heed of despair.... These are the two Millstones by which we are made pure bread.... One cannot work without the other."[56] Although Burgess and most of his Puritan colleagues gave the syllogisms a greater role in assurance than Calvin did,[57] all regarded the promises of God as the primary ground for assurance.[58]

The activity of the Spirit is essential in every part of assurance. As Burgess said, "As a man by the power of free-will is not able to do any supernatural good thing, so neither by the strength of natural light, can he discern the gracious privileges God bestoweth upon him, *1 Cor. 2.12.*"[59] Without the application of the Spirit, the promises of God lead to self-deceit and fruitless lives. Without the illumination of the Spirit, self-examination tends to introspection, bondage, and legalism. The witness of the Spirit, divorced from the promises of God and from scriptural inward evidences, can lead to unbiblical mysticism and excessive emotionalism.

18.3: The Cultivation of Assurance

This infallible assurance doth not so belong to the essence of faith, but that a true believer may wait long, and conflict with many difficulties, before he be partaker of it: yet, being enabled by the Spirit to know the things which are freely given him of God, he may, without extraordinary revelation, in the right use of ordinary means, attain thereunto. And therefore it is the duty of every one to give all diligence to make his calling and election sure, that thereby his heart may be enlarged in peace and joy in the Holy Ghost, in love and thankfulness to God, and in strength and cheerfulness in the duties of obedience, the proper fruits of this assurance; so far is it from inclining men to looseness.

Burgess addressed four practical issues on assurance contained in 18.3 of the Westminster Confession: the time involved in attaining assurance, the means of attaining assurance, the duty of pursuing assurance, and the fruits produced by assurance.

Concerning the issue of time, Burgess asserted that God is free and sovereign and is thus able to plant faith and full assurance simultaneously. Typically, however, Burgess said, "He works it by degrees,"[60] so that the believer's doubts about his own salvation diminish as he grows in grace. Grace usually grows with age, and, as faith increases, other graces increase.

God uses conflicts, doubts, and trials to mature the believer's faith. Assurance usually follows intense, spiritual warfare; it wears battle scars. Burgess wrote, "This privilege of Assurance is given to those who have a long time been acquainted with God, much exercised in his ways, and enduring much for him."[61] Assurance is the fruit of strengthened and seasoned faith. Not that age and experience guarantee assurance, however, or that new converts cannot be blessed with assurance. As Burgess wrote, "God doth to new Converts also many times discover the love of his Espousals to them, because they are most tender and need it, being much oppressed with sin. As Aristotle observeth it a special instinct of nature, whereby Parents are most tender of the youngest child, because that can least take care for itself."[62]

Burgess said the believer has a lifelong call to make diligent use of the means of grace in pursuit of ever greater degrees of assurance, because God uses both sovereignty and means to bequeath assurance.[63] Meditation on God's Word, participation in the sacraments, and perseverance in prayer are the usual means God uses to increase assurance. But though the Word and the promises of God remain primary in assurance, the sacraments are divine seals that confirm God's eternal commitments to His elect, thereby strengthening faith and multiplying assurance. "Although God has given us his Promise, and nothing can be surer than that," Burgess wrote, "yet he addeth Sacraments to seal and confirm his Promise unto us."[64] When the believer receives the sacraments by faith, he receives certification of that which is promised by God and renews covenant with Him. Covenant assurance and obligation then unite. The promises of God are made visible, cyclical, and personal in the sacraments. Finally, Word and sacrament must be accompanied by prayer. "We must give all diligence and heed to the obtaining of this privilege [of assurance]," Burgess wrote. "We must make it our business; it must be importunately begged for in prayer."[65] Those who would have assurance, therefore, must prayerfully use the ordinary means while walking with a good conscience before God. As a general rule, assurance so sought will be granted by God, though in varying degrees.[66]

Burgess affirmed the Confession's conviction that assurance must be pursued as a duty.[67] The concerned soul should never rest until he can say that God is his God. Moreover, this duty, when seriously engaged in, will assist the believer in other duties of the Christian life. The Puritan stress on duty reinforced the conviction that assurance must never be regarded as only the privilege of exceptional saints. The failure to believe that at least some degree of assurance is normative for the believer tends to leave people in a fruitless spiritual condition.

Assurance bears fruit. It produces holy living marked by spiritual peace, joyful love, humble gratitude, and cheerful obedience. Assurance distances itself from careless living and moral indifference. As Burgess wrote:

> [Assurance] keeps up excellent Fellowship and Acquaintance with God.... It will work a Filial and an Evangelical frame of heart.... [It] makes us also have the humble disposition of Sons; Hereby we are carried out to do him service for pure intentions and motives.... It will support, although there be nothing but outward misery and trouble.... It will much enflame in Prayer.... It makes a man walk with much tenderness against sin.... [The] heart will be impatient and earnest till the coming of Christ.... [And] a full acquiesency and resting in God and Christ, as sufficient for every kind of want.... The soul is more inflamed and enlarged to love God.... [It] will breed much spiritual strength and heavenly ability to all graces and duties, to go through all relations with much holiness and lively vigor.... [It] is a strong and mighty buckler against all those violent assaults and temptations, that the devil useth to exercise the godly with.... [It] is a special means to breed contentation [contentment] of mind, and a thankful, cheerful heart in every condition.... [It] is a sure and special antidote against death in all the fears of it.[68]

Far from making the believer proud, assurance keeps him humble and godly. The very nature of assurance, Burgess said, cannot "breed any arrogance, or neglect of God and godliness," since "it's only maintained and kept up by humility and holy fear: So that when a man ceaseth to be humble, to have an holy fear of God, his certainty likewise ceaseth, even as the lamp goeth out when the oil is taken away."[69]

18.4 Assurance Lost and Renewed

True believers may have the assurance of their salvation divers ways shaken, diminished, and intermitted; as, by negligence in preserving of it, by falling into some special sin which woundeth the conscience and grieveth the Spirit; by some sudden or vehement temptation, by God's withdrawing the light of His countenance, and suffering even such as fear Him to walk in darkness and have no light: yet are they never utterly destitute of that seed of God, and life of faith, that love of Christ and the brethren, that sincerity of heart, and conscience of duty, out of which, by the operation of the Spirit, this assurance may, in due time, be revived; and by the which, in the mean time, they are supported from utter despair.

This section of the Confession is a magnificent affirmation of the link between Reformed theology and Puritan piety. The reasons for a lack of assurance are found primarily in the believer. They include negligence in preserving assurance by exercise; falling into a special sin; yielding to sudden temptation. Burgess wrote, "It is true the most tender and exact godly ones, as *Job* and *David* are sometimes in desertions, and cry out God hath forsaken them, but ordinarily the more formal and careless we are in our approaches to God, the more are our doubts and fears."[70]

Burgess said that assurance may be hindered, even lost, for several reasons. (1) Assurance can be diminished when we deeply feel the guilt of sin, for then we tend to look upon God as one who will take vengeance rather than forgive. (2) Satan hates assurance, and will do everything he can to keep doubts and fears alive within us. (3) Most commonly, the hypocrisy of our hearts and the carelessness of our living hinders assurance.[71]

The Christian cannot enjoy high levels of assurance if he persists in low levels of obedience. Then "we chase away our assurance," Burgess explained.[72] "Nothing will darken thy soul more than dull, lazy and negligent walking."[73] This truth helps keep saints watchful in searching their souls.

Despite the great injury that ensues, God's people persevere. Their perseverance is secured by their persevering God. Divine perseverance is triunely worked, consisting of the perseverance of the Father's eternal good pleasure toward them, the perseverance of Christ in His sufferings and intercession for them, and the perseverance of the Spirit working within them. Election, covenant, providence, satisfaction, and perseverance are inseparable from each other and from assurance.[74] Thus, when the believer lacks assurance, the responsibility is his. No enemy shall keep him out of heaven, but he may well keep heaven out of his heart by sinning against God. Burgess concluded, "It is therefore an unworthy thing to speak of doubting, and complain of the loss of God's favour, and that thou hast no Assurance, when all thy Duties and Performances are careless and withered."[75]

Neither the Confession nor Burgess stopped here, however. They also emphasized the possibility of God's involvement in the believer's lack of assurance. They said lost assurance may also be the result of God's "withdrawing of the light of His countenance."

Does the Confession go beyond Scripture in maintaining that God has reasons to withhold assurance from some believers? Burgess said not. He first acknowledged, however, that it seemed senseless at first sight for God to withhold assurance from a believer, for assurance is "wings and legs in a man's service to God. It would enflame him more to promote God's glory."[76] Burgess went on to ask, "How frequently doth God keep his own people in darkness?" He then offered five reasons God might withhold assurance from His people:

> First, *That hereby we may taste and see how bitter sin is.*... If grace or the Assurance of it were in our power to have it when and as soon as we would, how sleighty and perfunctory would our thoughts be about sin?... Secondly, *Hereby God would keep us low and humble in ourselves.* That all such worms of pride may be killed in us, God hides his face from us, and thereby we see nothing but sin and weaknesses in us.... Thirdly, *God may therefore keep Assurance from our knowledge, that so when we have it, we may the more esteem it, and the more prize it, taking the greater heed how we lose it.* We see the Church in the *Canticles,* when she had despised her Spouse's love, how earnest she was to get it again, but it cost her much ere she could have it.... Dost thou therefore pray, and again pray for Assurance, yet can not obtain it? then think this delay may be to increase my appetite the more after it, the more to bless God when my soul shall enjoy it. Fourthly, *God doth it that thou mayest demonstrate thy obedience unto him, and give the greater honour to him.* For to rely upon God by faith, when thou hast no sensible testimonies of his love to thee, is the purest...act of obedience that can be.... The way of Assurance brings more comfort to thy self, but the way of believing gives more glory to God. When *Abraham* did not *stagger in his Faith,* though *Sarah's* womb was a *dead womb,* this was giving glory to God.... Fifthly, *God withholdeth the sense of pardon, that thou mayest be an experienced Christian able to comfort others in their distress....* Paul makes this end of God's comforts in his tribulations, that they might comfort others in the like case. He that is not tempted about the pardon of sin, wonders at those who are so afflicted, and therefore is altogether unskilful to apply fit remedies.[77]

We may be inclined to look askance at some of Burgess's reasons for the "withdrawment" of God, but bear in mind two things. First, to understand Burgess, we need to recognize that the Puritans believed that "withdrawment" on God's part was usually for holy reasons beyond the comprehension of the believer, who simply has to trust God's intentions. Second, those reasons were as many pieces of a jigsaw puzzle, possible and partial explanations which were experienced. Neither Burgess nor the Puritans offered a complete list of reasons. Rather, they grappled with the experimental and pastoral reality of times when they or their parishioners might not be backsliding, yet might lack assurance and feel distant from God. Burgess wanted to deal compassionately with those who earnestly sought greater assurance but had not obtained it.

According to the Confession, the loss of assurance does not destroy the germ of faith in the Christian, however, because even the believer's darkness cannot quench God's saving work. Even in his lowest spiritual condition, the Holy Spirit will keep the believer "from utter despair." Moreover, the Spirit will also revive assurance in the believer "in due time."

Assurance is revived the same way it was obtained the first time. Burgess told how this should be done. Believers should review their lives, confess their backsliding, and humbly cast themselves upon their covenant-keeping God and His gracious promises in Christ. They should use the means of grace diligently, pursue holiness, exercise tender watchfulness, and take heed of grieving or quenching the Spirit. In other words, they are to be converted afresh.[78] Spirit-worked conversion is a lifelong process of losing one's life and reviving assurance through nearness to Christ.

Conclusion

Burgess and the Westminster divines fleshed out the doctrine of assurance with precision. The terminology they developed, their treatises on assurance, their pastoral compassion for the weak in faith, and their pressing admonitions and invitations to grow in faith showed their great appreciation for vital union with Christ. Scholars today who attribute morbid introspection and man-centeredness to seventeenth-century Puritans have missed the mark. The majority of Puritan divines examined spiritual experience microscopically because they were eager to trace the hand of God in their lives so they could attribute glory to the Father who elects, the Son who redeems, and the Spirit who sanctifies.[79]

Moreover, those who advocate a radical cleavage of the Puritans from the Reformers on the issue of assurance are insensitive to the unique situation of first-generation Reformers who embraced the doctrines of grace with unparalleled zeal, and moved forward with special degrees of assurance.[80] Understandably, when subsequent generations emerged, that zeal for the truth cooled. Notwithstanding the inherent tensions of promoting the syllogisms from the sideline they occupied in

Calvin's thought to a mainline position, as Cornelis Graafland asserted, Burgess and his colleagues only enlarged for pastoral reasons the pores Calvin had already opened in allowing "signs which are sure attestations" of faith.[81] They tried with varying degrees of success to lead their flocks by the Spirit into "soundly bottomed assurance," and encouraged them not to rest short of experimental, vital union with the Lord Jesus Christ.

The seeds for the Puritan emphasis of assurance were already in the Reformers, for Calvin and the Puritans both agreed that assurance is organically a part of faith, though it may be possessed without the believer always being conscious of its possession.[82] Though the Puritans went beyond Calvin in emphasizing this, they both had the same goal in mind: *soli Deo gloria.*

The Confession's statements on assurance fleshed out by Burgess help the believer make his calling and election sure by going beyond himself to find everything necessary for time and eternity in the Spirit-applied grace of God in Jesus Christ. For Burgess, that is a worthy goal. Assurance is an excellent privilege because "(1) it keeps up excellent fellowship and acquaintance with God; (2) it will work a filial and an evangelical frame of heart; (3) it will support [a man, even when] there be nothing but outward misery and trouble; (4) it will much inflame [a man] in prayer; (5) it makes a man walk with much tenderness against sin; (6) his heart will be impatient and earnest till the coming of Christ; and (7) [it produces] a full acquiescency and resting in God and Christ, as sufficient for every kind of want."[83]

Is this also the goal of our lives? Are we experimentally acquainted with saving faith, and are we praying for increasing measures of assurance in Christ, even if, as Calvin said, "unbelief will not down"?

Let us remember that our measure of assurance is reflected in our daily life. We must daily learn the lessons Burgess and the Puritans taught. Our primary ground of assurance lies in the promises of God in Christ. Those promises must be applied to our hearts, bear fruit in our lives, and help us yearn for the Spirit's corroborating witness with our spirit that we are indeed children of God. We are called to live fruitful lives, to speak well of our great assuring God, and to serve as salt in the earth.

The practical message for the true Christian is simply this: Faith ultimately must triumph because it comes from the triune God and rests on His Word. Let us therefore not despair when, for a time, we do not feel its triumph. Let us embrace God's promise in Christ more fully, recognizing that our certainty, both objective and subjective, lies wholly in Christ, for faith is of Christ and rests in Him.

Christ shall ultimately win the day in believers, for it is He, Calvin wrote, who "wishes to cure the disease [of unbelief] in us, so that among us he may obtain full faith in his promises."[84] Let us take courage and seek grace to honor Christ, and through Christ, God Triune. That is what faith and assurance, Calvin and Reformed theology, Burgess and Puritanism, Scripture and life are all about—honoring the triune God through Jesus Christ. "For of him, and through him, and to him, are all things: to whom be glory for ever. Amen" (Rom. 11:36).

At the close of his first treatise on justification, Anthony Burgess put it this way: "Lord, who was more plunged into sin than I? whose diseases were greater than mine? It may be thousands and thousands for less and fewer sins then I have committed, are now taking their portion in hell. O Lord this thy overflowing goodness doth overcome me, oh that I had the hearts of all men and Angels to praise thee."[85]

---

[1] Anthony Burgess, *Spiritual Refining: or, A Treatise of Grace and Assurance* (London: A. Miller for Thomas Underhill, 1652), 43-44 [hereafter: *Spiritual Refining*].

[2] John Wallis, *Sermons* (London, 1791), 15.

[3] Anthony Burgess, *An Expository Comment, Doctrinal, Controversial and Practical Upon the whole First Chapter of The Second Epistle of St Paul to the Corinthians* (London: Abraham Miller for Abel Roper, 1661).

[4] William Young, "Anthony Burgess," in *The Encyclopedia of Christianity,* ed. Jay Green (Marshallton, Delaware: National Foundation for Christian Education, 1968), 2:228.

[5] Anthony Burgess, *Spiritual Refining: Part II Or, A Treatise of Sinne* (London: for Thomas Underhill, 1654), title page.

[6] Ibid., 1-64.

[7] *Spiritual Refining,* 3.

[8] Ibid., 19.

[9] Ibid., 27.

[10] Ibid., 27-32.

[11] Ibid., 33-34.

[12] Ibid., 2, 23-24, 676-77.

[13] Ibid., 17, 51, 54, 59, 671.

[14] Ibid., 20-21.

[15] Ibid., 1-11.

[16] Ibid., 24-25.

[17] Ibid., 672.

[18] Ibid., 25-26.

[19] Paul Helm, *Calvin and the Calvinists* (Edinburgh: Banner of Truth Trust), 28, 75.

[20] *Collected Writings* (Edinburgh: Banner of Truth Trust, 1980), 2:270.

[21] James Buchanan, *The Doctrine of Justification: An Outline of Its History in the Church and of Its Exposition from Scripture* (Edinburgh: T. & T. Clark, 1867), 184.

[22] *Spiritual Refining,* 51.

[23] Anthony Burgess, *The True Doctrine of Justification Asserted and Vindicated, From the*

Errors of Papists, Arminians, Socinians, and more especially Antinomians (London: Robert White for Thomas Underhil, 1648), 269-70.

[24] *Spiritual Refining,* 5-6.

[25] Edward Reynolds, *Three Treatises of the Vanity of the Creature. The Sinfulnesse of Sinne. The Life of Christ* (London: B. B. for Rob Bastocke and George Badger, 1642), 1:365.

[26] *Spiritual Refining,* 41.

[27] Ibid., 57.

[28] *The Works of Thomas Brooks* (reprint ed., Edinburgh: Banner of Truth Trust, 1980), 3:254-59.

[29] *The True Doctrine of Justification,* 272.

[30] *The Marrow of Theology,* trans. John D. Eusden (Boston: Pilgrim Press, 1968), 1.3.22.

[31] *The Works of John Flavel* (reprint ed., London: Banner of Truth Trust, 1968), 2:330.

[32] *Spiritual Refining,* 672.

[33] Cornelis Graafland, "Van *syllogismus practicus* naar *syllogismus mysticus,*" in *Wegen en Gestalten in het Gereformeerd Protestantisme,* ed. W. Balke, C. Graafland, and H. Harkema (Amsterdam: Ton Bolland, 1976), 105-122.

[34] Cornelius Burges, *A Chain of Graces drawn out at length for a Reformation of Manners. Or, A brief Treatise of Virtue, Knowledge, Temperance, Patience, Godliness, Brotherly kindness, and Charity, so far as they are urged by the Apostle, in 2 Pet. 1. 5, 6, 7* (London, 1622), 32.

[35] *Spiritual Refining,* 41.

[36] Graafland, "Van *syllogismus practicus* naar *syllogismus mysticus,*" 105.

[37] *Spiritual Refining,* 52-54.

[38] Ibid., 53.

[39] Ibid., 51, 54.

[40] Ibid., 59.

[41] Ibid., 56.

[42] Ibid., 57.

[43] Ibid., 44.

[44] *The Saints' Happiness, together with the several steps leading thereunto. Delivered in Divers Lectures on the Beatitudes* (reprint ed., Beaver Falls, Pa.: Soli Deo Gloria, 1988), 196.

[45] *A Treatise of Miscellany Questions* (Edinburgh: Gedeon Lithgovv, for George Svvinttum, 1649), 105-109.

[46] *Spiritual Refining,* 49.

[47] Ibid., 50.

[48] Ibid., 47-48.

[49] Ibid., 52.

[50] Rutherford, *The Covenant of Life Opened* (Edinburgh: Andro Anderson for Robert Broun, 1655), 65-67; Twisse, *The Doctrine of the Synod of Dort and Arles* (Amsterdam: G. Thorpe, 1631), 147-49; Scudder, *The Christian's Daily Walk* (reprint ed., Harrisonburg, Va.: Sprinkle, 1984), 338-42; *The Works of Thomas Goodwin* (reprint ed., Eureka, CA: Tanski, 1996), 6:27; 7:66; 8:351, 363.

[51] *Critical and Exegetical Hand-book to The Epistle of the Romans* (New York: Funk & Wagnalls, Publishers, 1889), 316. Cf. Robert Bolton, *Some General Directions for a Comfortable Walking with God* (Morgan, Pa.: Soli Deo Gloria, 1995), 326.

[52] *The Works of Thomas Goodwin,* 1:233; 8:366.

[53] *Catechism of the Second Reformation,* ed. Alexander Mitchell (London: Nisbet, 1866), 207; *The Trial and Triumph of Faith* (Edinburgh: Collins, 1845), 88ff.

[54] *Spiritual Refining,* 672.

[55] Ibid., 52.

[56] Anthony Burgess, *CXLV Expository Sermons upon the whole 17th Chapter of the Gospel According to St. John: or Christ's Prayer Before his Passion Explicated, and both Practically and Polemically Improved* (London: Abraham Miller for Thomas Underhill, 1656), 356.

[57] Graafland, "Van *syllogismus practicus* naar *syllogismus mysticus,*" 108, 120.

[58] Burgess, *Spiritual Refining,* 51.

[59] *The True Doctrine of Justification,* 273.

[60] Ibid., 152.

[61] *Spiritual Refining,* 35.

[62] Ibid.

[63] *CXLV Expository Sermons upon the whole 17th Chapter of St. John,* 356.

[64] *Spiritual Refining,* 53.

[65] Ibid., 673, 59; cf. *The True Doctrine of Justification,* 273.

[66] Ibid.

[67] *Spiritual Refining,* 673.

[68] Ibid., 26, 681-83.

[69] Ibid., 679-80.

[70] *CXLV Expository Sermons upon the whole 17th Chapter of St. John,* 356.

[71] *Spiritual Refining,* 25-26.

[72] Ibid., 672.

[73] Ibid., 673.

[74] Ibid., 34.

[75] Ibid., 34-35.

[76] Ibid., 35.

[77] Ibid., 35-36.

[78] Ibid., 673-75.

[79] Cf. J. I. Packer, "The Puritan Idea of Communion with God," in *Press Toward the Mark* (London: n.p., 1962), 7.

[80] Joel R. Beeke, *Assurance of Faith: Calvin, English Puritanism, and the Dutch Second Reformation* (New York: Peter Lang, 1994), 19-22, 54-72, 365-77.

[81] "'Waarheid in het Binnenste': Geloofszekerheid bij Calvijn en de Nadere Reformatie," in *Een Vaste Burcht,* ed. K. Exalto (Kampen: Kok, 1989), 69.

[82] Peter Lewis cited in Errol Hulse, *The Believer's Experience* (Haywards Heath, Sussex: Carey, 1977), 128-29.

[83] *Spiritual Refining,* 26.

[84] *Institutes of the Christian Religion,* 3.2.15.

[85] *The True Doctrine of Justification,* 275.

9

The Life and Writings of John Brown of Haddington

Eighteenth-century Scotland produced many noted ministers, scholars, and educators, but none greater or so greatly loved as John Brown of Haddington. He was a devout Christian, an able preacher, and a prolific theological writer. He was also a shining soldier of the cross who did not falter in the face of opposition. In the course of his life he saw his beloved church torn by painful conflicts, especially in the great breach that divided the Seceders, but he never lost faith that Jesus Christ is King of His church. As a faithful steward, Brown felt his highest calling was to shepherd Christ's flock and defend the truths of the Reformed faith.

Brown's life and career are all the more remarkable considering he began in obscurity and poverty, with no advantages of wealth, position, title, or education. Yet God favored him with unusual gifts and an enormous capacity for hard work, and providentially opened the way for him to use these gifts effectively. Best of all, God favored him with a profound experience of the truth of the Gospel as "the power of God unto salvation." That experience left its indelible stamp on every aspect of John Brown's many-sided ministry.

Early Life and Education

John Brown, named after his father, was born in 1722 in the village of Carpow, near Abernethy in the county of Perth, Scotland. His mother was Catherine Millie. His parents were poor (his father was a weaver) and could not afford an education for their son, though his father did teach him how to read. His parents also taught him the basics of true Christianity and conducted family worship every morning and evening.

The year of his birth is remembered in Scottish church history as the year in which the General Assembly of the Church of Scotland reaffirmed its 1720 condemnation of the book, *The Marrow of Modern Divinity*, and rebuked twelve ministers who had defended the book's theology. Included among the twelve was the minister of the parish church of

Abernethy, Alexander Moncrieff. Moncrieff and his colleagues were permitted to return to their charges, but the Marrow Controversy set in motion forces that would later divide the Scottish church. Born under the shadow of this controversy, Brown's faith and work were deeply impacted by all that resulted from it.

When Brown was eight years old, he pushed through a large Sabbath crowd outside the church at Abernethy and discovered that the Lord's Supper was going to be administered. Since non-communicants were excluded from such services, he was forced to leave, but not before he heard a minister who spoke highly of Christ. Brown later wrote, "This in a sweet and delightful manner captivated my young affections, and has since made me think that children should never be kept out of the church on such occasions."

Brown's formal training was meager, but he did study Latin. He also enjoyed memorizing catechisms. "I had a particular delight in learning by heart the Catechisms published by Vincent, Flavel, and the Westminster Assembly, and was much profited by them," he wrote later. His mother noted his eagerness to learn and envisioned him one day standing among Scotland's preachers.

In 1733, Ebenezer Erskine (1680-1754), James Fisher (1697-1775), Alexander Moncrieff (1695-1761), and William Wilson (1690-1741) seceded from the Church of Scotland. Banding together as the Associate Presbytery, they fathered a new organization which came to be known as the Secession Church. As a member of Moncrieff's flock in Abernethy, Brown joined the Secession Church early on and stayed in it until his death.

When Brown was eleven years old, his father died and shortly after his mother also, leaving him an orphan at the age of thirteen. He stayed with various families but was separated from his two brothers and sister. "I was left a poor orphan, and had nothing to depend on but the providence of God," he wrote, "and I must say that the Lord hath been 'the father of the fatherless, and the orphan's stay.'"

Shortly after his mother died, Brown himself became very ill and nearly died. Everyone but his sister thought he would not recover. While praying for her brother, the sister was struck with the promise, "With long life will I satisfy him, and show him my salvation," which set her mind at ease. Her brother became well again.

In his thirteenth and fourteenth years, Brown was irresistibly attracted to the gospel. He read the major religious books of the period, such as Joseph Alleine's *An Alarm to the Unconverted*, William Guthrie's

The Trial of a Saving Interest in Christ, William Gouge's *Christian Directions Shewing How to Walk with God All the Day Long*, and the letters of Samuel Rutherford. Though Brown profited by what he read, and was often convicted by it for several days, he resisted resting on free grace alone. "Such was the bias of my heart, under its convictions, that I was willing to do any thing rather than flee to Christ, and trust to his free grace alone for my salvation," he wrote.

A Teenage Shepherd Converted

John Ogilvie, an elderly man with little education, employed the teenage Brown to tend his sheep. Ogilvie asked Brown to read to him, and Brown did so on numerous occasions. They soon became friends and met often to read the Word of God, pray, and sing psalms. Brown treasured those times.

After a severe fever in 1741, Brown became greatly concerned about his soul's eternal welfare. While his sheep were resting in the fold, he went to hear a sermon two miles away, running to and from the church. He heard three sermons in this manner, the last of which was preached on John 6:64, "There are some of you that believe not." That sermon pierced his conscience. He was convinced that he was the greatest unbeliever in the world.

His anxiety was greatly eased the next morning when he heard a sermon on Isaiah 53:4, "Surely he hath borne our griefs, and carried our sorrows." "I was made, as a poor lost sinner, as the chief of sinners, to essay appropriating the Lord Jesus as having done all for *me*, and as wholly made over to *me* in the gospel, as the free gift of God; and as my all-sufficient Saviour, answerable to all my folly, ignorance, guilt, filth, slavery, and misery," he later wrote.

Through this sermon and another on Isaiah 45:24, "Surely in the Lord have I righteousness and strength," he was drawn to the Lord Jesus Christ. He was given a clearer view of the freeness of God's grace and the exercise of taking hold of the promises of God.

False Accusations

By age nineteen, through diligent self-study, Brown had acquired some fluency in Latin, Greek, and Hebrew. He had learned the Greek alphabet by poring over notes in his copy of the Latin poems of Ovid, which contained Hellenic words, and by analyzing the Greek forms in the English Bible. Some of the Seceding students were suspicious of Brown's amazing feat and accused him of having learned Greek from the devil!

Rumors about Brown and alleged dealings with the devil circulated for years. Brown agonized about them, though the Lord provided comfort. Brown especially found comfort in Psalm 42:8, "The Lord will command his loving-kindness in the day-time, and in the night his song shall be with me, and my prayer to the God of my life." In later years, he remarked that affliction is one of God's kindest blessings to the believer.

While still under suspicion, Brown went to a bookshop in St. Andrews and asked for a Greek New Testament. As the story goes, a professor in the university was struck with Brown, whose shabby clothes announced his deep poverty, asking for such a book. The professor declared that if Brown could read it, the professor would purchase the volume for him. Thus Brown obtained the New Testament at no cost.[1]

Peddler, Soldier, and Teacher

For several years, Brown was a peddler, shouldering a pack and traveling into neighboring counties to sell odds and ends at cottage doors. He did not have great success in this line. The books in people's homes and lengthy discussions would often divert him from selling merchandise.

During this time, Brown traveled great distances to attend Communion services. He once traveled over twenty-five miles to attend a Communion season at Ebenezer Erskine's church. It was customary at that time for the Lord's Supper to be administered only once or twice a year in a congregation, and many people would come from afar to take part in the several days of services devoted to the sacrament.

In 1745, Charles Edward Stuart, a staunch Roman Catholic, made an unsuccessful attempt to recover the British throne in Scotland. The Seceders were loyal to the Protestant faith, of course, and to the reigning House of Hanover. They took up arms to defend their church and country. John Brown fought alongside other Seceders in defense of Edinburgh Castle.

Afterwards, Brown returned to peddling but soon was dissatisfied with his work. From his earliest days, he had felt called to proclaim God's truth from the pulpit, but lacked a university education. The next logical step for him was to assume the role of teacher, which he did in 1748.

John Brown first taught at Gairney Bridge, near Kinross, then at Spittal, a village in the parish of Penicuik. One of his students during this time was Archibald Hall (1736-1778), who later became the well-respected minister of Wall Street, London.

During this period, Brown learned much about divinity and literature. He committed large portions of Scripture to memory. He acquired a working knowledge of Arabic, Syrian, Persian, Ethiopian, and major European languages, including French, Spanish, Italian, Dutch, and German. He studied long into the night, regularly sleeping no more than four hours. Much later he confessed the danger of such unhealthy habits.

The Breach in the Associate Synod

In April 1747, a division called "The Breach" took place in the Secession Church over the legitimacy of the Burgess oath. Citizens of Edinburgh, Glasgow, and Perth were required to take the oath in 1744. Taking this "loyalty oath" was a prerequisite to engaging in trade, belonging to one of the artisans' guilds, or voting in elections. Included in the oath was this clause: "Here I protest before God, and your Lordships, that I profess, and allow with my heart, the true religion presently professed within this realm, and authorized by the laws thereof…renouncing the Roman religion called papistry."

Those who condemned the oath believed that it was an endorsement of the Church of Scotland, with all its prevailing errors and corruptions. They were known as Antiburghers. Those who supported the oath were called Burghers, holding that the oath merely required one to profess to be a Protestant, over against Roman Catholicism. Brown and the Erskines sided with the Burghers. Twenty-three church leaders of the Antiburgher party, under the leadership of Alexander Moncrieff and Adam Gib (1714-88), declared that they were the rightful continuation of the Secession. They formed the General Associate Synod.

The secession of the General Associate Synod forced the Associate Synod to form a new seminary to train pastors for the ministry. The Associate Synod appointed Ebenezer Erskine to begin training students for the ministry at Stirling. Erskine accepted the appointment, though reluctantly, since he was already sixty-seven years old. The Synod therefore chose James Fisher of Glasgow as an alternate. Fisher is remembered for his *Exposition of the Shorter Catechism,* published in two parts beginning in 1753.

The first student to present himself at Stirling was John Brown. A university education was an entrance requirement, but Brown had already distinguished himself as a scholar through self-education. Some members of the Presbytery questioned his credentials, but Ralph Erskine (1685-1752), Ebenezer's younger brother, came to Brown's defense, saying, "I think the lad has a sweet savor of Christ about him."

Brown was approved for theological studies and started training for the Associate ministry under Ebenezer Erskine. The basic theology text used at the time was Francis Turretin's (1623-1687) *Institutes of Elenctic Theology*. Erskine's method was to read from Turretin and comment on its major doctrines. He excelled in teaching homiletics.

After two years, James Fisher took over the professorship. Brown moved to Glasgow to sit under Fisher's teaching. Fisher was often compared to an eagle, due to the keenness of his mental vision and the swiftness with which he swooped down upon fallacies and heresies. Brown learned much from Fisher and so refined his preaching skills that on November 14, 1750, at the age of twenty-eight, he received his license to preach from the Presbytery of Edinburgh.

Pastor in Haddington

A short time after his ordination, Brown received calls to be the minister of the Associate congregation of Haddington, the county town of East Lothian, and of Stow, Mid-Lothian. He accepted the call to Haddington, the smaller of the two congregations.

Brown served the small church in Haddington for thirty-six years, from 1751 until his death. He preached three times every Lord's Day, and visited and catechized his flock during the week. With all his learning, he tried to preach as if he had never read any book but the Bible. He often quoted Archbishop James Ussher's saying, "It will take all our learning to make things plain."

During the course of his pastorate, Brown suffered many trials in his

The church at Haddington

The manse at Haddington

personal life, including the loss of a wife and several children. He was married eighteen years to Janet Thomson, a God-fearing daughter of a Musselburgh merchant. They had eight children, of which only two survived. After his first wife died, Brown married Violet Croumbie, of Stenton, East Lothian, who outlived him by thirty-five years.

Brown often agonized that he was a trial to his congregation. He begged God to help him lead his flock, but if his ministry was not for God's glory, to remove him by death. He strongly disapproved of ministers who frequently switched pastorates.

On the other hand, he found great pleasure in studies that prepared him for the coming Sabbath. Personal spiritual experience also enriched his sermons. As he said, "Any little knowledge which I have had of my uncommonly wicked heart, and of the Lord's dealing with my own soul, hath helped me much in my sermons; and I have observed, that I have been apt to deliver that which I had experienced, in a more feeling and earnest manner, than other matters." Brown's main focus in preaching was the beauty and glory of Christ against the backdrop of man's wretched depravity. He wrote, "Now after near forty years preaching of Christ, and his great and sweet salvation, I think that I would rather beg my bread, all the labouring days of the week, for an opportunity of publishing the gospel on the Sabbath to an assembly of sinful men, than, without such a privilege, to enjoy the richest possessions on earth."

Brown loved to study the great theologians. He was particularly fond of the old divines—Francis Turretin, Benedict Pictet, Petrus VanMastricht, John Owen—and contemporary writers such as Thomas Boston, James Hervey, and Ebenezer and Ralph Erskine.

Brown was a lifetime scholar. As Thomas Brown noted, "He was never more in his element than when in his study, and here he spent the greater part of his time." He would often rise at four or five o'clock in the morning fervently praying for his dear flock before discharging the day's duties, though he often lamented his deficiency in prayer.

Brown delighted in prayer, often setting aside entire mornings for it. His tender love for God would often spring up spontaneously, such as his response to an extra loud peal of thunder. "That's the love-whisper of my God," he would say.

Brown also organized group prayer meetings. For some years, he held prayer meetings with seven or eight children in his parsonage. He also led a prayer meeting for adults from both the Church of Scotland and the Seceder congregations. In later years, he wrote guidelines for how prayer meetings should be conducted.

In 1758, Brown published his first book, *An Help for the Ignorant: Being an Essay Towards an Easy, Plain, Practical and Extensive Explication of the Assembly's Shorter Catechism, composed for the Young Ones of his own Congregation*. The book offers thousands of questions about the Shorter Catechism. The answers are succinct, practical, and supported by Scripture. Brown prefaces his book with an introduction to children, urging them to serve the Lord, flee the world, and trust in Christ alone for salvation.

For the most part, the book was well-received. Some Antiburghers, however, charged Brown with heresy because he wrote that, though Christ's righteousness is of infinite value in itself, it is imputed to believers only in proportion to their need. The Antiburghers maintained that the righteousness of Christ is imputed to believers in its full infinite value so that God's people are infinitely righteous in Christ.

The debate appeared more speculative than edifying. Nonetheless, Brown responded the following year with his *A Brief Dissertation concerning the Righteousness of Christ* (1759), in which he wrote, "Let them do to or wish me what they will, may their portion be redemption through the blood of Jesus.... [Let them] call me what they please, may the Lord call them 'the holy ones, the redeemed of the Lord.'"

That response was typical of Brown. He seldom spoke a negative word about anyone. He also treated rumor as rumor, saying that when it was spoken of those in public office, it usually was not true.

Brown once wrote to Rev. Archibald Bruce, a respected professor of divinity with the Antiburghers: "Our conduct on both sides of the Secession I have often thought to be like that of two travelers, both walking on the same road, not far from one another, but in consequence of a thick mist so suddenly come on they cannot see one another, and each supposes the other to be off the road. After some time the darkness is removed, and they are quite surprised to find that they are both on the road, and had been all along so near one another."

That proved true of the Burghers and the Antiburghers. In 1820, thirty-three years after Brown died, the two denominations were reconciled as the United Secession Church. In 1847, a union was forged between the United Secession Church and the Relief Church, founded in 1761. The new body was known as the United Presbyterian Church.

Brown's ministry was blessed by God. People in his congregation grew in grace under the Word and sacrament, as did others who heard him preach wherever he traveled. Many regarded him as their spiritual father.

Professor of Divinity

After the death of John Swanston of Kinross in 1767, Brown was appointed Professor of Divinity by the Associate Church Synod. For twenty years he filled that position with distinction. He taught theological students in the Associate Church for nine weeks each year, packing in 160 hours of instruction, examination, and student presentations.

Brown taught about thirty students a year in languages, theology, church history, and homiletics. Some of those lectures are included in his publications, such as *A General History of the Christian Church* (2 vols.; 1771), and most importantly, his systematic theology, *A Compendious View of Natural and Revealed Religion* (1782). This book, republished several times in the nineteenth century, is a work of great merit. Other lesser known works that grew out of his theological teaching are *Letters on Gospel Preaching* and *Ten Letters on the Exemplary Behaviour of Ministers,* printed in Brown's *Select Remains* (1789).

In his teaching, Brown continually stressed the necessity of heart-religion. He taught students as a father teaches his children, loving them and admonishing them for their good. After hearing a practice sermon, he said to one student, "I hope never to hear such a sermon again while I live." To another, he wrote, "I hope the Lord has let some of the wind out of you that I thought was in you when first I knew you. Beg of Him to fill its room with Himself and His grace." Such severity, however, was tempered with kindness. His concern for students earned their affection and respect. Many of his lectures stirred their souls. His annual closing address particularly searched their consciences. Here is an example:

> What state you are in, what are the reigning principles in your breasts, what are the motives by which you are influenced, and what are the ends you have in view—whether you are, indeed, what you profess, and what your outward appearance would indicate—all is known to God. To commend a Saviour for whom one has no love; to preach a gospel which one does not believe; to point out the way to heaven and never to have taken one step in that way; to enforce a saving acquaintance with religion, and to be an entire stranger to it one's self—how sad, how pre-posterous!

One biographer wrote of Brown, "Many of his sayings at those times, it is believed, will never be forgotten by those who heard him. The many able, useful, and acceptable ministers, both in Great Britain and Ireland, whom he trained up for the sacred office, evince the ample success with which the Lord crowned his labours." Some of the students Brown trained were George Lawson (1749-1820), John Dick (1764-1833), and his eldest son, John Brown (1754-1832), later minister of Whitburn.

During his years as professor, Brown was also busy in the work of his denomination. For the last twenty years of his life he served as clerk of the Synod. He missed only two of forty-one synodical meetings in those years. He also served on many denominational committees.

John Brown of Haddington

Sickness and Death

In early 1787, Brown suffered from indigestion, which became more acute as months passed. His health could no longer sustain the ruthless workload he had carried most of his life, but he was determined to keep working. "How can a dying man spend his last breath better than in preaching Christ?" he asked.

February 25, 1787, was his last Sabbath in the pulpit. In the morning, he preached from Luke 2:26, "It was revealed unto him by the Holy Ghost, that he should not see death, before he had seen the Lord's Christ." In the evening, his text was Acts 13:26, "To you is the word of this salvation sent." He told his congregation these were his last sermons and commended them to the grace of God.

While his health continued to decline, the man who had always been reluctant to speak of his own religious experience seemed to become as a little child. The doors of his affections sprung open. He said loving things to his children, urging them to persevere in the faith. Forty-five pages of deathbed expressions conclude his *Memoir* edited by his son William. Here is a sampling of what Brown said:

- If Christ be magnified in my life, that is the great matter I wish for.
- O! to be with God! to see him as he is in Christ! to know him even as we are known! It is worth not merely *doing* for, but *dying* for, to see a gracious God.
- I have served several masters; but none so kind as Christ. I have dealt with many honest men; but no creditor like Christ. Had I ten thousand hearts, they should all be given to Christ; and had I ten thousand bodies, they should all be employed in labouring for his honour.
- Oh! commend Jesus. I have been looking at him for these many years, and never yet could find a fault in him. Many a comely person I have seen, but none so comely as Christ.
- Oh! what must Christ be in himself, when he sweetens heaven, sweetens Scriptures, sweetens ordinances, sweetens earth, and sweetens even trials!
- Once I got a ravishing sight of the necessity of his loving me, *the sinner.* He said, "Other sheep I have; them also I *must* bring."

Brown had a powerful sense of his own sinfulness. He degraded his weakness as thoroughly as he exalted Christ. Here are some samples of that self-knowledge:

- My life is and has been a kind of almost perpetual strife between God and my soul. He strives to overcome my enmity and wickedness with his mercies, and I strive to overcome his mercy with my enmity and wickedness. Astonishingly kind on his side, but worse than diabolically wicked on mine! After all, I wish and hope that he, not I, may obtain the victory at last.

- I know the outrageous wickedness of my heart; such wickedness as would have provoked any but a God of infinite love to have cast me into hell.
- I have no more dependence on my labours than on my sins.
- It has been my comfort these twenty years, that not only *sensible* sinners, but the most stupid, are made welcome to believe in Christ.
- Since Christ came to save sinners, even the chief, why, thought I, should I except myself?

In a letter to his congregation, Brown wrote movingly of these two themes of a hellworthy sinner and a precious Christ:

I see such weakness, such deficiency, such unfaithfulness, such imprudence, such unfervency and unconcern, such selfishness, in all that I have done as a minister or a Christian, as richly deserves the deepest damnation of hell. I have no hope of eternal happiness but in Jesus' blood, which cleanseth from all sin—in "redemption through his blood, the forgiveness of my sins, according to the riches of his grace."

Ordinarily, Brown went to the congregation in Stow during June to take part in their Communion season. A friend who realized that the ailing Brown wasn't planning to go to Stow asked, "You are not journeying thither this year?" Brown answered, "No, I wish to be traveling to God, as my exceeding joy." On June 19, 1787, he uttered his last words, "My Christ," and died. He was sixty-five years old.

After Brown died, this "Solemn Dedication to the Lord," dated June 23, 1784, was found among his papers:

LORD! I am now entering on the 34th year of my ministry; an amazing instance of sovereign mercy and patience to a cumberer of the ground! How strange that thou shouldest have, for more than sixty years, continued striving to exercise mercy and loving-kindness upon a wretch that hath all along spoken and done all the evil that I could; nor ever would yield, but when the almighty influence of free grace put it out of my power to oppose it. Lord! how often have I vowed, but never grown better; confessed but never amended! Often thou hast challenged and corrected me, and yet I have gone on forwardly in the way of my heart. As an evil man, and seducer, I have grown worse and worse.

But where should a sinner flee but to the Saviour? Lord! all refuge faileth me, no man can help my soul. Nothing will do for me, but an uncommon stretch of thy almighty grace. To thee, O Jesus! I give up myself, as a foolish, guilty, polluted and enslaved sinner; and I hereby solemnly take thee as mine, as made of God to me wisdom, righteousness, sanctification, and redemption. I give up myself, as a poor, ignorant, careless and wicked creature, who hath been ever learning, and yet never able to come to the knowledge of the truth. To thee, O Lord! that thou mayest bestow gifts on the rebellious, and exalt thy grace, in showing kindness to the unworthy.

O Saviour! come down, and do something for me, before I die. I give up myself and family, wife, children, and servant, to thee, encouraged by thy promises, Gen. xvii. 7; Jer. xxxi. 1; Isa. xliv. 3, lix. 21. I commit my poor, weak, withered congregation, deprived by death of its pillars, that thou mayest strengthen, refresh and govern it. I commit all my students unto thee, that thou, O Lord! mayest train them up for the ministry. May never one of them be so unfit as I have been! Lord! I desire to take hold of thy new covenant, well ordered in all things, and sure. This is all my salvation, and all my desire.

A Prolific Writer

Brown published thirty books. He was best-known for his *Self-Interpreting Bible* (2 vols., 1778) and, to a lesser extent, *A Dictionary of the Holy Bible* (2 vols., 1769). "Brown's Bible" contains history, chronology, geography, summaries, explanatory notes, and reflections—in short, it is a miniature library that covers everything a typical reader desires. It was reprinted twenty-seven times in Britain and America, often increasing in size through editors' additions. The latest and best edition (4 vols., 1914) contains more than 2,200 pages; the numerous aids include a system of marginal cross-references. This library in itself became nearly as common in eighteenth-century Scottish households as Bunyan's

"Brown's Bible"

Pilgrim's Progress and Thomas Boston's *Fourfold State*. It incorporated material from the *Dictionary*, which explained English vocabulary and grammar, making it useful for home schooling, and it also applied the Scriptures practically and personally. The complete work is exemplary in its directness and accuracy.

Robert Mackenzie's book, *John Brown of Haddington*, devotes an entire chapter to commending *The Self-Interpreting Bible*. MacKenzie writes:

> No work carried the reputation of the author so far afield as his *Self-Interpreting Bible....* Its success from the first was extraordinary.... It will be evident that an extraordinary amount of valuable material was thus placed at the command of the ordinary reader. It was the information that a student of the Scriptures hungered for, who had not access to the learned works dealing with such subjects.... Brown states that his avowed aim in his publication is not to depreciate the valuable commentaries of these writers (referring to some of the most famous Reformed commentators of the past), but "to exhibit their principal substance with all possible advantage"...and in referring particularly to the New Testament, he adds that "there the explication is peculiarly extensive, and attempts to exhibit the substance of many learned and expensive commentaries."

Charles Simeon of Cambridge (1759-1836) used Brown's book in his morning devotions. He wrote to Brown, "Your *Self-Interpreting Bible* seems to stand in lieu of all other commentaries; and I am daily receiving so much edification and instruction from it, that I would wish it in the hands of all serious ministers."

Brown's audience was remarkably diverse. He wrote for children and young people. *The Young Christian; or, The Pleasantness of Early Piety* (1782) encourages the fear of God in youth. The catechism books for children that were first published under one cover as *Two Short Catechisms, mutually connected* (1764) came to be known as "Little Brown" and "Big Brown." "Little Brown" contains 202 questions, many of which are short, personal, and designed for young children; "Big Brown," written for older children, contains 743 questions based on the Shorter Catechism.

Brown also wrote a trilogy of books over a fifteen-year period on the figures, types, and prophecies of Scripture titled: *Sacred Tropology; or A Brief View of the Figures and Explication of the Metaphors contained in Scripture* (1768), *An Evangelical and Practical View of the Types and Figures of the Old Testament Dispensation* (1781), and *The Harmony of Scripture Prophecies, and history of their fulfillment* (1784). He wrote the books, he said, because "in the first, we observe the surprising eloquence of Heaven, and discern, in almost every form of nature, a guide to and an illustration of inspired truth. By the second, we perceive the whole substance of the Gospel of Christ, truly exhibited in ancient shadows, persons, and things: in laws apparently carnal and trifling. In the third, we observe how astonishingly inspired predictions, properly arranged, and compared with the history of nations and churches, do illustrate each other; and modern events, as with the evidence of miracles, confirm our faith in the oracles of God."

He also loved writing biographies and church history. For ministers, he wrote, *The Christian, the Student, and Pastor, exemplified in the lives of nine eminent Ministers* (1781). *Practical Piety Exemplified* (1783) presents the lives of thirteen eminent Christians, illustrating various cases of conscience. *Casuistical Hints, or Cases of Conscience* (1784) was originally written for personal use, but later Brown offered it as "an appended illustration of *Practical Piety Exemplified,* or an appendix to my system on the head of sanctification." It handles temptations, indwelling sin, heresy, and division in the church. His last published work was *The Most Remarkable Passages in the Life and Spiritual experiences of Elizabeth Wast, a Young Woman, sometime Matron of the Trades Hospital, Edinburgh* (1785). As for church history, in addition to his two-volume overview, he wrote *An Historical Account of the Rise and Progress of the Secession* (1766) and *A Compendious History of the British Churches in Scotland, England, Ireland, and America* (2 vols.; 1784).

At times, Brown wrote polemically to defend or attack a position. He

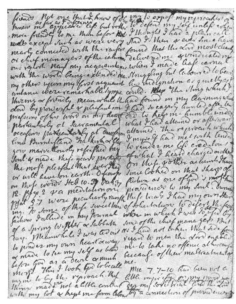

Facsimile of a page of Brown's "Short Memoir of My Life."

attacked the papacy in *The Oracles of Christ and the Abominations of Antichrist Compared; or, A Brief View of the Errors, Impieties, and Inhumanities of Popery* (1779) and *The Absurdity and Perfidy of All Authoritative Toleration of Gross Heresy, Blasphemy, Idolatry, and Popery in Britain* (1780). He defended the Burgher position in *The Re-exhibition of the Testimony vindicated, in opposition to the unfair account of given it by the Rev. Adam Gib* (1780). (Gib was a prominent anti-Burgher minister, who had written *An Account of the Burgher Re-exhibition of the Secession Testimony.*)

Brown also published the following sermons: *Religious Steadfastness Recommended* (1769), *The Fearful Shame and Contempt of those professed Christians who neglect to raise up spiritual Children to Christ* (1780), and *The Necessity and Advantage of Earnest Prayer for the Lord's Special Direction in the Choice of Pastors* (1783).

In 1765, Brown published his journal, titled *The Christian Journal; or, Common Incidents Spiritual Instructions*. The journal is divided into five parts: spring, summer, harvest, winter, and the day of rest. Lessons from nature and the Sabbath are applied to spiritual life. He also wrote a bit of fiction. *Letters on the Constitution, Government, and Discipline of the Christian Church* (1767) contains nineteen letters addressed to a fictitious person named Amelius, who lacks understanding of the constitution of the church and how members are accepted into the church. Brown offers the scriptural groundwork for promoting a strong view of the organized church and its Solemn League and Covenant.

The Psalms of David in Metre (1775), recently reprinted, include Brown's notes on the Psalms. *A Brief Concordance to the Holy Scriptures* (1783) was useful in its time. *Devout Breathings*, which emphasized experiential faith, was printed sixteen times by 1784. *The Awakening Call: Four Solemn Addresses, to Sinners, to Children, to Young Men and Women, and to Aged Persons*, sometimes bound with *Devout Breathings*, was also widely circulated.

By the time of his death, Brown's name was a household word among Presbyterians in Scotland and throughout the English-speaking world. His books, pamphlets, tracts, and catechisms were read by increasing numbers of people. Even after his death, additional works continued to be published. *Select Remains* (1789), which includes some of Brown's voluminous correspondence, a number of tracts, and his dying advice, was edited by his oldest son, John. *Posthumous Works* (1797) and *Apology for the more Frequent Administration of the Lord's Supper* (1804) were also published. In *Apology*, Brown argued for more frequent observation of the Lord's Supper, countering those who taught that infrequency safeguarded solemnity with, "Why not pray seldom, preach seldom, read God's Word seldom, that they may become more solemn too?"

A Spiritual Dynasty

Brown had many children, some of whom became prominent Christian leaders. His son John (1754-1832) was minister of Whitburn for fifty-five years and was a prolific devotional writer; Ebenezer (d. 1836) was a prominent preacher at Inverkeithing, Fife, for fifty-six years; Samuel (1779-1839) helped start circulating libraries; and William (1783-1863) was a historian of missions and an excellent biographer of his father. Grandson John Brown (1784-1858) served as pastor at Broughton Place United Presbyterian Church, Edinburgh, and was Professor of Exegetical Theology in the United Secession and United Presbyterian College, Edinburgh. Great-grandson Robert Johnston (d. 1918) was a professor in the United Presbyterian College, Edinburgh, and United Free Church College, Aberdeen. Another great-grandson, John (Rab) Brown (1810-82), became a medical doctor and writer. And great-great-grandsons John (1818-92) and David Cairns (1862-1946) became outstanding Presbyterian teachers and writers. Brown's descendants so respected him that some traveled to Scotland from the United States in 1987 for events marking the bicentennial of Brown's death.

Brown's *Compendious View*

Brown's systematic theology, printed in 1782 at the request of theological students, includes seven books and twenty-four chapters. It offers biblical focus, exegetical insights, a covenantal theme, experiential depth, and compelling applications. Brown's style is methodological and includes numerous divisions and sub-points to aid students.

Like Johannes Cocceius (1613-1669) and Herman Witsius (1636-1708), Brown felt that Reformed systematic theology should emphasize the historical activity of God in time rather than His eternal decrees. That activity was grounded pre-fall in the covenant of works and post-fall in the covenant of grace. Consequently, Brown's theology is organized around the doctrine of the covenant.

Address to Students of Divinity

In the 16-page prefix to the work, titled "Address to Students of Divinity," Brown says *A Compendious View* was not written "to make you read, but to make you *think much*," and "to impress your minds with the great things of God." He thus offers a plethora of Scripture verses and references (26,819 in all) in order to "render you mighty in the Scriptures, readily able to support the several articles of our holy religion by the self-evidencing and conscience-commanding testimony of the Holy Ghost, and accustomed to express the things of God in his own language." Brown expected students to move from paragraph to paragraph, committing as many texts as possible to memory.

With eternity in mind, Brown instructs students to do the following:

1. See that ye be *real Christians* yourselves.
2. Ponder much, as before God, what proper *furniture* you have for the ministerial work, and labour to increase it.
3. Take heed that your *call* from Christ and his Spirit to your ministerial work be not only *real* but *evident*.
4. See that your *end* in entering into, or executing your office, be single and disinterested.
5. See that your minds be deeply impressed with the *nature*, *extent*, and *importance* of your ministerial work.
6. See that ye take heed to your spirits, that ye deal not *treacherously* with the Lord.
7. See that ye, as workmen who need not be ashamed, earnestly labour *rightly to divide* the word of truth, according to the capacities, necessities, and particular occasions of your hearers, giving every one of them their portion in due season.
8. See that ye be judicious, upright, constant, and faithful in your profession.
9. Always improve and live on that blessed encouragement which is offered to you as Christians and ministers in the gospel.

Brown closes his preface with these words: "There is no master so kind as Christ; no service so pleasant and profitable as that of Christ; and no reward so full, satisfying, and permanent as that of Christ. Let us, therefore, begin all things from Christ; carry on all things with and through Christ; and let all things aim at and end in Christ."

The Regulating Standard of Religion

The first book in Brown's work provides the foundation for the rest of the work by addressing the prolegomena of theology. It consists of three chapters: the first, the law of nature; the second, the insufficiency of the law and nature to lead man to true and lasting happiness; the third, an elaborate treatment of the divine character of Scripture.

Brown's opening chapter covers the principles of natural religion as well as the elements of natural morality. In chapter two, he addresses ethics more directly, denouncing the slave trade as criminal, yet allowing for its lawfulness under prescribed circumstances. He also advocates limited monarchy over democracy. And he addresses issues that relate to family life, employers and employees, and wrongs inflicted on the weak.

Next, Brown discusses the insufficiency of natural theology. He meets the Deists on their own turf, crosses swords with David Hume, and exposes the weaknesses of Rationalism.

Brown is a master of examination. For example, commenting on the properties of memory, Brown writes, "The human memory is an intellectual power of *recollecting* or *retaining* our ideas, and is called *good*, when it quickly recollects and strongly retains them. Its condition much depends on that of our body, whether it be in health, free from sleep, etc."

Brown addresses issues that are rarely found in modern systematic theologies. Commenting on social virtues, he notes, "Humanity towards brutes, in carefully forbearing every form or degree of cruelty to them, is implied in social virtue. In this we imitate God, who is good to all, and show a proper regard to his creatures, and our fellow-partakers of his bounty in creation and providence."

Enlarging on the nature of revelation, Brown observes apologetically, "The contents of the Scriptures of the Old and New Testaments are *perfectly agreeable to reason.*" For Brown, scriptural doctrines, such as the Trinity and the mercy of God, transcend the most narrow and laborious search of reason. Brown's arguments, however, are weakened by the lack of a presuppositional apologetic, and by not allowing for the possibility of a gradual development of spiritual and ethical truth.

In his closing section on the doctrine of Scripture, Brown urges: "Ponder now, my soul! Are these oracles of God, these testimonies and testaments of Jesus Christ, my heritage, and the word upon which he hath caused me to hope? Are they my divine charter for my everlasting life?" He concludes, "Let me not dare to proceed to the contemplation of his nature and works, till I believe his word, and receive His *unspeakable gift*, that I may, on that ground, all along say of Him, *My Lord and my God*—my God and my All."

God, the Author, Object, and End of All Religion

The second book moves into theology proper. It includes four chapters on God's names, nature, and perfections; persons in the Godhead; the decrees of God; and the execution of His decree.

After discussing the knowledge, wisdom, power, sovereignty, holiness, justice, goodness, and truth of God, Brown challenges readers to say:

My Soul, stop thy contemplation of the Most High, and ask thyself, as in his presence: If God be a *Spirit*, am I spiritually minded, and a worshipper of Him in spirit and truth? Do I detest and banish every carnal imagination of him from my heart? Do I live in perpetual wonder, that his infinite equity can suffer such a sinner to live; nay, will save me? Do I reckon all things, as coming from His hand, as good—very good for me? Is He my Saviour, my Father, my Husband—my Friend, my Master, my Portion, my Pattern, my God—my All?

As a strong federal Calvinist, he says of God's decrees, "God acts on Himself in contemplating, loving, delighting in Himself; and in the persons of the Godhead, knowing, loving, delighting in, and consulting with each other." Brown then explains how providence works through election and reprobation. Election is always *in Christ,* who is the representative and covenant Head of the elect, Brown says. Like other federalists, Brown sees an essential connection between election and atonement, which limits the atonement to God's elect.

Concerning Brown's views on the debate between a supralapsarian and infralapsarian scheme of God's decrees, Richard Muller writes:

> Brown, I believe, has recognized a point that was latent in the entire debate from the point of its inception in the *Amica collatio* between Arminius and Junius and that had been stated more explicitly toward the close of the high orthodox era by Mastricht—namely, that the two perspectives need not be understood as mutually exclusive. The point that Brown makes is that God can be viewed legitimately as knowing the objects of his decree as creatable and fallible and, equally so, as created and fallen—in the former sense foreknowing human beings as possible objects for the manifestation of his glory; in the latter as actual objects of his mercy and justice. The former view corresponds with the divine "necessary knowledge" of all possibility; the latter with the divine "free" or "voluntary knowledge" of all divinely willed actuality. Both kinds of knowing are understood by the Reformed orthodox as belonging properly to God.[2]

In harmony with his federal Calvinistic forebears, Brown asserted that the "awful doctrine of Reprobation, as well as of the Election of men, ought, with great prudence and holy awe, be taught in the church." His reasons for doing so are as follows:

1. It hath been proved that the Holy Ghost hath plainly taught it in His Word.
2. Every thing taught in the Scripture, lawfully used, tends to promote men's holiness in heart and life.
3. Election and reprobation being so closely related and contrasted,

the former can neither be taught nor conceived of, separately from the latter.

4. In His providence, which every man ought to observe, God copies out of His decree of reprobation, in the life and in the death of the wicked.

5. A proper knowledge of this decree promotes right and reverential views of the sovereignty, power, wisdom, justice, and goodness of God.

6. The doctrine of reprobation, if duly taught, tends to alarm the wicked and render their conscience uneasy, till they obtain proper evidence that they are not included in it, and to render sin terrible to them: And it excites saints to self-examination, and to lively gratitude to God their Redeemer, in a course of gospel holiness.

Brown refutes eight objections against the doctrine of reprobation and concludes with a personal reflection.

The Covenant Bonds of Religious Connection between God and Men

Brown's theological work includes a notable explanation of God's covenantal relation to man. He says covenant is "an agreement made between different persons on certain terms" and that all covenants require a condition, a promise, and a penalty. For the sake of man's happiness, God exercises His providence toward His creatures "in the form of covenant-connection."

Book three, divided into two main chapters—the covenant of works and the covenant of grace—discusses this "covenant-connection." The first chapter examines in detail topics such as the freedom of Adam's will, the headship of Adam for all, and the curse of a broken covenant—all from a typical federalist perspective. In the second chapter, dealing with God's covenant of grace, Brown writes that the covenant of grace originates, "from the mere grace of God, and contracted between two divine persons, it was *made from all eternity.*"

The purpose of the covenant of grace, Brown says, is, "first, to display the glory of God's own perfections, wisdom, power, holiness, justice, and truth—especially the exceeding riches of His grace, and second, to bring elect men out of an estate of sin and misery into an estate of salvation."

Brown rejects the idea of a covenant of redemption separate from the covenant of grace. In characteristic *Marrow* fashion, he distinguishes between the contracting and administering of the covenant of grace. The former is accomplished in eternity, between the Father and the Son, and the latter in time, between the Triune God and fallen humanity, though in its secret decree with the elect only. Brown explains, "The covenant of grace is, in many things, administered indefinitely to men in general, without any consideration of them as either elect or as reprobates." Christ is granted to all as a warrant to those who believe, else men would have no more hope for faith than devils. If the covenant were not administered in such a general way, sinners could not be condemned for unbelief. This general administration of the covenant to all men, however, serves primarily for the salvation of the elect.

Brown teaches that the covenant of grace is essentially conditional in nature. Since Christ fulfils all its conditions, however, the covenant is entirely free to believers. God gives believers, in and through Christ and by His Spirit, whatever the covenant requires. All proper conditions, therefore, are satisfied through Christ's righteousness. Faith can only be spoken of as a condition of the covenant when it is understood to mean a "condition of connection" or an instrument through which we receive God's blessings. Even then, such language is risky. Neither faith nor repentance is a proper condition of the covenant, since, Brown says, "the admission of any act or quality of ours as the condition, would destroy the whole form and grace of" this covenant, which "stands opposed to the covenant of works."

Participation in the covenant of grace can only be understood in terms of spiritual union with Christ, Brown says. He stresses that only the elect are included in the covenant of grace. They come to a saving interest through Christ as their head. Brown fortifies his argument in this chapter with 1,792 Scripture references.

Christ, The Mediator of the Covenant of Grace
In book four, Brown considers Christ's role as Mediator of the covenant. He discusses Christ's mediatorial person, Christ's general and particular offices (such as prophet, priest, and king), and Christ's states of humiliation and exaltation.

Brown emphasizes the unique personhood of Christ, showing the essential incommunicability of any of the distinctively human properties to the divine nature, or of the distinctively divine attributes to the human nature. Next, he discusses the offices of Christ, marshalling hundreds of proof-texts to support limited atonement. His page on the intercession of Christ is comforting. His division of Christ's kingship into a kingdom of power, grace, and glory is succinct and scriptural.

Brown's chapter on Christ's states includes a remarkable list of twenty-four ways in which Christ's humiliation was attended by "honourable circumstances." He asserts that Christ's humiliation and exaltation were joined between His death and resurrection, His body lying in the grave (humiliation) while His soul fled to heavenly mansions (exaltation). He concludes by asking, "If God so exalt Jesus Christ, why hath he not an higher—a far higher place in my heart?"

The Principal Blessings of the Covenant of Grace
Book five discusses the blessings of the eternal covenant of grace in six chapters: union with Christ and effectual calling, justification, adoption, sanctification, spiritual consolation, and glorification.

Brown rightly considers union with Christ as preceding yet inseparable from effectual calling. Scripturally and experientially he explains the Spirit's work in establishing that union and making it effectual through an internal calling. He carefully refutes objections. But his chapters on justification and sanctification are the masterpieces of his soteriology.

Brown's emphasis on the "Surety righteousness" of Christ is clear and helpful. He shows how Christ fulfilled the broken covenant of works in the stead of believers, and how that becomes their justifying righteousness before God. Brown rejects faith as a condition of justification and asserts that justification as God's act is antecedent to the believer's faith.

Faith itself does not justify the believer, though he is justified through the instrument of faith. Faith is the believer's act—an act of his will that consents to the covenant of grace and receives Christ and His righteousness. Faith, which is seated in the will and the affections, is inseparably related to Christ. To walk by faith is to walk in union with Christ.

Brown carefully avoids preparationism. Evangelical repentance is the fruit of justification and never precedes it, he says. It is required of believers in sanctification but is never a ground for our justification.

Dr. George Lawson advised his theological students, "Read Brown on sanctification." MacKenzie also greatly admired this chapter. "The writer's life and character shine through every sentence of it," he said. "The study awakens admiration for the religious life which interpreted and expressed itself in the exposition here given of the secret source and mystic development of the divine life in the Christian soul. The survey of the mystery of divine grace in personal experience is the work of one who has searched the inner depths." Brown backs his points with 2,481 Scripture proofs.

Brown's chapter on spiritual consolation focuses on the perseverance of the saints, indwelling of the Spirit, assurance of God's love, peace of conscience, and joy in the Holy Ghost. Faith is always sure—hence assurance is of the essence of faith—but the believer's sense of having faith may waver. A solid sense of assurance, Brown asserts, comes when faith is repeatedly active in claiming the promises of the gospel, when there is earnest study of fellowship with God in Christ and of universal gospel holiness, and when there is a careful cherishing of the Spirit's activity and frequent exercises of self-examination. In proper self-examination, the Spirit bears witness of our heavenly adoption by directing us to "proper marks of grace." To make our calling and election sure, such examination must be "deliberate, judicious, impartial, earnest, and thorough," Brown says.

The External Dispensation of the Covenant of Grace by the Law and Gospel
Book six discusses the external dispensation of the covenant of grace through law and gospel. The book includes three parts: the law of God, the gospel of Christ, and the ordinances of the covenant of grace. Those ordinances include reading, meditation, preaching and hearing God's Word; spiritual conference, prayer, ministerial blessing, singing of psalms, vowing, fasting, thanksgiving, and the sacraments.

In a chapter that provides 3,133 proof-texts—more than any other—Brown explains each commandment, showing how it is conducive to spiritual life. He then shows how the gospel magnifies and vindicates the law, and provides an impressive double-column list which affirms that the gospel "promises preparation for, assistance in, and a gracious reward of every duty which the law, *as a rule*, requires." The Ten Commandments, he says, shouldn't be seen only as a law of nature or a reflection of the covenant of works, but as the law of Christ and rule of life.

One neglected ordinance today that Brown describes is "spiritual conference." On a personal level, that involves "communing with our own heart; putting serious questions to our conscience concerning our state, temper, and conduct, in order to have them compared with, and adjusted by God's word." Socially, it includes communing with other believers, formally or informally, and catechizing one's family. Ecclesiastically, it entails "ministerial visiting and catechizing persons and families, or the sick."

Brown's comment on the partaking of the Lord's Supper is notable: "*All professed Christians,* come to years of discretion, are *bound* by the law of God to *partake* of the Lord's Supper, and it is their sin, if they be incapable of regular admission to it." He lists three things necessary for a right partaking of the sacrament:

1. A worthy *state* of union with Christ as our husband, father, righteousness and strength.
2. A worthy *frame* in the actual exercise of all the graces of the Spirit, [such as] knowledge, faith, repentance, and love, etc.
3. A worthy *end* of honouring Christ, glorifying God, and receiving spiritual nourishment to our soul.

The Church Society, for, and to which, the Covenant of Grace is Dispensed
In his last book, Brown discusses ecclesiology. In chapter one, he deals with the nature, formation, and fellowship of the Christian church; in chapter two, the role of church power and where it resides within the church body; and in chapter three, the divine warrant, work, and accountability of ecclesiastical courts.

Brown defines the church as "a society of believers and holy persons whom God by the Gospel hath called from among mankind to fellowship with His Son, Jesus Christ." The church is called to be holy, spiritual, and orderly, Brown says, and orderliness is best seen in a carefully organized Presbyterian system of church government involving sessions, presbyteries, and synods.

"Doctrine is heaven!" Martin Luther wrote. Brown would concur. Doctrine was the lifeblood of his salvation. Brown's reflections at the end of nearly every chapter are a unique feature of his systematic theology. In these warm reflections he teaches us how to apply doctrine to our souls to examine whether God's grace and holiness truly shine in us. Only when this is done can we understand the beauty of sound biblical doctrine.

Brown's method of organization is attractive and his content full of evangelical piety. His systematic theology, said to be "one of the most profound, and at the same time perspicuous, views which have been given of the theology of the Westminster Confession," is an indispensable tool for the student, pastor, and professor of theology. It was used as a textbook in several colleges and seminaries, including the Countess of Huntingdon's college at Trevecca. Its Christ-centeredness is aptly reflected in Brown's last letter to the Countess:

There is none like Christ, none like Christ, none like Christ.... There is no learning nor knowledge like the knowledge of Christ; no life like Christ living in the heart by faith; no work like the service, the spiritual service of Christ; no reward like the free-graces wages of Christ; no riches nor wealth like "the unsearchable riches of Christ"; no rest, no comfort, like the rest, the consolation of Christ; no pleasure like the pleasure of fellowship with Christ. Little as I know of Christ, I would not exchange the learning of one hour's fellowship with Christ for all the liberal learning in ten thousand universities, during ten thousand ages, even though angels were to be my teachers.

Brown's last words, "my Christ," summarize his systematics, for his one great aim was to cultivate love for Christ in the soul of the believer. "If my soul love not this Lord Jesus, let me be Anathema, Maranatha, *accursed at his coming,*" are his closing words.

---

[1] This story has never been definitively verified. Robert Mackenzie, biographer of John Brown in the early twentieth century, considered it true. Brown's grandson, however, questioned its authenticity in his edition of his grandfather's *Memoirs.*

[2] *Calvin Theological Journal* 38, 2 (2003):363.

10

The Life and Theology
of Thomas Boston

"If Scotland had been searched during the earlier part of the eighteenth century, there was not a minister within its bounds who, alike in personal character, and in the discharge of his pastoral function, approached nearer the apostolic model than did this man of God. It is a fact that, even before he died, men and children had come to pronounce his name with reverence. It had become a synonym for holy living."[1] So wrote Andrew Thomson about Thomas Boston (1676-1732). Boston was an eminent Scottish divine and prolific theological writer. Ordained to the ministry of the Church of Scotland, he served two congregations, first in the parish of Simprin (1699-1707), then in the parish of Ettrick (1707-1732).

Birth, Conversion, and Education
Thomas Boston was born March 17, 1676, in Duns, Berwickshire, the youngest of seven children. His parents, who belonged to the lower middle class, sent Thomas to the grammar school in Duns, where he learned to love reading the Bible and was introduced to Latin and New Testament Greek.

John Boston, Thomas's father, was a cooper by trade and a strict Presbyterian. He was imprisoned for his faith when he refused to conform to the changes in worship and government imposed on the Church of Scotland by the Stuart kings.[2] One of Thomas's earliest memories was visiting his father in prison. After the Act of Toleration in 1687 permitted non-conforming Presbyterians to hold services in private houses, John Boston often traveled several miles with his family to Whitsome to hear Henry Erskine, the father of Ebenezer and Ralph Erskine.[3] Under Erskine's preaching from John 1:29 and Matthew 3:7, Thomas Boston was spiritually awakened at age eleven.[4]

Erskine's ministry continued to influence the Boston family. Regardless of the weather, Thomas would walk four or five miles each

Sabbath to obtain food for his soul. He later wrote, "In the winter sometimes it was my lot to go alone, without so much as a horse to carry me through Blackadder water, the wading whereof in sharp frosty weather I very well remember. But such things were then easy, for the benefit of the Word, which came with power."[5]

Boston's spiritual life was strengthened during his teenage years by regular Bible study and spiritual conversations with two boys from school. Before long he felt convicted, as did his father, that God was calling him to the ministry. To meet the cost of further studies, John Boston apprenticed his son to Alexander Cockburn, a notary in the town. That employment continued for two years. The skills acquired served Boston well in later years, both in study and as clerk of presbytery and synod.

Boston became a student at Edinburgh University in 1691. In addition to Greek and Latin, he studied logic, metaphysics, ethics, and general physics. He studied incessantly and lived on such scanty fare that his physical constitution was permanently weakened. After earning a master's degree in 1694, Boston received the bursary (a grant of financial aid) from the Presbytery of Duns. He spent the autumn in the private study of divinity, then began theological studies at Edinburgh

Covenanters worshipping by the banks of the Whitadder River.

under Dr. George Campbell, who occupied the theological chair.[6] Boston spent one semester there, then completed his studies under the oversight of his presbytery. During this time, he supported himself as a tutor for one year in the home of Andrew Fletcher, the stepson of Lieutenant Colonel Bruce of Kennet. That year was good preparation for the gospel ministry, as he "kept up family worship, catechized the servants, pressed the careless to secret prayer, reproved and warned against sinful practices, and earnestly endeavored the reformation of the vicious."[7]

Boston was licensed by the Presbytery of Duns and Chirnside on June 15, 1697. His preaching soon attracted attention. Ordinary people appreciated its power and freshness. However, Boston did not immediately settle in a parish because, though the people would have called him, the real power to do so was in the hands of the principal heritor, or landlord. In seven parishes where people would have chosen Boston, the landlord intervened to prevent it. He thus remained a probationer for more than two years. Finally, in 1699, the landlord and people of Simprin, Berwickshire, a small parish eight miles southeast of Duns, agreed to call Boston. Prior to being ordained, Boston renewed his covenant with God, confessing that he was "utterly lost and undone" in himself, stood in "absolute need of a Savior," and "cordially received Him in all His offices, consenting to the terms of the covenant."

Pastorates in Simprin and Ettrick

Thomas Boston's ministry at Simprin was challenging. The people of his congregation were largely ignorant of spiritual truth and needed to be instructed in the simplest things. They were primarily concerned with making a living rather than their souls. Boston was dismayed to learn that only one household observed family worship. Furthermore, the Lord's Supper had not been administered for several years because of general indifference to spiritual things.[8]

Within one year, Boston had reorganized his little flock. He reestablished two services on the Sabbath. He lectured on a chapter of the Bible in the morning and preached more freely in the afternoon. In the evening, Boston instructed people in the Shorter Catechism or on sermons preached that day. The young pastor learned much from questioning his people; it taught him about the needs of his flock and how to meet them.

He set apart Tuesday evening for prayer and praise. Every Thursday he conducted public worship. He regarded pastoral visitation as an integral part of his ministry and only laid it aside when his health failed

Thomas Boston

him. He spoke intimately with his people on those visits, urging the unconcerned to "close with Christ."

Personal organization was essential to the ministry, Boston believed, so he rose early each Monday morning and devoted hours to prayer and reflection. He was also a man of deep prayer throughout the week. On nearly every page of his autobiography, Boston refers to laying one matter or another before the Lord in prayer. He also established regular times for fasting as he strove for a life of habitual communion with God. "When his congregation saw him enter the pulpit on the morning of the Lord's day, they knew that they were looking into the face of one who had just come forth from intimate communion with God, and who at once was God's ambassador and their friend," wrote Thomson.[9]

Boston was hard on himself spiritually. A typical entry in his *Memoir* reads like this: "Having allotted the morning entirely for prayer and meditation, some worldly thoughts crept in…. In the afternoon I somewhat recovered my forenoon's loss."[10] Such entries are often followed by seasons of fasting, intense self-scrutiny, and passionate tears. "Oh, how my heart hates my heart!" he groaned.[11]

Boston remained an arduous student of theology and languages, though his library was modest. It contained less than 200 volumes at the time of his death, all of which were well-read and well-digested. [12] In addition to the classical languages, Boston mastered French and Dutch. To compare translations, he often read *De Staten Bijbel*—the Dutch Bible translation made by order of the Dutch parliament, the States General, in response to the decision of the Synod of Dort, 1618-19, and furnished with a renowned apparatus of explanatory glosses, notes, and cross references.

Boston's pastoral work, always performed with intense earnestness, bore fruit.[13] His flock grew until the church was unable to accommodate crowds, especially at communion seasons. After seven and one-half years of work there, not a single church family neglected family worship. Boston could write, "Simprin! O blessed be he for his kindness at Simprin.... I will ever remember Simprin as a field which the Lord had blessed."

When a call came from Ettrick, the low physical and spiritual condition there overcame Boston's reluctance to leave Simprin. When Boston arrived in Ettrick, the town had less than 400 people. The roads were nearly impassable. The parsonage was dilapidated. Church services were irregular. When a service was held, the people often talked throughout it. Spiritual barrenness, pride, deceit, swearing, and fornication abounded.

Boston had to rebuild and reorganize his parish. The first ten years were difficult. After eight years, he told his wife, "My heart is alienated from this place." Yet he couldn't leave.

Gradually, the Spirit began to bless Boston's work. His preaching affected increasing numbers of people. After one of his sermons was published, people in Edinburgh began to take notice. Visitors became common in the church. Ettrick finally became convinced that it had a pastor of note. When Boston received a call to Closeburn in 1716, the session at Ettrick called for a congregational fast. That proved to be the turning point for Boston's ministry. For the next sixteen years, he labored with new authority.[14]

At both Simprin and Ettrick, Boston was cautious in administering the Lord's Supper because of people's weak spiritual condition. He waited more than three years at Ettrick, then privately interviewed each candidate before recommending whether that person should partake of the Lord's Supper. The first communion had fifty-seven participants; however, by the time Boston last celebrated it in 1731, there were 777 communicants—which, to his joy, included all four of his surviving children.[15]

God sanctified heavy domestic trials in Boston's life. He lost his mother at age fifteen and his father a decade later, shortly after settling in Simprin. While in Simprin, Boston married Catherine Brown, the fifth daughter of Robert Brown of Barhill, Clackmannan, in whom Boston saw "sparkles of grace."[16] Boston considered his marriage a gift of the Lord, even though his wife suffered repeated bouts of acute depression and insanity. From 1720 on, she was often confined to an apartment called "the inner prison," where she spent months and years without relief, "an easy target for Satan's onslaughts, both concerning her assurance of salvation and her peace with God."[17] He also had to bury six of ten children, two while in Simprin and four at Ettrick. Then, too, Boston himself was often ill, suffering acute pain and weakness.

Though Boston groaned under all these domestic trials, he viewed them as coming from his heavenly Father's loving hand of discipline. That's why he could continue to describe his wife in glowing terms as "a woman of great worth, whom I therefore passionately loved, and inwardly honoured: a stately, beautiful, and comely personage, truly pious, and fearing the Lord,... patient in our common tribulations, and under her personal distresses."[18] He wrote to William Hog in Edinburgh, "It is a very sweet view of affliction, to view it as the discipline of the covenant; and so it is indeed; and nothing else to the children of our Father's family. In that respect it is medicinal; it shines with many gracious purposes about it; and, end as it will, one may have the confidence of faith, that it shall end well."[19] Boston felt that God's gracious purposes included "more heavenliness in the frame of my heart, more contempt of the world, more carefulness to walk with God, and more resolution for the Lord's work over the belly of difficulties."

Though able as a linguist, thorough as a theologian, and influential as an author, Boston never sought the limelight. He never taught in a university, yet his books and numerous published sermons expounded the basics of Christian theology. *An Illustration of the Doctrines of the Christian Religion,* his commentary on the Westminster Shorter Catechism, is a body of divinity in itself, giving one of the best systematic expositions of the catechism ever published. His *Human Nature in Its Fourfold State,* published in Edinburgh in 1720, traces the human condition through four states: man's original state of righteousness or innocence, man in the state of nature as a fallen creature, man in the state of grace as a redeemed and regenerated being, and finally, man in the eternal state, be it heaven or hell.

Philip G. Ryken refers to Boston as "a preacher to his dying day."[20] His entire life revolved around developing vigorous theological preaching with pointed application. His goals in preaching were to assure the regenerate of their salvation in Christ and to see the unregenerate converted to Christ.[21] To reach those goals, he preached a theology of grace: "grace in its sovereignty; grace in its freeness, offered to all without money and without price; grace in its fullness, pardoning, adopting, sanctifying, glorifying; grace in its simplicity, without works of law; grace in its security, ratified by an everlasting covenant; grace in its appointed channels, coming mainly through word and ordinance; grace in its practical fruit," wrote William G. Blaikie.[22]

Boston's last sermons, preached from 2 Corinthians 13:5 on the first two Sabbaths of April 1732, were on self-examination—typical of his preaching as well as his life as a pastor. He died at age fifty-six on May 20, 1732.

Theological Controversies

Boston was a reluctant participant in the theological controversies of his day.[23] Nevertheless, he was compelled at times to defend the truth. On different occasions he preached against the errors of the Cameronians, who willingly separated themselves from the body of other Christians.[24] In his sermon "The Evil and Danger of Schism," Boston pleaded for Christians to emulate Christ, who attended both temple and synagogue in spite of the corruptions of the day.

Boston refused to sign the Abjuration Oath, by which officers of church and state, and others, were required to abjure or renounce any claim of the Stuart pretender, James, to the British throne. The oath also reaffirmed previous acts of Parliament requiring that the reigning sovereign belong to the Church of England, and was therefore seen as an endorsement of episcopacy, or the government of the church by bishops. This prompted Boston to anonymously publish his pamphlet, *Reasons for refusing the Abjuration Oath in its latest form.*

The conflict that consumed most of Boston's time was the Marrow Controversy (1717-1723). Though this controversy will be dealt with in greater depth in the next chapter of this book, the basics of the debate in relation to Thomas Boston need to be mentioned here as well. The Marrow Controversy brought to a head differences between parties representing two strains, the legal and the evangelical, in Scottish theology.[25] The legal strain, led by Principal James Hadow (1670-1747) of St. Andrews,[26] sought to discredit the "antinomian" teachings of *The Marrow of Modern Divinity,* a book reputed to have been written by Edward Fisher[27] in 1645, which included extracts from the works of standard Reformed and Puritan writers. The evangelicals, or "Marrowmen," sought to correct the legalistic tendency in Scottish preaching by emphasizing God's free offer of grace and Christ's meritorious work for the sinner.

Tension grew as the General Assembly of the Church of Scotland debated the action of the Auchterarder presbytery. This presbytery, concerned for the doctrine of free grace, required students applying for license to adhere to certain propositions, known as the "Auchterarder Creed." One section read: "I believe that it is not sound and orthodox to teach that we must forsake our sins in order to our coming to Christ."[28] Boston saw these words as a muddled attempt to *defend* free grace rather than to promote antinomianism, but the Assembly rejected the proposition. Boston regarded the decision as a direct blow to the doctrine of free grace, and felt that it denied that saving faith precedes repentance in the Spirit's work of salvation.

Into this fray came the new edition of the *Marrow,* printed by James Hog (1658-1734), minister of Carnock in Fife.[29] It was immediately assailed by its opponents but well received by its adherents. Its wealth of paradoxical statements moved Principal Hadow, Alan Logan, and Robert Wodrow to proceed against it. They succeeded in convincing the General Assembly of 1720 that it taught universal atonement, that assurance is of the essence of faith, that holiness is not implicit in salvation, and that the believer is not under the law as a moral rule for life.

At the Assembly of 1721, the Marrowmen countered with a document titled "The Representation," which argued against the condemnation of the *Marrow* and the prohibition imposed on ministers that forbade them to circulate anything in its favor. The document was rejected and the Marrowmen rebuked. Boston wrote in his diary, "I received the rebuke and admonition as an ornament put upon me for the cause of truth."

Boston served as clerk of the Synod of Merse and Teviotdale and attended the General Assembly when needed. In 1728, he attracted attention when he stood during the Assembly to protest its leniency to John Simson, stating that Simson deserved deposition rather than a brief suspension. Simson, Professor of Divinity in the University of Glasgow, had been implicated in two heresy trials; the first (1715-1717) involved charges of Arminianism, and the second (1727-1729), charges of Arianism. Simson's family connections and friends shielded him from higher censure. Though he was permanently suspended in 1729, he remained on the Glasgow faculty until his death in 1740.

The growing hostility between legalists (known as "moderates") and evangelicals led to irreparable breaches in the Scottish church. In 1733, one year after Boston's death, most of the Marrowmen left the Church of Scotland to join the Associate Presbytery, giving birth to the Secession Church.

The Federal Theology of Thomas Boston

Thomas Boston was essentially a parish minister, but he was also a theologian. Perhaps his most significant contribution to theology was his clarification of the covenantal or "federal" (from the Latin *foedus*, meaning "covenant") theology of the Westminster Standards.[30] We shall briefly consider Boston's view of the covenants and the offer of the gospel.

The Covenant of Works
Boston's treatises on the covenants of works and of grace were written as correctives to the Pelagian and Arminian errors of his day.[31] Proper understanding of the two covenants is necessary because of their role in man's salvation, Boston said. The first covenant shows our lost estate in Adam and the second offers the remedy in Jesus Christ.

Boston said that the covenant of works is a prerequisite for a right understanding of Adam's federal headship, and thus the imputation of Adam's sin through disobedience. If the covenant of works is discarded as fictitious, as some covenant theologians maintain, then the imputation of Adam's sin to posterity is fictitious as well, since Adam would have ceased to be a proper federal head.[32] Boston writes, "If the covenant made with Adam was not a proper covenant [of works], he could not be a proper representing head; and if he was not, then there cannot be a proper imputation of Adam's sin unto his posterity." Boston is careful, however, to insist that God could have required absolute obedience from Adam without a covenant.[33] The emphasis here is on God's condescension (Confession of Faith, VII.I), not any obligation on God's part to enter into a covenant.

According to Boston, the covenant God made with Adam in the Garden of Eden was a trial of a *definite* length; for, "this state could not have been forever, without rendering the promise of life fruitless."[34] Two parties were involved in the covenant: the triune God as one party, and man, federally represented by Adam, as the other. God covenanted not only with Adam personally, but with all mankind in Adam. As Boston says, Adam covenanted "not only for himself, but for all his posterity, as the natural father of all, of whose one blood nations of men were to be made."[35]

The condition of the covenant was perfect obedience. For Boston, there were *moral* and *symbolical* aspects required of Adam. This moral law, according to Boston, included all of the Ten Commandments, for though they were not yet written on tablets of stone, they were written on Adam's heart.[36] The symbolic law consisted of the command not to eat of the tree of the knowledge of good and evil. The tree was neutral, but the act of eating was an act of disobedience; therefore, it was a law to try Adam's heart to see whether he would obey God.

The life promised to Adam for obedience, Boston says, was a holy and happy estate "beyond the hazard or possibility of sinning, or forfeiting it."[37] He adds, "After the time of his trial was over, he [Adam] would have been transported, soul and body, into the heavenly places, there to abide forever."[38]

Like other covenant theologians of his era, Boston speaks of signs and seals of the covenant. The tree of the knowledge of good and evil and the tree of life are two signs of the covenant.[39] They are signs because they point to the reality of the covenant.

Adam transgressed the covenant of works, however, thus putting all of his posterity into a state of spiritual death. The demands of the covenant of works are still binding upon man. Thus, all human beings are under the obligation of perfect obedience to the law, although they are unable to meet it. The only remedy is for man to be brought into the covenant of grace.

The Covenant of Grace

The first work of Boston to be published after his death was *A View of the Covenant of Grace* (published in 1734), in which he explains the doctrine of God's gracious covenant with man. The covenant of grace is intended only for the elect, and refers to God's response to man's breach of the covenant of works. He uses the terms "covenant of redemption" and "covenant of grace" to name the two sides of the covenant.[40] Boston did not believe the covenant of redemption was separate from the covenant of grace, or "a covenant within the covenant," as some theologians had taught. As with the covenant of works, there are two parties to this covenant: God the Father, representing the offended party, and Christ, the second (or last) Adam, representing the elect.

The covenant of grace was established in eternity, Boston says, in the council of the Trinity. The plan and the objects of salvation were settled before man was created. The Persons of the Godhead have different roles in the plan of salvation. All three Persons of the glorious Trinity are at work: the Father elects, or chooses, the objects of salvation; the Son redeems them; and the Spirit sanctifies them, applying redemption to them.

Christ is the representative head of His seed in the same way that Adam was of his seed, Boston says. The conditions of the covenant between the Father and the Son are the *principal* required in the first covenant—perfect obedience—and the *penalty* of Adam's disobedience to be paid in Christ. Thus, the second Adam entered into covenant with God on behalf of His elect; He stood where the first Adam stood but succeeded where the first Adam failed. Therefore, says Boston, the covenant for Christ's seed is *absolute* and not *conditional*, because the efficacy of the covenant rests in Christ's role, which He fulfilled.

What of the reprobate who are outside of God's gracious covenant with the elect? Boston says they have as good a warrant to take hold of the gospel as the elect and will in no wise be excused from everlasting punishment for their failure to do so. This deals more directly with Boston's concept of the offer of grace, more commonly known as the free offer of the gospel.

The Free Offer of the Gospel

In the last section of his treatise on the covenant of grace, Boston explains how sinners become part of that covenant. Most people are strangers to the covenant of grace and have no saving interest in Christ, Boston says, but we are called to offer the gospel of reconciliation to them. We indeed must endeavor to compel sinners to enter the covenant of grace. As support, Boston cites Luke 14:23, "Go out into the highways and hedges, and compel them to come in, that my house may be filled."

Our presentation of the gospel must be strictly covenantal, Boston says. We are to proclaim that there is a covenant between God and Christ, made for sinners of Adam's race ("mankind sinners"). It fully provides for salvation, for restoration of the sinner, and for happiness after a broken covenant of works.

Two things are necessary for entering a gracious state: the faith of the law prior to one's entrance into grace and the faith of the gospel by which one enters. According to Boston (and many Puritans), "faith of the law" is prerequisite to receiving Christ. Boston writes, "Whosoever…would enter into the covenant of grace, must in the first place have a faith of the law: for which cause, it is necessary, that the law as well as the gospel be preached unto sinners."[41] Accordingly, sinners must be uncovered, for by nature they hide in the deceits of their sin. Through the preaching of the law, Boston says, a sinner experiences three things: first, he comes to see himself as a sinner, whereas before he was righteous in his own eyes; second, he sees himself as a lost sinner; which, third, leads to believing he is utterly unable to attain a state of grace. Any form of evangelism that bypasses the law is a deterrent to true conversion.

"Faith of the gospel," on the other hand, is synonymous with saving faith, in which one takes hold of Christ. Saving faith has four components: first, faith in Christ's sufficiency, by which the sinner believes that Christ is fully able to save men from their sins; second, faith in the gospel offer, by which the sinner believes that Christ is offered to sinners such as himself; third, faith in one's right to Christ, whereby one is encouraged to go to Christ; and fourth, faith for salvation, whereby one appropriates Christ as his or her personal Savior. These different "faiths," as Boston calls them, are simply descriptions of a sinner's experience of salvation. The more one understands the operations of the Spirit in conversion, the more he is encouraged to discern those operations in his heart, and thus to embrace Christ as "a deed of gift and grant."

Additional Writings of Thomas Boston

Boston's *Memoirs,* published in 1776 by his grandson, Michael Boston, as *Memoirs of the Life, Time and Writings*, consist of two accounts written for Boston's posterity: *A General Account of My Life* and *Passages of My Life.* It remains the primary source of information about Boston's life and is based, as William Blaikie wrote, "on a faith in the particular providence of God, in the intimacy of His fellowship with His children, and in the closeness of the connection between their spiritual and their natural life, the like of which perhaps no man of equal intellectual power ever attained."[42]

Boston's most influential work, *Human Nature in its Fourfold State,* first published in 1720, consists of sermons preached at Simprin and amplified at Ettrick. A second, revised edition of this work appeared in 1729. *The Fourfold State* has been printed more than one hundred times and translated into several languages, including Gaelic and Welsh. John MacLeod wrote of it, "There is no book of practical divinity, not even William Guthrie's *Trial of Saving Interest in Christ,* nor Rutherford's *Letters,* that was more read in the godly homes of Scotland than this treatise. It did more to mold the thought of his countrymen than anything except the Westminster Shorter Catechism. It is of this work that Jonathan Edwards says that it 'showed Mr. Boston to have been a truly great divine.'"[43]

In the final months of his life, Boston completed *The Crook in the Lot,* subtitled, "The Sovereignty and Wisdom of God in the Afflictions of Men, together with a Christian Deportment under them." In this volume, Boston offers insight into a believer's conduct under pressing circumstances. The three themes of the book are: first, whatever crook there is in one's lot, it is of God's doing; second, whatever God mars, no one will be able to mend; and third, seeing the crook in one's lot as the work of God is the only way to true contentment.

Boston's *Soliloquy on the Art of Man-fishing* was written as a series of personal meditations. He was deeply impressed by Matthew 4:19, "Follow me and I will make you fishers of men." *Soliloquy* was first published in 1773, forty-three years after Boston's death.

Though Boston initially found the Hebrew language uninteresting, he later devoted much study to the accents in the text of the Hebrew Scriptures, calling it his "darling study." He came to believe that the accents were key to the Hebrew text and were themselves of divine inspiration. He completed a treatise on the subject and translated it into Latin. Published after his death as *Tractatus Stigmologicus, Hebraeo-Biblicus,* the book was embraced by many. With the insight he gained from his study of Hebrew, Boston prepared a translation and commentary on Genesis, but they were never published.

Boston's works were first collected and published in 1767, and later reprinted in 1773. *The Complete Works,* edited by Samuel McMillan and published in twelve volumes in 1853, were reprinted by Richard Owen Roberts in the twentieth century and by Tentmaker Publications in the twenty-first. "Rabbi" John Duncan wrote that "Thomas Boston was a common place genius—not a common place man but a common place genius," and someone else said that Boston did more "to fan the flame of true piety in Scotland than that of any other single minister in his generation."[44]

May God raise up servants in this third millennium of the Christian era motivated by that which made Boston such an effective ambassador of Christ: a humble spirituality, a high view of the Christian ministry, a compassionate zeal for souls, and unwearied preaching of Christ.

[1] *Thomas Boston of Ettrick: His Life and Times* (London: T. Nelson and Sons, 1895), 12.

[2] Nigel M. de S. Cameron, ed., *Dictionary of Scottish Church History and Theology* (Downers Grove, Ill.: InterVarsity Press, 1993), 88.

[3] Henry Erskine (1624-96) was ejected from the parish of Cornhill in Northumberland, England, by the Act of Uniformity in 1662. He then returned to his native Dryburgh in Scotland's Berwickshire. After the Revolution of 1688, he preached in the border parish of Whitsome, where Boston heard him for the first time. Cf. Joel R. Beeke, "Introduction," in *The Beauties of Ebenzer Erskine*, ed. Samuel McMillan (Grand Rapids: Reformation Heritage Books, 2001), i-ii.

[4] *Memoirs of the Life, Time and Writings of Mr. Thomas Boston* (London: Oliphant Anderson & Ferrier, 1899), 8.

[5] Ibid., 10.

[6] George Campbell (1635-1701), Professor of Divinity in the University of Edinburgh, "taught a large portion of the first generation ministers in the post-Revolution Church of Scotland" (*Dictionary of Scottish Church History and Theology*, 107).

[7] *Memoirs*, 25.

[8] Jean Watson, *The Pastor of Ettrick: Thomas Boston* (Edinburgh: James Gemmell, 1883), 34-45.

[9] *Thomas Boston of Ettrick*, 173. Cf. William Addison, *The Life and Writings of Thomas Boston of Ettrick* (Edinburgh: Oliver and Boyd, 1936).

[10] *Memoirs*, 97.

[11] Cited in D. J. Innes, "Thomas Boston of Ettrick," in *Faith and a Good Conscience* (London: Puritan and Reformed Conference, 1962), 36.

[12] For a list of Boston's library, see Philip Graham Ryken, *Thomas Boston as Preacher of the Fourfold State* (Carlisle: Paternoster Publishing, 1999), 312-19. Approximately one third of Boston's library consisted of Puritan literature.

[13] For Boston as a practitioner of pastoral care, see Stephen Albert Woodruff III, "The Pastoral Ministry in the Church of Scotland in the Eighteenth Century, with Special Reference to Thomas Boston, John Willison, and John Erskine" (Ph.D. dissertation, University of Edinburgh, 1966).

[14] Donald Macmillan, *Representative Men of the Scottish Church* (Edinburgh: T. & T. Clark, 1928), 106-107.

[15] John R. de la Haye, "Thomas Boston: At the Borders of Glory," *Banner of Truth* No. 431 (Aug-Sep, 1999):18.

[16] George H. Morrison, "Biographical Introduction," in Thomas Boston, *Human Nature in its Fourfold State* (London: Banner of Truth Trust, 1964), 14-15.

[17] For Catherine Boston's trials, see Faith Cook's *Singing in the Fire* (Edinburgh: Banner of Truth Trust, 1995), 122-31; Maureen Bradley, "A Brief Memorial of Thomas Boston," in Thomas Boston, *The Crook in the Lot* (Morgan, Pa.: Soli Deo Gloria, 2000), viii-ix.

[18] Cook, *Singing in the Fire*, 122.

[19] *Memoirs*, 499.

[20] Ryken, *Thomas Boston as Preacher of the Fourfold State*, 1.

[21] Ibid., 178.

[22] *The Preachers of Scotland: From the Sixth to the Nineteenth Century* (Edinburgh: Banner of Truth Trust, 2001), 201-202.

[23] *Dictionary of Scottish Church History and Theology*, 88.

[24] The Cameronians largely consisted of Covenanters in the southwest of Scotland

who attended the ministries of Donald Cargill, Richard Cameron (from whom their name is derived), and Patrick Walker. Cf. P. Walker, *Six Saints of the Covenant,* ed. D. Hay Fleming (London: Hodder and Stoughton, 1901), I:218-36.

[25] See John Macleod, *Scottish Theology* (London: Banner of Truth Trust, 1974), 139-66; John J. Murray, "The Marrow Controversy: Thomas Boston and the Free Offer," in *Preaching and Revival* (London: Westminster/Puritan Conference, 1984), 34-56; David C. Lachman, *The Marrow Controversy, 1718-1723: An Historical and Theological Analysis* (Edinburgh: Rutherford House, 1988); Thomas F. Torrance, *Scottish Theology from John Knox to John McLeod Campbell* (Edinburgh: T. & T. Clark, 1996), 204-220; A.T.B. McGowan, *The Federal Theology of Thomas Boston* (Carlisle, U.K.: Paternoster, 1997).

[26] Hadow, Professor of Divinity and Principal of St. Mary's College, sought to defend "orthodox" Scottish principles in opposing the *Marrow* (*Dictionary of National Biography* 23:437).

[27] When the *Marrow* was first published in 1645 only the author's initials E.F. appeared on the title page. Samuel Petite, one of several divines who added his testimony to the book, was the first to add a surname to the initials, saying, "God has endowed his Fisher with a net of trying understanding" (D.M. McIntyre, "First Strictures on the Marrow of Modern Divinity," *Evangelical Quarterly*, 10 [1938]: 61). Anthony à Wood mistakenly identifies the author as a gentleman commoner of Brazenose College, whereas the Edward Fisher who wrote the *Marrow* was probably a member of the guild of Barber Surgeons, who was converted through a conversation with Thomas Hooker (ibid., 64).

[28] When William Craig, applying for licensure in Auchterarder Presbytery in 1717, hesitated to assent to the Auchterarder propositions, the Presbytery licensed him but declined to give him an extract of the license. Craig's appeal to the General Assembly was successful, and the Assembly forbade the Auchterarder Presbytery to ask questions of candidates other than those prescribed by the General Assembly.

[29] Hog wrote a preface to his 1717 edition of the *Marrow*, which embroiled him for the rest of his life in the controversy. He engaged in several pamphlet wars between Hadow and James Adams of Kinnaird prior to the General Assembly's condemnation of the *Marrow* in 1720.

[30] Donald Jay Bruggink argues incorrectly that Boston's striving for a theology of grace was incompatible with what he views as "the legalistic federal theology of the Westminster Standards" ("The Theology of Thomas Boston, 1676-1732" [Ph.D. dissertation, University of Edinburgh, 1958], 84, 138).

[31] This is the view promoted by Boston's grandson, Michael Boston, in his introduction to the 1798 edition of *A View of the Covenant of Works*.

[32] The most notable example in Boston's day was Professor John Simson, whom Boston mentions in his treatise along with the Arminians. Two modern day examples are Herman Hoeksema and John Murray.

[33] *The Complete Works of Thomas Boston,* 11:181.

[34] Ibid., 1:232.

[35] Ibid., 1:230.

[36] Boston believed that the law given at Mount Sinai was a *renewal* of the covenant of works rather than the *instigation* of it. See ibid., 11:181-2.

[37] Ibid., 1:233.

[38] Ibid.

[39] The covenant theologian, Herman Witsius (1636-1708), taught there were four signs—the tree of the knowledge of good and evil, the tree of life, the Garden of Eden, and the Sabbath (*Economy of the Covenants* [London: Thomas Tegg & Son, 1838], 1:81.

[40] Boston wrote, "The covenant of redemption and the covenant of grace, are not two distinct covenants, but one and the same covenant. I know that many divines do express themselves otherwise in this matter; and that upon very different views, some of which are no ways injurious to the doctrine of free grace" (*The Complete Works of Thomas Boston,* 8:396-97).

[41] Ibid., 8:582.

[42] *The Preachers of Scotland,* 197.

[43] *Scottish Theology,* 146.

[44] In Thomas Boston, *A Soliloquy on the Art of Man-Fishing* (London: Alexander Gardner, 1900), 7.

11

The Lives of Ebenezer and Ralph Erskine: Dissenters with a Cause

"Sir, you have never heard the gospel in its majesty," said Adam Gib to a young minister who had never heard Ebenezer Erskine preach. Ebenezer Erskine and his younger brother, Ralph, were great eighteenth-century Scottish preachers. God used them to bring hundreds of people to conversion and thousands more to spiritual maturity through their lives, ministries, sermons, and writings.

I aim to show in two chapters that the Erskines have many lessons to teach the contemporary church. This chapter is biographical and historical, showing that the Erskines were dissenters with a cause. The next chapter is homiletical and theological, showing that the Erskines were preachers who focused on the promises of God.

Early Life and Ministry

Ebenezer Erskine was born in Dryburgh, Scotland, in 1680. Five years later, his brother, Ralph, was born in Monilaws, near Cornhill, Northumberland, the northernmost county of England. Their father, Henry, was a Puritan minister who had been forced to vacate his home and pastorate in Cornhill in 1662 by the Act of Uniformity. Their mother was Margaret Halcro, Henry Erskine's second wife. Both parents were of prestigious background and closely related to Scottish nobility.

The lives of the young boys were disrupted when their father refused to renounce the Solemn League and Covenant. The Scottish Assembly despised the preacher's Puritan principles. When Ebenezer was two years old, his father was arrested and sentenced to imprisonment on the Bass Rock for exercising his ministerial office illegally by "withdrawing from ordinances, keeping conventicles, and being guilty of disorderly baptisms." The Committee of Privy Council questioned Henry Erskine for hours, then finally asked if he would promise not to preach at any more conventicles. Erskine replied, "My lord, I have my commission from Christ, and, though I were within an hour of my death, I durst not lay it down at the feet of any mortal man."

Upon his plea of poor health, Erskine's sentence to Bass Rock was commuted to exile. He and his family moved to England and settled in Parkridge, near Carlisle. From there they went to Monilaws, where Erskine was arrested again and imprisoned for several months for preaching at conventicles. Erskine then preached in the border parish of Whitsome, where he helped lead Thomas Boston to Christ at age eleven. The king's indulgence of 1687 enabled him to continue his ministry without fear of arrest. In 1690, when Ebenezer was age ten and Ralph, five, their father was admitted to the parish of Chirnside, near Berwick, in southeastern Scotland, where he ministered until his death in 1696 at the age of seventy-two.

Ebenezer Erskine studied philosophy and the classics at Edinburgh University, then earned a master's degree in theology in 1697. He served as tutor and chaplain to the God-fearing family of the Earl of Rothes until he was licensed in 1703 by the Presbytery of Kirkcaldy and ordained to Portmoak, near Kinross, where he would minister for the next twenty-eight years. That same year, he married Alison Turpie, a God-fearing woman who had a profound spiritual influence on him.

Erskine's first years at Portmoak were difficult, mostly due to a spiritual battle that he had with himself after overhearing a conversation on the "deep things of God" between Ralph and his wife. The discussion convinced Ebenezer that he was not yet converted. After a year of spiritual struggle, he finally began to experience what he called "the true grace of God." In the summer of 1708, Erskine wrote in his voluminous diary that he finally "got his head out of Time into Eternity." On August 26, he said that God had "brought my heart to give a consent to him" and that he was now sure that God could never "deny his own covenant" with him. In turn, Erskine made a covenant with God. He wrote:

> Lord, if I have done iniquity, I am resolved through thy grace to do so no more. I flee for shelter to the blood of Jesus and his everlasting righteousness; for this is pleasing unto thee. I offer myself up, soul and body, unto God the Father, Son, and Holy Ghost. I offer myself unto Christ the Lord, as an object proper for all his offices to be exercised upon. I choose him as my prophet for instruction, illumination, and direction. I embrace him as my great priest, to be washed and justified by his blood and righteousness. I embrace him as my king to reign and rule within me. I take a whole Christ with all his laws, and all his crosses and afflic-

tions. I will live to him; I will die to him; I will quit with all I have in the world for his cause and truth.

Life Transformed

Erskine's encounter with God transformed his life and ministry. After that summer of 1708, Erskine's diary entries reveal a man who walked with God, was fully satisfied with Christ, and was deeply humbled by his sinfulness. They show us a man who knew the sanctifying power of Christ's death and who was constantly amazed at the generosity of God's sovereign grace. They show a man steeped in Scripture, immersed in fervent prayer, and fueled by lofty and biblical views of God.

From the time of his conversion, Erskine became more diligent than ever in preparing sermons. His delivery also improved; instead of fixing his attention on a stone in the rear wall of the church, he now looked straight into the eyes of his hearers. "The great desire and ambition of my soul, and that which I desire to aim and level at in all my ministerial work, is to commend Jesus Christ to immortal souls," he wrote.

The results were dramatic. Thousands of people flocked to hear him, coming from as far as sixty miles, particularly during times of Communion. Hundreds of people were converted to Christ. Many members of his congregation began to take notes of his sermons. Erskine sometimes addressed the note-takers publicly as his "scribes."

Early Commitment

Ebenezer's younger brother, Ralph, showed evidence of piety at a very early age. According to the notebooks he kept, Ralph believed the Lord began His saving work within him when he was age eleven and his father died. "Lord, put thy fear in my heart," the young boy wrote. "Let my thoughts be holy, and let me do for thy glory, all that I do. Bless me in my lawful work. Give a good judgment and memory—a belief in Jesus Christ, and an assured token of thy love."

Ralph experienced a profound sense of sin and of deliverance in Christ, as well as remarkable answers to prayer. With this conviction, he made excellent progress at school. He entered Edinburgh University at the age of fifteen to study theology. During his holidays, Ralph stayed with his brother Ebenezer at Portmoak. After earning a master's degree in theology in 1704, Ralph worked for five years as a private chaplain for his relative, Colonel John Erskine. The Colonel had written to Ralph, saying, "I beg earnestly, that the Lord may bless your good designs to my children; and am fully persuaded, that the right impressions that children get of God and the ways of God, when they are young, is a great help to them in life." The Colonel's son, John, would later become a professor of Scots law.

By 1709, Ralph was old enough to be licensed as a preacher, but he felt unworthy of the task. The Colonel did all in his power to persuade him to become licensed. So did his brother, Ebenezer, who had secretly heard Ralph practice preaching. The Dunfermline Presbytery agreed to try Ralph Erskine out, and after a short time its members became convinced that this young man was sent by God to preach the gospel. Erskine was ordained to the second charge in Dunfermline in 1711 and promoted to the first charge in 1716.

After Erskine was settled in Dunfermline, he was overcome by doubts about his Christian witness and calling. He began scouring the works of godly men to find comfort. Thomas Boston's work on the covenant of grace finally brought him relief. After reading Boston, Erskine was able to plead the promises of God and regain peace of heart.

The assurance gleaned from that experience energized his ministry. So intent was Erskine on studying the Word, praying, and preaching that he ignored sleep and worked long into the night. His motto became, "In the Lord have I righteousness and strength." A typical entry in his diary during this time reads like this: "This morning, after reading, I went to prayer, under a sense of my nothingness and naughtiness, vileness and corruption, and acknowledged myself 'a beast before God.' Yet looking to God as an infinite, eternal and unchangeable Spirit, who from everlasting to everlasting is God, and always the same, and who manifests himself in Christ…he allowed me some communion with him in a way of believing, and I was made to cry with tears, 'Lord, I believe, help thou mine unbelief.' I was led, in some suitable manner, under a view of my nothingness, and of God's all-sufficiency, to renounce all confidence in the flesh, and to betake myself solely to the name of the Lord, and there to rest and repose myself."

Fruitful Ministries

Ralph Erskine would serve the Dunfermline congregation for more than forty years until his death in 1752. God mightily blessed that work. Within two years of Erskine's ordination, the Spirit was working so powerfully through his preaching that worshipers filled the church and church yard. A previously dead church came alive. After the evening service, prayer and thanksgiving went on in small groups, sometimes until after midnight. One seeker rose at 2:00 a.m. to pray in secret and found so many people in town on their knees that the countryside hummed like a gigantic hive of bees. Hundreds of penitent sinners were pouring out their hearts to God. The revival proved to be genuine and abiding, though it remained largely confined to Dunfermline.

Ralph Erskine married Margaret Dewer, a gentleman's daughter, in 1714. Margaret was noted for her kindness. She served at Ralph's side for sixteen years, bearing him ten children, five of whom died in infancy. Erskine was shattered by her death at the age of thirty-two. He wrote to a friend: "Her last words expressed the deepest humiliation, and greatest submission to the sovereign will of God, that words could manifest, and thereafter, she concluded all with — 'O death, where is thy sting? O grave, where is thy victory? Thanks be to God who giveth us the victory through Jesus Christ our Lord!' — which she repeated two or three times over. And yet, even at this time, I knew not that they were her dying words, till instantly I perceived the evident symptoms of death; in view whereof I was plunged, as it were, into a sea of confusion, when she, less than an hour after, in a most soft and easy manner, departed this life."

He did not remain alone for long, however. Two years later, he married Margaret Simson of Edinburgh. In June 1732 Erskine wrote, "I was made to bless the Lord for his goodness in providing me a wife whose character was so pleasant and peaceable." He and his wife were greatly blessed as they taught their children of the mercies of God in Christ, but they also experienced sorrow. Three of four sons born to them died in childhood.

While Ralph's ministry was thriving, his brother Ebenezer Erksine was called to a new charge in Stirling (1731), where he would serve for twenty-two years. Andrew Muirhead, who wrote a master's thesis on social and ecclesiastical life in the town of Stirling, concluded that Erskine's "religious impact was great...and permeated every facet of life in Stirling." Hundreds of people from neighboring parishes joined Erskine's congregation. Professions of faith became so numerous and the Lord's Table so crowded in the churches of both Erskines that the brothers began to admonish the people in order to remove the chaff from the wheat. Very little chaff existed, however; most of the converts proved to be genuine, as evidenced by the fruits that their lives brought forth.

The Erskines sometimes served more than thirty tables at Communion. Ralph wrote on July 18, 1734, "There being such a multitude of people, and thirty-three tables, the service was not over at twelve o'clock [midnight,] and I began to preach betwixt twelve and one on that text, 'Behold, thy time was the time of love,' and the congregation was dismissed betwixt one and two in the morning." A year later he administered the Lord's Supper to thirty-eight tables of communicants. The Erskines longed for more fruit on their preaching, however. They grieved over how many of their parishioners remained unconverted, even apathetic. After thirty years of preaching in Dunfermline, Ralph Erskine wrote to his flock: "Where is the fruit that might be expected to follow thirty years of labor? Who has believed our preaching? How few among you were drawn to Christ!" When preaching about the "tabernacle of David that is fallen" (Amos 9:11), Ebenezer Erskine complained, "Oh, what barrenness and unfruitfulness is found under the preaching of the gospel!"

Those whom God greatly blesses He also tries, to keep them humble, or, as Elihu put it, to "hide pride from man" (Job 33:17). The troubles for the Erskines would come in four major waves, beginning in the early 1720s and continuing for more than two decades.

The Marrow Controversy

The first major trial, which became known as the Marrow Controversy, stirred up the Scottish church from 1717 to 1723. The controversy centered on the Auchterarder Creed. In 1717, William Craig, a divinity student, took issue with the General Assembly about one of the propositions that the Presbytery of Auchterarder required all candidates for ordination to sign. The proposition, which was intended as a guard against Arminianism, said: "I believe that it is not sound and orthodox to teach that we must forsake sin in order to our coming to Christ, and instating us in covenant with God." The Assembly sided with Craig, declaring the proposition to be "unsound and most detestable." It also said the statement tended to "encourage sloth in Christians and slacken people's obligation to gospel holiness."

The Assembly's commission somewhat softened the harshness of the General Assembly's pronouncement by stating in its report to the 1718 Assembly that the Presbytery was sound and orthodox in its intent, though the word choice was "unwarrantable" and should not be used again. In the context of that debate, Thomas Boston told John Drummond of Crieff that he had received aid years ago on the disputed issue from a relatively unknown book titled *The Marrow of Modern Divinity,* written in 1645 by Edward Fisher, a Presbyterian from London. Drummond mentioned the book to James Webster of Edinburgh, who told

James Hog of Carnock about it. Hog prefaced a reprinting of the book in 1718.

Fisher's book reflected the orthodox Reformed thought of its time. It emphasized an immediate offer of salvation to sinners who looked to Christ in faith. That was avidly supported by Boston and the Erskines, who were leaders among the church's evangelical minority. Fisher's emphasis, however, raised the opposition of the controlling party of the church, who as neonomians held that the gospel is a "new law" *(neonomos),* replacing the Old Testament law with the legal conditions of faith and repentance that must be met before salvation can be offered. These neomomians, later known as the Moderates, maintained the necessity of forsaking sin before Christ could be received, whereas the Erskines and their evangelical friends said that only union with Christ could empower a sinner to become holy.

The Moderates considered a call to immediate trust in Christ and to full assurance to be dangerously antinomian. James Hadow, of St. Mary's College in St. Andrews, identified a number of supposed antinomian statements in Fisher's book, including one that he thought stated that the believer is not subject to the divine law as a rule of life and another that seemed to suggest that holy living was not essential to salvation. Hadow also said that the book taught that assurance is of the essence of faith, and that the fear of punishment and the hope of reward are not proper motives of a believer's obedience. Finally, Hadow claimed that Fisher's book taught universal atonement because it asserted that Christ's death was "the deed of gift and grant to mankind lost."

Led by Hadow, the church's General Assembly condemned *The Marrow of Modern Divinity* in 1720 and required all ministers of the church to warn their people against reading it. The Erskines, Boston, and nine of their colleagues, known as the Marrowmen or Marrow Brethren for their defense of Fisher's book, protested this action but without avail. They were formally rebuked by the General Assembly in 1722.

The Marrow Controversy quieted down by 1723, but its effects lingered. The Marrow Brethren suffered continuing rejection in the Church of Scotland. They lost many friends and opportunities to move to more important parishes. In 1724, Ebenezer Erskine was a candidate for a call to the first charge in Kirkcaldy, but when people opposed his candidacy because of his participation in the Marrow controversy, the Assembly's commission of 1725 refused to let his name stand. In some presbyteries, approval of Assembly acts against Fisher's book was even made a qualification for ordination.

The Erskines and the other Marrow Brethren continued to teach and write on the doctrines the Assembly had condemned, however. Thomas Boston published his copious notes on *The Marrow of Modern Divinity* in the 1726 edition, and Ralph Erskine wrote several tracts defending Marrow theology. The Marrow Brethren also presented additional formal protests in vain to the Assembly to reverse its judgment on Fisher's book.

The Marrowmen were convinced that the Assembly, in condemning Fisher's book, condemned gospel truth. Doctrinally, the controversy centered around various aspects of the relationship between God's sovereignty and human responsibility in the work of salvation. The Marrow Brethren emphasized God's grace, and the Assembly insisted on what must be done in order to obtain salvation. The Marrow Brethren described the covenant of grace as a testament containing God's promises of grace in Christ, which is freely offered to all. Assurance is found primarily in Christ and His work. A believer's response to this is love and gratitude, they said. Their opponents viewed the covenant as a contract with mutual obligations. The gospel is offered only to the prepared or "sensible" sinner, and assurance focuses on the good works of the believer. Obedience is a response to threats of God's wrath as much as it is to His love.

Theological divisions in the Marrow controversy reflected similar divisions in Reformed thought. The Marrow Brethren were more in harmony with the Reformed orthodoxy of the sixteenth and early seventeenth centuries, codified in the Westminster Confession of Faith and catechisms. Marrow opponents, though representative of the majority of ministers in the early eighteenth-century Church of Scotland, reflected the legalistic tendencies of a part of Reformed theology that developed in the late seventeenth century.

Patronage and Secession

The second major trial that affected the Erskines centered on the issue of patronage. The 1731 Assembly, dealing with an overture "concerning the Method of Planting Vacant Churches," legalized the appointment of ministers by patrons (wealthy landowners) rather than by the vote of church members. Both of the Erskines spoke out against the proposal, arguing strenuously for the right of the people to choose their ministers. Ralph Erskine refused to acquiesce in the settlement of a minister at Kinross against the will of the people, and took an active part in defending the Presbytery before the Commission for having refused to ordain the minister.

The 1732 Assembly reaffirmed support of patronage, even though the majority of presbyteries that responded had problems with it or firmly opposed it. In this, the Assembly violated the so-called Barrier Act of the 1697 Assembly, which protected inferior church courts from the imposition of superior church courts by stating that "before any General Assembly shall pass any Acts which are to be binding [they were] to be remitted to the consideration of the several Presbyteries [and] their opinion and consent reported to the next General Assembly." Furthermore, the 1732 Assembly refused to receive one petition signed by 2,000 people and another signed by forty-two ministers, including the Erskines, against the evils of patronage.

Ebenezer Erskine preached against the 1732 Act when he returned to his own congregation in Stirling. He also preached a strong sermon titled, "The Stone rejected by the Builders, Exalted as the Head-Stone of the Corner," before the Synod of Perth and Stirling, which denounced the evil of patronage and the growing defects in the church in matters of doctrine and government. Erskine drew a parallel between the wicked conduct of the priests and rulers during Christ's earthly ministry and the recent transactions of the General Assembly. Though carefully worded, the sermon roused so much discussion that the Synod voted to rebuke Erskine. Synod took issue with Erskine's statement that "God's promise of guidance is given not to heritors or patrons, but to the Church as the body of Christ."

"As it is a natural privilege of every house or society of men to make the choice of its own servants or officers," Erskine said, "so it is the privilege of the house of God in a particular manner." When the 1733 Assembly supported the rebuke of the Synod, Erskine and three of his colleagues lodged a protest. The Assembly responded by insisting that the four repent of the protest. If they refused to do so, a higher censure would be passed against them.

The Assembly later that year carried out that threat by a majority of one. It suspended Erskine and three other ministers from their parishes, declared their churches vacant, and prohibited them from being employed by any Church of Scotland ministers.

The four ministers (Ebenezer Erskine, James Fisher, Alexander Moncrieff, and William Wilson) met at Gairney Bridge, near Kinross, in December of 1733, where they formed the Associate Presbytery, giving birth to the Scottish Secession Church. They then drafted "A Testimony to the doctrine, worship, government, and discipline of the Church of Scotland," which set forth five reasons for the Secession:

- The prevailing party in the church was pursuing measures that undermined the presbyterian constitution of the church.
- The measures adopted by the majority "do actually corrupt, or have the most direct tendency to corrupt, the doctrine contained in our excellent Confession of Faith."
- "Sinful and unwarrantable terms of ministerial communion are imposed, by restraining ministerial freedom and faithfulness in testifying against the present course of defection and backsliding."
- "These corrupt courses are carried on with a high hand, notwithstanding that the ordinary means have been used to reclaim them, and to stop the current of the present defection."
- The seceding ministers were "excluded from keeping up a proper testimony against the defections and backslidings of the prevailing party, by being denied ministerial communion with them."

Ralph Erskine, who was at the Gairney Bridge meeting, continued to fellowship and correspond with the other ministers, though he did not join the Associate Presbytery at that time. Meantime, his brother, Ebenezer, maintained a major role in the affairs of the Presbytery of the Established Church and carried on his ministerial duties as if no sentence had been passed. Most people in the Presbytery of Stirling responded sympathetically to Ebenezer Erskine and felt alienated from the church courts. Many ministers, including his brother, allowed Ebenezer to preach from their pulpits.

Fathers of the Secession (left to right): Thomas Mair, Ebenezer Erskine, Ralph Erskine, Alexander Moncrieff, James Fisher, William Wilson

In 1734, the General Assembly softened its stand against the suspended ministers. In 1735, it invited Ebenezer Erskine to serve again as moderator of the Presbytery of Stirling. Unfortunately, that was "too little, too late," according to Ebenezer Erskine. After lengthy deliberations, Erskine and his three friends declined to return, stating that none of their grievances had been addressed. Moreover, several parishes had been filled by heritors and patrons over the heads of the people. The main issue for Erskine was the honoring of Christ's sole headship of the church and the sanctity of the relation between pastor and people. Erskine felt that sanctity could only be created by Christ Himself. He differentiated between the established Church of Scotland and the Church *of Christ* in Scotland, stating that "the last is in a great measure driven into the wilderness by the first." When his colleagues pleaded with him to return to the Church of Scotland, he said they would better preserve the Lord's work and testimony if they would leave the church as well.

After much inner conflict, Ralph Erskine formally joined his brother in the Secession. He wrote in his diary on February 16, 1737, "I gave in an adherence to the Secession, explaining what I meant by it. May the Lord pity and lead."

On May 12, 1740, both of the Erskines and their colleagues were deposed by the General Assembly. The Seceders protested that they had not broken from the Church of Scotland, but only from the current prevailing party in the established church.

Most of Ralph Erskine's congregation left the established church with him. "I know not of seven or eight persons, among all the 8,000 examinable people of this parish, but seem to be still satisfied to subject themselves to my ministry in peace," he wrote. For nearly two years, he preached one sermon each Sabbath under a tent and one sermon unmolested by civic authorities in the parish church. A new building seating 2,000 was completed in 1741. In 1742, a new minister was ordained in the parish church, all ties were broken, and several hundred people drifted back to the parish church.

In the end, fourteen of Erskine's twenty-six elders and deacons joined the Secession, five continued in the established church, and seven stayed neutral. Ralph Erskine's church grew quickly, however. He continued to be the leading minister in the community.

Unlike Ralph, Ebenezer Erskine was immediately shut out of his church after he was deposed. Instead of letting his congregation break down the doors, Erskine began preaching outdoors. His congregation grew rapidly in the ensuing months. The Erskines became busier and busier. As they ministered to their own large churches and a variety of other parishes throughout Scotland, the Secession cause grew dramatically, promoting Marrow theology.

The Assembly continued to criticize the Erskines and the Seceders for making justification the goal of faith rather than Christ, and showing disrespect to those placed in authority. The Erskines, in turn, felt that the Assembly mistook anti-Baxterism and anti-neonomianism for antinomianism and showed too much respect for "persons of quality" by endorsing patronage. For the Erskines, both the heart of the gospel and the effectiveness of church government were at stake. Marrow theology became the hallmark of the Secession churches, which continued to grow and exert their influence in Scotland and in the colonies.

Whitefield and the Erskines

The next trial for the Erskines was their quarrel with George Whitefield. In 1739, Ralph Erskine and Whitefield began corresponding after Whitefield spoke of Erskine as "a field preacher of the Scots Church, a noble soldier of Jesus Christ, a burning and shining light who had appeared in the midnight of the Church." The two men highly respected, encouraged, and prayed for one another.

Ralph Erskine proposed that Whitefield visit Scotland and advised him how to proceed with ministry there. He said it would be best to join with the Associate Presbytery; to do otherwise would unduly comfort the Seceders' opponents. Whitefield replied that he could not do that, for he was coming as a visiting preacher to any who would hear him regardless of denominational affiliation.

On July 30, 1741, Whitefield arrived in Dunfermline, and the next day he preached for Ralph Erskine. The two of them then went into Edinburgh, where Whitefield preached at Orphan-house Park and Canongate Church. The following week, Whitefield met with the Associate Presbytery at Dunfermline.

According to Whitefield's account, he and the Presbytery discussed church government and the covenants. Whitefield said that he was not interested in those subjects but only in preaching. Ralph Erskine said Whitefield should be given time to become better acquainted with those subjects since he had been reared in England and was not familiar with them. But others, who were not so charitable, argued that Whitefield should have correct views on church government since every pin in the tabernacle was important. Whitefield became frustrated with the prolonged discussion on church government. He laid his hand on his heart and said, "I do not find it here." Alexander Moncrieff responded, rapping on an open Bible, "But I find it here."

Whitefield asked what the Presbytery wanted him to do. He was told that he didn't have to immediately subscribe to the covenants but only to preach for them until he had further light. "Why preach only for you?" Whitefield asked. Ralph Erskine's answer, according to Whitefield, was "We are the Lord's people." Whitefield then said that if others were the devil's people, he had more need to go to them. The meeting was adjourned.

That account, which hardly flatters Ralph Erskine, was based on misunderstanding. Whitefield apparently attributed to Erskine what was said by someone else. Erskine sought to right the injustice the next Sunday by condemning an opinion he had heard that "none have Christ's image who have not just our image." Moreover, in a letter to Whitefield that Erskine wrote ten days later, he said: "Your refusing a close communing on this head seemed to me so far unlike the disposition which our former correspondence made me think you were of, that I was willing to ascribe it rather to the hurry of temptation for the time, amidst the ringing of bells for sermon, and some rash words uttered in your hearing, than to any contrary bias that now you have got." Erskine went on to express anxiety that Whitefield might gain such a wrong impression of the Secession so as to be lost to them. He also congratulated Whitefield on the welcome he was receiving and on the liberality being shown towards his burden for orphanages.

George Whitefield

Whitefield continued to associate with the ministers of the established church, however, so the break with the Associate Presbytery was inevitable. Both condemned each other. In *Faith No Fancy* and *Fraud and Falsehood Discovered,* Ralph Erskine denounced the Cambuslang Revival and its emotionalism as the devil's work and Whitefield as the devil's agent. Whitefield, in response, accused the Erskines of building a Babel. He wrote to Gilbert Tennent, "The associate brethren are much to be blamed; I never met with such narrow spirits."

Though tension was high for a time, the Erskines and Whitefield later reached a peaceable accord of sorts. Whitefield later wrote in his *Journal,* "I have met and shaken hands with Mr. Ralph Erskine. Oh when will God's people learn war no more!" The following year, when Ralph Erskine died, Whitefield cited him in a sermon as one of "God's triumphant saints."

The Burgher Conflict

The last major trial for the Erskines involved the so-called Burgher conflict. This proved to be more heart-breaking and bitter than any previous dispute. The Burgess Oath of 1744, which endorsed the religion of the realm, was required of all citizens of Edinburgh, Glasgow, and Perth. The oath stated, "Here I protest before God, and your lordships, that I profess, and allow with my heart, the true religion presently professed within this realm, and authorized by the laws thereof: I shall abide thereat, and defend the same to my life's end; renouncing the Roman religion called papistry."

The oath was important because only burgesses were permitted to vote, engage in commerce, or belong to a trade guild. Some members of the Associate Synod (the Seceders) objected to the oath, saying it endorsed practices in the established Church of Scotland that the Seceders had found objectionable. Others, including the Erskine brothers, regarded the oath as an approbation of the Reformed faith, intended only to exclude Roman Catholics from becoming burgesses. The Erskines affirmed the right to take the burgess oath, believing that an antiburgher position would lead to the abandonment of civic and political duty. Ralph Erskine wrote a greater number of pamphlets than any other member of the Burgher Synod in defense of this position.

After three years of synodical meetings, the issue split the young denomination. Twenty-three church leaders of the Antiburgher party, under the leadership of Adam Gib and Alexander Moncrieff, started a new denomination, commonly known as the Antiburgher Synod, avowing that they were the rightful continuation of the Secession. Gib and Moncrieff were godly and conscientious men, but at times they were overly zealous in their conservatism. As one of Moncrieff's children put it, "Father hates everything new except the New Testament."

What made the split particularly heart-breaking for Ralph Erskine was that his son John sided with the Antiburghers and even participated in their Synod's decision to excommunicate the Erskines along with other members of the Burgher Synod. The Antiburgher Synod declared that the Erskines should be "holden by the faithful as heathen men and publicans."

Excommunication prompted Ralph Erskine to do some serious soul-searching, particularly on how the Seceders had behaved toward those left behind in the Church of Scotland. In examining how God must be regarding this new denominational split, Erskine admitted "untenderness towards those we left in the judicatories, when we made secession from them, without dealing more kindly with them, praying more for them, and bearing more with them, especially such as were friends to the same Reformation cause, though not enlightened in the same manner of witnessing for it."

That kind of soul-searching bore fruit. In the years following the controversy, the Burgher Synod redefined its position (in a Revised Testimony), gradually dropped the practice of covenanting, and resumed friendly relations with evangelical ministers in the established church. When John Willison of Dundee was dying, Ralph Erskine was with him. A woman tried to revive the old quarrel by saying there would be no Secession in heaven, but Erskine would have no part of it. "Madam, in heaven there will be a complete Secession—from sin and sorrow," he said. Willison nodded assent.

The Work Goes On

Though they were deeply affected by them, controversies were not a priority for the Erskines. Their work centered on winning souls, and, for a time, on training young ministers. When Alexander Moncrieff joined the Antiburgher Synod, Ebenezer Erskine was asked to teach divinity for the Associate Synod; he served in that capacity only until 1749, when he resigned for health reasons. Ralph Erskine spent more time training men for the ministry. His vision of the ministry is compelling. Typical of his views are the comments he made on Luke 14:23 relative to the evangelistic work of ministers:

Their work is not only driving work, while they preach the law as the schoolmaster to lead to Christ; but it is also drawing work, while they preach the Gospel of Christ, who was lifted up to draw men to Him by His love and grace. Their work is winning work, seeking to win souls to Christ, compelling them to come in; and their work is filling work, that their Master's house may be filled; and that every corner, every seat, every chamber, every story of His house may be filled. As long as the gospel is preached, His house is filling; and as long as there is room in His house, there is work for the minister; his work is never over, so long as His Master's house is empty; compel them to come in, that my house may be filled.

In the autumn of 1752, Ralph Erskine's wife begged him to slow down and to spend more time with the family, for he was now sixty-seven years old. He promised to do so, but in October he became convinced that his work was nearing an end and that he should prepare to depart in peace. The following month he became very ill. His last sermon was on the text, "All her paths are peace." He was so weak that most of his death-bed words were difficult to understand, but people near him heard him say: "I will be forever a debtor to free grace." His final words were unmistakably clear. He shouted for all to hear, "Victory, victory, victory!"

When Ebenezer Erskine heard of his brother's death, he said quietly, "He has twice got the start of me; he was first in Christ, and now he is first in glory."

Ebenezer would soon follow, however. Because of his frail health, Erskine had already ordained his nephew James Fisher as his sucessor in January 1752. The Sunday after his brother's departure, Erskine struggled out of bed to preach his last sermon. His text was, "I know that my Redeemer liveth" (Job 19:25).

Erskine lived eighteen months longer. As death became imminent, one of his elders asked him, "Sir, you have given us many good advices; may I ask what you are now doing with your own soul?" Erskine replied, "I am just doing with it what I did forty years ago; I am resting on that word, 'I am the Lord thy God.'"

When a friend asked him if he, like Samuel Rutherford, was now and then receiving a "blink" (a brief glance from Christ) to bear him up in pain, Erskine said, "I know more of words than blinks. 'Though he slay me, yet will I trust in him.'" He went on to say, "The covenant is my charter. If it had not been for the blessed Word, my hope and strength had perished from the Lord. I have known more of God since I came to this bed than through all my life."

Erskine's last words were to his daughter. When he asked what she was reading, she said, "Your sermon on 'I am the Lord thy God.'"

"Oh," he said, "that is the best sermon ever I preached." With that, he passed into the presence of the Lord his God. He died on June 1, 1754, at the age of seventy-three, after nearly fifty-one faithful years in the ministry and twenty years of guiding town affairs in Stirling.

Lessons for Today

The lives of the Erskines have many lessons for us:

1. The value of cultivating a growing relationship with God. In all the busyness of their ministries, the Erskines didn't forget to seek nourishment for their own spiritual lives. They prayed morning, noon, and evening. Ralph Erskine made it his practice to read a portion of Scripture, often on his knees, before every private prayer. On occasion, he would appoint a special day for prayer or humiliation in his family, keeping his children home from school on those days. The family would pray, talk, and walk together, and he would speak with them about the gospel and the ways of God with His people.

Whatever their faults, the Erskines radiated warm, experiential, Christ-centered Christianity. That was the heartbeat of their ministry. Their diaries affirm that there was no disparity between their personal relationship with God and the message they proclaimed. They lived in obedience to Paul's injunction to Timothy, "Take heed unto thyself and unto the doctrine; continue in them: for in doing this thou shalt both save thyself, and them that hear thee" (1 Tim. 4:16).

Will others also say of us that there is no disparity between our lips and our lives, between the doctrine we profess and the doctrine we act out in our daily lives? Scripture clearly assumes a cause-and-effect relationship between the character of a Christian's life and the fruitfulness of his life. That is particularly true for those of us who are ministers. We as ministers must seek grace to build the house of God with two hands—the hand of sound preaching and doctrine, and the hand of a sanctified heart. The Old School Presbyterians used to say, "Truth is in order to godliness." Our doctrine must direct our life, and our life must adorn our doctrine. We as preachers must live what we preach and teach. As Gardiner Spring wrote, "Our hearts must be transcripts of our sermons."

Ebenezer Erskine once said, "The ministers of the gospel, when dispensing the truths of God, must preach home to their own souls as well as to others; and truly it can never be expected that we should apply the truth with any warmth or liveliness to others unless we make a warm application thereof to our souls. And if we do not feed upon these doctrines, and practice the duties which we deliver to you, though we preach to others, we ourselves are but castaways."

Our sermons will not be dry or insipid if they are infused with the freshness of our own growing relationship with God. Let us never forget that we preach most when we live best. "Our ministry is as our heart is," wrote Thomas Wilson. "No man rises much above the level of his own habitual godliness." John Owen put it negatively: "If a man teach uprightly and walk crookedly, more will fall down in the night of his life than he built in the day of his doctrine."

Perhaps Robert Murray M'Cheyne said it best: "A minister's life is the life of his ministry.... In great measure, according to the purity and perfections of the instrument will be the success. It is not great talents that God blesses so much as likeness to Jesus. A holy minister is an awful weapon in the hand of God."

2. The way Christians should face affliction. The Erskines endured much tribulation before they entered into glory. In addition to the religious controversies that dampened their joy in ministry for twenty-five years, they endured much domestic grief. Ebenezer Erskine buried his first wife when she was thirty-nine; his second wife, three years before his own death. He also lost six of fifteen children. Ralph Erskine buried his first wife when she was thirty-two and nine of thirteen children. The three sons who reached maturity all entered the ministry, but one helped to depose his own father.

The Erskines well understood that God has only one Son without sin but none without affliction. Their diaries are filled with Christ-centered submission in the midst of affliction. Here is what Ebenezer Erskine wrote when his first wife was on her deathbed and he had just buried several children:

> I have had the rod of God laying upon my family by the great distress of a dear wife, on whom the Lord hath laid his hand, and on whom his hand doth still lie heavy. But O that I could proclaim the praises of his free grace, which has paid me a new and undeserved visit this day. He has been with me both in secret and public. I found the sweet smells of the Rose of Sharon, and my soul was refreshed with a new sight of him in the excellency of his person as Immanuel, and in the sufficiency of his everlasting righteousness. My sinking hopes are revived by the sight

of him. My bonds are loosed, and my burdens of affliction made light, when he appears…. "Here am I, let him do to me as seemeth good unto him." If he call me to go down to the swellings of Jordan, why not, if it be his holy will? Only be with me, Lord, and let thy rod and staff comfort me, and then I shall not fear to go through the valley of trouble, yea, through the valley of the shadow of death.

We have much to learn today about learning to live with affliction. We need affliction to humble us (Deut. 8:2), to teach us what sin is (Zeph. 1:12), and to bring us to God (Hosea 5:15). "Affliction is the diamond dust that heaven polishes its jewels with," wrote Robert Leighton. Let us view God's rod of affliction as writing Christ's image more fully upon us so that we may be partakers of His righteousness and holiness (Heb. 12:10-11). Let our afflictions move us to walk by faith and to wean us from the world. As Thomas Watson wrote, "God would have the world hang as a loose tooth which, being twitched away, does not much trouble us." May we, like the Erskines, allow affliction to elevate our souls to heaven and pave our way to glory (2 Cor. 4:7).

If you are a Christian presently undergoing profound trials, don't overestimate those trials. Remember that life is short and eternity is forever. Your days on earth are nearly over. Think more of your coming crown and your eternal communion with the Triune God, saints, and angels. As John Trapp wrote, "He that rides to be crowned need not think much of a rainy day."

You are merely renters here; a mansion awaits you in glory. Don't despair. The Shepherd's rod is held by a fatherly hand of love, not a punitive hand of judgment. Consider Christ in your afflictions—were they not much more than yours, and was not He not wholly innocent? Consider how He perseveres for you, how He prays for you, how He helps you toward the goals He has for you. In the end, He will be glorified through your afflictions.

(3) The importance of Christ's rule over His church. Today, patronage no longer rules in our church circles. But do we really wish Christ to rule in the church? Do we wish for unanimity in our churches in Christ, or is Christ's rule impeded by church politics? Do some congregations exalt their ministers into a position that only Christ should occupy—and don't some ministers enjoy such treatment? Do some elders think they have been called to run the church as they think best without asking what Christ thinks best? And do many people in a congregation vote

for office-bearers according to worldly standards rather than according to the criteria stated by Paul in 1 Timothy 3 and Titus 1?

What about the relationship between the minister and his congregation—isn't it violated by search committees and congregations who seek to fulfill human expectations rather than God's? Are too many churches today disregarding the need for God to send a particular minister to their congregation, even though neither may be initially attracted to each other? Have we lost sight of the supremacy of Christ in calling and sending His ambassadors to whomsoever He will?

(4) The value of conducting regular family visitation, catechetical training, and prayer meetings. It was Ralph Erskine's custom, with a colleague, to visit every home in his parish, which consisted of 5,000 people, once a year for spiritual examination and instruction. He also taught catechism to young children every week and wrote a catechism for their use. The catechism was direct and personal. It began with these questions: "Are you so young that you may not be sick and die?" and "Are you so young that you may not go to hell?" He also encouraged fellowship meetings for prayer and fellowship.

Ebenezer Erskine had the same pastoral concerns as his brother. At Portmoak, he met with the children of the parish each Sunday to instruct them in the catechism as well as the day's sermons. He raised the standards of the parish school and started prayer meetings in various parts of the parish. In 1714, he wrote guidelines for praying societies that all members were expected to observe. During his many pastoral visitations, he began by saying, "Peace be to this house," then proceeded to question the adults about their spiritual condition. He also examined and encouraged the children. Then he closed with warm and affectionate prayer.

Do we who are ministers show such devotion to our flocks? Do we realize the value of habitual family visitation—often called "soul visitation" by our forefathers—to meet individually with members of our congregation? Richard Baxter came to the painful conclusion that "some ignorant persons, who have been so long unprofitable hearers, have got more knowledge and remorse of conscience in half an hour of close [private] disclosure, than they did from ten years of public preaching." Do we keep our hearts and homes open for people who may need such disclosure?

Do we, like the Erskines, use the catechism to examine our parishioners' spiritual condition and to encourage them to flee to Christ? When we teach the young, do we, like the Erskines, explain the fundamental teachings of the Bible and urge young people to commit the Bible to memory? Do we make sermons and the sacraments more understandable to prepare covenant children for confession of faith and to teach them how to defend their faith against error?

Do we encourage our people to meet regularly for prayer? Do we lead them in those meetings, patiently guiding them to deeper levels of prayer and supplication?

Let us carry on our pastoral work patiently, not looking for quick and easy conversions with people. Rather, like the Erskines, we should be committed to build up believers so their hearts, minds, and souls are won to the service of Christ.

5. The importance of Christlike thinking in controversy. Augustine once wrote, "In essentials, unity; in nonessentials, liberty; and in all things, charity." During the Marrow controversy and the patronage controversy, the Erskines defended the gospel heroically, but at times an uncharitable, sectarian attitude crept into that defense.

Surely there was fault on both sides of the Whitefield-Erskine conflict. It was difficult for the Erskines and Seceders, who had developed strong views of church government during their difficult experiences with the Assembly, to tolerate Whitefield's indifference to church government. Whitefield's biographer, Erasmus Middleton, even recognized that in Whitefield. He wrote, "Most certainly, he did not care for all the outward church government in the world, if men were not brought really to the knowledge of God and themselves. Prelacy and presbytery were indeed matters of indifference to a man, who wished 'the whole world to be his diocese' and that men of all denominations might be brought to a real acquaintance with Jesus Christ."

Sadly, in campaigning for their own right to dissent, the Erskines refused Episcopalian dissenters the same right. In denouncing the prevailing evils, the Erskines lost a measure of propriety. At times, their zeal ran ahead of their charity. They certainly failed to distinguish essentials from nonessentials in contributing to the Associate Presbytery's official tract of 138 pages which listed the Church of Scotland's sins in 1744. The tract included the statement: "The sins and provocations of this land are further increased by the kind reception that many, both ministers and people, have given Mr. George Whitefield, a professed member and priest of the superstitious Church of England; and by the great entertainment that has been given to latitudinarian tenets, as propagated by him and others; whereby any particular form of church government is denied to be of divine institution." In the heat of debate, the Erskines forgot John Howe's warning that "the main inlet of all the distractions, confusions and divisions of the Christian world hath been by adding other conditions of Church communion than Christ hath done."

On the other hand, Whitefield showed little tolerance for the difficulties that the Erskines were experiencing in the church. By moving back and forth from Seceder to established church, Whitefield added to the pain of pastors and congregations who had recently separated from each other. The Seceders had been maligned and wounded in the house of friends. They had experienced the profound cost of holding to their principles. They had stood against a disorderly church government that threatened the pure preaching of the Word and had lost much in the process. Whitefield did not comprehend the ecclesiastical battles of the Erskines against the growing evil of Moderatism that was casting spiritual death over the Established Church. In view of that, Whitefield's response lacked compassion and understanding. To his credit, Whitefield acknowledged that the Erskines were more charitable in their opposition to him than most of their colleagues. Whitefield wrote to one of Ebenezer Erskine's sons, "I wish all [the ministers of the Associate Presbytery] were like-minded with your honoured father and uncle; matters then would not be carried on with so high an hand."

When the conflict between the Erskines and Whitefield is viewed in terms of church history, the Erskines represented the Reformers, Puritans, and Covenanters. They emphasized confessional fidelity, purity of worship, and biblical church polity. As true evangelicals, they contended for the true gospel and preached it fervently. At the same time, they believed that the mission of the gospel required a Reformed and biblically faithful church.

George Whitefield shared the Erskines' passion for the gospel. He also held to a Reformed soteriology. He had less interest in the reformation of the church, however. With the Wesleys, he pioneered that characteristic feature of modern evangelicalism, the para-church movement.

The agenda of the Methodists therefore was considerably shorter than that of the Reformers and the Puritans. They too often built their movement around themselves and their personalities. They tended to reduce Christianity to a matter of the personal experience of the new birth and subsequent sanctification.

These men lived and died adhering to the Church of England. As such, they tolerated the kind of doctrinal indifference, prelatism, and ritualistic worship which had been rejected by the Scottish Reformers and resisted so steadfastly by the Covenanters and the Seceders.

The issues that divided the Erskines from Whitefield have not gone away. They have lived on in America and have surfaced repeatedly in movements led by evangelists such as Charles Finney, Dwight Moody, Billy Sunday, and Billy Graham. In each case the question of the reformation of the church has been left unaddressed. In fact, these movements have contributed to the doctrinal confusion and corruption of worship in the churches of our country.

Let us attempt to take the high road in church conflicts—the road of principle that defends *with Christ-like charity* confessional fidelity and purity of worship and polity. It is not Christ-like to see only the worst faults of our opponents. True humility magnifies our own flaws and diminishes the sins of others. Let us pray for love that covers a multitude of evils as we stand for the essentials of the faith.

We must avoid two extremes. The call to unity and charity in Christ should help us avoid the kind of denominationalism produced by splits over nonessential doctrines and egotistic differences. Such splits violate the unity of the body of Christ. As Samuel Rutherford warned, "It is a fearful sin to make a rent and a hole in Christ's mystical body because there is a spot in it." Such discord offends the Father who longs to see His family living in harmony; it offends the Son who died to break down walls of hostility; and it offends the Spirit who dwells within believers to help them live in unity.

On the other hand, we should avoid the kind of unity that a church claims at the expense of her confessions of faith and purity of worship. Some divisions are essential to keep the true church separate from the false. "Division is better than agreement in evil," George Hutcheson once said. Those who support spurious unity by tolerating heresy forget that a split based on biblical essentials helps to preserve the true unity of the body of Christ.

In the final analysis, the Erskines were dissenters with a cause. They challenge us, for the most part, to better things. They challenge us to consider Christ in all our afflictions. They challenge us to crown the Redeemer of the church and to have a high view of the calling of the ministry. They challenge us to pursue intimate acquaintance with God. We would do well to make Ebenezer Erskine's personal covenant our own: "I will live to Christ; I will die to him; I will quit with all I have in the world for his cause and truth." But perhaps most of all, they challenge us to proclaim and live a rich gospel message centered on the promises of God in Jesus Christ. As the next chapter explains, the Erskines were preeminently preachers with a message of promise.

12

Ebenezer and Ralph Erskine:
Preachers With a Message of Promise

When Samuel M'Millan published *The Beauties of Ralph Erskine* in 1812, followed by *The Beauties of Ebenezer Erskine* in 1830, he culled spiritual gems from their Christ-centered sermons. The three volumes of Ebenezer Erskine's sermons, the six volumes of Ralph Erskine's sermons (referenced by volume and page number throughout this chapter), together with Ralph's volume of *Gospel Sonnets,* profoundly influenced ministers and lay people in the Reformed faith in several countries. These sermons deserve to be more influential today, and their recent publication makes this possible.

After showing how influential the preaching and writing of the Erskine brothers have been over the years, I will then offer highlights of their preaching derived from its major paradigm: God's promises in the gospel to sinners.

Influence in Scotland

The preaching and writings of the Erskines affected tens of thousands of people in Scotland for over a century. Their preaching gave direction to the Secession movement. It assimilated and passed on the essence of Marrow theology to subsequent generations. Ebenezer Erskine's *Whole Works,* first printed in Edinburgh in 1761, was reprinted six more times in Scotland. Ralph Erskine's writings, first published in 1764, were reprinted four times in Scotland, and his *Gospel Sonnets* forty times in the eighteenth century. The American preacher William Taylor, a Scot who lectured at Yale in 1886 on the history of Scottish preaching, said that the poems of Ralph Erskine were cited at communion celebrations when he was young. And John Ker wrote in 1887 that the sermons of the Erskines were scattered throughout Scotland "in almost every farm-house and cottage where there was an interest in religion."

The Free Church of Scotland, which started in 1843, was also influenced by the Erskines. George Smeaton, an eminent Free Church

scholar, warmly introduced a reprinting of *The Beauties of Ralph Erskine.*
Robert Candlish, a leading preacher in the Free Church, recommended
reading the Erskines, as did the Free Church minister and theologian
Hugh Martin, who wrote in 1875 that the Erskines were still loved by
the Scottish people.

Influence in England, Wales, and Ireland
In England, men of such stature as George Whitefield, Augustus
Toplady, and James Hervey lauded the Erskines for preaching the gospel
freely without sacrificing experimental depth. Throughout his lifetime
Hervey kept a copy of *Gospel Sonnets* on his desk for study. One of Hervey's last tasks was to dictate a preface to a new edition, in which he
wrote that he had found in his lifetime no human works "more evangelical, more comfortable, or more useful" than those of Ralph Erskine.
A Dutch scholar, P. H. van Harten, who wrote his doctoral dissertation
on the preaching of Ebenezer and Ralph Erskine, said the writings of
the Erskines helped strengthen Reformed thinking in and beyond the
Anglican Church. This chapter leans heavily upon his work. Ralph Erskine's literary works were so treasured that, as late as 1879, they were
still the best-selling religious books in London.

Many of the sermons of the Erskines, as well as the *Gospel Sonnets,*
were translated into Welsh. Those writings helped shape the preaching
of two eighteenth-century Welsh preachers, Howell Harris and Daniel
Rowland, whose messages were instrumental in the conversion of thousands. The Methodists in Wales "read, borrowed, translated, used and
commended the Erskine brothers," wrote Eifion Evans. The Erskines
influenced people in Ireland as well, particularly through the ministries
of John Erskine, Ralph Erskine's son, and James Fisher, Ebenezer Erskine's son-in-law, who both labored there for some years.

Influence in the Netherlands and America
From 1740 on, the writings of the Erskines were translated into Dutch
and received a ready reception throughout the Netherlands. On a typi-
cal eighteenth-century market day in Rotterdam, farmers inquired at
bookstalls for sermons of *Erskeyna*. Alexander Comrie and Theodorus
Van der Groe, two great leaders of the *Nadere Reformatie* (the Dutch vari-
ant of seventeenth- and eighteenth-century pietism, usually translated as
Dutch Second Reformation), were greatly influenced by the Erskines.
Comrie was catechized by both Erskines as a boy and later referred to
Ralph Erskine as "my faithful old friend, whom God used as the guide

of my youth." Van der Groe introduced several translated books of the Erskines, though he had a more restricted view of the promises of God than the Erskines. By the time of VanderGroe's death in 1784, the sermons of the Erskines were outselling those of any English or Scottish divine in the Netherlands.

In the 1830s, Hendrik Scholte, a well-known Secession leader who immigrated to Pella, Iowa, published a number of Ralph Erskine's sermons. In the mid-nineteenth century, volumes of the Erskines' sermons were published three times, finding a ready market among Dutch Reformed Church believers as well as among those who had seceded. Among the Seceders, those who approved of the sermons of the Erskines defended an unconditional, free offer of grace; those who opposed the sermons judged them to be tainted by Arminianism. In 1904, Herman Bavinck, a prominent Dutch theologian and professor at Kampen and the Free University of Amsterdam, wrote a largely commendatory foreword to a compilation of Ebenezer and Ralph Erskine's sermons.

Throughout the twentieth century, the writings of the Erskines have been reprinted frequently in the Netherlands. They continue to prompt discussion in Dutch Reformed circles, particularly in subjects such as how to preach grace to the unsaved and how to teach people about God's promises.

In America, the ministry of the Erskines bore considerable fruit. Benjamin Franklin saw several of their writings through the press. Converts of the Great Awakening became avid readers of the Erskines. Jonathan Edwards acknowledged the *Gospel Sonnets* in a letter to James Robe in Kilsyth. About 30,000 copies of the Erskine-Fisher *Catechism* for children were sold in America by the Presbyterian Board in Philadelphia. John Mason, Scottish preacher in New York and leader in the Associate Reformed Church, which he helped establish, was nourished by the Erskines.

Ecclesiastical Influence

The ecclesiastical body founded by the Erskines and their colleagues quickly grew in size. What began as the Associate Presbytery soon became the Associate Synod. Congregations were established in many parts of Scotland and then in Northern Ireland. The Secession churches remained a factor in Scottish Church life until the mid-1900's.

From these two homelands, members of the Associate Church, sometimes called the Secession Church, and its people, the Seceders, migrated to the new world. Their influence was to be felt in many places. Some Associate Presbyterians held steadfastly to their own course, and as late as the 1960s there were some remaining Associate Presbyterian (AP) congregations. They united with the Reformed Presbyterian Churches in North America (RPCNA) at the end of that decade.

Other Associate Presbyterians joined forces with the Reformed Presbyterians early on to form the Associate Reformed Presbyterian Church (ARP) in 1782. The synod of the South separated from the main body in the 1820s, and continues to the present day as the ARP Church. In 1837, the ARP founded a seminary in South Carolina in honor of the Erskine brothers.

In 1858, the ARPs in the North joined forces with the largest part of the remaining APs to form the United Presbyterian Church of North America (UP). For one hundred years this small but vital denomination spread over the country, establishing churches, schools, colleges, seminaries and other institutions, as well as supporting a vigorous foreign missions program. The UPs were prominent in the cause of abolition before the Civil War, and in missions among the freed men afterwards. For many years the UPs adhered to exclusive Psalmody and took the lead in producing *The Psalter* of 1912, still used today in many Reformed churches.

The influence of the Associate Presbyterians was a potent factor in the history of Christianity in Canada as well. They were the first preachers on the field in many parts of Ontario and the Maritime Provinces. They were leaders in the movement which gave birth to the Presbyterian Church in Canada in 1872.

The missionary work of the ARPs and UPs led to the planting of the ARP Church of Pakistan, the UP Church of Pakistan, the United Evangelical Church of Egypt, and the ARP Church of Mexico. Churches were also planted in Ethiopia and the Sudan.

Prominent AP, ARP, and UP scholars and writers include such men as John Brown of Haddington, John Dick, George Lawson, John Eadie, John Anderson, John Mitchell Mason, John T. Pressly, James Harper, William Moorehead, John McNaugher, Melvin Kyle, James Kelso, John Gerstner, G.I. Williamson, and Jay Adams. Presbyterians such as James R. Miller, Andrew Blackwood, John Calvin Reid, and John Leith were UPs or ARPs by birth and upbringing.

Why have the Erskines been so influential? Why are they still important for us to read today? Answers to these questions should become clear as we examine the content of Ebenezer and Ralph Erskine's sermons.

Ralph Erskine

Two as One

In a sense, the sermons of Ebenezer and Ralph Erskine could have been written by the same hand. The brothers differed, of course. Ebenezer's gifts were not as striking as Ralph's, but Ebenezer had a calm, sure strength that made him a better leader. Ralph was more self-effacing, more devout, and more experimental than his brother, and looked more to the Puritans for guidance. Nevertheless, the substance and spirit of their sermons are so similar—and remained so throughout their careers —that examining them together does no disservice to either.

The Erskines began to publish sermons and other writings in the 1720s to illustrate Reformed doctrines of grace, to explain Marrow theology, and to guard against legalism. Their writings include the Reformation's emphasis on the promises of God, the Puritan emphasis on experimental piety, and the Scottish Second Reformation's emphasis on covenant theology. Their sermons glow with teachings on the love of God and indiscriminate offers of Christ.

Exegesis and Homiletics

The Erskines leaned on the Reformers and Puritans for exegetical help. Luther and Calvin were their favorite commentators among the Reformers and James Durham and Matthew Henry among the Puritans. Some scholars have critiqued the Erskines for focusing more on the doctrines flowing out of a text than on the exegesis of a text, wandering at times beyond the boundaries of the text so that they lost its original intent. More commonly, however, the Erskines showed considerable exegetical skill in their sermons, particularly in expounding texts about salvation in Jesus Christ.

Homiletically, the Erskines followed the Puritan "plain" style of preaching. This style of preaching, according to William Perkins, did three things:

1. It gave the basic meaning of a text of Scripture within its context;
2. It explained points of doctrine gathered from the natural sense of the text;
3. It applied the doctrines "rightly collected to the life and manners of men."

The first part of an Erskine sermon was therefore exegetical, usually providing a short analysis of the text; the second, doctrinal, stating and expounding some doctrine or "observation"; and the third, applicatory. The Erskines usually divided the third part, often referred to as the "uses" of doctrine derived from a text, into sections such as information, trial (self-examination), comfort, exhortation, and advice. For example, in a sermon titled "Present Duty Before Approaching Darkness," based on Jeremiah 13:16 ("Give glory to the Lord your God, before he cause darkness"), Ralph Erskine offered six points of information, two points of self-examination, five points of exhortation, and six points of advice. Because of the nature of the text, no section was offered for comfort.

This homiletical method often led to a lengthy series of sermons on one text. For example, Ralph Erskine delivered fourteen sermons on prayer based on Romans 12:12, thirteen sermons on Christian living based on Colossians 2:6, nine sermons on self-conceit based on Proverbs 30:12, and eight sermons on "The Happy Congregation" based on Genesis 49:10.

The Erskine sermons combined doctrinal and experimental exposition. Doctrinally, they focused on the great, central themes of Christianity: the person and work of Christ, sin and salvation, faith and hope, and God's grace. Experimentally, they dealt with such matters as comfort, assurance, assistance in trials, and the privileges of being a Christian.

Centered on the Promises

The Erskines are best known for sermons that, in keeping with Scottish tradition, focus on the promises of God. The Scots Confession of 1560 spoke of an "assured faith in the promises of God." Writings such as

George Hutcheson's *Exposition of the XII Small Prophets*, Andrew Gray's *Great and Precious Promises*, and Thomas Halyburton's *Great Concern of Salvation* made much of God's promises. "God binds Himself to us with His promises," Halyburton had written.

But the Erskines emphasized the promises even more than those writers. "What is the gospel but a word of promise?" Ebenezer Erskine asked (1:262). "Take away the promise out of the Bible," wrote Ralph Erskine, "and you take away the gospel" (5:118), for "the gospel and the promise is one and the same thing" (5:235).

The Erskines never tired of preaching on the promises of Scripture. Ralph Erskine wrote, "I will look to the promise, and lay stress upon it, and upon a God that promises" (5:236). They found promises everywhere in the Bible, even in texts such as John 17:17, which says, "Sanctify them through thy truth; thy word is truth" (5:103). As Ebenezer Erskine wrote, "All the histories, prophecies and shadows, and types of the Word—what are they but an opening and an exposition of the promises?" (1:512).

This focus on God's promises impacted the theology of the Erskines in a variety of key doctrines.

1. Eternal Promises

The Erskines preached about promises from eternity past to eternity future. Ebenezer Erskine defined God's promises as the "revelation of his counsel and purpose of grace before the world began" (1:431). Ralph Erskine personalized that, saying God's promises are a "revelation of his grace and good-will to sinners in Christ" (5:192).

All of God's promises proceed from an act of His sovereign will. "Hence, all the promises of the new covenant are so many *I wills*," said Ralph Erskine. "'I will be your God; I will take away the heart of stone; I will put my Spirit within you'" (5:375). From God's eternal perspective, those promises can only be claimed by the elect; but from man's perspective, they must be preached to all men, for whoever responds to the promises in faith will become recipients of them. The promises are made to the elect but are endorsed or directed to all "who hear the gospel, with their seed," the Erskines said. Every hearer has *the right of access* to the promises, therefore, but only the elect have *the right of possession*. They alone will embrace the promises of God by faith (*Exposition of the Shorter Catechism,* Questions 81-84 on Question 20).

The God who makes promises from eternity also fulfills them in time. "God is not a speaker only, but a doer," wrote Ralph Erskine

(2:308), "giving a being [or existence] to his promises" (5:382) in this life through His Word. The Erskines were fond of quoting Romans 10:6-8 to stress that sinners do not have to ascend into heaven to lay hold of the promises because the Word is near us, even in our mouth and heart (EE, 1:435-36; RE, 5:278). Ralph Erskine illustrated this by saying that as water flows from a distant source to a city by water mains and is brought so close to people's mouths that they can drink it from a faucet, so the water of life flows from the fountainhead, the Triune God, through the pipes of His promises in the gospel right to our mouths (5:278).

The nearness of God's promises eliminates any excuse for unbelief. In his sermon on John 3:18 ("Unbelief Arraigned and Condemned at the Bar of God"), Ebenezer Erskine said, "I am convinced that if sinners would know how closely Christ is brought to us by the gospel in the salvation he has wrought, there would not be so many unbelieving sinners among us" (1:358).

The promise endures into the future. The glorified Christ is God's eternal promise for now and the future, for He has ascended and will reign forever. Heaven is where God's promise will reach full perfection (RE, 2:519ff).

2. The Gospel as Promise

The promises of God are a means of salvation, the Erskines taught. Since the promise and the gospel coincide, the promise is as powerful for salvation as is the gospel. Ralph Erskine explained this in his sermons on Galatians 4:28, titled "The Pregnant Promise." He said that just as Isaac was born more of the power of promise than of nature, so believers are "children of promise" through God's eternal promise in Christ (5:96). God's "powerful and prolific promise" is thus the channel of saving power (5:108). In God's mind, spiritual conception took place in eternity, since the elect were Christ's seed promised to Him in the Counsel of Peace (Is. 53:10), but spiritual birth takes place in time. The pregnant womb of God's promise, which can never be aborted, is opened in the hour of regeneration by His own power. While God's pleasure is the ultimate "moving cause" of that new birth, the promise of God is its means—the "instrumental cause."

3. Promises in Christ

The promises are inseparable from Jesus Christ, the Erskines taught. The promises were made to Christ in the Counsel of Peace, but He is also their content. Ralph Erskine illustrated the relation of Christ to the promises by saying the promise is like a cup, but Christ is the drink held by the cup. Faith doesn't just take hold of the cup of promise and look into it; it is satisfied only when it drinks Christ. Sipping the cup of Christ by Spirit-worked faith enlightens the mind and moves the will to seek after Christ more, Ralph Erskine said (1:126). The glory of Christ fills the soul as Christ appears in all His beauty as Savior and Lord. Natural enmity is broken, the will and affections are renewed, and the sinner cries out that Christ is altogether lovely, the chief among ten thousand.

The Erskines' preaching was thus thoroughly Christ-centered, in keeping with pristine Reformation preaching. Preaching for them was "the chariot that carries Christ up and down the world," as Richard Sibbes wrote. "Christ is the Head, and centre of all gospel-truth, and we ought to hold by the Head; and so we shall hold by the truth," Ralph Erskine proclaimed (4:491). Elsewhere he said, "Whatever manifold articles of truth there be, yet truth itself is but one; and Christ the center is but one" (4:246).

The Bible is a wellspring for preaching Christ, the Erskines believed. To be Word-centered and Christ-centered are synonymous since the Word proclaims Christ and Christ proclaims the Word. As Ebenezer Erskine said to his congregation: "All prophecies, promises, histories, and doctrines of the Word point us to him, as the needle in the mariner's compass points to the pole-star…. Our preaching, and your hearing, is in vain, unless we bring you to the knowledge of Christ and an acquaintance with him…. All the lines of religion meet in him as their centre" (2:7-8).

The Erskines presented Christ in His ability and willingness to save, and preciousness as the Redeemer of lost sinners. Preaching Christ with theological articulation, divine grandeur, and winsome passion was their greatest burden and most essential task. Thus they chose to preach on texts from both testaments that centered on Christ and the gospel (RE, 5:88). They believed that every text led to Christ, either directly or indirectly, but it was the minister's responsibility to focus on the texts most full of Christ, for "the more of Christ [there] be in any text, the more marrow and fatness, the more savour and sweetness, will be in [the sermon] to the soul that knows him," Ebenezer Erskine wrote (2:8).

4. Promises in the Father and Spirit
The promises are also inseparable from the Father and the Holy Spirit, the Erskines taught. In Christ, God Himself comes to us as the Triune Redeemer, declaring "I am the LORD thy God." In such promises, the

Father gives Himself with all of His divine attributes to save and help us. So does the Spirit, for Christ promised to send the Spirit to believers to abide with them (John 16:7; RE, 5:101).

Notwithstanding their christocentricity, the Erskines also devoted considerable attention to the person and work of the Father, whose attributes are represented in Christ, and to the presence and work of the Holy Spirit, through whom Christ works what He has merited for believers. They extolled the Triune God and abased man the sinner. They did not worry about injuring the self-esteem of their listeners in the process, for they were far more concerned with esteeming the Triune God: the Father who created us in His image, the Son who restores that dignity to us through redemption and adoption, and the Holy Spirit who indwells us and makes us His temple. The Erskines would have viewed messages that build up self-esteem rather than center upon the Triune God as messages of self-deceit. We have nothing to esteem in ourselves apart from God and His grace; apart from Him, we are fallen, unworthy, and hell-bound.

5. Promises of Every Kind

God comes to us in Christ, and Christ comes to us in a dazzling wealth of promises. Those promises meet any condition of any believer. In one sermon, Ralph Erskine listed fifty aspects of salvation contained in the promises and claimed that he could list a thousand more (5:259-60). "What can you desire that is not in the promise?" he asked. He then answered:

> The promise contains salvation from sin, from the guilt of sin, from the filth of sin, from the power of sin, from the sting of sin, from the stain of sin, from the fruit of sin, from the fountain of sin, and from the very being of sin at length. Here are promises of salvation from wrath, from the law, from justice, from death, from hell, from the world, and from the devil and unreasonable men. Salvation from troubles, and reproaches, and fears, and doubts, and faintings; salvation from desertion and despondency, from wants and weakness, from wrongs and injuries done to your names or otherwise; salvation from all woes and weariness; salvation from backsliding and apostasy; salvation from plagues and all imperfections; innumerable positive salvations and mercies; pardoning mercy, sin-subduing mercy, healing mercy, conquering mercy, comforting mercy, upholding mercy, grace increasing mercy, and perfecting mercy; sanctifying mercy, to sanctify all providences, all crosses, all relations; defending mercy, strengthening mercy, helping mercy, following mercy, enlightening, enlivening, enlarging mercy; mercy for supplying your wants, dispelling your fears, covering your infirmities, hearing

your prayers, ordering all things for your good; and salvation to everlasting life, glory and immortality (5:259).

Ebenezer Erskine was also impressed by the variety of God's promises. In preaching on Revelation 22:2 ("the leaves of the tree were for the healing of the nations"), Erskine said that the promises, like leaves on a tree, are so diverse, that there is no ailment that they cannot heal. "What is your disease, O sinner? Whatever it may be, you will find a leaf on this tree that can heal you," he said (1:502). Ralph Erskine concurred: "Tell me one case that the promise does not reach," he asked (5:118).

People must be caught like fish by gospel promises. Ralph Erskine said that the preacher, who is a "fisher of men," must let down "a bundle of promises" as hooks on a line to catch people. The hooks are of various sizes to catch every kind of person. "Do you say, 'I am a poor insignificant worm?' Well, there is a hook for you. 'Fear not, worm Jacob, I will help thee.' Are you poor and needy? There is a hook for you: 'When the poor and needy seek water...I the Lord will hear them.' Are you a poor, blind creature, that knows not what way to go? There is a hook for you, 'I will bring the blind by a way they know not.'

"If one promise does not fit you, go to another," Erskine went on. "If one hook is too large for you, another will suit you better. O happy soul, if you be taken! For the hook will not hurt you, but only hale you to the same happy shore with all the children of promise" (5:128-30).

6. Unconditional Promises

To encourage sinners to grasp hold of the promises, the Erskines stressed the unconditional nature of those promises. In opposition to growing forms of legalism, neominianism, and Arminianism, Ralph Erskine had complained already in 1720 that "the glorious gospel is much clouded at this day, with legal terms, conditions, and qualifications" for coming to Christ and embracing the promises (1:52). He recognized that hearts inclined toward legalism reach for the law or other conditions, including faith, repentance, mourning, and prayer, in hope of pleasing God and effecting peace with Him (1:168).

All conditions of the promises are already met by God, the Erskines argued. Either Christ meets those conditions for the sinner, or the condition of a promise is offered by God in some other promise. In every case, God meets the conditions for sinners who come to the promises by faith. Thus no sinner may reject any promise of God due to conditions he cannot meet. As Ralph Erskine wrote, "There is no conditional form put upon any promise in the Bible, to keep back a soul from applying and taking hold of the promise, but [rather] to draw it in to embrace the condition, either by taking Christ for the condition, or running to an absolute promise, where that condition is promised" (5:129).

To teach otherwise is to mingle the covenant of works with the covenant of grace, or to mix law and gospel, the Erskines said. The distinction between the law and the gospel must be guarded like a treasure. The law is a precept; the gospel is a promise (RE, 5:164-65). "How miserable are you that are gospel hearers, if you can never come to understand what is the gospel, and what is the law!" warned Ralph Erskine. "The law runs always in a mandatory strain; that is, in commands and threatenings: but the gospel runs in a promissory strain; the law begets fear and dread, and the gospel begets hope; and happy they, who, being terrified by the law, are made to flee away to the gospel...for there lies all your salvation" (5:193).

7. Faith: No Condition for the Promises

Even faith is not a condition for the gospel. The Erskines concurred with Robert Traill, who wrote: "Faith in Jesus Christ in justification is neither condition nor qualification, but in its very act a renouncing of all such pretences." Hence the Erskines wrote of "the grace of faith." Faith is one of the primary effects in the elect when they are effectually called (RE, 1:257). As a seal leaves an impression on wax, so faith responds to the call of the gospel (RE, 4:453).

Faith is "the way of the gospel," given by God, not a condition merited by man. The receiving hand of faith presupposes the giving hand of God (RE, 3:9; 5:16). Faith does nothing but receive Jesus as He is offered in the gospel, the Shorter Catechism says. As Ralph Erskine wrote, faith is the "most uniting grace.... It makes us spiritually and mystically one with Christ" (3:475, 477). Because of faith's intimate union with Christ, the believer has a right to Christ and all His mediatorial work (RE, 2:172). Faith brings Christ and His salvation home to the soul; it is a "leading and commanding grace," yet in its receiving character "it seems the poorest and weakest grace, the most beggarly of all the graces."

In describing the woman who anointed Jesus (Luke 7:36-50), Ralph Erskine wrote, "Love brings ointment to Christ's head, and repentance tears to wash his feet; but faith gives nothing, and brings nothing to Christ; yet it is designed to a higher office than any other grace: [for] it is the hand that receives Christ, and receives all from him" (3:476).

Faith is not conditional to the gospel; rather, faith itself is promised in the promises of God, such as Psalm 110:3 ("Thy people shall be willing in the day of thy power"). Such texts, Ralph Erskine said, are "absolute" that is, they have no conditions attached to them (5:239). Were this not so, no one would be able to believe. If faith was a condition, people could object against the gospel by saying, "But I cannot believe!" If faith was itself not unconditionally promised, the gospel would not be good news for sinners who mourn their lack of faith (5:107).

Ralph Erskine was aware that preachers such as Robert Rollock, Samuel Rutherford, and David Dickson spoke of faith as a condition. But he argued that when they did, they did not view faith as a condition in the proper sense of that word (5:107). Ralph Erskine would have approved of what Robert Shaw would later write: "Some worthy divines have called faith a condition, who were far from being of the opinion that it is a condition properly so called, on the performance of which men should, according to the gracious covenant of God, have a right to justification as their reward. They merely intended, that without faith we cannot be justified—that faith must precede justification in the order of nature. But as the term *condition* is very ambiguous, and calculated to mislead the ignorant, it should be avoided."

According to the Erskines, the act of faith, by which we receive Christ, is an act that utterly renounces all our works and righteousness as a condition of salvation. Faith is the cessation of all merit and utter abandonment to and acceptance of what Christ has done for us. It is staking our soul, understanding, will, affections, and very life upon the blood of Christ alone (RE, 1:116, 301).

The Erskines used the word *condition* in a carefully defined context. Along with Andrew Gray, they taught that some promises had conditions or were conditional. Conditional promises, however, do not detract from the unconditional character of the gospel; rather, one covenant blessing is bound to another as links in a chain. There is an order in God's covenant blessings. Faith is given as a part of God's promise (RE, 4:128), then other blessings are received by faith through conditional promises. If conditional promises, such as Malachi 4:2 ("But unto you that fear my name shall the Sun of righteousness arised with healing in his wings") frighten us, we should flee by faith to the absolute promises of God such as John 12:32 ("And I, if I be lifted up from the earth, will draw all men unto me") to obtain the condition of the conditional promise (5:106).

We must never confuse the right to believe and the power to believe, Ralph Erskine taught. The right to believe is based upon the offer of grace and the command of the gospel to believe. The power to believe is the gift of the Holy Spirit. Thus, whoever believes credits his faith to the internal work of the Spirit as a result of God's electing grace.

The believer must thus pray for the work of the Spirit. Nevertheless, as Ralph Erskine said, that does not mean that the sinner must feel the Spirit's power in order to believe. When the gospel call is pressed upon our heart, we may believe without feeling the Spirit's internal power. Such faith is not audacious, for how could obeying God's command ever be audacious? It is more audacious to say that a sinner cannot believe until he feels the power to believe. True faith, by contrast, confesses, "I have no power; hence I flee from myself to Christ and the Word of promise to embrace his promised power" (2:307-322).

To the sinner who asked, "What if I am not elected?" Ralph Erskine responded: Don't meddle with that secret. If your heart goes out to the offer of grace, and you make Christ your choice by faith, then your election is sure. If you say, "All shall not be saved—and perhaps not I?," we answer, "Some shall be saved, and why not you?" (1:55, 157).

"Why is it that all who hear the gospel are not saved?" Erskine asked. "Is it not because they will not give employment to Christ to save them by faith? If you do not receive Christ, you will be damned for your neglect of him—not because you were not elected (1:99; 2:408). We cannot say you are an elect man or woman, therefore believe. We have no such commission. God says by this gospel, 'Whosoever will, let him take,' and in taking he shall have proof of his being an elect vessel (2:182-83). But you say, 'If I am not elected, I will not get grace to come.' We answer that you could better begin on the other end: if you have no will to come, you have no grace to come. And if you have no will to come, who can you blame but yourself that you will not come? Will you complain that you have no grace to come and still reject the gospel of grace which alone can make you willing? If you end in hell one day, it will be because of your unbelieving rejection of the gospel. Non-election, therefore, can be no hindrance to you, for it is a secret with which you are not now to be concerned" (3:312-13; 5:224-25). The Erskines concurred with George Whitefield who advised, "Go to the grammar school of faith and repentance before you attend the university of election."

8. Repentance, Conviction, and the Promises

Repentance is not a condition of salvation, either, the Erskines said. Like Calvin, the Erskines taught that repentance is not a cause of grace, nor a condition of grace, but always a consequence of grace. Repentance is derived from faith, not vice versa. If repentance preceded faith, then sanctification, of which repentance is a part, would be indispensable for justification, as Roman Catholicism teaches. Rather, repentance is a turning from sin to God through Christ by faith.

When perceived by faith, the goodness of God produces evangelical repentance. That, not legal repentance, is the kind of repentance we need. Legal repentance tries to qualify the heart before God by remorse not rooted in the gospel and its promises. It must be distinguished from "gospel repentance," which by faith views Christ as totally qualified for sinners and grieves that the heart has sinned against the gospel and its promises. Whatsoever is not of faith is sin (1:433-34).

The convicting power of the law in the soul is certainly not superfluous, however. The Erskines taught that God normally uses the law to convict a sinner prior to comforting him with the gospel. The Spirit of God uses the law to persuade the sinner of how deeply he has broken its commands and how utterly unable he is to obey it (RE, 2:279-81; 3:10). The sinner loses all hope of being justified by the law or his own works (RE, 1:134), and confesses that God could rightly send him to hell (RE, 1:70).

Under the tutelage of the Spirit, conviction of sin by the law augments rather than detracts from free grace, the Erskines taught. Conviction is not a condition for the gospel, however, nor does it fit the sinner for the gospel. Here is why:

1. Genuine humiliation under the law's curse and God's judgment makes us less fit in our own estimation for salvation. This is God's way of leading the sinner to a more profound need for Christ. Since the Spirit's purpose in bringing sinners to despair is to prompt them to flee to Christ, ministers must blow on two trumpets, Ralph Erskine said. The trumpet of the law must be blown so that the trumpet of the gospel may be heard (RE, 2:648-49). Preaching must convict the sinner of the wrath of God and the torments of hell that are due to him if he persists in unbelief and impenitence. Conviction under the law then leads the sinner to receive the gospel by sheer grace. Erskine wrote, "The needle of the law is followed by the thread of the gospel" (2:41).

Conviction is not preparatory grace as much as it is humbling, stripping, killing grace. It puts self-righteousness to death and pronounces a curse upon the sinner (Gal. 3:10). The law is a hard, merciless taskmaster. It terrifies us and drives us to Christ Jesus, who is our only righteousness before God (Gal. 3:24). The law does not lead us to a saving knowledge of God in Christ; rather, the Spirit uses the law as a mirror to show us our guilt and hopelessless and to induce repentance, thereby creating and sustaining the spiritual need that He uses to give birth to faith in Christ.

The Spirit thus uses the law to lead the sinner to renounce all assets and to flee to Christ—to turn all merits into demerits before the meriting Redeemer. The Spirit does not use the law to prompt a certain degree of conviction of sin, which is then used as an asset for pleading for grace. Conviction is adequate if the sinner flees to Christ, Ralph Erskine said. "The soul is sufficiently melted, when it runs into the mould. What is the gospel-mould? It is Christ; and when the melted soul runs into this mould, there does it get the right shape and form, and there only," he explained (4:526).

2. Conviction of sin under the law is not a condition for salvation because it is not a human work. It is sown in the heart by the Word and Spirit. The sinner's acceptance of the curse of the law is an act of Spirit-worked faith (RE, 2:197). Humiliation through the law usually precedes the sinner's knowledge of salvation through the gospel, but it does not precede the manifestation of Christ's grace. Christ, as the executor of the covenant of grace, convicts men of sin through the law, thereby paving the way for Himself (RE, 5:26).

Sinners, then, must flee to Christ with all their sin. They must be told that the gospel is free to sinners. The Erskines taught that the Lord wants us to relinquish all conditions for coming to Christ for full salvation. "He seeks that you come down from all terms, conditions, and personal qualifications; to a renunciation of your all, which is nothing, and to an embracing of Christ's all, which is 'all in all,'" Ralph Erskine wrote (6:470-71). He added that if you wait to enter into covenant with God "till you be in a better condition…you will wait to the day of judgment, and in the mean time inevitably perish at death; and all your terms, conditions, and good qualifications, will perish with you" (1:148).

9. The Free Offer and God's Promises

Like the Reformers, the Erskines advocated for the free offer of the gospel. The gospel was extended to everyone without conditions or reserve. Ebenezer Erskine wrote, "Oh, invite others to come to the Tree of Life and to see that his fruit is good, pleasant, profitable and plenteous. Tell the hungry what excellent fruit is here; tell the weary what glorious rest is here; tell the diseased souls what healing leaves are here. Let your resentment run against those who would hew down the Tree of Life."

Ralph Erskine added, "There are many pipes full of water for refreshing, full of wine for cheering, full of milk for nourishing souls. And we are come to set the pipe to your mouth: 'Ho, everyone that thirsteth, come to the waters.' Here is a pipe for every mouth, by which you may draw Christ to your heart, though he be in heaven, and you on earth."

Biographer A. R. MacEwen wrote of Ebenezer Erskine's preaching: "Of all the sermons which have been preserved by his 'scribes,' as he affectionately styled the short-hand writers who clustered round his pulpit, not one fails to repeat the free offer of grace to all without distinction." The Erskines protested against the kind of extreme Calvinism that offered the gospel only to the elect. They believed that such a limited offer displaced the heart of the gospel message. As Ralph Erskine wrote to John Wesley: "The true spirit of God within a believer leads him to a dependence upon Christ *without* him, and not upon a Christ *within* him, not upon any created or communicated graces, gifts, experiences, tears, sorrows, joys, frowns, feelings, or whatever else."

The finished work of Christ is the heart of the gospel, the Erskines said. And that work must be freely and unconditionally offered to sinners. The Erskines offered the whole Christ—prophet, priest, and king—to all who would have Him. They did not separate Christ's benefits from His person or present Him as Savior from sin apart from His claims as Lord. They encouraged listeners to appropriate, or "close with," a freely offered Christ by faith, then to enter into "covenant with God" by drafting a document in which they promised to surrender their entire lives to Him. The Erskines would have been appalled at the contemporary notion of rescuing sinners from hell without demanding their immediate submission to the sovereign lordship of Christ.

Predestination is no obstacle in proclaiming the gospel, the Erskines said. They opposed Moderates who confessed a doctrine of unconditional election but preached a doctrine of conditional grace that contradicted the fullness and freeness of the gospel. Syllogistically, the major premise of such Moderates was that the grace of God in Christ saves the elect. Their minor premise was that the elect are known by their forsaking of sin. They therefore concluded that grace is given to those who forsake sin. Sinclair Ferguson says that such teaching includes four errors:

♦ Such preaching separates the benefits of the gospel from Christ, who is the gospel. These Moderates reasoned that since the benefits of Christ's works belong only to the elect and no one else appropriates them, they must therefore be offered only to those to whom they belong, namely, the elect. The elect are thus known by signs that show they belong to the elect, such as their forsaking sin. How different such preaching is from that of the Erskines, John Calvin, and most Puritans who offer Christ with all His benefits to the greatest of sinners.

• Such preaching promotes a conditional offer of the gospel. If Christ's benefits are offered without Christ, those benefits must be offered on condition. For example, you may receive forgiveness *if* you have sufficiently forsaken sin. You may know grace *if* you have received a certain degree of conviction. Such conditions turn the gospel upon its head. The Erskines were adamant that only the grace of Jesus Christ enables a sinner to forsake sin.

• Such preaching distorts the character of God and the salvation that He offers. The Erskines taught that the free offer of salvation emphasizes the great work that God has done, out of which flows the imperatives on how we are to respond. They said that to make the offer of grace dependent on anything, even upon graces received, distorts the true nature of grace. It distorts salvation because no man, dead in trespasses and sins, can ever meet a single condition of God. It also distorts the character of God because our God deals with man on the basis of free, unmerited grace rather than presenting conditions to lost sinners by which they may be saved.

• Finally, such preaching distorts the nature of pastoral ministry. One who has only a conditional gospel to offer knows only conditional grace. And one who knows only conditional grace knows only a conditional God. And one who knows only a conditional God will, in the final analysis, only be able to offer others a conditional ministry. He will give his heart, life, time, and devotion to people, but only on condition. He may master the mechanics of the great doctrines of grace, but until grace in God Himself masters him, that grace will not flow from him to his people. He will be a modern Jonah, sitting under his tree with a heart closed to sinners because he thinks of God in conditional terms.

The Erskines' teaching is illustrated in the parable of the prodigal son, or as we might call it, the parable of the father of free grace. The homebound prodigal might have asked himself, "Have I felt sufficient sorrow for my sin and repented enough for my father to take me back?" Yet the knowledge of the grace in the house and heart of his father brought the young man to himself in the first place, and then began to draw him home. Any possible conditions of qualifying for his father's love were silenced by his father's loving embrace.

Ministers must treat sinners like the father treated his wayward son. They must view people with eyes of mercy, approach them with feet of mercy, evangelize them with words of mercy, and love them with the

Father's heart of mercy. Surely the beginning and end of the pastoral vocation is simply this: to know and love Christ, then to strive to be like Him by loving those whom He has entrusted to its care.

The father who loved the prodigal son was still concerned about his firstborn son, however. When the eldest son complained, "Didn't I meet all the conditions? Haven't I merited the ring, the robe, the fatted calf, and the feast?" the father responded as if to say, "It is all yours, unconditionally and freely, but your legalistic heart won't free you to enjoy my gifts. You will only accept grace on the condition that you merit it. On that condition, you can never have it."

May God prevent us from allowing the spirit of the Moderates, the neonomians, and the legalists to affect our preaching of God's free grace and the application of that grace to the flock of God. The offer must be presented to sinners without conditions. The Erskines agreed with Samuel Rutherford who stated, "The reprobate have the same warrant to believe in Christ as the elect." God presents His gospel offer to sinners, even to sinners whose hands are filled with the blood of Jesus Christ.

Ebenezer Erskine wrote, "God speaks to every sinner as particularly as though he named him by his name and surname" (1:265). The gospel is God's letter of promise to every sinner. It says, "To you is this word of salvation come," and the word is Jesus Christ who has come to save sinners. God is not willing that any should perish; hence His gospel offer to all is sincere. "God is hearty and in good earnest when he offers us Christ and salvation in him; it pains him at his heart when sinners don't come to him," Ebenezer Erskine said (2:497).

There is no excuse for rejecting such an invitation. Unbelief is always the culprit. Ralph Erskine stated in a post-communion sermon: "Christ as the covenant is offered to you, man; to you, woman; to you that are before me, and behind me, and round about, in every corner of this place.... God's giving him in this gospel is your warrant for taking him: and if you will not hearken to this gospel offer of Christ for a covenant to you, I charge you, in God's name, and as you will answer at his tribunal, to declare before him and your own consciences, what ye have to say against him" (1:182).

The Erskines appealed to sinners, yes, even commanded them (1 John 3:23), to flee to Christ and His promises, knowing that the Holy Spirit blesses such preaching. "The promises are flying about your heads and ears," Ralph Erskine said to listeners. "Is there none of them flying into your hearts? Have you no use for any of these promises? If you be for the promise, then take it, and God's blessing with it, and Christ in the bosom of it; for the promise is the place where the Lord lies" (5:120).

When some parishioners pleaded their inability to embrace the promises, Erskine acknowledged that "faith is not a flower that grows in nature's garden" (4:321), but then advised them to attempt the impossible. Ebenezer Erskine used two illustrations to reinforce that advice. As Jesus told the lame man to stretch out his hand and the Lord gave him strength to do so, so sinners must attempt to believe in Jesus, trusting that God will give them the strength to do what is natively impossible for them to do. Likewise, as a child who is too young to read is sent to school with a primer, is asked to read, and does so as he learns how to read, so God commands us to believe, then helps us to do so.

Sinners must seek God by waiting on Him. They must strive to remove every impediment to faith and diligently use the means of grace, such as the preaching of the Word, learning the Scriptures, meditation, prayer, conversing with the godly, reading orthodox literature, and self-examination (RE, 3:195; 5:248). Those who neglect such means are so far out of God's way that they exclude themselves, Ralph Erskine said (3:467; 4:125). The poor beggar who stays at the wayside where the king passes is closer to God than the man who ascends a distant mountain where the king never passes (4:315).

Erskine advised sinners to neglect no duty or ordinance in which God may be found (6:426). "We never heard of any that got this disposition, but they found their waiting on the Lord was not in vain; the Lord pitied them, and gave them a heart to believe and receive Christ," he said (4:37).

10. Self-examination and the Promises

The Erskines were well aware that the promises of God can be abused. As Ralph Erskine said, "People may take and apply a promise amiss, and ruin themselves in their way of taking, when they take the promise to themselves, not of faith, [or] not out of God's hand, [or] not for the end and design for which it is given" (5:247).

How should the minister address this problem? Not by restricting the invitation of the gospel, the Erskines said, but by calling sinners to self-examination. Ralph Erskine explained that as a gardener waters both good plants and weeds, so a minister must water the garden of God's church, including the good plants of the elect as well as the weeds of the reprobate. The offer of grace comes to both so that no one has any excuse for unbelief, and the Holy Spirit will bless it to deliver the elect from condemnation (5:109).

The faithful minister must offer grace to all his hearers, but he must also explain what a life of faith consists of, separating the precious from the vile. According to Ralph Erskine, he must ask questions, such as:

- What think ye of Christ? Has the Holy Spirit ever worked within you to extol Christ and to debase you at His feet?
- Have you experienced the promises of God?
- Have you partaken of Christ's humiliation, exaltation, righteousness, and strength? (5:193-235)

The faithful preacher must also present the clear marks of grace that meet the test of the Word of God. According to Ralph Erskine, you are a child of God if:

- You strive to walk as Christ walked (1:134-36);
- Your heart is rent by and away from sin (1:104-105);
- You long for Christ's second coming (1:138);
- You diligently use the means of grace (1:357);
- You are making progress in the Christian life (1:356);
- You no longer enjoy the company of sinners (2:46);
- You seek to bring others to Christ (3:445);
- You regularly have God in your thoughts (3:94);
- You strive against temptation (5:219).

Such marks of grace are offered not to destroy but to strengthen the faith of the believer. Self-examination must be done in faith, depending on Scripture, Christ Jesus, and the Holy Spirit for enlightenment. If the believer can embrace by faith only a few evidences of salvation, he has good reason to be satisfied, Ralph Erskine said. By implication, the rest of the evidences will be there, for God does a full work in His people even when they can't see it. "If a child cannot go, yet if it can suck; if it cannot suck, yet if it can cry; if it cannot cry, yet if it can breathe, it is a mark of life: so, there may be breathings in the soul, that are evidences of life and faith, when other things are hid," Erskine explained (4:270).

Self-examination is crucial for the believer. As Ralph Erskine said, if all that you owned in the world was one precious stone, you would not regard its examination by a competent jeweler with indifference. Rather, you would wonder, "Can it withstand the blow of a hammer, or will it be smashed to powder?" Likewise, all that we have in this world and the next depends on whether or not we are saved in Christ. So we must examine ourselves to see whether our faith in Christ can endure the hammer blows of God's Word or if it will be smashed to pieces by those blows (4:522).

Proper self-examination is helpful for checking false assurance, which rests outside of Christ. It will also assure the true believer that his salvation is based on the right foundation, Jesus Christ. Self-examination should be a positive, growing experience. In seeing our faults, we will look more to Christ.

11. Assurance and the Promises

Proper self-examination helps the believer grow in assurance and sanctification. The Erskines differentiated between the assurance of faith that rests in the promises of God and the assurance of sense, or feeling, that rests in inward evidences of God's grace. The former works justification; the latter, consolation. By assurance of faith, we receive Christ as ours; by assurance of sense, we know Him to be ours. Assurance of faith says, "I am sure because God says it," while assurance of sense says, "I am sure because I feel it."

Ralph Erskine said that every believer must experience some assurance of faith but that not every believer has assurance of sense (RE, 3:28-29, 348; 4:184). In his famous sermon "The Assurance of Faith," Ebenezer Erskine said,

> There is a great difference betwixt the assurance of *faith,* and the assurance of *sense,* which follows upon faith. The assurance of faith is a *direct,* but the assurance of sense is a *reflex* act of the soul. The assurance of faith hath its object and foundation from *without,* but that of sense has them *within.* The object of the assurance of faith is *a Christ revealed, promised, and offered in the word;* the object of the assurance of sense is *a Christ formed within us by the Holy Spirit.* The assurance of faith is the *cause,* that of sense is the *effect;* the first is the *root,* and the other is the *fruit.* The assurance of faith eyes the promise in its *stability,* flowing from the *veracity* of the promiser; the assurance of sense, it eyes the promise in its *actual accomplishment.* By the assurance of faith, Abraham believed that he should have a son in his old age, because God who cannot lie had promised; but by the assurance of sense, he believed it when he got Isaac in his arms (1:254).

Assurance of sense, experiential piety, sanctification, and communion with God were highly treasured by the Erskines. Ralph Erskine spoke of "experimental sense and feeling" as a foretaste of heaven and an important means of glorifying God on earth. But he also warned against making the assurance of sense and experimental feelings the ground of faith, saying, "They are ebbing and flowing, up and down, it may be twenty times, in the space of one sermon; and your faith that is built thereupon, will be up and down therewith" (5:35). If we depend on our feelings rather than upon God's promises, the water in our cistern will soon be used up, Ebenezer Erskine said. We must go daily to the spring for fresh water; what we receive today cannot help us tomorrow (2:155). That means that if we wish to recover our certainty and comfort if it should be lost, we must go out of ourselves by a direct act of faith, taking "Christ a-new" (1:166).

Thus, the Erskines stressed a life of faith. The believer cannot live without some assurance of sense, they said, but he finds true stability through faith in Christ. The supreme act of faith is the appropriation of God's promises in Christ. That is the nature and marrow of faith (RE, 2:200ff). As Ralph Erskine said, "The sinner must be brought off from confidence in, or dependence upon frames, enlargements, influences and attainments, to a solid life of faith, upon the grounds that are unchangeable." Ebenezer Erskine offered nine points of comparison between a life of faith and a life of sense:

1. Sense regards only what a man presently enjoys, whereas faith regards what a man has in Christ and in a well-ordered covenant.

2. Sense tends to judge the love of God by circumstances or conditions, and whenever God seems to frown or hide, it cries out, "The Lord hath forgotten to be gracious." Faith sees the love of God in the face of Christ Jesus and in the declarations, offers, and promises of the Word. "In his word will I hope," faith says.

3. Sense and sight vary and fluctuate, but faith is steady and fixed, like Abraham, "who against hope believed in hope, and staggered not at the promise through unbelief."

4. Sense and sight focus on things that are present, whereas faith, like a prophet, looks at things to come.

5. Sense and sight are superficial and easily deceived with appearances, but faith is a meditative grace that goes deeply into things.

6. Faith is the leader, while sense is a follower; faith is the duty, and sense the privilege connected with it.

7. Sense is hasty in judgment, whereas faith patiently waits to the end. Sense draws rash conclusions in the midst of difficulties, but faith waits until the cloud passes.

8. A life of sense is dangerous, but a life of faith is safe and sure.

9. The foundation of sense is within; it trades in the shallow waters of created grace, experimental attainments, marks of grace, and the like. The foundation of faith, by contrast, is in Christ, God's covenant, and the great and precious promises of God's Word. When the mariner keeps his ship in shallow waters, he continually fears rocks and sand-

banks, but when he launches out into deep waters, he is safe. Likewise, faith trades in the deep waters of God's fulness in Christ, rising above doubts and fears of shipwreck (1:254ff.).

Where do we who are ministers lead people in our preaching? Do we keep them in shallow water by focusing on the assurance of sense, or do we lead them into deeper waters to challenge them to trust Christ and His promises? Spiritual experience is important, but experience is not the foundation of our salvation. Rather, faith in the promises of God in Christ should be the foundation of spiritual experiences. Like Richard Baxter, we should say, "For every look you take inside yourself, be sure that you take ten looks to Christ."

12. Sanctification and God's Promises
Faith alone justifies, but justifying faith is never alone. As surely as the rising sun brings forth light, faith in God's promises produces holiness, love, and obedience, Ralph Erskine said (2:36). Sanctification is the native, necessary, and inseparable fruit of justification; it is the justified man's way of living or walking to heaven (RE, 2:318, 3:240). To illustrate, Erskine said the believer is like a woman spinning at the wheel. One of her hands holds and the other works. One holds the thread and draws it down, and the other goes round and about the wheel. The holding hand is the hand of faith that clings to God's promises, and the working hand is the hand of obedience (3:425).

Christ in His obedience purchased the Holy Spirit to work both faith and sanctification in believers (1:150-51). The believer is like a ship, Ralph Erskine said. The sails of grace are not enough to move the ship; they must be filled with the winds of the Spirit in order to progress towards the heavenly port (3:109).

Sanctification receives Christ not only as Savior from hell but also as Lord of deliverance from sin. Sanctification carries faith beyond the cross to heaven, Ralph Erskine said (3:15; 1:96). No one can know Jesus as Savior who does not also receive Him as Lord of sanctification (3:38).

In sanctification the Spirit transforms a believer's nature into the image of God through Jesus Christ (6:6; 1:312, 318). The believer is freed from the power and dominion of sin (2:269). A new heart produces a new walk (6:335). Sanctification bends the will, inclining it to obey God's will (1:361). The believer's goal is to be purged from sin, to kill sin, and be done with it once and for all (1:68), and to serve God forever (2:306). He sees the law as a rule of life to be obeyed out of love to God (2:269; 1:406) but realizes he will never fully obey that law in this life. Sin and corruption, darkness and ignorance, rebellion and unbelief will not be completely removed this side of the grave. We will still sin, but we will hate it more and more (1:102, 105).

The believer dies daily to sin and strives to live in grateful obedience to the promises of Christ. He cannot cease repenting until he has ceased sinning, and he cannot cease sinning until he has ceased living. Sanctification will become complete only when we die and enter into the presence of Christ (4:389; 1:326).

Concluding Lessons

The Erskines never lost confidence in the plain interpretation of Scripture. Neither should we. They believed in the perspicuity of Scripture, never forcing Christ into a text where He is not. But they did go into each text as if with a flashlight to look for Him and draw Him out. So should we. Let us preach Christ from the Old Testament and the New, from the law and the gospel, from warning texts and texts of encouragement, from the Psalms and history and prophecy and epistles. Let us preach Christ to sinners even if we cannot preach sinners to Christ.

The Erskines preached Scripture with an incredible array of illustrations. So should we. After all, Scripture is fascinating. It is attractive. It elevates, stimulates, challenges, and exhorts. Let its text ruminate in your mind and soul and live in your thoughts, words, and actions.

The Erskines preached the big texts of Scripture with warmth and freshness. So should we. As Henry Venn wrote to his son, "I am persuaded we are very negligent in selecting our texts. Some of the most weighty and striking are never brought before the people, yet they are the texts that speak for themselves. You no sooner repeat them, then you appear in your high and holy character as a messenger of the Lord of hosts."

Like the Erskines, let us preach the whole counsel of God. Let us preach every doctrine to the full. Preach man's depravity and the spirituality of the law. Show people the fearful nature of their human predicament. Unveil their bad hearts and their bad records before God. Do not offer a quick fix—let the sinner know his plight, and offer him no escape from his dire need for Jesus Christ. Do not comfort him short of Christ.

Preach the love of God expressed through His promises. The love of God is the most powerful message that people can ever hear. Liberal preachers may steal fruit from our trees with that message, but do not neglect to preach it yourself. The heart of the gospel is God's immeasurable love. Show your people what God is like. Show them Jesus on His knees with a basin of water and a towel over his arm, washing the feet of men who are too proud to humble themselves. That is the heart of God. Tell your people that their Supreme Maker is so loving a God that through Jesus Christ He is willing to wash sinners from their filth and adopt them into His family as children of God. Teach them about the Triune heart of love.

Then, too, be sure to plead for the power of the Holy Spirit to speak about the things of God. We need the Spirit twice in every sermon— once in the study and once again on the pulpit. The Erskines worked hard and long on sermon preparation. With few exceptions, their sermons were fully written, wrestled out, and prayed over. They stayed close to their notes on the pulpit. Ralph Erskine is often portrayed with a sermon book in hand.

Later in life, the Erskines learned to speak more extemporaneously. At times, however, they struggled for a text. Ralph Erskine wrote in his diary one Sunday in 1731, "My eyes were towards the Lord for a word this day, having to preach, and not yet knowing what to think of for the subject." When they had little time to prepare, they leaned heavily on the Spirit. "Though I had studied little," Ralph Erskine wrote in 1739, "I preached on that word Zechariah 8:19, 'Love the truth and peace.'"

We need to work hard at sermon preparation. We need to agonize for souls in our studies if our ministries are to be blessed from the pulpit. Of course there are times when God knows that we don't have adequate time for preparation—not because of slothfulness, but because of a multitude of pastoral duties that press us throughout the week. During such times, we will experience, after heart-felt prayer, that the Lord will intervene for us, enabling us to preach with little preparation, sometimes better than we do with much preparation. But the Erskines would warn us not to make that the norm. There is little excuse for not preparing for the pulpit. Pulpit ministry is our primary task. Fail in that, and we fail in all. God will not keep assisting a lazy preacher.

Once on the pulpit, we should not overly rely on our notes. Regardless of how many notes you take to the pulpit, allow yourself freedom to deviate from them under the promptings of the Spirit of God, and pray for wisdom to know when to revert to your notes. One of the greatest problems that many of us have in preaching is that when we move spontaneously from our notes, we fail to understand when to return. We are prone to begin extemporaneous speaking in the Spirit and to end in the flesh.

Finally, the Erskines challenge us to ask ourselves what is the heart of our evangelistic message. We are called to proclaim to all the inexhaustible riches of God's grace; to declare that in the cross and the resurrection of Christ, God has won the victory over everything that could keep sinners from Him. Sin and grace are vanquished only because of God's free grace, not because of our merit. Do we preach that? The Erskines proclaimed the gospel message indiscriminately to all. Do we? They preached the richness of Christ to bankrupt sinners. Do we?

The Erskines also spoke to the hearts of God's people. An aged saint said of Ebenezer Erskine's preaching: "Mr. Erskine had a peculiar talent of entering into the heart and conscience of sinners, and into all the hopes and fears, the joys and griefs, the very life and death of saints; I never heard one preach, who could so well as he, bring, as it were, the Savior and the sinner together."

The Erskines viewed the inner chamber and the pulpit as a wrestling arena. Everything they wrote or preached had a compelling, earnest, beseeching, inviting power. Listen to one of Ralph Erskine's closing appeals after preaching Christ to his flock:

> Woe will be to you, if you live and die without a due improvement of this glorious gospel, which is the doctrine of a God in Christ reconciling the world to himself. God worshipped out of Christ is an idol, and all hope of acceptance out of Christ is a dream. O then let Christ, above all things, have the preeminence among you. What doth God care for your coming to church, if you will not hearken to what he says, and come to his Son?... The Lord is my witness, that it is the desire of my soul that you may be convinced and converted, and brought to Christ.... Little matter what you think of me or my preaching. Let me decrease in your esteem as much as you will, but let Christ increase among you, and then in the close of the day, I shall have you, and you will have advantage.... O go to God this night, and never give him rest, till you be brought, in some measure, to behold his glory in the face of Jesus, who is the "image of the invisible God."

The Erskines were no armchair petitioners, pulpiteers, or theologians. Do we likewise wrestle with God and men for the souls of men and women, boys and girls? Like the Erskines, let us take the kingdom of heaven by violence and the souls of men by divine allurement.

13

Assurance of Faith:
A Comparison of English Puritanism
and the *Nadere Reformatie*

This chapter will compare assurance of faith in two movements, English Puritanism and the *Nadere Reformatie*. I will first present working definitions of the terms *Puritanism* and *Nadere Reformatie,* then compare assurance of faith in both movements. Finally, I will offer some lessons the church can learn from those movements.

Puritanism

Puritanism and *Nadere Reformatie* are difficult to define. Originally, the term *Puritan* was pejorative. As Leonard Trinterud says, "Throughout the sixteenth century it was used more often as a scornful adjective than as a substantive noun, and was rejected as slanderous in whatever quarter it was applied."[1] For William Perkins (1558-1602), often called the father of Puritanism, it was "a vile term" that described people with perfectionist tendencies.[2]

The essence of Puritanism has been variously defined. William Haller sees the central dogma of Puritanism as an "all-embracing determinism, theologically formulated as the doctrine of predestination."[3] Perry Miller finds covenant at the "marrow of Puritan divinity";[4] Alan Simpson, the concept of conversion.[5] Christopher Hill emphasizes the social and political ideas of Puritanism.[6] John Coolidge views Puritanism as a repudiation of the Anglican doctrine of adiaphora, or "things indifferent."[7] R.M. Hawkes addresses the quandary by asking, "Was [English Puritanism] essentially a theological movement, emphasizing covenant theology, predestination, and a reformed church service? Or was the heart of the matter political, asserting the inalienable rights of conscience before God, the rule of natural law over arbitrary prerogative courts, the dependency of the king in parliament, the foundation of state authority in the people? Some modern research has pointed to a third possibility, that the essence of Puritanism was its piety, a stress on conversion, on existential, heartfelt religion."[8]

This paper agrees with Hawkes in viewing Puritans as people who desired to reform and purify the Church of England and were concerned about living a godly life as the outworking of the Reformed doctrines of grace. As Peter Lewis says, "Puritanism grew out of three great areas: the New Testament pattern of personal piety, sound doctrine and a properly ordered Church-life."[9]

Nadere Reformatie

Less is known about the *Nadere Reformatie* than about English Puritanism; hence a more detailed explanation is in order. The Dutch Reformation may be divided into four periods: the Lutheran period (1517-26), the Sacramentarian period (1526-31), the Anabaptist period (1531-45),[10] and, the most influential, the period of Calvinist infiltration.[11] The Calvinist penetration into the Netherlands (southern Netherlands, c. 1545; northern, c. 1560) was far more influential from the start than its number of adherents might suggest. However, Dutch Calvinism did not flower profusely until the seventeenth century, cultivated by the Synod of Dort (1618-19) and fortified by the *Nadere Reformatie*, a primarily seventeenth- and early eighteenth-century movement paralleling English Puritanism both in time and in substance. The *Nadere Reformatie* dates from Willem Teellinck (1579-1629),[12] often called the father of the movement, to its last brilliant contributors, Alexander Comrie (1706-74)[13] and Theodorus Van der Groe (1705-84).[14]

Episcopius addressing the members of the Synod of Dort.

The term *Nadere Reformatie* is a problem because it allows for no standard English translation of "nadere."[15] Literally, *Nadere Reformatie* means a nearer, more intimate, or more precise Reformation. Its emphasis is the working out of the Reformation more intensely in people's lives, in the church's worship, and in society.

Those who attempt to translate the term *Nadere Reformatie* inevitably color the translation with their own judgments of its significance. For example, the term has been translated as "Further Reformation," which is not accurate because it implies that the first Reformation did not go far enough. The *Nadere Reformatie* divines did not intend that. Rather, they sought to *apply* Reformation truths to practical, daily living. To avoid that false implication, Cornelis Graafland suggests the terms *Continuing Reformation* or *Second Reformation*. The term *continuing* has disadvantages, however: it does not distinguish the *Nadere Reformatie* from the Reformation proper, besides sounding awkward.[16]

I have chosen to use "Dutch Second Reformation" or "Second Reformation." While this translation misses the emphasis on the Reformation as a work in progress,[17] it has a long pedigree and appears to be gaining acceptance among scholars.[18] Moreover, "Second Reformation" was a term already used by some early Dutch divines of that era. For example, Jacobus Koelman (1632-1695), who had much contact with Scotland's Second Reformation, spoke of the Dutch movement as a "second reformation" and a "second purging."[19] Historically, there were second Reformation movements in the Netherlands, England, and Scotland to consolidate the gains and further the work of the Reformation.

I prefer not to use "Dutch Precisianism," "Dutch Pietism," or "Dutch Puritanism," because of the following reasons. Dutch Precisianism makes *Nadere Reformatie* sound too legalistic (*wettisch*). It is true that most Second Reformation divines promoted a negative ethic. Gisbertus Voetius, for example, forbade such practices as "visiting public houses, playing with dice, the wearing of luxurious clothes, dancing, drunkenness, revelry, smoking and the wearing of wigs." Nevertheless, such precisianism was not an end in itself. Rather, it was cultivated in the face of the "alleged worldliness then prevailing" and as a means of sustaining and developing individual faith and conduct against spiritual shallowness.[20]

Dutch Pietism might initially seem to be an acceptable translation of *Nadere Reformatie*. It has been widely used to show the movement's pietistic emphasis. However, that term is also problematic, for two reasons: First, it suggests an intimate connection with German Pietism.[21]

The *Nadere Reformatie* predates Spener's appeal for reform by nearly half a century and was more extensive as a movement than German Pietism. Additionally, Pietism among German Lutherans was more concerned with the believer's inner life than with transforming society, whereas most *Nadere Reformatie* divines were concerned with both.[22] And second, pietism is usually regarded as a protest against Protestant scholastic theology and doctrinal precision, whereas many *Nadere Reformatie* divines helped formulate Reformed orthodoxy and analyze doctrine.[23]

The *Nadere Reformatie* has also been called "Dutch Puritanism." But how accurate or helpful is such a description?

English Puritanism and the *Nadere Reformatie*

The *Nadere Reformatie* is the Dutch counterpart to English Puritanism. The link between those movements is strong, historically and theologically.[24] Keith Sprunger has shown that during the seventeenth century tens of thousands of Anglo-Scottish believers of Puritan persuasion lived in the Netherlands. Those believers represented about forty congregations and 350 ministers.[25] The Dutch government allowed the believers to organize churches and form an English classis within the Dutch Reformed Church. Cornelis Pronk notes that the presence of so many English and Scottish Puritans was bound to have some influence upon the Dutch churches. "Many Dutch Reformed ministers were impressed by the practical divinity of the English Puritans," Pronk says. "They saw it as a healthy corrective to the dry intellectualistic sermonizing that was becoming the trend in their churches."[26]

The divines of English Puritanism and the *Nadere Reformatie* respected each other. They enriched each other through personal contact and their writings, both their Latin treatises and the many books translated from English into Dutch.[27] More Reformed theological books were printed in the seventeenth century in the Netherlands than in all other countries combined.[28]

English Puritan and *Nadere Reformatie* divines had similar ideals: to foster God-glorifying experiential piety and ethical precision in individuals, churches, and nations. However, only England had the opportunity to fully work out those ideals, during the Cromwellian years.

Despite similar outlooks, English Puritanism and the *Nadere Reformatie* developed historically and theologically distinct identities. Hendrikus Berkhof is too simplistic in saying that the *Nadere Reformatie* resulted merely from "the practical piety of the English Calvinists blowing over to the Netherlands."[29] Though English Puritanism was a primary influence on the *Nadere Reformatie*—particularly in its stress on the need for a personal and congregational life of practical godliness (as Willem op't Hof has ably emphasized)[30]—it was not an exclusive influence. Non-English factors also contributed.[31] In some respects, the Dutch movement was more Puritan than English Puritanism itself. As Jonathan Gerstner says, "In England from an orthodox Reformed perspective, for all but a short period under Cromwell, there were always grossly unbiblical things to fight: the presence of bishops, superstitious rites in the Book of Common Prayer, vestments, etc. In the Netherlands none of these were present, and the task was all the more subtle. Defenders of the *status quo* were not so clearly unreformed as in England. In this context the true spirit of Puritanism came to the fore."[32]

Divines of the Dutch Second Reformation were less interested in reforming the government and church than were their English brethren. Their theological emphases also varied on doctrines such as assurance of faith. Also, the Dutch were more inclined to emphasize theology as a science, whereas the English emphasized the practical aspects of theology.[33] Sprunger notes that William Ames found the Dutch too intellectual and not sufficiently practical, and therefore promoted Puritan piety "in an effort to make Dutchmen into Puritans."[34] Those variations are not sufficiently respected when the Dutch movement is narrowly defined as Dutch Puritanism.[35]

Nevertheless, the essence of the Dutch Second Reformation does match the emphasis of English Puritanism on Reformed spirituality. S. van der Linde, a leading scholar on the Dutch Second Reformation, says the goal of the movement, like that of Puritanism, was to wed doctrine to the whole of daily life.[36] Van der Linde notes: "The Second Reformation sides entirely with the Reformation and levels criticism not so much against the *reformata* (the church which is reformed), but rather against the *reformanda* (the church which needs to be reformed)."[37]

Though the Second Reformation is preeminently concerned with spiritual life and experience, that concern is expressed in various ways. As van der Linde writes: "In Voetius we have the church-organizer, in Ames a very original theologian, in Teellinck and Brakel, divines of practical religion, and in Lodensteyn and Saldenus, the men of 'mysticism,' cross-bearing, and meditation upon the life to come."[38] Despite those differing emphases, van der Linde concludes there is an underlying element of precision in the Second Reformation that is inseparable from a fervent desire to counteract impiety with a piety that "con-sciously consecrates all of life to God."[39]

Scholars responsible for the periodical *Documentatieblad Nadere Reformatie*[40] offer two, well-stated definitions of the Dutch Second Reformation. The first definition, formulated in 1983, is the following:

> This movement within the Nederduits Gereformeerde Kerk (Dutch Reformed Church), while opposing generally prevailing abuses and misconceptions and pursuing the broadening and progressive advance-ment of the sixteenth-century Reformation, urges and strives with prophetic zeal for both the inner experience of Reformed doctrine and personal sanctification, as well as the radical and total sanctification of all spheres of life.[41]

The second definition, formulated in 1995, is more refined:

> The Dutch Second Reformation is that movement within the Neder-duits Gereformeerde Kerk (Dutch Reformed Church) during the seven-teenth and eighteenth centuries, which, as a reaction to the declension or absence of a living faith, made both the personal experience of faith and godliness matters of central importance. From that perspective the movement formulated substantial and procedural reformation initia-tives, submitting them to the proper ecclesiastical, political, and social agencies, and/or in conformity therewith pursued in both word and deed a further reformation of the church, society, and state.[42]

These definitions of the versatile Dutch Second Reformation are necessarily somewhat simplistic. As Graafland points out, the Second Reformation had no organizational structure beyond a strong feeling of spiritual kinship among its divines. At times this led to small organiza-tions such as the "Utrecht Circle" under the leadership of Voetius, or to programs for action, such as those promoted by Willem Teellinck and Jacobus Koelman. For the most part, however, each divine of the Sec-ond Reformation stressed the necessity of reform to his own parish-ioners. That call to reform naturally varied according to each locality and generation.[43]

Like English Puritanism, the preaching of the Second Reformation was experimental, featuring a well wrought-out theology of Christian experience. M. Eugene Osterhaven defines that theology as "that broad stream of Reformed teaching which, accepting the creeds of the church, emphasized the new birth, the conversion, and the sanctification of the believer so that he might acquire an experiential or personal knowledge of Christ's saving grace."[44] Religion, doctrine, and theological proposi-tions are not enough; feeling, experience, spiritual warfare, and prayer are also essential for faith and practice. The head knowledge of doctrine, albeit necessary, must be accompanied by the heart knowledge of scriptural experience.[45] For Second Reformation adherents, as well as for Puritans, formal Christianity (a Christianity that exhausted itself in externals) was only slightly better than none at all. For that reason they emphasized the importance of the inward response to God.[46] Struggles of faith thus were primary.[47]

Assurance of Faith

The relationship of faith and assurance became a focal point in both English Puritanism and the Dutch Second Reformation. The theologians of that age recognized that understanding their relationship required a delicate balance between objectivity and subjectivity, Scripture and experience, Word and Spirit.

In dealing with assurance, Puritan and Second Reformation divines sought to be faithful to the authority of Scripture as they wrestled with biblical data, exegesis, and hermeneutics. Because Scripture displays a formidable tension between vital faith and some kind of normative assurance, conjoined with the possibility of lacking assurance, the real question was: How could that scriptural tension be fleshed out in a pastoral context? In a meticulous addition to early Reformation doctrinal principles, English Puritan and Second Reformation divines decided that assurance was more complex than simply resting on the promises of God in Christ. When properly set in the context of Scripture, Christ, and the Trinity, the inward evidences of grace and the witness of the Spirit have a valid place as secondary grounds in the believer's assurance. Those foundations of assurance were codified in the confessions of both English Puritanism and the Dutch Second Reformation. The Dutch divines included it in the Canons of Dort (1619), stating that the foundations of assurance were "(1) faith in God's promises…(2) the testimony of the Holy Spirit witnessing with our spirit that we are children and heirs of God…(3) a serious and holy desire to preserve a good conscience and to perform good works" (Head 5, art. 10). And English Puritans included it in the Westminster Confession of Faith (1647), stating that the foundations of assurance were "the divine truth of the promises of salvation, the inward evidences of those graces unto which these promises are made, [and] the testimony of the Spirit of adoption witnessing with our spirits that we are the children of God" (chap. 18, par. 2).[48]

The grounds of assurance acquired a particular intensity in English

Puritanism and the Dutch Second Reformation as divines developed terminology and treatises on assurance. Their pastoral overtones of compassion for the weak in faith, pressing admonitions and invitations to grow in faith, and dissecting of temporary faith and other false forms of faith show how they relished communion with God in Christ. By elevating the importance of the secondary grounds of assurance (i.e., the inward evidences of grace and the witness of the Spirit) to a "mainline" from the "sideline" they occupied in Calvin's thought, the English Puritans and Second Reformation divines only enlarged, for pastoral reasons, as Graafland asserts, the "pores" that Calvin had already opened in allowing "signs which are sure attestations" of faith.[49] People who accuse the Puritans and Second Reformation divines of morbid intro- spection and anthropocentrism have simply missed the mark. The truth is, contemporary Christians have much to learn from the English Puri- tans and Second Reformation divines. They carefully examined per- sonal, spiritual experience because they were eager to trace the hand of God Triune in their lives and then return all glory to the electing Father, redeeming Son, and applying Spirit.

As an outgrowth of Calvin and the early Reformers' views on assur- ance, the Puritans and Second Reformation divines further developed the doctrine of assurance both pastorally and theologically, moving it from a Christological to a Trinitarian framework. The Reformers and post-Reformers may have different emphases, but they are one in this: Assurance of salvation ought to be regarded as the possession of all Christians in principle, despite varying measures of consciousness.[50] The "despite" clause is essential, for passages such as Psalm 88 warn us not to deny our redemption if we lack assurance. The clause also shows the pastoral sensitivity of Scripture by confirming that what is normal should not be equated with what is necessary in the matter of assurance.

For the Puritans and Second Reformation divines, assurance was a gift of God that involved the whole man, including his understanding and his will. Because the human will is incapable of choosing or cleav- ing to God in its own strength, the divines felt a great need to develop a clear doctrine of assurance. They knew the deceitfulness of their own hearts, and trembled to assume what God had not applied. On the other hand, they also detested unbelief. God was worthy of being trusted, they knew. So their goal, duty, and desire were faith and assurance in Him.[51]

In one sense, assurance was the most crucial issue of the post-Refor- mation. And the churches, for the most part, benefited by it. Puritan and Second Reformation expositions of assurance contributed to the spiritual health of churches, as long as they did not degenerate into unbiblical mysticism. As a rule, the divines exemplified a healthy, Pauline mysticism that was Word-regulated within a Christocentric and Trinitarian matrix. Out of that grew their strong emphasis on experimental religion that did not lead *from* but *to* Christ for increased faith and assurance. By sincerely believing that sound experimental religion was from Christ and by His Spirit, they aimed to rest that experience in the objective gospel.

The divines made no attempt to divorce subjective religion from the objective. Nor would they have endorsed such. That kind of religion, they would have said, may produce a full head but an empty heart. The post-Reformers aimed for whole-souled, intelligent piety. They wanted the kind of faith and assurance that feels the power of God's grace and rests on its foundations. Some of the post-Reformers probably should have tied the experiential emphases more thoroughly to the Word and to Christ, but their teaching leaves little doubt that this was what they intended.

What the English Puritans and Dutch Second Reformation divines believed on assurance far exceeded their differences. Both groups taught that full assurance of personal salvation is the fruit of faith rather than the essence of faith. Both taught that assurance may not be divorced from a scriptural, Trinitarian, and Christological framework. Both taught that assurance comes from the Holy Spirit. The Holy Spirit directs the believer to rest in the promises of God, enlightens him to conclude from the marks of grace that he is a child of God, and applies the Word to his conscience that Christ is *his* Savior.

Some leaders in both groups may have inappropriately ranked the importance of those modes of assurance and failed to recognize that various forms of assurance may be applied with various degrees of benefit. Some said the direct testimony of the Spirit is superior to assurance gleaned from reflecting by faith on inward evidences of grace. Others, recognizing that danger, combined these two forms of assurance. All agreed on the essence of assurance, saying the primary ground of assurance lies in the promises of God, though some in both groups chose to focus more on Spirit-enlightened, syllogistic reasoning.[52]

Divines in both groups recognized that the believer finds himself in constant flux in regard to his personal, experiential milieu. They taught that the Spirit knows best which kind of assurance to apply to the believer at any given time. Both groups acknowledged that assurance is covenantally based, sealed with the blood of Christ, and grounded ultimately in eternal election. Both affirmed that though assurance remains incomplete in this life, varies in degree, and is often weakened by affliction and doubt, its riches must never be taken for granted. It is always the sovereign gift of God Triune. Nevertheless, it must be diligently sought through the means of grace. And it only becomes well-grounded when it evidences fruits, such as love to God and for His kingdom, filial obedience, godly repentance, hatred for sin, brotherly love, and humble adoration.[53]

The English Puritans and the Dutch Second Reformation divines did differ generally on some aspects of assurance. The following represent the most significant:

As a whole, the English Puritans tended to emphasize the *marks of grace* more than the Dutch Second Reformation divines, who, in turn, stressed the *steps of grace* more than their brethren across the channel.[54] In this respect, it appears that the English had more influence on the Dutch than vice versa.[55] Jacobus Koelman, a notable Second Reformation divine and translator of numerous Puritan works, confessed that "books concerning the practice of godliness are rare; consequently, we are dependent upon England since the theologians there are very well exercised in this respect."[56]

The Dutch were more prone to schematize God's work of grace than the English,[57] placing a higher premium on the Spirit's advanced steps of grace.[58] For example, the Dutch stressed the Spirit's immediate internal witness and distanced that witness from syllogistic conclusions more than the English.[59] They regarded the sealing of the Spirit as a special work above and beyond a normal experience of faith.[60] They paid more attention to justification in the court of conscience as an experience of assurance being sealed rather than as a metaphor of how assurance is received.

The greater emphasis the Dutch had on the advanced steps in grace and lesser emphasis on normal steps is a major reason why the English Puritans made greater allowance for various degrees of assurance. The English had greater hope for assurance by means of the promises and syllogisms. No English Puritan taught, as Teellinck did, that scarce one in ten rises even to these forms of assurance.[61]

The Dutch emphasized receiving assurance as a sovereign gift, whereas the English emphasized seeking assurance as a solemn duty. Hence, the English often provided elaborate directions, even entire treatises, on how to obtain assurance and why the believer must strive for it.[62]

Accordingly, the Puritan stress was on the act (*actus*) of faith; the Dutch, on the principle or habit (*habitus*) of faith. Many divines in both groups, however, worked for balance between the habit and act of faith. They recognized that if the *habitus* was neglected, voluntarism might be encouraged; if the *actus* was minimized, a lethargic brand of antinomianism, which viewed faith as something to *have* rather than to *exercise*, might result.

The English emphasized the need for the fruits of assurance.[63] The English leaned more toward the practical syllogism; the Dutch increasingly leaned toward the mystical syllogism.[64] Graafland and van der Linde are sharply critical of that transition, but van der Linde fails to note that the mystical syllogism is also inseparable from the enlightening of the Spirit.[65] Moreover, an underlying emphasis on the activity of faith influenced the English toward a greater evangelistic thrust[66] and greater use of sense perception[67] in describing assurance of faith.

The varying emphases of the English and Dutch divines should not be exaggerated. Both movements contained such varying emphases that whatever was true of their differences as groups was not true of each individual. For example, the English and Dutch divines who stressed predestination and the monopleuric character of the covenant also tended to emphasize assurance apart from ourselves (*extra nos*) in the promises of God. Those who stressed conditionality in the covenant emphasized assurance found within (*intra nos*) by means of the syllogisms and the direct testimony of the Spirit.[68] The different emphases of Puritans, such as John Owen and Richard Baxter, and Second Reformation

Thomas Goodwin

John Owen

divines, such as Alexander Comrie and Wilhelmus à Brakel, show considerable differing emphases within a broad consensus.

Some divines, such as Thomas Goodwin, offered a mix of emphases of English Puritanism and the Dutch Second Reformation. Goodwin promoted both the marks and steps of grace. He schematized grace more than Owen but less than Comrie. He stressed the Spirit's internal witness but allowed a role of "comfortable believing" to the syllogisms. While affirming the expectation for assurance, he stressed the rarity of full assurance. He presented assurance as a solemn duty as well as a sovereign gift. He emphasized both the habit and the acts of faith.[69]

The message that emerges from both Puritans and Second Reformation divines is this: Assurance is the cream of faith; it is inseparable from each of its exercises. Assurance grows by faith in the promises of God, by inward evidences of grace, and by the witness of the Spirit. Each of those means should be diligently prayed for and pursued; none should be separated from the others, for undue emphasis on one will lead to a distortion of others.[70] The believer is dependent upon the application of the Holy Spirit for each of them.

Lessons for the Church

In conclusion, here are some lessons that English Puritanism and the Dutch Second Reformation have for the contemporary church:

First, we learn from the Puritan and Dutch Second Reformation divines that we should retrench ourselves in the great truths of Holy Scripture. The divines of both movements found all they needed in the Bible. Here was a system of doctrine, a manual for worship, and a church order that was God-breathed, comprehensive, all-sufficient, and utterly compelling. We too must relish that authority and protect it from erosion.

Puritanism and the Second Reformation call us to cherish once again the vision of God in the compelling self-revelation of His majestic, yet tender, attributes. That will help us love the Lord Jesus in His fullness far more than we do. Puritan and Second Reformation pastors would have all men bow before Christ as Lord and Judge of all flesh. They would have every sinner come to Him for cleansing, healing, and life.

Second, even as English Puritanism and the Dutch Second Reformation show us the reality of our desperately wicked hearts and the corruption of this polluted world, they provide balance by calling us to savor the liberty of worship under the new covenant. Likewise, we need to restore a dread sense of sin and a sorrow over our poverty in sanctification in God's people, and call believers to a royal priesthood through

Christ and His Spirit. Puritanism and the Second Reformation have much to teach about the discipline of mortification and the unending riches of experiencing communion with the divine persons of the blessed Trinity—and the contemporary church has much to learn from such teaching.

Third, as the doctrine of sanctification inevitably flows out of the doctrine of justification, so English Puritanism and the Second Reformation grew out of the Reformation. The relationship between the Reformation and the two movements is a kind of illustration, as it were, of the inseparable relationship between justification and sanctification. Aiming for more sanctification in our churches thus calls for more lucid teaching of justification by faith.

In this, two extremes must be avoided: doctrinal precision in justification at the expense of the piety of biblical sanctification, which was generally true of Dutch orthodoxy prior to the Second Reformation; and sanctification at the expense of doctrinal precision relative to justification, a tendency of a few Puritans like Richard Baxter. Like most Puritan and Second Reformation divines, we must strive for a balance of doctrinal precision and biblical piety, thereby acknowledging the inseparable union of the two.

We must vigorously promote a biblically experiential religion that stresses the experience of both justification and sanctification. As essential as experiential knowledge of Christ is in justification, so it is essential that we know Him experientially through sanctification. We must know Him as a "priest after the order of Melchizedek" who rules us as King. The experiential religion of the Puritan and Second Reformation movements was filled with vitality because it stressed both through scriptural meditation, the cultivation of humility, and the profit of affliction.

Fourth, as the Reformers labored to return to apostolic teaching via Augustine, so the Puritans and Second Reformation divines labored to return to the apostolic teaching and practice expounded by the Reformers. Likewise, we must also labor to perpetuate their work, which originated in Christ (who is the crowning piece and fulfillment of Old Testament truth) and was perpetuated by the apostles, Augustine, the Reformers, the Puritans, and Second Reformation divines. The church today must cultivate the simplicity of biblical, theocentric, and Christocentric worship.

We must labor for the continual reforming of doctrine and life in the church. This reformation must, as the Puritan and Dutch Second Reformation divines never tired of telling us, commence with us as individuals. As the Reformation, Puritan, and Second Reformation movements started at the grassroots level of influencing individual hearts, so we must strive to reform our pulpits and congregations to bring about a reformation in our day. Let us use the means of grace prayerfully and diligently to improve the spirituality of ourselves and our families, and to bring us all back to the kind of daily worship practiced by the Second Reformation and Puritan divines.

The Puritan and Second Reformation divines struggled for spiritual balance in their lives. In their consciences, in their families, at work, and in church, they sought *soli Deo gloria*. They saw no separation between sacred and secular; their entire lives were devoted to divine service. We must learn from them that all we do must be done to the glory of God.

Finally, like the Puritan and Second Reformation divines, we must strive for theological scholarship that is subservient to God's kingdom in this world. We must thus avoid the pursuit and practice of theology as a mere academic enterprise. Like the divines of a former day, we must strive for the kind of scholarship that says: "Hallowed be Thy Name; Thy kingdom come; Thy will be done." As J. I. Packer says concerning the Puritans (and can also be applied to their counterparts in the Netherlands):

> The Puritans made me aware that all theology is also spirituality, in the sense that it has an influence, good or bad, positive or negative, on its recipients' relationship or lack of relationship to God. If our theology does not quicken the conscience and soften the heart, it actually hardens both; if it does not encourage the commitment of faith, it reinforces the detachment of unbelief; if it fails to promote humility, it inevitably feeds pride. So one who theologizes in public, whether formally in the pulpit, on the podium or in print, or informally from the armchair, must think hard about the effect his thoughts will have on people—God's people, and other people.[71]

On the other hand, we must not abandon theological scholarship, which nearly became the norm in Dutch experiential Christianity during the nineteenth century after the Second Reformation subsided. The academic credentials of Puritan and Second Reformation divines unquestionably influenced their ability to exegete and expound the Scriptures. The Holy Spirit used those gifts mightily in that time, and He is able to do so as well today. In this day of small things and weak men, may God enable us to become the kind of spiritual giants those Puritan and Second Reformation divines once were.

---

[1] *Elizabethan Puritanism* (New York: Oxford, 1971), 3.

[2] *The Workes of That Famovs and VVorthy Minister of Christ in the Vniuersitie of Cambridge, Mr. William Perkins* (London: John Legatt, 1612-13)[hereafter: *Works of Perkins*], 1:342, 3:15.

[3] *The Rise of Puritanism* (New York: Columbia, 1938), 83.

[4] *Errand into the Wilderness* (Cambridge: Belknap Press, 1956), 48-89.

[5] *Puritanism in Old and New England* (Chicago: University of Chicago Press, 1955), 2.

[6] *Society and Puritanism* (New York: Schocken, 1967).

[7] *The Pauline Renaissance in England: Puritanism and the Bible* (Oxford: University Press, 1970).

[8] "The Logic of Assurance in English Puritan Theology," *Westminster Theological Journal* 52 (1990):247.

[9] *The Genius of Puritanism* (Haywards Heath, Sussex: Carey, 1975], 11ff. For additional difficulties involved in defining Puritanism, see Ralph Bronkema, *The Essence of Puritanism* (Goes: Oosterbaan and LeCointre, 1929); Leonard J. Trinterud, "The Origins of Puritanism," *Church History* 20 (1951):37-57; Jerald C. Brauer, "Reflections on the Nature of English Puritanism," *Church History* 23 (1954):98-109; Basil Hall, "Puritanism: The Problem of Definition," in G. J. Cumming, ed., *Studies in Church History*, vol. 2 (London, 1965), 283-96; Charles H. George, "Puritanism as History and Historiography," *Past and Present* 41 (1968):77-104; William Lamont, "Puritanism as History and Historiography: Some Further Thoughts," *Past and Present* 42 (1969):133-46; Lionel Greve, "Freedom and Discipline in the Theology of John Calvin, William Perkins, and John Wesley: An Examination of the Origin and Nature of Pietism" (Ph.D. dissertation, Hartford Seminary Foundation, 1976), 151ff.; Richard Greaves, "The Nature of the Puritan Tradition," in R. Buick Knox, ed., *Reformation, Conformity and Dissent: Essays in Honour of Geoffrey Nuttall* (London: Epworth Press, 1977), 255-73; D. M. Lloyd-Jones, "Puritanism and Its Origins," *The Puritans: Their Origins and Successors* (Edinburgh: Banner of Truth Trust, 1987), 237-59; J. I. Packer, "Why We Need the Puritans," in *A Quest for Godliness: The Puritan Vision of the Christian Life* (Wheaton: Crossway Books, 1990), 21ff.

[10] Dutch Anabaptists continued to be martyred, however, until the 1570s in the Netherlands, despite the fact that the movement itself lost impetus by 1545.

[11] Mention should also be made of the followers of Erasmus who precipitated the Dutch Second Reformation in a negative sense. Cf. W. Robert Godfrey, "The Dutch Reformed Response," in *Discord, Dialogue, and Concord*, ed. by Lewis W. Spitz and Wenzel Lohff (Philadelphia: Fortress Press, 1977), 166-67. Godfrey also gives a succinct overview of the Calvinist aspect in "Calvin and Calvinism in the Netherlands," in *John Calvin: His Influence in the Western World*, ed. by W. Stanford Reid (Grand Rapids: Zondervan, 1982), 95-122. Also, see Walter Lagerway, "The History of Calvinism in the Netherlands," in *The Rise and Development of Calvinism*, ed. John Bratt (Grand Rapids: Eerdmans, 1959), 63-102; Jerry D. van der Veen, "Adoption of Calvinism in the Reformed Church in the Netherlands" (B.S.T. thesis, Biblical Seminary in New York, 1951).

[12] What William Perkins was to English Puritanism, Willem Teellinck was to the Dutch Second Reformation; hence these divines are often denominated as "the fathers" of these respective movements (Joel R. Beeke, *Assurance of Faith: Calvin, English Puritanism, and the Dutch Second Reformation* [New York: Peter Lang, 1991], 105-138).

[13] Ibid., 281-320.

[14] For a concise introduction to the leading *Nadere Reformatie* divines, see B. Glasius, ed., *Godgeleerd Nederland: Biographisch Woordenboek van Nederlandsche Godgeleerden*, 3 vols. ('s-Hertogenbosch: Gebr. Muller, 1851-56); Sietse Douwes van Veen, *Voor tweehonderd jaren: Schetsen van het leven onzer Gereformeerde Vaderen*, 2nd ed. (Utrecht: Kemink & Zoon, 1905); J. P. de Bie and J. Loosjes, eds., *Biographisch Woordenboek Protestantische Godgeleerden in Nederland*, 5 vols. ('s-Gravenhage: Martinus Nijhoff, 1907-1943); *Christelijke Encyclopedie*, 6 vols., 2nd ed. (Kampen: J. H. Kok, 1959); K. Exalto, *Beleefd Geloof: Acht schetsen van gereformeerde theologen uit de 17e Eeuw* (Amsterdam: Ton Bolland, 1974), and *De Kracht der Religie: Tien schetsen van Gereformeerde 'Oude Schrijvers' uit de 17e en 18e Eeuw* (Urk: De Vuurtoren, 1976); H. Florijn, ed., *Hollandse Geloofshelden* (Utrecht: De Banier, 1981); W. van Gorsel, *De Ijver voor Zijn Huis: De Nadere Reformatie en haar belangrijkste vertegenwoordigers* (Groede: Pieters, 1981); C. J. Malan, *Die Nadere Reformasie* (Potchefstroom: Potchefstroomse Universiteit vir CHO, 1981); H. Florijn, *100 Portretten van Godgeleerden in Nederland uit de 16e, 17e, 18e Eeuw* (Utrecht: Den Hertog, 1982); D. Nauta, et al., *Biografisch Lexicon voor de Geschiedenis van het Nederlandse Protestantisme*, 4 vols. (Kampen: Kok, 1978-98); W. van't Spijker, et al., *De Nadere Reformatie. Beschrijving van haar voornaamste vertegenwoordigers* ('s-Gravenhage: Boekencentrum, 1986), and *De Nadere Reformatie en het Gereformeerd Pietisme* ('s-Gravenhage: Boekencentrum, 1989); Joel R. Beeke, "Biographies of Dutch Second Reformation Divines," *Banner of Truth* 54, 2 (1988) through 56, 3 (1990)—a series of twenty-five articles representing the major divines of the movement.

For bibliography of the Dutch Second Reformation, see P. L. Eggermont, "Bibliographie van het Nederlandse Pietisme in de zeventiende en achttiende eeuw," *Documentatie-blad 18e eeuw* 3 (1969):17-31; W. van Gent, *Bibliotheek van oude schrijvers* (Rotterdam: Lindebergs, 1979); J. van der Haar, *Schatkamer van de Gereformeerde Theologie in Nederland (c. 1600-c.1800): Bibliografisch Onderzoek* (Veenendaal: Antiquariaat Kool, 1987).

Cf. F. Ernest Stoeffler, *The Rise of Evangelical Pietism* (Leiden: Brill, 1971), 109-68, covering twelve Second Reformation divines in varying depth and quality; Cornelis Graafland, *De Zekerheid van het Geloof: Een onderzoek naar de geloofsbeschouwing van enige vertegenwoordigers van reformatie en nadere reformatie* (Wageningen: H. Veenman & Zonen, 1961), 138-244, concentrating on the doctrine of faith and assurance in fourteen Second Reformation theologians; Johannes de Boer, *De Verzegeling met de Heilige Geest volgens de opvatting van de Nadere Reformatie* (Rotterdam: Bronder, 1968), which examines the soteriological thought of fourteen Second Reformation divines.

Monographs have also been published in Dutch on the following divines of Dutch Second Reformation persuasion (the author's surname is within parentheses): Baudartius (Roelofs); Bogerman (van Itterzon; van der Tuuk); W. à Brakel (Los); Colonius (Hoek); Comrie (Honig; Verboom); Dathenus (Ruijs); Gomarus (van Itterzon); Haemstedius (Jelsma); Helmichius (Hania); Hommius (Wijminga); Hoornbeeck (Hofmeyr); Junius (de Jonge, Reitsma, Venemans); Koelman (Janse, Krull); Lodenstein (Proost; Slagboom); Lubbertus (van der Woude); Marnix (van Schelven); Maresius (Nauta); Rivetus (Honders); Saldenus (van den End); Schortinghuis (Kromsigt; de Vrijer); Smytegelt (de Vrijer); Taffin (van der Linde); Teellinck (Engelberts; Bouwman); Trigland (ter Haar); Voetius (Bouwman, Duker, Janse, McCahagan, Steenblok); Udemans (Meertens, Vergunst); Walaeus (van

Wijngaarden); Wittewrongel (Groenendijk). For bibliographical information on these studies, see Beeke, *Assurance of Faith*, 451-500.

[15] The term was used as early as Jean Taffin (1528-1602). Cf. L. F. Groenendijk, "De Oorsprong van de uitdrukking 'Nadere Reformatie,'" *Documentatieblad Nadere Reformatie* 9 (1985):128-34; S. van der Linde, "Jean Taffin: eerste pleiter voor 'Nadere Reformatie' in Nederland," *Theologia Reformata* 25 (1982):7ff.; W. van't Spijker, in *De Nadere Reformatie en het Gereformeerd Pietisme*, 5ff.

[16] Jonathan Neil Gerstner, *The Thousand Generation Covenant: Dutch Reformed Covenant Theology and Group Identity in Colonial South Africa, 1652-1814* (London: E. J. Brill, 1991), 75ff.

[17] Ibid., 75n.

[18] J. W. Hofmeyr, "The Doctrine of Calvin as Transmitted in the South African Context by Among Others the *Oude Schrijvers*," in *Calvinus Reformator: His contribution to Theology, Church and Society* (Potchefstroom: Potchefstroom University for Christian Higher Education, 1983), 260.

[19] *Christelijke Encyclopedie*, 5:128.

[20] Martin H. Prozesky, "The Emergence of Dutch Pietism," *Journal of Ecclesiastical History* 28 (1977):33.

[21] Stoeffler (*The Rise of Evangelical Pietism*, which attempts to define "Pietism" as embracing English Puritanism, the Dutch Second Reformation, and German Pietism, 1-23) and James Tanis (*Dutch Calvinistic Pietism in the Middle Colonies: A Study in the Life and Theology of Theodorus Jacobus Frelinghuysen* [The Hague: Martinus Nijhoff, 1967] and "The Heidelberg Catechism in the Hands of the Calvinistic Pietists," *Reformed Review* 24 [1970-71]:154-61) follow German church historians in using the term, "Dutch Pietism," notably Heinrich Heppe (*Geschichte des Pietismus und der Mystik in der Reformierten Kirche, namentlich der Niederlande* [Leiden: Brill, 1879]) and Albrecht Ritschl (*Geschichte des Pietismus*, 3 vols. [Bonn: Marcus, 1880-86]).

For the influence of German Pietism on the Dutch Second Reformation, see Graafland, "De Gereformeerde Orthodoxie en het Pietisme in Nederland," *Nederlands Theologisch Tijdschrift* 19 (1965):466-79; J. Steven O'Malley, *Pilgrimage of Faith: The Legacy of the Otterbeins* (Metuchen, N.J.: The Scarecrow Press, 1973); Willem Balke, "Het Pietisme in Oostfriesland," *Theologia Reformata* 21 (1978):308-327.

[22] S. van der Linde, *Vromen en Verlichten: Twee Eeuwen Protestantse Geloofsbeleving 1650-1850* (Utrecht: Aartsbisschoppelijk Museum Utrecht, 1974), 2; Gerstner, *Thousand Generation Covenant*, 76.

[23] Ibid., 76.

[24] Cf. *Dutch Puritanism: A History of English and Scottish Churches of the Netherlands in the Sixteenth and Seventeenth Centuries* (Leiden: Brill, 1982), and *The Learned Doctor William Ames: Dutch Backgrounds of English and American Puritanism* (Chicago: University of Illinois Press, 1972); Douglas MacMillan, "The Connection between 17th Century British and Dutch Calvinism," in *Not by Might nor by Power*, 1988 Westminster Conference papers, 22-31.

[25] Willem op't Hof points out the influence of Dutch refugee congregations in England, noting that "it can be justifiably concluded that it is chiefly the Dutch congregations in England which are in the background of the Puritanization of spiritual life in the Netherlands" (*Engelse pietistische geschriften in het Nederlands, 1598-1622* [Rotterdam: Lindenberg, 1987], 639).

[26] "The Dutch Puritans," *Banner of Truth*, nos. 154-55 (July-August, 1976):3.

[27] Speaking of English Puritan writings translated into Dutch from 1598 to 1622, op't Hof says, "A total of 114 editions were issued of a total of 60 translations. These 60 translations concerned works by…twenty-two English authors…. Two authors are numerically preeminent among them: Cowper (18 editions of 10 translations) and Perkins (71 editions of 29 translations). Indeed, Perkins alone eclipses all the others taken together…. Auction catalogues show that Udemans possessed 20 Puritan books in Latin and 57 in English. Similarly, Voetius possessed 30 Puritan works in Latin and 270 in English…. A rough estimate for the period from 1623-1699 gives 260 new translations, 580 editions and 100 new translators" (*Engelse pietistische geschriften in het Nederlands,* 636-37, 640, 645).

[28] Sprunger, *Dutch Puritanism,* 307.

[29] *Geschiedenis der Kerk* (Nijkerk: G. F. Callenbach, 1955), 228.

[30] *Engelse pietistische geschriften in het Nederlands,* 583-97, 627-35, 645-46. Cf. Cornelis Graafland, "De Invloed van het Puritanisme op het Ontstaan van het Gereformeerd Pietisme in Nederland," *Documentatieblad Nadere Reformatie* 7, 1 (1983):1-19. Graafland also details influences on preaching, the art of meditation, casuistry, covenanting, the administration of the Lord's Supper, and eschatology.

[31] Ibid., 2, 15-16.

[32] Gerstner, *Thousand Generation Covenant,* 77-78.

[33] Pronk, *The Banner of Truth,* nos. 154-55 (July-August, 1976):6. Gerstner explains: "As orthodox Reformed in their doctrine as the English Puritans were, they were primarily pastors, not formal theologians. Thus one finds a remarkable scarcity of systematic theologies. Dutch Reformed thought while retaining a strong emphasis on the pulpit, produced a remarkable number of theological works, the majority addressed to the average person. Catechism preaching was perhaps part of the reason, but it seems they possessed a greater tendency towards system building. So the Continuing Reformation pastor strove for his parishioner's conversion, and at the same time to make him a dogmatician" (*Thousand Generation Covenant,* 78).

[34] *The Learned Doctor Ames: Dutch Backgrounds of English and American Puritanism,* 260. Cf. Hugo Visscher, *Guilielmus Ames, Zijn Leven en Werken* (Haarlem: J. M. Stap, 1894).

[35] This term has been used more accurately to depict English-speaking Puritan churches in the Netherlands (cf. Douglas Campbell, *The Puritan in Holland, England, and America*, 4th ed., 2 vols. [New York: Harper and Brothers, 1892]; Sprunger, *Dutch Puritanism*; T. Brienen, *De prediking van de Nadere Reformatie* [Amsterdam: Ton Bolland, 1974]). Van der Linde prefers "English Puritanism in the Netherlands" to "Dutch Puritanism," since the English Puritans in the Netherlands confined themselves largely to their own circles (cf. "Jean Taffin: eerste pleiter voor 'Nadere Reformatie' in Nederland," *Theologie Reformata* 25 [1982]: 6ff.).

[36] "De Godservaring bij W. Teellinck, D. G. à Brakel en A. Comrie," *Theologia Reformata* 16 (1973):205.

[37] "De betekenis van de Nadere Reformatie voor Kerk en Theologie," *Kerk en Theologie* 5 (1954):216.

[38] Ibid., 218.

[39] *Het Gereformeerde Protestantisme* (Nijkerk: G. F. Callenbach, 1957), 9.

[40] Those scholars have an officially organized society in the Netherlands, *Stichting Studie der Nadere Reformatie*. The express goal of the SSNR is to promote in-depth study of the Dutch Second Reformation.

[41] *Documentatieblad Nadere Reformatie* 7 (1983):109.

[42] *Documentatieblad Nadere Reformatie* 19 (1995):108, translated by Bartel Elshout in his *The Pastoral and Practical Theology of Wilhelmus à Brakel* (Grand Rapids: Reformation Heritage Books, 1997), 9.

[43] Graafland, "Kernen en contouren van de Nadere Reformatie," in *De Nadere Reformatie: Beschrijving van haar voornaamste vertegenwoordigers*, 350.

[44] "The Experiential Theology of Early Dutch Calvinism, " *Reformed Review* 27 (1974):180.

[45] Ibid., 183-84.

[46] Stoeffler, *The Rise of Evangelical Pietism*, 14.

[47] Van der Linde, "De betekenis van de Nadere Reformatie voor Kerk en Theologie," in *Opgang en voortgang der reformatie*, 146.

[48] For detailed exposition of how those movements worked out these foundations of assurance, and for primary source proof of the generalizations that follow with regard to their views on assurance of faith, see Beeke, *Assurance of Faith*, chaps. 5-9.

[49] Graafland faults the Second Reformation divines for allowing the subjective line of assurance to "overrule" the objective, but recognizes that this accentuation of subjective assurance was an outgrowth of combatting various forms of pseudo-faith. He asserts that when subjective assurance is prominent as in the Second Reformation, assurance itself becomes problematical and is prone to be viewed as a scarce entity belonging to the quintessence rather than the essence of faith. The post-Reformers, Graafland concludes, "end where Calvin begins" ("Waarheid in het Binnenste," pp. 69ff.). Though Graafland's presentation is largely accurate, he overstates his conclusions, since the post-Reformers still retained the priority of the promises of God. He neglects to point out that the post-Reformers made more use of the secondary grounds of assurance than Calvin in order to validate that the promises of God were intended particularly for the believer. Though Graafland asserts that the post-Reformers remain relatively close to Calvin notwithstanding their varying emphases, they are still closer than he is willing to admit (cf. Beeke, *Assurance of Faith*, 72-78).

[50] "Reformed theology is fond of insisting that, while full assurance is frequently experienced, it is never inevitable, never continuously sustained and certainly does not patently characterise every degree of Christian stature here below" (G. Thomson, "Assurance," *The Evangelical Quarterly* 14 [1942]:7).

[51] Hence Bunyan has Christian walking over a narrow precipice with the yawning cavern of presumption on one side and unbelief on the other (*The Complete Works of John Bunyan*, 2:38).

[52] Graafland argues that this represents the majority of Second Reformation divines (cf. note 7 above).

[53] Cf. Donald MacLeod, "Christian Assurance 2," *Banner of Truth*, no. 133 (November 1974):1-7.

[54] Cf. Beeke, *Assurance of Faith*, 310ff.

[55] E.g., William Ames, professor in theology at Franeker University (1622-33). "Through missionaries like Ames, the Dutch precisionist movement was fed with choice Puritan doctrines. From the English sprang forth practical divinity 'as from a perennial spring,' praised Voetius" (Sprunger, *Dutch Puritanism*, 359). According to Matthias Nethenus, Voetius's colleague at the University of Utrecht: "In England...the study of practical theology has flourished marvelously; and in the Dutch

churches and schools, from the time of Willem Teellinck and Ames it has ever more widely spread, even though all do not take to it with equal interest" (introduction to Ames, *Omnia Opera*, trans. and ed. by Douglas Horton, in *William Ames* [Harvard: Harvard Divinity School Library, 1965], 15).

56 Cited by Graafland, "De Invloed van het Puritanisme op het Ontstaan van het Gereformeerd Pietisme in Nederland," *Documentatie blad Nadere Reformatie* 7 (1983):5. As Sprunger notes: "The translation into Dutch and printing of Puritan books in Holland was an enterprise for spreading the Puritan doctrines of godliness among the Dutch. Writings of William Perkins, William Ames, William Whately, Lewis Bayly, William Whitaker, Thomas Hooker, Richard Sibbes, Paul Baynes, Robert Bolton, Richard Baxter, Daniel Dyke, Thomas Adams, William Prynne, Thomas Cartwright, Henry Ainsworth, and Thomas Goodwin are a few of the Puritan books put into Dutch. The traffic in books also went the other way [but not to the same degree, JRB], worthy Dutch books being put into English" (*Dutch Puritanism*, 359-60). Cf. VanderHaar, *Van Abbadie tot Young*; Schoneveld, *Intertraffic of the Mind*.

57 Cf. Beeke, *Assurance of Faith,* 363ff., 212ff.

58 Ibid., 211ff. A notable exception in this regard is experimental communion with the distinct Persons of the Trinity (ibid., 191, 215, 343ff.).

59 Ibid., 127, 303ff., 349ff.

60 Ibid., 245ff., 340, 358ff.

61 Ibid., 124, 234, 364ff.

62 Ibid., 167, 231, 240ff., 341, 362.

63 Ibid., 359ff.

64 Ibid., 148, 310ff.; Graafland, "Van *syllogismus practicus* naar *syllogismus mysticus*," in *Wegen en Gestalten in het Gereformeerd Protestantisme*, 105-122.

65 "De Godservaring bij W. Teellinck, D. G. à Brakel en A. Comrie," *Theologia Reformata* 16 (1973):202-203. Cf. van der Linde, *Opgang en voortgang der reformatie*, 146.

66 Cf. Beeke, *Assurance of Faith*, 331-32n.

67 Ibid., 354ff.

68 Cf. Letham, "Saving Faith and Assurance in Reformed Theology," 1:362ff., who argues that this distinction is traceable back to the sixteenth century as well. Cf. Stephen Strehle, *Calvinism, Federalism, and Scholasticism: A Study of the Reformed Doctrine of Covenant* (New York: Peter Lang, 1988), 137ff., 188ff., 386-92.

69 E.g., Goodwin emphasizes the Spirit's implanting of faith in *The Work of the Holy Spirit*, but stresses the acts of faith in *The Objects and Acts of Justifying Faith* (*Works of Thomas Goodwin*, vols. 6 and 8).

70 Ernest Reisinger asserts that to hold to assurance by means of the first (i.e., the promises of God) without affirming the second (i.e., Christian character and conduct) and third (i.e., the Spirit's witness), is *antinomianism*. To hold exclusively to the second without the first and third is *legalism*; to maintain the third at the expense of the first two, is "either *hypocrisy* or the *deepest self-delusion or fantasy*" (*Today's Evangelism: Its Message and Methods* [Phillipsburg, N.J.: Craig Press, 1982], 127ff.).

71 *A Quest for Godliness: The Puritan Vision of the Christian Life* (Wheaton: Crossway, 1990), 15.

Willem Teellinck (1579-1629)

14

Willem Teellinck and
The Path of True Godliness

Christians know that the practice of godliness is no easy task. They want to glorify God, but often do not know how to go about it. They know they need "to put on the whole armour of God" (Eph. 6:11), but often have little understanding of what it is or how to use it. For example, how does the believer use the Word of God to arm himself, to uncover the schemes of the enemy, and to press on to victory? How do we use prayer in this battle? Should we tell God in prayer how strong our enemies are, how weak we are, and how desperately we need His Son to help us? How do believers flee from temptation? What can they do to purge their mind of blasphemous thoughts and selfish pride? How should they battle a sense of despair when affliction strikes? How can they learn from mature Christians how to fight the good fight of faith? What is the proper role of self-examination in this fight? How does the believer open his heart to God's promises?

These are questions that Willem Teellinck answers in *The Path of True Godliness*. The book is packed with scriptural and practical guidance for Christians who earnestly desire to live holy lives focused on God and His glory.

Teellinck is often called "the father of the Dutch *Nadere Reformatie*," usually translated as the "Further" or "Second Reformation," much as William Perkins is called the father of English Puritanism. As discussed in the previous chapter, the *Nadere Reformatie* was primarily a seventeenth- and early eighteenth-century movement that roughly paralleled English Puritanism, dating from such early representatives as Jean Taffin (1528/9-1602) and Willem Teellinck (1579-1629) to its last major contributors, Alexander Comrie (1706-1774) and Theodorus Van der Groe (1705-1784). Like English Puritanism, it stressed the necessity of a vital Christian piety, true to the teachings of Scripture and the Reformed confessions, and consistently worked out in all aspects of one's daily life.

The Banbury church in the eighteenth century.

Education and Family Life

Willem Teellinck was born January 4, 1579, in Zerikzee, the main town on the island of Duiveland, Zeeland, to a godly, prominent family. He was the youngest of eight children. His father, Joost Teellinck (1543-1594), who served as mayor of Zerikzee two years prior to Willem's birth, died when Willem was fifteen years old. His mother, Johanna de Jonge (1552-1609), survived her husband by fifteen years but was often sickly when Willem was young. Willem was well educated in his youth; he studied law at St. Andrews in Scotland (1600) and at the University of Poitiers in France, where he earned a doctorate in 1603.

The following year he spent nine months with the Puritan community in England. His lodging with a godly family in Banbury and his exposure to Puritan godliness—lived out through extensive family worship, private prayer, sermon discussions, Sabbath observance, fast days, spiritual fellowship, self-examination, heartfelt piety, and good works—profoundly impressed him. At that time, Psalm-singing could be heard everywhere a person walked in Banbury, particularly on Sabbath days. These Puritans did not feel at home in the established church; they believed that the Reformation had been shortchanged in England, and greatly admired Calvin's Genevan model for church, society, and family life. Godly Puritans in England such as John Dod (d. 1645) and

Arthur Hildersham (1563-1632) were their mentors, and the people lived what these divines taught. Teellinck would later write about the fruits of their holy living: "Their Christian walk was such that it convinced even their most bitter foes of the sincerity and wholeheartedness of their faith and practice. The foes saw faith working powerfully through love, demonstrated in their straightforward business dealings, charitable deeds to the poor, visiting and comforting the sick and oppressed, educating the ignorant, convincing the erring, punishing the wicked, reproving the idle, and encouraging the devout. And all this was done with diligence and sensitivity, as well as joy, peace, and happiness, such that it was obvious that the Lord was truly with them."

Teellinck believed the Lord converted him in England. A zeal for God's truth and Puritan piety that was never quenched was born in his heart. He surrendered his life to the Lord and considered changing his field of studies to theology. After consulting some astute theologians in England and holding a day of prayer and fasting with his friends, Teellinck decided to study theology at Leiden. He trained there for two years under Lucas Trelcatius (1542-1602), Franciscus Gomarus (1563-1641), and James Arminius (1560-1609). He felt most attached to Trelcatius and tried to stay neutral in the tensions that had developed between Gomarus and Arminius.

While in England, Teellinck met Martha Greendon, a young Puritan woman from Derby, who became his wife. She shared Teellinck's life goal of living out the Puritan *praxis pietatis* (practice of piety) in family life as well as in their parish work. Their first son, Johannes, died in infancy. They were then blessed with three sons—Maximiliaan, Theodorus, and Johannes—all of whom became Reformed ministers with emphases similar to their father's. They also had two daughters: Johanna, who married an English minister; and Maria, who married a political official at Middelburg. The oldest son, Maximiliaan, became pastor of the English-speaking church at Vlissingen in 1627, then served at Middelburg until his death in 1653. Willem Teellinck did not live to see his younger sons ordained into the ministry. None of the sons became as renowned as their father, although Johannes drew some attention as pastor at Utrecht through his book *Den Vruchtbaarmakende Wijnstock* [Christ, the Fructifying Vine] and a sermon on God's promises. In both he tried to move the Second Reformation in a more objective direction.

Teellinck edified his family by his godly example. He was hospitable and philanthropic, yet stressed simplicity in furnishings, clothing, and food. He generally steered conversation at mealtimes in a spiritual direction. Foolish conversation was not tolerated. Family worship was scrupulously practiced the Puritan way. Once a week, Teellinck invited a few of the godliest members of his congregation to join his family for devotions. Overnight guests were always welcome and were expected to participate in family worship. Once or twice a year, the Teellincks observed a family day of prayer and fasting. Teellinck regarded this practice as helpful for moving himself and his family to dedicate themselves entirely to God.

Pastoral Ministry and Friendships

Willem Teellinck was ordained into the pastoral ministry in 1606 and served the Burgh-Haamstede parish, on the island of Duiveland, for seven fairly fruitful years. There were several conversions, but Teellinck, much like his predecessor, Godfridus Udemans (c. 1580-1649), struggled with village life, which was rough and undisciplined. The classis minutes of that time frequently address the problems of alcohol abuse, Sabbath desecration, fighting, carnival attendance, and a general disorderly spirit.

During this pastorate, Teellinck wrote his first books. In his first publication, *Philopatris ofte Christelijke Bericht* (1608; [The Love of Fatherland, or A Christian Report]), he stressed the Dutch government's need to implement strict laws to combat the sins and faults of the populace. Teellinck also translated one of William Perkins's books from English

John Dod (d. 1645)   *Arthur Hildersham (1563-1632)*

into Dutch. In 1610, Teellinck visited England again to renew ties with his Puritan colleagues Thomas Taylor, Dod, and Hildersham. During that stay, he preached to the Dutch congregation in London. In 1612, he was delegated by Zeeland to go to The Hague to lobby the National Estates General to call a national synod for resolving the growing problems associated with Arminianism.

From 1613 until his death in 1629, Teellinck served as pastor in Middelburg, a flourishing city that had six Reformed churches—four Dutch, one English, and one French. People were drawn to his ministry

The interior of the Reformed church at Haamstede. Teellinck preached from this pulpit, which was installed in 1610 during his ministry there.

by his sincere conversation and preaching, faithful visiting and catechizing, godly walk and selfless demeanor, and simple and practical writings. He demonstrated the conviction that a pastor ought to be the godliest person in the congregation—and his godliness involved self-denial. When a pestilence swept through Middelburg in 1624, for example, Teellinck called people to public and private repentance, but also visited numerous infected homes, even as he urged others not to put themselves at risk by doing so.

Teellinck's hard work in Middelburg bore fruit. Five years after his arrival, he wrote to his congregation in *Noodwendig Vertoogh:* "We have every reason to thank the Lord. You come to church in large numbers each Sunday; our four church buildings cannot contain all the people. Many of your families may be called 'little churches.' There is good order according to good rules. Many of you use the means of grace diligently and you gladly listen to our admonitions to exercise godliness."

Yet Teellinck remained burdened by the indifference in and beyond his flock. The "constant hurt and pain" that he carried in his heart because of the spiritual laxity and carnality that prevailed in church and society moved him to use his prodigious energies and gifts in speaking and writing to bring about a comprehensive reformation in every sphere of life.

Teellinck was known for his friendliness, warmth, and humility. He was tolerant and loving toward his colleagues. Three of his closest colleagues at Middelburg served as delegates at the Synod of Dort (1618-1619): Hermannus Faukelius (1560-1625), a gifted preacher, active churchman, and author of *The Compendium,* a simplified version of the Heidelberg Catechism; Antonius Walaeus (1573-1639), pastor and professor of theology, a primary composer of the Canons of Dort, and author of numerous books, including an influential work on the Sabbath; and Franciscus Gomarus, Teellinck's former professor at Leiden, an able polemicist and a prominent leader of the orthodox Calvinists during the Arminian controversy.

Meanwhile, Teellinck maintained close contact with England through family ties and visits as well as his keen interest in English churches in the Netherlands. He periodically conducted services in the English parish of Middelburg. He also translated two more English Puritan books into Dutch.

Near the end of his life, Teellinck developed a mystical emphasis that had surfaced only occasionally in his earlier writings. That mysticism became evident in the posthumously published *Soliloquium* [Soliloquy] and *Het Nieuwe Jeruzalem* (1635; [The New Jerusalem]). This latter

The new church at Middelburg

book is reminiscent of the writings of Bernard of Clairvaux. Feelings and emotions are accented more than faith; the believing soul becomes one with Christ in tender communion. In its introduction, Gisbertus Voetius wrote that in this book Teellinck "could rightly be regarded as a second Thomas à Kempis," albeit Reformed in his theology.

Teellinck battled ill health for most of his ministry. He passed away on April 8, 1629, at the age of fifty. He was mourned by thousands. He was buried in the churchyard of St. Pieters Church in Middelburg.

Sermons

In preaching, Teellinck infiltrated the Dutch scene with English Puritan pathos. His sermons focused on the practice of godliness. He preached often on the necessity of repentance. He had the gifts to rebuke sin and pronounce God's impending judgments while simultaneously drawing people to the love of God and wooing them to Christ. He despised trivialities in the pulpit, which included flowery expressions and petty illustrations. He was blunt and forthright in expressing himself, even to the point of coarseness. Not everyone appreciated his reference to God as the "first tailor" or to Paul as a *voor-vrijer* of Christ—that is, one who would deliver a suitor's overture to a young woman.

Teellinck was a practical preacher who addressed current events. For example, when Admiral Piet Hein captured the Spanish Silver-fleet and all of the Netherlands rejoiced, Teellinck preached from 1 Timothy 6:17-19, stressing that the riches of this world are counterfeit and that only the riches of Christ are authentic.

Teellinck also addressed the current trends and fashions of the day. At times, he was criticized for being legalistic in his sermons against luxury in dress, amorous literature, excessive drinking, dancing, traveling on the Sabbath, overindulgence in feasting, and the neglect of fasting. However, that was only one strand of a complex web of practical godliness that Teellinck sought to weave in the hearts and lives of his parishioners. Though he castigated the ethical insensibilities of some professing believers and deplored spiritual deadness in the church, his overarching emphasis was to build up the believer's "most holy faith" and to move the church toward a "new life in Christ."

Homiletically, Teellinck was influenced by William Perkins (1558-1602) who advocated the Puritan "plain method" of preaching. After exegeting a text, Teellinck drew out various doctrines from the text, explained how these doctrines should benefit the hearer by means of comfort and admonition, then applied wisdom gleaned from the text to various kinds of saved and unsaved hearers. Though not an eloquent orator, Teellinck was an effective preacher. After hearing Teellinck preach on a few occasions, Gisbertus Voetius wrote, "Since that time my heart's

William Perkins (1558-1602)

desire has been that I and all other preachers of this land could duplicate this kind of powerful preaching."

The Netherlands was not as ready for Teellinck as England had been
for Perkins, however. Teellinck's insistence on connecting the fruits of
love with the acts of justifying faith did not appeal to some of his peers.
They found his call for renewal in church, school, family, government,
and society too intense. So, on the one hand, Teellinck's preaching
against dead Reformed orthodoxy brought him under suspicion by the
orthodox Reformed, while, on the other hand, Arminians censored him
for his devotion to that same Reformed orthodoxy and resented his
popularity with lay people.

Writing Ministry

Teellinck's goals for the reformation of the church are most evident in
his writings. His numerous works sought to build people up in the faith
by moving the Reformed Church beyond reformation in doctrine and
polity to reformation in life and practice. Even more than Perkins,
Teellinck stressed godly living, fruits of love, marks of grace, and the
primacy of the will.

Teellinck produced 127 manuscripts in all, sixty of which were
printed. Those sixty included twenty full-length books. Franciscus Rid-
derus published a representative anthology of Teellinck's works in 1656
titled *Uyt de Geschriften en Tractaten van Mr. Willem Teellinck* [From the
Writings and Tracts of Mr. Willem Teellinck]. Three years later
Teellinck's sons began printing his works, but they never got beyond
three folio volumes titled *Alle de wercken van Mr. Willem Teellinck*
(1659–64; [The Works of Mr. Willem Teellinck]). Most of Teellinck's
writings can be divided into five categories:

• *Exegetical.* Teellinck's exegesis of Romans 7 was published posthumously as *De Worstelinghe eenes Bekeerden Sondaers* [The Wrestling of a
Converted Sinner]. He published commentaries on Malachi, Judges
13–16, and Isaiah 9:5. His commentary on the Pentateuch, *Verklaringe
Over de Vijf Boecken Moses* [Exposition of the Five Books of Moses],
which was ready for print shortly before his death, was lost. All of his
exegetical works were written on a popular level. His concern was always for the genuine practice of Christianity.

• *Catechetical.* Teellinck's catechetical writings include his *Huysboeck*
[Family Manual], a commentary on the Compendium of the Heidelberg Catechism intended for family devotions, and *Sleutel der Devotie*

openende de Deure des Hemels voor ons [The Key of Devotion Opening the Door of Heaven for Us], a two-volume work of dialogues that addresses many questions about spiritual and practical Christian living.

• *Edificatory.* The majority of Teellinck's books were written to edify and instruct believers. They usually focus on a single theme. Only a few examples can be mentioned here. *Een getrouwe Bericht hoe men sich in geval van Sieckte Dragen Moet* [A Faithful Account of How One Should Conduct Oneself in Time of Sickness] provides practical guidance for coping with affliction. *Den Christelijcken Leidsman, Aanwijzend de Practycke der Warer Bekeeringhe* [The Christian Guide, Showing the Practice of True Conversion], dedicated to the city fathers of Rotterdam, was written to challenge Calvinists spiritually and to warn them about Arminian ideas. In this book, Teellinck discusses three categories of people: (1) the unwilling and sluggish who have no desire for the work of conversion; (2) conceited and slow learners who persuade themselves that they are already converted when they are not; and (3) those who lack courage and are ignorant. They would like to be involved in the work of conversion but do not know how to go about it.

In 1620, Teellinck published several books, including *Beurenkout* [Neighborly Discussions], which contains twelve discussions about practical Christianity; *Lusthof der Christelijcker Gebeden* [A Pleasurable Garden of Christian Prayers], which contains sixty-seven prayers suitable for a variety of occasions; and *Davids Wapentuig* [The Armor of David], which is dedicated to Prince Maurice and which urges him to follow Nehemiah's example. This book demonstrates Teellinck's warm love for the House of Orange and the ease with which he moved among the highest ranks of society.

In *Noodwendigh Vertoogh Aengaende de Tegenwoordigen Bedroefden Staet van Gods Volck* [Urgent Discussion Regarding the Present Sad State of God's People]—one of his most important books, written in 1627 shortly before his death—Teellinck strongly emphasizes the need for reform of Christian life. The condition of the church grieves him deeply, so he urges everyone to repent. He zealously opposes all kinds of abuses that have crept into the church, especially the lack of holiness and devotion and the abuse of Sabbath-keeping and the sacraments. His tone is loving and earnest. Voetius calls this book a "golden treatment" and highly recommends it to his theological students.

Teellinck was an early and enthusiastic proponent of foreign missions in the Netherlands. That is particularly shown in his *Ecce Homo, ofte ooghen-salve voor die noch sitten in blintheydt des ghemoedts* [Behold the Man, or Eye-salve for Those Whose Hearts are Still Blinded] and *Davids danckbaerheyt voor Gods weldadicheyt* [David's Thankfulness for God's Lovingkindness], which stress the Reformed Church's duty to bring Christianity to all the pagans with whom the Dutch East and West India companies trade. He tells the directors of these companies that God did not give the discovery of new continents for them to obtain earthly treasure so much as to send his eternal treasures to these continents.

After Teellinck's death, his son Maximiliaan edited and published a large practical work on anthropology titled *Adam, Rechtschapen, Wanschapen, Herschapen: Eene Naackte Ontdeckinge van de Gelegenheydt des menschen in Sijn Drieërley Staet, m.l. der onooselheyt, der Verdorvenheyt ende der Wede Oprechtinge* [Adam, Formed, Deformed, Reformed: A plain treatise concerning the threefold state of man—innocence, depravity, and regeneration]. *Corte Samensprekinge Leerende hoe Wij Bidden Moeten* [A Short Dialogue Teaching How We Should Pray] exhorts readers to simplicity and sincerity in a life of earnest prayer.

• *Admonitory.* In *Wraeck-Sweert* [Sword of Revenge], Teellinck warns the Netherlands of divine judgments that will descend upon the people who fail to repent and turn to God. In *Zions Basuijne* [The Trumpet of Zion], he tells representatives of the provinces that the Netherlands cannot be saved without a spiritual and moral reformation. In *Balsam Gileads voor Zions wonde* [The Balm of Gilead for Zion's Wounds], he warns political leaders that they cannot truly serve the Netherlands unless they obey God and view all faithful ministers as watchmen stationed on the walls. If the watchmen give no alarm when danger threatens, they should be regarded as traitors. And in *Zephaniae waerschouwinge, om te Voorkomen de Ondergang Jerusalems* [Zephaniah's Warning of How to Prevent the Overthrow of Jerusalem], he warns the aristocracy about their greed and stinginess toward the poor and admonishes every citizen to examine themselves as to what they think of Christ and of God's commandments.

Teellinck often wrote short books to warn against specific sins. In *Timotheus* [Timothy], he warns about the use of images, and in *Den Spiegel der Zedicheyt* [The Mirror of Morality], he opposes immodesty and extravagance in dress. In *Gesonde Bitterheit voor den Weeldirigen Christen die Geerne Kermisse Houdt* [A Healthy Antidote for the Luxuriating Christian Who Gladly Keeps Carnival], he castigates worldly carnivals which are like "goring beasts that wound many."

• *Polemical.* In *Balaam,* Teellinck warns against Roman Catholicism, and in *Den Volstandigen Christen* [The Mature Christian], against Arminianism. In *Eubolus,* which is earnest in tone but mild in rebuke, Teellinck opposes Arminians for their man-centered doctrine, though he also points out faults of the Calvinists. Teellinck believed that most Calvinists focused on sound doctrine at the expense of practical godliness. He thought that Calvinists should read practical writers *(practijk-scribenten)* such as William Perkins and Jean Taffin. He also stressed that staunch orthodoxy is worthless if confession is not made from the heart. Because of this emphasis, some Reformed leaders charged Teellinck with being too emotionally subjective and put him in league with the Arminians. Teellinck responded to these charges by saying that he emphasized both soundness of doctrine and godliness of life.

In his sermons and writings, Teellinck stressed the practice of godliness. His driving purpose was to reform the life of the people and the church. In the years when the followers of Arminius and Gomarus became increasingly hostile towards each other and every leader was compelled to choose sides, Teellinck sided with the Calvinists. Nevertheless, he regularly challenged the Calvinists to live what they believed. This made some Calvinists suspicious of him. Some accused him of not sufficiently emphasizing doctrinal matters while overemphasizing the practical dimensions of Christian living.

Sanctification, Devotion, Sabbath-Keeping, the Lord's Supper
Teellinck's writings focused on four major themes: sanctification, devotion, the Lord's Supper, and Sabbath-keeping. *The True Path of Godliness* is his major work on sanctification.

Teellinck's most extensive work, *Sleutel der Devotie* [The Key of Devotion], offers nearly 800 pages on the subject of devotion, which is, for Teellinck, one aspect of sanctification. This book is divided into six sections. Teellinck's preface explains *devotion* as commitment to God in Christ, which is man's highest calling. The first section covers communion with and love for Christ. The Christian "must receive, keep, and increase in the communion and love of Christ," Teellinck says. His great desire for the Lord Jesus will mortify all other lusts and desires. The believer will be humble and volunteer "to suffer the Christian life"; he will serve the Lord alone, meditate on eternity, and have communion with Christ.

The second section stresses the importance of self-denial. The third section shows "how we must use all spiritual means, and especially heed well the movements of the Spirit, in order really to deny ourselves, and to be one with Christ." The fourth section explains the "modesty and lowliness, which one must observe in the use of the means to receive the gracious gifts of God." The fifth section shows how faith can discern the many errors of the day. The sixth section speaks about divine grace, without which the Christian life is impossible.

Teellinck wrote extensively about the Lord's Supper, particularly in his *Het Geestelijk Sieraad van Christus' Bruiloftskinderen, of de Praktijk van het H. Avondmaal* [The Spiritual Ornament of Christ's Children of the Bridechamber, or the Use of the Holy Supper], which was reprinted eleven times from 1620 to 1665. The book consists of four lengthy sermons, the first of which details a believer's duty toward the Lord's Supper; the second, preparation for the supper; the third, partaking of the supper; and the fourth, our conduct after the supper. Teellinck balances sharp rebukes of neglecting the supper with earnest calls for probing self-examinations.

Teellinck also wrote extensively on Sabbath-keeping. He was offended by how easily the Lord's Day was profaned in the Netherlands. He and Godefridus Udemans, who also wrote on the subject, introduced the Puritan Sabbath to the Netherlands. Their conservative views of Sabbath-keeping led to serious differences among ministerial brothers in Zeeland, which were later brought to the Synod of Dort. Dort established six guidelines for Sabbath-keeping, found in the post-acta of the Synod (1619). But those guidelines were by no means conclusive.

In 1622, Teellinck wrote *De Rusttijdt, ofte Tractaet van d'onderhoudinge des Christelijcke Rustdachs, diemen gemeynlijck den Sondach Noemt* [The Time of Rest, or A Tract about Maintaining the Christian Day of Rest, which is generally called the Sunday]. Divided into seven books, *De Rustijdt* urges strict observance of the Sabbath. It includes details from Teellinck's own experience on how to prepare beforehand for the Sabbath on Saturday. In Teellinck's home, most work activities were completed on Friday so that all members of the household, including the maids, could prepare themselves on Saturday for a serious keeping of the Sabbath. Teellinck said the Sabbath should be spent in godly pursuits such as reading God's Word, which Teellinck calls "studying God's journal," or "stepping into the cabinet meeting of the heavenly King," where we read the minutes that he himself has kept. On the Sabbath, believers should meditate more on divine subjects than on other days. Government leaders should set a good example, and if necessary, use their authority to compel the sanctifying of Sunday, because government operates *in loco Dei* (in God's place) and rules by the grace of God.

With Franciscus Gomarus's support, Rev. Jacobus Burs of Tholen accused Teellinck of reintroducing the Jewish Sabbath in his *Threnos ofte Weeclaghe* [Threnos or Lamentation]. Even Gisbertus Voetius had to agree that Teellinck "pulled the ropes too tight." In 1627, Teellinck responded to this criticism in *Noodwendigh Vertoogh* [Urgent Discourse], an important volume that synthesizes his main ideas for a total reformation of life. In this volume, written two years before he died, Teellinck said that he was grieved about being misunderstood and wished to enlarge upon his Sabbath convictions as a day of rest. He then listed activities that are permissible on the Sabbath, including natural activities, such as eating or making one's bed; religious activities, such as preaching, studying for sermons, and bell-ringing for church services; works of necessity, such as bringing grain into a barn when it would otherwise be lost; works of mercy, such as milking cows; works of civil politeness expected in unusual circumstances, such as purchasing a necessity for a friend who unexpectedly drops in for a visit; and recreational activities that refresh a person without hindering religious devotion. Apparently, the opposition he encountered for strict Puritan Sabbath-keeping from *De Rusttijdt* moved Teellinck to embrace a milder position five years later in *Noodwendigh Vertoogh*.

Voetius wrote a rebuttal of Burs's *Threnos* in the form of a satire entitled *Lacrimae Crocodilli Abstersae* [Wiping Away the Tears of a Crocodile]. Though that did not end the debate, Voetius succeeded in developing a view of the Sabbath that was stricter than the earlier Protestant view and milder than Puritan teaching, and which would become widely accepted among the orthodox Reformed in the Netherlands.

Teellinck's first love was to promote the Puritan ideal of the sanctification of life in all its aspects, nurtured by heartfelt devotion. That is why *The Path of True Godliness* was chosen to be the first of his writings to be translated into English.

The Path of True Godliness

The Path of True Godliness, originally titled *Noord-Sterre, aanwijzende de juiste richting van de ware godzalighed* [The North Star, showing the right direction of true godliness], was printed four times in Dutch: in 1621, at Middelburg by Hans van der Hellen; in 1636, at Groningen by Nathanael Rooman; in 1642, at Groningen by Jan Claesen; and in 1971, at Dordrecht by J.P. van den Tol. This last edition, edited by J. van der

Haar (from the 1636 edition), was used as the basis for the English translation, published by Baker in 2003. In the address to the reader, Teellinck says that we must be real Christians and not just pose as Christians. He stresses that he wrote to promote godliness and concludes with the exhortation, "Let us concentrate for the remainder of our lives upon our souls, and serve God by practicing blessed godliness."

The Path of True Godliness, Teellinck's major work on sanctification, is a Puritan-style manual on how to practice godliness. Teellinck divided this work into nine sections which he called "books," then subdivided the books into eighty-one "chapters."

Teellinck divided each chapter into three main parts, then frequently subdivided these parts into paragraphs. For the most part, these divisions and subdivisions give the work a sense of balance and organization. On rare occasions, the subdivisions appear somewhat artificial, as Teellinck himself admits, but he quickly justifies himself in his preface by pointing out that a similar kind of organization is also found in some of the Psalms, particularly Psalm 119—under the inspiration of the Spirit!

Book 1. Since many people boast of their faith but have no saving knowledge of the truth, Teellinck feels a need to address three matters in writing *The Path of True Godliness*: (1) what true godliness is, (2) how believers should conduct themselves in practicing godliness, and (3) why the exercise of true godliness is of utmost importance.

Teellinck defines true godliness as a gift of God by which people are made willing and able to serve God's will as revealed in His Word. True godliness reveals itself in three sets of three things. The first set of three consists of resolving to live in accord with God's Word, doing one's utmost to carry out that resolve, and preparing to be what God intends us to be. That preparation includes submission to God's will in every trial. The second set relates to one's behavior after having fallen into sin. Those who practice godliness promptly forsake sin, search for reconciliation with God, and strive to obtain spiritual gain from their fall. The third set teaches us that we should do God's will abundantly, firmly, and steadfastly.

Book 2. The second book discusses the realm of darkness that opposes the practice of godliness. The three main powers of this realm are our own depraved flesh, the world, and the devil. Our depraved flesh is active through our carnal mind, our evil desires, and our depraved consciences. The evil world works through sinful customs, wrong role models, and an erroneous premise of reward and recompense. The

devil is active through evil temptations, false doctrines, and fierce persecutions. The devil presents sins as virtues, turns virtues into sins, and
draws false conclusions from true data. Teellinck's point is unavoidable:
we must be on guard against the realm of darkness.

Book 3. Teellinck shows how the kingdom of grace, in contrast to the
realm of darkness, promotes godliness. The kingdom of grace also possesses three powers: the renewed spirit, which wars against the depraved
flesh; the church of God, which fights against the world; and the Spirit
of God, who opposes the devil. Each of these powers possesses three
gifts that oppose and overcome its enemy in the realm of darkness. The
renewed spirit, or new creature, overcomes the depraved flesh by an
enlightened mind, a holy desire, and a tender conscience. The church
of God overcomes the world by the Word of God, the examples of the
saints, and the keys of the kingdom of heaven. The Holy Spirit overcomes the devil by holy and heavenly operations, the truth of God, and
various comforts of the Spirit, including His wisdom, patience, and
holiness. Teellinck concludes that the kingdom of grace will be victorious over the realm of darkness.

Book 4. The fourth book shows us how to respond to these two realms.
We must at all times keep life's three major purposes before us: the glory
of God, the salvation of our own souls, and the promotion of the salvation of others. Based on 1 John 2:12-14, Teellinck divides those who
pursue right goals into three levels of spiritual maturity—little children,
young men, and fathers—and describes what is distinctive about each.
He then explains how the realm of darkness tries to divert people from
life's real purposes by influencing them to live without ever knowing
those purposes, to pursue wrong purposes, or to only half-heartedly
pursue the right purposes.

Book 5. This book describes the means of achieving the true purposes
of life: God's holy ordinances, God's works, and God's promises. It also
describes people upon whom it is especially incumbent to use those
means: civil authorities, church office-bearers (especially pastors), and
ordinary Christians. Civil authorities must set a good example, exercise
criminal punishment with discernment, and revere godliness. Pastors
must rightly divide the Word, rightly administer discipline, and model
godly living. Ordinary Christians should help each other to live right,
edify each other with godly conversation in fellowship gatherings, and
obey those in authority over them.

Book 6. This book shows how Christians must attain the right purposes of life through the assistance of the right means described in the last book, all the while living consistently, watching diligently, and struggling against every hindrance. Consistent living involves establishing fixed times for all our duties, assigning priority to those duties that are most critical, and examining daily how we have fared in practicing godliness. Watching diligently means knowing what to guard against, being aware of the deceitfulness of one's heart, and staying alert by prayerfully watching what may be approaching.

Teellinck expounds in detail on the Christian's warfare against sin. Ephesians 6:10-20 teaches us that spiritual warfare compels us to remain courageous, to put on good armor, and to be much in prayer. Given Teellinck's emphasis on the inward life of the believer, it is understandable that this book is the longest of the nine.

Book 7. Here Teellinck provides us with a variety of God-centered motivations for practicing godliness. These include the Father's wisdom, omnipotence, and lovingkindness; the Son's incarnation, exemplary life, and kind invitations to come to Him; and the Spirit's promise to give new hearts, to overlook weaknesses, and to graciously reward the practice of godliness.

Book 8. This book contains motivations for practicing godliness and is divided into three major sections: our natural condition, the manifold blessings of God, and the promises we make to God. Motivations from our natural condition include the vanity of life, the horrors of the ungodly life, and the certainty of death and damnation for all who do not practice godliness. Motivations from God's blessings include His past, present, and future mercies to us. Motivations from our promises to God include the vows we make when we use the sacraments, in prayer, and on other occasions.

Book 9. The last book presents motivations for practicing godliness from the excellence of the godly life, including the glorious God we serve, the glorious work that is accomplished, and the glorious fruits that result; the misery of the godless life, including the awful master that is served, the detestable work that is accomplished, and the shameful fruits that result; and the emptiness of material things with regard to this life, to death, and to life after death.

Throughout *The Path of True Godliness*, Teellinck insists on the need for personal religious experience and the detailed regulation of Christian conduct in life, especially in prayer, fasting, Christian education, and Sabbath observance, but also extending to mealtimes, clothing, dancing, carnivals, and card-playing. Notwithstanding his intensely spiritual and practical emphasis on inward godliness, the modern reader may be somewhat taken aback by his repeated negative references to a number of these outward things. To understand Teellinck in these cases, one must understand two things:

First, Teellinck's stress on external sanctification must be understood against the backdrop of the numerous sins and faults of his generation that deeply troubled him. According to Teellinck and like-minded contemporaries, both the society and the church were plagued by lasciviousness that was promoted by dancing, immoral jokes, amorous literature, and card-playing that was often accompanied by gambling. Games involving dice were seen as challenging God's providence, hence Teellinck's warnings against them.

Teellinck also complained about the abuse of worship by church members. Preaching was not highly respected. Many attended church only out of custom. A fair number extended their dinner hour so that they could not attend the evening service. When they did come, some slept or yawned openly, and a few talked to each other during worship. Sacraments fared no better. Some people unnecessarily postponed the baptism of their children. Others would enter the service late, have their child baptized, and leave before the service concluded. Scores of parents were not fulfilling their baptismal vows to instruct their children in the doctrines of Scripture. Some church members presented themselves at the Table of the Lord without knowing the fundamental doctrines of the Christian faith. Or, they entered church after the sermon was over just in time to partake of the Supper and then left. Few sacrificed in giving to the church; their offerings were usually meager and given thoughtlessly.

Sabbath days were ill-spent by many. Many people attended church only once on Sunday, even if they had no other obligations for the day. The remainder of the day was not spent in personal Bible study, self-examination, holy meditation, and spiritual conversation. Many would work at unnecessary occupations or take pleasure trips. Some would frequent taverns, even after attending the Lord's Supper.

Family life often followed little or no order. Discipline was minimal at best. Family and private worship was often neglected. Parents did not talk to their children about the sermons or about their catechism class. Some let their children dance, sing sinful love songs, and exchange risqué jokes. There was little waging of war against the devil, the world, and self. Self-denial was almost unheard of. Fast days were abused and fasting was often regarded as "popish."

Christian education was neglected. In many towns the teachers themselves were ignorant of the basics of vital Christianity. Universities were corrupt. Many young people from the church married unbelieving, worldly friends, staging grandiose wedding receptions, at which guests would drink too much. Wearing of immodest clothing was on the increase—even in the church. Many had an inordinate desire for keeping up with the latest fashions. The poor and the orphans were oppressed. Selfishness and idleness abounded.

These, then, were some of Teellinck's complaints that are repeated throughout his writings. Did he exaggerate his case? Many today might think so, but to understand history rightly we must always place ourselves in the era in which the author lived. We must not forget that many of Teellinck's contemporaries voiced similar complaints. As we read Teellinck's lists of admonitions against various evils, we must bear in mind the pastoral context in the midst of which he labored.

Second, like most Reformed forefathers who focused on a practical, vital religion of experience, Teellinck believed that true spirituality is inseparable from an outward walk of life that flees all kinds of worldliness. Whatever one may think of Teellinck's warnings against external forms of worldly behavior, of one thing we may be certain: he was motivated by a zealous desire for God's glory, not by legalism. Teellinck and nearly all who stressed Reformed spirituality in the seventeenth century believed that serious admonitions against a worldly spirit were a natural outgrowth of the scriptural teachings that "By their fruits ye shall know them" (Matt. 7:20); "Out of the abundance of the heart, the mouth speaketh" (Matt. 12:34); "Be not conformed to this world: but be ye transformed by the renewing of your mind" (Rom. 12:2); "Whether therefore ye eat, or drink, or whatsoever ye do, do all to the glory of God" (1 Cor. 10:31); "These all died in faith, having embraced [the promises], and confessed that they were strangers and pilgrims on the earth" (Heb. 11:13); and "Love not the world, neither the things that are in the world, [for] if any man love the world, the love of the Father is not in him" (1 John 2:15).

In Teellinck's day, the only way to travel long distances was by sea. Sea travel involved many dangers and problems of navigation. It was easy to lose one's way. Travelers looked to the north star (also called *polaris,* "the pole star") as a fixed point to help them keep to a true course. Teellinck intended *The Path of True Godliness* to be a North Star to those laboring to practice godliness as they traversed the seas of life.

Influence

Teellinck's major influence was injecting Puritan color into the Dutch Second Reformation. Though he never taught theology at a university, was no scholar at heart, and was not eloquent, his life, sermons, and writings helped shape the piety of the entire movement, as his contemporaries William Ames and Gisbertus Voetius acknowledged. In his preface to Teellinck's work on Romans 7, Voetius wrote, "The sermons of Willem Teellinck—how scriptural, how profound, powerful and moving they were, all those godly souls who heard him can best testify, to whom he was so often a sweet savor of Christ, and is so still!"

Teellinck was one of the most influential "old writers" (*oude schrijvers*) of the seventeenth century. More than 150 editions of his books were printed in Dutch. Moreover, his practical piety was carried on and reshaped by other major Dutch Second Reformation writers, such as Voetius.

Four of his books were translated into English in the 1620s but never reprinted, and are now scarce titles: *The Balance of the Sanctuary, Showing How We Must Behave Ourselves When We See and Behold the People of God in Misery and Oppression Under the Tyranny of Their Enemies* (1621); *Paul's Complaint Against His Natural Corruption* (1621)—two sermons on Romans 7:24; *The Christian Conflict and Conquest* (1622); *The Resting Place of the Mind, that is, a Propounding of the Wonderful Providence of God whereupon a Christian Man Ought to Rest and Repose Himself when Outward Means Fail Him* (1622)—three messages on Genesis 2:4-6. One of Teellinck's last writings, *Redeeming the Time,* consisting of thirty-one short devotionals, was published in 1975 as a booklet by Zoar Publications.

Several of Teellinck's books were also translated into German. One of Germany's most influential Pietists, Friedrich Adolph Lampe (1683-1729), often used Teellinck to promote the practice of godly living. Thus, Teellinck left his mark on both continental and American pietism.

Teellinck's influence waned in the Netherlands in the eighteenth century when the Dutch Second Reformation became more of an introspective movement that stressed passivity rather than activity in practical Christian living. Only his *Het Nieuwe Jeruzalem* (The New Jerusalem) was reprinted in 1731. Some divines, especially those who thrived on conventicles, began to question Teellinck's Reformed orthodoxy and to disparage his writings.

Four of Teellinck's smaller works were reprinted in the nineteenth century, two in 1841 and two in 1884. His writings drew the attention of Heinrich Heppe in 1879, Albrecht Ritschl in 1880, and Willem Engelberts, who wrote a doctoral dissertation on Teellinck in 1898. H. Bouwman's *Willem Teellinck en de practijk der godzalighed* (1928; [Willem Teellinck and the Practice of Godliness]) defends Teellinck from the somewhat negative views of Heppe and Ritschl. More of Teellinck's major titles were reprinted in the twentieth century, beginning in 1969. Some scholars associated with the *Stichting Studie der Nadere Reformatie*—Willem op't Hof in particular—are now studying and writing extensively about Teellinck's life and writings. Teellinck is being increasingly read in the Netherlands today, especially by conservative Reformed believers.

Teellinck's positive emphasis in promoting biblical, Reformed spirituality serves as a corrective to much false spirituality being marketed today. It also serves as an important corrective to orthodox teaching that presents truth to the mind but does not apply it to the heart and daily life. Teellinck helps us link together a clear mind, a warm heart, and helping hands, to serve God with the whole person, which is our reasonable service. He fleshes out James's emphasis, saying to us, "Show me your faith by your works" (cf. James 2:18).

Herman Witsius (1636-1708)

15

The Life and Theology of
Herman Witsius (1636-1708)

Herman Wits (Latinized as Witsius) was born on February 12, 1636, at Enkhuizen to God-fearing parents who dedicated their firstborn to the Lord. His father, Nicholas Wits (1599-1669), was a man of some renown, having been an elder for more than twenty years, a member of Enkhuizen's city council, and an author of devotional poetry.[1] Witsius's mother, Johanna, was a daughter of Herman Gerard, pastor for thirty years of the Reformed church in Enkhuizen. Herman was named after his grandfather with the prayer that he might emulate his godly example.[2]

Education

Witsius was an avid learner. He began Latin studies at age five. Three years later, noticing the boy's gifts, his uncle, Peter Gerard, began to tutor him. By the time Witsius took up theological studies in Utrecht at age fifteen, he could speak Latin fluently. He could read Greek and Hebrew, and had memorizied numerous Scriptures in their original languages. At Utrecht, he studied Syriac and Arabic under Johannes Leusden and theology under Johannes Hoornbeeck, whom he called "my teacher of undying memory." He also studied under Andreas Essenius, whom he honored as "my father in the Lord," and Gisbertus Voetius, whom he called "the great Voetius."[3] From Voetius he learned how to wed precise Reformed orthodoxy to heartfelt, experiential piety.[4]

After studying theology and homiletics with Samuel Maresius at Groningen, Witsius returned to Utrecht in 1653, where he was profoundly influenced by the local pastor, Justus van der Bogaerdt. According to Witsius's later testimony, van der Bogaerdt's preaching and fellowship brought him to understand experientially the difference between theological knowledge gleaned from study and the heavenly wisdom taught by the Holy Spirit through communion with God, love, prayer, and meditation. Witsius wrote that he was born again in "the bosom of the Utrecht church by the living and eternal Word of God."

Through this godly pastor's influence, Witsius said, he was preserved "from the pride of science, taught to receive the kingdom of heaven as a little child, led beyond the outer court in which he had previously been inclined to linger, and conducted to the sacred recesses of vital Christianity."[5]

Witsius demonstrated his gifts in public debate already as a teenager. In 1655, he defeated some of the leading debaters at the University of Utrecht by showing that the doctrine of the Trinity could be proven from the writings of ancient Jews. When Witsius thanked the moderator for his assistance, the moderator replied, "You neither had, nor stood in need of, any assistance from me."[6]

In 1656, Witsius passed his final examinations and was declared a candidate for the ministry. Due to the abundance of ministers, he had to wait a year before receiving a pastoral call. During that time he applied to the authorities of the French Church in Dort for a license to preach in French-speaking Reformed churches. Witsius often preached in French at Utrecht, Amsterdam, and elsewhere.

Pastorates

On July 8, 1657, Witsius was ordained into the ministry at Westwoud. Though his catechizing of young people bore special fruit, he encountered opposition because of the congregation's ignorance of their Reformed heritage. Medieval customs such as praying for the dead were still evident in the people. These problems convinced Witsius early in his ministry of the need for further Reformation among the people. It also prompted him to publish his first book, *'t bedroefde Nederlant* (The Sorrowing Netherlands).[7]

In 1660, Witsius married Aletta van Borchorn, daughter of a merchant who was an elder in Witsius's church. They were blessed with twenty-four years of marriage. Aletta said she could not tell what was greater—her love or her respect for her husband. The couple had five children—two sons, who died young, and three daughters: Martina, Johanna, and Petronella.

In 1661, Witsius was installed in the church at Wormer—one of Holland's largest churches—where he succeeded in uniting factions and training the people in divine knowledge. He and his colleague, Petrus Goddaeus, took turns teaching a doctrinal class on weekday evenings to "defend the truth of our teachings against false doctrines" and to inculcate "the sanctity of our teachings in terms of God-fearing conduct." The class began in private homes, then outgrew that space and moved to the church. Eventually people had to stand outside the church due to lack of room.[8]

These class lectures were eventually published in a book titled *Practycke des Christendoms* (The Practice of Christianity), to which Witsius appended *Geestelycke Printen van een Onwedergeborenen op syn beste en een Wedergeborenen op syn slechste* (A Spiritual Picture of the Unregenerate at His Best and the Regenerate at His Worst).

Practycke des Christendoms explains the primary grounds of godliness, while the appended work applies those grounds by teaching what is laudable in the unregenerate and what is culpable in the regenerate. John Owen said he hoped he could be as consistent as Witsius's unregenerate man at his best and that he would never fall so deeply as Witsius's regenerate man at his worst.

In his writings, Witsius demonstrates the convictions of the *Nadere Reformatie* (Dutch Second Reformation or "Further Reformation").[9] This is particularly true in his attempts to merge Reformed, doctrinal knowledge with heartfelt practical piety.

Witsius accepted a call to Goes in 1666, where he labored for two years. In the preface to *Twist des Heeren met syn Wijngaert* (The Lord's Controversy with His Vineyard), published in Leeuwarden in 1669, he said he had labored with much peace in this congregation together with three colleagues, "two of whom were venerated as fathers, and the third was loved as a brother." Of these four ministers working together in one congregation, Witsius noted: "We walked together in fellowship to God's house. We did not only attend each other's services, but also each other's catechism classes and other public services, so that what one servant of God might have taught yesterday, the others confirmed and recommended to the congregation the next day." Under the influence of these four ministers, "all sorts of devotional practices blossomed, piety grew, and the unity of God's people was enhanced," Witsius wrote.[10]

After serving Goes, Witsius went to his fourth pastoral charge, Leeuwarden, where he served for seven years (1668-1675). In 1672, called the "year of miracles" because the Dutch Republic survived the onslaught of four enemies who had declared war on the Netherlands (France, England, and the German electorates of Cologne and Munster), Witsius gained renown for faithful ministry in the midst of crisis. Johannes à Marck, a future colleague, said of Witsius that he knew of no other minister whose labors were so owned of God.[11]

In 1673, Witsius again teamed up with a renowned colleague—this time, Wilhelmus à Brakel, with whom he served two years. At Leeuwarden, Witsius played a critical role mediating disputes between Voetius and Maresius.

Professorships

In 1675, Witsius was called to be a professor of theology. He served in this capacity for the rest of his life, first at Franeker (1675-1680), then at Utrecht (1680-1698), and finally at Leiden (1698-1707).

Shortly after his arrival at Franeker, the university there awarded Witsius a doctorate in theology. His inaugural address, *On the character of a true theologian* (1675), which was attended by scholars from all over the province, stressed the difference between a theologian who knows his subject only scholastically and a theologian who knows his subject experientially.[12]

Under Witsius's leadership the university began to flourish as a place to study theology, especially after the arrival of the twenty-one-year-old professor, Johannes à Marck, in 1678. It soon attracted students from all over Europe.

During his professorship at Franeker, tension between the Voetians and the Cocceians escalated. Gisbertus Voetius (1589-1676), a renowned Reformed scholastic theologian and professor at Utrecht, represents the mature fruit of the *Nadere Reformatie,* much as John Owen does for English Puritanism. Voetius unceasingly opposed Johannes Cocceius (1603-1669), the Bremen-born theologian who taught at Franeker and Leiden, and whose covenant theology, in Voetius's opinion, overempha-

Wilhelmus à Brakel   *Gisbertus Voetius*

sized the historical and contextual character of specific ages. Voetius believed that Cocceius's new approach to the Scriptures would undermine both Reformed dogmatics and practical Christianity. For Voetius, Cocceius's devaluing of practical Christianity culminated in his rejection of the Sabbath as a ceremonial yoke no longer binding on Christians. The Voetian-Cocceian controversy racked the Dutch Reformed Church long after the death of both divines, splitting theological faculties into factions. Eventually both factions compromised, agreeing in many cities to rotate their pastors between Voetians and Cocceians.[13]

Witsius's concern about this controversy moved him to publish *De Oeconomia Foederum Dei cum Hominibus* (1677), first printed in English in 1736 as *The Oeconomy of the Covenants between God and Man, comprehending a Complete Body of Divinity.* It was reprinted numerous times, most recently in two volumes in 2004. In governing his systematic theology by the concept of covenant, Witsius uses Cocceian methods while maintaining essentially Voetian theology.

In his work on the covenants, Witsius argued against Roman Catholicism, Arminianism, Socinianism, and those Dutch Protestant theologians, who, with Hugo Grotius, had exchanged a *sola scriptura* theology for an institutionalized, sacramental view of the church based on traditions that paved the way back to Rome. Witsius opposed Grotians "who spoke of a 'law' which was not the law of Moses, a 'satisfaction' which was not through punishment and a 'substitution' which was not of necessity and not vicarious."[14]

Witsius next went to Utrecht, where he labored for eighteen years as professor and pastor. Students from all over the Protestant world attended his lectures; magistrates attended his sermons. On two occasions, his colleagues honored him with the headship of the university (1686, 1697).

In 1685, the Dutch Parliament appointed Witsius as a delegate to represent the Dutch government at the coronation of James II and to serve as chaplain to the Netherlands Embassy in London.[15] While there he met the archbishop of Canterbury as well as several leading theologians. He studied Puritan theology and enhanced his stature in England as a peacemaker. The English church later called on him to serve as a mediating figure between antinomians and neonomians—the former accusing the latter of overemphasizing the law, the latter accusing the former of minimizing the law. Out of this came his *Conciliatory Animadversions,* a treatise on the antinomian controversy in England. In this treatise, Witsius argued that God's starting point in His eternal decrees did not demean His activity in time. He also helped facilitate the translation into Dutch of some of the works of Thomas Goodwin, William Cave, and Thomas Gataker and wrote prefaces for them.[16]

Witsius's years at Utrecht were not free from strife. He felt obliged to oppose the theology of Professor Herman A. Roell, who advocated a unique mixture of the biblical theology of Johannes Cocceius and the rationalistic philosophy of René Descartes. Witsius felt that this combination threatened the authority of Scripture. Witsius taught the superiority of faith over reason to protect the purity of Scripture. Reason lost its purity in the fall, he said. Though reason is a critical faculty, it remains imperfect, even in the regenerate. It is not an autonomous judge, but a servant of faith.

Clearly, Witsius's understanding of who God is affected his understanding of how we know what we know and that Scripture is the final standard of truth rather than our reason. His knowledge of God through the Scriptures shaped all his thinking. How evident this is in his defense of the penal substitution of Christ against the rationalist Socinus.[17]

Subsequently, Witisus opposed rationalism in the teachings of Balthasar Bekker as well as the popular, separatistic ideas of Jean de Labadie. He admitted that the Reformed churches were seriously flawed, but he strongly opposed separating from the church.

At Utrecht, Witsius published three volumes of *Exercitationes Sacrae* (Sacred Exercises), two on the Apostles' Creed (1681) and one on the Lord's Prayer (1689). Second in importance only to his *Economy of the Covenants,* these books stress the truths of the gospel in a pure, clear manner. The three works birthed in a seminary setting are known as Witsius's trilogy.

In the midst of his busy years at Utrecht (1684), Witsius's wife died. His daughter Petronella, who never married, remained with her father, faithfully caring for him through twenty-four years as a widower.

When he was sixty-two years old, Witsius accepted a call to serve at the university at Leiden as professor. His inaugural address was on "the modest theologian." At Leiden he trained men from Europe, Great Britain, and America, including several native Americans who had been converted through the work of John Eliot (1604-90).[18]

Within a year (1699), Holland and West Friesland appointed Witsius inspector of the University's theological college. It was a position he held until he retired in 1707 because of ill health. In his last six years he suffered painful bouts of gout, dizziness, and memory lapses.[19] After a serious attack in October 1708, he told friends that his homecoming was near. Four days later, he died at the age of seventy-two, after nearly fifty-two years of ministry. During his last hour, he told his close friend, Johannes à Marck, that he was persevering in the faith that he had long enjoyed in Christ.

All his life Witsius was a humble biblical and systematic theologian, dependent on the Scriptures. He was also a faithful preacher. For him, Christ—in the university, on the pulpit, and in daily living—took pre-eminence. "Free and sovereign grace, reigning through the person and righteousness of the great Immanuel, he cordially regarded at once as the source of all our hope, and the grand incitement to a holy practice," Fraser wrote of Witsius.[20]

Despite all his learning, Witsius remained concerned about the soundness and piety of the church. All his writing and learning was employed to promote the church's well-being. After his death, his writings were collected in six volumes. We shall briefly look at Witsius's most influential books.

Twist des Heeren (The Lord's Controversy)

In *Twist des Heeren* (1669), Witsius calls for "a holy reformation." Basing his work on Isaiah 5:4, Witsius equates the Netherlands with a second Canaan. Just as God cared for Israel as a vinedresser by providing numerous means of grace, but Israel responded with the wild grapes (Dutch: *stinkende druiven,* "stinking grapes") of sinful indulgence rather than the good grapes of gratitude, so God still expends much care upon His people and His church in the Netherlands despite people's sinful response.

God had led a hundred thousand Reformed Dutch forebearers out of bondage to the tyranny of the papacy and the fury of the Spaniards and planted them as a noble vine. The axe of the Inquisition could not destroy that vine, for God Himself protected the Dutch churches. He granted them peace, edified and multiplied them, and enabled them to walk in the fear of the Lord and the comfort of the Holy Ghost. The Synod of Dort dethroned heresy and enthroned truth. Preachers "eloquent and mighty in the Scriptures" as Apollos (Acts 18:23-24) were given to the churches, though they were now rare in the land, Witsius said.

Shouldn't God expect good grapes from the Dutch churches? If not, where could vital, spiritual godliness be found? Only a few clusters of the grapes of Canaan could be seen. Witsius, like Willem Teellinck before him, complained that "the first love" of the Reformation had largely dissipated due to the lack of Spirit-empowered preaching, lack of godliness, and lack of church discipline. Instead, novel, dangerous opinions were beginning to grow on God's vine, Witsius said. Those opinions included facets of Descartes's philosophy that promoted reason as the interpreter of Scripture, Cocceius's view of the Lord's Day, which viewed the fourth commandment as ceremonial for the Israelites rather than moral for all ages, and a host of other erroneous innovations.[21]

Another Reformation was needed, Witsius said. The sixteenth-century Reformation did not go far enough because of the disobedience, worldliness, and hard-heartedness of the people. "What a blot it is on the Reformation that we Reformed remain so deformed in our lives," Witsius wrote.[22] Through natural disasters, wars, and quarrels—even among ministers—God was declaring that a new Reformation must begin.

A second Reformation called for the renewal of genuine piety and the abandoning of unrighteousness. Promoting a kind of theocratic idealism, Witsius said that rulers should lead their subjects by renewing their covenant with the Lord. Ministers in particular should live a God-fearing life. They could not reform people until they had reformed themselves, their consciences, conduct, company, and homes. Everyone must examine themselves, repent of sin, and return to the Lord, using God's Word as their guide for life. Witsius wrote, "I plead with you, readers, to turn yourselves sincerely to the Lord…. Begin that holy reformation of your unholy life, which has long been urged upon you, but which, until now, you have obstinately postponed. Begin that reformation now, this very hour. Today, if you hear the Lord's voice, harden not your heart."[23]

Personal reformation begins with an experiential knowledge of sin, self, and God, Witsius explained. The spiritually-minded will find rest only in Jesus Christ. The truly pious love God more than themselves, His honor more than their own salvation. They yearn to please God and surrender themselves to God. They see their own sinfulness, and, in light of divine holiness, come to view themselves as less than nothing. They seek to hide themselves behind Christ so that God may view them only through Christ. They want grace to live only for God so they can say with Paul, "I live, yet not I, but Christ liveth in me" (Gal. 2:20).

Such people radiate Christ. The mind in them was also in Christ Jesus (Phil. 2:5). A renewed believer conducts himself like a "little Christ" on earth. He sees Christ in others and loves others in Christ. His life radiates the holiness and glory of God.

Few people in the Netherlands believe such experiential truth,

Witsius laments. Christianity is far below the norm. Few die to their own righteousness, live to the glory of Christ, and show sincere love to the brethren.

Witsius taught that only a renewed Reformation could keep the faltering state and church from destroying themselves. Only when purity of doctrine was accompanied by purity of life could the state and church expect God's blessing. Then God would approve the good grapes, and not complain of the wild grapes the Netherlands brought forth.

Economy of the Covenants

Witsius wrote his *magnum opus* on the covenants to promote peace among Dutch theologians who were divided on covenant theology. Witsius sought to be a theologian of synthesis; he strove to lessen tension between the Voetians and the Cocceians. He wrote in his introduction that "the enemies of our church...secretly rejoice that there are as many and as warm disputes amongst ourselves, as with them. And this, not very secretly neither: for they do not, nor will ever cease to cast this reproach upon us; which, I grieve to say is not so easily wiped away. O! how much better would it be to use our utmost endeavours, to lessen, make up, and, if it could be, put an end to all controversy!"[24]

Economy of the Covenants is not a complete systematic theology, though its title claims that it comprehends "a complete body of divinity." Several major doctrines not addressed here, such as Trinity, creation, and providence, were dealt with later in Witsius's exposition of the Apostles' Creed.

For Witsius, the doctrine of the covenants is the best way of reading Scripture. The covenants are for him what J. I. Packer calls "a successful hermeneutic," or a consistent interpretative procedure yielding a proper understanding of Scripture, both law and gospel.[25] Witsius's work is divided into four books:
- Book I: The Covenant of Works (120 pages)
- Book II: The Covenant of Redemption, or The Covenant of Grace from Eternity Between the Father and the Son (118 pages)
- Book III: The Covenant of Grace in Time (295 pages)
- Book IV: Covenant Ordinances Thoughout the Scriptures (356 pages)

Throughout his exposition of covenant theology, Witsius corrected inadequacies of the Cocceians and infused Voetian content. He treated each topic analytically, drawing from other Reformed and Puritan systematicians to move the reader to clarity of mind, warmth of heart, and godliness of life.

In Book I, Witsius discusses divine covenants in general, focusing on etymological and exegetical considerations related to them (*berîth* and *diathēkē*). He notes promise, oath, pledge, and command as well as a mutual pact that combines promise and law. He concludes that covenant, in its proper sense, "signifies a mutual agreement between parties with respect to something."[26] Then he defines covenant as "an agreement between God and man, about the method of obtaining ultimate blessedness, with the addition of a threat of eternal destruction, against anyone contemptuous of this blessedness."[27] The essence of the covenant, then, is the relationship of love between God and man.

Covenants between God and man are essentially monopleuric (one-sided) covenants in the sense that they can only be initiated by God and are grounded in "the utmost majesty of the most high God." Though initiated by God, these covenants call for human consent to the covenant, to exercise the responsibility of obedience within it and to acquiesce in punishment in case of violation. In the covenant of works, that responsibility is partly gracious and partly meritorious, whereas in the covenant of grace, it is wholly gracious in response to God's election and Christ's fulfillment of all conditions of the covenant.[28]

Nevertheless, all covenants between God and man are dipleuric (two-sided) in administration. Both aspects are important. Without the monopleuric emphasis on God's part, covenant initiation and fulfillment would not be by grace alone; without the dipleuric emphasis of divine initiation and human responsibility, man would be passive in covenant administration. The attempt made by contemporary scholars to force seventeenth-century federal theologians into either a monopleuric or dipleuric concept of the covenant misses the mark, as Richard Muller has shown, both with Witsius as well as his popular, younger contemporary, Wilhelmus à Brakel (1635-1711), whose *De Redelijke Godsdienst (The Christian's Reasonable Service)* was first printed in Dutch in 1700.[29] Muller concludes, "It is not the case, as some have argued that covenant language cuts against election and grace and that covenant doctrine either relaxes the strict doctrine of the decrees or is itself rigidified by contact with the doctrine of predestination during the scholastic era of Reformed theology."[30]

According to Witsius, the covenant of works consists of the contracting parties (God and Adam), the law or condition (perfect obedience), the promises (eternal life in heaven for unqualified veneration to divine law), the penal sanction (death), and the sacraments (Paradise, the tree of life, the tree of knowledge of good and evil, the Sabbath).[31] Throughout, Witsius stressed the relationship of the covenant of parties in terms of the Reformed concept of covenant. Denying the covenant of works causes serious Christological and soteriological errors, he said.[32]

For example, the violation of the covenant of works by Adam and Eve rendered the promises of the covenant inaccessible to their descendants. Those promises were abrogated by God, who cannot lower His standard of law by recasting the covenant of works to account for fallen man's unrighteousness. Divine abrogation, however, does not annul the demand of God for perfect obedience. Rather, because of the stability of God's promise and His law, the covenant of grace is made effective in Christ, the perfect Law-fulfiller. In fulfilling all the conditions of the covenant of grace, Christ fulfilled all the conditions of the covenant of works. Thus "the covenant of grace is not the abolition, but rather the confirmation of the covenant of works, inasmuch as the Mediator has fulfilled all the conditions of that covenant, so that all believers may be justified and saved according to the covenant of works, to which satisfaction was made by the Mediator," Witsius wrote.[33]

Witsius outlined the relationship of the covenant of works to the covenant of grace in his second book. He discussed the covenant of grace from eternity, or, the covenant of redemption as the *pactum salutis* between God the Father and God the Son.[34] In the eternal *pactum,* the Father solicited from the Son acts of obedience for the elect, while pledging ownership of the elect to the Son. This "agreement between God and the Mediator" makes possible the covenant of grace between God and His elect. The covenant of grace "presupposes" the covenant of grace from eternity and "is founded upon it," Witsius said.[35]

The covenant of redemption established God's remedy for the problem of sin. The covenant of redemption is the answer for the covenant of works abrogated by sin. The Son binds Himself to work out that answer by fulfilling the promises and conditions and bearing the penalties of the covenant on behalf of the elect. Ratified by the covenant of redemption, "conditions are offered to which eternal salvation is annexed; conditions not to be performed again by us, which might throw the mind into despondency; but by him, who would not part with his life, before he had truly said, 'It is finished,'" Witsius explained.[36]

This covenant of grace worked out in time (Book 3) is the core of

Witsius's work, and covers the entire field of soteriology. By treating the *ordo salutis* within the framework of the covenant of grace, Witsius asserted that former presentations of covenant doctrine were superior to newer ones. He showed how covenant theology binds theologians together rather than drives them apart.

Election is the backdrop of the covenant. Election, as the decree or counsel of God, is God's unilateral, unchangeable resolve that does not depend on human conditions. Here the covenant of grace parts ways with the covenant of works. In the covenant of works, God promised man life on the condition of complete obedience without promising that He would work that obedience in man. In the covenant of grace, God promised to give everything to the elect—eternal life and the means to it: faith, repentance, sanctification, and perseverance. Every condition of salvation is included in God's promises to His elect. Faith is not, properly speaking, a condition, but the way and means through which believers receive the promises of eternal life.[37]

Though the "*internal,* mystical, and spiritual *communion*" of the covenant is established within the elect, there is also an external economy or administration of the covenant. Those who are baptized and raised with the means of grace are in the covenant externally, though many of them "are not in the testament of God" in terms of being saved.[38]

Effectual calling is the first fruit of election, which in turn works regeneration. Regeneration is the infusion of new life in the spiritually dead person. Thus the incorruptible seed of the Word is made fruitful by the Spirit's power. Witsius argued that so-called "preparations" to regeneration, such as breaking of the will, serious consideration of the law and conviction of sin, fear of hell and despairing of salvation, are fruits of regeneration rather than preparations when the Spirit uses them to lead sinners to Christ.[39]

The first act of this new life is faith. Faith, in turn, produces various acts: (1) knowing Christ, (2) assenting to the gospel, (3) loving the truth, (4) hungering and thirsting after Christ, (5) receiving Christ for salvation, (6) reclining upon Christ, (7) receiving Christ as Lord, and (8) appropriating the promises of the gospel. The first three acts are called preceding acts; the next three, essential acts; the last two, following acts.[40]

In the last two acts, the believer promises to live in the obedience of faith and obtains assurance through the reflective act of faith which reasons syllogistically like this: "[Major premise:] Christ offers himself as a full and complete Saviour to all who are weary, hungry, thirsty, to all who receive him, and are ready to give themselves up to him. [Minor premise:] But I am weary, hungry, etc. [Conclusion:] Therefore Christ has offered himself to me, is now become mine, and I his, nor shall any thing ever separate me from his love."[41]

Witsius referred to this conclusion of faith, later called the practical or mystical syllogism, whenever he discussed assurance of faith. In this, he followed Puritan and Dutch Second Reformation thinking.[42] Aware of the dangers of relying upon personal sanctification for assurance— particularly the objections of the antinomians that syllogisms can provide no sure comfort and may lead to "free-will" thinking, Witsius took pains to keep the syllogism within the confines of the doctrines of grace. Like the Puritans, he taught that the syllogism is bound to the Scriptures, flows out of Jesus Christ, and is ratified by the Holy Spirit. The Spirit witnesses to the believer's spirit, not only by direct testimony from the Word, but also by stirring up the believer to observe scriptural marks of grace in his own soul and in the fruits of his life. Those marks of grace lead to Jesus Christ. The syllogism is always scriptural, christological, and pneumatological.

For Witsius, assurance by syllogism is more common than assurance by the direct testimony of the Spirit. Consequently, careful self-examination as to whether one is in the faith and Christ in him is critical (2 Cor. 13:5). If justification issues in sanctification, the believer ought to reason syllogistically from sanctification back to justification—i.e., from the effect to the cause. That is what the apostle John does in his First Epistle General (2:2, 3, 5; 3:14, 19; 5:2).[43]

Witsius is solidly Reformed on justification by faith alone. He speaks of the elect being justified not only in Christ's death and resurrection, but already in the giving of the first gospel promise in Genesis 3:15. Applications of justification to the individual believer occur at his regeneration, in the court of his conscience, in daily communion with God, after death, and on the Judgment Day.[44]

Witsius went on to discuss the immediate results of justification: spiritual peace and the adoption of sonship. These chapters excel in showing the friendship and intimacy between the believer and the Triune God. They place a large measure of responsibility on the believer to be active in preserving spiritual peace and the consciousness of his gracious adoption.[45]

Typical of Puritan and Dutch Second Reformation divines, Witsius devoted the longest chapter in his *ordo salutis* to sanctification. Sanctification is the work of God by which the justified sinner is increasingly "transformed from the turpitude of sin, to the purity of the divine image."[46] Mortification and vivification show the extensiveness of sanctification. Grace, faith, and love are motives for growing in holiness. The goals and means of sanctification are explained in detail. Nevertheless, because believers do not attain perfection in this life, Witsius concluded by examining the doctrine of perfectionism. God does not grant perfection to us in this life for four reasons: to display the difference between earth and heaven, warfare and triumph, toil and rest; to teach us patience, humility, and sympathy; to teach us that salvation is by grace alone; and to demonstrate the wisdom of God in gradually perfecting us.[47]

After explaining the doctrine of perseverance, Witsius ended his third book with a detailed account of glorification. Glorification begins in this life with the firstfruits of grace: holiness, the vision of God apprehended by faith and an experimental sense of God's goodness, the gracious enjoyment of God, full assurance of faith, and joy unspeakable. It is consummated in the life to come.

The focus of glorification is the enjoyment of God, Witsius said. For example, the joy in the intermediate state is the joy of being with God and Christ, the joy of loving God, and the joy of dwelling in glory.[48]

Book 4 presents covenant theology from the perspective of biblical theology. Witsius offered some aspects of what would later be called progressive redemption, emphasizing the faith of Abraham, the nature of the Mosaic covenant, the role of the law, the sacraments of the Old Testament, and the blessings and defects of the Old Testament. Some of his most fascinating sections deal with the Decalogue as a national covenant with Israel rather than as a formal covenant of works or covenant of grace;[49] his defense of the Old Testament against false charges; his explanation of the ceremonial law's abrogation and the relationship between the covenant of works and the covenant of grace. He then explained the relationship between the testaments and the sacraments of the New Testament era. He strongly supported the restoration of Israel according to Romans 11:25-27.[50] He set Christian liberty in the context of freedom from the tyranny of the devil, the reigning and condemning power of sin, the rigor of the law, the laws of men, things indifferent, and death itself. By including things indifferent, he dispelled the charge that the precisianism of the Puritans and Dutch Second Reformation divines allowed no room for the adiaphora.

In summary, Witsius was one of the first theologians among Dutch Second Reformation divines who drew close ties between the doctrines of election and covenant. He aimed for reconciliation between orthodoxy and federalism, while stressing biblical theology as a proper study in itself.

The Cocceians did not respond kindly to Witsius's efforts to reconcile them and the Voetians. They accused him of extending the covenant of grace back into eternity, thereby helping the Reformed orthodox negate the Cocceian principle of the historical development of redemption.[51]

Witsius's work on covenant theology became a standard work in the Netherlands, Scotland, England, and New England. Throughout this work, he stressed that the motto "the Reformed church needs to be ever reforming" *(ecclesia reformata, semper reformanda)* should be applied to the church's life and not to doctrine since Reformation doctrine was foundational truth. His stress was on experiencing the reality of the covenant with God by faith and on the need for godly, precise living—often called "precisianism" somewhat pejoratively by many historians. Few realize, however, that precisianism avoids the medieval ideal of perfection and the pharisaical ideal of legalism. Witsius's emphasis on precise living is characterized by the following:

- Precisianism emphasizes what God's law emphasizes; the law serves as its standard of holiness.
- Precisianism is accompanied by spiritual liberty, rooted in the love of Christ.
- Precisianism treats others mildly but is strict toward one's self.
- Precisianism focuses primarily on heart motivations and only secondarily on outward actions.
- Precisianism humbles the godly, even as they increase in holiness.
- Precisianism's goal is God's glory.[52]

For Witsius precisianism was essentially the practice of experiential piety, for its core was hidden, heartfelt communion with the faithful covenant-keeping God. In Witsius we have theology that is pious in itself rather than theology to which piety is added. [53]

Witsius emphasized Scripture, faith, experience, and the saving work of the Holy Spirit. Scripture was the norm for all belief. The true believer is a humble student of Scripture, reads Scriptures through the glasses of faith, and subjects all his experiences to the touchstone of Scripture for confirmation. True experience flows from the "star light" of Scripture and the "sunlight" of the Holy Spirit, both of which illumine the soul.[54] These two are inseparable from each other and are both received by faith. Students of Scripture are also students of the Holy Spirit.[55] They experience in the Spirit's heavenly academy the forgiveness of sin, adoption as sons, intimate communion with God, love of God poured into the soul, hidden manna, the kisses of Jesus' mouth, and the assurance of blessedness in Christ. The Spirit leads His pupils to feast with God and to know in His banqueting house that His banner over them is love.[56]

The Apostles' Creed and *The Lord's Prayer*

More than a century after Witsius's death, two of his most significant works were translated into English: *Sacred Dissertations on what is commonly called The Apostles' Creed,* translated by Donald Fraser, 2 vols. (Glasgow, 1823), and *Sacred Dissertations on the Lord's Prayer,* translated by Rev. William Pringle (Edinburgh, 1839). Both of these works are judicious, practical, pointed, and edifying. They are meat for the soul.

Witsius's two-volume work on the Apostles' Creed, originally published in Latin at Franeker in 1681, grew out of lectures he gave to his students at the University of Franeker on what he called "the principal articles of our religion." These lectures affirmed Witsius's maxim: "He alone is a true theologian who adds the practical to the theoretical part of religion." Like all of Witsius's writings, these volumes combine profound intellect with spiritual passion.[57]

Witsius's exposition begins with studies that discuss the title, authorship, and authority of the creed; the role of fundamental articles; and the nature of saving faith. The creed's authority is great but not supreme, Witsius said. It contains fundamental articles that are limited to those truths "without which neither faith nor repentance can exist" and "to the rejection of which God has annexed a threatening of destructions." It is scarcely possible to determine the number of fundamental articles. Some are not contained in the creed but are taken up in lengthier doctrinal standards.[58]

Witsius again addressed the acts of saving faith, affirming that the "principal act" of faith is the "receiving of Christ for justification, sanctification, and complete salvation." He stressed that faith receives "a whole Christ," and that "he cannot be a Saviour, unless he be also a Lord."[59] He reasserted the validity of obtaining assurance of faith by syllogistic conclusions and distinguished temporary faith from saving faith. Because temporary faith can remain until the end of a person's life, Witsius preferred to call it presumptuous faith. These kinds of faith differ in their knowledge of the truth, their application of the gospel, their joy, and their fruits.[60]

The remainder of the work follows a phrase-by-phrase 800-page exposition of the creed, accompanied by more than 200 pages of notes added by the translator. Throughout, Witsius excels in exegesis, remains faithful to Reformed dogmatics without becoming overly scholastic, applies every article of the creed to the believer's soul, and, when occasion warrants, exposes various heresies. His closing chapter on life everlasting is perhaps the most sublime. His concluding applications summarize his approach:

- From this sublime doctrine, let us learn the Divine origin of the Gospel
- Let us carefully inquire whether we ourselves have a solid hope of this glorious felicity
- Let us labor diligently, lest we come short of it
- Let us comfort ourselves with the hope of it amidst all our adversities
- Let us walk worthy of it by leading a heavenly life in this world.[61]

Like Witsius's work on the Apostles' Creed, *Sacred Dissertations on the Lord's Prayer* was based on lectures delivered to his theological students. As such, it is a bit heavy with Hebrew and Greek words; however, Pringle's translation includes a rendering of most words of the original languages into English.

The Lord's Prayer contains more than its title reveals. In his preface to a 230-page exposition of the Lord's Prayer, Witsius devoted 150 pages to the subject of prayer: "First, to explain what is prayer; next, in what our obligation to it consists; and lastly, in what manner it ought to be performed."[62] Though parts of this introduction seem a bit dated (especially chapter 4), most of it is practical and insightful. For example, Witsius's dissertation "On the Preparation of the Mind for Right Prayer" contains valuable guidance on a subject seldom addressed today.

Throughout this introduction, Witsius established that genuine prayer is the pulse of the renewed soul. The constancy of its beat is the test of spiritual life. For Witsius, prayer is rightly deemed, in the words of John Bunyan, "a shield to the soul, a sacrifice to God, and a scourge for Satan."

Witsius stressed the two-part channel of prayer: those who would have God hear them when they pray must hear Him when He speaks. Prayer and work must both be engaged in. To pray without working is to mock God; to work without praying is to rob Him of His glory.

Witsius's exposition of the individual petitions of the Lord's Prayer is a masterpiece. In many instances, the questions receive greater instruction from Witsius's pen than anyone else to date. For example, where else can such insight be found on whether the infant believer and the unregenerate should use the name Father in addressing God?[63]

Gifts and Influence

Witsius had many gifts, as even this outline of *Economy of the Covenants* reveals. As an exegete, he exhibited scriptural simplicity and precision, though at times he leaned toward questionable typological and mystical interpretations.[64] As a historian, he measured movements against the ideal, apostolic church, bringing history and theology from numerous sources to bear upon his reasoning. As a theologian, he grounded spiritual life in regeneration and covenantally applied the entire *ordo salutis* to practical, experiential living. As an ethicist, he set forth Christ as the perfect example in probing the heart and guiding the believer in his walk of life. As a polemicist, he opposed Cartesianism, Labadism, antinomianism, neonomianism, and the excesses of Cocceianism. As a homiletician, he, like William Perkins, stressed the marks of grace to encourage believers and convict nominal Christians.[65]

Throughout his life as pastor and professor, Witsius mediated disputes. Formally a Cocceian and materially a Voetian, he managed to remain friends with both sides. His motto, taken from Augustine, was: "In essentials, unity; in non-essentials, liberty; in all things, prudence and charity." He was noted for meekness and patience and stressed that, despite the church's condition, a believer had no right to separate from the church. One biographer wrote of Witsius: "With him it was a fundamental maxim, that Christ 'in all things must have the preeminence'; and free and sovereign grace, reigning through the person and righteousness of the great Immanuel, he cordially regarded as at once the source of all our hope, and the grand incitement to a holy practice."[66]

Witsius influenced many theologians in his lifetime: Campegius Vitringa and Bernardus Smytegelt in the Netherlands; Friedrich Lampe in Germany; Thomas Boston and the Erskine brothers (Ralph and Ebenezer) in Scotland. James Hervey commended him as "a most excellent author, all of whose works have such a delicacy of composition, and such a sweet savour of holiness, [like] the golden pot which had manna, and was outwardly bright with burnished gold, inwardly rich with heavenly food." John Gill described Witsius as "a writer not only eminent for his great talents and particularly solid judgment, rich imagination, and elegance of composition, but for a deep, powerful, and evangelical spirituality, and savour of godliness."[67]

In the nineteenth century, the Free Church of Scotland translated, published, and distributed 1,000 copies of Witsius's *On the character of a true theologian,* free of charge to its divinity students.[68] William Cunningham said in a prefatory note to that work, "He [Witsius] has long been regarded by all competent judges as presenting a very fine and remarkable combination of the highest qualities that constitute a 'true' and consummate theologian—talent, sound judgment, learning, orthodoxy, piety and unction."[69] Witsius's translator, William Pringle, wrote that his writings "are destined to hold an enduring place among the stores of Christian theology. In extensive and profound acquaintance with the doctrines of scripture, powerful defence of the truth against attacks of adversaries, and earnest exhortations to a holy and devout life, he has few equals."[70]

Rabbi John Duncan described Witsius as "perhaps the most tender, spiritually-minded and richly evangelical as well as one of the most learned of the Dutch divines of the old school." He said Witsius had special influence upon him. Duncan's biographers stated "that the attraction proved so strong that for some time he could hardly theologize or preach out of that man's groove."[71]

Witsius's influence continues today. "Learned, wise, mighty in the Scriptures, practical and 'experimental,'" J.I. Packer wrote in 1990, "[Witsius] was a man whose work stands comparison for substance and thrust with that of his British contemporary John Owen, and this writer, for one, knows no praise higher than that!"[72]

Witsius's trilogy is the cream of Reformed theology. Sound biblical exegesis and practical doctrinal substance abound. Oh, to be more centered upon our covenant LORD Himself—confessing His truth, hallowing His name, longing for the coming of His kingdom, doing His will!

---

[1] B. Glasius, ed., *Godgeleerd Nederland: Biographisch Woordenboek van Nederlandsche Godgeleerden* (Leiden: E. J. Brill, 1861), 3:611.

[2] For biographical detail on Witsius, see especially the standard work on his life and thought, J. van Genderen, *Herman Witsius: Bijdrage tot de kennis der gereformeerde theologie* ('s-Gravenhage: Guido de Bres, 1953), 1-107.

[3] J. van Genderen, "Herman Witsius (1636-1708)," in *De Nadere Reformatie: Beschrijving van haar voornaamste vertegenwoordigers,* ed. Willem van 't Spijker ('s-Gravenhage: Boekencentrum, 1986), 193.

[4] Joel R. Beeke, *Gisbertus Voetius: Toward a Reformed Marriage of Knowledge and Piety* (Grand Rapids: Reformation Heritage Books, 1999).

[5] Donald Fraser, "Memoir of Witsius" prefaced to Herman Witsius, *Sacred Disserta-*

tions, on what is commonly called the Apostles' Creed, trans. Donald Fraser (1823; reprint Phillipsburg, N.J.: Presbyterian and Reformed, 1993), 1:xiv.

[6] Erasmus Middleton, *Biographica Evangelica* (London: R. Denham, 1786), 4:158.

[7] The full title is *'t Bedroefde Nederlant, ofte Betooninge van den elendigen toestant onses Vanderlants* (Utrecht, 1659). For a study of this scarce work, see K. Slik, "Het oudste geschrift van Herman Witsius," in *NAKG,* Nieuwe serie, deel 41 (1956):222-41.

[8] J. van der Haar, "Hermannus Witsius," in *Het blijvende Woord,* ed. J. van der Haar, A. Bergsma, L.M.P. Scholten (Dordrecht: Gereformeerde Bijbelstichting, 1985), 243.

[9] For a summary of the *Nadere Reformatie,* see Joel R. Beeke, *The Quest for Full Assurance: The Legacy of Calvin and His Successors* (Edinburgh: Banner of Truth Trust, 1999), 286-309.

[10] Van der Haar, *Het blijvende Woord,* 244.

[11] Fraser, *Apostles' Creed,* xvii.

[12] Herman Witsius, *On the character of a true theologian,* ed. J. Ligon Duncan, III (Greenville, S.C.: Reformed Academic Press, 1994).

[13] For further study, see Charles McCoy, "The Covenant Theology of Johannes Cocceius" (Ph.D. dissertation, Yale, 1957); idem, "Johannes Cocceius: Federal Theologian," *Scottish Journal of Theology* 16 (1963):352-70; idem, *History, Humanity, and Federalism in the Theology and Ethics of Johannes Cocceius* (Philadelphia: Center for the Study of Federalism, Temple University, 1980); C. Steenblok, *Gisbertus Voetius: zijn leven en werken,* 2nd ed. (Gouda: Gereformeerde Pers, 1976); idem, *Voetius en de Sabbat* (Hoorn, 1941); Willem van't Spijker, "Gisbertus Voetius (1589-1676)," in *De Nadere Reformatie: Beschrijving van haar voornaamste vertegenwoordigers* ('s-Gravenhage: Boekencentrum, 1986), 49-84.

[14] George M. Ella, *Mountain Movers* (Durham, England: Go Publications, 1999), 157.

[15] John Macleod, *Scottish Theology* (reprint London: Banner of Truth Trust, 1974), 140.

[16] Cornelis Pronk, "The Second Reformation in the Netherlands," *The Messenger* 48 (Apr. 2001), 10.

[17] *The Economy of the Covenants Between God and Man* (1736; reprint Phillipsburg, N.J.: Presbyterian and Reformed, 1990), 1.2.16; 2.5.8.

[18] Ella, *Mountain Movers,* 158.

[19] William Crookshank, biographical preface to Herman Witsius, *The Economy of the Covenants,* 1:39.

[20] Fraser, *Apostles' Creed,* xxvii.

[21] See Thomas Arthur McGahagan, "Cartesianism in the Netherlands, 1639-1676: The New Science and the Calvinist Counter-Reformation" (Ph.D. dissertation, University of Pennsylvania, 1976); H. B. Visser, *Geschiedenis van den Sabbatstrijd onder de Gereformeerden in de Zeventiende Eeuw* (Utrecht: Kemink en Zoon, 1939).

[22] *Twist des Heeren met syn Wijngaert* (Utrecht, 1710), 393.

[23] Cited by Van Genderen, *De Nadere Reformatie,* 200.

[24] *Economy of the Covenants,* 1:22-23.

[25] Ibid., first page of Packer's unnumbered preface.

[26] Ibid., Book 1, Chapter 1, Paragraphs 3-5 [hereafter 1.1.3-5].

[27] Ibid., 1.1.9.

[28] Ibid., 1.1.15; 1.4.

[29] Wilhelmus à Brakel, *The Christian's Reasonable Service,* trans. Bartel Elshout, ed. Joel R. Beeke, 4 vols. (Grand Rapids: Reformation Heritage Books, 1999-2001).

[30] "The Covenant of Works and the Stability of Divine Law in Seventeenth-Century

Reformed Orthodoxy: A Study in the Theology of Herman Witsius and Wilhelmus à Brakel," *Calvin Theological Journal* 29 (1994):86-87.

[31] Stephen Strehle, *Calvinism, Federalism, and Scholasticism: A Study of the Reformed Doctine of Covenant* (New York: Peter Lang, 1988), 288.

[32] *The Economy of the Covenants*, 1.2.13-15; 1.3.9-10; 1.4.4-7.

[33] Ibid., 1.11.23.

[34] Ibid., 2.2-4.

[35] Ibid., 2.2.1.

[36] Ibid., 2.1.4; cf. Gerald Hamstra, "Membership in the Covenant of Grace," unpublished research paper for Calvin Theological Seminary (1986), 10.

[37] *The Economy of the Covenants*, 3.1-4; 3.8.6.

[38] Ibid., 3.1.5.

[39] Ibid., 3.6.11-15.

[40] Cornelis Graafland, *De Zekerheid van het Geloof: Een onderzoek naar de geloofsbeschouwing van enige vertegenwoordigers van reformatie en nadere reformatie* (Wageningen: H. Veenman & Zonen, 1961), 162-63.

[41] *The Economy of the Covenants*, 3.7.24.

[42] Joel R. Beeke, *Assurance of Faith: Calvin, English Puritansim, and the Dutch Second Reformation* (New York: Peter Lang, 1991), 113-15, 124-26, 159-69, 247-48.

[43] For the views of Calvin and the Puritans on the syllogisms in assurance, see Beeke, *Quest for Full Assurance*, 65-72, 130-42.

[44] *Economy of the Covenants*, 3.8.57-64.

[45] Ibid., 3.9-11.

[46] Ibid., 3.12.11.

[47] Ibid., 3.12.121-24.

[48] Ibid., 3.14.

[49] Here Witsius follows the minority of the seventeenth-century English Puritans, e.g. Samuel Bolton (*True Bounds of Christian Freedom* [Edinburgh: Banner of Truth Trust, 1994], 99) and John Owen (Sinclair Ferguson, *John Owen on the Christian Life* [Edinburgh: Banner Of Truth Trust, 1987], 28).

[50] *Economy of the Covenants*, 4.15.7.

[51] Charles Fred Lincoln, "The Development of the Covenant Theory," *Bibliotheca Sacra*, #397 (Jan. 1943):161-62.

[52] Adapted from Van Genderen, *De Nadere Reformatie*, 206.

[53] I. van Dijk, *Gezamenlijke Geschriften* (Groningen, 1972), 1:314.

[54] *Twist des Heeren*, 167.

[55] Witsius, *On the character of a true theologian*, 35-38.

[56] Herman Witsius, *Miscelleanorum Sacrorum tomus alter* (Lugd. Bat., 1736), 671-72.

[57] Sinclair Ferguson, preface to *Apostles' Creed*, iv.

[58] Witsius, *Apostles' Creed*, 1:16-33.

[59] Ibid., 1:49, 51.

[60] Ibid., 1:56-60.

[61] Ibid., 2:xvi, 470-83.

[62] Herman Witsius, *The Lord's Prayer* (1839; reprint Phillipsburg, N.J.: Presbyterian and Reformed, 1994), 1. The following summary is adapted from my preface in this reprint.

[63] Ibid., 168-70.

[64] J. van Genderen shows how Witsius revealed some mystical tendencies in his

enthusiasm for speaking about contemplation, ecstasy, and mystical marriage with Christ, which surfaces especially in his exegesis of the Song of Solomon and some of the Psalms (*Herman Witsius,* 119-23, 173-76, 262). See also Witsius's discussion of the "mystery" of the manna (*Economy of the Covenants,* 4.10.48).

65 Ibid., 261-63.

66 Fraser, *Apostles' Creed,* xxvii.

67 Ibid., ii; Thomas K. Ascol, "Preface," *Economy of the Covenants.*

68 Michael W. Honeycutt, introduction to *On the character of a true theologian,* 7.

69 Ibid., 19.

70 *The Lord's Prayer,* frontispiece.

71 Pronk, "The Second Reformation in the Netherlands," *The Messenger* 48 (Apr. 2001), 10.

72 *The Economy of the Covenants,* back cover.

Theodorus Jacobus
Frelinghuysen (1691-1747):
Precursor of the Great Awakening

Major historical movements, whether religious, political, or social, are the product of a period of fermentation. Spokesmen for these movements often seem to appear suddenly on the scene, but in most cases lesser-known individuals pave the way for great leaders. Thus Martin Luther and the Reformation cannot be understood apart from forerunners like John Wycliffe and Jan Hus. Similarly, the Great Awakening, while associated with such great leaders as Jonathan Edwards and George Whitefield, had its precursors. One was Theodorus Jacobus Frelinghuysen, whom Whitefield referred to as "the beginner of the great work." Who was this relatively unknown harbinger whose ministry made such an impact and to whom many church historians trace the seeds of the revivals of the 1740s? Why did Frelinghuysen create so much controversy? What can we learn from him today?

Family and Educational Background

The Frelinghuysen family supported the Reformation from the sixteenth century. Theodorus's great-grandfather pioneered the Lutheran Reformation in the German village of Ergste. His grandfather introduced the family to the Reformed tradition in 1669; they joined a small Reformed church in nearby Schwerte. His father, Johan Henrich, became pastor of a newly established German Reformed church in 1683 at Hagen, Westphalia, an area adjacent to the eastern part of the Netherlands. Shortly after Johan was ordained, he married Anna Margaretha Bruggemann, daughter of a Reformed pastor. He baptized their fifth child, Theodorus Jacobus, on November 6, 1692.

God blessed the solid Reformed education Theodorus received at home and school and brought him to conversion. After Theodorus became a communicant member of his father's congregation at age seventeen, he attended the Reformed *gymnasium* at Hamm for two years to study philosophy and theology. The faculty at Hamm imbibed the teachings of Johannes Cocceius (1603-1669), a Bremen-born linguist and biblical theologian who taught at Franeker and Leiden, and whose covenant theology emphasized the historical and contextual character of specific ages. Upon completion of his pre-seminary education at Hamm, Theodorus enrolled at the University of Lingen for theological study. The faculty there adhered to the theology of Gisbertus Voetius (1589-1676), a professor at Utrecht who promoted a Reformed blend of knowledge and piety. Voetius represents the mature fruit of the Dutch Second Reformation. At Lingen, Theodorus became thoroughly committed to Reformed piety and the experimental divinity of the Voetian rather than Cocceian mode. There, too, he mastered the Dutch language and learned to preach in Dutch.

Ordination and Last Years in the Old World

After his classical examination, Frelinghuysen was ordained to the ministry in 1717 at Loegumer Voorwerk in East Friesland, near Emden. By that time the *Nadere Reformatie* had taken a firm hold on the Reformed community in East Friesland through the preaching and writing of Jacobus Koelman, Eduard Meiners, and Johan Verschuir. Those Reformed pietists emphasized the necessity of the new birth and holy living, or the practice of piety, as its inevitable fruit. That experiential theology had a profound, abiding impact on Frelinghuysen.

Frelinghuysen's pastorate in Loegumer Voorwerk lasted only fourteen months. A flood on Christmas Eve swept over the area and devastated much of East Friesland, reducing his parishioners to such poverty that they no longer could support a minister. The young pastor accepted a position at Enkhuizen, North Holland, as co-regent of the Latin school. But only a few months after taking that position, he was approached by Classis Amsterdam of the Reformed Church and asked if he was willing to accept a pastorate in Rarethans. He responded affirmatively, but thought that Rarethans (Raritan) was in one of the adjoining Dutch provinces rather than in America. When he realized he was actually being called by four, small, Dutch Reformed congregations in New Jersey's Raritan Valley (Raritan, Six Mile Run, Three Mile Run, and North Branch), Frelinghuysen felt convicted by Psalm 15:4 to keep his word of acceptance: "[God] honoureth them that fear the LORD. He that sweareth to his own hurt, and changeth not." He was also influenced by what he felt was a providential meeting with Sicco Tjadde (1693-1736), a pietist minister who was searching for young ministers adhering to Reformed experimental theology to recommend for service in America. Being deeply impressed with Frelinghuysen's orthodoxy and godliness, Tjadde encouraged him "to give up the prospect of a successful career in the Old World in order to spread vital religion in the New." After bidding farewell to relatives and friends, Frelinghuysen sailed to New York and the New World in September 1719.

The Dutch Reformed Church in North America

Unlike the English Pilgrims and Puritans who came to the New World primarily for religious reasons, the Dutch who settled in North America were largely motivated by economic factors. Early in the seventeenth century, the Dutch West India Company had established trading posts on Manhattan Island and at other strategic locations near the Hudson and Delaware rivers. The population of the Dutch colony grew steadily, but little was done to promote its religious life. In 1623, when the settlement of Manhattan had grown to 200, two *ziekentroosters* (comforters of the sick) arrived and undertook some pastoral duties. Two years later the colony received its own pastor, Jonas Michaelius, who organized the first Dutch-speaking Reformed church in the New World. In 1633, a second pastor, Everard Bogardus, arrived from Holland.

The chronic shortage of ministers posed a problem for the new

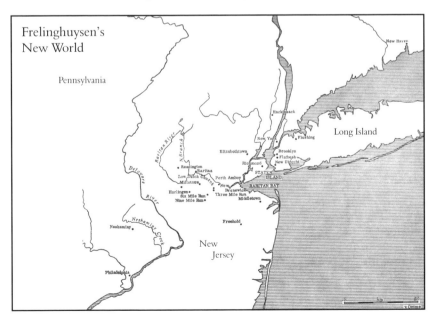

Dutch churches in North America. The shortage reflected the short-sightedness of the mother church, which insisted that ministers for the New World be educated and ordained in the Netherlands under the auspices of Classis Amsterdam. Consequently, the spiritual life and moral tone of the colony was adversely affected.

Doctrinally, these American churches were consistent with their mother church in the Netherlands. Their standards were the Three Forms of Unity adopted by the Synod of Dort: the Belgic Confession of Faith (1561), the Heidelberg Catechism (1563), and the Canons of Dort (1618-19). Practically, however, most members lived on a low spiritual plane. Dead orthodoxy had been a serious problem from the beginning and had only grown worse by the eighteenth century. Abraham Messler, who translated several of Frelinghuysen's sermons and eventually became one of his successors, noted: "The necessity of a new heart had almost entirely been lost sight of…formalism and self-righteousness almost universally prevailed. Christians were not ashamed to ridicule Christian experience, and many had become very resolute in opposing it."

The time was ripe for the waves of revival that would sweep over the Dutch and British colonies. And the minister who played a key role in initiating those revivals was Theodorus Frelinghuysen.

Arrival in New York

When the twenty-eight-year-old Dominie Frelinghuysen arrived in New York in January 1720, his honeymoon of adjustment in America was short-lived. He and a young helper, Jacobus Schureman, who had come to serve as schoolmaster and *voorlezer* (lay reader) in the church, were welcomed by two prominent ministers of the Dutch Reformed Church in New York City, Gualtherus DuBois (1671-1751) and Henricus Boel (1692-1754). They invited the new minister to conduct worship on the following Sunday. The reaction of the parishioners, who were accustomed to long, unemotional, and impersonal sermons, was discouraging. Many objected to Frelinghuysen's stress on regeneration, his experiential style of preaching, and what some called his "howling prayers." Moreover, when Boel asked Frelinghuysen why he omitted the Lord's Prayer in worship, Frelinghuysen replied that he was willing to follow the practice of the Reformed Church but he did not care for using form prayers in corporate worship. Right from the beginning of his ministry in the New World, Frelinghuysen's preaching style and his preference for free prayers over form prayers became sore points that would later develop into major issues.

Henricus Boel   *Gualtherus DuBois*

Nor did Frelinghuysen endear himself to Dominie DuBois when he was invited to the senior pastor's home. Upon entering, Frelinghuysen asked his colleague why he had such a large wall mirror and remarked that it was not justified "by the most far-stretched necessity." This ascetic tendency would also cause considerable friction between Frelinghuysen and others in the church.

Settlement in the Raritan Valley

The Raritan Valley area in New Jersey was settled mostly by Dutch Reformed farmers who were attracted to its rich soil. Though most of them showed more interest in improving their economic condition than in pursuing spiritual growth, the farmers still looked forward to the arrival of their new minister. But they soon perceived that they had received no ordinary Reformed preacher. Frelinghuysen preached his inaugural sermon on January 31, 1720, from 2 Corinthians 5:20: "Now then we are ambassadors for Christ, as though God did beseech you by us: we pray you in Christ's stead, be ye reconciled to God." The sermon caused quite a stir as the new minister made it abundantly clear that he intended to labor among them "in Christ's stead"—that is, with earnestness and personal examination as if Christ Himself stood among them.

If the Dutch Reformed parishioners of New Jersey's Raritan Valley were surprised by their minister's probing sermons and intense pastoral work, Frelinghuysen was no less surprised by his placid parishioners.

Though he had anticipated their low level of spirituality because of the rumors he had heard in the Netherlands, he soon discovered that the situation was far worse than he had thought. Messler noted:

> He found that great laxity of manners prevailed throughout his charge... that while horse-racing, gambling, dissipation, and rudeness of various kinds were common, the [church] was attended at convenience, and religion consisted of the mere formal pursuit of the routine of duty.

Bluntly put, Frelinghuysen realized that many of his parishioners showed no fruits of conversion. Practical spirituality—"the life of God in the soul of man"—was largely absent. General ignorance and blatant godlessness abounded. William Tennent, Jr. later wrote of the sad condition of the people at Raritan Valley during Frelinghuysen's early years of ministry there:

> Family prayer was unpracticed by all, a very few excepted; ignorance so overshadowed their minds, that the doctrine of the New Birth when clearly explained, and powerfully pressed upon them, as absolutely necessary to salvation, by that faithful preacher of God's Word, Mr. Theodorus Jacobus Frelinghousa.... [The new birth] was made a common game of; so that not only the preachers but professors of that truth were called in derision "new-born" and looked upon as holders forth of some new and false doctrine. And indeed their practice was as bad as their principles, viz. loose and profane.

Consequently, Frelinghuysen's preaching focused on the conversion of sinners rather than on the nurture of believers. He taught that an outward confession and upright life are not sufficient for salvation. The Holy Spirit must reveal to a sinner his sinful state and lost condition before God, which in turn drives the convicted sinner to Christ for mercy and salvation. In a sermon on Isaiah 66:2, "The Poor and Contrite Are God's Temple," he said:

> In a contrite spirit are found: a deep sense and clear perception of sin. . . . Heart-felt disquietude and sadness. . . . An open and free confession of sin. By reason of a sense of the greatness of his sins, he knows not whither to look or turn: but, notwithstanding, places his dependence upon the grace which God can exercise through his Son. Hence, the contrite in spirit flees from the curse of the law to the Gospel. . . . Thus he is driven out of himself, to the sovereign grace of God in Christ, for reconciliation, pardon, sanctification, and salvation.

Frelinghuysen taught that only those are truly saved who have *experienced* conversion, which includes, according to the Heidelberg Catechism, not only the knowledge of sin and misery, but also the experience of deliverance in Christ, resulting in a lifestyle of gratitude to God. In his sermon "The Way of God with His People in the Sanctuary," Frelinghuysen invited sinners to come to Christ as strongly as he warned them against sin: "If thou be but weary of sin, if thou be sincerely desirous of drawing near to God in the right way, which is only through Christ, then come." Later in the same sermon, he presented God as running to meet those who have repented, just as the father of the prodigal ran to meet his returning son. In another sermon he said, "Jesus still stands with extended arms to gather you." He urged listeners "to be willing, and to arise and come to Jesus." He said a true experience of joyous salvation in Christ, however, will necessarily reap a Christian life of gratitude, a life of total submission to God's Word, "marked by a new and hearty service." Progress in grateful sanctification is only possible when the believer continually flees to Christ for strength in his war against indwelling sin and in striving to regulate his life by God's Word. The Voetian themes of the narrow gate and the hard way, the life of precision and the scarcity of salvation, the priority of internal motives which effect external observance—all this and more consistently reappear in Frelinghuysen's sermons as inevitable fruits of the life of Christian gratitude.

Though members in Frelinghuysen's church did not object to such scriptural and Reformed doctrines in themselves, many resented the forceful manner in which the pastor applied this experiential theology. Had he referred to people outside of the church as unregenerate, self-righteous hypocrites, church members might have concurred. But Frelinghuysen made it clear that he was speaking to his own parishioners. In one sermon, he applied the lesson of an earthquake in no uncertain terms:

> Come hither, ye careless, at ease in sin, ye carnal and earthly minded, ye unchaste whoremongers, adulterers, ye proud, haughty men and women, ye devotees of pleasure, drunkards, gamblers, ye disobedient, ye wicked rejectors of the Gospel, ye hypocrites and dissemblers, how suppose ye it will go with you?... Be filled with terror, ye impure swine, adulterers, and whoremongers, and consider that without true repentance ye shall soon be with the impure devils; for I announce a fire better than that of Sodom and Gomorrah to all that burn in their lusts.

He addressed the wealthy with extra admonitions, based on James 5:1-6:

> Ye have lived in pleasure on the earth and been wanton. Ye have nourished your hearts as in a day of slaughter. Ye have condemned and killed the just, and he doth not resist you. Know then, that ye unrighteous and covetous, who are idolaters, shall not inherit the kingdom of God.

Frelinghuysen clearly viewed most of his members as unregenerate and hell-bound. This was a bitter pill for them to swallow, especially when he warned against their casual attendance at the Lord's Supper. In his sermon, "The Acceptable Communicant," he said:

> Much loved hearers, who have so often been at the Lord's table, do you know that the unconverted may not approach? Have you then, with the utmost care examined, whether you be born again?... Reflect, therefore, upon, and bear in mind this truth; and remember, that though morally and outwardly religious, if you still be unregenerate and destitute of spiritual life, you have no warrant for an approach to the table of grace.

For Frelinghuysen, the evidences of a true, personal conversion—which are repentance, faith, and holiness—are tests for admission to the Lord's Supper. Since, in his judgment, lack of the fruits of godliness revealed that most of his members were unregenerate, he felt obliged to warn them against coming to the communion table. In a few cases, he even forbade them to do so. For Frelinghuysen, this was in keeping with the calling of the minister and elders to faithfully and solemnly examine church members prior to each celebration of the Lord's Supper. If such members have departed from the faith or behaved unworthily, they "may be rebuked or admonished, and if necessary [be] suspended from the privilege of the Lord's Table" (*The Constitution of the Reformed Church in America,* section 70).

There were good reasons to maintain such examination, Frelinghuysen believed. Unworthy participants dishonored the Head of the Church, profaned God's covenant, kindled God's wrath against the entire congregation, and rendered themselves liable to a severe doom. Consequently, during one communion service, when Frelinghuysen saw some approach the table whom he had admonished not to partake, he exclaimed, "See! See! even the people of the world and the impenitent are coming, that they may eat and drink judgment to themselves!" Several people who were approaching thought the minister meant them and returned to their seats.

Predictably, the disciplinary actions of Frelinghuysen and his consistory upset many in the congregation, particularly the wealthy. They complained to influential Reformed ministers in New York whose views differed from those of Frelinghuysen. Some of the ministers sided with the complainants—most notably, DuBois and Boel—who had had negative impressions of Frelinghuysen from the outset. They levied serious accusations at Frelinghuysen, who responded in kind. Matters became extremely tense when Frelinghuysen openly referred to

colleagues who opposed him, including DuBois and Boel, as "unconverted ministers."

Supportive Colleagues and Family

Other pastors supported Frelinghuysen, although they cautioned him
not to be too harsh in judging the spiritual lives of his people. Among
those who supported Frelinghuysen was Guiliam Bartholf (1656-1726),
an itinerant, pioneer pastor who was responsible for organizing all but
two of the New Jersey churches north of the Raritan before 1702, including the four congregations to which Frelinghuysen was called.
Bartholf had grown up in the Dutch village of Sluis, near Middelburg in
the Province of Zeeland, and had been greatly influenced by his childhood minister, Jacobus Koelman (1632-1695), who is now considered by
historians of the *Nadere Reformatie* to be one of the premier representatives of that movement. After Bartholf came to the New World, he so
promoted his mentor's views, that by the time Frelinghuysen arrived,
the roots of Dutch experiential Calvinism had been planted. As Frelinghuysen had also been influenced by Koelman's writings, the preparatory work done by Bartholf proved to be most helpful. Both men stood
in the tradition of the *Nadere Reformatie* and shared its emphases, but
Bartholf had a more irenic and tactful disposition than Frelinghuysen.

Two New York ministers who also held Reformed experiential views
and would eventually publish booklets in Frelinghuysen's defense were
Bernardus Freeman (1660-1743) of Long Island and Cornelius Van
Santvoord (1687-1752) of Staten Island. Frelinghuysen developed a
warm friendship with Freeman, a German pietist, who shared his evangelistic convictions and carried on an effective ministry among the
Mohawk Indians while ministering to Dutch Reformed churches. Van
Santvoord had been a favorite student of Johannes à Marck (1656-
1731), an able Voetian theologian at Leiden, and remained friends with
him in the New World.

Shortly after his arrival in the New World, Frelinghuysen married
Eva Terhune. An orphan daughter of a well-to-do Long Island farmer,
Eva had been cared for by Freeman after her parents' death. Their union
was a happy one and was blessed with five sons and two daughters. All
five sons became ministers, and both daughters married ministers.

The Opposition Grows

The majority of the Reformed pastors in the Middle Colonies held
decidedly anti-pietist views. They viewed the members of their congre-

gations as regenerate and rejected the experiential emphases of the Dutch Second Reformation as being too subjective and introspective.

By the end of the first spring, the situation in the Raritan Valley had become so tense that even Freeman, though basically supportive of Frelinghuysen, became alarmed and started to question his colleague's actions. When, for instance, Frelinghuysen turned the wife of a prominent member away from the Lord's Supper, Freeman became alarmed. He believed that she was a God-fearing member of the church. Other issues soon arose that confirmed Freeman and others in their opinions that Frelinghuysen was tactless and too unrealistic about his standards for admission to the Lord's Supper.

As attacks upon his ministry increased, Frelinghuysen took steps to defend himself. In a gesture of defiance, he had the following poem written on the back of his sleigh:

> No one's tongue, and no one's pen
> Can make me other than I am.
> Speak slanderers! Speak without end;
> In vain you all your slanders send.

He published three sermons that counteracted reports that he was "a maker of divisions and a teacher of false doctrines." In one sermon he wrote: "Men chatter a lot about my way of serving the Lord's Supper, but that I teach nothing different here than has always been taught by the Reformed Church can easily be seen by any unprejudiced person." It is important to note that these sermons were published with the approval of Frelinghuysen's friends, Bartholf and Freeman, who considered them to be soul-searching sermons in full harmony with Scripture and the Heidelberg Catechism. Frelinghuysen's sermons only intensified the conflict that swirled around his ministry. Boel and his supporters viewed the sermons as an attack rather than a defense and took sharp issue with Bartholf and Freeman for endorsing them.

Another source of contention was Frelinghuysen's use of the Frisian Catechism written by followers of Koelman as a supplement to the Heidelberg Catechism. Koelman had been deposed from his congregation at Sluis, partly for his opposition to Christian feast days and the use of prescribed liturgical forms, but also for his scathing criticism of colleagues whom he viewed as unconverted. Frelinghuysen's opponents, who suffered similar aspersions from the Raritan Valley pastor, viewed Koelman as the real instigator and referred to him as "the arch heretic." What was there about this little book that so upset Frelinghuysen's opponents? Basically, they took issue with Frelinghuysen's emphasis on the need for vital Christian experience. In their view, the Heidelberg Catechism addresses this need in a more balanced way. For the composers of the Frisian Catechism, however, personal experience of what was taught doctrinally was critical, and any writing that enhanced this emphasis was welcome. For Frelinghuysen and his supporters, opposition to the Frisian Catechism only augmented their suspicions that most of their opponents had no vital Christian experience.

The Battle Lines Are Drawn

On March 12, 1723, several disgruntled members of Frelinghuysen's congregation asked Freeman for support against their pastor. They charged Frelinghuysen with preaching false doctrines. Freeman refused to take their side. Although he agreed that Frelinghuysen had his faults, this did not make him a preacher of false doctrines. After listening to their complaints, he responded, "I perceive that you are all affected by the spirit of hatred and revenge. Because he sharply exposes sin, you try to help the devil and to cause him to trample upon the Church of Christ." He advised them to draw up a list of complaints and present them to their consistory, warning them that if they took their complaints elsewhere they would be regarded as schismatics.

The *Klagers* (Complainants), as they came to be called, ignored Freeman's advice and turned to Dominie Boel and his brother Tobias, an attorney, for aid and advice. Instead of advising the *Klagers* to follow the principles of Matthew 18:15-17 and the Church Order in dealing with their grievances, the Boel brothers showed sympathy, which evoked the anger of Frelinghuysen's consistories. The consistories drew up a summons *(daagbrief)*, which they sent to the *Klagers*. In this summons the *Dagers* (Summoners), as they became known, listed the errors of their opponents and warned that if they did not withdraw their accusations they would be excommunicated. Later in the spring of 1723, Frelinghuysen's consistories issued two additional summons to the agitators. Each summons threatened to excommunicate those who did not repent and return to the church. When no replies were received by September, the consistories controlled by the *Dagers* unanimously excommunicated four ringleaders of the opposition: Peter DuMont, Simon Wyckoff, Hendrick Vroom, and Daniel Sebring.

This action sent shock waves throughout the entire Dutch Reformed community. Classis Amsterdam, which had to tread cautiously as arbitrator, was thousands of miles away. Classis forwarded a careful letter of caution to Frelinghuysen, to which he responded in detail. Classis wrote back:

> We have already referred to the harsh expressions which you have used in your reply. . . . Also in your manner of exercising discipline, even excommunication, on certain guilty persons, did you act as prudently as is becoming to a minister in such an important matter?. . . Would it not have been safer not to take such an important step without first consulting the Classis?

In 1725, the *Klagers* finally responded to the summons in a *Klagte* (Complaint)—a document of 146 pages addressed to Classis Amsterdam. The *Klagte* was presumably written by the Boel brothers and signed by sixty-four heads of households, which represented close to one quarter of Frelinghuysen's four congregations. The *Klagte* details every conceivable criticism of Frelinghuysen that might rouse the disaffection of Classis and lead to his dismissal. Many of the charges are petty or based on false rumor and reveal the bitter mindset of the *Klagers*. Frelinghuysen is presented as a tyrant with homosexual tendencies. The *Klagers* state that Frelinghuysen would not admit to the Lord's Supper those who could not give a satisfactory account of their conversion, that he insisted strenuously on a change of heart experienced as a result of conviction of sin, that he violated the Church Order by reserving the right of nominating elders and deacons to the consistory rather than to the congregation and by excommunicating members without the advice of Classis, and that he preached pietistic doctrines that were contrary to the Three Forms of Unity. The *Klagte* charges Frelinghuysen with "straying from the pure doctrine and discipline, not wholly unlike those of Labadie, Koelman, and other Schismatics."

To add fuel to the fire, the *Klagers* decided to frustrate Frelinghuysen's efforts by locking him out of two churches. He responded by calling the *Klagers* "impious" and "the scum of these four congregations." He and his supporters maintained that they were only trying to keep the church pure by exercising the keys of discipline—both the key of preaching and the key of excommunication—as Lord's Day 31 of the Heidelberg Catechism directed them to do. They said that more than half of the signatories of the *Klagte* had never made a profession of faith and warned that, "the wrath of God and eternal damnation abide on them." Consequently, even though Article 76 of the Church Order states that "no person shall be excommunicated without the previous advice of Classis," Frelinghuysen defended his actions by appealing to

Article 86, which declares that changes could be made in the Church Order if the well-being of the church required it.

The fierce opposition took its toll on Frelinghuysen's mental health. He suffered from what his major biographer, James Tanis, describes as "mild psychoses." In a sermon on Paul's "thorn in the flesh," Frelinghuysen suggested that the apostle's affliction may have been *morbus hypochondriacus*, a mental breakdown brought on by emotional stress, which Frelinghuysen felt had also afflicted him periodically for several years. The breakdowns, which occurred most frequently in the early 1730s, often left him incapacitated for several months.

Between breakdowns, Frelinghuysen continued to spread his experiential and controversial teachings by the printed and spoken word. One booklet that caused quite a stir was *Een Spiegel die niet vleyt* (A Mirror That Does Not Flatter), based on Proverbs 14:12: "There is a way which seems right unto a man, but the end thereof are the ways of death." Though no names were mentioned, the *Klagers* must have known that this sermon targeted them. Remarkably, Classis Amsterdam, which usually supported the *Klagers,* approved this pamphlet for publication. After carefully examining *Een Spiegel*, classis had found nothing in it that conflicted with God's Word and the Three Forms of Unity.

The controversy between the *Dagers* and the *Klagers* raged intermittently until, through the prodding of Classis Amsterdam, they reached a compromise. On November 18, 1733, the churches served by Frelinghuysen adopted eleven "Peace Articles," which were read from the pulpits on the first three Sundays of 1734, then forwarded to Amsterdam for final approval. The articles, to which the *Klagers* subscribed, stated that the consistories should forgive the shortcomings of the *Klagers* and rescind their excommunication, providing the *Klagers* accept Frelinghuysen as an orthodox Reformed minister and return to the church. Though Boel's opposition to Frelinghuysen and the revivals continued, DuBois inaugurated a movement to join the revival party in a petition for independence from Classis Amsterdam. Two parties emerged by mid-century, the Coetus and the Conferentie. The Coetus party was composed largely of ministers who represented Frelinghuysen's pro-revivalist, progressive piety. The Conferentie party represented anti-revivalist, traditional orthodoxy and consisted of those who desired to remain "in conference" with Classis Amsterdam. For decades, the two parties exchanged a series of pamphlets. In the end, the goals of Frelinghuysen and the Coetus were reached: preaching in

English was sanctioned, ministers were trained and ordained in America, and the American church was granted full autonomy.

Influence In and Beyond The Dutch Reformed Community

Despite relentless criticism, Frelinghuysen faithfully carried on his labors. While some people were offended by his searching preaching, others were convicted by it and came to a saving knowledge of Christ. Abraham Messler, one of Frelinghuysen's successors, wrote that his predecessor's banner years were 1726, 1729, 1734, 1739, and 1741, during which 16 to 122 persons made confessions of faith. It appears that more than 300 persons were converted under Frelinghuysen's ministry in New Jersey. That does not include the effect of Frelinghuysen's preaching beyond his own congregations. Those numbers become more significant when one considers that the total number of communicants in 1726 was approximately twenty. Messler exaggerated when he said that the numbers evidence "a great revival," though we may conclude that there were at least several mini-revivals under Frelinghuysen's ministry that paved the way for the Great Awakening.

Although Frelinghuysen remained firmly committed to the Dutch Reformed faith in which he had been nurtured, he ventured freely outside the confines of his Dutch constituency. From the commencement of his ministry in North America, he sought contact with Christians from other backgrounds. Among his close associates were clergymen of Presbyterian, German Reformed, and Anglican persuasions. Due to these contacts, he was able to influence the English-speaking community in the Middle Colonies and thereby augment his contribution to the Great Awakening.

In 1726, one year after the publication of the *Klagte*, Gilbert Tennent, a young Presbyterian minister, came to New Brunswick to labor among the English-speaking colonists. He had been trained for the ministry by his father, William Tennent, an Episcopalian-turned-Presbyterian. Convinced of the necessity of sound biblical and experimental preaching, William Tennent began a program for preparing godly young men for the ministry. A log house was built at Neshaminy, New Jersey to accommodate the eager students, including three of Tennent's sons. This small, unpretentious theological institution, derisively referred to by its opponents as the "Log College," produced twenty preachers who played key roles in the Great Awakening.

William Tennent's oldest son, Gilbert, enthusiastically undertook his pastoral duties in New Brunswick. The young preacher soon won the admiration and friendship of his neighbor, Dominie Frelinghuysen. Tennent was impressed by the soundness of the numerous conversions that were taking place under his Dutch colleague's preaching and felt discouraged by his own, seemingly unfruitful labors. In his journal he wrote:

> When I came here I had the privilege of seeing much of the fruits of Frelinghuysen's ministry. . . . This, together with a kind letter which he sent me respecting the necessity of dividing the Word aright and giving to every man his portion in due season through the divine blessing, excited me to great earnestness in ministerial labours.

Tennent's friendship with Frelinghuysen proved beneficial as a rebuke and as an inspiration. Tennent implemented his more experienced colleague's advice on how to preach and soon began to witness significant numbers of conversions. The revival begun under Frelinghuysen in the Dutch community now spread to the English-speaking settlers under Tennent's ministry.

What was it in Frelinghuysen's style of preaching that led, with the Spirit's blessing, to so many conversions? Hendrik Visscher, Frelinghuysen's friend and assistant, described it as "his exceeding talent of drawing one matter out of another, thereby discovering the state and condition of his auditors to themselves." Frelinghuysen, in other words, excelled in *discriminatory preaching*. As he stated in an ordination sermon of a colleague:

> Preaching must be structured to the differing conditions of our hearers. In the church there are godless and unconverted persons; civil, false, and pretending Christians. . . . There are also converted persons in the church, and little children and those more advanced. Each one . . . must be spoken to and handled according to his state and frame.

Tennent was a fast learner and soon excelled in discriminatory preaching. Emphasizing the necessity of regeneration, he challenged his hearers to examine whether they possessed the scriptural evidence of the new birth.

Tennent's ministry became increasingly bound up with Frelinghuysen's. On occasion they held combined worship services in the Dutch and English languages. The *Klagers* charged that by allowing "this English Dissenter" (i.e., Tennent) to preach and administer the sacraments in his church, Frelinghuysen was violating the Dutch Church Order and liturgy, and thereby undermining the authority of Classis Amsterdam. Viewing themselves as the guardians of Dutch orthodoxy, they deplored his ecumenicity as inimical to the true, Dutch Reformed religion. As orthodox traditionalists they appealed to Classis Amsterdam, saying, "We must be careful to keep things in a Dutch way in our churches."

Frelinghuysen's goal, on the other hand, was the conversion of sinners. Whoever shared this vision was his friend, regardless of denominational attachments, ethnic and linguistic backgrounds, parish boundaries, and social distinctions.

In June 1729, Classis Amsterdam charged Frelinghuysen with deepening the rift in the churches by moving beyond his denominational boundary and linguistic background:

> You did permit a dissenting candidate [Gilbert Tennent], in one of the churches where you preached, at the Communion, to offer a prayer in English before a Dutch congregation. . . . Also, you had no objection to letting him preach in our Dutch churches. . . . Is there to be no accounting for this before Divine and Ecclesiastical judgment seats?. . . Then there is also that which was done against the order of the established Consistory of Navesink, and against the wish of Rev. Morgen their pastor. Did you not go there and preach in a barn? And did you not also go and preach at Joris Ryerson's in the Rev. Coen's congregation, where there is an established Consistory and pastor?

Critics and Classis notwithstanding, Frelinghuysen continued to accept invitations to preach in barns and churches in New York, Staten Island, Long Island, and as far west as Neshaminy, Pennsylvania. He could not keep up with all the demands for his services, but responded as a man of vision. He published a number of his sermons in order to reach a wider audience. To foster the communion of saints and maintain a high level of spirituality, he held private devotional meetings of fellowship (conventicles or *gezelschappen*) for those whom he regarded to be God's people. He transformed "helpers" (*voorlezers*) into lay preachers, several of whom he trained to assume the full duties of pastors, with the exception of administering the sacraments. During his absences to preach elsewhere, those lay preachers would lead services and preside over the *gezelschappen*. Most notable among them was the first translator of Frelinghuysen's sermons, Hendrik Visscher. Those sermons were published and cherished for years by Reformed pietists in Raritan Valley.

Frelinghuysen also trained several men for ordained ministry (including Samuel Verbryck, John Goetachius, and Thomas Romeyn), advocated the establishment of a colonial theological seminary, and helped lay the groundwork that ultimately led to the ecclesiastical independence of the American churches from Classis Amsterdam.

The result of Frelinghuysen's preaching and contacts with ministers and lay people of kindred spirits was that revivals gradually spread until much of New Jersey and New York was caught up in what was later called "The Great Awakening." When this revival was in full swing, George Whitefield came to preach in New Brunswick and met Frelinghuysen. Later he wrote in his *Journals*:

> Among those who came to hear the Word were several ministers whom the Lord has been pleased to honour in making them instruments of bringing many sons to glory. One was a Dutch Calvinistic minister, named Freeling Housen, pastor of a congregation about four miles from New Brunswick. He is a worthy old soldier of Jesus Christ, and was the beginner of the great work which I trust the Lord is carrying on in these parts. He has been strongly opposed by his carnal brethren, but God has always appeared for him in a surprising manner, and made him more than conqueror, through his love. He has long since learnt to fear him only who can destroy both body and soul in hell.

Whitefield not only acknowledged Frelinghuysen as God's instrument for the commencement of the revivals of the 1740s, but also was influenced by Frelinghuysen's method of preaching with which he became acquainted through Gilbert Tennent.

Frelinghuysen's Place in American Church History

Frelinghuysen has been called the father of American pietism, but this title needs further explanation. The words *pietist* and *pietism* mean different things to different people. For many, these terms are negative. In fact, they were originally used as derogatory terms, just as *puritan* originally downgraded those who desired to reform and "purify" the Church of England and were pastorally concerned about living a biblical, godly life within the scope of the Reformed doctrines of grace. All of these terms evoked images, real or imagined, of sanctimonious and hypocritical persons who went too far with their religious zeal. But people like Frelinghuysen used terms like piety to mean *vroomheid* or godliness.

We have to distinguish historically between Lutheran, Reformed, Moravian, and other forms of pietism. All those forms of pietism emphasize personal, experiential religion. Pietism with a capital "P" arose in German Lutheran circles as a protest against the dead orthodoxy and formalism in the established church. Similar pietistic, protest movements (*Nadere Reformatie* and Puritanism) arose against the same abuses in the national churches of the Netherlands and England. Despite these similarities, there were important differences in these movements, especially with regard to the doctrines of grace. Frelinghuysen was a Calvinist; his pietism was of a distinctly Reformed variety. The Dutch Reformed pietism that he championed was more closely related to English Puritanism than to German Pietism. The Dutch learned much from the English in practical, daily sanctification. One of the first Puritan treatises translated into Dutch was Lewis Bayly's *The Practice of Piety*. But the Dutch pietists also contributed to the English Puritans and their successors, especially in their understanding of preaching. As we have shown, Frelinghuysen influenced Tennent's preaching, and Tennent's preaching impacted Whitefield's. Though Tennent and Whitefield were molded by generations of Puritan divines whose reputation was largely based on their pulpit work, they found in Frelinghuysen an ability to preach to different classes of hearers that went beyond most Puritans. This type of preaching has been designated by historians as "the classification method."

The Classification Method of Preaching

Frelinghuysen excelled in distinguishing between true and false religion. He developed this skill with the assistance of Dutch, pietistic mentors who divided a congregation into various states and conditions of soul and then made personal applications in preaching to each group. Pioneers of this classification method in Dutch pietism were Jean Taffin (1528-1602), Godefridus Udemans (1581-1649), and Willem Teellinck (1579-1629). This practice of classification expanded and developed under the Voetian circle of preachers, such as Jodocus VanLodenstein (1620-1677), Wilhelmus à Brakel (1635-1711), and Bernardus Smytegelt (1665-1739). Those *Nadere Reformatie* divines represented the cream of Dutch pietism. Frelinghuysen's foremost mentor, Johannes Verschuir (1680-1737), belonged to this Voetian circle of preachers. Verschuir was born and raised in Groningen and spent his entire ministry in that northern province. He is known mainly for his *Waarheit in het Binnenste, of Bevindelyke godtgeleertheit* (Truth in the Inward Parts, or Experimental Divinity). In that treatise, Verschuir argued that true Christianity is a rare thing; many who think they are believers are deceiving themselves. Since ministers must be able to distinguish between what is true and false in religion, Verschuir wrote especially for young pastors to help them deal with souls entrusted to their care. Verschuir distinguished between several categories of churchgoers, all of whom need to be addressed by the preacher: (1) the strong Christian (*sterk Christen*) who is converted and has reached a degree of maturity in spiritual life; (2) the concerned Christian *(bekommerde Christen)* who is also converted but struggles with many doubts and lacks assurance of faith; (3) the "letter-learned" (*letterwyse*) who are unconverted but instructed and conversant in truth though not knowing its experience or power; (4) the ignorant (*onkunde*) who are unconverted and unlearned but who may still be persuaded to learn because they have native intelligence. Further distinctions are made among the various types of the wicked.

Frelinghuysen's sermons show that he usually followed Verschuir's method of classification. More preaching is devoted to counselling the concerned Christian than the strong Christian. Because of the time he spent on encouraging this class of hearers, we may conclude that Frelinghuysen believed that most of the true believers in his congregation belonged to this category. Most of his warnings are directed to the "letter-learned." They are viewed as being in great danger because they are "almost Christians," not far from the kingdom of God. They walk with Christians and talk like Christians, but they do not possess the new birth. Despite their outward morality and profession of truth, they will perish if death overtakes them.

Frelinghuysen's conviction that the one thing needful is regeneration constitutes the heart of his theology and that of the *Nadere Reformatie*. In a typical sermon, he exhorts his hearers to examine whether they possess the evidences of the new birth. Closely related to this is the call to conversion, by which Frelinghuysen usually does not mean the daily conversion of the believer but the initial conversion of the unsaved. He used conversion in that sense interchangeably with regeneration or the new birth.

Frelinghuysen preached that the new birth must be experimental. That is to say, a convert had to know how he had passed from death to life and was expected to be able to relate what God had done for his soul. Particularly these two things—a heavy emphasis on the necessity of the new birth and on classifying churchgoers into various categories—impressed Tennent, Whitefield, and other revival preachers.

All of this is consistent with Frelinghuysen's philosophy of preaching. In the application to a sermon, "Duties of Watchmen on the Walls of Zion," he reflects upon his duty as a preacher:

> Though I would prescribe a method of preaching to no one, I am yet of the opinion that the application should be discriminating, adapted to the various states of all hearers (Jude 20, 21; Jeremiah 15). In the church are wicked and unconverted persons, moral persons, Christians in appearance and profession: and these constitute the greater number for many are called but few are chosen. Also are there in the church converted

persons: little children and those more advanced. Each one longs and calls, each one must be addressed and dealt with according to his state and frame (Jer. 15:19). How pernicious are general applications, has been shown by many zealous divines (Ezekiel 13:19-20).

According to Teunis Brienen, who wrote his doctoral dissertation on the subject of the classification method used by preachers of the *Nadere Reformatie (The prediking van de Nadere Reformatie)*, this approach varies from the method of Calvin and other early Reformers who simply divided church members into two categories, believers and unbelievers. Not that Calvin was unaware of differences between strong and weak believers and that there are various kinds and degrees of unbelief, but he did not draw such detailed distinctions as did the later representatives of the *Nadere Reformatie*. The difference between early Reformers like Calvin and post-Reformation divines like Frelinghuysen are due in part to the different settings in which they preached. The Reformers preached, as John Macleod pointed out, to "a generation of believers on which the Gospel of the free grace of God in Justification burst in all its wonder as something altogether new." Post-Reformers like Frelinghuysen preached in a setting in which mere assent to the given truths of Scripture without a believing response from the soul was regarded as sufficient for salvation. Against this background, it became essential to distinguish clearly between saving faith and historical faith by placing a heavier emphasis on self-examination, the marks of grace, and the classification of hearers into various groups.

Brienen said that the English Puritans did not go as far as their Dutch counterparts in making distinctions among various hearers. That explains why Tennent and Whitefield were impressed by Frelinghuysen's preaching. His method of classifying hearers and his soul-searching applications went beyond what they had been accustomed to hearing. Tanis concluded:

> Tennent's preaching was Frelinghuysen's method perfected. . . . Whitefield's own method of preaching was greatly affected by this instruction, and so the torch which Frelinghuysen bore from East Friesland passed to Tennent, on to Whitefield.

Was Frelinghuysen's classification method of preaching biblical in every respect? Brienen goes too far in rejecting the classification method, but is he not correct in pointing out the danger of its going beyond Scripture? The Bible *generally* draws only one distinction between hearers; it says people respond in either faith or unbelief. While the Scriptures do recognize different stages in the life of faith, as well as varying degrees of unbelief, they do not support a detailed system by which everyone is *habitually* placed in a separate category.

On the other hand, we should not forget that the positive, scriptural purposes of categorizing were to focus on the necessity of the new birth; to foster growth in grace through specific instruction, encouragement, and warning; and to point out the danger of deceiving oneself for eternity. The classification method has its place, providing it is not overdone by forcing itself beyond the text it is expounding. If the preacher is controlled by his text, the classification method yields specificity and a rich harvest of diverse applications. When applications in preaching are not controlled by the text, the classification method tends to produce repetition or, even worse, promotes the preacher's criteria for self-examination rather than the criteria of Scripture.

Calvin and Frelinghuysen on the New Birth and the Covenant of Grace

The classification method of preaching brings to light another difference in emphasis between Frelinghuysen and Calvin: the manner in which they preached about the new birth. Both agreed that regeneration was essential to salvation. But while Frelinghuysen stressed the necessity of looking for evidences of the new birth through Word-centered and Spirit-directed self-examination, Calvin emphasized faith in the promises of the gospel. He said such promises addressed the whole congregation or covenant community.

Calvin viewed the covenant of grace as established by God with believers and their children. He taught that all are under the promise of salvation. Though he distinguished two kinds of covenant children—those who were savingly united to Christ by faith and those who were only outwardly connected to Him—both are in covenant with God, the Isaacs as well as the Ishmaels.

Frelinghuysen's view of the covenant had a somewhat different focus. For him and for most of the *Nadere Reformatie* theologians, the covenant of grace was established only with the elect, and therefore the promises of the covenant were meant only for them. For such theologians the emphasis on marks of grace as evidences of the new birth and election played a larger role than for Calvin. Frelinghuysen said a person could appropriate the promises of the gospel and entertain hope that he was in the state of grace only when he, by the light of the Spirit, was able to conclude from these marks that he belonged to God's elect.

Frelinghuysen's view of the covenant naturally had consequences for his view of the church and the sacraments. Frelinghuysen believed that the church was essentially a congregation of believers to which only those should be admitted who could give an account of their conversion. This was the view of Jean de Labadie for whom Frelinghuysen had some sympathy, though he realized that a perfect church cannot be expected in an imperfect world. But if a pure church could not be attained, at least a pure communion table must be sought. That is why Frelinghuysen set very high standards for admission to the Lord's Supper.

We can appreciate Frelinghuysen's concern for the sanctity of the sacrament. In an environment in which many church members lived immoral lives, he had to apply strict rules. The problem is that he also may have kept from the Lord's Supper some whose lives were exemplary but who, in his estimation, did not possess the marks of grace. Here he went too far because he assumed the right to judge the heart, God's exclusive prerogative, and this increased tension in the congregations he served.

Concluding Observations

The Great Awakening and similar revival movements have been used mightily by God to bring sinners to Christ and into His kingdom. But they have their downside as well, due to the sinful tendencies of human nature. In some instances they have led to rampant individualism and have contributed to divisions in congregations and denominations. It is not difficult to see why this was so. The revivalists' emphasis on new birth and sudden conversion caused some who experienced such radical change to think of themselves as the true church. This led to the desire to organize into exclusive fellowships of visible saints, fostering conventicles (*gezelschappen*). While these conventicles helped believers edify each other and experience the communion of saints, they also tended, if not carefully monitored, to split congregations into various factions or "churches within the church" (*ecclesiolae in ecclesia*). Frelinghuysen realized this danger of exclusivity in his latter years, and, in 1745, opened his conventicles to anyone who desired to attend.

Despite his weaknesses and shortcomings, Frelinghuysen was used powerfully by the Lord in building his church in America. Heinrich Melchior Mühlenberg, a Lutheran pietist who toured the Middle Colonies in 1759, referred to Frelinghuysen as "a converted Dutch preacher who was the first in these parts to insist upon true repentance, living faith, and sanctification, and who had much success." God is sovereign and accomplishes His purposes through a great variety of instruments. Though Frelinghuysen did not have an irenic character, he was a man of profound spiritual conviction and of tremendous courage. He personified the concluding words of the preface to a collection of his sermons, *"Laudem non quæro; culpam non tiemo"* (I seek not praise; I fear not blame). When matters concerned the truth, he would not waver: "I would sooner die a thousand deaths," he declared to his flock, "than not preach the truth." He was an eloquent speaker, a vigorous writer, an able theologian, and a zealous, experiential preacher. "By the fervor of his preaching," Leonard Bacon wrote, "he was to win the signal glory of bringing in the Great Awakening." Jonathan Edwards regarded him to be one of the greatest divines of the American church and, under God, attributed the success of the revival in New Jersey to his instrumentality. Throughout his long tenure in New Jersey, he served as God's man of the hour to herald a number of bountiful harvests which promoted Reformed, spiritual piety. Tanis concluded:

> His influence in the developing structures of American theology was enormous. His role was that of a transmitter between the Old World and the New; his great contribution was his infusing into the Middle Colonies that Dutch evangelical pietism which he carried within himself.

Age often mellows, matures, and sanctifies people. In his later years, Frelinghuysen became more aware of his character flaws. He became less judgmental of others and realized that he at times had made life unnecessarily difficult for himself and others. It troubled him increasingly that he had treated some of his colleagues with disdain, and he apologized for calling some of them unconverted. Reconciliation efforts between Frelinghuysen and DuBois were successful; at a revival meeting in 1741, at which Whitefield preached, both dominies sat together on the platform. In our divisive day, may we experience more spiritual unity with all who love the Lord Jesus Christ in sincerity and who long for revivals like those given by God in the days of Frelinghuysen, Tennent, and Whitefield.

Few could remain neutral to Frelinghuysen; his searching theology of regeneration, his demand that the converted live in a holy and precise manner, and his zeal to keep the church pure produced many friends and many foes. In the end, however, Frelinghuysen's indefatigable work, zeal, and piety won the day; even many of his former enemies came to accept him, for they could not deny the fruits of his ministry. His ministry underscores for us the importance of enduring hardship as good soldiers of Jesus Christ and of keeping our hand on the plow in kingdom work.

Justification *By* Faith Alone:
The Relation of Faith to Justification

The concept of justification by faith alone was a great spiritual and theological breakthrough for Martin Luther. Realizing this truth did not come easily, however. Luther had tried everything to find peace with God from sleeping on hard floors and fasting to climbing a staircase in Rome while kneeling in prayer. Monasteries, disciplines, confessions, masses, absolutions, good works all proved fruitless: peace with God eluded the monk. Yet the thought of the righteousness of God pursued him. Luther hated the word *righteousness*, which he believed indicated a divine mandate to condemn him.

Light finally dawned for Luther as he meditated on Romans 1:17, "For therein is the righteousness of God revealed from faith to faith: as it is written, The just shall live by faith." He saw for the first time that the righteousness Paul had in mind was not a punitive justice that con-

Martin Luther discovering justification by faith.

demns sinners but a perfect righteousness which God freely grants to sinners on the basis of Christ's merits and which sinners receive by faith. Luther saw that the doctrine of justification by grace alone *(sola gratia)* through faith alone *(per solam fidem)* because of Christ alone *(solus Christus)* was the heart of the gospel. It became for him "an open door into paradise...a gate to heaven."

The phrase *justification by faith alone* was the key that unlocked the entire Bible for Luther.[1] He came to understand each of those four words in relation to the others by the light of Scripture and the Spirit. The word *by* may appear at first glance to be elementary, yet around this simple preposition has waged the great debate between Roman Catholics and Protestants. Let's address several issues regarding this critical preposition, highlighting the relationship of faith to justification. We will consider the preposition *by* from four perspectives:

1. *Scripturally.* The basic teaching of justification by faith, together with exegetical and etymological implications of the preposition.
2. *Theologically.* The issue of faith as a possible condition of justification.
3. *Experientially.* How a sinner appropriates Christ by faith.
4. *Polemically.* A defense of the Protestant view of justification by faith against the views of Roman Catholicism, Arminianism, and Antinomianism.

What Does the Bible Teach about Justification *by* Faith?

The Old Testament affirms that justification is "by faith." Of Abraham's faith, Genesis 15:6 states, "And he believed in the LORD; and he counted it to him for righteousness." Roman Catholics have traditionally used this verse to support the doctrine of justification by grace-empowered works, but not one word of work or merit is mentioned here. Rather, in Genesis 15:6, God grants righteousness to Abraham as a free gift. Paul confirms in Romans 4 and Galatians 3:6-14 that the imputed (i.e., reckoned) righteousness of Genesis 15:6 is to be understood in terms of "*by* or *through* faith." The Hebrew verb in Genesis 15:6 is also interpreted as "was counted" in Romans 4:3 (cf. Galatians 3:6, which uses "accounted" in the text and "imputed" in the marginal notes). This verb most often indicates "what a person, *considered by himself*, is not, or does not have, but is reckoned, held or regarded to be, or to have."[2] It is clear, then, that when Abraham was justified by faith, the righteousness that was reckoned or "charged to his account" was not his own but that of another— namely, the righteousness of Christ (Gal. 3:16).

You might ask: If Abraham's "faith is counted *for* righteousness... faith was reckoned to Abraham *for* righteousness...it was imputed to him *for* righteousness," does not the Greek preposition *eis* used in Romans 4:5, 9, 22 imply that the act of believing is imputed to the believer *for* righteousness? In these verses, *eis* does not signify "in the stead of," but means "with a view to," or "in order to." It could be translated "towards" or "unto." Its meaning is clear from Romans 10:10, "with the heart man believeth *unto [eis]* righteousness." Therefore, faith moves toward and lays hold of Christ Himself.[3] J. I. Packer summarizes this well: "When Paul paraphrases this verse [Gen. 15:6] as teaching that Abraham's faith was reckoned for righteousness (Rom. 4:5, 9, 22), all he intends us to understand is that faith—decisive, whole-hearted reliance on God's gracious promise (vv. 18ff.)—was the occasion and means of righteousness being imputed to him. There is no suggestion here that faith is the ground of justification."[4]

In explaining Romans 4, Theodore Beza comments: "Abraham was not justified, and made the father of the faithful, by any of his own works, either preceding or following his faith in Christ, as promised to him; but merely by faith in Christ, or the merit of Christ by faith imputed to him for righteousness. Therefore all his children become his children and are justified, not by their works, either preceding or following their faith; but by faith alone in the same Christ."[5]

Habakkuk 2:4 also supports justification by faith in saying, "The just shall live by his faith," or, as some scholars would say, "The just by faith shall live." Paul makes clear that this verse, quoted in Romans 1:17, Galatians 3:11, and Hebrews 10:38, is ultimately fulfilled in the righteousness that comes by faith in the gospel of Christ, for which the law itself teaches us to look (Rom. 3:21-22; 10:4). Paul's explanation of Habakkuk has inspired Martin Luther and other believers to place their faith in a righteousness not their own but in Jesus Christ, who is called "THE LORD OUR RIGHTEOUSNESS" (Jer. 23:6).

The New Testament also clearly teaches justification by faith: "Even the righteousness of God which is by faith of Jesus Christ unto all and upon all them that believe.... It is one God, which shall justify the circumcision by faith, and uncircumcision through faith" (Rom. 3:22, 30). Romans 11:20 says, "Thou standest by faith." And Galatians 3:24 says, "Wherefore the law was our schoolmaster to bring us unto Christ, that we might be justified by faith."

If Scripture clearly affirms justification by faith, what then is the relationship of faith to justification? How does faith cause the believer's justification? The answer lies in the preposition *by.* Few things are more necessary for a correct understanding of the New Testament than a precise acquaintance with the common prepositions," wrote J. Gresham Machen.[6] The New Testament writers commonly employ three prepositions: *pistei, ek pisteos,* and *dia pisteos.* The Christian is justified "by faith" (*pistei* or *ek pisteos*) or "through faith" (*dia pisteos*). *Pistei* (the dative case of the noun *pistis*) is used in Romans 3:28: "Therefore we conclude that a man is justified *by faith* without the deeds of the law." *Ek pisteos* is used in Romans 5:1: "Therefore being justified *by faith*, we have peace with God through our Lord Jesus Christ." *Dia pisteos* is used in Ephesians 2:8: "For by grace are ye saved *through faith*; and that not of yourselves: it is the gift of God" (emphasis added).

Each of these prepositions has its own emphasis. The simple dative (*pistei*) calls attention to the necessity and importance of faith. The preposition *dia* ("through" or "by means of") describes faith as the *instrument* of justification, or means by which the righteousness of Christ is received and appropriated by the sinner for justification. The preposition *ek* ("from," "out of," or "by") describes faith as the *occasion* of justification, though never as the efficient or ultimate cause of justification.[7]

Note that in none of these cases, nor anywhere else in Scripture, does faith (or any other grace) earn justification. This is all the more remarkable when one considers that *dia* with the accusative would mean "on the ground of" or "on account of." Thus, *dia ten pistin* would convey the notion of "on the ground of or on account of faith," thereby making faith the basis for a believer's acceptance with God. Yet such is the precision of the Spirit's overseeing of the New Testament Scriptures that nowhere does a writer slip into using this prepositional phrase. On every occasion, faith is presented as the *means* of justification. Justification by faith alone is never justification on account of faith *(propter fidem)*, but always justification on account of Christ *(propter Christum).* It is on account of the blood-satisfaction of the Lamb of God that is graciously imputed to and received by an undeserving sinner (Gal. 3:6; James 2:23). Ultimately, the only ground of justification is Christ and His righteousness.[8]

In the Reformed tradition, various theological terms or expressions have been used to capture this biblical relationship of faith to justification. For example, the *Belgic Confession of Faith* (1561, Article 22) and the *Westminster Confession of Faith* (1647, Chapter 11.2) present faith as "only an *instrument*" and "the alone *instrument* of justification."[9] Faith is not an agent (an efficient cause) but an instrument (a means) of justification. It is the believer's sole means by which he receives justification. The means is not mechanical, as "instrument" implies; rather, the means is the saving work of the Holy Spirit through the Word whereby a sinner is brought into a living, personal relationship with the Triune God.

The *Heidelberg Catechism* (1563, Question 61) states that Christ's righteousness becomes ours by "no other way" *(nicht anders)* than faith. God did not ordain faith to be the instrument of justification because of some peculiar virtue in faith but because faith is self-emptying and has no merit in itself: "Therefore it is of faith, that it might be by grace," says Romans 4:16.

John Calvin compares faith to an empty container. "We compare faith to a kind of vessel; for unless we come empty and with the mouth of our souls open to seek Christ's grace, we are not capable of receiving Christ."[10] The vessel cannot be compared in value to the treasure it contains (2 Cor. 4:7).

The Puritan Thomas Goodwin uses strong language to describe faith. He says it is "eyes, and hands, and feet, yea, and mouth, and stomach, and all."[11] And nineteenth-century Bishop J. C. Ryle writes: "Saving faith is the hand...the eye...the mouth...and the foot of the soul."[12] Yet faith lives by the Living Bread alone, not by the mouth that feeds on the bread (John 6:35-58). The sinner is justified by Christ's sacrifice alone, not by the act of feasting upon or believing in that sacrifice by faith.

Is Faith a Condition of Justification?

Given the meaning of "by faith" in the original Greek, it is more accurate to speak of faith as an *instrument* rather than as a *condition* of justification and salvation, for a condition generally denotes a merit for the sake of which a benefit is conferred. We are justified by faith in Christ—not because of what faith *is*, but because of what faith lays hold of and receives. We are not saved *for* believing but *by* believing. In the application of justification, faith is not a builder but a beholder; it has nothing to give or achieve, but has all to receive. Faith is neither the ground nor substance of our justification, but the hand, the instrument, the vessel that receives the divine gift offered to us in the gospel. As Herman Kuiper wrote, "As little as a beggar, who puts forth his hand to receive a piece of bread, can say that he has earned the gift granted him, so little can believers claim that they have merited justification, just because they have embraced the righteousness of Christ, graciously offered them in the Gospel."[13]

The distinction between these two views is critical. It is fatal to regard faith as a prerequisite that a sinner can fulfill by an act of his own will in order to be saved. In such a case, man becomes his own savior. Worse yet, everything then depends on the purity and strength or perfection of the sinner's faith. Instead, Scripture teaches that the very character of faith is at stake. Is faith a work of man or the gift of God? The Apostle Paul's answer to that is decisive: "For unto you it *is given* in the behalf of Christ, *not only to believe on Him,* but also to suffer for His sake" (Phil. 1:29; see also Eph. 2:8; emphasis added). Justification is received in faith because it pleases God to justify a sinner by *giving* him faith.[14]

Though faith is the means through which God works salvation, faith is not a human condition—that is, if condition implicates more than the necessary order of salvation. If faith were the conditional ground of justification, salvation would in part be due to human merit. That would dishonor divine grace and subvert the gospel by reducing it to one more version of justification by works (Gal. 4:21-5:12). Moreover, since we cannot be accepted by God with less than perfect righteousness, our faith would have to be perfect. No one's faith is perfect; it is impaired by sin. Nothing in us, including our faith, could possibly succeed as a condition for salvation. Faith knows no human merit and needs no human merit (Eph. 2:8), for the very nature of faith is to rely wholly on the merit and righteousness of Christ, and that is "more than sufficient to acquit us of our sins" (*Belgic Confession*, Article 22). We are not justified by our imperfect faith but by the perfect righteousness of Christ. All the conditions of salvation must be fulfilled by Jesus through His obedience in the state of His humiliation (Rom. 5:19). No conditions for salvation can be laid upon man because salvation is entirely of God. "So then it [salvation] is not of him that willeth, nor of him that runneth, but of God that showeth mercy" (Rom. 9:16).

As A. A. Hodge succinctly writes: "Justifying faith terminates on or in Christ, in his blood and sacrifice, and in the promises of God; in its very essence, therefore, it involves trust, and, denying its own justifying value, affirms the sole merit of that on which it trusts (Rom. 3:25-26; 4:20, 22; Gal. 3:26; Eph. 1:12-13; 1 John 5:10)."[15]

Some theologians have called faith a condition in a non-meritorious sense. Robert Shaw's response to that is: "Some worthy divines have called faith a condition, who were far from being of the opinion that it is a condition properly so called, on the performance of which men should, according to the gracious covenant of God, have a right to justification as their reward. They merely intended that without faith we cannot be justified—that faith must precede justification in the order of time or of nature. But as the term 'condition' is very ambiguous, and calculated to mislead the ignorant, it should be avoided."[16]

Robert Traill is even stronger. He writes, "Faith in Jesus Christ...in the office of justification, is neither condition nor qualification...but in its very act a renouncing of all such pretences."[17] The faith by which we receive Christ is an act of utter renunciation of all our own works and righteousness as a condition or ground of salvation. As Horatius Bonar remarks: "Faith is not work, nor merit, nor effort; but the cessation from all these, and the acceptance in place of them of what another has done—done completely, and forever."[18] John Girardeau also notes, "Faith is emptiness filled with Christ's fullness; impotency lying down upon Christ's strength."[19]

But if faith is essential in uniting a sinner to Christ but not in any way a conditional merit for salvation, is it proper to regard faith as the "hand" that receives Christ? Doesn't the natural man have some hand in this process? Since faith is both God's gift (Eph. 2:8) and God's work ("This is the work of God, that ye believe on him whom he hath sent" [John 6:29]), how can faith be described as a hand?

Man indeed does not have the ability to reach out for salvation in Christ. He is so dead in trespasses and sins (Eph. 2:1) that he will never accept Christ of his own free will (Matt. 23:37; John 5:40). Scripture teaches that the sinner does not move first toward God, but God first moves toward the sinner to unite him with Christ by faith, for a sinner would never of his own will turn to Christ in faith (Rom. 9:16). Even when tormented with the terror of divine judgment, natural man cannot be persuaded to flee to God by saving faith for salvation (Prov. 1:24-27).

In regeneration, however, the Holy Spirit grants the gift of a living, empty hand that can turn nowhere else than to Jesus. "But as many as received him, to them gave he power to become the sons of God, even to them that believe on his name: which were born, not of blood, nor of the will of the flesh, nor of the will of man, but of God" (John 1:12-13; cf. Psalm 110:3).

Faith is not called a hand because it merits justification in any way, but because it receives, embraces, and appropriates Christ upon divine imputation. Faith is not a creative hand but a receptive hand. As Abraham Booth notes, "In justification we read of the precious faith in the righteousness of our God and Saviour Jesus Christ (2 Pet. 1) and of 'faith in His blood' (Rom. 3:25), and believers are described as 'receiving the atonement' and receiving 'the gift of righteousness' (Rom. 5:11, 17)."[20]

Faith is passive in justification but becomes active in accepting Christ after He is offered to the sinner.[21] Indeed, when Christ is given, faith cannot refrain from being active, moving the believer to rejoice in the imputed righteousness of Christ with profound joy. Nevertheless, this joy can boast no human merit for it is not the hand that produces joy but the gift received by the hand of faith, Jesus Christ.

The hand of faith graciously and unconditionally rests upon Christ and His righteousness alone. Faith lives out of Christ, in whom all of our salvation is to be found (John 15:1-7). B. B. Warfield explains: "It is from its *object* [Jesus Christ] that faith derives its value.... The *saving power* of faith resides thus not in itself, but in the Almighty Savior on whom it rests.... It is not faith that saves, but faith in Jesus Christ.... It is not strictly speaking, even faith in Christ that saves, but Christ that saves through faith."[22]

How Does Faith Appropriate Christ and His Righteousness?

The concept of receiving Christ by faith, usurped today by Arminianism, needs to be recovered. Many sincere Reformed Christians are afraid to speak of "receiving Christ" simply because of the false way modern evangelists define it as an act of the "free will" of the sinner to fulfill a condition for salvation. Believing that it seems wrong and "Arminian" to receive Christ, their liberty to respond to the gospel is inhibited.

Denying faith as the foundation of justification does not minimize faith or the need for personally receiving Christ by faith. Though Scripture never ascribes merit to faith itself, it clearly establishes the necessity of faith (Heb.11:6). The imputed righteousness of Christ must be personally received by faith if a sinner is to be grafted into Christ (John 3:36; Rom. 5:11, 17). The Holy Spirit uses faith to work out sovereign grace. G. C. Berkouwer states: "The way of salvation is the way of faith just because it is only in faith that the exclusiveness of divine grace is recognized and honored.... Faith is no competitor of *sola gratia* [by grace alone]; but sovereign grace is confirmed by faith.... *Sola gratia* and *sola fide* [by faith alone], thus, remain the be all and end all of the relation between faith and justification."[23]

Faith is a holy command, a personal necessity, and a pressing urgency (2 Kings 17:14, 18, 21). There is only faith or damnation (Mark 16:16; John 3:18). Faith is indispensable. As John Flavel writes, "The soul is the life of the body; faith is the life of the soul; Christ is the life of faith."

By the Spirit and Word of God, justifying faith is saving grace that, first, convicts us of sin and misery; second, assents to the gospel from the heart; third, receives and rests upon Christ and His righteousness for pardon and salvation; and fourth, lives out of Christ, who is the hallmark of appropriating faith (Heb. 10:39; Rom. 10:14, 17; John 16:8-9; Rom. 10:8-10; Acts 10:43; Phil. 3:9; Gal. 3:11; cf. *Westminster Larger Catechism*, Questions 72-73). Let us examine these marks of faith so that we may more clearly understand the experiential dimensions of "by" in *justification by faith alone.*

1. *Faith is an experiential, convicting, soul-emptying grace.* To lay hold of Christ and to treasure His righteousness necessitates losing my own righteousness. Faith teaches utter humility, the total emptiness of all within the sinner when viewed outside of Christ.[24] Faith means the utter despair of everything except Christ. To that end, faith makes a sinner conscious of the desperate situation he is in and the tragic judgment he deserves. Sin must become sin if grace is to become grace. Far from being a work of merit, faith makes me realize my demerit, negates all hope of merit, and makes me cling to the hope of divine mercy. The spiritual character of the law which demands perfect love to God and my neighbor must condemn me if I am to appreciate the beauty of my Savior who, for the ungodly, perfectly obeyed the law and bore the penalty of sin (Rom. 5:6-10). My unrighteousness must be uncovered if Christ's righteousness is to be discovered (Ps. 71:16).

2. *Faith wholeheartedly assents to the truth of the gospel* (*Westminster Larger Catechism*, Question 73). Faith is not merely intellectual assent. Rather, faith believes from the heart what the Scriptures teach about self, the holiness of God, and the saving nature of Christ. Before God's holiness, faith repudiates self-righteousness and brings the sinner to need Christ as revealed in the Scriptures and given by the Spirit. Faith abandons all self-merit as it is increasingly allured to Christ and His merits (Rom. 7:24-25). Faith surrenders to the evangel and falls into the outstretched arms of God. As Berkouwer says, "The act of faith is as much being held by God as holding Him; the power of faith is exercised as much in capitulation as in conquering—the faith that overcomes the world is capitulation to Christ's great victory."[25] Faith looks away from self to Christ, moving entirely from and in grace.[26] Faith flees with all the soul's poverty to Christ's riches. It moves with all the soul's guilt to Christ as reconciler, with all the soul's bondage to Christ as liberator. Faith confesses with Augustus Toplady:

Nothing in my hand I bring,
Simply to thy cross I cling;
Naked, come to thee for dress;
Helpless, look to thee for grace;
Foul, I to the fountain fly;
Wash me, Saviour, or I die.

3. *Justifying faith lays hold of Christ and His righteousness and experiences pardon and peace that passes understanding* (Phil. 4:7). Faith is nothing more than the means that unites a sinner with his Savior. As Calvin says, "Faith justifies in no other way than as it introduces us into a participation of the righteousness of Christ." It apprehends (*fides apprehensiva*), closes with, and grasps Christ in a believing embrace, surrendering all of self, clinging to His Word, and relying on His promises. Christ is not only the object of faith but is Himself present in faith. Faith rests in the person of Christ—coming, hearing, seeing, trusting, taking, embracing, knowing, rejoicing, loving, and triumphing. It leaves its case in the hands of Christ as the great Physician, taking His prescriptions, following His directions, and trusting in His finished work and ongoing intercessions. As Luther writes, "Faith clasps Christ as a ring clasps its jewel." Faith wraps the soul in Christ's righteousness. It appropriates with a believing heart the perfect righteousness, satisfaction, and holiness of Christ. It tastes the efficacy of Christ's blood-righteousness as the righteousness of God Himself (Rom. 3:21-25, 5:9, 6:7; 2 Cor. 5:18-21). It weds the soul to Christ, experiences divine pardon and acceptance in the Beloved, and makes the soul partake of every covenant mercy. Faith and Christ become inseparable in justification. As Daniel Cawdray explains: "As the act of healing through the eyes of the Israelites and the brazen serpent went together; so, in the act of justifying, these two, faith and Christ, have a mutual relation, and must always concur—faith as the action which apprehendeth, Christ as the object which is apprehended; so that neither the passion of Christ saveth without faith, nor doth faith help unless it be in Christ, its object."[27]

William Gurnall puts it this way: "With one hand faith pulls off its own righteousness and throws it away; with the other it puts on Christ's." The Heidelberg Catechism best explains the personal appropriation of Christ's righteousness:

Question 60: How art thou righteous before God?
Answer: Only by a true faith in Jesus Christ (Rom. 3:22ff.; Gal. 2:16); so that, though my conscience accuse me, that I have grossly transgressed

all the commandments of God, and kept none of them (Rom. 3:9ff.), and am still inclined to all evil (Rom. 7:23); notwithstanding, God, without any merit of mine (Rom. 3:24), but only of mere grace (Tit. 3:5; Eph. 2:8-9), grants (Rom. 4:4-5; 2 Cor. 5:19) and imputes to me (1 John 2:1) the perfect satisfaction, righteousness, and holiness of Christ (Rom. 3:24-25); even so, as if I never had had, nor committed any sin; yea, as if I had fully accomplished all that obedience which Christ has accomplished for me (2 Cor. 5:21), inasmuch as I embrace such benefit with a believing heart (Rom. 3:28; Jn. 3:18).

Question 61 Why sayest thou that thou art righteous by faith only?
Answer: Not that I am acceptable to God on account of the worthiness of my faith (Ps. 16:2; Eph. 2:8-9), but because only the satisfaction, righteousness, and holiness of Christ, is my righteousness before God (1 Cor. 1:30; 2:2); and that I cannot receive and apply the same to myself any other way than by faith only (1 John 5:10).

4. *Faith lives out of Christ.* Being united to Christ by faith, the believer possesses all of Christ's benefits and experiences them abundantly as the Spirit applies them. Since grace and faith are given in Christ, the essential righteousness of the believer remains extrinsic to him even as Christ is present within him, effecting daily conversion. "Christ without" is the ground of justification; "Christ within" is the fruit of justification and the evidence of vital union with Christ.[28] For faith, Christ—both in glory as ascended Lord and in the believer's soul—is chief among ten thousand, white and ruddy, altogether lovely (Song of Sol. 5:10, 16). Faith can say, like the queen of Sheba, when gazing and feasting upon His blessed person and benefits, "Behold, the one half of the greatness of thy wisdom was not told me: for thou exceedest the fame that I heard" (2 Chron. 9:6). Faith then exclaims, "Christ is all, and in all" (Col. 3:11)!

This Christ-centeredness is the hallmark of faith. It is the very nature and fountain of faith. Faith does not look at itself. Many today are too preoccupied with looking at their faith rather than faith's object. The Reformers spoke much about faith, but their concern was object-centered rather than subject-centered. It was Christocentric rather than anthropocentric, theological rather than psychological. It is not faith in our faith, nor faith in the faith, nor faith in our justification, but faith in Christ. The Puritans understood this well. As George Swinnock writes, "First, Faith must look out for Christ; secondly, Faith must look up to Christ for grace; thirdly, Faith must take Christ down, or receive him and grace."[29]

"Faith has two hands," Thomas Manton writes. "With one it stretches out for Christ; with the other, it pushes away all that comes all the commandments of God, and kept none of them (Rom. 3:9ff.), and am still inclined to all evil (Rom. 7:23); notwithstanding, God, without any merit of mine (Rom. 3:24), but only of mere grace (Tit. 3:5; Eph. 2:8-9), grants (Rom. 4:4-5; 2 Cor. 5:19) and imputes to me (1 John 2:1) the perfect satisfaction, righteousness, and holiness of Christ (Rom. 3:24-25); even so, as if I never had had, nor committed any sin; yea, as if I had fully accomplished all that obedience which Christ has accomplished for me (2 Cor. 5:21), inasmuch as I embrace such benefit with a believing heart (Rom. 3:28; Jn. 3:18).

Question 61 Why sayest thou that thou art righteous by faith only?
Answer: Not that I am acceptable to God on account of the worthiness of my faith (Ps. 16:2; Eph. 2:8-9), but because only the satisfaction, righteousness, and holiness of Christ, is my righteousness before God (1 Cor. 1:30; 2:2); and that I cannot receive and apply the same to myself any other way than by faith only (1 John 5:10).

4. *Faith lives out of Christ.* Being united to Christ by faith, the believer possesses all of Christ's benefits and experiences them abundantly as the Spirit applies them. Since grace and faith are given in Christ, the essential righteousness of the believer remains extrinsic to him even as Christ is present within him, effecting daily conversion. "Christ without" is the ground of justification; "Christ within" is the fruit of justification and the evidence of vital union with Christ.[28] For faith, Christ—both in glory as ascended Lord and in the believer's soul—is chief among ten thousand, white and ruddy, altogether lovely (Song of Sol. 5:10, 16). Faith can say, like the queen of Sheba, when gazing and feasting upon His blessed person and benefits, "Behold, the one half of the greatness of thy wisdom was not told me: for thou exceedest the fame that I heard" (2 Chron. 9:6). Faith then exclaims, "Christ is all, and in all" (Col. 3:11)!

This Christ-centeredness is the hallmark of faith. It is the very nature and fountain of faith. Faith does not look at itself. Many today are too preoccupied with looking at their faith rather than faith's object. The Reformers spoke much about faith, but their concern was object-centered rather than subject-centered. It was Christocentric rather than anthropocentric, theological rather than psychological. It is not faith in our faith, nor faith in the faith, nor faith in our justification, but faith in Christ. The Puritans understood this well. As George Swinnock writes, "First, Faith must look out for Christ; secondly, Faith must look up to Christ for grace; thirdly, Faith must take Christ down, or receive him and grace."[29]

"Faith has two hands," Thomas Manton writes. "With one it stretches out for Christ; with the other, it pushes away all that comes

Thomas Manton

between Christ and the soul." Faith not only ventures to Christ with the demanding law at its heels and upon Christ with all the soul's guilt, but it also ventures for Christ despite all difficulties and discouragements.

"Without faith it is impossible to please God" (Heb. 11:6). God is pleased with faith because faith is pleased with Christ. Faith continually takes refuge, as the Belgic Confession states, "in the blood, death, passion, and obedience of our Lord Jesus Christ" (Article 29).

Christ is faith's only object and expectation. Faith enables the soul to enjoy the whole salvation of Christ, for by faith Christ becomes the soul's wisdom, righteousness, sanctification, and redemption (1 Cor. 1:30). Faith commits the total person to the total person of Christ. This Christ-centeredness, more than anything else, makes faith inseparable from justification and superior to all other graces in justification.[30] Small wonder, then, that faith has been called the captain of all spiritual graces. As Thomas Watson writes, "Love is the crowning grace in heaven, but faith is the conquering grace upon earth.... Faith is the master-wheel; it sets all the other graces running.... Other graces make us like Christ, faith makes us members of Christ."[31] "Call forth first that commander-in-chief," George Swinnock adds, "and then the private soldiers, the other graces, will all follow."[32]

388 Puritan Reformed Spirituality

How Does the Protestant View of Justification by Faith Contradict Roman Catholic Teaching?

When leaders of the Roman Catholic Church met to combat Protestantism at the Council of Trent (1545-1563), one of their major purposes was to deal with the doctrine of justification by faith. They wanted to condemn the new Protestantism and the distinctive teachings of Luther,[33] particularly the doctrine of justification. The Tridentine Decree (Sixth Session, finalized January 13, 1547) contains a detailed exposition of Romanist teaching in sixteen "chapters" (each containing one or two lengthy paragraphs), followed by thirty-three specific opinions, called "canons" (one short paragraph each).[34] The final part of the Sixth Decree explains the Romanist notion of three states of justification: the first state (chapters 1-9) describes the sinner's transition from a state of sin to a state of righteousness; the second state (chapters 10-13) how the justified sinner might increase in righteousness; and the third (chapters 14-16), the recovery of justification through the sacrament of penance by those who have fallen from grace. The thirty-three appended canons condemning specific heretical opinions deal largely with Protestantism. Unfortunately, Protestant teachings are so severely caricatured in these canons that most of them are unrecognizable as Protestant doctrines. Or they are mingled with real heresies, which Protestants themselves would condemn as severely as Rome. Trent did make clear, however, that Romanists and Protestants differ substantially on the doctrine of justification in the following ways.

First, traditional Roman Catholic teaching regards justification as the process in which a sinner is made righteous. Rome claims that the verb "to justify" means to make righteous. Justification follows sanctification; it is dependent upon an inner change in a sinner's nature that makes him a righteous person. Theologically, that results in the commingling of justification and sanctification. Justification results from being *made* righteous; justification is righteousness *infused (iustitia infusa,* chapter 7). Therefore, righteousness is actualized rather than imputed. The believer is justified on the basis of internal righteousness *(iustitia in nobis),* so justification is granted to the righteous rather than to the sinner. According to Trent, faith is the beginning of human salvation, the foundation and root of all justification (chapter 8). Faith justifies as it is animated by love; hence faith is never alone, but "worketh by love" (Gal. 5:6). Therefore its own virtues merit some degree of divine acceptance (chapter 7). Canon 11 states: "If anyone says that men are justified either by the sole imputation of the justice of Christ or by the sole remission of sins, to the exclusion of the grace and the charity which is poured forth in their hearts by the Holy Ghost, and remains in them, or also that the grace by which they were justified is only the good will of God, let him be anathema."

Recently, Jesuit scholar John Bligh joined other Roman Catholic scholars in affirming that "to justify" often occurs in judicial contexts and can mean to acquit as a declarative act on God's part. Bligh continues to mix justification and sanctification, however, by stating that "justification is more than forgiveness; it is forgiveness plus transformation."[35] This mix is also evident in the statement on justification by faith issued by the Anglican-Roman Catholic International Commission: "Justification and sanctification are two aspects of the same divine act."[36]

Contrary to Trent, Scripture and Protestant theology teach that in justification, righteousness is imputed *(iustitia imputata)* or reckoned to the sinner's account solely by the good will of God. Justification is a declaration that a sinner is reckoned righteous by God. It justifies the ungodly "apart from ourselves" *(iustitia extra nos),* i.e., by the external or alien righteousness of Christ (Isa. 45:24-25; Acts 13:39; 1 Cor. 6:11; Eph. 1:7). The sinner's sin is not reckoned; Christ's righteousness is (Rom. 4:5-8) and is received by faith alone. Justification and sanctification are not mixed together, and justification by inward transformation is not the way to salvation. As Luther states in his Galatians commentary, "We are justified, not by faith furnished with charity, but by faith only and alone."

Faith does not justify because it produces the fruit of love for Christ but because it receives the fruit of Christ's love. As James teaches (2:14ff.), such faith will indeed bear fruits of love, good works, and every Christian grace. A good tree will bear good fruit, which testifies to, rather than causes, its good nature.

"Works are not taken into consideration when the question respects justification," Luther continues. "But true faith will no more fail to produce them, than the sun can cease to give light." Justification without sanctification is impossible, for sanctification confirms that justification has taken place. Conversely, if works do not follow faith, that faith is not a living faith in Christ.[37]

For the historic Protestant faith, justification and sanctification, which are key ingredients in the believer's salvation, are distinct though inseparable. Both proceed from free grace because both are rooted in the sovereign good pleasure of the Triune God. Both are made possible only through the head of the eternal covenant, Jesus Christ. Both are necessary for salvation and are evident from the moment of regeneration.

Still, there are distinctions: Justification is extrinsic to the saved sinner, while sanctification is intrinsic. Justification declares the sinner righteous and holy in Christ while sanctification makes the sinner righteous and the bearer of holy fruit from Christ. Justification, which has to do with legal status, removes the guilt of sin, while sanctification, which deals with spiritual condition, subdues the love and power of sin. Justification restores the sinner to God's favor, while sanctification restores God's image in the sinner. Justification is a complete, perfect once-and-for-all act; sanctification is a progressive process that is not perfected until death. Justification grants the redeemed the title for heaven and the boldness to enter it; sanctification gives them the preparation necessary to enjoy it. Justification gives the right of salvation; sanctification grants the beginning of salvation. By grace the justified are what they are in justification; by grace they do what they will in sanctification. Justification is the criminal pardoned; sanctification, the patient healed. The union of both constitutes salvation. As John Angel James writes: "Conceive of a man in prison under sentence of death, and at the same time dangerously ill [with] jail fever. If the monarch pardons him, this is not enough for his safety and happiness, for he will die soon of his disease, unless it be cured. On the other hand, if the physician cures his disease, it is of little consequence unless the monarch gives him a reprieve; for though he get well of his disorder, he must soon suffer the penalty of the law; but if he be both pardoned and cured, he will be *completely* saved."[38]

The Roman Catholic is taught to come to faith by good works, the Protestant to come to good works by faith. Trent reasons that if salvation is given freely, regardless of works, justification by faith will reap complacency. Virtue and good works will serve no purpose.

In response, Protestant Reformers argue that the believer, having been justified by free grace, is reborn with a will inclined to good and the glory of God. Faith must bear fruit. As Luther writes, "Let us conclude that faith alone justifies and that faith alone fulfils the law.... Faith is a living, restless thing. It cannot be inoperative."[39] The Reformers and their successors insist that though we are justified by faith, our faith must be validated by our works (James 2:17). Hence they speak often of "the obedience of faith" (Rom. 16:26), stressing that faith leads to obedience. "By faith Abraham...obeyed" (Heb. 11:8). As Thomas Watson says: "Faith believes as if it did not work, and it works as if it did not believe."[40]

The *Westminster Confession of Faith* (11.1-2) succinctly summarizes the Protestant position in the following:

Those whom God effectually calleth, He also freely justifieth (Rom. 8:30; 3:24): not by infusing righteousness into them, but by pardoning their sins, and by accounting and accepting their persons as righteous, not for any thing wrought in them, or done by them, but for Christ's sake alone; nor by imputing faith itself, the act of believing, or any other evangelical obedience to them, as their righteousness, but by imputing the obedience and satisfaction of Christ unto them (Rom. 3:22-28; 4:5-8; 5:17-19; 2 Cor. 5:19, 21), they receiving and resting on Him and His righteousness by faith, which faith they have not of themselves, it is the gift of God (Acts 10:44; Gal. 2:16; Phil. 3:9; Eph. 2:7-8).

Faith, thus receiving and resting on Christ and His righteousness, is the alone instrument of justification (John 1:12; Rom. 3:28; 5:1); yet is it not alone in the person justified, but is ever accompanied with all other saving graces, and is no dead faith, but worketh by love (James 2:17, 22, 26; Gal. 5:6).

Justification is a sister to imputation. As a judicial term, justification is the act of God's sovereign grace whereby He imputes to the guilty and condemned sinner the perfect righteousness of Christ. The sinner is acquitted on the ground of Christ's merits of all guilt and punishment, is granted the right to eternal life, and is enabled to appropriate to himself Christ and His benefits. Imputation credits something to someone's account; God transfers the perfect righteousness of Christ to the elect sinner as a gracious gift and transfers all of the sinner's unrighteousness to Christ, who has paid the full price of satisfaction for that unrighteousness.[41] By means of that mutual transfer, God views the sinner as if he "never had had, nor committed any sin," but had himself "fully accomplished all that obedience which Christ has accomplished" (*Heidelberg Catechism*, Q. 60; cf. Rom. 4:4-6; 5:12-19; 2 Cor. 5:21).[42]

Second, Roman Catholicism teaches that Christ's righteousness must be buttressed by the sinner's own righteousness in justification. Chapter 16 of Trent on justification asserts that the believer, by cooperating with grace, is entitled to merit in justification. If he perseveres until the end, he will be rewarded with God's gift to persevering believers. But that was just the error of the Jews in Romans 10:3-4, who thought to find something in themselves that could help establish righteousness before God. As Romans 10:3-4 says: "For they being ignorant of God's righteousness, and going about to establish their own righteousness, have not submitted themselves unto the righteousness of God. For Christ is the end of the law for righteousness to every one that believeth."

Protestant theology teaches that Christ's merited righteousness will not tolerate human addition. All our works are a stench in God's nostrils in meriting any righteousness in His holy sight (Isa. 64:6). Neither our sweetest experiences of God's love and grace, nor our faith itself granted by the Holy Spirit, can add one stitch of merit to the white robe of Christ's righteousness. Nothing will satisfy the justice of God except the righteousness of Christ Jesus. We are only "justified freely by his grace through the redemption that is in Christ Jesus" (Rom. 3:24; cf. Job 25:4-6).

Roman Catholicism mixes grace and works in justification. Both are required in preparation for justification. The Council of Trent stresses the role of grace in the believer's merits and says that those merits are to be considered the believer's own and true merits due to free will and inherent grace. Scripture and Protestantism assert that justification is by sovereign grace only through faith, without any merit on the believer's part (Jon. 2:9). The ultimate foundation of our justification is God's sovereign election. As 2 Timothy 2:19 says, "Nevertheless the foundation of God standeth sure, having this seal, The Lord knoweth them that are his." In justification, God's eternal decree is worked out through His eternal covenant of grace, which, in turn, is grounded in Christ's meritorious satisfaction. That is the satisfaction the elect sinner receives through grace by faith (Rom. 9-10).

Third, Roman Catholicism advocates degrees in justification and implicit faith in the church's teaching. Scripture and Protestantism do not. We are either justified or not justified, either totally under grace or totally under wrath. In Luke 18, the publican returns home justified, while the Pharisee remains unjustified. As verse 14 says, "I tell you, this man went down to his house justified rather than the other." The faith that justifies the publican is not implicit faith in the teaching of the church but personal trust in and reliance on the sheer mercy of God (Luke 18:13). Such justification is grounded in the absolute favor of God to a sinner rather than to a quality at work within his soul, as Trent advocates (Chapter 16).

Finally, Roman Catholicism connects receiving God's grace with receiving the sacraments. In scholastic terminology, the Council of Trent teaches that baptism (rather than faith) is the instrumental cause of justification, and personal righteousness (rather than imputed righteousness) the formal cause.[43] Thus, it is impossible, according to Trent, to be justified outside of the visible church, or without being baptized. That not only is contrary to biblical example (Luke 23:39-43), but it also deprives the believer of his direct relation to Christ by faith because the sacraments are allowed to come between himself and Christ. With its ceremonial rituals, automatic communications of grace, and reliance on the church, the sacramental system can easily become a surrogate savior. All forms of sacramentalism obscure the honor of Christ in becoming a condition of salvation.

Protestantism, on the other hand, maintains that faith is the instrumental cause of justification while the alien righteousness of Christ, external to the believer and imputed to him, is the formal cause and the ground upon which God justifies sinners. "For he hath made him to be sin for us, who knew no sin; that we might be made the righteousness of God in him" (2 Cor. 5:21; cf. Rom. 3:26). It is critical to maintain that this formal cause of justification is in Christ's righteousness alone, for all the Scriptures on the depraved nature of man make clear that there is no righteousness inherent in natural man upon which a divine verdict of justification could be based. Psalm 14:3 says, "They are all gone aside, they are all together become filthy: there is none that doeth good, no, not one." For the Reformers, faith is the conscious, personal, immediate reliance of a sinner on Christ alone. Such faith brings the sinner into Christ's church and makes him a member of the body even if he has never heard of the visible church. Sacraments are not essential for salvation but for the consummation of discipleship.[44] The sacraments are signs and seals of grace that is received by faith; they are no part of justifying faith.

If the church is the dispenser of the sacraments, and the sacraments are necessary for salvation, the church becomes the dispenser of salvation. Thus we arrive at Roman Catholicism's ultimate error: the church replaces Christ in salvation. That is one of the many unavoidable consequences of her defective views of justification. Notwithstanding Vatican II, Rome has yet to repudiate the Council of Trent's errors on the doctrine of justification by faith. Until that takes place, as Martin Smyth concludes, there can be "no honest compromise between the Roman and Reformed doctrine of justification."[45] Cooperation can only be based on evasion rather than on explanation, as has been witnessed yet again in the March 29, 1994 document, *Evangelicals and Catholics Together: The Christian Mission in the Third Millenium*, signed by forty evangelical Protestants and Roman Catholics.

How are Arminianism and Antinomianism Refuted by Justification by Faith Alone?

Arminianism errs in saying that part of the foundation of justification is faith.[46] By advocating conditional predestination and conditional faith in justification (God elects and saves those who believe), Arminianism is a cruel hoax. John Owen ridicules the Arminian condition of salvation by faith as an impossibility, saying it is "as if a man should promise a blind man a thousand pounds upon condition that he will see." Owen views the Christ of the Arminian as "but a half-mediator" because He procures the end of salvation but not the means to it.[47]

Charles Spurgeon is more graphic. He likens Arminianism and Calvinism to two bridges. The Arminian bridge is wide and easy but does not bring its traveler safely to the opposite shore of the river. It stops short of eternal communion with God because something is left for the depraved will of the natural man to accomplish—exercising faith in Christ. The Calvinist bridge is narrow but spans the entire river, for Christ Jesus is the alpha and omega of salvation and justification. Arminianism *looks* promising, but it cannot live up to its promises because it depends upon depraved humanity to act. In doing so, it deceives myriads of souls who think they accept Christ by a simple act of their own will but do not bow under Christ's lordship. They imagine they have saving faith while their lives evidence that they remain spiritually dead. Calvinism *is* promising, for it places the entire weight of justification and salvation upon the sufficiency of Christ and the operation of His Spirit who bestows and sustains saving faith.

In the final analysis, if we base our justification on human faith, works, or anything else, the very foundations of justification crumble. For inevitably, the agonizing, perplexing, and hopeless questions of having enough of anything would surface: Is my faith strong enough? Are the fruits of grace in my life enough? Are my experiences deep enough, clear enough, persistent enough? Every inadequacy in my faith will shake the very foundations of my spiritual life. My best believing is always defective. I am too ungodly, even in my faith. Apart from Christ, the best of my best is "as filthy rags" (Isa. 64:6).

Too many Christians despair because they cannot distinguish between the rock on which they stand and the faith by which they stand upon it. Faith is not our rock; Christ is our rock. We do not get faith by having faith in our faith or by looking to faith, but by looking to Christ. Looking to Christ is faith.

Perfect faith, great faith, fruitful faith, or strong faith do not justify. If we start qualifying our faith, we destroy the gospel. Our faith may be weak, immature, timid, even indiscernible at times, but if it is real faith, it is justifying faith (Matt. 6:30). Our degree of faith affects sanctification and assurance but not justification. Faith's value in justification does not lie in any degree but in uniting us to Christ and His glorious achievement. As George Downame says: "A small and weak hand, if it be able to reach up the meat to the mouth, as well performs its duty for the nourishment of the body as one of greater strength, because it is not the strength of the hand but the goodness of the meat which nourishes the body."[48]

Far too often we look at the quality of our faith, the quality of our conviction of sin, the quality of our evangelical repentance, or the quality of our love for the brethren for confirmation of our justification, forgetting that Christ alone saves by gracious faith alone. Horatius Bonar states: "It is not the strength of faith, but the perfection of the sacrifice, that saves; and no feebleness of faith, no dimness of eye, no trembling of hand, can change the efficacy of our burnt-offering."[49]

Christ is the solid rock who is the same yesterday, today, and forever (Heb. 13:8). As the old hymn says:

> *My hope is built on nothing less*
> *Than Jesus' blood and righteousness;*
> *I dare not trust the sweetest frame,*
> *But wholly lean on Jesus' name.*
> *On Christ the solid rock I stand;*
> *All other ground is sinking sand.*

We must also reject Antinomian or hyper-Calvinistic tendencies that negates the need for actual justification in time through becoming personal partakers of Christ by faith.[50] For example, Abraham Kuyper went beyond the Synod of Dort in describing justification by faith as merely "becoming conscious" that we were already justified by God from eternity and in the resurrection of Christ. William Gadsby, J. C. Philpot, and most of the Strict Baptists speak similarly by affirming that the believer is justified in time only with respect to his own conscience by the Spirit's witness. This erroneous view already existed in Puritan times. Thomas Goodwin responded to the Antinomians of his day by writing: "It is vain to say I am justified only in respect to the court of mine own conscience. The faith that Paul and the other apostles were justified by, was their believing on Christ that they *might be* justified (Gal. 2:15, 16), and not a believing they were justified already."[51]

The view that actual justification by faith in time does not exist for the believer faces three additional obstacles: First, it is contrary to Romans 4:6-8, which clearly affirms the imputation of Christ's righteousness in time. Second, time itself would then be a mere parenthesis, for God's people would not be viewed prior to regeneration as being "children of wrath, even as others" (Eph. 2:3). If justification by faith does not transfer a sinner from the state of wrath to grace and is merely recognition of justification from eternity, all historical relevance of justification by faith alone is swept away. Third, if justification by faith is not a personal and historical necessity, the fruits of justification in deadness to sin and aliveness to Christ would likewise be unimportant. One could then ask in all seriousness, "Shall we continue in sin, that grace may abound?" (Rom. 6:2). Paul strenuously opposes this in Romans 6.

We have shown that the absence of works is impossible for a true Christian. Faith which justifies is a working faith. "Faith without works is dead" (James 2:21)—yes, *dead*, not just sick or dying. Saving faith does not exist unless it is accompanied by good works. Where Christ saves, He will also exercise His lordship. This is contrary to the primary tenet of Antinomianism that the believer may disregard the law altogether (*anti*=against; *nomos*= law) because he is freed from its demands as a means of salvation. Rather, Scripture teaches that Christ sends the saved believer, who was condemned by the law prior to being justified by faith, back to the law to live in gratitude under His lordship in obedience to His Word. As Luther says, the law is like a stick that God first uses to beat us to Christ, but later we use it as a cane to help us walk the Christian life.

Today, as Christians confront various forms of Roman Catholicism, Antinomianism, Arminianism, and Modernism, the doctrine of justification by faith too often fails to receive its biblical and rightful place. Alister McGrath notes, "The present century has witnessed a growing tendency to relate the doctrine of justification to the question of the meaning of human existence, rather than the more restricted sphere of man's justification *coram Deo* [before God]. It is this trend which underlies the existentialist reinterpretation of the doctrine."[52] But when justification by faith alone is presented in all the freeness of the evangel, are not some bound to say, "This is dangerous teaching"?

Of course they will, and in one sense they are right. Rightly understood and rightly preached, the doctrine of justification by faith alone exposes the natural enmity of carnal man to the exclusivity and freeness of the gospel. Therefore, this doctrine is distorted and wrested to the destruction of souls, both by "can-do" Arminianism and "won't-do" Antinomianism. Faith is overemphasized when viewed as a condition of salvation (Arminianism), but underemphasized when denied as a necessary fruit of salvation (Antinomianism). We are not transferred from death to life by faith as a joint effort with works (Romanists), by faith as an act of grace in us (Arminians), by faith as it receives the Spirit's witness (Antinomians), nor by faith as it relates to the meaning of human existence (modern existentialists), but only by Christ's righteousness received by faith.

The doctrine of justification by faith alone, when biblically preached and rightly balanced, is not a denominational or sectarian peculiarity. It is the heart of the evangel, the kernel of the glorious gospel of the blessed Triune God, and the key to the kingdom of heaven. As John Murray writes, "Justification by faith is the jubilee trumpet of the gospel because it proclaims the gospel to the poor and destitute whose only door of hope is to roll themselves in total helplessness upon the grace and power and righteousness of the Redeemer of the lost."[53]

In our decadent and desperate day, there is a crying need to defend the scriptural proclamation of this doctrine. The relevance of this doctrine is critical to the identity of the church, the essence of Christian theology, and the proclamation of the gospel, as well as to the scriptural, experiential foundations of the Christian faith. Not only is justification by faith still, in Luther's words, "the article by which the church stands or falls" *(articulus stantis et cadentis ecclesiae)*, but by this doctrine each of us will personally stand or fall before God.[54] *Justification by faith alone* must be confessed and experienced by you and me; it is a matter of eternal life or eternal death.

---

[1] *D. Martin Luthers Werke* (hereafter: WA), ed. J. C. F. Knaake, et al. (Weimar: Herman Bohlaus, 1883ff.), 40I, 33, 7-9. For the development of Luther's theology of justification, see Johann Heinz, *Justification and Merit: Luther vs. Catholicism* (Berrien Springs, Mich.: Andrews University Press, 1981), 45-81; Alister E. McGrath, *Iustitia Dei: A History of the Christian Doctrine of Justification* (Cambridge: Cambridge University Press, 1986), 2:3ff.

[2] William Hendriksen, *Romans* (Grand Rapids: Baker, 1982), 147.

[3] Arthur W. Pink, *The Doctrines of Election and Justification* (Grand Rapids: Baker, 1974), 234. In noting the Holy Spirit's precision in using Greek prepositions, Pink adds: "Never do we find Him employing *eis* in connection with Christ's satisfaction and sacrifice in our room and stead, but only 'anti' or 'huper,' which means *in lieu of.* On the other hand, 'anti' and 'huper' are *never* used in connection with our believing, for faith is *not* accepted by God *in lieu of* perfect obedience. Faith must either be the ground of our acceptance with God, or the means or instrument of our becoming interested in the righteousness of Christ; it cannot stand in both relations to our justification" (ibid., 235).

[4] "Justification," *Evangelical Dictionary of Theology*, ed. Walter A. Elwell (Grand Rapids: Baker, 1984), 596.

[5] Quoted by Wm. S. Plumer, *The Grace of Christ, or Sinners Saved by Unmerited Kindness* (1853; repr. Keyser, West Virginia: Odom, n.d.), 244.

[6] *New Testament Greek for Beginners* (New York: MacMillan, 1923), par. 88.

[7] Some texts employ *ek pisteos* and *dia pisteos* in one sentence (Rom. 3:30).

[8] Cf. G. Abbott-Smith, *A Manual Greek Lexicon of the New Testament*, 3rd ed. (Edinburgh: T. & T. Clark, 1937), 105, 492.

[9] Cf. also the *Westminster Larger Catechism*, Question 73 (emphasis added).

[10] *Institutes of the Christian Religion*, ed. J. T. McNeill, trans. Ford Lewis Battles (Philadelphia: Westminster Press, 1960), 3.11.7.

[11] *The Works of Thomas Goodwin*, ed. John C. Miller (Edinburgh: James Nichol, 1864), 8:147.

[12] *Home Truths*, Second Series (repr. Keyser, West Virginia, n.d.), 102.

[13] *By Grace Alone: A Study in Soteriology* (Grand Rapids: Eerdmans, 1955), 109.

[14] Cf. Peter Toon's exposition of Luther's view, *Justification and Sanctification* (Westchester, Illinois: Crossway Books, 1983), 58.

[15] *Outlines of Theology* (Chicago: Bible Institute Colportage Ass'n., 1878), 504.

[16] *The Reformed Faith: An Exposition of the Westminster Confession of Faith* (1845; repr. Inverness: Christian Focus, 1974), 131. For one such "worthy divine," see Francis Turretin, *Institutes of Elenctic Theology*, trans. George Musgrave Giger, ed. James T. Dennison, Jr. (Phillipsburg, N.J.: Presbyterian and Reformed, 1994), 2:675. Cf. *The Works of John Owen* (1851; repr. London: Banner of Truth Trust, 1965), 5:113; Thomas Ridgley, *A Body of Divinity...on the Assembly's Larger Catechism* (Philadelphia: William Woodward, 1815), 3:108-109.

[17] "A Vindication of the Protestant Doctrine Concerning Justification...from the Unjust Charge of Antinomianism," *The Works of Robert Traill* (1810; repr. Edinburgh: Banner of Truth Trust, 1975), 1:252-96.

[18] *The Everlasting Righteousness* (1874; repr. Edinburgh: Banner of Truth Trust, 1993), 75.

[19] *Calvinism and Evangelical Arminianism: Compared as to Election, Reprobation, Justification, and Related Doctrines* (1890; repr. Harrisonburg, Va.: Sprinkle, 1984), 522-66.

[20] *The Reign of Grace from Its Rise to Its Consummation* (Boston: Lincoln & Edmands, 1820), 180-81.

[21] Heinrich Heppe, *Reformed Dogmatics,* trans. by G. T. Thomson (London: George Allen and Unwin, 1950), quoting Guilielmus Bucanus (XXXI, 34): "In what sense are we said to be justified by faith? It is not regarded in its own intrinsic dignity or merit, nor as a work or a new quality in us, nor in its force and efficacy minus love; nor because it has love added to it or works through love; nor because faith imparts the Spirit of Christ, by whom the believer is rendered just because we are bidden seek righteousness not in ourselves but in Christ; but because it seeks and embraces the righteousness offered in the Gospel" (554).

[22] *Biblical and Theological Studies* (Philadelphia: Presbyterian and Reformed, 1968), 423-25.

[23] *Faith and Justification* (Grand Rapids: Eerdmans, 1954), 185-89, 200.

[24] Ibid., 172-75.

[25] Ibid., 190.

[26] John Calvin, *Commentary on Romans* (Edinburgh: Calvin Translation Society, 1843), 147-49.

[27] *Selfe-examination required in everyone for the Worthy Receiving of the Lord's Supper*, 2nd ed. (London: T. Walkley, 1648), 55.

[28] Joel R. Beeke, *Assurance of Faith: Calvin, English Puritanism, and the Dutch Second Reformation* (New York: Peter Lang, 1991), 158ff. Grave danger results from interchanging the ground and fruit of justification, as William Gurnall points out (*The*

Christian in Complete Armour [1655-62; repr. Edinburgh: Banner of Truth Trust, 1974], 2:145). Cf. James Ussher, *A Body of Divinity* (1645; repr. London: R. B. Seeley and W. Burnside, 1841), 244.

29 *The Works of George Swinnock* (1868; repr. Edinburgh: Banner of Truth Trust, 1992), 1:203.

30 James Buchanan, *The Doctrine of Justification* (Edinburgh: T. & T. Clark, 1867), 385.

31 *The Select Works of the Rev. Thomas Watson* (New York: Robert Carter & Brothers, 1856), 150-51.

32 *The Works of George Swinnock*, 1:202.

33 Hubert Jedin, *A History of the Council of Trent*, trans. Dom Ernest Graf (St. Louis: B. Herder, 1961), 2:309. Jedin's work is the definitive study of the Council by a Roman Catholic.

34 Philip Schaff, *The Creeds of Christendom* (New York: Harper & Brothers, 1878), 2:77-206, provides parallel Latin and English columns.

35 *Galatians: A Discussion of St. Paul's Epistle* (London, St. Paul Publications, 1969), 42.

36 *Salvation and the Church* (1987), para. 15.

37 *WA* 69, 254, 27-30; 69, 46, 20.

38 *Pastoral Addresses* (New York: Robert Carter, 1853), 309.

39 *WA* 69, 46, 20.

40 *A Body of Divinity*, 151. Cf. Berkouwer, *Faith and Justification,*195-96.

41 Wilhelmus à Brakel, *The Christian's Reasonable Service*, trans. Bartel Elshout, ed. Joel R. Beeke (Ligonier, Pa.: Soli Deo Gloria, 1993), 2:375.

42 For numerous biblical proofs of divine imputation, see John Bunyan, "Justification by an Imputed Righteousness," *The Works of John Bunyan* (Marshallton, Delaware: National Foundation for Christian Education, 1968), 382-414.

43 Chapter 7. For scholastic Roman Catholic and Protestant views on a fourfold schema of causality in salvation, see Richard A. Muller, *Dictionary of Latin and Greek Theological Terms* (Grand Rapids: Baker, 1985), 61.

44 John Murray, *Christian Baptism* (Grand Rapids: Baker, 1974), 45.

45 "Differences between the Roman and Reformed Doctrines of Justification," *Evangelical Quarterly* 36 (1964):47.

46 Cf. *The Works of James Arminius*, trans. James Nichols and W. R. Bagnall, 3 vols. (1825-28; repr. Grand Rapids: Baker, 1956).

47 *The Works of John Owen*, 5:323. Cf. Belgic Confession, Article 22.

48 *A Treatise of Justification* (London: Felix Kyngston, 1633), 142.

49 *The Everlasting Righteousness*, 23.

50 See Peter Toon, *The Emergence of Hyper-Calvinism* (London: The Olive Tree, 1967).

51 *The Object and Acts of Justifying Faith* (repr. Marshallton, Delaware: National Foundation for Christian Education, n.d.), 325.

52 *Iustitia Dei*, 2:185.

53 *Collected Writings of John Murray* (Edinburgh: Banner of Truth Trust, 1977), 2:217.

54 Johann Heinrich Alsted, *Theologia scholastica didactica* (Hanover, 1618), 711; John H. Gerstner, *A Primer on Justification* (Phillipsburg, N.J.: Presbyterian and Reformed, 1983), 1.

Cultivating Holiness

The godly farmer who plows his field, sows seed, fertilizes, and cultivates is acutely aware that, in the final analysis, he is utterly dependent
on outside forces for an assured crop. He knows he cannot cause the
seed to germinate, the rain to fall, or the sun to shine. But he pursues
his task with diligence nonetheless, looking to God for blessing and
knowing that if he does not fertilize and cultivate, his crop will be meager at best.

Similarly, the Christian life is like a garden that must be cultivated in
order to produce the fruits of holy living unto God. "Theology is the
doctrine or teaching of living to God," wrote William Ames in the opening words of his classic, *The Marrow of Theology*.[1] God Himself exhorts
His children, "Be ye holy; for I am holy" (1 Pet. 1:16). Paul instructs the
Thessalonians, "God hath not called us unto uncleanness, but unto holiness" (1 Thes. 4:7). And the author of Hebrews writes, "Follow peace
with all men, and holiness, without which no man shall see the Lord"
(Heb. 12:14). The believer who does not diligently cultivate holiness
will neither have much genuine assurance of his own salvation nor be
obeying Peter's call to seek it (2 Pet. 1:10).[2] In this chapter I will focus
on the Christian's scriptural call to cultivate Spirit-worked holiness by
diligently using the means God has provided to assist him.

The Call to Cultivate Holiness

Holiness is a noun that relates to the adjective *holy* and the verb *sanctify*,
which means to "make holy."[3] In both biblical languages *holy* means
separated and set apart for God. For the Christian, to be set apart means,
negatively, to be separate from sin, and, positively, to be consecrated
(i.e., dedicated) to God and conformed to Christ. There is no disparity
between Old Testament and New Testament concepts of holiness,
though there is a change in emphasis on what holiness involves. The
Old Testament stresses ritual and moral holiness; the New Testament

stresses inward and transforming holiness (Lev. 10:10-11; 19:2; Heb. 10:10; 1 Thes. 5:23).[4]

Scripture presents the essence of holiness primarily in relation to God. The focus of Scripture's sacred realm is God Himself. God's holiness is the very essence of His being (Isa. 57:15);[5] it is the backdrop of all else the Bible declares about God. His justice is holy justice; His wisdom is holy wisdom; His power is holy power; His grace is holy grace. No other attribute of God is celebrated before the throne of heaven as is His holiness: "Holy, holy, holy, is the LORD of hosts" (Isa. 6:3). "Holy" is prefixed to God's name more than any other attribute.[6] Isaiah alone calls God the "Holy One" twenty-six times. God's holiness, John Howe wrote, "may be said to be a transcendental attribute that, as it were, runs through the rest, and casts lustre upon them. It is an attribute of attributes,... and so it is the very lustre and glory of His other perfections."[7] God manifests His majestic holiness in His works (Ps. 145:17), in His law (Ps. 19:8-9), and especially at the cross of Christ (Matt. 27:46). Holiness is His permanent crown, His glory, and His beauty. It is "more than a mere attribute of God," says Jonathan Edwards. "It is the sum of all His attributes, the outshining of all that God is."[8]

God's holiness denotes two critical truths about Himself: first, it denotes the "separateness" of God from all His creation and from all that is

Jonathan Edwards

unclean or evil. God's holiness testifies of His purity, His absolute moral perfection or excellence, His separateness from all outside of Him, and His complete absence of sin (Job 34:10; Isa. 5:16; 40:18; Hab. 1:13).[9]

Second, since God is holy and set apart from all sin, sinners cannot approach Him apart from holy sacrifice (Lev. 17:11; Heb. 9:22). He cannot be the Holy One and remain indifferent to sin (Jer. 44:4); He must punish it (Ex. 34:6-7). Since all mankind are sinners through both our tragic fall in Adam and our daily transgressions, God can never be appeased by our efforts. We creatures, once made after the image of our holy Creator, voluntarily chose in our covenant-head Adam to become unholy and unacceptable in the sight of our Creator. Atoning blood must be shed if remission of sin is to be granted (Heb. 9:22). Only the perfect, atoning obedience of a sufficient Mediator, the God-man Christ Jesus, can fulfill the demands of God's holiness on behalf of sinners (1 Tim. 2:5). And blessed be God, Christ agreed to accomplish that atonement by the initiation of His Father and accomplished it with His full approbation (Ps. 40:7-8; Mark 15:37-39). "For he hath made him to be sin for us, who knew no sin; that we might be made the righteousness of God in him" (2 Cor. 5:21). As the Dutch Reformed Lord's Supper Form states, "The wrath of God against sin is so great, that (rather than it should go unpunished) He hath punished the same in His beloved Son Jesus Christ with the bitter and shameful death of the cross."[10]

By free grace, God regenerates sinners and causes them to believe in Christ alone as their righteousness and salvation. Those of us who are among these blessed believers are also made partakers of Christ's holiness by means of divine discipline (Heb. 12:10). As Christ's disciples, we are called by God to be more holy than we shall ever become by ourselves during this life (1 John 1:10).[11] He calls us to separate from sin and to consecrate and assimilate ourselves to Himself out of gratitude for His great salvation. These concepts—separation from sin, consecration to God, and conformity to Christ—make holiness comprehensive. Everything, Paul tells us in 1 Timothy 4:4-5, is to be sanctified, that is, made holy.

In the first place, personal holiness demands total consecration. God never calls us to give Him only a piece of our hearts. The call to holiness is a call for our entire heart: "My son, give me thine heart" (Prov. 23:26).

Second, holiness of heart must be cultivated in every sphere of life: in privacy with God, in the confidentiality of our homes, in the competitiveness of our occupation, in the pleasures of social friendship, in relation with our unevangelized neighbors and the world's hungry and unemployed, as well as in Sunday worship. Horatius Bonar writes:

> Holiness...extends to every part of our persons, fills up our being, spreads over our life, influences everything we are, or do, or think, or speak, or plan, small or great, outward or inward, negative or positive, our loving, our hating, our sorrowing, our rejoicing, our recreations, our business, our friendships, our relationships, our silence, our speech, our reading, our writing, our going out and our coming in—our whole man in every movement of spirit, soul, and body.[12]

The call to holiness is a daily task and an absolute, radical call involving the core of religious faith and practice. John Calvin put it this way: "Because they have been called to holiness, the entire life of all Christians must be an exercise in piety."[13] In short, holiness is the commitment of a whole life to live "God-ward" (2 Cor. 3:4), to be set apart to the lordship of Jesus Christ.

Thus, holiness must be inward, filling our entire heart, and outward, covering all of life. "And the very God of peace sanctify you wholly; and I pray God your whole spirit and soul and body be preserved blameless unto the coming of our Lord Jesus Christ" (1 Thes. 5:23). "Holiness," Thomas Boston maintained, "is a constellation of graces."[14] In gratitude to God, a believer cultivates the fruits of holiness, such as meekness, gentleness, love, joy, peace, patience, kindness, goodness, mercy, contentment, gratitude, purity of heart, faithfulness, the fear of God, humility, spiritual-mindedness, self-control, and self-denial (Gal. 5:22-23).[15]

This call to holiness is not a call to merit acceptance with God. The New Testament declares that every believer is sanctified by the sacrifice of Christ: "By the which will we are sanctified through the offering of the body of Jesus Christ once for all" (Heb. 10:10). Christ is our sanctification (1 Cor. 1:30); therefore, the church, as the bride of Christ, is sanctified (Eph. 5:25-26). The believer's *status* before God is one of sanctity in Christ, on account of His perfect obedience which has fully satisfied the justice of God for all sin.

The believer's status, however, does not infer that he has arrived at a wholly sanctified *condition* (1 Cor. 1:2). Several attempts have been made to express the relationship between the believer's status and his condition before God, foremost among them being Luther's well-known *simul justus et peccator* ("at once righteous and a sinner"). That is to say, the believer is both righteous in God's sight because of Christ and remains a sinner as measured according to his own merits.[16] Though from the onset of Christian experience (which coincides with regeneration) the believer's status makes an impact on his condition, he is never in a perfectly sanctified condition in this life. Paul prays that the Thessalonians may be sanctified wholly, something that still had to be accomplished (1 Thes. 5:23). Sanctification received is sanctification well and truly begun, though not yet perfected.

This explains the New Testament's emphasis on holiness as something to be cultivated and pursued. New Testament language stresses vital, progressive sanctification. The believer must strive for sanctity, for holiness (Heb. 12:14). Growth in holiness must and will follow regeneration (Eph. 1:4; Phil. 3:12).

Thus, true believer, you are holy before God in Christ, and yet you must cultivate holiness in the strength of Christ. Your status in holiness is conferred; your condition in holiness must be pursued. Through Christ you are made holy in your standing before God, and through Him you are called to reflect that standing by being holy in daily life. Your context of holiness is justification through Christ; your route of holiness is to be crucified and resurrected with Him, which involves the continual "mortification of the old, and the quickening of the new man" (*Heidelberg Catechism*, Question 88). You are called to be in life what you already are in principle by grace.

The Cultivation of Holiness

Concretely, then, what must you cultivate? Three things:

1. *Imitation of the character of the Jehovah.* God says, "Be ye holy; for I am holy" (1 Pet. 1:16). The holiness of God Himself ought to be your foremost stimulus to cultivate holy living. Seek to be like your Heavenly Father in righteousness, holiness, and integrity. In the Spirit, strive to think God's thoughts via His Word, to be of one mind with Him, and to live and act as God Himself would have you do.[17] As Stephen Charnock concludes: "This is the prime way of honouring God. We do not so glorify God by elevated admirations, or eloquent expressions, or pompous services for him, as when we aspire to a conversing with him with unstained spirits, and live *to* him in living *like* him."[18]

2. *Conformity to the image of Christ.* This is a favorite Pauline theme, of which one example must suffice: "Let this mind be in you, which was also in Christ Jesus: who...made himself of no reputation, and took upon him the form of a servant...and...humbled himself, and became obedient unto death, even the death of the cross" (Phil. 2:5-8). Christ was humble, willing to give up His rights in order to obey God and serve sinners. If you would be holy, Paul is saying, be like-minded.

Stephen Charnock

Do not aim for conformity to Christ as a condition of salvation, however, but, rather, as a fruit of salvation received by faith. We must look to Christ for holiness, for He is the fount and path of holiness. Seek no other path. Follow the advice of Augustine who contended that it is better to limp on the path than to run outside of it.[19] Do as Calvin taught: Set Christ before you as the mirror of sanctification, and seek grace to mirror Him in His image.[20] Ask in each situation encountered: "What would Christ think, say, and do?" Then trust Him for holiness. He will not disappoint you (James 1:2-7).

There is unending room for growth in holiness because Jesus is the bottomless well of salvation. You cannot go to Him too often for holiness, for He is holiness *par excellence*. He lived holiness; He merited holiness; He sends His Spirit to apply holiness. "Christ is all, and in all" (Col. 3:11)—holiness inclusive. As Luther profoundly set forth, "We in Christ = justification; Christ in us = sanctification."[21]

3. *Submission to the mind of the Holy Spirit.* In Romans 8:6, Paul divides people into two categories—those who let themselves be controlled by their sinful natures (i.e., the carnally minded who follow fleshly desires) and those who follow after the Spirit (i.e., those who *mind* "the things of the Spirit," Rom. 8:5).

The Holy Spirit was sent to bring the believer's mind into submission to His mind (1 Cor. 2). He was given to make sinners holy; the most holy increasingly bow as willing servants under His control. Let us beg for grace to be willing servants more fully and more consistently.

How does the Spirit work this holy grace of submission to His mind, thereby making us holy?

- He shows us our need for holiness through conviction of sin, righteousness, and judgment (John 16:8).
- He implants the desire for holiness. His saving work never leads to despair but always to sanctification in Christ.
- He grants Christ-likeness in holiness. He works upon our whole nature, molding us after Christ's image.
- He provides strength to live a holy life by indwelling and influencing our soul. If we live by the Spirit, we will not gratify the desires of our sinful nature (Gal. 5:16); rather, we will live in obedience to and dependence on that Spirit.
- Through humble feeding on Scripture and the exercise of prayer, the Spirit teaches us His mind and establishes an ongoing realization that holiness remains essential to being worthy of God and His kingdom (1 Thes. 2:12; Eph. 4:1) and for fitness in His service (1 Cor. 9:24-25; Phil. 3:13).

Ephesians 5:18 says, "Be not drunk with wine, wherein is excess; but be filled with the Spirit." Thomas Watson writes: "The Spirit stamps the impression of his own sanctity upon the heart, as the seal prints its likeness upon the wax. The Spirit of God in a man perfumes him with holiness, and makes his heart a map of heaven."[22]

How to Cultivate Holiness

That believers are called to holiness is indisputably clear. But the cardinal question remains: How does the believer cultivate holiness? Here are seven directions to assist us.

1. *Know and love Scripture.* This is God's primary road to holiness and to spiritual growth—the Spirit as Master Teacher blessing the reading and searching of God's Word. Jesus prayed, "Sanctify them through thy truth: thy word is truth" (John 17:17). And Peter advised, "Desire the sincere milk of the word, that ye may grow thereby" (1 Pet. 2:2).

If you would not remain spiritually ignorant and impoverished, read through the Bible at least annually. Even more importantly, memorize the Scriptures (Ps. 119:11), search (John 5:39) and meditate upon them (Ps. 1:2), live and love them (Ps. 119; 19:10). Compare Scripture with Scripture; take time to study the Word. Proverbs 2:1-5 sets before us the following principles involved in serious personal Bible study: teachability (receiving God's words), obedience (storing God's commandments), discipline (applying the heart), dependence (crying for knowledge), and perseverance (searching for hidden treasure).[23] Do not expect growth in holiness if you spend little time alone with God and do not take His Word seriously. When plagued with a heart prone to be tempted away from holiness, let Scripture teach you how to live a holy life in an unholy world.

Develop a scriptural formula for holy living. Here is one possibility drawn from 1 Corinthians. When hesitant over a course of action, ask yourself:

- Does this glorify God? (1 Cor. 10:31)
- Is this consistent with the lordship of Christ? (1 Cor. 7:23)
- Is this consistent with biblical examples? (1 Cor. 11:1)
- Is this lawful and beneficial for me—spiritually, mentally, physically? (1 Cor. 6:9-12)
- Does this help others positively and not hurt others unnecessarily? (1 Cor. 10:33; 8:13)
- Does this bring me under any enslaving power? (1 Cor. 6:12)

Let Scripture be your compass to guide you in cultivating holiness, in making life's decisions, and in encountering the high waves of personal affliction.

2. Use the sacraments of baptism and the Lord's Supper diligently as means of grace to strengthen your faith in Christ. God's sacraments complement His Word. They point us away from ourselves. Each sign—the water, the bread, the wine—directs us to believe in Christ and His sacrifice on the cross. The sacraments are visible means through which He invisibly communes with us and we with Him. They are spurs to Christlikeness and therefore to holiness.

The grace received through the sacraments is not different from that received through the Word. Both convey the same Christ. But as Robert Bruce put it, "While we do not get a better Christ in the sacraments than we do in the Word, there are times when we get Christ better."[24]

Flee often to Christ by Word and sacrament. Faith in Christ is a powerful motivator for holiness, since faith and the love of sin cannot mix. Be careful, however, not to seek your holiness in your experiences of Christ, but in Christ Himself. As William Gurnall admonishes: "When thou trustest in Christ *within* thee, instead of Christ *without* thee, thou settest Christ against Christ. The bride does well to esteem her husband's picture, but it were ridiculous if she should love it better than himself, much more if she should go to it *rather than to him to supply her wants*. Yet thou actest thus when thou art more fond of Christ's image in thy soul than of him who painted it there."[25]

3. *Regard yourself as dead to the dominion of sin and as alive to God in Christ* (Rom. 6:11). "To realize this," writes Dr. Martyn Lloyd-Jones, "takes away from us that old sense of hopelessness which we have all known and felt because of the terrible power of sin.... I can say to myself that not only am I no longer under the dominion of sin, but I am under the dominion of another power that nothing can frustrate."[26] That does not imply that because sin no longer reigns over us as believers, we have license to forego our duty to fight against sin. Bridges rightly admonishes us, "To confuse the *potential* for resisting sin (which God provided) with the *responsibility* for resisting (which is ours) is to court disaster in our pursuit of holiness."[27] Westminster's *Shorter Catechism* balances God's gift and our responsibility when stating, "Sanctification is the work of God's free grace, whereby we are renewed in the whole man after the image of God, and are enabled more and more to die unto sin, and live unto righteousness" (Question 35).

Seek to cultivate a growing hatred of sin *as sin*, for that is the kind of hatred against sin that God possesses. Recognize that God is worthy of obedience not only as the Judge, but especially as a loving Father. Say with Joseph in temptation, "How then can I do this great wickedness, and sin against God?" (Gen. 39:9).

Look for heart-idols. Pray for strength to uproot them and cast them out. Attack all sin, all unrighteousness, and all devices of Satan.

Strive for daily repentance before God. Never rise above the publican's petition, "God be merciful to me a sinner" (Luke 18:13). Remember Luther's advice that God would have His people exercise "lifelong repentance."

Believe that Christ is mighty to preserve you alive by His Spirit. You live through union with Christ, therefore live unto His righteousness. His righteousness is greater than your unrighteousness. His power to save is greater than your sinfulness. His Spirit is within you: "Ye are of God, little children, and have overcome them: because greater is he that is in you, than he that is in the world" (1 John 4:4). Do not despair: you are strong in Him, alive in Him, and victorious in Him. Satan may win many skirmishes, but the war is yours, the victory is yours (1 Cor. 15:57; Rom. 8:37). In Christ, the optimism of divine grace reigns over the pessimism of human nature.

4. *Pray and work in dependence upon God for holiness.* No one but God

is sufficient to bring a clean thing out of an unclean (Job 14:4). Hence, pray with David, "Create in me a clean heart, O God" (Ps. 51:10). And as you pray, work.

The Heidelberg Catechism (Question 116) points out that prayer and work belong together. They are like two oars, which, when both utilized, will keep a rowboat moving forward. If you use only one oar—if you pray without working or you work without praying—you will row in circles.

Holiness and prayer have much in common. Both are central to the Christian life and faith; they are obligatory, not optional. Both originate with God and focus upon Him. Both are activated, often simultaneously, by the Spirit of God. Neither can survive without the other. Both are learned by experience and through spiritual battles.[28] Neither is perfected in this life, but must be cultivated lifelong; they are easier to talk and write about than to exercise. The most prayerful often feel themselves to be prayerless; the most holy often regard themselves as unholy.

Holiness and work are also closely related, especially the work of nurturing and persevering in personal discipline. Discipline takes time and effort. Paul exhorted Timothy, "Exercise thyself rather unto godliness" (1 Tim. 4:7). Holiness is not achieved sloppily or instantaneously.[29] Holiness is a call to a disciplined life; it cannot live out of what Dietrich Bonhoeffer called cheap grace—that is, grace which forgives without demanding repentance and obedience. Holiness is costly grace—grace that cost God the blood of His Son, cost the Son His own life, and costs the believer daily mortification so that, like Paul, he dies daily (1 Cor. 15:31).[30] Gracious holiness calls for continual commitment, continual diligence, continual practice, and continual repentance.[31] "If we sometimes through weakness fall into sin, we must not therefore despair of God's mercy, nor continue in sin, since…we have an eternal covenant of grace with God" (*Baptism Form*).[32] Rather, resolve with Jonathan Edwards: "Never to give over, nor in the least to slacken, my fight with my corruptions, however unsuccessful I may be."[33]

These two things, fighting against sin and lack of success, appear contradictory but are not. Failing and becoming a failure are two different matters. The believer recognizes he will often fail. Luther said that the righteous man feels more often like "a loser than a victor" in the struggle against sin, "for the Lord lets him be tested and assailed to his utmost limits as gold is tested in a furnace."[34] This too is an important component of discipleship. Nevertheless, the godly man will persevere even through his failures. Failure does not make him quit; it makes him repent all the more earnestly and press on in the Spirit's strength. "For a just man falleth seven times, and riseth up again: but the wicked shall fall into mischief" (Prov. 24:16). As John Owen wrote, "God works in us and with us, not against us or without us; so that his assistance is an encouragement as to the facilitating of the work, and no occasion of neglect as to the work itself."[35]

Let us never forget that the God we love, loves holiness. Hence the intensity of His fatherly, chastising discipline (Heb. 12:5-6, 10)! Perhaps William Gurnall says it best: "God would not rub so hard if it were not to fetch out the dirt that is ingrained in our natures. God loves purity so well He had rather see a hole than a spot in his child's garments."[36]

5. *Flee worldliness.* We must strike out against the first appearance of the pride of life, the lusts of the flesh and eye, and all forms of sinful worldliness as they knock on the door of our hearts and minds. If we open the door and allow them to roam about in our minds and take foothold in our lives, we are already their prey. "Daniel purposed *in his heart* that he would not defile himself with the portion of the king's meat, nor with the wine which he drank: *therefore* he requested of the prince of the eunuchs that he might not defile himself" (Dan. 1:8; emphasis added). The material we read, the recreation and entertainment we engage in, the music we listen to, the friendships we form, and the conversations we have all affect our minds and ought to be judged in the context of Philippians 4:8: Whatsoever things are true, honest, just, pure, lovely, and of good report, "think on these things." We must live *above* the world and not be *of* the world while yet *in* the world (Rom. 12:1-2).

6. *Seek fellowship in the church; associate with mentors in holiness* (Eph. 4:12-13; 1 Cor. 11:1).[37] The church ought to be a fellowship of mutual care and a community of prayer (1 Cor. 12:7; Acts 2:42). Converse and pray with fellow believers whose godly walk you admire (Col. 3:16). "He that walketh with the wise shall be wise" (Prov. 13:20). Association promotes assimilation. A Christian life lived in isolation from other believers will be defective; usually such a believer will remain spiritually immature.

Such conversation, however, ought not exclude the reading of godly treatises of former ages which promote holiness. Luther said that some of his best friends were dead ones. For example, he questioned if anyone could possess spiritual life who did not feel kinship with David pouring out his heart in the psalms. Read classics that speak out vehemently against sin. Let Thomas Watson be your mentor in *The Mischief*

A conventicle meeting on a hillside.

of Sin, or Jeremiah Burroughs in *The Evil of Evils*.[38] But also read J. C. Ryle's *Holiness* and Octavius Winslow's *Personal Declension and Revival of Religion in the Soul*.[39] Let these divines of former ages become your spiritual mentors and friends.

7. *Live present-tense, total commitment to God.* Form habits of holiness. Pursue harmony and symmetry in holy living. By the grace of the Spirit, root out all inconsistencies and enjoy godly activities. Be committed to not being sullied by this world's temptations and to remain clean by forgiveness from and consecration to your perfect Savior.

Don't fall prey to the "one-more-time" syndrome. Postponed obedience is disobedience. Tomorrow's holiness is impurity *now*. Tomorrow's faith is unbelief *now*. Aim to not sin at all (1 John 2:1); ask for divine strength to bring every thought into captivity to Christ (2 Cor.

10:5), for Scripture indicates that our "thought-lives" ultimately determine our character: "For as he thinketh in his heart, so is he" (Prov. 23:7a). An old proverb says it this way:

> *Sow a thought, reap an act;*
> *Sow an act, reap a habit;*
> *Sow a habit, reap a character.*
> *Sow a character, reap a destiny.*

Encouragements for Cultivating Holiness

The cultivation of holiness is demanding. Thomas Watson called it "sweating work." Happily, God provides us with several motivations to holiness in His Word. To encourage us in the pursuit of holiness, we need to keep our eyes focused on the following biblical truths.

1. *God has called you to holiness for your good and His glory.* "For God hath not called us unto uncleanness, but unto holiness" (1 Thes. 4:7). Whatever God calls us to is necessary. His call itself, as well as the benefits which we experience from holy living as described below, should induce us to seek and practice holiness.

Holiness augments our spiritual well-being. God assures us that "no good thing will he withhold from them that walk uprightly" (Ps. 84:11). "What health is to the heart," John Flavel noted, "that holiness is to the soul."[40] In Richard Baxter's scarce work on holiness, the very chapter titles are enlightening: "Holiness is the only way of safety. Holiness is the only honest way. Holiness is the most gainful way. Holiness is the most honourable way. Holiness is the most pleasant way."[41]

But most importantly, holiness glorifies the God you love (Isa. 43:21). As Thomas Brooks affirmed, "Holiness makes most for God's honour."[42]

2. *Holiness makes you resemble God and preserves your integrity.* Watson wrote: "We must endeavour to be like God in sanctity. It is a clear glass in which we can see a face; it is a holy heart in which something of God can be seen."[43] Christ serves here as a pattern of holiness for us—a pattern of holy humility (Phil. 2:5-13), holy compassion (Mark 1:41), holy forgiveness (Col. 3:13), holy unselfishness (Rom. 15:3), holy indignation against sin (Matt. 23), and holy prayer (Heb. 5:7). Holiness cultivated, to resemble God and be patterned after Christ, saves us from much hypocrisy and from resorting to a "Sunday only" Christianity. It gives vitality, purpose, meaning, and direction to daily living.

3. *Holiness gives evidence of your justification and election, and fosters assurance.* Sanctification is the inevitable fruit of justification (1 Cor. 6:11). The two may be distinguished, but never separated; God Himself has

married them. Justification is organically linked to sanctification; new birth infallibly issues in new life. The justified will walk in "the King's highway of holiness."[44] In and through Christ, justification gives God's child the *title* for heaven and the boldness to enter; sanctification gives him the *fitness* for heaven and the preparation necessary to enjoy it. Sanctification is the personal appropriation of the fruits of justification. B. B. Warfield notes, "Sanctification is but the execution of the justifying decree. For it to fail would be for the acquitted person not to be released in accordance with his acquittal."[45] Consequently, the justifying decree of Christ in John 8, "Neither do I condemn thee," is immediately followed by the call to holiness, "Go, and sin no more" (v. 11).

Election is also inseparable from holiness: "God hath from the beginning chosen you to salvation through sanctification of the Spirit" (2 Thes. 2:13). Sanctification is the earmark of Christ's elect sheep. That is why election is always a comforting doctrine for the believer, for it is the sure foundation that explains the grace of God working within him. No wonder our Reformed forebears deemed election to be one of the believer's greatest comforts.[46]

Calvin insisted that election should discourage none, for the believer receives comfort from it and the unbeliever is not called to consider it—rather, he is called to repentance. Whoever is discouraged by election or relies upon it without living a holy life is falling prey to a satanic misuse of this precious, encouraging doctrine (cf. Deut. 29:29). As Ryle asserts, "It is not given to us in this world to study the pages of the book of life, and see if our names are there. But if there is one thing clearly and plainly laid down about election, it is this—that elect men and women may be known and distinguished by holy lives."[47] Holiness is the visible side of their salvation. "Ye shall know them by their fruits" (Matt. 7:16).

Consequently, holiness fosters assurance (1 John 2:3; 3:19). "Everyone may be assured in himself of his faith by the fruits thereof" (*Heidelberg Catechism*, Question 86). Reformed divines agree that most of the forms and degrees of assurance experienced by true believers—especially daily assurance—are reached gradually in the path of sanctification through careful cultivation of God's Word, the means of grace, and corresponding obedience.[48] An increasing hatred of sin, by means of mortification, and a growing love for obeying God by means of vivification, accompany the progress of faith as it grows into assurance. Christ-centered, Spirit-worked holiness is the best and most sound evidence of divine sonship (Rom. 8:1-16).

The way to lose a daily sense of assurance is to forego the daily pursuit of holiness. Many believers live too carelessly. They treat sin lightly or neglect daily devotions and study of the Word. Others live too inactively. They do not cultivate holiness, but assume the posture that nothing can be done to foster sanctification, as if holiness were something *outside* of us except on rare occasions when something very special "happens" *inside*. To live carelessly or inactively is to ask for daily spiritual darkness, deadness, and fruitlessness.

4. *As a believer, holiness alone can purify you.* Conversely, "unto them that are defiled is nothing pure" (Titus 1:15). Holiness cannot be exercised where the heart has not been fundamentally transformed through divine regeneration. Through the new birth, Satan is deposed, the law of God is written upon the heart of the believer, Christ is crowned Lord and King, and the believer made "willing and ready, henceforth, to live unto Him" (*Heidelberg Catechism*, Question 1). Christ in us *(Christus in nobis)* is an essential complement to Christ for us *(Christus pro nobis).*[49] The Spirit of God not only teaches the believer what Christ has done, but actualizes the holiness and work of Christ in his personal life. Through Christ, God sanctifies His child and makes his prayers and thanksgivings acceptable. As Thomas Watson said: "A holy heart is the altar which sanctifies the offering; if not to satisfaction, to acceptation."[50]

5. *Holiness is essential for your effective service to God.* Paul joins sanctification and usefulness together: "If a man therefore purge himself, he shall be a vessel unto honour, sanctified and meet for the master's use, and prepared unto every good work" (2 Tim. 2:21). God uses holiness to assist the preaching of the gospel and to build up the credit of the Christian faith, which is dishonored by the carelessness of Christians and hypocrites who often serve as Satan's best allies.[51] Our lives are always doing good or harm; they are an open epistle for all to read (2 Cor. 3:2). Holy living preaches reality. It influences and impresses like nothing else can; no argument can match it. It displays the beauty of religion; it gives credibility to witness and to evangelism (Phil. 2:15).[52] "Holiness," writes Hugh Morgan, "is the most effective way of influencing unconverted people and creating within them a willingness to listen to the preaching of the gospel" (Matt. 5:16; 1 Pet. 3:1-2).[53]

Holiness manifests itself in humility and reverence for God. Such are those whom God looks to and uses (Isa. 66:2). As Andrew Murray notes:

> The great test of whether the holiness we profess to seek or to attain is truth and life will be *whether it be manifest in the increasing humility it pro-*

duces. In the creature, humility is the one thing needed to allow God's holiness to dwell in him and shine through him. In Jesus, the holy one of God who makes us holy, a divine humility was the secret of his life and his death and his exaltation; the one infallible test of our holiness will be the humility before God and men which marks us. Humility is the bloom and the beauty of holiness.[54]

6. *Holiness fits you for heaven* (Rev. 21:27). Hebrews 12:14 says, "Follow [literally: *pursue*]...holiness, without which no man shall see the Lord." As John Owen wrote:

> There is no imagination wherewith man is besotted, more foolish, none so pernicious, as this—that persons not purified, not sanctified, not made holy in their life, should afterwards be taken into that state of blessedness which consists in the enjoyment of God. Neither can such persons enjoy God, nor would God be a reward to them. Holiness indeed is perfected in heaven: but the beginning of it is invariably confined to this world. God leads none to heaven but whom He sanctifies on the earth. This living Head will not admit of dead members.[55]

Obstacles to Cultivating Holiness

The cultivation of holiness will inevitably meet with numerous obstacles. Much impedes holiness. Five common problems against which we need to be on guard are these:

1. Our attitude to sin and life itself is prone to be *more self-centered than God-centered*. We are often more concerned about the consequences of sin or victory over sin than about how our sins grieve God. The cultivation of holiness necessitates hating sin as God hates sin. Holiness is not merely loving God and our neighbor; it also involves hatred. The hatred of sin is elemental to holiness. Those who love God hate sin (Prov. 8:36). We must cultivate an attitude that views sin as always being preeminently against God (Ps. 51:4).[56]

Low and distorted views of sin reap low and distorted views of holiness. "Wrong views about holiness are generally traceable to wrong views about human corruption," J. C. Ryle asserted. "If a man does not realize the dangerous nature of his soul's diseases, you cannot wonder if he is content with false or imperfect remedies."[57] Cultivating holiness demands a rejection of the pride of life and the lusts of the flesh as well as the prayer, "Give me the single eye, Thy Name to glorify" (Psalter 236, stanza 2).

We fail when we do not live with our priorities consciously centered on God's Word, will, and glory. In the words of the Scottish theologian, John Brown, "Holiness does not consist in mystic speculations, enthusiastic fervours, or uncommanded austerities; it consists in thinking as God thinks, and willing as God wills."[58]

2. Our progress is hindered when we misunderstand "living by faith" (Gal. 2:20) to imply that *no effort towards holiness is commanded of us.* Sometimes we are even prone to consider human effort sinful or "fleshly." Bishop Ryle provides us with a corrective here:

> Is it wise to proclaim in so bald, naked, and unqualified a way as many do, that the holiness of converted people is by faith only, and not at all by personal exertion? Is this according to the proportion of God's Word? I doubt it. That faith in Christ is the root of all holiness no well-instructed Christian will ever think of denying. But surely the Scriptures teach us that in following holiness the true Christian needs personal exertion and work as well as faith.[59]

We are responsible for holiness. Whose fault is it but our own if we are not holy? As Ralph Erskine counsels, we need to implement the *fight-or-flight* attitude with regard to sinful temptations. Sometimes we simply need to heed Peter's plain injunction, "Dearly beloved, I beseech you as strangers and pilgrims, abstain from fleshly lusts, which war against the soul" (1 Pet. 2:11). *Abstain*—often it is that simple.

If you have put off the old man and put on the new (Eph. 4:22-32), live accordingly (Col. 3:9-10). Mortify your members (i.e., unholy habits) and seek those things which are above (Col. 3:1-5)—not as a form of legalism, but as a repercussion of divine blessing (Col. 2:9-23).[60] Make a covenant with your eyes and feet and hands to turn from iniquity (Job 31:1). Look the other way; walk the other way. Put away uncontrolled anger, gossip, and bitterness. Put sin to death (Rom. 8:13) by the blood of Christ. "Set faith at work on Christ for the killing of thy sin," wrote Owen, "and thou wilt…live to see thy lust dead at thy feet."[61]

3. On the other hand, we fail miserably when we *take pride in our holiness and think that our exertions can somehow produce holiness* apart from faith. From beginning to end holiness is the work of God and His free grace (*Westminster Confession of Faith*, Chapter 13). As Richard Sibbes maintained, "By grace we are what we are in justification, and work what we work in sanctification."[62] Holiness is not partially God's work and partially our work. Holiness manufactured by our heart is not holiness after God's heart. All working out of the Christian life on our part is the fruit of God working in us and through us: "Work out your own salvation with fear and trembling, for it is God which worketh in you both to will and to do of his good pleasure" (Phil. 2:12-13). "The regenerate have a spiritual nature within that fits them for holy action, other-

wise there would be no difference between them and the unregenerate," wrote A.W. Pink.[63] Nevertheless, self-sanctification, strictly speaking, is non-existent.[64] "We do good works, but not to merit by them (for
what can we merit?), nay, we are beholden to God for the good works
we do, and not He to us" (*Belgic Confession of Faith*, Article 24). As Calvin
explained, "Holiness is not a merit by which we can
attain communion with God, but a gift of Christ which enables us to
cling to him and to follow him."[65] John Murray put it this way: "God's
working in us is not suspended because we work, nor our working suspended because God works. Neither is the relation strictly one of cooperation as if God did his part and we did ours.... God works in us and
we also work. But the relation is that *because* God works we work."[66]

> *And every virtue we possess,*
> *And every conquest won,*
> *And every thought of holiness,*
> *Are His alone.*

Kenneth Prior warns: "There is a subtle danger of speaking of sanctification as essentially coming from our own effort or initiative. We can
unconsciously do this even while acknowledging our need for the
power of the Holy Spirit, by making the operation of that power dependent upon our surrender and consecration."[67]

Our dependence on God for holiness ought to humble us. Holiness
and humility are inseparable.[68] One of the most common traits they
share is that neither one recognizes itself. The most holy complain of
their impurity; the most humble, of their pride. Those of us called to be
teachers and examples of holiness must beware of subtle and insidious
pride working its way into our supposed holiness.

Holiness is greatly impeded by any number of wrong views of holiness in its relation to humility; for example:

- As soon as we think, speak, or act as if our own holiness will somehow suffice without being clothed with Christ's humility, we are
  already enveloped in spiritual pride.
- When we begin to feel complacent about our holiness, we are far
  from both holiness and humility.
- When self-abasement is lacking, holiness is lacking.
- When self-abasement does not make us to flee to Christ and His
  holiness for refuge, holiness is lacking.
- Without a life dependent on Christ, we shall possess no holiness.

4. *Embracing unscriptural, erroneous views about holiness* can greatly impede
our holiness. The need to experience "the second blessing," or various

charismatic gifts such as speaking in tongues or faith healing, an earnest search for our own special gift of the Spirit, and the acceptance of Jesus as Savior but not as Lord—these are but a few of many erroneous interpretations of Scripture that can skew a proper understanding of holiness in our personal lives. Though addressing these issues lies beyond the scope of this chapter, allow me to provide three summary statements. Concerning the first error mentioned above, it is not just *the* second blessing that the believer needs, but he needs *a* second blessing, as well as a third and fourth and fifth—yes, he needs the continual blessing of the Holy Spirit in order to progress in holiness so that Christ may increase and he may decrease (John 3:30). Concerning the second error mentioned above, John Stott wisely comments that "when Paul wrote to the Corinthians that they were not lacking in spiritual gifts (1 Cor. 1:7), he makes it clear that the evidence of the Spirit's fullness is not the exercise of His gifts (of which they had plenty), but the ripening of His fruit (of which they had little)."[69] And with regard to the third error of separating the Savior from His lordship, the Heidelberg Catechism provides a summary corrective in Question 30: "One of these two things must be true, that either Jesus is not a complete Savior or that they, who by a true faith receive this Savior, must find all things in Him necessary to their salvation."

5. We are prone to shirk *the battle of daily spiritual warfare.* No one likes war. The believer is often blind to his own real enemies—to a subtle Satan, to a tempting world, and especially to the reality of his own ongoing pollution which Paul so poignantly expresses in Romans 7:14-25. To be holy among the holy takes grace; to be holy among the unholy is great grace. Maintaining personal holiness in an unholy world with a heart prone to backslide necessitates a perpetual fight. It will involve conflict, holy warfare, struggle against Satan, a battle between the flesh and the spirit (Gal. 5:17). A believer not only has peace of conscience, but also war within (Rom. 7:24 – 8:1). As Samuel Rutherford asserts, "The devil's war is better than the devil's peace."[70] Hence the remedies of Christ's holiness (Heb. 7:25-28) and of His Spirit-supplied Christian armor (Eph. 6:10-20) are ignored at our peril. True holiness must be pursued against the backdrop of an acute awareness of the indwelling sin that continues to live in our hearts and to deceive our understanding. The holy man, unlike others, is never at peace with indwelling sin. Though he may backslide far, he will again be humbled and ashamed because of his sin.

The Joy of Holiness Cultivated

A holy life ought to be one of joy in the Lord, not negative drudgery (Neh. 8:10). The idea that holiness requires a gloomy disposition is a tragic distortion of Scripture. On the contrary, Scripture asserts that those who cultivate holiness experience true joy. Jesus said, "If ye keep my commandments, ye shall abide in my love; even as I have kept my Father's commandments, and abide in his love. These things have I spoken unto you that my joy might remain in you, and that your joy might be full" (John 15:10-11). Those who are obedient—who are pursuing holiness as a way of life—will know that the joy which flows from communion with God is a supreme joy, an ongoing joy, and an anticipated joy.

1. *The supreme joy: fellowship with God.* No greater joy can be had than that of communion with God. "In thy presence is fulness of joy" (Ps. 16:10). True joy springs from God as we are enabled to walk in fellowship with Him. When we break our fellowship with God by sin, we need to return, like David, with penitential prayer to Him: "Restore unto me the joy of thy salvation" (Ps. 51:12). The words Jesus spoke to the thief on the cross represent the chief delight of every child of God: "To day shalt thou be with me in paradise" (Luke 23:43).

2. *The ongoing joy: abiding assurance.* True holiness obeys God, and obedience always trusts God. It believes, "And we know that all things work together for good to them that love God" (Rom. 8:28)—even when it cannot be seen. Like faithful workers on a Persian carpet, who blindly hand up all colors of strand to the overseer working out the pattern above them, God's intimate saints are those who hand Him even the black strands He calls for, knowing that His pattern will be perfect from above, notwithstanding the gnarled mess underneath. Do you know this profound, childlike trust in believing the words of Jesus: "What I do thou knowest not now: but thou shalt know hereafter" (John 13:7)? Such ongoing, stabilizing joy surpasses understanding. Holiness reaps joyous contentment; "godliness with contentment is great gain" (1 Tim. 6:6).

3. *The anticipated joy: eternal, gracious reward.* Jesus was motivated to endure His sufferings by anticipating the joy of His reward (Heb. 12:1-2). Believers too may look forward to entering into the joy of their Lord as they pursue holiness in the strength of Christ throughout their lives. By grace, they may joyously anticipate their eternal reward: "Well done, thou good and faithful servant.... Enter thou into the joy of thy Lord"

(Matt. 25:21, 23). John Whitlock noted: "Here is the Christian's way and his end—his way is holiness, his end, happiness."[71]

Holiness is its own reward, for everlasting glory is holiness perfected. "The souls of believers are at their death made perfect in holiness" (*Westminster Shorter Catechism*, Question 37). Also their bodies shall be raised immortal and incorruptible, perfect in holiness and complete in glorification (1 Cor. 15:49, 53). The believer shall finally be what he has desired to become ever since his regeneration—perfectly holy in a triune God. He shall enter into the eternal glory as a son of God and fellow-heir with Jesus Christ (Phil. 3:20-21; Rom. 8:17). He shall finally be like Christ, holy and without blemish (Eph. 5:25-27), eternally magnifying and exalting the unfathomable bounties of God's sovereign grace. Truly, as Calvin stated, "the thought of the great nobility God has conferred upon us ought to whet our desire for holiness."[72]

Concluding Application

I once read of a missionary who had in his garden a shrub that bore poisonous leaves. At that time, he had a child who was prone to put anything within reach into his mouth. Naturally, he dug the shrub out and threw it away. The shrub's roots, however, went very deep. Soon the shrub sprouted again. Repeatedly, the missionary had to dig it out. There was no solution but to inspect the ground every day and to dig up the shrub every time it surfaced. Indwelling sin is like that shrub. It needs constant uprooting. Our hearts need continual mortification. As John Owen warns us:

> We must be exercising [mortification] every day, and in every duty. Sin will not die, unless it be constantly weakened. Spare it, and it will heal its wounds, and recover its strength. We must continually watch against the operations of this principle of sin: in our duties, in our calling, in conversation, in retirement, in our straits, in our enjoyments, and in all that we do. If we are negligent on any occasion, we shall suffer by it; every mistake, every neglect is perilous.[73]

Press on in the uprooting of sin and the cultivation of holiness. Continue to fight the good fight of faith under the best of generals, Jesus Christ; with the best of internal advocates, the Holy Spirit; by the best of assurances, the promises of God; for the best of results, everlasting glory.

Have you been persuaded that cultivating holiness is worth the price of saying "no" to sin and "yes" to God? Do you know the joy of walking in God's ways? The joy of experiencing Jesus' easy yoke and light burden? The joy of not belonging to yourself, but belonging to your "faithful Savior Jesus Christ," who makes you "sincerely willing and ready, henceforth, to live unto Him" (*Heidelberg Catechism*, Question 1)? Are you holy? Thomas Brooks gives us sixteen marks on "how we shall know whether we have real holiness," which include marks like these: The holy believer "admires the holiness of God,... possesses diffusive holiness that spreads itself over head and heart, lip and life, inside and outside,... stretches himself after higher degrees of holiness,... hates and detests all ungodliness and wickedness,... grieves over his own vileness and unholiness."[74] It is a daunting list, yet a biblical one. No doubt we all fall far short, but the question remains: Are we striving for these marks of holiness?

Perhaps you respond, "Who is sufficient for these things" (2 Cor. 2:16)? Paul's ready answer is, "Not that we are sufficient of ourselves to think any thing as of ourselves; but our sufficiency is of God" (2 Cor. 3:5). "Would you be holy?... Then you must *begin with Christ....* Would you continue holy? Then *abide in Christ.*"[75] "Holiness is not the way to Christ; Christ is the way of holiness."[76] Outside of Him, there is no holiness. Then every list of marks of holiness must condemn us to hell. Ultimately, of course, holiness is not a list; it is much more—it is a life, a life in Jesus Christ. Holiness in believers proves that they are joined to Christ, for sanctified obedience is impossible without Him. But in Christ, the call to holiness remains within the context of *sola gratia* (grace alone) and *sola fide* (faith alone).[77] "If thou, LORD, shouldest mark iniquities, O Lord, who shall stand? But there is forgiveness with thee, that thou mayest be feared" (Ps. 130:3-4).

"Since Christ cannot be known apart from the sanctification of the Spirit," Calvin writes, "it follows that faith can in no wise be separated from a devout disposition."[78] Christ, the Holy Spirit, the Word of God, holiness, grace, and faith are inseparable. Make it your prayer: "Lord, grant that I might cultivate holiness today—not out of merit, but out of gratitude, by Thy grace through faith in Christ Jesus. Sanctify me by the blood of Christ, the Spirit of Christ, and the Word of God." Pray with Robert Murray M'Cheyne, "Lord, make me as holy as a pardoned sinner can be."[79]

---

[1] *The Marrow of Theology*, trans. and ed. John D. Eusden (1629; Boston: Pilgrim Press, 1968), 77.

[2] Jerry Bridges, *The Pursuit of Holiness* (Colorado Springs: Navpress, 1978), 13-14.

[3] This is apparent from the Dutch word for sanctification, *heiligmaking* (literally: "holy-making").

[4] Cf. Lawrence O. Richards, *Expository Dictionary of Bible Words* (Grand Rapids: Zondervan, 1985), 339-40.

[5] See especially Rudolf Otto, *The Idea of the Holy*, trans. J. W. Harvey (London: Oxford University Press, 1946).

[6] Stephen Charnock, *The Existence and Attributes of God* (repr. Evansville, Ind.: Sovereign Grace, 1958), 449.

[7] *The Works of the Rev. John Howe* (1848; repr. Ligonier, Pa.: Soli Deo Gloria, 1990), 2:59.

[8] *The Works of Jonathan Edwards* (1834; repr. Edinburgh: Banner of Truth Trust, 1974), 1:101; cf. R. C. Sproul, *The Holiness of God* (Wheaton, Ill.: Tyndale House, 1985).

[9] R. A. Finlayson, *The Holiness of God* (Glasgow: Pickering and Inglis, 1955), 4.

[10] *The Psalter* (Grand Rapids: Eerdmans, 1991), 136.

[11] Stephen C. Neill, *Christian Holiness* (Guildford, England: Lutterworth, 1960), 35.

[12] Horatius Bonar, *God's Way of Holiness* (repr. Pensacola, Fla.: Mt. Zion Publications, 1994), 16.

[13] Quoted in Donald G. Bloesch, *Essentials of Evangelical Theology* (New York: Harper & Row, 1979), 2:31.

[14] Quoted in John Blanchard, *Gathered Gold* (Welwyn, England: Evangelical Press, 1984), 144.

[15] Cf. George Bethune, *The Fruit of the Spirit* (1839; repr. Swengel, Pa.: Reiner, 1972); W. E. Sangster, *The Pure in Heart: A Study of Christian Sanctity* (London: Epworth Press, 1954); John W. Sanderson, *The Fruit of the Spirit* (Grand Rapids: Zondervan, 1972); Jerry Bridges, *The Practice of Holiness* (Colorado Springs: NavPress, 1983); Roger Roberts, *Holiness: Every Christian's Calling* (Nashville: Broadman Press, 1985).

[16] Cf. *Heidelberg Catechism*, Question 1 (the believer's status) and Question 114 (the believer's condition).

[17] A. W. Pink, *The Doctrine of Sanctification* (Swengel, Pa.: Bible Truth Depot, 1955), 25.

[18] Charnock, *The Existence and Attributes of God*, 453.

[19] Aurelius Augustine, *Against Two Letters of the Pelagians*, 3.5.14, in *A Select Library of the Nicene and Post-Nicene Fathers*, first series, ed. P. Schaff (repr. Grand Rapids: Eerdmans, 1982), 5:404.

[20] John Calvin, *Institutes of the Christian Relgion*, ed. John T. McNeill, trans. Ford Lewis Battles (Philadelphia: Westminster Press, 1960), 3.14.4ff.; cf. Thomas Goodwin, *The Works of Thomas Goodwin*, ed. John C. Miller (Edinburgh: James Nichol, 1864), 6:220.

[21] Quoted in John Blanchard, *More Gathered Gold* (Welwyn, England: Evangelical Press, 1986), 147.

[22] Thomas Watson, *A Body of Divinity* (1856; repr. Grand Rapids: Sovereign Grace Publishers, 1970), 173.

[23] Bridges, *Practice of Holiness*, 52.

[24] Robert Bruce, *The Mystery of the Lord's Supper*, trans. and ed. Thomas F. Torrance (Richmond: John Knox Press, 1958), 82.

[25] Quoted in Joel R. Beeke, *Holiness: God's Call to Sanctification* (Edinburgh: Banner of Truth Trust, 1994), 18-19.

[26] D. Martyn Lloyd-Jones, *Romans: An Exposition of Chapter 6—The New Man* (Edinburgh: Banner of Truth Trust, 1972), 144.

[27] Bridges, *Pursuit of Holiness*, 60.

[28] James I. Packer, *Rediscovering Holiness* (Ann Arbor: Servant, 1992), 15.

[29] Cf. Jay Adams, *Godliness Through Discipline* (Grand Rapids: Baker, 1973), 3.

[30] Dietrich Bonhoeffer, *The Cost of Discipleship*, trans. R. H. Fuller (London: SCM Press, 1959).

[31] Bridges, *Practice of Holiness*, 41-56.

[32] *The Psalter*, 126.

[33] For Edwards's seventy resolutions to promote holiness made at nineteen years of age, see *The Works of Jonathan Edwards*, 1:xx-xxii.

[34] *Luther: Lectures on Romans*, trans. and ed. William Pauck (Philadelphia: Westminster Press, 1961), 189.

[35] Owen, *Works*, 6:20.

[36] Quoted in I. D. E. Thomas, *The Golden Treasury of Puritan Quotations* (Chicago: Moody Press, 1975), 140.

[37] See *Belgic Confession of Faith*, Article 28.

[38] Thomas Watson, *The Mischief of Sin* (1671; Pittsburgh: Soli Deo Gloria, 1994); Jeremiah Burroughs, *The Evil of Evils; or The Exceeding Sinfulness of Sin* (1654; Pittsburgh: Soli Deo Gloria, 1992).

[39] John Charles Ryle, *Holiness: Its Nature, Hindrances, Difficulties, and Roots* (repr. Greensboro, N.C.: Homiletic Press, 1956); Octavius Winslow, *Personal Declension and Revival of Religion in the Soul* (1841; repr. London: Banner of Truth Trust, 1960).

[40] Blanchard, *Gathered Gold*, 144.

[41] "The Spiritual and Carnal Man Compared and Contrasted; or, The Absolute Necessity and Excellency of Holiness," *The Select Practical Works of Richard Baxter* (Glasgow: Blackie & Son, 1840), 115-291.

[42] Blanchard, *More Gathered Gold*, 149.

[43] Watson, *A Body of Divinity*, 172.

[44] Owen, *Works*, 11:254ff.; Joel R. Beeke, *Jehovah Shepherding His Sheep* (Grand Rapids: Reformation Heritage Books, 1997), 186-88.

[45] B. B. Warfield, *Perfectionism* (Phillipsburg, N.J.: Presbyterian and Reformed, 1958), 100.

[46] Cf. Walter Marshall, *The Gospel Mystery of Sanctification* (repr. Grand Rapids: Reformation Heritage Books, 2000), 220-221.

[47] Ryle, *Holiness*, 27.

[48] Joel R. Beeke, *Assurance of Faith: Calvin, English Puritanism, and the Dutch Second Reformation* (New York: Peter Lang, 1991), 160ff.; cf. *Westminster Confession*, Chapter 18, and the *Canons of Dort*, Head 5, for an appreciation of the intertwining of holiness and assurance.

[49] Cf. Bonar, *God's Way of Holiness*, chapter 2.

[50] Watson, *A Body of Divinity*, 167.

[51] Ryle, *Holiness*, 62.

[52] Leonard J. Coppes, *Are Five Points Enough? Ten Points of Calvinism* (Manassas, Va.: Reformation Educational Foundation, 1980), 94-96.

[53] Hugh D. Morgan, *The Holiness of God and of His People* (Bridgend, Wales: Evangelical Press of Wales, 1979), 9.

[54] Andrew Murray, *Humility: The Beauty of Holiness* (Old Tappan, N.J.: Revell, n.d), 40.

[55] Thomas, *Puritan Quotations*, 141.

[56] William S. Plumer, *Psalms* (1867; repr. Edinburgh: Banner of Truth Trust, 1975), 557.

57 Ryle, *Holiness*, 1-2.

58 John Brown, *Expository Discourses on 1 Peter* (1848; repr. Edinburgh: Banner of Truth Trust, 1978), 1:106.

59 Ryle, *Holiness*, viii.

60 Sinclair Ferguson, "The Reformed View," in *Christian Spirituality: Five Views of Sanctification*, ed. Donald L. Alexander (Downers Grove, Ill.: InterVarsity Press, 1988), 64.

61 Owen, *Works*, 6:79.

62 Blanchard, *More Gathered Gold*, 152.

63 Ibid., 149.

64 Peter Toon, *Justification and Sanctification* (Westchester, Ill.: Crossway, 1983), p. 40.

65 Blanchard, *More Gathered Gold*, 148.

66 John Murray, *Redemption Accomplished and Applied* (Grand Rapids: Eerdmans, 1955), 184-85.

67 Kenneth Prior, *The Way of Holiness: A Study in Christian Growth* (Downers Grove, Ill.: InterVarsity Press, 1982), 42.

68 Cf. G. C. Berkouwer, *Faith and Sanctification*, trans. John Vriend (Grand Rapids: Eerdmans, 1952), chapter 6.

69 John Stott, *The Baptism and Fullness of the Holy Spirit*, 2nd ed. (Downers Grove, Ill.: InterVarsity Press, 1975), 50.

70 Samuel Rutherford, *The Trial and Triumph of Faith* (Edinburgh: William Collins, 1845), 403.

71 Thomas, *Puritan Quotations*, 140.

72 Blanchard, *More Gathered Gold*, 153.

73 Owen, *Works*, 3:310.

74 "The Crown and Glory of Christianity: or Holiness, The Only Way to Happiness," in *The Works of Thomas Brooks* (1864; repr. Edinburgh: Banner of Truth Trust, 1980), 4:103-150. I have summarized Brooks's marks. His entire treatise on holiness (446 pages) is an invaluable classic, but has been strangely neglected in contemporary studies on holiness.

75 Ryle, *Holiness*, 71-72.

76 Blanchard, *Gathered Gold*, 146.

77 Cf. Berkouwer, *Faith and Sanctification*, chapter 2.

78 *Institutes*, 3.2.8.

79 Blanchard, *Gathered Gold*, 146.

The Lasting Power of Reformed Experiential Preaching

While I was on active duty in the U.S. Army Reserves, a big, black sergeant laid his hand on my shoulder one day and said, "Son, if you ever have to go to war, there are three things you must remember in battle: what tactics you need to use, how the fight is going (which is usually very different from how it ought to go), and what the goal of the battle is."

That sergeant gave me an experiential approach to fighting. His three points also provide insight into how experiential religion and preaching ought to go. There are five questions I would like to consider as we address the important subject of Reformed experiential preaching:

- What is experiential religion and preaching?
- Why is the experiential aspect of preaching necessary?
- What are the essential characteristics of experiential preaching?
- Why must a minister be experientially prepared for the ministry?
- What practical lessons on Christian living can we learn from the experiential preaching of our predecessors?

The Definition of Experiential Religion and Preaching

The term *experimental* comes from the Latin *experimentum*, meaning trial. It is derived from the verb *experior*, meaning to try, prove, or put to the test. That same verb can also mean to find or know by experience, thus leading to the word *experientia*, meaning knowledge gained by experiment. John Calvin used experiential and experimental interchangeably, since both words in biblical preaching indicate the need for measuring experienced knowledge against the touchstone of Scripture.

Experiential or experimental preaching addresses the vital matter of how a Christian experiences the truth of biblical, Christian doctrine in his life. A working definition of experimental preaching might be: Experimental preaching seeks to explain in terms of biblical truth how matters ought to go, how they do go, and what the goal is of the Christian life. It aims to apply divine truth to the whole range of the believer's personal experience, including his relationships with family, the church, and the world around him.

Paul Helm wrote about such preaching: "The situation [today] calls for preaching that will cover the full range of Christian experience, and a developed experimental theology. The preaching must give guidance and instruction to Christians in terms of their actual experience. It must not deal in unrealities or treat congregations as if they lived in a different century or in wholly different circumstances. This involves taking the full measure of our modern situation and entering with full sympathy into the actual experiences, the hopes and fears, of Christian people."[1]

Experimental preaching is discriminatory preaching, meaning that it clearly defines the difference between a Christian and non-Christian, opening the kingdom of heaven to one and shutting it against the other. Discriminatory preaching offers the forgiveness of sins and eternal life to all who by a true faith embrace Christ as Savior and Lord, but it also proclaims the wrath of God and His eternal condemnation upon those who are unbelieving, unrepentant, and unconverted. Such preaching teaches that unless our religion is experiential, we will perish, not because experience itself saves, but because the Christ who saves sinners must be experienced personally as the foundation upon which our eternal hope is built (Matt. 7:22-27; 1 Cor. 1:30; 2:2).

Experimental preaching is applicatory. It applies the text to every aspect of a listener's life, promoting a religion that is truly a power and not mere form (2 Tim. 3:5). Robert Burns defined such religion as "Christianity brought home to men's business and bosoms" and said the principle on which it rests is "that Christianity should not only be known, and understood, and believed, but also felt, and enjoyed, and practically applied."[2]

Experiential preaching, then, teaches that the Christian faith must be experienced, tasted, and lived through the saving power of the Holy Spirit. It stresses the knowledge of scriptural truth "which is able to make us wise unto salvation through faith in Christ Jesus" (2 Tim. 3:15). Specifically, such preaching teaches that Christ, the living Word (John. 1:1) and the very embodiment of the truth, must be experientially known and embraced. It proclaims the need for sinners to experience who God is in His Son. As John 17:3 says, "And this is life eternal, that they might know thee the only true God, and Jesus Christ, whom thou hast sent." The word *know* in this text, as well as other biblical usages, does not indicate casual acquaintance but a deep, abiding relationship. For example, Genesis 4:1 uses the word *know* to suggest marital intimacy: "And Adam knew Eve his wife; and she conceived, and bare Cain." Experiential preaching stresses the intimate, personal knowledge of God in Christ.

Such knowledge is never divorced from Scripture. According to Isaiah 8:20, all of our beliefs, including our experiences, must be tested against Holy Scripture. "If I can't find my experiences back in the Bible, they are not from the Lord but from the devil," Martin Luther once said. That is really what the word *experimental*, derived from experiment, intends to convey. Just as scientific experiment means testing a hypothesis against a body of evidence, so experimental preaching involves examining experience in the light of the teaching of the Word of God.

Reformed experimental preaching grounded in the Word of God is theocentric rather than anthropocentric. Some people accuse the Puritans of being man-centered in their passion for godly experience. But as J. I. Packer argues, the Puritans were not interested in tracing the experience of the Spirit's work in their souls to promote their own experience but to be driven out of themselves into Christ, in whom they could then enter into fellowship with the Triune God.

This passion for fellowship with the Triune God means that experimental preaching not only addresses the believer's conscience but also his relationship with others in the church and the world. If experimental preaching led me only to examine my experiences and my relationship with God, it would fall short of affecting my interaction with family, church members, and society. It would remain self-centered. Instead, true experimental preaching brings a believer into the realm of vital Christian experience, prompting a love for God and His glory as well as a burning passion to declare that love to others around him. A believer so instructed cannot help but be evangelistic since vital experience and a heart for missions are inseparable.

In sum, Reformed experimental preaching addresses the entire range of Christian living. With the Spirit's blessing, its mission is to transform the believer in all that he is and does so that he becomes more and more like the Savior.

Until early in the 19th century many Reformed ministers preached experimentally. Francis Wayland wrote in 1857 in his *Notes on the Principles and Practices of the Baptist Churches*:

> From the manner in which our ministers entered upon the work, it is evident that it must have been the prominent object of their lives to convert men to God. They were remarkable for what was called experimental preaching. They told much of the exercises of the human soul

under the influence of the truth of the gospel. The feeling of a sinner while under the convicting power of the truth; the various subterfuges to which he resorted when aware of his danger; the successive applications of truth by which he was driven out of all of them; the despair of the soul when it found itself wholly without a refuge; its final submission to God, and simple reliance on Christ; the joys of the new birth and the earnestness of the soul to introduce others to the happiness which it has now for the first time experienced; the trials of the soul when it found itself an object of reproach and persecution among those whom it loved best; the process of sanctification; the devices of Satan to lead us into sin; the mode in which the attacks of the adversary may be resisted; the danger of backsliding, with its evidences, and the means of recovery from it.... These remarks show the tendency of the class of preachers which seem now to be passing away.[3]

How different experiential preaching is from what we often hear today. The Word of God is preached too often in a way that will not transform listeners because it fails to discriminate and fails to apply. Such preaching is reduced to a lecture, a demonstration, a catering to what people want to hear, or the kind of subjectivism that is divorced from the foundation of Scripture. It fails to biblically explain what the Reformed called vital religion: how a sinner must be stripped of his righteousness, driven to Christ alone for salvation, and led to the joy of simple reliance upon Christ. It fails to show how a sinner encounters the plague of indwelling sin, battles against backsliding, and gains victory by faith in Christ.

By contrast, when God's Word is preached experimentally, it is "the power of God unto salvation" (Rom. 1:16) that transforms men and nations. Such preaching proclaims from the gates of hell, as it were, that those who are not born again will walk through those gates to dwell there eternally unless they repent (Luke 13:1-9). And such preaching proclaims from the gates of heaven that those who by God's grace persevere in holiness will walk through those gates into eternal glory, where they will dwell in unceasing communion with the Triune God.

Such preaching is transforming because it accurately reflects the vital experience of the children of God (cf. Rom. 5:1-11), clearly explains the marks and fruits of the saving grace necessary for a believer (Matt. 5:3-12; Gal. 5:22-23), and sets before believer and unbeliever alike their eternal futures (Rev. 21:1-9).

The Necessity of Experimental Preaching

Preaching today must be experiential for the following reasons:

1. *Scripture commands it.* Preaching is rooted in grammatical and historical exegesis, but also involves spiritual, practical, and experimental application. In 1 Corinthians 2:10-16, Paul says that good exegesis is spiritual. Since the Spirit always testifies of Jesus Christ, sound exegesis finds Christ not only in the new covenant but also in the old. As all roads in the ancient world once led to Rome, so the preaching of all texts today must ultimately lead to Christ. Jesus Himself said, "Search the scriptures; for in them ye think ye have eternal life: and they are they which testify of me" (John 5:39). Likewise, when He spoke with the travelers to Emmaus, Jesus said, "These are the words which I spake unto you, while I was yet with you, that all things must be fulfilled, which were written in the law of Moses, and in the prophets, and in the psalms, concerning me" (Luke 24:44-45). Spiritual exegesis is thus Christological exegesis, and, through Christ, it will be theological exegesis, bringing all glory to the Triune God.

Exegesis offers sound analysis of the words, grammar, syntax, and historical setting of Scripture. Experiential preaching does not minimize these aspects of interpretation, but neither is it content with them. Words, grammar, syntax, and historical setting serve God in exegeting the Word of God, but they are not enough.

Preaching is not exposition alone. A minister who only presents the grammatical and historical meaning of God's Word may be lecturing or discoursing, but he is not preaching. The Word must also be applied. This application is an essential characteristic of Reformed preaching. Without it, vitality is quenched.

Jesus shows us how to preach experientially in the Sermon on the Mount. He begins the sermon by describing the true citizens of the kingdom of heaven through the beatitudes, which also are a beautiful summary of the Christian experience. The first three beatitudes (spiritual poverty, mourning, and meekness) focus on the inward disposition of the believer, the fourth (hungering and thirsting after righteousness) reveals the heartbeat of experiential faith, and the last four (merciful, pure in heart, peacemakers, persecuted) show faith in the midst of the world. The beatitudes thus reveal the marks of genuine piety. The remainder of Jesus' sermon shows the fruits of grace in a believer's life.

2. *True religion is more than notion.* Because true religion is experimental, preaching must relate to the vital experience of the children of God. Consider the experience of affliction. Romans 5:3-5 says, "We glory in tribulations also: knowing that tribulation worketh patience; and

patience, experience; and experience, hope: and hope maketh not ashamed." In this passage, Paul regards experience as an important link to the blessings that flow out of sanctified affliction.

Paul's epistles are filled with experiential truth. Romans 7, for example, shows that human depravity forces a believer to groan, "Oh wretched man that I am!" and Romans 8 leads a believer to the heights of divine riches in Christ, revealed by the Spirit in all its comfort and glory. Paul concludes by saying that nothing we experience in this life can separate believers from the love of God in Christ Jesus.

Experiential preaching shows the comfort of the living church and the glory of God. How could a minister preach the opening words of Isaiah 40 without an experiential emphasis? "Comfort ye, comfort ye my people, saith your God. Speak ye comfortably to Jerusalem, and cry unto her, that her warfare is accomplished, that her iniquity is pardoned: for she hath received of the Lord's hand double for all her sins" (vv. 1-2). An unexperiential sermon fails to offer life and power and comfort to the believer. It also fails to glorify God as Isaiah so eloquently does in the remainder of the chapter.

3. *Without such preaching, we will everlastingly perish.* Experience itself does not save. We cannot have faith in our experience or faith in our faith. Our faith is in Christ alone, but that faith is experiential. Unless we build on the Rock of Christ Jesus (Matt. 7:22-27), our house of hope will crash. Some preachers may not know what it means personally, vitally, and experientially to build upon that Rock. Yet if they are to lead others to Christ, they above all must understand experientially what Paul declares in 1 Corinthians: "But of him [God the Father] are ye in Christ Jesus, who of God is made unto us wisdom, and righteousness, and sanctification, and redemption.... For I determined not to know any thing among you, save Jesus Christ, and him crucified" (1:30; 2:2).

The Characteristics of Experiential Preaching
Experiential preaching includes the following characteristics:

1. *God's Word is central in it.* Preaching flows out of the scriptural passage by expounding it in accord with sound exegetical and hermeneutical principles. As Jeremiah 3:15 says, God has given preachers to His church to "feed them with knowledge and understanding." Proper preaching does not add an experiential part to the text being preached; rather, with the Spirit's light, it draws the true experience of believers from the text. The minister must bring the sincere milk of the Word in

John Knox preaching.

order that, by the Spirit's blessing, experiential preaching will foster true growth (1 Pet. 2:2; Rom. 10:14).

Centering on the Word preserves experiential preaching from unbiblical mysticism. Mysticism separates experience from the Word of God, whereas historic Reformed conviction demands Word-centered, God-glorifying, Spirit-wrought experiential Christianity. That kind of preaching is essential to the health and prosperity of the church. As Calvin says, God begets and multiplies His church only by means of His Word (James 1:18).

2. *It is discerning.* A faithful minister rightly divides the Word of truth to separate the precious from the vile (Jer. 15:19), emphasizing law and gospel as well as death in Adam and life in Christ for that purpose. Grace is to be offered indiscriminately to all (Matt. 13:24-30); however, the divine acts, marks, and fruits of grace that God works in His people must be explained to encourage the elect and uncover the false hopes of the hypocrite.

Biblical experiential preaching stresses what God does in, for, and through His elect. As Philippians 2:13 says, "For it is God which worketh in you both to will and to do of his good pleasure." Expounding the divine acts, marks, and fruits of grace is critical in our day when so much passes for genuine Christianity that is man-glorifying. We must preach about the fruits of grace that distinguish true belief from counterfeit Christianity. We must be obedient to 2 Corinthians 13:5, which says, "Examine yourselves, whether ye be in the faith; prove your own selves," as well as to James 2:17, which says, "Faith, if it hath not works, is dead, being alone."

3. *It explains how things go in the lives of God's people and how they ought to go* (Rom. 7-8). Telling how matters go without indicating how they should go lulls the believer into ceasing from pressing on in his spiritual pilgrimage. He will not press forward to grow in the grace and knowledge of Christ (2 Pet. 3:18). Only telling how matters should be rather than how they really are discourages the believer from being assured that the Lord has ever worked in his heart. He may fear that the marks and fruits of grace are too high for him to claim. The true believer thus needs to hear both: he must be encouraged in spite of all his infirmities not to despair for Christ's sake (Heb. 4:15). He must also be warned against assuming that he has reached the end of his spiritual pilgrimage and be urged to "press toward the mark for the prize of the high calling of God in Christ Jesus" (Phil. 3:14).

Every Christian is a soldier. To win the war against evil, a believer must put on the whole armor of God (Eph. 6:10-20). Experiential preaching brings the believer to the battlefield, shows him how to fight, tells him how to win skirmishes, and reminds him of the victory that awaits him in which God will receive the glory. "For of him, and through him, and to him, are all things: to whom be glory for ever. Amen" (Rom. 11:36).

4. It stresses inward knowledge. The old divines were fond of stressing the difference between head knowledge and heart knowledge in Christian faith. Head knowledge is not enough for true religion; it also demands heart knowledge. "Keep thy heart with all diligence; for out of it are the issues of life," says Proverbs 4:23. Romans 10:10 adds, "For with the heart man believeth unto righteousness."

To illustrate, consider the minister who went to a Christian bookstore where a book he had written was being sold. The storekeeper asked the minister whether he knew the book's author. When the man said yes, the storekeeper said that he also was acquainted with the author. The minister disputed that; the storekeeper looked puzzled and asked why he was being questioned. The minister replied, "Sir, if you knew the author, you would have greeted me as such when I entered your store!"

The storekeeper's acquaintance with the author was mere head knowledge. Despite his claims, he did not truly know the author; he did not even recognize the man when he met him. His knowledge of the author was not experiential; it was not the fruit of personal communion with the author. It lacked the kind of heart knowledge that would have made it authentic.

Heart knowledge of God in Christ results from a personal, experiential encounter with Christ through the wondrous work of the Spirit. Such knowledge transforms the heart and bears heavenly fruit. It savors the Lord and delights in Him (Job 34:9; Ps. 34:7; Isa. 58:14). It tastes and sees that God in Christ loves lost, depraved, hell-worthy sinners (Ps. 34:8). Heart knowledge includes an appetite for tasting and digesting God's truth. As Jeremiah says, "Thy words were found, and I did eat them; and thy word was unto me the joy and rejoicing of mine heart" (Jer. 15:16). Heart knowledge feasts on God, His Word, His truth, and His Son (Ps. 144:15; 146:5).

Heart knowledge does not lack head knowledge, but head knowledge may lack heart knowledge (Rom. 10:8-21). Some people pursue religion as an objective study or to appease their conscience without ever allowing it to penetrate their heart. They have never felt guilty and condemned before the holy justice of God. They have not experienced deliverance in Christ, so they are unaware of the kind of gratitude for such deliverance that masters a believer's soul, mind, and strength. By contrast, those who experience saving heart knowledge find sin such an unbearable burden that Christ is altogether necessary. The grace of deliverance through the Savior is then so overwhelming that their lives shine forth with gratitude.

Head knowledge is not evil in and of itself. Most of our Reformed and Puritan forefathers were highly educated; they never tired of stressing the value of Christian education. But this education must be empowered by the Holy Spirit and applied to the heart. Head knowledge is insufficient without the Spirit's application to the inward man.

5. *It must be centered in Jesus Christ* (John 1:29, 36). According to 1 Corinthians 2:2, a true preacher must be "determined not to know anything... save Jesus Christ, and him crucified." Or, as William Perkins once said, the heart of all preaching is "to preach one Christ, by Christ, to the praise of Christ."[4]

Christ must be the beginning, middle, and end of every sermon (Isa. 61:1-3; 1 John 1:1-4). Preaching must exalt Christ for awakening, justifying, sanctifying, and comforting sinners (Eph. 5:4; 1 Cor. 1:30; Isa. 61:2). As John says, "In him was life; and the life was the light of men.... The word was made flesh, and dwelt among us, (and we beheld his glory, the glory as of the only begotten of the Father), full of grace and truth" (John 1:4, 14; cf. Ps. 36:9; Eph. 5:1-2).

Experiential preaching must stress what Rowland Hill calls the "three Rs" of preaching: Ruin by the fall, Righteousness by Christ, and Regeneration by the Spirit. Experience does not save the sinner, but Christ saves in an experiential way (Phil. 1:6). Christ is the divine fulcrum upon which genuine experience pivots.

Experiential preaching teaches that a Christian must not be separated from Christ. Though conviction of sin cannot save us, it is nonetheless critical. Under the Spirit's tutelage, conviction of sin and misery lead us to the Savior, where we cry out, "Give me Jesus else I die." As Martin Luther once said, "Being saved is going lost at Jesus' feet."

6. *Its aim is to glorify the Triune God:* the Father's eternal love and good pleasure, Christ's redemptive and mediatorial work, and the Spirit's sanctifying and preserving ministry. The minister's goal in preaching is

Covenanters worshipping in the open field.

to help people fall in love with each person of the Trinity. As Samuel Rutherford said, "I know not which divine person I love the most, but this I know, I need and love each of them."

Experiential preaching stresses the God-centered nature of each benefit of salvation: internal calling, regeneration, faith, justification, sanctification, and perseverance. It differentiates between what is of man and what is of God. It exalts what is of God and abases what is of man (John 3:30).

Let us seek grace daily to experience the saving work of the Triune God. We can offer no better petition than the simple prayer of Moses, "Show me now thy way, that I may know thee" (Ex. 33:13). As Sukey Harley prayed, "Lord, make me to know myself; make me to know Thyself." Knowing the Triune God is the marrow of genuine Christian experience (cf. Jer. 9:23-24; John17:3).

Preparation for the Ministry

It is impossible to separate godly, experiential living from true experiential ministry. The sanctification of a minister's heart is not merely ideal; it is absolutely necessary both personally and for his calling as a minister of the gospel.

Scripture says there should be no disparity between the heart, character, and life of a man who is called to proclaim God's Word and the content of his message. "Take heed unto thyself, and unto the doctrine; continue in them: for in doing this thou shalt both save thyself, and them that hear thee" (1 Tim. 4:16).

Jesus condemned the Pharisees and scribes for not doing what they proclaimed. He faulted them for the difference that existed between their words and deeds, between what they professionally proclaimed and how they acted in their daily life. Professional clerics, more than anyone else, should consider the scathing words of Christ: "The scribes and the Pharisees sit in Moses' seat. All therefore whatsoever they bid you observe, that observe and do; but do not ye after their works: for they say, and do not" (Matt. 23:2-3). As ministers, we are called to be as holy in our private relationship with God, in our role as husbands and fathers at home, and as shepherds among our people as we appear to be in the pulpit. There must be no disjunction between our calling and our living, our confession and our practice.

Scripture says there is a cause-and-effect relationship between the character of a man's life as a Christian and his fruitfulness as a minister (Matt. 7:17-20). A minister's work is usually blessed in proportion to the sanctification of his heart before God. Ministers must therefore seek grace to build the house of God with sound experiential preaching and doctrine as well as with a sanctified life. Our preaching must shape our life, and our life must adorn our preaching. As John Boys wrote, "He doth preach most who doth live best."

We must be what we preach, not only applying ourselves to our texts but applying our texts to ourselves. Our hearts must be transcripts of our sermons.[5] Otherwise, as John Owen warned, "If a man teach uprightly and walk crookedly, more will fall down in the night of his life than he built in the day of his doctrine."

Lessons from the Experiential Preachers

The old experimental preachers were masters at applying truth to their own hearts as well as to those of others. Here are some lessons from the divines that will serve us well today.

1. *Live close to God.* You can't fake Reformed, experiential living anymore than you can fake Reformed, experiential preaching. As people see through ministers who don't live up to what they preach, so we must live close to God in order to show others that Christianity is real and experiential. For our words and actions to convey godly piety, our very

thoughts must pulsate with that piety which only flows out of a close life with God. As a man thinketh, so is he.

2. *Pursue godliness in dependence on the Holy Spirit.* The way to godly living is surprisingly simple: We are to walk with God in His appointed way (Mic. 6:8), diligently using the means of grace and the spiritual disciplines, and waiting on the Holy Spirit for blessing. Note that godly living involves both discipline and grace. This emphasis on duty and grace is fundamental to Reformed, experiential perspective on godly living. [6] As John Flavel wrote, "The duty is ours, though the power be God's. A natural man has no power, a gracious man hath some, though not sufficient; and that power he hath depends upon the assisting strength of Christ."[7]

Likewise, John Owen wrote, "It is the Holy Ghost who is the immediate peculiar sanctifier of all believers, and the author of all holiness in them." The Spirit supplies what we lack so that we may press toward the mark of holiness, enabling us as believers to "yield obedience to God… by virtue of the life and death of Jesus Christ."[8]

The believer then is empowered, as Flavel said, with "a diligent and constant use and improvement of all holy means and duties, to preserve the soul from sin, and maintain its sweet and free communion with God."[9] We can also be encouraged by Owen's advice: "If thou meanest to enlarge thy religion, do it rather by enlarging thy ordinary devotions than thy extraordinary."

Reformed experiential preachers frequently advised listeners to exercise spiritual disciplines that would promote experiential and practical Christian living. Specifically, they advised to:

• *Read Scripture diligently and meditatively* (1 Tim. 4:13). Richard Greenham said that we ought to read our Bibles with more diligence than men dig for hidden treasure. Diligence makes the rough places plain, the difficult easy, and the unsavory tasty.[10]

After reading Scripture, we must ask God for light to scrutinize our hearts and lives, then meditate upon the Word. Disciplined meditation on Scripture helps us focus on God. Meditation helps us view worship as a discipline. It involves our mind and understanding as well as our heart and affections; it works Scripture through the texture of the soul. Meditation helps prevent vain and sinful thoughts (Matt. 12:35) and provides inner resources on which to draw (Ps. 77:10-12), including direction for daily life (Prov. 6:21-22). It fights temptation (Ps. 119:11,

15), provides relief in afflictions (Isa. 49:15-17), benefits others (Ps. 145:7), and glorifies God (Ps. 49:3).

• *Pray without ceasing.* We must sustain the habit of secret prayer if we are to live experientially before God. The only way to learn the art of holy argument with God is to pray. Prayer helps us cling to the altar of God's promises by which we lay hold of God Himself.

Failing to pray is the downfall of many Christians today. "A family without prayer is like a house without a roof, open and exposed to all the storms of heaven," wrote Thomas Brooks. If the giants of church history dwarf us today, perhaps it is not because they were more educated, more devout, or more faithful as much as because they were men of prayer. They were possessed with the Spirit of supplication. They were Daniels in the temple of God.

Let us cling to the refuge of the inner prayer chamber, for there experiential Christianity is either established or broken. Let us refuse to be content with the shell of religion without the inner core of prayer. When we grow drowsy in prayer, let us pray aloud, or write down our prayers, or find a quiet place outside to walk and pray. Above all, let us continue to pray.

We should not give up regular times of prayer, but we should also be open at the slightest impulse to pray. Conversing with God through Christ is our most effective antidote to spiritual backsliding and discouragement. Discouragement without prayer is an open sore ripe for infection, whereas discouragement with prayer is a sore lifted to the balm of Gilead.

Keep prayer a priority in your personal and family life. As John Bunyan said, "You can do more than pray after you have prayed, but you cannot do more than pray until you have prayed…. Pray often, for prayer is a shield to the soul, a sacrifice to God, and a scourge to Satan."[11]

• *Study Reformed experiential literature.* Books that promote godly living are a powerful aid to experiential living. Read the spiritual classics, inviting great writers to be your spiritual mentors and friends. The Puritans excel in such writing. "There must scarcely be a sermon, a treatise, a pamphlet, a diary, a history, or a biography from a Puritan pen, which was not in one way or another aimed at fostering the spiritual life," said Maurice Roberts.[12]

Read sound experiential books on various topics to meet a variety of needs. To foster experiential living by remaining sensitized to sin, read

Ralph Venning's *The Plague of Plagues*. To be drawn closer to Christ, read Isaac Ambrose's *Looking Unto Jesus*. To find peace in affliction, read Samuel Rutherford's *Letters*. To gain relief from temptation, read John Owen's *Temptation and Sin*. To grow in holiness, read John Flavel's *Keeping the Heart*.

Read as an act of worship. Read to be elevated into the great truths of God so that you may worship the Trinity in Spirit and in truth. Be selective about what you read, however. Measure all your reading against the touchstone of Scripture. So much of today's Christian literature is froth, riddled with Arminian theology or secular thinking. Time is too precious to waste on nonsense. Read more for eternity than time, more for spiritual growth than professional advancement. Think of John Trapp's warning: "As water tastes of the soil it runs through, so does the soul taste of the authors that a man reads."

Before picking up a book, ask yourself: Would Christ approve of this book? Will it increase my love for the Word of God, help me to conquer sin, offer abiding wisdom, and prepare me for the life to come? Or could I better spend time reading another book?

Speak to others about the good books that you read. Conversation about experiential reading promotes experiential living.

• *Keep a journal.* Keeping a thoughtful record of your spiritual journey can promote godliness. It can help us in our meditation and prayer. It can remind us of the Lord's faithfulness and work. It can help us understand and evaluate ourselves. It can help us monitor our goals and priorities, as well as maintain other spiritual disciplines.[13]

• *Keep the Lord's Day holy.* We ought to view the Sabbath as a joyful privilege, not as a tedious burden. This is the day on which we may worship God and practice spiritual disciplines without interruption. As J. I. Packer says, "We are to rest from the business of our earthly calling in order to prosecute the business of our heavenly calling."[14]

• *Serve others and tell them about Christ.* Jesus expects us to evangelize and serve others (Matt. 28:19-20; Heb. 9:14). We are to do so out of obedience (Deut. 13:4), gratitude (1 Sam. 12:24), gladness (Ps. 100:2), humility (John 13:15-16), and love (Gal. 5:13). Serving others may be difficult at times, but we are called to do so, using every spiritual gift that God has granted us (cf. Rom. 12:4-8; 1 Cor. 12:6-11; Eph. 4:7-13). One of our greatest rewards as Christians is to serve people. If it allows us to see them drawing closer to Christ through the Spirit's blessing upon God's

Word and our efforts, what more could we possibly ask for? It is a profoundly humbling experience that can only draw us closer to God.

3. *Aim for balanced thinking*. The great Reformed experiential preachers aimed for balance in Christian living in three important ways:

• *Between the objective and subjective dimensions of Christianity*. The objective is the food for the subjective; thus the subjective is always rooted in the objective. For example, the Puritans stated that the primary ground of assurance is rooted in the promises of God, but those promises must become increasingly real to the believer through the subjective evidences of grace and the internal witness of the Holy Spirit. Without the Spirit's application, the promises of God lead to self-deceit and carnal presumption. On the other hand, without the promises of God and the illumination of the Spirit, self-examination tends to introspection, bondage, and legalism. Objective and subjective Christianity must not be separated from each other.

We must seek to live in a way that reveals Christ's internal presence based on His objective work of active and passive obedience. The gospel of Christ must be proclaimed as objective truth, but it must also be applied by the Holy Spirit and inwardly appropriated by faith. We therefore reject two kinds of religion: one that separates subjective experience from the the objective Word, thereby leading to mysticism; and one that presumes salvation on the false grounds of historical or temporary faith.[15]

• *Between the sovereignty of God and the responsibility of man*. Nearly all of our Reformed forefathers stressed that God is fully sovereign and man is fully responsible. How that can be resolved logically is beyond our finite minds. When Spurgeon was once asked how these two grand, biblical doctrines could be reconciled, he responded, "I didn't know that friends needed reconciliation."

He went on to compare these two doctrines to the rails of a track upon which Christianity runs. Just as the rails of a train, which run parallel to each other, appear to merge in the distance, so the doctrines of God's sovereignty and man's responsibility, which seem separate from each other in this life, will merge in eternity. Our task is not to force their merging in this life but to keep them in balance and to live accordingly. We must thus strive for experiential Christianity that does justice both to God's sovereignty and to our responsibility.

• *Between doctrinal, experiential, and practical Christianity.* Just as Reformed preachers taught that experiential preaching must offer a balance of doctrine and application, Christian living also involves more than experience. Biblical Christian living is grounded in sound doctrine, sound experience, and sound practice.

4. *Communicate experiential truth to others.* Reformed and Puritan experiential preachers applied their sermons to every part of life, all of Scripture to the entire man. They were unashamedly doctrinal. We can learn much from them on how to evangelize, such as:

• *Speak the truth about God.* That seems obvious. But how often do we speak to others about God's majestic being, His Trinitarian personality, and His glorious attributes? How often do we tell others about His holiness, sovereignty, mercy, and love? Do we root our evangelism in a robust biblical theism, or do we take our cues from modern evangelism which approaches God as if He were a next-door neighbor who adjusts His attributes to our needs and desires? How often do we speak to others about how God and His majestic attributes have become experientially real to us?

• *Speak the truth about man.* Do you talk to others about our depraved nature and our desperate need for salvation in Jesus Christ? Do you say that you are no better than they are by nature; that we are all, apart from grace, sinners with a terrible record, which is a legal problem, as well as a bad heart, which is a moral problem? Do you talk to them about the dreadful character of sin; that sin is something that stems back to our tragic fall in Adam and affects every part of us, so dominating our mind, heart, will, and conscience that we are slaves to it? Do you describe sin as moral rebellion against God? Do you say that the wages of sin is death, now and for all eternity?

• *Speak the truth about Christ.* Do we present the complete Christ to sinners, not separating His benefits from His person or offering Him as a Savior while ignoring His claims as Lord? Do we offer Christ as the grand remedy for the great malady of sin and repeatedly declare His ability, willingness to save, and preciousness as the exclusive Redeemer of lost sinners?

Do you exhibit the way of salvation in Christ in your faith and repentance? Paul said, "I testified to you publicly and from house to house repentance toward God, and faith toward our Lord Jesus Christ" (Acts

20:20-21). Do you likewise evangelize your friends and neighbors when God offers that opportunity? Do you explain to them what faith and repentance are in a born-again sinner?

• *Speak the truth about sanctification.* Do you tell others how a Christian must walk the King's highway of holiness in gratitude, service, obedience, love, and self-denial? Do you tell how he must learn the art of meditation, of fearing God, and of childlike prayer? How he must press on by God's grace, seeking to make his calling and election sure? Do you disciple your associates in the need for habitual, experiential faith, repentance, and godliness?[16]

• *Speak the truth about eternal consequences.* Do not be afraid to speak about the consequences of despising the blood of Jesus Christ. Do not flinch from describing damnation and hell. As one Puritan wrote, "We must go with the stick of divine truth and beat every bush behind which a sinner hides, until like Adam who hid, he stands before God in his nakedness."

We must speak urgently to people around us because many are on their way to hell. We must confront sinners with the law and gospel, with death in Adam and life in Christ. Let us use every weapon we can to turn sinners from the road of destruction so they may, through grace, experience a living, experiential relationship with God in Jesus Christ. We know from Scripture and by experience that an omnipotent Christ can bless our efforts and rescue a dead sinner, divorce him from his sinful lusts, and make him willing to forsake his wicked ways and turn to God, fully resolved to make God his goal and his praise. Acts 5:31 says, "Him hath God exalted with his right hand to be a Prince and a Saviour, for to give repentance to Israel, and forgiveness of sins." Praise God for the experience of His amazing grace toward us in Christ.

---

[1] "Christian Experience," *Banner of Truth,* no. 139 (April 1975):6.

[2] *Works of Thomas Halyburton* (London: Thomas Tegg, 1835), xiv-xv.

[3] Cited in Iain Murray, *Revival and Revivalism* (Edinburgh: Banner of Truth Trust, 1994), 321-22.

[4] *Works of William Perkins* (London: John Legatt, 1613), 2:762.

[5] Gardiner Spring, *The Power of the Pulpit* (reprint Edinburgh: Banner of Truth Trust, 1986), 154.

[6] Daniel Webber, "Sanctifying the Inner Life," in *Aspects of Sanctification,* 1981 Westminster Conference Papers (Hertfordshire: Evangelical Press, 1982), 44-45.

[7] *The Works of John Flavel* (reprint London: Banner of Truth Trust, 1968), 5:424.

[8] *The Works of John Owen* (reprint Edinburgh: Banner of Truth Trust, 1976), 3:385-86.

[9] *Works of Flavel,* 5:423.

[10] *The Works of the Reverend and Faithfvll Servant of Jesvs Christ, M. Richard Greenham,* ed. H[enry] H[olland] (London: Felix Kingston for Robert Dexter, 1599), 390.

[11] *Prayer* (reprint Edinburgh: Banner of Truth Trust, 1999), 23ff.

[12] "Visible Saints: the Puritans as a Godly People," in *Aspects of Sanctification,* 1981 Westminster Conference Papers (Hertfordshire: Evangelical Press, 1982), 1-2.

[13] Donald S. Whitney, *Spiritual Disciplines for the Christian Life* (Colorado Springs: NavPress, 1991), 196-210.

[14] *A Quest for Godliness: The Puritan Vision of the Christian Life* (Wheaton, Ill: Crossway Books, 1990), 239; Errol Hulse, "Sanctifying the Lord's Day: Reformed and Puritan Attitudes," in *Aspects of Sanctification,* 1981 Westminster Conference Papers (Hertfordshire: Evangelical Press, 1982), 78-102.

[15] Joel R. Beeke, *Quest for Full Assurance: The Legacy of Calvin and His Successors* (Edinburgh: Banner of Truth Trust, 1999), 125, 130, 146.

[16] Joel R. Beeke, *Puritan Evangelism: A Biblical Approach* (Grand Rapids: Reformation Heritage Books, 1999), 15-16.

Selected Bibliographies

Chapter 1: Calvin on Piety

Primary Sources

Calvin, John. *Commentaries of Calvin*. 46 vols. Various translators. Edinburgh: Calvin Translation Society, 1843-55; reprint ed. in 22 vols., Grand Rapids: Baker, 1979.

_____. *Concerning the Eternal Predestination of God*. Trans. J. K. S. Reid. London: James Clarke, 1961.

_____. *Institutes of the Christian Religion*. Ed. John T. McNeill. Trans. Ford Lewis Battles. 2 vols. Library of Christian Classics, no. 20-21. Philadelphia: Westminster Press, 1960.

_____. *Joannis Calvini Opera Selecta*. Ed. Peter Barth, Wilhelm Niesel, and Dora Scheuner. Munich: Chr. Kaiser, 1926-52.

_____. *Letters of John Calvin*. Ed. Jules Bonnet; trans. David Constable and Marcus Robert Gilchrist. 4 vols. Philadelphia: Presbyterian Board, 1858.

_____. *New Testament Commentaries*. Ed. David W. Torrance and Thomas F. Torrance. 12 vols. Grand Rapids: Eerdmans, 1960-72.

_____. *Opera quae supersunt omnia*. Ed. Guilielmus Baum, Eduardus Cunitz, and Eduardus Reuss. 59 vols. *Corpus Reformatorum: Volumen XXIX-LXXXVII*. Brunsvigae: C. A. Schwetschke et filium, 1863-1900.

_____. *Sermons from Job*. Trans. Harold Dekker. Grand Rapids: Eerdmans, 1952.

_____. *Sermons of M. John Calvin, on the Epistles of S. Paule to Timothie and Titus*. Trans. L. T. London: Imprinted for G. Bishop and T. Woodcoke, 1579; reprint ed., Edinburgh: Banner of Truth Trust, 1983.

_____. *Sermons of Master John Calvin upon the Fifthe Book of Moses called Deuteronomie*. Trans. Arthur Golding. London, 1583; reprint ed., Edinburgh: Banner of Truth Trust, 1987.

_____. *Sermons on the Epistle to the Ephesians*. Trans. Arthur Golding. London, 1577; reprint ed., Edinburgh: Banner of Truth Trust, 1973.

_____. *Sermons on Isaiah's Prophecy of the Death and Passion of Jesus Christ*. Trans. T. H. L. Parker. London: James Clarke, 1956.

_____. *Sermons on the Ten Commandments*. Ed. and trans. Benjamin W. Farley. Grand Rapids: Baker, 1980.

_____. *Sermons on the Saving Work of Christ*. Trans. Leroy Nixon. Grand Rapids: Eerdmans, 1950.

_____. *Tracts and Treatises*. Trans. Henry Beveridge. 3 vols. Grand Rapids: Eerdmans, 1958.

Secondary Sources

Armstrong, Brian. "The Nature and Structure of Calvin's Thought According to the *Institutes*: Another Look." In *John Calvin's Magnum Opus*, 55-82. Potchefstroom, South Africa: Institute for Reformational Studies, 1986.

_____. "The Role of the Holy Spirit in Calvin's Teaching on the Ministry." In *Calvin and the Holy Spirit*, ed. by P. DeKlerk, 99-111. Grand Rapids: Calvin Studies Society, 1989.

Battles, Ford Lewis. *The Piety of John Calvin*. Grand Rapids: Baker, 1978.

_____. "True Piety According to Calvin." In *Interpreting John Calvin*, ed. R. Bene-detto, 289-306. Grand Rapids: Baker, 1996.

Beeke, Joel R. "Making Sense of Calvin's Paradoxes on Assurance of Faith." In *Calvin Studies Society Papers,* ed. David Foxgrover, 13-30. Grand Rapids: CRC, 1998.

_____. *The Quest for Full Assurance: The Legacy of Calvin and His Successors.* Edinburgh: The Banner of Truth Trust, 1999.

Benoît, Jean-Daniel. "The Pastoral Care of the Prophet." In *John Calvin: Comtemporary Prophet*, ed. J.T. Hoogstra, 51-67. Grand Rapids: Baker, 1959.

Bouwsma, William. "The Spirituality of John Calvin." In *Christian Spirituality: High Middle Ages and Reformation*, ed. Jill Raitt, 318-33. New York: Crossroad, 1987.

DeJong, James A. "'An Anatomy of All Parts of the Soul': Insights into Calvin's Spirituality from His Psalms Commentary." In *Calvinus Sacrae Scripturae Professor,* ed. Wilhelm H. Neuser, 1-14. Grand Rapids: Eerdmans, 1994.

DeKlerk, Peter, ed. *Calvin and Christian Ethics*. Grand Rapids: Calvin Studies Society, 1987.

_____. *Calvin and the Holy Spirit*. Grand Rapids: Calvin Studies Society, 1989.

_____. *Renaissance, Reformation, Resurgence*. Grand Rapids: Calvin Theological Semi-nary, 1976.

DeKoster, Lester R. "Living Themes in the Thought of John Calvin: A Bibliographical Study." Ph.D. dissertation, University of Michigan, 1964.

Evans, William Borden. "Imputation and Impartation: The Problem of Union with Christ in Nineteenth-Century American Reformed Theology." Ph.D. dissertation, Vanderbilt University, 1996.

Foxgrover, David. "John Calvin's Understanding of Conscience." Ph.D. dissertation, Claremont, 1978.

_____, ed. *Calvin Studies Society Papers, 1995-1997*. Grand Rapids: CRC, 1998.

_____. *The Legacy of John Calvin: Calvin Studies Society Papers, 1999*. Grand Rapids: CRC, 2000

Gamble, Richard C. "Calvin and Sixteenth-Century Spirituality." In *Calvin Studies Society Papers, 1995-1997,* ed. David Foxgrover, 31-51. Grand Rapids: CRC, 1998.

_____, ed. *Articles on Calvin and Calvinism*, vol. 1, *The Biography of Calvin*. New York: Garland, 1992.

_____. *Articles on Calvin and Calvinism, vol. 4, Influences upon Calvin and Discussion of the 1559 Institutes*. New York: Garland, 1992.

Garside, Charles. *The Origins of Calvin's Theology of Music: 1536-1543*. Philadelphia: American Philosophical Society, 1979.

George, Timothy, ed. *John Calvin and the Church: A Prism of Reform*. Louisville: West-minster/John Knox Press, 1990.

Gerrish, Brian A. "Calvin's Eucharistic Piety." In *Calvin Studies Society Papers, 1995-1997*, ed. David Foxgrover, 52-65. Grand Rapids: CRC, 1998.

_____. *Grace and Gratitude: The Eucharistic Theology of John Calvin*. Minneapolis: Fortress Press, 1993.

Gleason, Randall C. *John Calvin and John Owen on Mortification: A Comparative Study in Reformed Spirituality.* New York: Peter Lang, 1995.

Greve, Lionel. "Freedom and Discipline in the Theology of John Calvin, William Perkins and John Wesley: An Examination of the Origin and Nature of Pietism." Ph.D. dissertation, The Hartfod Seminary Foundation, 1976.

Gründler, Otto. "John Calvin: Ingrafting in Christ." In *The Spirituality of Western Christendom*, ed. E. Rozanne Elder, 172-87. Kalamazoo, Mich.: Cistercian, 1976.

Hall, T. Hartley. "The Shape of Reformed Piety." In *Spiritual Traditions for the Contemporary Church*, ed. Robin Maas and Gabriel O'Donnell. Nashville: Abingdon Press, 1990.

Harman, Allan. "The Psalms and Reformed Spirituality." *The Reformed Theological Review* [Australia] 53:2 (1994): 53-62.

Hateman, Howard G. "Reformed Spirituality." In *Protestant Spiritual Traditions*, ed. F.C. Senn, 55-79. Mahwah, N.J.: Paulist Press, 1986.

Hesselink, I. John. *Calvin's Concept of the Law*. Allison Park, Pa.: Pickwick, 1992.

_____. "Governed and Guided by the Spirit: A Key Issue in Calvin's Doctrine of the Holy Spirit." In *Das Reformierte Erbe: Festschrift für Gottfried W. Locher*, ed. Heiko A. Oberman *et al.*, Part 2:161-71. Zürich: TVZ, 1992.

Hoogstra, Jacob T., ed. *John Calvin, Contemporary Prophet*. Grand Rapids: Baker, 1959.

Hulse, Erroll. "The Preacher and Piety." In *The Preacher and Preaching,* ed. Samuel T. Logan, Jr. Phillipsburg, N.J.: Presbyterian and Reformed, 1986.

Johnson, Merwyn S. "Calvin's Ethical Legacy." In *The Legacy of John Calvin*, ed. David Foxgrover. Grand Rapids: CRC 2000.

Jones, Serene. *Calvin and the Rhetoric of Piety*. Louisville: Westminster/John Knox, 1995.

Kingdon, Robert M. "The Genevan Revolution in Public Worship." *Princeton Seminary Bulletin* 20:3 (1999): 264-80.

Kolfhaus, Wilhelm. *Christusgemeinschaft bei Johannes Calvin*. Neukirchen Kreis Moers: Buchhandlung der Erziehungsvereings, 1939.

Krusche, Werner. *Das Wirken des Heiligen Geistes nach Calvin*. Göttingen: Vandenhoeck & Ruprecht, 1957.

Lambert, Thomas A. "Preaching, Praying, and Policing the Reform in Sixteenth Century Geneva." Ph.D. dissertation, University of Wisconsin-Madison, 1998.

Lee, Sou-Young. "Calvin's Understanding of *Pietas*." In *Calvinus Sincerioris Religionis Vindex*, ed. Wilhelm H. Neuser & Brian G. Armstrong, 225-39. Kirksville, Mo.: Sixteenth Century Studies, 1997.

Leith, John. *John Calvin's Doctrine of the Christian Life*. Louisville: Westminster/John Knox, 1989.

_____, ed. *John Calvin: The Christian Life*. San Francisco: Harper & Row, 1984.

Loggie, R.D. "Chief Exercise of Faith: An Exposition of Calvin's Doctrine of Prayer." *Hartford Quarterly* 5 (1965):65-81.

Maurer, H.W. "An Examination of Form and Content in John Calvin's Prayers." Ph.D. dissertation, Edinburgh, 1960.

McKee, Elsie Anne. "Contexts, Contours, Contents: Towards a Description of Calvin's Understanding of Worship." In *Calvin Studies Society Papers, 1995-1997*, ed. David Foxgrover, 66-92. Grand Rapids: CRC, 1998.

_____. *Diakonia in the Classical Reformed Tradition and Today*. Grand Rapids: Eerdmans, 1989.

_____. *John Calvin on the Diaconate and Liturgical Almsgiving*. Geneva: Droz, 1984.

_____, ed. and trans. *John Calvin: Writings on Pastoral Piety*. New York: Paulist Press, 2001.

Muller, Richard A. *The Unaccommodated Calvin: Studies in the Foundation of a Theological Tradition*. New York: Oxford University Press, 2000.

Neuser, Wilhelm H., ed. *Calvinus Sacrae Scripturae Professor: Calvin as Confessor of Holy Scripture*. Grand Rapids: Eerdmans, 1994.

Neuser, Wilhelm H. & Armstrong, Brian G. *Calvinus Sincerioris Religionis Vindex: Calvin as Protector of the Purer Religion*. Kirksville, Mo.: Sixteenth Century Journal, 1997.

Oberman, Heiko A. "The Pursuit of Happiness: Calvin Between Humanism and Reformation." In *Humanity and Divinity in Renaissance and Reformation*, ed. J.W. O'Malley, T. Izbicki, and G. Christianson, 251-83. Leiden: E.J. Brill, 1993.

Old, H.O. *The Shaping of the Reformed Baptismal Rite in the Sixteenth Century*. Grand Rapids: Eerdmans, 1992.

_____. "What is Reformed Spirituality? Played Over Again Lightly." In *Calvin Studies VII*, ed. J.H. Leith, 61-68. Davidson, N.C., 1994.

Parker, T.H.L. *Calvin's Preaching*. Louisville: Westminster/John Knox, 1992.

Partee, Charles. "Calvin's Central Dogma Again." *Sixteenth Century Journal* 18, 2 (1987):19-28.

_____. "Prayer as the Practice of Predestination." In *Calvinus Servus Christi*, ed. Wilhelm H. Neuser, 241-56. Budapest: Pressabteilung des Raday-Kollegiums, 1988.

Pitkin, Barbara. "Imitation of David: David as a Paradigm for Faith in Calvin's Exegesis of the Psalms." *The Sixteenth Century Journal* 24:4 (1993): 843-63.

_____. *What Pure Eyes Could See: Calvin's Doctrine of Faith in Its Exegetical Context*. New York: Oxford University Press, 1999.

Raitt, Jill, ed. *Christian Spirituality: High Middle Ages and Reformation*. New York: Crossroad, 1988.

Reid, W. Stanford. "The Battle Hymns of the Lord: Calvinist Psalmody of the Sixteenth Century." In *Sixteenth Century Essays and Studies,* ed. C.S. Meyer, 2:36-54. St. Louis: Foundation for Reformation Research, 1971.

Richard, Lucien. *The Spirituality of John Calvin*. Pittsburgh: Pickwick Press, 1974.

Senn, Frank, ed. *Protestant Spiritual Traditions*. New York: Paulist, 1986.

Simpson, H.W. "*Pietas* in the *Institutes* of Calvin." In *Reformational Tradition: A Rich Heritage and Lasting Vocation,* 179-91. Potchefstroom: Potchefstroom University for Christian Higher Education, 1984.

Tamburello, Dennis. *Union with Christ: John Calvin and the Mysticism of St. Bernard*. Louisville: Westminster/John Knox, 1994.

Tripp, Diane Karay. "Daily Prayer in the Reformed Tradition: An Initial Survey." *Studia Liturgica* 21 (1991): 76-107, 190-219.

VanderWilt, Jeffrey T. "John Calvin's Theology of Liturgical Song." *Christian Scholar's Review* 25 (1996): 63-82.

Walchenbach, John. "The Influence of David and the Psalms on the Life and Thought of John Calvin." Th.M. thesis, Pittsburgh Theological Seminary, 1969.

Wallace, Ronald S. *Calvin's Doctrine of the Christian Life*. London: Oliver and Boyd, 1959.

_____. *Calvin's Doctrine of the Word and Sacrament*. London: Oliver and Boyd, 1959.

Willis-Watkins, David. "Calvin's Theology of Pastoral Care." In *Calvin Studies VI*, ed. J.H. Leith, 36-46. Davidson, N.C., 1992.

_____. "The Third Part of Christian Freedom Misplaced." In *Later Calvinism: International Perspectives,* ed. W. Fred Graham, 471-88 (Kirksville, Mo.: Sixteenth Century Journal, 1994).

_____. "The *Unio Mystica* and the Assurance of Faith According to Calvin." In *Calvin Erbe und Auftrag: Festschrift für Wilhelm Heinrich Neuser zum 65. Geburtstag,* ed. Willem van't Spijker. Kampen: Kok, 1991.

Witvliet, John. "The Spirituality of the Psalter: Metrical Psalms in Liturgy and Life in Calvin's Geneva." In *Calvin Studies Society Papers, 1995-1997,* ed. David Foxgrover, 93-117. Grand Rapids: CRC, 1998.

Zachman, Randall C. *The Assurance of Faith: Conscience in the Theology of Martin Luther and John Calvin.* Minneapolis: Fortress Press, 1993.

Chapter 4: The Puritan Practice of Meditation

Primary Sources

Alleine, Richard. *Vindiciae Pietatis. A Vindication of Godlinesse.* London, 1663.

Ambrose, Isaac. "Of the Nature and Kinds of Meditations." In *The Compleat Works Of that Eminent Minister of God's Word Mr. Isaac Ambrose.* London: for R. Chiswel, B. Tooke, T. Sawbridge, 1689, 135-155.

Ball, John. *Treatise of Divine Meditation.* London: Printed for Tho. Parkhurst, 1650.

Bates, William. "On Divine Meditation." In *The Works of William Bates.* Harrisonburg, Va.: Sprinkle, 1990, 3:113-65.

Baxter, Richard. *The Saints' Everlasting Rest.* Ross-shire, Scotland: Christian Focus unabridged reprint, 1998, 547-658.

Bayly, Lewis. *The Practice of Piety.* Morgan, Pa.: Soli Deo Gloria, 1996.

Boston, Thomas. "Duty and Advantage of Solemn Meditation." In *The Complete Works of the Late Rev. Thomas Boston.* Wheaton, Ill.: Richard Owen Roberts, 1980, 4:453-57.

Bridge, William. "The Sweetness and Profitableness of Meditation" (Sermon #7) and "The Work and Way of Meditation" (Sermon #8). In *The Works of William Bridge.* Beaver Falls, Pa.: Soli Deo Gloria, 1989, 3:124-60.

Bunyan, John. *Complete Works.* 3 vols. Marshallton, Del.: National Foundation for Christian Education, 1968.

Bury, Edward. *The Husbandmans Companion: Containing One Hundred Occasional Meditations, Reflections, and Ejaculations, Especially Suited to Men of that Employment. Directing them how they may be Heavenly-minded while about their Ordinary Calling.* London: for Tho. Parkhurst, 1677.

Calamy, Edmund. *The Art of Divine Meditation. Or, A Discourse of the Nature, Necessity,and Excellency thereof. With Motives to, and Rules for the better performance of that most Important Christian Duty. In Several Sermons on Gen. 24.63.* London: Printed for Tho. Parkhurst, 1680.

Case, Thomas. "Mount Pisgah; or A Prospect of Heaven," the second book in *The Select Works of Thomas Case.* Ligonier, Pa.: Soli Deo Gloria, 1993.

Culverwell, Ezekiel. *Time Well Spent in Sacred Meditation.* London: for Tho. Parkhurst, 1634.

Fenner, William. *Christs Alarm to Drowsie Saints.* London: for John Rothwell, 1650, 236-60.

_____. *The Use and Benefit of Divine Meditation.* London: E.T. for John Stafford, 1657.

Flavel, John. "The Mystery of Providence." In *The Works of John Flavel.* London: Banner of Truth Trust, 1968, 4:336-497.

Gouge, Thomas. *Christian Directions, shewing How to walk with God All the Day long.*
London: R. Ibbitson and M. Wright, 1661, 63-73.

Greenham, Richard. "Grave Covnsels and Godly Observations." In *The Works of the
Reverend and Faithfvll Servant of Iesvs Christ M. Richard Greenham*, ed. H. H. London:
Felix Kingston for Robert Dexter, 1599, 37-42.

Heywood, Oliver. "Concerning Meditation, with some Helps to Furnish the Thoughts
with Suitable and Profitable Subjects." In *The Works of Oliver Heywood*. Morgan,
Pa.: Soli Deo Gloria, 1997, 2:246-82.

Hooker, Thomas. *The Application of Redemption. The Ninth and Tenth Books*. London:
Peter Cole, 1657.

Horneck, Anthony. *The Fire of the Altar: or, Certain directions how to raise the soul into holy
flames before, at, and after the receiving the blessed sacrament of the Lord's Supper*. London:
J. Dawks for Sam. Lownds, 1702.

Howe, John. "Delighting in God." In *The Works of John Howe*. Ligonier, Pa.: Soli Deo
Gloria, 1990, 1:474-664.

Huntley, Frank Livingstone. *Bishop Joseph Hall and Protestant Meditation in Seventeenth-
Century England: A Study With the texts of* The Art of Divine Meditations *(1606) and*
Occasional Meditations *(1633)*. Binghamton, N.Y.: Center for Medieval & Early
Renaissance Studies, 1981.

Lukin, Henry. *An Introduction to the Holy Scriptures*. London, 1669.

Manton, Thomas. "Sermons Upon Genesis XXIV.63." In *The Works of Thomas Manton*.
London: James Nisbet & Co., 1874, 17:263-348. Also see in vols. 6-9 on Psalm
119 sermons no. 16, 54, 87, 102, 105, and 166.

Owen, John. "The Grace and Duty of Being Spiritually Minded." In *The Works of John
Owen*. London: Banner of Truth Trust, 1965, 7:262-497.

Ranew, Nathanael. *Solitude Improved by Divine Meditation*. Morgan, Pa.: Soli Deo
Gloria reprint, 1995.

Reynolds, Edward. *Meditations on the Holy Sacrament of the Lord's Last Supper*, vol. 3 of the
Works. Morgan, Pa.: Soli Deo Gloria, 1999.

Rogers, Richard. *Seven Treatises Containing Such Direction As Is Gathered Out of The Holy
Scriptures*. London: Felix Kyngston for Thomas Man, 1603.

Scougal, Henry. *The Works of Henry Scougal*. Morgan, Pa.: Soli Deo Gloria, 2002,
256-77.

Scudder, Henry. "On Meditation." In *The Christian Man's Calling*. Philadelphia: Presbyterian Board of Publication, n.d., 102-109.

Sibbes, Richard. "Divine Meditations and Holy Contemplations." In *The Works of
Richard Sibbes*. Edinburgh: Banner of Truth Trust, 2001, 7:179-228.

Spurstowe, William. *The Spiritual Chymist: or, Six Decads Of Divine Meditations*. London:
n.p., 1666.

Swinnock, George. "The Christian Man's Calling." In *The Works of George Swinnock*.
Edinburgh: Banner of Truth Trust, 1992, 2:417-29.

Taylor, Thomas. *Meditations from the Creatures*. London, 1629.

Ussher, James. *A Method for Meditation: or, A Manuall of Divine Duties, fit for every
Christians Practice*. London: for Joseph Nevill, 1656.

Watson, Thomas. "A Christian on the Mount; Or, A Treatise Concerning Meditation."
In *The Sermons of Thomas Watson*. Ligonier, Pa.: Soli Deo Gloria, 1990, 197-291.

_____. *Heaven Taken by Storm*. Morgan, Pa.: Soli Deo Gloria, 2000, 23-29.

_____. "Meditation." In *Gleanings from Thomas Watson*. Morgan, Pa.: Soli Deo Gloria, 1995, 103-113.

White, Thomas. *A Method and Instructions for the Art of Divine Meditation with Instances of the several Kindes of Solemn Meditation*. London: for Tho. Parkhurst, 1672.

Secondary Sources

Chan, Simon. "The Puritan Meditative Tradition, 1599-1691: A Study of Ascetical Piety." Ph.D. dissertation, Cambridge University, 1986.

Dabney, Robert L. "Meditation A Means of Grace." In *Discussions: Evangelical and Theological*. London: Banner of Truth Trust, 1967, 1:643-53.

Foster, Richard J. "The Discipline of Meditation," chap. 2. In *Celebration of Discipline*. San Francisco: Harper & Row, 1978, 13-29.

Huntley, Frank Livingstone. *Bishop Joseph Hall 1574-1656: A biographical and critical study*. Cambridge: D. S. Brewer, 1979, chap. 6.

Kaufmann, U. Milo. *The Pilgrim's Progress and Traditions in Puritan Meditation*. New Haven: Yale University Press, 1966.

Martz, Louis. "Problems in Puritan Meditation." In *The Poetry of Meditation*. New Haven: Yale, 1954, chap. 4.

Shedd, William G. T. "Religious Meditation" (sermon no. 1). *Sermons to the Spiritual Man*. London: Banner of Truth Trust, 1972, 1-18.

Smith, Edmond. *A Tree by a Stream: Unlock the Secrets of Active Meditation*. Ross-shire, Scotland: Christian Focus, 1995.

Toon, Peter. *From Mind to Heart: Christian Meditation Today*. Grand Rapids: Baker, 1987.

_____. *Meditating as a Christian*. London: Collins Religious Division, 1991.

Chapters 11-12: The Lives and Ministries of Ebenezer and Ralph Erskine

Addison, William. *The Life and Writings of Thomas Boston of Ettrick*. Edinburgh: Oliver and Boyd, 1936.

Baker, Frank. "The Erskines and the Methodists." *The London Quarterly and Holborn Review* 27 (1958): 36-45.

Barnett, T. Ratcliffe. *The Makers of the Kirk*. Boston: T.N. Foulis, 1913, 243-55.

Bavinck, Herman. Introduction to *Levengeschiedenis en Werken van Ralph en Ebenezer Erskine*, 1-13. Doesburg: J.C. van Schenk Brill, 1904.

Beaton, Donald. "'The Marrow of Modern Divinity' and the Marrow Controversy." *The Princeton Theological Review* IV, 3 (1906): 317-338.

Bell, M. Charles. *Calvin and Scottish Theology: The Doctrine of Assurance*. Edinburgh: Handsel Press, 1985.

Blaikie, W.G. *The Preachers of Scotland from the sixth to the nineteenth century*. Edinburgh: T. & T. Clark, 1888.

Boorman, David. "Ebenezer Erskine and Secession." In *Diversities of Gifts*, 86-101. The Westminster Conference, 1980. Swansea: Howard Jones, 1981.

Boston, Thomas. *The Complete Works of the Late Rev. Thomas Boston, Ettrick*. 12 vols. Ed. Samuel M'Millan. London: William Tegg, 1855; reprint, Wheaton, Ill.: Richard Owen Roberts, 1980. (See especially, "The Marrow of Modern Divinity, with notes by Thomas Boston," vol. 7.)

Brienen, Teunis. "Het Avondmaal in de Gereformeerde Schotse Kerken, speciaal in de preken van de Erskines." In *Bij Brood en Beker,* ed. Willem van't Spijker. Kampen: De Groot Goudriaan, 1980, 226-47.

Brown, James Campbell. *The Annals of Portmoak during the Ministry of the Rev. Ebenezer Erskine from 1703 to 1731, gathered from the Session Book*, published in Kinross-shire Advertiser, 1889.

Brown, John (of Whitburn), ed. *Gospel Truth Accurately Stated and Illustrated, by the Rev. Mess. James Hog, Thomas Boston, Ebenezer and Ralph Erskine, and Others. Occasioned by the Republication of the Marrow of Modern Divinity.* Edinburgh: J. Pillans and Sons, 1817.

Bruggink, Donald J. "The Theology of Thomas Boston, 1676-1732." Ph.D. dissertation, University of Edinburgh, 1956.

Burleigh, J. H. S. *A Church History of Scotland.* Edinburgh: Hope Trust, 1988.

Cowan, Henry. "Erskine, Ebenzer." In *The New Schaff-Herzog Encyclopedia of Religious Knowledge,* ed. Samuel Macauley Jackson, IV:171. Reprint, Grand Rapids: Baker, 1977.

Cunningham, John. *The Church History of Scotland, from the commencement of the christian era to the present century*, vol. II. Edinburgh: Adam & Charles Black, 1882.

Drummond, A. L., and Bulloch, J. *The Scottish Church 1688-1843. The Age of the Moderates.* Edinburgh: The Saint Andrew Press, 1973.

Erskine, Ebenezer. *God's Little Remnant Keeping their Garments Clean in an Evil Day.* Edinburgh: Patrick Walker, 1725.

_____.*The Whole Works of Ebenezer Erskine.* 3 vols. Philadelphia: Wm. S. & A. Young, 1836. (Includes memoir by Donald Fraser, iii-xxx.)

Erskine, Ralph. *Faith no Fancy, or Treatise of Mental Images.* Edinburgh, 1745.

_____.*The Sermons and Other Practical Works of Ralph Erskine.* 7 vols. Aberdeen: George and Robert King, 1862; reprint vols. 1-6, Glasgow: Free Presbyterian, 1991. (Vol. 7, which contains Erskine's *Poetical Works,* includes memoir by John Brown of Whitburn, v-xxxvi.)

Fawcett, Arthur. *The Cambuslang Revival, the Scottish Evangelical Revival of the Eighteenth Century*, London: Banner of Truth Trust, 1971.

Fraser, Donald. *The Life and Diary of the Reverend Ebenezer Erskine.* Edinburgh: William Oliphant, 1831.

_____. *The Life and Diary of the Reverend Ralph Erskine.* Edinburgh: William Oliphant, 1834.

Gentleman, Ebenezer. "Memorials of Erskine Church." In *Stirling Natural History and Arch. Soc. Transactions* XXX-XXXI (1907-1908).

Gib, Adam. *The Present Truth: A Display of the Secession-Testimony in the three periods of the rise, state and maintenance of that Testimony.* 2 vols. Edinburgh, 1774.

Gordon, Alexander. "Erskine, Ebenezer" and "Erskine, Ralph." In *Dictionary of National Biography,* ed. Leslie Stephen and Sidney Lee, VI: 822-25, 851-52. London: Oxford, 1921.

Graafland, Cornelis. "De spiritualiteit van de Puriteinen (inzonderheid van Ebenezer en Ralph Erskine en haar invloed in Nederland)." In *Spiritualiteit,* ed. Willem van't Spijker. Kampen: De Groot Goudriaan, 1993, 209-229.

_____. *Van Calvijn tot Comrie. Oorsprong en ontwikkeling van de leer van het verbond in het Gereformeerd Protestantisme.* Zoetermeer, 1993.

Grier, W.J. "Erskine, Ebenezer" and "Erskine, Ralph." In *The Encyclopedia of Christianity,* IV: 89-90. Ed. Philip E. Hughes. Marshallton, Del.: National Foundation for Christian Education, 1972.

Harper, James, et al. *Lives of Ebenezer Erskine, William Wilson, and Thomas Gillespie, Fathers of the United Presbyterian Church.* Edinburgh: A. Fullarton, 1849. (On Ebenezer Erskine, 1-88.)

Hetherington, W.M. *History of the Church of Scotland from the introduction of Christianity, to the period of the Disruption, May 18, 1843.* Edinburgh: Johnstone and Hunter, 1852.

Jenkins, Gordon, F.C. "Establishment and Dissent in the Dunfermline Area 1733-1883." Ph.D. dissertation, University of Edinburgh, 1988.

Ker, John. "The Erskines: Ebenezer and Ralph." In *Scottish Nationality and other Papers.* Edinburgh: Andrew Elliot, 1887, 64-108.

Lachman, David. "Erskine, Ebenezer" and "Erskine, Ralph." In *Dictionary of Scottish Church History & Theology,* ed. Nigel M. de S. Cameron. Downers Grove, Ill.: InterVarsity Press, 1993, 298-302.

_____. *The Marrow Controversy, 1718-1723: An Historical and Theological Analysis.* Rutherford Studies Series One: Historical Theology. Edinburgh: Rutherford House, 1988.

_____."The Marrow Controversy: An Historical Survey with special reference to the Free Offer of the Gospel, the Extent of the Atonement, and Assurance and Saving Faith." Th.M. thesis, Westminster Theological Seminary, 1973.

Leckie, J.H. *Secession Memories, the United Presbyterian Contribution to the Scottish Church.* Edinburgh: T & T Clark, 1926.

McCain, Charles Rodgers. "Preaching in Eighteenth Century Scotland: A Comparative Study of the Extant Sermons of Ralph Erskine, John Erskine, and Hugh Blair." Ph.D. dissertation, Edinburgh, 1949.

M'Clintock, John, and Strong, James, eds. "Erskine, Ebenezer" and "Erskine, Ralph." In *Cyclopedia of Biblical, Theological, and Ecclesiastical Literature,* III: 282-83. New York: Harper & Brothers, 1894.

M'Crie, C.G. *The Church of Scotland her Divisions and her Reunions,* Edinburgh: Mac-Niven & Wallace, 1901.

_____. *The Confessions of the Church of Scotland, their Revolution in History.* Edinburgh: MacNiven & Wallace, 1907.

M'Crie, Thomas, Jr. "Account of the Controversy respecting the Marrow of Modern Divinity." *The Edinburgh Christian Instructor* XXX (August, October, December 1831); New Series, I, (February 1832).

_____."'The Marrow' Controversy: with Notices of the State of Scottish Theology in the beginning of last Century." *The British and Foreign Evangelical Review* II (June 1853):411-40.

_____.*The Story of the Scottish Church from the Reformation to the Disruption.* Glasgow: Bell and Bain Ltd., 1875.

MacEwen, A.R. *The Erskines.* Edinburgh: Oliphant Anderson & Ferrier, 1900.

McIntyre, D.M. "First Strictures on 'The Marrow of Modern Divinity.'" *The Evangelical Quarterly* X (January 1938): 61-70.

MacKenzie, Robert. *John Brown of Haddington,* London: Hodder and Stoughton, 1964.

M'Kerrow, John. *History of the Secession Church.* 2 vols. Edinburgh: William Oliphant and Son, 1839.

Macleod, John. *Scottish Theology.* Reprint, London: Banner of Truth Trust, 1974.

M'Millan, Samuel, ed. *The Beauties of the Rev. Ebenezer Erskine, being a Selection of the Most Striking Illustrations of Gospel Doctrine Contained in His Whole Works*. Glasgow: Blackie & Son, 1850. (Includes memoir, ix-xxiv.)

M'Millan, Samuel, ed. *The Beauties of the Rev. Ralph Erskine, being a Selection of the Most Striking Illustrations of Gospel Doctrine Contained in His Whole Works*. 2 vols. Edinburgh: A. Fullarton, 1850. (Includes memoir, xiii-xxxvi.)

Mathieson, William Law. *The Awakening of Scotland: A History from 1747 to 1797*. Glasgow, 1910.

Mechie, Stewart. "The Marrow Controversy Reviewed." *The Evangelical Quarterly* XXII (January 1950): 20-31.

Mitchell, James. "Ebenezer Erskine." In *Scottish Divines 1505-1872*, 149-88. Edinburgh: Macniven and Wallace, 1883.

Muirhead, Andrew T. N. "Religion, Politics and Society in Stirling during the ministry of Ebenezer Erskine, 1731-1754." M.Litt. thesis, University of Stirling, 1983.

———. "A Secession Congregation in its Community: The Stirling Congregation of the Rev. Ebenezer Erskine, 1731-1754." *Records of the Scottish Church History Society*, XXII (1989): 211-223.

———. "Stirling 1734." *Forth Naturalist and Historian*, 11 (1986): 105-120.

Murray, John J. "The Marrow Controversy—Thomas Boston and the Free Offer." In *Preaching and Revival*, 34-56. The Westminster Conference. London, 1984. Colchester, Essex: Christian Design & Print, 1985.

Philip, Adam. *The Devotional Literature of Scotland*, London: James Clarke & Co.,n.d.

Philpot, J.C. *Reviews*, 2:483-91. London: Frederick Kirby, 1901.

Scott, David. *Annals and Statistics of the Original Secession Church: till its disruption and union with the Free Church of Scotland in 1852*. Edinburgh: Andrew Elliot, 1886.

Scott, E. Erskine. *The Erskine-Halcro Genealogy. The ancestors and descendants of Henry Erskine, minister of Chirnside, his wife, Margaret Halcro of Orkney, and their sons, Ebenezer and Ralph Erskine*. Edinburgh, 1895.

Scott, Hew. *Fasti Ecclesiae Scoticanae. The Succession of Ministers in the Church of Scotland from the Reformation*. 7 vols. Edinburgh, 1915-1928.

Scott, Kenneth B. *Ebenezer Erskine, the Secession of 1733, and the Churches of Stirling*. Edinburgh, n.d.

Sell, Alan. "The Message of the Erskines for Today." *Evangelical Quarterly* 60, 4 (1988): 299-316.

Small, Robert. *History of the Congregations of the United Presbyterian Church*. 2 vols. Edinburgh, 1904.

Smeaton, George. "The suitableness of Erskine's writings to a period of religious revivals." In *The Beauties of Ralph Erksine*, ed. Samuel M'Millan. Edinburgh: A. Fullarton, 1829, xxxi-xxxviii.

Stewart, Alexander. *Reminiscences of Dunfermline and neighbourhood*. Edinburgh, 1886.

Taylor, William M. *The Scottish Pulpit from the Reformation to the Present Day*. London: Harper and Brothers, 1887.

Thomson, Andrew. *Historical Sketch of the Origin of the Secession Church*. Edinburgh: A. Fullarton, 1848.

———. "On the characteristics of Ralph Erskine's ministry." In *The Beauties of Ralph Erskine*, ed. S. M'Millan. Edinburgh: A. Fullarton, 1829, xv-xxx. Reprinted in *Free Presbyterian Magazine* XXXVIII, 11-12 (1934):459-64, 493-99.

_____. *Thomas Boston of Ettrick: His life and Times.* Edinburgh: T. Nelson and Sons, 1895.

Tyerman, Luke. *The Life of the Rev. George Whitefield.* 2 vols. London: Hodder and Stoughton, 1890.

Van der Groe, Theodorus. "Voorrede, handelende over het schadelijke misbruik van eene algemeene overtuiging, tot een valschen grond van rust voor de ziel." In *Al de werken van R. en E. Erskine,* deel 8, stuk 1. Amsterdam, 1855, iii-xxiv.

_____. "Voorrede aan den christelijken lezer." In *Al de werken van R. en E. Erskine,* deel 7, stuk 1. Amsterdam, 1855, iii-xxxi.

_____. "Voorrede, waarin omstandig gehandeld wordt over de noodige voorbereid-selen, wezenlijke eigenschappen en onafscheidelijke gevolgen van het ware zalig-makende geloof." In *Al de werken van R. en E. Erskine,* deel 5, stuk 1. Amsterdam, 1854, iii-lxxxvi.

_____. "Voorrede handelende over het opregt geloovig aannemen en gebruik maken van de beloften des H. Evangelies, tot ontdekking van de tijd- en waan-geloovigen, en tot bevestiging van de ware geloovigen." In *Al de werken van R. en E. Erskine,* deel 4, stuk 1. Amsterdam, 1854, iii-xlvi.

_____. "Voorrede of verhandeling over den pligt van het lezen der H. Schrift en andere godgeleerde boeken." In *Al de werken van R. en E. Erskine,* deel 3, stuk 1. Amsterdam, 1854, iii-lxviii.

Van der Linde, Simon. "Ebenezer en Ralph Erskine." In *Christelijke Encyclopedie,* 2:630-31. Kampen: J.H. Kok, 1957.

Van Harten, Pieter Hendrik. *De Prediking van Ebenezer en Ralph Erskine: Evangeliever-kondiging in het spanningsveld van verkiezing en belofte.* 's-Gravenhage: Boekencen-trum, 1986.

Van Valen, L.J. *Herauten van het kruis: Leven en werk van Ralph en Ebenezer Erskine.* Houten: DenHertog, 1995.

_____. *Thomas Boston: een visser der mensen.* Houten: Den Hertog, 1990.

Walker, James. *The Theology and Theologians of Scotland.* Edinburgh: T. & T. Clark, 1888.

Watson, Jean L. *Life of Ralph Erskine.* Edinburgh: James Gemmell, 1881.

Watt, Hugh. "Ebenezer Erskine, 1680-1754." In *Fathers of the Kirk: Some Leaders of the Church in Scotland from the Reformation to the Reunion,* ed. R. S. White. Oxford: University Press, 1960, 106-118.

Webber, F. *A History of Preaching in Britain and America,* 2:168-76. Milwaukee: North-western Publishing House, 1952.

Woodside, D. *The Soul of a Scottish Church, of the Contribution of the United Presbyterian Church to Scottish Life and Religion.* Edinburgh, n.d.

Young, D., and Brown, J. *Memorials of Alexander Moncrieff, M.A., and James Fisher, Fathers of the United Presbyterian Church.* Edinburgh, 1849.

Chapter 16: Theodorus Jacobus Frelinghuysen: Precursor of the Great Awakening
Annotated Bibliography

Primary Sources

Beeke, Joel R., ed. *Forerunner of the Great Awakening: Sermons by Theodorus Jacobus Frelinghuysen.* The Historical Series of the Reformed Church in America, No. 36. Grand Rapids: Eerdmans, 2000. Contains an updated translation of all twenty-two of Frelinghuysen's extant sermons.

Boel, Tobias. *Boel's Complaint Against Frelinghuysen.* Trans. and ed. by Joseph Anthony Loux, Jr. Rensselaer, New York: Hamilton, 1979. Includes first full translation of *Klagte van Eenige Leeden der Nederduytse Hervormde Kerk…* (New York: William Bradford and J. Peter Zenger, 1725). Introductory essay by Loux is biased against Frelinghuysen.

Frelinghuysen, Theodorus Jacobus. *A Clear Demonstration of a Righteous and Ungodly Man, in Their Frame, Way and End.* Trans. Hendrick Fischer. New York: John Peter, 1731. Contains five sermons, all of which are included in Demarest's translated *Sermons,* with the exception of one sermon on Proverbs 14:12 (which is printed as Appendix 1 in James Tanis, *Dutch Calvinistic Pietism*).

_____. *Sermons,* ed. and trans. William Demarest. New York: Board of Publication of the Reformed Protestant Dutch Church, 1856. This scarce work contains twenty-one of Frelinghuysen's sermons, translated from Dutch in mid-Victorian English. Includes *Drie Predicatien* (New York: William Bradford, 1721); *Een Trouwhertig Vertoog van Een waare Rechtveerdige, in Tegenstellinge van Een Godloose Sondaar* (New York: John Peter Zenger, 1729); *Een Bundelken Leer-redenen* (Amsterdam, 1736); *Versamelinge van Eenige Keur-Texten* (Philadelphia: W. Bradford, 1748).

Hastings, Hugh. *Ecclesiastical Records of the State of New York.* 7 vols. Albany, New York: James B. Lyon, 1901-1916. Volumes III and IV contain considerable primary source material dealing with Frelinghuysen's controversial ministry; an invaluable source.

Messler, Abraham. *Forty Years at Raritan: Eight Memorial Sermons, with Notes for a History of the Reformed Dutch Churches in Somerset County, New Jersey.* New York: A. Lloyd, 1873. Written by a Reformed church historian, and a successor and defender of Frelinghuysen. Contains eight of Messler's own memorial sermons preached at five-year intervals of his forty-year ministry at Raritan, as well as 175 pages of historical notes on the Dutch Reformed churches of Somerset County, New Jersey. For valuable material on Frelinghuysen's ministry, see the second memorial sermon and pages 162-212 of the historical notes.

Roberts, Richard Owen. *Salvation in Full Color: Twenty Sermons by Great Awakening Preachers.* Wheaton, Ill.: International Awakening Press, 1994. Contains Frelinghuysen's sermon, "The Righteous Are Scarcely Saved" (pp. 77-94).

Secondary Sources

Balmer, Randall H. *A Perfect Babel of Confusion: Dutch Religion and English Culture in the Middle Colonies.* New York: Oxford University Press, 1989. Chapter 5, "Flames of Contention: The Raritan Dispute and the Spread of Pietism," disparages Frelinghuysen's ministry and motives.

_____. "The Social Roots of Dutch Pietism in the Middle Colonies." *Church History* 53 (1984):187-99. Downplays Frelinghuysen's experiential emphases and exaggerates his being motivated by social roots.

Beardslee, John W., III. "Orthodoxy and Piety: Two Styles of Faith in the Colonial Period," in *Word and World: Reformed Theology in America,* ed. James W. Van Hoeven. Grand Rapids: Eerdmans, 1986, pages 1-14. Contrasts the styles of faith of Gisbertus Voetius and Johannes Cocceius. Confirms that Frelinghuysen was Voetian in his theology and preaching.

Brienen, Teunis. *De prediking van de Nadere Reformatie.* Amsterdam: Ton Bolland, 1974.

Examines and criticizes the classification method of *Nadere Reformatie* preaching that Frelinghuysen popularized in America.

Chambers, Talbot W. *Memoir of the Life and Character of the late Hon. Theo. Frelinghuysen, LL.D.* New York: Harper & Brothers, 1863. Chapter 1 sheds light on Rev. Frelinghuysen's children and grandchildren.

Coalter, Milton, Jr. *Gilbert Tennent, Son of Thunder: A Case Study of Continental Pietism's Impact on the First Great Awakening in the Middle Colonies.* Westport, Connecticut: Greenwood Press, 1986, pages 12-25. Underscores Frelinghuysen's influence on Tennent.

DeJong, Gerald F. *The Dutch Reformed Church in the American Colonies.* Ed. Donald J. Bruggink. The Historical Series of the Reformed Church in America, No. 5. Grand Rapids: Eerdmans, 1978. Focuses on the internal discord and controversy surrounding Frelinghuysen's ministry (pp. 170-179).

Frelinghuysen, Joseph S. "The Church in the Raritan Valley." In *Tercentenary Studies, 1928: Reformed Church in America, A Record of Beginnings.* New York: General Synod, 1928, pages 209-226. Strongly supportive of Frelinghuysen.

Frelinghuysen, Peter Hood Ballantine, Jr. *Theodorus Jacobus Frelinghuysen.* Princeton: privately printed, 1938. A 90-page, pro-Frelinghuysen work. Relies on English sources.

Hardman, K. "Theodore Jacob Frelinghuysen in the Middle Colonies." *Christian History* 8, 3, 23 (1989):10-11. Views Frelinghuysen as an important source of the Great Awakening.

Harmelink III, Herman. "Another Look at Frelinghuysen and His 'Awakening.'" *Church History* 37 (1968):423-38. Argues for disaffection rather than an awakening under Frelinghuysen's ministry.

Lodge, Martin Ellsworth. "The Great Awakening in the Middle Colonies." Ph.D. dissertation, University of California, Berkeley, 1964, chapters 8-9. Helpful, but sheds little new light.

Klunder, Jack Douglas. "The Application of Holy Things: A Study of the Covenant Preaching in the Eighteenth Century Dutch Colonial Church." Th.D. dissertation, Westminster Theological Seminary, 1984. Based on the extant sermons of four representative Dutch ministers: Theodorus Frelinghuysen, Archibald Laidlie, John H. Livingston, and William Linn. Argues too strongly for a covenantal framework in Frelinghuysen's sermons. Excursus II examines the historical and theological context for the complaints raised against Frelinghuysen.

Luidens, John Pershing. "The Americanization of the Dutch Reformed Church." Ph.D. dissertation, University of Oklahoma, 1969. Chapter 3 contains an excellent summary of Frelinghuysen's ministry and of the subsequent development of the Coetus and Conferentie parties in the Dutch Reformed Church.

Maxson, Charles Hartshorn. *The Great Awakening in the Middle Colonies.* Chicago: University of Chicago Press, 1920, chapter 2. A condensed, supportive, and helpful chapter on Frelinghuysen; relies largely on Messler and the *Ecclesiastical Records of the State of New York.*

McFarland, George Kennedy. "Clergy, Lay Leaders, and the People: An Analysis of 'Faith and Works' in Albany and Boston, 1630-1750." Unpublished manuscript. Pages 287-93 present a helpful summary of conflicts that swirled around Frelinghuysen. Drawn from *Ecclesiastical Records of the State of New York.*

Messler, Abraham. "Theodorus Jacobus Frelinghuysen," in *Annals of the American*

Reformed Dutch Pulpit by William Sprague. New York: Robert Carter & Brothers, 1869, pages 8-15. General overview; also contained in *Forty Years at Raritan.*

Osterhaven, M. Eugene. "Experiential Theology of Early Dutch Calvinism." *Reformed Review* 27 (1974):180-89. Focuses on William Ames and Frelinghuysen to get at the heart of Dutch Reformed experiential theology.

Pals, Daniel L. "Several Christologies of the Great Awakening," *Anglican Theological Review* 72 (1990):412-27. Examines christologies of Frelinghuysen, Tennent, Edwards, and Whitefield; argues that Frelinghuysen's christology balances the Reformed emphases of dogma and devotion.

Pointer, Richard W. *Protestant Pluralism and the New York Experience: A Study of Eighteenth-Century Religious Diversity.* Indianapolis: Indiana University Press, 1988. Views Frelinghuysen as a "radical Pietist," but acknowledges that the awakenings under his ministry spilled over into the Great Awakening.

Rollins, John William. "Frederick Theodore Frelinghuysen, 1817-1885: The Politics and Diplomacy of Stewardship." 2 vols. Ph.D. dissertation, University of Wisconsin, 1974. Chapter 1, "The Garden of the Dutch Church," accents the Dutch commitment of piety that Theodorus Frelinghuysen brought to America (pp. 25-59).

Schrag, F.J. "Theodorus Jacobus Frelinghuysen, the Father of American Pietism." *Church History* 14 (1945):201-216. The best over-all article on Frelinghuysen; stresses the influence of German Pietism.

Swanson, Thomas Lee. "A Critical Analysis of the Reformed Piety of Theodore Frelinghuysen." Th.M. thesis, Dallas Theological Seminary, 1983. Examines Frelinghuysen's doctrines of soteriology and ecclesiology, and concludes that he was a Reformed orthodox minister notwithstanding his deviations from a strict observance of church order.

Tanis, James. *Dutch Calvinistic Pietism in the Middle Colonies: A Study in the Life and Theology of Theodorus Jacobus Frelinghuysen.* The Hague: Martinus Nijhoff, 1967. The premier work on Frelinghuysen's life and theology; contains considerable fresh study. Free of hagiography and caricature.

_____. "Frelinghuysen, the Dutch Clergy, and the Great Awakening in the Middle Colonies." *Reformed Review* 28 (1985):109-118. Proves that Frelinghuysen was influenced by the *Nadere Reformatie* divines.

_____. "Reformed Pietism in Colonial America," in *Continental Pietism and Early American Christianity,* ed. F. Ernest Stoeffler. Grand Rapids: Eerdmans, 1976, pages 34-74. Examines the influence of the Huguenots, Labadism, the *Nadere Reformatie,* and German Pietism in colonial America. Frelinghuysen is set in the context of Reformed experiential divines.

Trinterud, Leonard J. *The Forming of an American Tradition: A Re-examination of Colonial Presbyterianism.* Philadelphia: Westminster Press, 1949, pages 54-56. Argues that Frelinghuysen was influenced by the Reformers and *Nadere Reformatie* divines rather than by German Pietists.

Vincent, Lorena Cole. *Readington Reformed Church, Readington, New Jersey, 1719-1969.* Somerville, N.J.: Somerville Press, 1969. A balanced treatment of Frelinghuysen (pp.5-18).

Index of Names and Subjects

Index of Biblical References

A wide range of excellent books on spiritual subjects is available from Evangelical Press. Please write to us for your free catalogue or contact us by e-mail.

Evangelical Press
Faverdale North, Darlington, Co. Durham, DL3 OPH, England
email: sales@evangelicalpress.org

Evangelical Press USA
P. O. Box 825, Webster, NY 14580, USA
email: usa.sales@evangelicalpress.org

web: http://www.evangelicalpress.org